Selected
English Critical Texts

With Excerpts from Classical Criticism

Edited
by
Sang-sup Lee

Shina-sa

• CONTENTS •

서설 : 영미 비평의 특징

한 사회집단이 처한 특수한 문화적 환경으로 말미암아 그 집단의 문학이 특수성을 띄우게 된다. 문학의 특수성은 또한 문학 비평의 특수성을 가져온다.

영미 비평—궁극적으로는 영국과 미국의 비평이 서로 갈라서는 지점이 있겠지만—이 기타 다른 유럽 국가들의 비평과 다른 점이 있으리라는 것은 쉽게 짐작할 수 있다. 유럽 비평은 궁극적으로는 그리이스·로마의 고전 비평을 공동의 조상으로 하여 생겨났고, 따라서 많은 공동의 관심사를 가지고 있으나, 나라마다 구체적 정황, 특히 모국어로 창작되는 문학이 서로 다름에 따라 비평 또한 달라질 수 밖에 없었던 것이다.

아래에서 영미 비평의 몇 가지 특수성을 열거하되, 그런 성격을 띄우게 된 원인과 배경은 논의하지 않기로 한다. 먼저 유의해 둘 것은 영미 비평의 특수성이 유독 영미 비평에 국한되어 있다는 말은 아니라는 것이다. 강조의 중심이 다소 다르다는 것이지 공통의 조상으로부터 연유한 유럽 각국의 비평이 각각 독특한 성질만은 노정할 수는 없을 것이다.

1. 변호적 성격

영미 비평사에서 처음 문학의 문제를 신중하게 논의한 사람은 Sir Thomas Elyot(1499?-1549)이라는 영국 초기 르네상스의 지식인으로서, 당대의 명저인 *The Governor*(1531)에서 부분적으로 문학의 교육적 효과를 논하고 있다. 그는 문학인은 아니었지만 근대 국가로 발돋움하는 영국의 지도자를 양성하기 위한 청소년 교육 문제를 다루는 과정에서 필수교양과목으로서의 문학을 적극 권장하고 있다.

그는 문학이 당시의 일부 도덕론자들에게 부도덕하다는 부당한 평가를 받고 있다면서, 문학의 교육적 효과를 옹호하는 입장이다. 즉 영국 최초의 신중한 문학론에 이와 같은 문학에 대한 옹호적, 변호적 자세를 보이고 있는 것이다. 자연히 문학의 도덕적, 교훈적 효용을 기리는 말투와 논리가 의식적으로 동원될 수 밖에 없다.

Elyot 보다 두 세대나 뒤떨어져서 활약한 Sir Philip Sidney는 너무나도 잘 알려진 *An Apology for Poetry*(또는 *Defence of Poesy*)를 쓸 때 Elyot 의 어휘와 논리를 많이 빌려다 썼다. 제목부터 그것이 「변호」임을 공언하고 있다. 청교도를 비롯한 도덕론자들이 물론 문학을 공격한 것이 사실이지만, Sidney는 단지 그들에게 답변하기 위해서만 그렇게도 포괄적이고 종합적인 문학론을 전개한 것은 아니다. 그는 실상 르네상스 유럽의 문학관을 요약하면서, 그 작업을 「변호」의 구실 아래에서 해내고 있는 것이다.

실상 청교도인 Stephen Gosson 의 공격에 직접 맞서서 대답한 사람은 Thomas Lodge (1558-1625)였다(1580). 그는 Gosson의 공격에 하나씩 하나씩 대답하면서, 그에 그치지 않고 문학의 숭고한 이념, 그 문학적 중요성을 강조하는 것을 잊지 않았다.

그러나 Sidney 의 변호는 Gosson-Lodge 의 공방전을 훨씬 초월하여 문학의 창조성, 도덕성, 및 근본정신을 권위있게 논한 것이다. 변호의 입장인 까닭에 매우 설득력이 있는 수사법을 발휘하며, 또한 문학을 예찬하는 입장인 까닭에 찬양의 진지하고 화려한 말씨가 동원된다.

Sidney 이후 영국의 르네상스는 전성기를 맞았는데, 느닷없이 일류 시인이던 Thomas Campion(1567-1620)이 *Observations in the Art of English Poesy*(1602)를 발표하여 영시의 운율이 고전시의 그것보다 비천하므로 특히 중세의 유물인 압운을 버리고 고전적 운율을 모방하여야 하겠다는 충격적 비판을 가했다.

이에 맞서서 역시 시인인 Samuel Daniel(1562-1619)이 *Defence of Rhyme*(1603)에서 압운(rhyme)은 영어가 가진 언어적 특성에 알맞으므로 결코 버릴 수 없으며 고전 운율은 고전어에나 맞지 영어에도 맞을 수는 없다는 주장을 했다.

이와같이 영국 문학에 대한 경멸, 비판, 공격이 영국 비평사를 점철하는 것을 보게 된다. 섬나라 영국은 유럽대륙과 일종의 문화적 긴장 관계를 유지하면서 발전했다.

Dryden의 *An Essay of Dramatic Poesy*는 그리이스·로마의 고전문학과 유럽 문학에 대한 영국 문학(Shakespeare)의 비교 우위론을 펼쳤다. 영문학에 대한 옹호론인 셈이다. 같은 시대에 Thomas Rymer가 프랑스의 입법비평을 받아들여 합리성의 이름으로 Shakespeare를 매도한 것과 크게 대조된다.

18세기 후반에 Samuel Johnson이 다시금 대륙의 문학과 Shakespeare를 비교하여 후자의 우수성을 옹호했다. 그 과정에서 입법비평의 오류를 통렬히 공격했다. 이것은 입법비평의 기초가 되는 합리주의의 전횡에 대한 경험론적 반발을 뜻한다.

Shelley의 *Defence of Poetry*는 그가 Sidney의 후예임을 그 제목에서도 알아볼 수 있다. 이글에는 영문학에 대한 옹호가 아니라 문학 자체에 대한 위기의식이 깔려 있다. 간단히 말해서 과학에 비하여 문학의 인식적 기능이 문제가 되어 있다. 이 시대로부터 문학과 과학은 충돌관계에 있게 되는 것을 본다.

과학이 진리에 대한 독점권을 주장함에 대처하여 Arnold는 "Literature and Science"에서 문학을 옹호했고, "The Study of Poetry"에서는 문학이 궁극적으로 인간성의 지주로서의 역할을 독점할 것이라고 주장했다.

I. A. Richards는 과학적 세계관을 일단 받아들이고 나서 문학이 할 수 있는 일을 면밀히 고찰함으로써 과학적 세계에서의 문학의 존재 이유를 옹호하고자 하였다. 그에 의하면 문학은 사람의 심리적 조화라는 막중한 일을 떠맡고 있다는 것이다.

이처럼 영국 비평사는 문학 옹호론의 색채가 짙고 또한 그 전통은 계속 이어지고 있다고 볼 수 있다.

2. 시인 겸 비평가의 전통

영미의 대표적 비평가, 다시 말하자면 오늘날에도 일반 문학론에서 거론되고 교실의 강의 내용에 포함되는 비평가들은 거의 모두 창작가였다는 사실은 다른 나라 문학에서 별로 찾아볼 수 없는 사실이다. Sidney, Jonson, Dryden, Pope, Johnson, Wordsworth, Coleridge, Shelley, Keats, Arnold, Poe, James, Eliot 등은 모두 창작가(James만 빼면 모두 시인)였다. Johnson만 빼면 실상 영미의 일급 창작가들인 것이다. (Johnson의 시도 상당한 수준이다.)

T. S. Eliot에 이르기까지 영국과 미국에 창작 말고 비평에만 손을 댄 이른바 전문직 비평가가 없었던 것이 아니다. 수를 헤아릴 수 없이 많았다. 특히 18세기에 문학 저널리즘이 왕성해지면서 영국은 유례없는 비평의 시대를 맞았다. 19세기에는 저널리즘이 더욱 기세를 부렸다. Keats가 비평을 쓴다는 의식 없이 친지들에게 보낸 편지는 영미 비평사에 남지만, Keats를 절망케 하여 일찍 죽음으로 몰아갔다는 그의 *Endymion*에 대

한 비평은 지금 읽히지 않고 있다. Wordsworth의 이름난 서문은 비평 논문이라기보다는 20세기에 그리도 흔해빠진 새로운 유파의 선언(manifesto)과도 같은 것이지만, 영미 비평사의 가장 중요한 문헌으로 귀중히 취급되고 있다. 더욱 놀라운 사실은 Pope의 *Essay on Criticism*이 시로서가 아니라 비평적 문헌으로 더 중요시된다는 것이다. 그 시대에 산문으로 된 고전주의 문학론이 적지 않지만, 영국 비평사는 Pope의 기지의 운문을 채택하고 정작 비평적 산문은 도외시하다시피 한다. Coleridge나 Arnold가 우수한 시를 남기지 않았다면 지금처럼 읽히지는 못할 것이라는 가정이 전혀 무리스럽지는 않다.

이것은 무엇을 뜻하는가?

첫째로, 아마도, 영미문학은 적어도 Eliot 전까지는 비평 주도의 문학이 아니었음을 뜻할 것이다(이 점에 대해서는 뒤에서 다시 논의한다).

둘째로, 영미인들은 시인, 소설가, 곧 창작 당사자들의 말에 권위를 부여하는 전통이 있음을 말할 것이다. Pope와 Eliot은 창작을 못하는 자들은 비평도 삼가라는 뜻의 말을 했다. 당사자가 아니고서는 그 사실, 사건에 대한 진실된 말을 하기 힘들다는 생각은 영국적 경험주의의 일단일지도 모른다.

세째로, 그런 까닭에 영미비평은 사변적이거나 이론적이거나 체계적이기보다는 상식적이고 사실적이고 구체적이기 쉽다.

그 밖에 이에 관련된 여러 사항을 추론할 수 있을 것이다.

3. 상상론, 창작 심리에 대한 관심

시인들이 쓴 비평 또는 문학론은 자신의 창작 경험을 근거로 하기 쉽다. 따라서 창작 과정과 창작 심리에 대한 경험적 발언은 영미 비평의 근간을 이루게 된다. 게다가 일찌감치 Bacon

은 문학을 인간 능력의 기본영역인 이성, 기억, 상상 중 상상의 소관이라 못박고, 상상은 이성과 기억의 지배를 벗어나서 욕망에 부합되는 "가짜 역사", 즉 꾸며낸 이야기를 만든다고 하였다. Hobbes, Locke, Shaftesbury, Hartley 등 영국의 인성철학자들은 사람의 정신작용 중 상상, 또는 환상, 또는 연상 등 이성작용과는 다른 정신작용에 대하여 전통적으로 깊은 관심을 보였다. Coleridge의 상상론은 그러한 영국적 인성철학 내지는 심리학에 근거하고 있는 것이다.

대륙의 경우, *phantasia*와 *imaginatio*는 동일한 뜻으로 사용되었는데 유독 영국에서는 공상(환상)과 상상으로 구별될 만큼, 영국의 시인, 비평가들은 상상의 문제를 세밀히 다루었다.

Eliot의 「백금 촉매론」은 영미 비평의 주관심사인 창작 과정 내지 상상작용에 대한 현대적 표현인 것이다. 그리고 오늘날의 최대 비평가의 한 사람인 Northrop Frye의 비평은 전적으로 인간의 상상에 관한 것이라 할 수 있다.

4. 처방적 비평에 대한 불신

비평이 경험적이라 함은 자연히 주관적이고 개인적임을 암시한다. 주관적이고 개인적인 비평은 이론적이든가 이론적 근거를 빙자한 처방이 되지 않는다.

물론 영미의 문학사를 보면 시 짓는 법, 희곡 짓는 법 등 창작의 처방 내지 명령이 얼마든지 많았지만, 비평사에서 귀중히 여기지 않는다. 또한 문학에 대한 합리적, 철학적 논의, 즉 이론이 적지 않았지만 역시 대체로 시대의 유물로 제쳐놓여져 있다. Pope의 *Essay on Criticism*은 다분히 처방스럽지만, 그 처방스러움 때문에 지금껏 귀중히 여겨지는 것이 아니라 신고전주의의 이념을 기지와 해학이 가득한 세련된 운문으로 표현한 까닭이다. 합리성을 표방하면서 Shakespeare를 공격한 17세기 말의 Thomas Rymer는 똑똑한 체하는 바보로 취급되고 있다. Johnson은 이론적 비평은 언제나 실제 경험을 참조할 수 있도록 열려져 있어야 한다고 주장했다.

처방적 비평이 불신당하는 반면에 실제 비평이 왕성할 것은 당연한 일이다. 작품에 대한 실제 비평의 전통은 Richards를 거쳐 New Criticism에 이르러 그 전성기를 맞은 것 같다.

오늘날의 영미 비평에서 유럽의 영향을 받아 이론 비평이 성행하고 있는 것은 사실이나, 실제 비평이 압도당할 정도는 아니며, 유럽의 여타 비평과 비교할 때 영미 비평은 훨씬 덜 이론적, 독단적이다.

마지막으로 한가지 특징을 덧붙이자면, 영미 비평은 영어 문화의 세계적 전파와 더불어 비평의 대상과 방법에 있어 세계의 어느 나라 비평보다도 다양하고 포괄적이라는 것이다. 프랑스 문학, 스페인 문학, 러시아 문학, 심지어 중국, 한국의 문학까지 영미 비평이 대상으로 삼지 않는 문학이 없다고 할 수 있으며, 그 수준도 대체로 최고에 속한다. 또한 각국에서 개발된 이론이나 방법을 수용하여 다각적으로 실험, 검토하여 쓸 만한 것으로 다듬는 일도 잘 해낸다. 예컨대 프랑스를 중심하여 생겨난 구조주의 비평은 영미의 학자들에 의하여 재해석되고 실제 비평에 응용될 수 있도록 재정비되고 있다.

이런 의미에서 영미 비평은 세계 문학 비평에의 길이 되는 것이다.

Sir Philip Sidney

(1554—1586)

명문 귀족 출신으로 옥스포드 대학에서 수학한 후 오랜 대륙 여행, 특히 이탈리아 체재를 통하여 르네상스 지성인으로 성장하였다. 엘리자베드 여왕의 총애를 받는 외교관으로 활약했고, 영국군 사령관으로 네덜란드에서 스페인군과 전투 중 부상으로 사망했다. 소넷집 *Astrophel and Stella*, 전원 로만스 *Arcadia*, 문학론 *An Apology for Poetry* 등을 남겼다.

*An Apology for Poetry*는 1583년경에 집필되어 당시 상류 식자층에 원고 형태로 돌려 가며 읽히다가 저자가 죽은 훨씬 후인 1595년에 두 상업 출판업자에 의하여 거의 동시에 출간되었다. 그 중 조금 먼저 나온 책의 제목이 *The Defence of Poesy*이고, 여기에 약간의 수정을 가하여 출판한 것이 *An Apology for Poetry*인 것이다.

Sidney는 물론 근대적 의미의 비평가는 아니며 Spenser나 Shakespeare처럼 직업적 문필가도 아니었다. 그는 르네상스의 모범적인 Christian humanist로서, 열렬한 종교인인 동시에 정력적인 사회인이요, 또한 인간적인 지식에 강렬한 호기심을 가진 전인적인 사람이었다. 그의 문학은 인간적인 지식의 탐구의 한 결과였던 것이다. 중세의 기사나 승려와는 달리, 르네상스의 이 신사는 쓸만한 인간적인 지식——그것은 주로 그리이스와 로마의 고전에서 얻는 것인데——은 사람의 개인적 및 사회적 덕을 기르고 궁극적으로는 종교적인 삶에 보탬이 된다고 믿어 마지 않았다.

1579년에 Stephen Gosson이라는 사람이 *The School of Abuse*란 책자를 내면서 그것을 Sir Philip Sidney에게 바친다고 했다. 본인에게 허락을 받지 않고 한 짓이었다. Gosson은 옥스포드 재학 중에 시와 극을 써본 경험이 있고, 문학에 대해서도 배워 알고 있어서 비교적 쉽게, 또한 능란한 필치로 문학을 공격하였는데, 요컨대, 문학은 부도덕하며, 거짓말이며, 최대의 철인인 플라톤이 배격한 물건이라는 것이었다. (이런 내용의 책을 두 권 더 내고 나중에 그는 영국 교회의 목사가 되었다. 항간에 알려졌듯이 「청교도」는 아니었다.)

하필이면 왜 당시 일류 소넷 작가로 발돋움하던 시드니에게 반문학론을 헌정하였는지 알 수 없지만, 시드니는 직업 의식에서가 아닌 순수한 지성인의 입장에서 이에 답변할 책임을 느꼈던 것같다.

*An Apology for Poetry*는 문학(poetry)이 인간에게 처음으로 문명의 빛을 가져다 주었음을 주장함으로써 시작한다. 그 후에 나타난 철학, 과학, 역사 등의 학문은 모두 문학을 모태로 하여 생겨난 것이다.

다음으로 시드니는 다른 모든 학문이 이 세상의 사물에 종속되어 있는데 반하여 시는 이 세상과 자연을 능가하는 이상적인 세계를 구축한다는 플라톤주의적 사상을 전개한다.

이러한 이상주의적 입장에서 그는 아리스토텔레스의 모방의 이론을 확대 해석하여 결국 모방을 이상적인 형상의 창조로 규정한다.

모든 학문은 사람의 도덕을 함양하는 것이 목적이라는 고전적인 사상에서 그는 철학, 역사, 문학의 3대 학문의 우열을 가리는데, 철학은 추상적인 도덕율을, 역사는 개체적인 실례를 가르치므로 추상적 도덕율을 개체적 실례를 통하여 가르치는 문학에 모두 뒤떨어진다고 주장한다. 특히 흥미있는 것은, 역사가 불완전하고 타락한 세상의 일을 통하여 완전한 덕을 가르치려는 거의 불가능한 작업을 수행함에 반하여, 문학은 역사적 사실에 얽매이지 않고 그것을 바꾸어 완전한 형상으로 꾸밀 수 있는 권리를 향유한다는 것과, 도덕율에 대한 정의, 분류, 단계, 논리 등을 벌여놓는 데에만 능란한 철학에 반하여, 문학은 도덕적 행위의 완전한 형상을 즐겁게 보여줄 뿐 아니라 실제로 실행할 수 있도록 감동(move)시킨다는 것이다. 문학은 즐겁게 가르치는 특유한 방법이라는 생각은 로마의 호라티우스 이래 고전주의적 문학관의 한 초석이 되어 있다.

문학의 일반적 옹호를 끝내고 시드니는 문학의 각 장르의 도덕적 내지 교육적 효용성을 들어 그 각각을 옹호한다. 이것은 효용론적 장르론이라 하겠다.

그는 문학이 거짓말이라는 공격에 대해서 문학은 자기가 하는 말을 정말이라고 잡아떼지 않으므로 거짓말을 한다고 할 수 없다고 변호한다. 즉 그는 문학의 솔직한 허구성을 강조한다. 이어서 문학은 올바른 생활에 방해가 된다는 플라톤의 주장에 대하여, 그것은 진정한 문학이 아닌 남용된(abused) 가짜 문학을 두고 하는 말이라고 한다. 남용 때문에 진정이 송두리째 부인될 수는 없다는 것이다.

마지막 부분에서 시드니는 당시 영국에서 문학이 공격받는 이유의 하나를 못난 문인들의 탓으로 돌린다. 그는 Chaucer, Spenser 등의 작품을 찬양하고, 이어 당시 영국 문인들, 특히 극작가들이 이탈리아 이론가들에 의해 확정된 삼일치의 법칙, 어울림(decorum)의 법칙을 어기고 있음을 비판한다. 영어는 시를 지을 만한 언어로서 손색이 없으나 문인들이 스스로 연마하지 않음을 탓한다.

전체적으로 보아 *An Apology for Poetry*는 플라톤, 아리스토텔레스, 호라티우스 및 르네상스 이탈리아의 이론가들의 문학관을 매우 포괄적으로 다룬 당대 유럽의 대표적 문헌인 동시에, 논리의 전개와 수사법에 있어서도 우수한 하나의 산문이라 하겠다.

An Apology for Poetry (1595)

When the right virtuous Edward Wotton* and I were at the Emperor's court together, we gave ourselves to learn horsemanship of John Pietro Pugliano, one that with great com-

---

***Edward Wotton:** 16-17세기의 영국의 외교관, 정치가.

mendation had the place of an esquire in his stable; and he, according to the fertileness of the Italian wit, did not only afford us the demonstration of his practice, but sought to enrich our minds with the contemplations therein* which he thought most precious. But with none I remember mine ears were at any time more laden, than when—either angered with slow payment,* or moved with our learner-like admiration—he exercised his speech in the praise of his faculty. He said soldiers were the noblest estate of mankind, and horsemen the noblest of soldiers. He said they were the masters of war and ornaments of peace, speedy goers and strong abiders, triumphers both in camps and courts. Nay, to so unbelieved a point he proceeded, as that no earthly thing bred such wonder to a prince as to be a good horseman; skill of government was but a *pedanteria** in comparison. Then would he add certain praises, by telling what a peerless beast the horse was, the only serviceable courtier without flattery, the beast of most beauty, faithfulness, courage, and such more, that if I had not been a piece of a logician before I came to him, I think he would have persuaded me to have wished myself a horse. But thus much at least with his no few words he drove into me, that self-love is better than any gilding to make that seem gorgeous wherein ourselves be parties.*

Wherein if Pugliano's strong affection and weak arguments will not satisfy you, I will give you a nearer example of myself, who, I know not by what mischance, in these my not old years and idlest times, having slipped into the title of a poet, am provoked to say something unto you in the defence of that my unelected vocation,* which if I handle with more good will

---

***of**: from (16세기 영어에서 of 는 종종 from 또는 by 의 뜻으로 쓰임).
***therein**: in horsemanship (승마술에 관한).
***angered with slow payment**: 「학습효과가 빨리 나타나지 않아 성이 나서 (보답이 늦어 화가 나서)」.
****pedanteria***: pedantry. 「실효성이 없는 단순한 지식」.
***wherein ourselves be parties**: in which...parties. 「우리가 관여하고 있는 것」.
***unelected vocation**: 「직업적으로 선택한 일이 아닌 일」. 「취미」.

than good reasons, bear with me, since the scholar is to be pardoned that followeth the steps of his master.

And yet I must say that, as I have just cause to make a pitiful defence of poor poetry, which from almost the highest estimation of learning is fallen to be the laughing-stock of children, so have I need to bring some more available proofs, since the former* is by no man barred of his deserved credit;* the silly latter* hath had even the names of philosophers used to the defacing of it, with great danger of civil war among the Muses.*

And first, truly, to all them that, professing learning, inveigh against poetry, may justly be objected that they go very near to ungratefulness, to seek to deface that which, in the noblest nations and languages that are known, hath been the first light-giver to ignorance, and first nurse, whose milk by little and little enabled them to feed afterwards of tougher knowledges. And will they now play the hedgehog,* that, being received into the den, drove out his host? Or rather the vipers,* that with their birth kill their parents? Let learned Greece in any of her manifold sciences be able to show me one book before Musaeus, Homer, and Hesiod,* all three nothing else but poets. Nay, let any history be brought that can say any writers were there before them, if they were not men of the same skill, as Orpheus, Linus,* and some other are named, who, having

---

***the former**: 전자, 즉 learning(학문).

***of his deserved credit**: 「그 본래의 합당한 명망으로부터」. of는 from, his는 its. (16세기 영어에는 grammatical gender가 상당히 살아 있었다.)

***the silly latter**: 「못난 후자」. 즉 poetry(시).

***with...the Muses**: 「학예의 신들 사이에 내분이 일어날 위험을 안고」. 아홉 명의 Muses는 보통 시의 신들로 알려져 있지만, 실제로는 아홉 가지의 예술과 학문들을 대표한다. 그러므로 시를 멸시하는 것은 Muses 사이에 내분을 조성시키는 것이다.

***the hedgehog, the viper**: 불쌍해서 집안에 들여놓으니까 주인을 몰아냈다는 고슴도치와 알에서 깨어나자 어미를 잡아먹는다는 독사는 둘 다 배은망덕한 자의 전형으로, 인류문화를 처음 창시한 시를 나중에 와서 타박하는 태도도 그와 같다는 것.

***Musaeus, Homer, and Hesiod**: 이들 세 시인은 그리이스의 최초의 저술가들인데, 그리이스의 최초의 저술가들이 모두 시인이었다는 사실은 모든 학문의 시초가 시였음을 증명한다.

been the first of that country that made pens deliverers of their knowledge to their posterity, may justly challenge to be called their fathers in learning. For not only in time they had this priority (although in itself antiquity be venerable) but went before them as causes, to draw with their charming sweetness the wild untamed wits to an admiration of knowledge. So as Amphion* was said to move stones with his poetry to build Thebes, and Orpheus to be listened to by beasts, indeed stony and beastly people. So among the Romans were Livius Andronicus and Ennius; so in the Italian language the first that made it aspire to be a treasure-house of science were the poets Dante, Boccaccio, and Petrarch; so in our English were Gower* and Chaucer, after whom, encouraged and delighted with their excellent foregoing, others have followed to beautify our mother-tongue, as well in the same kind as in other arts.

This did so notably show itself, that the philosophers of Greece durst not a long time appear to the world but* under the masks of poets.* So Thales, Empedocles, and Parmenides sang their natural philosophy in verses; so did Pythagoras and Phocylides their moral counsels; so did Tyrtaeus in war matters, and Solon* in matters of policy; or rather they, being poets, did exercise their delightful vein* in those points of highest knowledge which before them lay hid to the world. For that wise Solon* was directly a poet it is manifest, having written in

---

***Orpheus, Linus**: 둘 다 시신 Apollo와 Muse 사이에서 태어난 음악가. 이들은 음악으로 야만인들을 승화시켜 문명을 일으켰다고 한다.

***Amphion**: Zeus의 아들로, 신이 내려준 악기를 연주하여 돌을 움직여서 Thebes성을 쌓았다.

***Gower, John**: (1325?-1408), Chaucer와 동시대 시인. *Confessio Amantis*의 저자.

***but**: except.

***the Philosophers of Greece...under the masks of poets**: 「그리이스 초창기의 철인들은 시인의 탈을 쓰고서야 세상에 나타났다」.

***Thales, Empedocles, Parmenides, Pythagoras, Phocylides, Tyrtaeus, Solon**: 그리이스 문명 황금기의 초창기에 속하는 과학자, 철학자, 군사학자, 정치학자들. 모두 운문으로 글을 썼다.

***vein**: 「(시적) 기질(을 발휘했다)」.

verse the notable fable of the Atlantic Island which was continued by Plato. And truly even Plato whosoever well considereth, shall find that in the body of his work, though the inside and strength were philosophy, the skin, as it were, and beauty depended most of poetry. For all standeth upon dialogues; wherein he feigneth many honest burgesses of Athens to speak of such matters that, if they had been set on the rack, they would never have confessed them, besides his poetical describing the circumstances of their meetings, as the well-ordering of a banquet, the delicacy of a walk, with interlacing mere tales, as Gyges' Ring and others, which who knoweth not to be flowers of poetry did never walk into Apollo's garden.

And even historiographers, (although their lips sound of things done, and verity be written in their foreheads,) have been glad to borrow both fashion and perchance weight of poets. So Herodotus entitled his history by the name of the nine Muses;* and both he and all the rest that followed him either stole or usurped of poetry their passionate describing of passions, the many particularities of battles which no man could affirm, or, if that be denied me, long orations put in the mouths of great kings and captains, which it is certain they never pronounced.

So that truly neither philosopher nor historiographer could, at the first, have entered into the gates of popular judgements, if

---

*Solon: (638–559 B.C.), 아테네의 정치가였는데, 이상국 Atlantis에 관한 저술을 남겼다는 전설이 있다. Plato도 그 나라에 관해 언급했다.

***And truly even Plato...into Apollo's garden**: Plato는 그의 철학을 모두 아테네의 실제 지식인이 등장하는 대화를 통해 전개하였다. 그 대화들은 단순한 말의 오고감뿐 아니라, 연극처럼 재미있게 꾸며져 있다. Gyges' Ring은 〈이상국가론〉에 나오는 신비로운 전설인데, 그런 것들이 바로 시의 꽃이라는 것을 모르는 자는 시신 Apollo의 동산을 거닐어 보지 못한자, 즉 시가 무엇인지를 모르는 자인 것이다.

***although their lips...in their foreheads**: 역사가들이 사실을 기술한다면서 소설처럼 감정을 묘사하고 말을 인용함으로써, 허구 즉 문학을 흉내낸다는 것.

***Herodotus...nine Muses**: 그리이스의 역사가 헤로도투스(기원전 5세기)는 아홉 명의 시신들의 이름으로 〈역사〉의 각 장의 명칭을 삼았다.

they had not taken a great passport of poetry;*which in all nations at this day, where learning flourisheth not, is plain to be seen, in all which they have some feeling of poetry. In Turkey, besides their lawgiving divines they have no other writers but poets. In our neighbour-country Ireland, where truly learning goeth* very bare, yet are their poets held in a devout reverence. Even among the most barbarous and simple Indians, where no writing is, yet have they their poets, who make and sing songs (which they call *areytos*)*, both of their ancestors' deeds and praises of their gods. A sufficient probability that, if ever learning come among them, it must be by having their hard dull wits softened and sharpened with the sweet delights of poetry; for until they find a pleasure in the exercises of the mind, great promises of much knowledge will little persuade them that know not the fruits of knowledge. In Wales, the true remnant of the ancient Britons* as there are good authorities to show the long time they had poets, which they called bards, so through all the conquests of Romans, Saxons, Danes, and Normans, some of whom did seek to ruin all memory of learning from among them, yet do their poets even to this day last; so as it is not more notable in soon beginning, than in long continuing.

But since the authors of most of our sciences were the Romans, and before them the Greeks, let us a little stand upon their authorities, but even so far as to see what names they have given unto this now scorned skill* Among the Romans a poet was called *vates*, which is as much as a diviner, foreseer, or prophet, as by his*conjoined words, *vaticinium* and *vaticinari*, is

---

***a great passport of poetry**: 「시라는 위대한 여권」. 형식상 시라는 표시가 있어야 사람들이 읽어주었다는 뜻.

***goeth**: is 로 읽을 것.

****areytos***: 인디안의 춤과 노래.

***Wales...Britons**: 영국 서부 Wales 지방 사람들은 영국의 원주민 Briton 의 후예로서, Celt 어계의 고유언어를 가지고 있었고, bard 라 불리는 음유시인이 있었다.

***this now scorned skill**: 지금은 멸시받는 시예술.

***his**: its (*vates* 란 낱말의).

manifest; so heavenly a title did that excellent people bestow upon this heart-ravishing knowledge.* And so far were they carried into the admiration thereof, that they thought in the chanceable hitting upon any such verses great foretokens of their following fortunes were placed; whereupon grew the word of *Sortes Virgilianae*,* when by sudden opening Virgil's book they lighted upon any verse of his making; whereof the Histories of the Emperors' Lives are full: as of Albinus, the governor of our island, who in his childhood met with this verse,

> Arma amens capio, nec sat rationis in armis,*

and in his age performed it; which although it were a very vain and godless superstition, as also it was to think that spirits were commanded by such verses—whereupon this word charms,* derived of *carmina*, cometh—so yet serveth it to show the great reverence those wits were held in, and altogether not without ground, since both the oracles of Delphos and Sibylla's prophecies* were wholly delivered in verses; for that same exquisite observing of number and measure in words, and that high-flying liberty of conceit proper to the poet, did seem to have some divine force in it.

And may not I presume a little further to show the reasonableness of this word *vates*, and say that the holy David's Psalms* are a divine poem? If I do, I shall not do it without the

---

***heart-ravishing knowledge**: 「마음을 사로잡는 지식, 즉 시」. Sidney 는 시의 매력을 강조하기 위해 이와 유사한 말을 여러 곳에서 쓰고 있다.

****Sortes Virgilianae***: 로마의 대시인 Vilgil 의 작품 *Aeneid* 를 펼쳐봄으로써 운수를 점치는 일. 시를 거룩한 예언서로 생각하는 태도.

***Arma...in armis**: "격한 감정으로 무기를 잡도다. 무기를 잡을 만큼 충분한 이유는 없도다" (*Aeneid* 제 2 권, 314행). 이 부분을 읽고 영국의 로마 총독이었던 Albinus 가 군인이 되기로 결심했다고 한다.

***charms**: 「주문」. 라틴어의 *carmina*(노래)에서 온 말.

***the oracles of Delphos and Sibylla's prophecies**: 그리이스 Delphos 섬의 Apollo 신전에서 신의 말씀(oracles: 명령, 예언 등)을 들을 수 있었다 함. Sibylla 는 예언하는 여자. 신의 말씀이나 여자 예언자의 말은 모두 운문으로 되어 있었다.

***David's Psalms**: 고대 유태인의 영웅 David(다윗 왕)은 정치가일 뿐만 아

testimony of great learned men, both ancient and modern. But even the name Psalms will speak for me, which, being interpreted, is nothing but Songs; then, that it is fully written in metre, as all learned Hebricians agree, although the rules be not yet fully found; lastly and principally, his handling his prophecy, which is merely poetical. For what else is the awaking his musical instruments, the often and free changing of persons, his notable *prosopopoeias*,* when he maketh you, as it were, see God coming in His majesty, his telling of the beasts' joyfulness and hills' leaping, but a heavenly poesy, wherein almost he showeth himself a passionate lover of that unspeakable and everlasting beauty to be seen by the eyes of the mind, only cleared by faith? But truly, now, having named him, I fear me* I seem to profane that holy name, applying it to poetry, which is among us thrown down to so ridiculous an estimation. But they that with quiet judgements will look a little deeper into it, shall find the end and working of it such as,* being rightly applied, deserveth not to be scourged out of the church of God.

But now let us see how the Greeks named it and how they deemed of it. The Greeks called him a Poet, which name hath, as the most excellent, gone through other languages. It cometh of this word *poiein*, which is 'to make';* wherein I know not whether by luck or wisdom we Englishmen have met with the Greeks in calling him a maker. Which name, how high and incomparable a title it is, I had rather were known by marking the scope of other sciences than by my partial allegation.*

니라 신과 인간의 관계를 노래한 시인이기도 한데, 구약에 수록된 시편 Psalms 중 다수가 그의 작품이다. 성경의 일부를 세속적인 시의 장르에 속한다고 말하는 데 Sidney 는 약간 주저하고 있다.

prosopopoeias: 「의인화」(personifications). Psalms 가 시의 요건을 다 충족시키는 가운데 의인법도 많이 사용했다는 것.

I fear me: I am afraid. fear 는 재귀동사로 쓰이기도 했었다.

find the end...it such...: 「시의 목적과 작용이 ...한 것임을 알게 된다」.

poiein...'to make': 그리이스 말의 *poiein* 은 maker 란 뜻이니까, 그 명사형 poet 는 maker 란 뜻이 되는데, 영어에서 한 때는 maker 란 말이 poet 란 뜻으로 쓰였었다.

Which name, ...I...allegation: 「maker 란 이름이 얼마나 고상하고 다른 것

There is no art delivered unto mankind that hath not the works of nature for his*principal object, without which they could not consist, and on which they so depend as they become actors and players, as it were, of what nature will have set forth. So doth the astronomer look upon the stars, and, by that he seeth, set down what order nature hath taken therein. So do the geometrician and arithmetician in their divers sorts of quantities. So doth the musician in times* tell you which by nature agree, which not. The natural philosopher* thereon hath his name, and the moral philosopher* standeth upon the natural virtues, vices, and passions of man; and 'follow nature', saith he, 'therein, and thou shalt not err.' The lawyer saith what men have determined; the historian what men have done. The grammarian speaketh only of the rules of speech, and the rhetorician and logician, considering what in nature will soonest prove and persuade, thereon give artificial rules, which still* are compassed within the circle of a question, according to the proposed matter. The physician weigheth the nature of man's body, and the nature of things helpful or hurtful unto it. And the metaphysic, though it be in the second and abstract notions, and therefore be counted supernatural, yet doth he, indeed, build upon the depth of nature.*

Only the poet, disdaining to be tied to any such subjection, lifted up with the vigour of his own invention, doth grow, in effect, into another nature, in making things either better than nature bringeth forth, or, quite anew, forms such as never were in nature, as the heroes, demi-gods, cyclops, chimeras,

---

과 비교할 수 없는 것인지를 나 혼자만의 주장으로보다는 다른 학문들의 영역을 고찰함으로써 깨닫게 하고자 한다」. which는 관계지시대명사(that name의 뜻). I had rather were=I would like it (how high...is) would be.

***his:** its(이하에서도 언제나 유의할 것).

***times:** 「박자」(화음도 포함되어 있다).

***natural philosopher:** 「자연과학자」. *cf*. moral philosopher: '정신'철학자.

***still:** always

*모든 학문은 자연에 대해 종속적인 관계에 있지만, 시만은 자연을 능가하여, 자연보다 더 아름답다든가, 자연에 없는 것을 창조한다는 신플라톤 사상이 표현되고 있다.

furies, and such like; so as he goeth hand in hand with Nature, not enclosed within the narrow warrant of her*gifts, but freely ranging only within the zodiac of his own wit. Nature never set forth the earth in so rich tapestry as divers poets have done; neither with pleasant rivers, fruitful trees, sweet-smelling flowers, nor whatsoever else may make the too-much-loved earth more lovely; her world is brazen, the poets only deliver a golden.*

But let those things alone, and go to man—for whom as the other things are, so it seemeth in him her uttermost cunning is employed—and know whether she have brought forth so true a lover as Theagenes;* so constant a friend as Pylades;* so valiant a man as Orlando;* so right a prince as Xenophon's Cyrus;* so excellent a man every way as Virgil's Aeneas?* Neither let this be jestingly conceived, because the works of the one be essential, the other in imitation or fiction;* for any understanding knoweth the skill of the artificer standeth in*that idea, or fore-conceit of the work, and not in the work itself. And that the poet hath that idea is manifest, by delivering them forth in such excellency as he hath imagined them. Which delivering forth, also, is not wholly imaginative, as we are wont to say by them that build castles in the air; but so far substantially it worketh, not only to make a Cyrus, which had been but a particular excellency, as nature might have done,

---

***her:** Nature's. (만물이 사람을 위해 있고, 또한 사람 안에서 자연의 최고의 재간이 발휘되어 있다.)

***Theagenes, Pylades, Orlando, Cyrus, Aeneas:** 르네상스 시대 사람들이 애독하던 작품들 속의 주인공들.

***Neither...imitation or fiction:** 자연 (the one)의 작품 (즉 실제의 사실)은 실질적이나, 시 (the other)의 작품은 모방 또는 허구로 되어 있다고 해서 이 말을 우스개로 여기지 말라.

***standeth in:** consists in. 기술자나 제작자의 진짜 능력은 구체적인 공작물이 아니라 그 공작물에 대한 idea (또는 fore-conceit)에 있다는 생각은 실제보다 관념을 중시하는 플라톤 사상의 일단이다. 시인이 작품에서 영웅의 idea를 보여주면, 그를 본받아 많은 개별적 영웅이 생길 수 있다고 Sidney는 믿는다. 반면에 자연은 한번에 개별적 영웅을 하나씩밖에 낳을 수 없다.

but to bestow a Cyrus upon the world to make many Cyruses, if they will learn aright why and how that maker made him. Neither let it be deemed too saucy a comparison to balance the highest point of man's wit with the efficacy of nature; but rather give right honour to the Heavenly Maker* of that maker, who, having made man to His own likeness, set him beyond and over all the works of that second nature. Which in nothing he showeth so much as in poetry, when, with the force of a divine breath, he bringeth things forth far surpassing her doings, with no small argument to the incredulous of that first accursed fall of Adam,*—since our erected wit maketh us know what perfection is, and yet our infected will keepeth us from reaching unto it. But these arguments will by few be understood, and by fewer granted; thus much I hope will be given me, that the Greeks, with some probability of reason, gave him the name above all names of learning.

Now let us go to a more ordinary opening* of him, that the truth may be the more palpable; and so, I hope, though we get not so unmatched a praise as the etymology of his names will grant, yet his very description, which no man will deny, shall not justly be barred from a principal commendation.

Poesy, therefore, is an art of imitation, for so Aristotle termeth it in his word *Mimesis*,* that is to say, a representing, counterfeiting, or figuring forth; to speak metaphorically, a speaking picture, with this end, to teach and delight.*

Of this have been three several kinds. The chief, both in antiquity and excellency, were they that did imitate the incon-

---

***the Heavenly Maker:** 시인 (maker)을 만드신 거룩한 창조주, 즉 하느님. 하느님의 형상으로 사람을 만들어 자연을 다스리게 하셨다는 것이 기독교 신앙임.

***with no small argument...fall of Adam:** 불신자들에게 최초의 저주스런 아담의 타락을 증명하는 큰 증거 (argument)를 제공하며, 우리의 영혼은 타락 이전의 상태를 동경할 수 있으나 우리의 병든 의지로 말미암아 완전해질 수 없다는 기독교 사상.

***opening:** 「설명」.

****mimesis*:** [maimísis], imitation. Aristotle, *Poetics*, ch. 1.

*Horace, *Art of Poetry* 333—347.

ceivable excellencies of God. Such were David in his Psalms; Solomon in his Song of Songs, in his Ecclesiastes and Proverbs; Moses and Deborah in their Hymns;* and the writer of Job; which, beside other, the learned Emanuel Tremellius* and Franciscus Junius* do entitle the poetical part of the Scripture. Against these none will speak that hath the Holy Ghost in due holy reverence. In this kind, though in a full wrong divinity, were Orpheus, Amphion, Homer in his Hymns;* and many other, both Greeks and Romans. And this poesy must be used by whosoever will follow St. James's counsel* in singing psalms when they are merry; and I know is used with the fruit of comfort by some, when, in sorrowful pangs of their death-bringing sins, they find the consolation of the never-leaving goodness.

The second kind is of them that deal with matters philosophical: either moral, as Tyrtaeus, Phocylides, and Cato; or natural, as Lucretius and Virgil's Georgics; or astronomical, as Manilius and Pontanus; or historical, as Lucan;* which who mislike,* the fault is in their judgement, quite out of taste, and not in the sweet food of sweetly uttered knowledge.

But because this second sort is wrapped within the fold of the proposed subject, and takes not the free course of his own invention, whether they properly be poets or no let grammarians dispute, and go to the third, indeed right poets, of whom chiefly this question ariseth. Betwixt whom and these second is such a kind of difference as betwixt the meaner sort of

---

*Moses and Deborah in their Hymns: 모세의 찬송은 출애굽기 (Exodus) 15장, 신명기 (Deuteronomy) 32장, 33장에, 여자 판관 드보라의 찬송은 판관기 (Judges) 5장에 나옴.

*Emanuel Tremellius, Franciscus Junius: 히브리어 학자들. 16세기 후반에 성서를 라틴어로 번역함. 구약의 「욥기」를 〈시〉라고 칭했다.

*Homer in his Hymns: 호머의 것으로 전해지는 찬양시가 있으나 실은 후세의 작품임.

*St. James's counsel: 야고보는 그의 서한에서 찬송 부를 것을 권고하고 있다. 「야고보서」 5장 13절.

*Tyrtaeus, ..., Lucan: 이들 고대시인들은 정치나 윤리, 우주론, 농사법, 역사 등을 운문으로 읊고 있다.

*which who mislike: which if there are those who do not like.

painters, who counterfeit only such faces as are set before them, and the more excellent, who having no law but wit, bestow that in colours upon you which is fittest for the eye to see; as the constant though lamenting look of Lucretia, when she punished in herself another's fault; wherein he painteth not Lucretia, whom he never saw, but painteth the outward beauty of such a virtue.* For these third be they which most properly do imitate to teach and delight; and to imitate borrow nothing of what is, hath been, or shall be; but range, only reined with learned discretion, into the divine consideration of what may be and should be.* These be they that, as the first and most noble sort, may justly be termed *vates*;* so these are waited on in the excellentest languages and best understandings with the fore-described name of poets. For these, indeed, do merely* make to imitate, and imitate both to delight and teach, and delight to move men to take that goodness in hand, which without delight they would fly as from a stranger; and teach to make them know that goodness whereunto they are moved; which being the noblest scope to which ever any learning was directed, yet want there not idle tongues to bark at them.*

These be subdivided into sundry more special denominations. The most notable be the heroic, lyric, tragic, comic, satiric, iambic, elegiac, pastoral, and certain others, some of these being termed according to the matter they deal with, some by the sorts of verses they liked best to write in,—for indeed the greatest part of poets have apparelled their poetical

---

***Betwixt...Lucretia...the outward beauty of such a virtue:** Lucretia (Lucrece)는 남편에 대한 정절을 지키기 위해 자살한 로마의 열녀. 여기서 Sidney는 있는 그대로를 그릴 뿐인 평범한(mean) 화가와 상상력(wit)이 가는 대로 감동적으로 그리는 보다 훌륭한 화가를 비교하고 있다. 그래서 전설의 Lucretia를 그리려면, 단지 예쁜 여인을 그려서는 안되고 정절 자체의 아름다운 모습을 그려야 한다는 것이다.

*Aristotle, *poetics* 9장.

****vates*:** 라틴어로 예언자 및 시인을 뜻함.

***merely:** 「전적으로, 순전히」.

***yet...them:** 「'즐겁게 가르치는 시인'들을 향해 짖어대는 하릴없는 혓바닥들이 없지 않다」.

inventions in that numberous* kind of writing which is called verse. Indeed but apparelled, verse being but an ornament and no cause to poetry, since there have been many most excellent poets that never versified, and now swarm many versifiers that need never answer to the name of poets. For Xenophon, who did imitate so excellently as to give us *effigiem justi imperii*—the portraiture of a just empire, under the name of Cyrus* (as Cicero says of him) made therein an absolute heroical poem; so did Heliodorus in his sugared invention of that picture of love in Theagenes and Chariclea;* and yet both these writ in prose. Which I speak to show that it is not rhyming and versing that maketh a poet (no more than a long gown maketh an advocate, who, though he pleaded in armour, should be an advocate and no soldier,) but it is that feigning notable images of virtues, vices, or what else, with that delightful teaching, which must be the right describing note to know a poet by. Although indeed the Senate of Poets* hath chosen verse as their fittest raiment, meaning, as in matter they passed all in all, so in manner to go beyond them; not speaking, (table-talk fashion, or like men in a dream,) words as they chanceably* fall from the mouth, but peizing* each syllable of each word by just proportion, according to the dignity of the subject.

Now, therefore, it shall not be amiss, first to weigh this latter sort of poetry by his works, and then by his parts; and if in neither of these anatomies he be condemnable, I hope we shall obtain a more favourable sentence. This purifying of wit, this enriching of memory, enabling of judgement, and enlarging of

---

***numberous:** metrical(운율적인).

***Cyrus:** 고대 그리이스의 역사가요 전략가인 Xenophon이 쓴 Persia 대왕 Cyrus 전기 (*Cyropaedia*)를 말한다. Verse가 시의 요건은 아니라는 생각은 Aristotle에게서도 보인다.

***Theagenes and Chariclea:** 기원 4세기 Heliodorus가 그리이스어로 쓴 소설 *Aethiopica*의 남녀 주인공.

***the Senate of Poets:** 시인들 대다수의 의견이란 뜻.

***chanceably:** 「우연히」(내용이 우수한 만큼 형식도 우수할 필요가 있어서, 우연히 하는 말처럼 하지 않고 verse를 쓴다는 것).

***peizing:** weighing.

conceit, which commonly we call learning, under what name soever it come forth or to what immediate end soever it be directed, the final end is to lead and draw us to as high a perfection as our degenerate souls, made worse by their clayey lodgings, can be capable of. This, according to the inclination of man, bred many-formed impressions. For some that thought this felicity principally to be gotten by knowledge, and no knowledge to be so high or heavenly as acquaintance with the stars, gave themselves to astronomy; others, persuading themselves to be demi-gods if they knew the causes of things, became natural and supernatural philosophers. Some an admirable delight drew to music, and some the certainty of demonstration to the mathematics; but all, one and other, having this scope: to know, and by knowledge to lift up the mind from the dungeon of the body to the enjoying his own divine essence. But when by the balance of experience it was found that the astronomer, looking to the stars, might fall into a ditch, that the inquiring philosopher might be blind in himself, and the mathematician might draw forth a straight line with a crooked heart; then lo! did proof, the overruler of opinions, make manifest, that all these are but serving sciences, which, as they have each a private end in themselves, so yet are they all directed to the highest end of the mistress-knowledge, by the Greeks called *architektonikē*,* which stands, as I think, in the knowledge of a man's self, in the ethic and politic consideration, with the end of well-doing, and not of well-knowing only; even as the saddler's next* end is to make a good saddle, but his further end to serve a nobler faculty, which is horsemanship; so the horseman's to soldiery; and the soldier not only to have the skill, but to perform the practice of a soldier. So that the ending end of all earthly learning being virtuous action, those skills that most serve to bring forth that have a most just title to be princes over all the rest; wherein, if we can show, the poet is worthy to have it

---

architektonikē: 「옳은 판단력」. 선한 마음씨와 행위를 즐기는 것과 같은 정신적 함양.

next: nearest, immediate.

before any other competitors.

Among whom as principal challengers step forth the moral philosophers; whom, me thinketh,* I see coming toward me with a sullen gravity, (as though they could not abide vice by daylight,) rudely clothed, for to witness outwardly their contempt of outward things; with books in their hands against glory, whereto they set their names; sophistically speaking against subtlety; and angry with any man in whom they see the foul fault of anger. These men, casting largess* as they go of Definitions, Divisions, and Distinctions, with a scornful interrogative do soberly ask whether it be possible to find any path so ready to lead a man to virtue, as that which teacheth what virtue is, and teacheth it not only by delivering forth his very being, his causes and effects, but also by making known his enemy, Vice, which must be destroyed, and his cumbersome servant, Passion, which must be mastered, by showing the generalities that containeth it, and the specialities that are derived from it; lastly, by plain setting down how it extendeth itself out of the limits of a man's own little world, to the government of families, and maintaining of public societies?

The historian scarcely giveth leisure to the moralist to say so much, but that he, laden with old mouse-eaten records, authorizing himself for the most part upon other histories, whose greatest authorities are built upon the notable foundation of hearsay; having much ado to accord differing writers, and to pick truth out of partiality; better acquainted with a thousand years ago than with the present age, and yet better knowing how this word goeth than how his own wit runneth; curious for antiquities and inquisitive of novelties, a wonder to young folks and a tyrant in table-talk; denieth, in a great chafe, that any man for teaching of virtue and virtuous actions is comparable to him. 'I am *testis temporum, lux veritatis, vita memoriae, magistra vitae, nuntia vetustatis*,* etc. The philosopher,'

***me thinketh:** it seems to me.

***largess:** 다음에 of definitions...를 붙여서 읽을 것.

*'the light of life, the master of the times, the life of memory, the messenger of antiquity' (Cicero, De Oratore, II, 9, 36).

saith he, 'teacheth a disputative virtue, but I do an active. His virtue is excellent in the dangerless Academy of Plato, but mine showeth forth her honourable face in the battles of Marathon, Pharsalia, Poitiers, and Agincourt.* He teacheth virtue by certain abstract considerations, but I only bid you follow the footing of them that have gone before you. Old-aged experience goeth beyond the fine-witted philosopher; but I give the experience of many ages. Lastly, if he make the song-book, I put the learner's hand to the lute; and if he be the guide, I am the light.' Then would he allege you innumerable examples, conferring story by story, how much the wisest senators and princes have been directed by the credit of history, as Brutus, Alphonsus* of Aragon (and who not, if need be?). At length the long line of their disputation maketh a point in this, that the one giveth the precept, and the other the example.

Now whom shall we find, since the question standeth for the highest form in the school of learning, to be moderator? Truly, as me seemeth, the poet; and if not a moderator, even the man that ought to carry the title from them both, and much more from all other serving sciences. Therefore compare we the poet with the historian and with the moral philosopher; and if he go beyond them both, no other human skill can match him. For as for the divine,* with all reverence it is ever to be excepted, not only for having his scope as far beyond any of these as eternity exceedeth a moment, but even for passing each of these in themselves. And for the lawyer, though *Jus* be the daughter of Justice, and Justice the chief of virtues, yet because he seeketh to make men good rather *formidine poenae* than *virtutis amore*;* or, to say righter, doth not endeavour to make men good, but that their evil hurt not others; having no care, so he be a good citizen, how bad a man he be; therefore, as our wicked-

---

***Marathon, Pharsalia, Poitiers, Agincourt:** 모두 다 이름난 격전지들.

***Brutus, Alphonsus:** 15세기 Aragon과 Sicily의 현명하고 용감한 군주.

***divine:** 신학자(Sidney는 신학과 법학을 논외로 한다).

*'by fear of punishment rather than love of virtue' (Horace, *Epistles* I, 16, 52).

ness maketh him necessary, and necessity maketh him honourable, so is he not in the deepest truth to stand in rank with these, who all endeavour to take naughtiness away, and plant goodness even in the secretest cabinet of our souls. And these four are all that any way deal in that consideration of men's manners, which being the supreme knowledge, they that best breed it deserve the best commendation.

The philosopher therefore and the historian are they which would win the goal, the one by precept, the other by example; but both, not having both, do both halt. For the philosopher, setting down with thorny argument the bare rule, is so hard of utterance and so misty to be conceived, that one that hath no other guide but him shall wade in him till he be old, before he shall find sufficient cause to be honest. For his knowledge standeth so upon the abstract and general, that happy is that man who may understand him, and more happy that can apply what he doth understand. On the other side, the historian, wanting the precept, is so tied, not to what should be but to what is, to the particular truth of things and not to the general reason of things, that his example draweth no necessary consequence, and therefore a less fruitful doctrine.

Now doth the peerless poet perform both; for whatsoever the philosopher saith should be done, he giveth a perfect picture of it in some one by whom he presupposeth it was done, so as* he coupleth the general notion with the particular example. A perfect picture, I say; for he yieldeth to the powers of the mind an image of that whereof the philosopher bestoweth but a wordish description, which doth neither strike, pierce, nor possess the sight of the soul so much as that other doth. For as, in outward things, to a man that had never seen an elephant or a rhinoceros, who* should tell him most exquisitely all their shapes, colour, bigness, and particular marks; or of a gorgeous palace, the architecture, with declaring the full beauties, might well make the hearer able to repeat, as it were by rote,

---

***so as:** so that.

***who:** he who.

all he had heard, yet should never satisfy his inward conceit with being witness to itself of a true lively knowledge; but the same man, as soon as he might see those beasts well painted, or that house well in model, should straightways grow, without need of any description, to a judicial comprehending of them: so no doubt the philosopher, with his learned definitions, be it of virtues or vices, matters of public policy or private government, replenisheth the memory with many infallible grounds of wisdom, which notwithstanding lie dark before the imaginative and judging power, if they be not illuminated or figured forth by the speaking picture of poesy.

Tully* taketh much pains, and many times not without poetical helps, to make us know the force love of our country hath in us. Let us but hear old Anchises* speaking in the midst of Troy's flames, or see Ulysses, in the fullness of all Calypso's delights, bewail his absence from barren and beggarly Ithaca.* Anger, the Stoics said, was a short madness. Let but Sophocles bring you Ajax* on a stage, killing or whipping sheep and oxen, thinking them the army of Greeks, with their chieftains Agamemnon and Menelaus, and tell me if you have not a more familiar insight into anger, than finding in the schoolmen* his* genus and difference. See whether wisdom and temperance in Ulysses and Diomedes, valour in Achilles,* friendship in Nisus and Euryalus,* even to an ignorant man carry not an apparent shining. And, contrarily, the remorse of conscience in Oedipus; the soon-repenting pride of Agamemnon; the self-devouring cruelty in his father Atreus*; the violence of ambition

---

***Tully:** Cicero를 가리킴. *De Oratore* 196행 참조.

***Anchises:** Virgil의 *Aeneid*에 나오는 영웅 Aeneas의 부친.

***Ulysses...Ithaca:** Ulysses는 Calypso란 여신의 사랑을 받으나, 고향 Ithaca를 그리워한다 (*Odyssey*, 5).

***Ajax:** Sophocles의 희곡의 주인공.

***schoolmen:** 중세의 스콜라 철학자들.

***his:** its (=anger's).

***Diomedes, Achilles:** *Iliad*에 나오는 영웅.

***Nisus, Euryalus:** *Aeneid*에 나오는 인물.

***Agamemnon, Atreus:** Atreus의 두 아들 Agamemnon과 Menelaus에 대한 언급.

in the two Theban brothers;* the sour sweetness of revenge in Medea; and, to fall lower, the Terentian Gnatho and our Chaucer's Pandar,* so expressed that we now use their names to signify their trades; and finally, all virtues, vices, and passions so in their own natural states laid to the view, that we seem not to hear of them, but clearly to see through them.

But even in the most excellent determination of goodness, what philosopher's counsel can so readily direct a prince, as the feigned Cyrus in Xenophon? Or a virtuous man in all fortunes, as Aeneas in Virgil? Or a whole commonwealth, as the way of Sir Thomas More's Utopia? I say the way, because where Sir Thomas More erred, it was the fault of the man, and not of the poet; for that way of patterning a commonwealth was most absolute,* though he, perchance, hath not so absolutely performed it. For the question is, whether the feigned image of poesy, or the regular instruction of philosophy, hath the more force in teaching. Wherein if the philosophers have more rightly showed themselves philosophers than the poets have attained to the high top of their profession, (as in truth,

Mediocribus esse poetis
Non Di, non homines, non concessere columnae,)*

it is, I say again, not the fault of the art, but that by few men that art can be accomplished.

Certainly, even our Saviour Christ could as well have given the moral commonplaces of uncharitableness and humbleness as the divine narration of Dives and Lazarus*; or of disobedience and mercy, as that heavenly discourse of the lost child and the

---

***two Theban brothers:** Atreus와 그의 형제 Thyestes.

***Gnatho:** 로마의 극작가 Terence의 *Eunuchus*에 나오는 인물로, 이는 남에게 붙어 사는 기생충같은 인물의 대명사로 쓰인다.

***Pandar:** Chaucer의 *Troilus and Criseyde*에 나오는 인물로, 「뚜장이 남자」란 뜻으로 쓰인다.

***absolute:** perfect.

*'Mediocre poets are not endured by gods, men, or booksellers' (Horace, *Art of Poetry*, 372—3).

***Dives and Lazarus:** 부자 다이비즈와 걸인 나자로(누가복음 16 : 19—31).

gracious father;* but that his through-searching wisdom knew the estate of Dives burning in hell, and of Lazarus in Abraham's bosom, would more constantly, as it were, inhabit both the memory and judgement. Truly, for myself, me seems I see before mine eyes the lost child's disdainful prodigality turned to envy a swine's dinner; which by the learned divines are thought not historical acts, but instructing parables.

For conclusion, I say the philosopher teacheth, but he teacheth obscurely, so as the learned only can understand him; that is to say, he teacheth them that are already taught. But the poet is the food for the tenderest stomachs; the poet is indeed the right popular philosopher. Whereof Aesop's tales give good proof; whose pretty allegories, stealing under the formal tales of beasts, make many, more beastly than beasts, begin to hear the sound of virtue from those dumb speakers.

But now may it be alleged that if this imagining of matters be so fit for the imagination, then must the historian needs surpass, who bringeth you images of true matters, such as indeed were done, and not such as fantastically or falsely may be suggested to have been done. Truly, Aristotle himself, in his Discourse of Poesy,* plainly determineth this question, saying that poetry is *philosophoteron* and *spoudaioteron*, that is to say, it is more philosophical and more studiously serious than history. His reason is, because poesy dealeth with *katholou*, that is to say with the universal consideration, and the history with *kathekaston*, the particular. 'Now,' saith he, 'the universal weighs what is fit to be said or done, either in likelihood or necessity, which the poesy considereth in his imposed names; and the particular only marketh whether Alcibiades did, or suffered, this or that': thus far Aristotle. Which reason of his, as all his, is most full of reason.

For, indeed, if the question were whether it were better to have a particular act truly or falsely set down, there is no doubt which is to be chosen, no more than whether you had

*the lost child and the gracious father: 탕자의 비유(누가복음 15 : 11—32).
*Discourse of Poesy: Aristotle, *Poetics*, 9장.

rather have Vespasian's picture right as he was, or, at the painter's pleasure, nothing resembling. But if the question be for your own use and learning, whether it be better to have it set down as it should be or as it was, then certainly is more doctrinable the feigned Cyrus of Xenophon than the true Cyrus in Justin*; and the feigned Aeneas in Virgil than the right Aeneas in Dares Phrygius;* as to a lady that desired to fashion her countenance to the best grace, a painter should more benefit her to portrait a most sweet face, writing Canidia* upon it, than to paint Canidia as she was, who, Horace sweareth, was foul and ill-favoured.

If the poet do his part aright, he will show you in Tantalus,* Atreus, and such like, nothing that is not to be shunned; in Cyrus, Aeneas, Ulysses, each thing to be followed. Where the historian, bound to tell things as things were, cannot be liberal (without*he will be poetical,) of a perfect pattern, but, as in Alexander, or Scipio himself, show doings, some to be liked, some to be misliked; and then how will you discern what to follow, but by your own discretion, which you had without reading Quintus Curtius? And whereas a man may say, though in universal consideration of doctrine the poet prevaileth, yet that the history, in his saying such a thing was done, doth warrant a man more in that he shall follow, the answer is manifest: that if he stand upon that *was*,* as if he should argue, because it rained yesterday therefore it should rain today, then

---

***Cyrus in Justin, Aeneas in Dares Phrygius:** Cyrus에 관한 역사적 기술은 4세기경의 역사가 Justinius가 했고, Aeneas에 대해서도 사실적 진술은 Dares Phrygius가 했다. 역사적 사실을 알려면 역사서를 보아야 하겠지만, 인간에 대한 보편적 사실을 알려면 Xenophon과 Virgil의 작품을 보아야 한다.

***Canidia:** old witch in Horace, *Satires*, I. 8.

***Tantalus:** Atreus의 할아버지. 둘 다 친족의 살을 잘라 음식을 만든 죄인.

***without:** otherwise(역사를 도덕적으로 변경시키면 시인이 된다는 것).

***Quintus Curtius:** 연대 미상. Alexander의 전기를 씀.

***Alexander, Scipio:** 두 사람 다 좋은 점과 나쁜 점을 함께 가진 영웅들이므로, 그들의 전기에서 도덕을 배우려면 판단력이 온전치 못한 한 힘들다는 것.

****was*:** 과거의 사실.

indeed it hath some advantage to a gross conceit. But if he know an example only informs a conjectured likelihood, and so go by reason, the poet doth so far exceed him as he is to frame his example to that which is most reasonable, be it in warlike, politic, or private matters; where the historian in his bare *was* hath many times that which we call fortune* to over-rule the best wisdom. Many times he must tell events whereof he can yield no cause; or if he do, it must be poetically.

For, that a feigned example hath as much force to teach as a true example, (for as for to move, it is clear, since the feigned may be tuned to the highest key of passion,) let us take one example wherein a poet and a historian do concur. Herodotus* and Justin do both testify that Zopyrus, king Darius' faithful servant, seeing his master long resisted by the rebellious Babylonians, feigned himself in extreme disgrace of his king; for verifying of which he caused his own nose and ears to be cut off, and so flying to the Babylonians, was received, and for his known valour so far credited, that he did find means to deliver them over to Darius. Much like matter doth Livy record* of Tarquinius and his son. Xenophon excellently feigneth such another strategem, performed by Abradates in Cyrus' behalf. Now would I fain know, if occasion be presented unto you to serve your prince by such an honest dissimulation, why do you not as well learn it of Xenophon's fiction as of the other's verity? and, truly, so much the better, as you shall save your nose by the bargain; for Abradates did not counterfeit so far.

So, then, the best of the historian is subject to the poet; for whatsoever action or faction, whatsoever counsel, policy, or war-stratagem the historian is bound to recite, that may the poet, if he list,* with his imitation make his own, beautifying it both for further teaching and more delighting, as it pleaseth

---

***forfune:** 「우연」(합리적 · 도덕적으로 설명할 수 없는).

***Herodotus:** 그리이스의 역사가(B.C. 5세기경). 그의 역사서 3권에 다음의 이야기가 실려 있다.

***Livy record:** 로마의 역사가 Livy(Livius)의 역사서 1권.

***list:** pleases, likes.

him; having all, from Dante's Heaven to his Hell, under the authority of his pen. Which if I be asked what poets have done so? as I might well name some, yet say I, and say again, I speak of the art, and not of the artificer.

Now, to that which commonly is attributed to the praise of histories, in respect of the notable learning is gotten by marking the success, as though therein a man should see virtue exalted and vice punished, truly that commendation is peculiar to poetry and far off from history. For, indeed, poetry ever setteth virtue so out in her best colours, making Fortune* her well-waiting handmaid, that one must needs be enamoured of her.* Well may you see Ulysses in a storm, and in other hard plights; but they are but exercises of patience and magnanimity, to make them shine the more in the near following prosperity. And, of the contrary part, if evil men come to the stage, they ever go out, (as the tragedy writer answered to one that misliked the show of such persons) so manacled, as they little animate folks to follow them. But the historian, being captived to the truth of a foolish world, is many times a terror from well-doing, and an encouragement to unbridled wickedness. For see we not valiant Miltiades* rot in his fetters? The just Phocion* and the accomplished Socrates* put to death like traitors? The cruel Severus live prosperously? The excellent Severus* miserably murdered? Sylla and Marius dying in their beds? Pompey and Cicero slain then, when they would have thought exile a happiness? See we not virtuous Cato driven to kill himself, and rebel Caesar so advanced that his name yet, after sixteen hundred years, lasteth in the highest honour? And mark but even Caesar's own words of the forenamed Sylla, (who in that

---

***poetry...Fortune...of her:** 공평치 못한 이 세상 현실의 주인인 Fortune을 시에서는 마음대로 부리는 하녀로 삼아, 선한 자에게는 상을, 악한 자에게는 벌을 준다는 것.

*여기의 인물들은 고전 세계에서 선함에도 불구하고 억울하게 죽었든가, 악함에도 불구하고 행복하게 산 인물들. 즉 역사가 공평하지 못함을 증거하는 인물들이다. 특히 Severus는 동명이인으로, 선한 Severus와 악한 Severus가 있었다.

only did honestly, to put down his dishonest tyranny), *literas nescivit*:* as if want of learning caused him to do well. He meant it not by poetry,* which, not content with earthly plagues, deviseth new punishments in hell for tyrants; nor yet by philosophy, which teacheth *occidendos esse*;* but, no doubt, by skill in history, for that indeed can afford you Cypselus, Periander, Phalaris, Dionysius,* and I know not how many more of the same kennel, that speed well* enough in their abominable injustice or usurpation.

I conclude, therefore, that he excelleth history, not only in furnishing the mind with knowledge, but in setting it forward to that which deserveth to be called and accounted good; which setting forward, and moving to well-doing, indeed setteth the laurel crown upon the poet as victorious, not only of the historian, but over the philosopher, howsoever in teaching it may be questionable. For suppose it be granted, (that which I suppose with great reason may be denied,) that the philosopher, in respect of his methodical proceeding, doth teach more perfectly than the poet, yet do I think that no man is so much *philophilosophos** as to compare the philosopher in moving with the poet. And that moving is of a higher degree than teaching, it may by this appear, that it is well nigh both the cause and the effect of teaching; for who will be taught, if he be not moved with desire to be taught? And what so much good doth that teaching bring forth (I speak still of moral doctrine,) as that it moveth one to do that which it doth teach? For, as Aristotle saith, it is not *gnosis* but *praxis** must be the fruit; and how *praxis* can be, without being moved to practise, it is

---

**literas nescivit:* 'Sylla did not know literature' (Caesar가 Sylla를 비꼬아서 한 말. Sylla는 '무식해서' 권력을 스스로 양보하고 노년을 잘 살았음).

*'they are to be killed'; '악한 인물은 마땅히 죽여야 한다'는 Seneca의 생각에서 더 나아가, '문학은 악당을 지옥에 빠뜨려 징벌한다' (Dante의 지옥편).

***Cypselus, Periander, Phalaris, Dionysius:** 역대 악명높은 폭군들.

***speed well:** 「잘 살아가다」.

****philophilosophos:*** 'a lover of philosophers.'

***not *gnosis* but *praxis*:** not 'knowing' but 'doing'.

no hard matter to consider. The philosopher showeth you the way, he informeth you of the particularities, as well of the tediousness of the way, as of the pleasant lodging you shall have when your journey is ended, as of the many by-turnings* that may divert you from your way; but this is to no man but to him that will read him, and read him with attentive, studious painfulness; which constant desire whosoever hath in him, hath already passed half the hardness of the way, and therefore is beholding to the philosopher but for the other half. Nay, truly, learned men have learnedly thought, that where once reason hath so much overmastered passion as that the mind hath a free desire to do well, the inward light each mind hath in itself is as good as a philosopher's book; since in nature we know it is well to do well, and what is well and what is evil, although not in the words of art which philosophers bestow upon us; for out of natural conceit* the philosophers drew it. But to be moved to do that which we know, or to be moved with desire to know, ***hoc opus, hic labor est.****

Now therein of all sciences, (I speak still of human, and according to the human conceit,) is our poet the monarch. For he doth not only show the way, but giveth so sweet a prospect into the way as will entice any man to enter into it. Nay, he doth, as if your journey should lie through a fair vineyard, at the very first give you a cluster of grapes, that full of that taste you may long to pass further. He beginneth not with obscure definitions, which must blur the margin* with interpretations, and load the memory with doubtfulness. But he cometh to you with words set in delightful proportion, either accompanied with, or prepared for, the well-enchanting skill of music; and with a tale, forsooth, he cometh unto you, with a tale which holdeth children from play, and old men from the chimney-corner; and, pretending no more, doth intend the winning of

---

***by-turnings:** wrong roads.

***conceit:** idea (타고난 생각).

*'That is work, this is labor' (Virgil, *Aeneid*, Ⅵ. 129).

***margin:** 「책의 여백」(주석이 붙는 자리).

the mind from wickedness to virtue; even as the child is often brought to take most wholesome things, by hiding them in such other as have a pleasant taste,—which, if one should begin to tell them the nature of the aloes or rhubarb they should receive, would sooner take their physic at their ears than at their mouth. So is it in men, (most of which are childish in the best things, till they be cradled in their graves,) glad they will be to hear the tales of Hercules, Achilles, Cyrus, Aeneas; and, hearing them, must needs hear the right description of wisdom, valour, and justice; which, if they had been barely, (that is to say philosophically,) set out, they would swear they be brought to school again.

That imitation whereof poetry is, hath the most conveniency to nature of all other;* insomuch that, as Aristotle saith,* those things which in themselves are horrible, as cruel battles, unnatural monsters, are made in poetical imitation delightful. Truly, I have known men, that even with reading Amadis de Gaule,* (which, God knoweth, wanteth much of a perfect poesy,) have found their hearts moved to the exercise of courtesy, liberality, and especially courage. Who readeth Aeneas carrying old Anchises on his back, that wisheth not it were his fortune to perform so excellent an act? Whom do not those words of Turnus move, the tale of Turnus having planted his image in the imagination?

Fugientem haec terra videbit?
Usque adeone mori miserum est?*

Where the philosophers, as they scorn to delight, so must they be content little to move, saving wrangling whether virtue be the chief or the only good, whether the contemplative or the

---

***the most...other:** 「다른 무엇보다도 자연에 가장 잘 어울림」.

***those things...imitation delightful:** Aristotle, *Poetics*, 4 장.

***Amadis de Gaule:** 14세기 스페인의 Castille어로 쓰여진 Vasco de Lobeyra의 명작 로망스.

*'Shall this land see Turnus fleeing away? Is it so wretched a thing to die as that?' (Virgil, *Aeneid*, XII, 645—6).

active life do excel, which Plato and Boethius* well knew, and therefore made Mistress Philosophy very often borrow the masking raiment of Poesy. For even those hard-hearted evil men who think virtue a school-name,* and know no other good but *indulgere genio*,* and therefore despise the austere admonitions of the philosopher, and feel not the inward reason they stand upon, yet will be content to be delighted, which is all the good-fellow poet seemeth to promise; and so steal to see the form of goodness (which seen, they cannot but love) ere themselves be aware, as if they took a medicine of cherries.*

Infinite proofs of the strange effects of this poetical invention might be alleged; only two shall servé, which are so often remembered as I think all men know them. The one of Menenius Agrippa,* who, when the whole people of Rome had resolutely divided themselves from the senate, with apparent show of utter ruin, though he were, for that time, an excellent orator, came not among them upon trust either of figurative speeches or cunning insinuations, and much less with far-fetched maxims of philosophy, which, (especially if they were Platonic,) they must have learned geometry before they could well have conceived; but, forsooth, he behaves himself like a homely and familiar poet. He telleth them a tale, that there was a time when all the parts of the body made a mutinous conspiracy against the belly, which they thought devoured the fruits of each other's labour; they concluded they would let so unprofitable a spender starve. In the end, to be short—for the tale is notorious, and as notorious that it was a tale—with punishing the belly they plagued themselves. This, applied by him, wrought such effect in the people, as I never read that ever words brought forth but then so sudden and so good an

***Boethius:** 중세의 철학자. 그의 *Consolation of Philosophy*는 중세와 르네상스를 통해 애독되었다.

***a school-name:** schola 철학에서 논하는 명사.

******indulgere genio:*** 'to indulge one's nature.'

***a medicine of cherries:** 「앵두즙에 탄 쓴 약」. 오늘날의 코푸시럽같은 것.

***Menenius Agrippa:** 로마의 정치가. 원로원 회원.

alteration; for upon reasonable conditions a perfect reconcilement ensued.

The other is of Nathan the prophet,* who, when the holy David had so far forsaken God as to confirm adultery with murder, when he was to do the tenderest office of a friend, in laying his own shame before his eyes, (sent by God to call again so chosen a servant,) how doth he it but by telling of a man whose beloved lamb was ungratefully taken from his bosom? The application most divinely true, but the discourse itself feigned; which made David (I speak of the second and instrumental cause) as in a glass to see his own filthiness, as that heavenly Psalm of Mercy* well testifieth.

By these, therefore, examples and reasons, I think it may be manifest that the poet, with that same hand of delight, doth draw the mind more effectually than any other art doth. And so a conclusion not unfitly ensueth: that as virtue is the most excellent resting-place for all worldly learning to make his end of, so poetry, being the most familiar to teach it, and most princely to move towards it, in the most excellent work is the most excellent workman.

But I am content not only to decipher him by his works, (although works in commendation or dispraise must ever hold a high authority,) but more narrowly will examine his parts; so that, as in a man, though all together may carry a presence full of majesty and beauty, perchance in some one defectious piece we may find a blemish.

Now in his parts, kinds, or species, (as you list to term them,) it is to be noted that some poesies have coupled together two or three kinds, as tragical and comical, whereupon is risen the tragi-comical; some, in the like manner, have mingled prose and verse, as Sannazzaro* and Boethius; some have mingled matters heroical and pastoral; but that cometh all to one in this question, for, if severed they be good, the conjunction cannot

---

***Nathan the prophet:** 이 이야기는 구약 Samuel 상 12장 1—7절에 있음.
***Psalm of Mercy:** 다윗왕이 죄를 뉘우치고 지은 시편 51편.
***Sannazzaro, Giacopo:** 15-16세기 이탈리아의 pastoral romance 작가.

be hurtful. Therefore, perchance forgetting some, and leaving some as needless to be remembered, it shall not be amiss in a word to cite the special kinds, to see what faults may be found in the right use of them.

Is it then the pastoral poem which is misliked?—for perchance where the hedge is lowest they will soonest leap over.* Is the poor pipe* disdained, which sometimes out of Meliboeus'* mouth can show the misery of people under hard lords and ravening soldiers, and again, by Tityrus,* what blessedness is derived to them that lie lowest from the goodness of them that sit highest? sometimes, under the pretty tales of wolves and sheep, can include the whole considerations of wrong-doing and patience; sometimes show that contention for trifles can get but a trifling victory; where perchance a man may see that even Alexander and Darius, when they strove who should be cock of this world's dunghill, the benefit they got was that the after-livers may say:

> Haec memini et victum frustra contendere Thyrsim;
> Ex illo Corydon, Corydon est tempore nobis.*

Or is it the lamenting elegiac, which in a kind heart would move rather pity than blame; who bewaileth, with the great philosopher Heraclitus,* the weakness of mankind and the wretchedness of the world; who surely is to be praised, either for compassionate accompanying just causes of lamentation, or for rightly painting out how weak be the passions of woefulness?

Is it the bitter but wholesome iambic,* who rubs the galled

***where the hedge...leap over:** '울타리가 낮으면 뛰어넘기 쉽다.' 전원시 (pastoral)는 「미천한」 장르이므로 얕잡아보기 쉽다는 것.

***poor pipe:** 「시골의 피리」, 즉 전원시란 뜻.

***Meliboeus, Tityrus:** 둘 다 Virgil의 전원시에 나오는 인물. 유럽의 전원시에는 농민, 목동의 입을 통하여 현실을 비판하는 전통이 있었다. 때때로 동물우화가 등장하기도 한다.

*'I recall those things, and that the conquered Thyrsis strove in vain: From that time Corydon for us is Corydon.' (Virgil, *Eclogue* VII, 69—70).

***Heraclitus:** B.C. 6세기 초의 그리이스의 철인.

***iambic:** 영시의 약강보격을 말하지 않고, 이 운률로 표현된 강한 풍자시를 뜻함.

mind, in making shame the trumpet of villainy with bold and open crying out against naughtiness?

Or the satiric? who

> Omne vafer vitium ridenti tangit amico;*

who sportingly never leaveth till he make a man laugh at folly, and at length ashamed to laugh at himself, which he cannot avoid without avoiding the folly; who, while *circum praecordia ludit*,* giveth us to feel how many headaches a passionate life bringeth us to,—how, when all is done,

> Est Ulubris, animus si nos non deficit aequus.*

No, perchance it is the comic; whom naughty play-makers and stage-keepers have justly made odious. To the argument of abuse I will answer after. Only thus much now is to be said, that the comedy is an imitation of the common errors of our life, which he representeth in the most ridiculous and scornful sort that may be, so as it is impossible that any beholder can be content to be such a one. Now, as in geometry the oblique must be known as well as the right and in arithmetic the odd as well as the even; so in the actions of our life who seeth not the filthiness of evil, wanteth a great foil to perceive the beauty of virtue. This doth the comedy handle so, in our private and domestical matters, as with hearing it we get, as it were, an experience what is to be looked for of a niggardly Demea,* of a crafty Davus,* of a flattering Gnatho, of a vain-glorious Thraso;* and not only to know what effects are to be expected, but to know who be such, by the signifying badge given them by the comedian. And little reason hath any man to say that men learn evil by seeing it so set out, since, as I said before, there is

*'The rogue touches every vice while causing his friend to laugh' (Persius, *Satires* I, 116).

*'He plays around the heart-strings' (*Ibid*)

*'Happiness is found in Ulubrae if we have a sane mind' (Horace, *Epistles* I, ii. 30)

***Demea, Davus, Thraso:** Demea 는 수전노, Davus 는 꾀장이 하인, Thraso 는 허풍선이 군인. 모두 Terence 의 희극에 나오는 인물들.

no man living, but by the force truth hath in nature, no sooner seeth these men play their parts, but wisheth them *in pistrinum*,* although perchance the sack of his own faults lie so behind his back, that he seeth not himself to dance the same measure,—whereto yet nothing can more open his eyes than to find his own actions contemptibly set forth.

So that the right use of comedy will, I think, by nobody be blamed, and much less of the high and excellent tragedy, that openeth the greatest wounds, and showeth forth the ulcers that are covered with tissue; that maketh kings fear to be tyrants, and tyrants manifest their tyrannical humours; that with stirring the effects of admiration and commiseration teacheth the uncertainty of this world, and upon how weak foundations gilden roofs are builded; that maketh us know:

> Qui sceptra saevus duro imperio regit,
> Timet timentes, metus in auctorem redit.*

But how much it can move, Plutarch yieldeth a notable testimony of the abominable tyrant Alexander Pheraeus;* from whose eyes a tragedy, well made and represented, drew abundance of tears, who without all pity had murdered infinite numbers, and some of his own blood; so as he that was not ashamed to make matters for tragedies, yet could not resist the sweet violence of a tragedy. And if it wrought no further good in him, it was that he, in despite of himself, withdrew himself from hearkening to that which might mollify his hardened heart. But it is not the tragedy they do mislike, for it were too absurd to cast out so excellent a representation of whatsoever is most worthy to be learned.

Is it the lyric that most displeaseth, who with his tuned lyre and well-accorded voice, giveth praise, the reward of virtue, to

---

***pistrinum:** 로마의 인력 방앗간. 노예가 벌로 돌림.

*'The savage ruler who wields the sceptre with a hard hand fears his frightened subjects, and fear thus returns to the author of it' (Seneca, *Oedipus*, 705—6)

***Alexander Pheraeus:** 고대 그리이스의 폭군. Plutarch의 *Life of Pelopidas* 29장에 나옴.

virtuous acts; who giveth moral precepts and natural problems; who sometimes raiseth up his voice to the height of the heavens, in singing the lauds of the immortal God? Certainly I must confess mine own barbarousness; I never heard the old song of Percy and Douglas* that I found not my heart moved more than with a trumpet; and yet it is sung but by some blind crowder,* with no rougher voice than rude style; which being so evil apparalled in the dust and cobwebs of that uncivil age, what would it work, trimmed in the gorgeous eloquence of Pindar?* In Hungary I have seen it the manner at all feasts, and other such meetings, to have songs of their ancestors' valour, which that right soldier-like nation think the chiefest kindlers of brave courage. The incomparable Lacedaemonians* did not only carry that kind of music ever with them to the field, but even at home, as such songs were made, so were they all content to be singers of them; when the lusty men were to tell what they did, the old men what they had done, and the young men what they would do. And where a man may say that Pindar many times praiseth highly victories of small moment, matters rather of sport than virtue; as it may be answered, it was the fault of the poet, and not of the poetry, so indeed the chief fault was in the time and custom of the Greeks, who set those toys at so high a price that Philip of Macedon* reckoned a horserace won at Olympus among his three fearful felicities. But as the inimitable Pindar often did, so is that kind most capable and most fit to awake the thoughts from the sleep of idleness, to embrace honourable enterprises.

There rests the heroical, whose very name, I think, should daunt all backbiters. For by what conceit can a tongue be directed to speak evil of that which draweth with it no less

---

***Percy and Douglas:** 두 사람은 스콧틀랜드의 용감한 군인들로, 그들에 관한 "Chevy Chase"란 ballad가 전해진다.

***crowder:** fiddler. 또는 떠돌이 노랫꾼.

***Pindar:** B.C. 5세기 경의 그리이스의 서정시인.

***Lacedaemonians:** 고대 그리이스의 Lacedaemónia (Sparta)의 주민들.

***Philip of Macedon:** Alexander 대왕의 부친.

champions than Achilles, Cyrus, Aeneas, Turnus, Tydeus, Rinaldo?* who doth not only teach and move to a truth, but teacheth and moveth to the most high and excellent truth; who maketh magnanimity and justice shine through all misty fearfulness and foggy desires; who, if the saying of Plato and Tully be true, that who could see virtue would be wonderfully ravished with the love of her beauty, this man setteth her out to make her more lovely, in her holiday apparel, to the eye of any that will deign not to disdain until they understand. But if anything be already said in the defence of sweet poetry, all concurreth to the maintaining the heroical, which is not only a kind, but the best and most accomplished kind of poetry. For, as the image of each action stirreth and instructeth the mind, so the lofty image of such worthies most inflameth the mind with desire to be worthy, and informs with counsel how to be worthy. Only let Aeneas be worn in the tablet of your memory, how he governeth himself in the ruin of his country; in the preserving his old father, and carrying away his religious ceremonies; in obeying the gods' commandment to leave Dido,* though not only all passionate kindness, but even the human consideration of virtuous gratefulness, would have craved other* of him; how in storms, how in sports, how in war, how in peace, how a fugitive, how victorious, how besieged, how besieging, how to strangers, how to allies, how to enemies, how to his own; lastly, how in his inward self, and how in his outward government;* and I think, in a mind not prejudiced with a prejudicating humour, he will be found in excellency fruitful. Yea, even as Horace saith, *melius Chrysippo et Crantore*.* But, truly,

---

***Archilles, Cyrus, Aeneas, Turnus, Tydeus, Rinaldo:** 이들은 모두 heroic poetry의 영웅들.

***Dido:** *Aeneid*에 나오는 Carthago의 여왕. Aeneas가 사랑에 빠졌으나, 새 나라를 건설해야 하는 책임을 완수하기 위해 버리고 떠나자 자살한다.

***other:** otherwise.

***government:** 「행위」.

*'Better than do Chrysippus and Crantor' (*Epistles*, I, 2, 4). 이 두 사람은 3류 철학자. 따라서 그들에게서 배우기보다는 시인에게서 배우는 게 낫다는 말.

I imagine it falleth out with these poet-whippers as with some good women who often are sick, but in faith they cannot tell where. So the name of poetry is odious to them, but neither his cause nor effects, neither the sum that contains him* nor the particularities descending from him, give any fast handle* to their carping dispraise.

Since, then, poetry is of all human learnings the most ancient and of most fatherly antiquity, as from whence other learnings have taken their beginnings; since it is so universal that no learned nation doth despise it, nor no barbarous nation is without it; since both Roman and Greek gave divine names unto it, the one of prophesying, the other of making, and that indeed that name of making is fit for him, considering that whereas other arts retain themselves within their subject, and receive, as it were, their being from it, the poet only, bringeth his own stuff, and doth not learn a conceit out of a matter, but maketh matter for a conceit; since neither his description nor his end containeth any evil, the thing described cannot be evil; since his effects be so good as to teach goodness, and delight the learners of it; since therein (namely in moral doctrine, the chief of all knowledges,) he doth not only far pass the historian, but for instructing is well nigh comparable to the philosopher, and for moving leaveth him behind him; since the Holy Scripture, (wherein there is no uncleanness,) hath whole parts in it poetical, and that even our Saviour Christ vouchsafed to use the flowers* of it; since all his kinds are not only in their united forms, but in their several dissections fully commendable; I think, and think I think rightly, the laurel crown appointed for triumphing captains doth worthily, of all other learnings, honour the poet's triumph.

But because we have ears as well as tongues, and that the

***falleth out:** happens.

***poet-whippers:** 「시인을 공격하는 자들」.

***the sum...him:** the total of its(poetry's) value.

***handle:** 「근거」.

***flowers:** 「시의 정수」(비유적 표현법).

lightest reasons that may be will seem to weigh greatly, if nothing be put in the counter-balance, let us hear, and, as well as we can, ponder, what objections be made against this art, which may be worthy either of yielding or answering.

First, truly, I note not only in these *misomousoi*,* poet-haters, but in all that kind of people who seek a praise by dispraising others, that they do prodigally spend a great many wandering words in quips and scoffs, carping and taunting at each thing which, by stirring the spleen, may stay the brain from a through-beholding the worthiness of the subject. Those kind of objections, as they are full of a very idle easiness (since there is nothing of so sacred a majesty but that an itching tongue may rub itself upon it), so deserve they no other answer, but, instead of laughing at the jest, to laugh at the jester. We know a playing wit can praise the discretion of an ass, the comfortableness of being in debt, and the jolly commodity of being sick of the plague. So of the contrary side, if we will turn Ovid's verse,

Ut lateat virtus proximitate mali,*

'that good lie hid in nearness of the evil,' Agrippa* will be as merry in showing the vanity of science, as Erasmus* was in commending of folly; neither shall any man or matter escape some touch of these smiling railers. But for Erasmus and Agrippa, they had another foundation than the superficial part would promise. Marry,* these other pleasant fault-finders, who will correct the verb before they understand the noun, and confute others' knowledge before they confirm their own, I would have them only remember that scoffing cometh not of wisdom; so as the best title in true English they get with their merriments is to be called good fools, for so have our grave

---

**misomousoi:* poet-haters. 괜히 시인을 미워하는 사람. 좋은 것을 보면 흉보지 않고는 못배기는 사람들의 일종.

*Ovid, *Ars Amatoria*, 2, 662

***Agrippa:** 16세기 초 프랑스의 기발한 학자. 〈지식의 불확실성과 허무에 대하여〉 저술.

***Erasmus:** 르네상스 시대 화란의 학자. 〈우신예찬〉을 저술.

***Marry:** 「진정！」(감탄사).

forefathers ever termed that humorous kind of jesters.

But that which giveth greatest scope to their scorning humours is rhyming and versing. It is already said, (and as I think truly said,) it is not rhyming and versing that maketh poesy. One may be a poet without versing, and a versifier without poetry. But yet presuppose it were inseparable (as indeed it seemeth Scaliger* judgeth,) truly it were an inseparable commendation. For if *oratio* next to *ratio*, speech next to reason, be the greatest gift bestowed upon mortality, that cannot be praiseless which doth most polish that blessing of speech; which considereth each word, not only, (as a man may say,) by his forcible quality, but by his best-measured quantity; carrying even in themselves a harmony, without,* perchance, number, measure, order, proportion be in our time grown odious.

But lay aside the just praise it hath by being the only fit speech for music (music, I say, the most divine striker of the senses,) thus much is undoubtedly true, that if reading be foolish without remembering, memory being the only treasurer of knowledge, those words which are fittest for memory are likewise most convenient for knowledge. Now that verse far exceedeth prose in the knitting up of the memory, the reason is manifest; the words, (besides their delight, which hath a great affinity to memory,) being so set, as one cannot be lost but the whole work fails; which, accusing itself, calleth the remembrance back to itself, and so most strongly confirmeth it. Besides, one word so, as it were, begetting another, as, be it in rhyme or measured verse, by the former a man shall have a near guess to the follower. Lastly, even they that have taught the art of memory have showed nothing so apt for it as a certain room divided into many places, well and throughly known;

***Scaliger:** 16세기 이탈리아의 군인, 평론가.

***without:** unless.

*운율이 없이도 산문의 시가 있을 수 있으나, 운문은 아름다움을 더해주고 또한 기억을 돕는 효과가 있다는 것으로, 일정한 가락을 기억하면 그 운율에 실린 말도 따라서 기억된다는 것이다. 예컨대 「구구단」은 운율이랄 수 있다.

now that hath the verse in effect perfectly, every word having his natural seat, which seat must needs make the word remembered. But what needeth more in a thing so known to all men? Who is it that ever was a scholar that doth not carry away some verses of Virgil, Horace, or Cato, which in his youth he learned, and even to his old age serve him for hourly lessons? as:

> Percontatorem fugito, nam garrulus idem est.
>
> Dum sibi quisque placet, credula turba sumus.

But the fitness it hath for memory is notably proved by all delivery of arts, wherein, for the most part, from grammar to logic, mathematic, physic, and the rest, the rules chiefly necessary to be borne away are compiled in verses. So that verse being in itself sweet and orderly, and being best for memory, the only handle of knowledge, it must be in jest that any man can speak against it.

Now, then, go we to the most important imputations laid to the poor poets: for aught I can yet learn they are these.

First, that there being many other more fruitful knowledges, a man might better spend his time in them than in this.*

Secondly, that it is the mother of lies.

Thirdly, that it is the nurse of abuse,* infecting us with many pestilent desires, with a siren's sweetness drawing the mind to the serpent's tail of sinful fancies, and herein especially comedies give the largest field to ear,* as Chaucer saith; how, both in other nations and in ours, before poets did soften us, we were full of courage, given to martial exercises, the pillars of manlike liberty, and not lulled asleep in shady idleness with poets' pastimes.

And, lastly and chiefly, they cry out with an open mouth, as if they had overshot Robin Hood, that Plato* banished them

---

***this:** poetry.

***abuse:** corruption 의 뜻.

***ear:** plough. 속담으로, "가장 많은 기회를 제공한다"는 뜻. Chaucer 의 *Knight's Tale* 29에 이 속담이 인용되어 있다.

*Plato, *The Republic*, X

out of his Commonwealth. Truly this is much, if there be much truth in it.

First, to the first: that a man might better spend his time is a reason indeed; but it doth, (as they say,) but *petere principium.** For if it be, as I affirm, that no learning is so good as that which teacheth and moveth to virtue, and that none can both teach and move thereto so much as poesy, then is the conclusion manifest that ink and paper cannot be to a more profitable purpose employed. And certainly, though a man should grant their first assumption, it should follow, (me thinks,) very unwillingly, that good is not good because better is better. But I still and utterly deny that there is sprung out of earth a more fruitful knowledge.

To the second, therefore, that they should be the principal liars, I answer paradoxically, but truly, I think truly, that of all writers under the sun the poet is the least liar, and though he would, as a poet, can scarcely be a liar. The astronomer, with his cousin the geometrician, can hardly escape when they take upon them to* measure the height of the stars. How often, think you, do the physicians lie, when they aver things good for sicknesses, which afterwards send Charon a great number of souls drowned in a potion before they come to his ferry?* And no less of the rest which take upon them to affirm. Now, for the poet, he nothing affirmeth, and therefore never lieth. For, as I take it, to lie is to affirm that to be true which is false; so as the other artists, and especially the historian, affirming many things, can, in the cloudy knowledge of mankind, hardly escape from many lies. But the poet, as I said before, never affirmeth. The poet never maketh any circles about your imagination* to conjure you to believe for true what he writeth. He citeth not authorities of other histories, but even for his entry* calleth the

---

**petere principium:* 'Beg the question'(그 전제부터가 문제된다).

***take...to...:** 「...의 책임을 떠맡다」.

***which...potion:** 의사가 약(potion)을 잘못 써서 지옥 황천나루터의 사공 Charon에게 보내는 사람(즉, 죽은 자)이 무수하다는 뜻.

***The poet...imagination:** 「당신의 상상을 속이려고 요술을 부리지 않는다」.

***entry:** introduction:

sweet Muses to inspire into him a good invention; in troth, not labouring to tell you what is or is not, but what should or should not be. And therefore, though he recount things not true, yet because he telleth them not for true, he lieth not; without* we will say that Nathan lied in his speech, before alleged, to David; which, as a wicked man durst scarce say, so think I none so simple would say that Aesop lied in the tales of his beasts; for who thinketh that Aesop wrote it for actually true, were well worthy to have his name chronicled among the beasts he writeth of. What child is there that, coming to a play, and seeing Thebes written in great letters upon an old door, doth believe that it is Thebes? If then a man can arrive, at that child's-age, to know that the poet's persons and doings are but pictures what should be, and not stories what have been, they will never give the lie to things not affirmatively, but allegorically and figuratively written. And therefore, as in history looking for truth, they may go away full-fraught with falsehood, so in poesy looking for fiction, they shall use the narration but as an imaginative ground-plot of a profitable invention. But hereto is replied that the poets give names to men they write of, which argueth a conceit of an actual truth, and so, not being true, proveth a falsehood. And doth the lawyer lie then, when, under the names of John a Stile, and John a Noakes,* he putteth his case? But that is easily answered. Their naming of men is but to make their picture the more lively, and not to build any history. Painting men, they cannot leave men nameless. We see we cannot play at chess but that we must give names to our chess-men; and yet, me thinks, he were a very partial champion of truth that would say we lied for giving a piece of wood the reverend title of a bishop.* The poet nameth Cyrus and Aeneas no other way than to show

---

***without:** unless.

***John a Stile, John a Noakes:** 재산 관계 재판에서 원고를 가상적으로 부르는 익명. 우리말에서 김 아무개, 또는 홍 길동 따위로 부르는 것과 같은 예. 현재는 Doe, Roe 등으로 쓰임.

***bishop:** 서양장기의 말의 하나 (Knight, Bishop, 등등).

what men of their fames, fortunes, and estates should do.

Their third is, how much it abuseth men's wit, training it to wanton sinfulness and lustful love. For indeed that is the principal, if not the only, abuse I can hear alleged. They say the comedies rather teach than reprehend amorous conceits. They say the lyric is larded with* passionate sonnets, the elegiac weeps the want of his mistress, and that even to the heroical Cupid hath ambitiously climbed. Alas! Love, I would thou couldst as well defend thyself as thou canst offend others! I would those on whom thou dost attend could either put thee away, or yield good reason why they keep thee! But grant love of beauty to be a beastly fault, (although it be very hard, since only man, and no beast, hath that gift to discern beauty); grant* that lovely name of Love to deserve all hateful reproaches, (although even some of my masters the philosophers spent a good deal of their lamp-oil* in setting forth the excellency of it): grant, I say, whatsoever they will have granted,—that not only love, but lust, but vanity, but, (if they list,) scurrility, possesseth many leaves of the poets' books; yet think I, when this is granted, they will find their sentence may with good manners put the last words foremost, and not say that poetry abuseth man's wit, but that man's wit abuseth poetry. For I will not deny, but that man's wit may make poesy, (which should be *eikastikē*,* which some learned have defined, figuring forth good things), to be *phantastikē*,* which doth contrariwise infect the fancy with unworthy objects; as the painter that should give to the eye either some excellent perspective, or some fine picture fit for building or fortification, or containing in it some notable example, as Abraham sacrificing his son Isaac, Judith* killing

---

***lard with:** 「...으로 장식하다」.

***grant:** 「설사 ...을 인정하더라도」.

***spend lamp-oil:** 「밤에 연구하느라고 등유를 소비하다」.

******Eikastike, Phantastike:*** 앞의 것은 사물을 정확하고 유익하게 모방하는 능력, 뒤의 것은 환상적으로 또는 눈속임으로 모방하는 능력 (Plato, *Sophists*).

***Judith:** 앗수르의 장군 Holofernes를 죽인 유태인 여걸 (구약, 외경 「유딧」).

Holofernes, David fighting with Goliath, may leave those, and please an ill-pleased eye with wanton shows of better-hidden matters.* But what! shall the abuse of a thing make the right use odious? Nay, truly, though I yield that poesy may not only be abused, but that being abused, by the reason of his sweet charming force, it can do more hurt than any other army of words, yet shall it be so far from concluding that the abuse should give reproach to the abused, that contrariwise it is a good reason, that whatsoever, being abused, doth most harm, being rightly used—and upon the right use each thing receiveth his title—doth most good. Do we not see the skill of physic,* (the best rampire* to our often-assaulted bodies,) being abused, teach poison, the most violent destroyer? Doth not knowledge of law, whose end is to even and right all things, being abused, grow the crooked fosterer of horrible injuries? Doth not, (to go to the highest,) God's word abused, breed heresy; and his Name abused, become blasphemy? Truly a needle cannot do much hurt, and as truly (with leave of ladies be it spoken,) it cannot do much good. With a sword thou mayst kill thy father, and with a sword thou mayst defend thy prince and country. So that, as in their calling poets the fathers of lies they say nothing, so in this their argument of abuse they prove the commendation.

They allege herewith, that before poets began to be in price* our nation hath set their hearts' delight upon action, and not upon imagination; rather doing things worthy to be written, than writing things fit to be done. What that before-time was, I think scarcely Sphinx can tell; since no memory is so ancient that hath the precedence of poetry. And certain it is that, in our plainest homeliness, yet never was the Albion nation* without poetry. Marry, this argument, though it be levelled against

---

***better hidden matter:** 「감추는 게 더 좋을 사실들」.

***physic:** 「의학」.

***rampire:** rampart, 「보루」.

***to be in price:** to be valued.

***Albion nation:** 영국. 영국의 가장 오랜 이름.

poetry, yet is it indeed a chain-shot* against all learning, or bookishness, as they commonly term it. Of such mind were certain Goths, of whom it is written that, having in the spoil of a famous city taken a fair library, one hangman (belike* fit to execute the fruits of their wits) who had murdered a great number of bodies, would have set fire on it. 'No,' said another very gravely, 'take heed what you do; for while they are busy about these toys, we shall with more leisure conquer their countries.' This, indeed, is the ordinary doctrine of ignorance, and many words sometimes I have heard spent in it; but because this reason is generally against all learning, as well as poetry, or rather all learning but poetry; because it were too large a digression to handle, or at least too superfluous, (since it is manifest that all government of action is to be gotten by knowledge, and knowledge best by gathering many knowledges, which is reading;) I only, with Horace, to him that is of that opinion

Jubeo stultum esse libenter;*

for as for poetry itself, it is the freest from this objection, for poetry is the companion of the camps. I dare undertake, Orlando Furioso* or honest King Arthur will never displease a soldier; but the quiddity of *ens*, and *prima materia*,* will hardly agree with a corselet. And therefore, as I said in the beginning, even Turks and Tartars are delighted with poets. Homer, a Greek, flourished before Greece flourished; and if to a slight conjecture a conjecture may be opposed, truly it may seem, that as by him their learned men took almost their first light of knowledge, so their active men received their first motions of courage. Only Alexander's example may serve, who by

***chain-shot:** 쇠줄을 서로 연결시킨 공격용 포환.
***belike:** perhaps.
*'I ask him to be as much of a fool as he wishes' (*Satires*, I, i. 63).
***Orlando Furioso:** 16세기 이탈리아 서사시인 Ariosto의 동명 작품의 영웅.
****ens, prima materia:*** 존재, 근본질료 등 중세철학의 개념. (군인과 부합되지 않는 것은 시가 아니라 철학이라는 뜻).

Plutarch is accounted of such virtue, that Fortune was not his guide but his footstool;* whose acts speak for him, though Plutarch did not; indeed the phoenix of warlike princes. This Alexander left his schoolmaster, living Aristotle, behind him, but took dead Homer with him. He put the philosopher Callisthenes* to death, for his seeming philosophical, indeed mutinous, stubbornness; but the chief thing he was ever heard to wish for was that Homer had been alive. He well found he received more bravery of mind by the pattern of Achilles, than by hearing the definition of fortitude. And therefore if Cato misliked Fulvius for carrying Ennius with him to the field,* it may be answered that if Cato misliked it, the noble Fulvius liked it, or else he had not done it. For it was not the excellent Cato Uticensis, (whose authority I would much more have reverenced;) but it was the former, in truth a bitter punisher of faults, but else a man that had never well sacrificed to the Graces. He misliked and cried out upon all Greek learning; and yet, being fourscore years old, began to learn it, belike fearing that Pluto understood not Latin.* Indeed, the Roman laws allowed no person to be carried to the wars but he that was in the soldiers' roll. And therefore though Cato misliked his unmustered person,* he misliked not his work. And if he had, Scipio Nasica,* judged by common consent the best Roman,

---

***Fortune...footstool:** 운수의 여신은 그의 인도자가 아니라 발등이었다. 즉, Alexander는 운수에 끌려다닌 게 아니라, 오히려 운수를 타눌렀다.

***Callisthenes:** Alexander와 함께 Aristotle의 제자 노릇을 했던 철학자. 나중에 Alexander의 부하가 되었다가 모반에 가담한 죄로 처형됨.

***Cato...the field:** 로마의 장군 Fulvius가 시인 Ennius를 전쟁에 데리고 간 것을 정치가 Cato가 반대했었다. Cato는 냉혹한 인물, 즉 Grace가 없는 인물이었다. 뒤에 나오는 Cato Ulticensis는 그의 손자.

***Pluto...Latin:** 「지옥의 대왕 Pluto가 Latin어를 모를까봐」(그는 늙어서 그리이스어를 공부했다).

***unmustered person:** 「군적에 없는 평민으로, 즉 불법적으로 종군한 자」. Ennius를 지칭.

***Scipio Nasica:** B.C. 2, 3세기 로마의 존경받은 인물. 뒤에 나오는 아시아의 Scipio, 아프리카의 Scipio라는 두 형제는 다른 인물들로, 이름난 장군들.

loved him. Both the other Scipio brothers, who had by their virtues no less surnames than of Asia and Afric, so loved him that they caused his body to be buried in their sepulchre. So as Cato's authority being but against his person, and that answered with so far greater than himself, is herein of no validity.

But now, indeed, my burden is great, that Plato's name is laid upon me, whom, I must confess, of all philosophers I have ever esteemed most worthy of reverence; and with great reason, since of all philosophers he is the most poetical. Yet if he will defile the fountain out of which his flowing streams have proceeded, let us boldly examine with what reasons he did it.

First, truly, a man might maliciously object that Plato, being a philosopher, was a natural enemy of poets. For, indeed, after the philosophers had picked out of the sweet mysteries of poetry the right discerning true points of knowledge, they forthwith, putting it in method,* and making a school-art* of that which the poets did only teach by a divine delightfulness, beginning to spurn at their guides, like ungrateful prentices* were not content to set up shops for themselves, but sought by all means to discredit their masters; which by the force of delight being barred them, the less they could overthrow them the more they hated them. For, indeed, they found for Homer seven cities* strove who should have him for their citizen; where many cities banished philosophers, as not fit members to live among them. For only repeating certain of Euripides' verses,* many Athenians had their lives saved of the Syracusans, when the Athenians themselves thought many philosophers unworthy to live.

***putting it in method:** 「시에서 얻은 지식을 체계화하여」.

***school-art:** 「학교에서 배우는 따분한 학문」.

***prentices:** apprentices. 주인집에 기거하며 기술을 배우는 직공. 나중에 독립하여 사업을 차림 (set up shops for themselves). 철학은 시의 apprentice 라는 것.

***seven cities:** Homer 가 자기네 도시 출신이라고 주장한 7개의 도시 (시인에 대한 존경을 나타냄).

***Euripides' verses:** Athene 군대가 Sicily 섬의 Syracuse 를 점령하러 갔다가 패했을 때, Euripides 를 읊을 줄 아는 포로는 죽이지 않았다는 일화가 있다.

Certain poets as Simonides and Pindar,* had so prevailed with Hiero the First, that of a tyrant they made him a just king; where Plato could do so little with Dionysius, that he himself of a philosopher was made a slave.* But who should do thus, I confess, should requite the objections made against poets with like cavillations against philosophers; as likewise one should do that should bid one read Phaedrus or Symposium in Plato,* or the Discourse of Love in Plutarch, and see whether any poet do authorize abominable filthiness, as they do.

Again, a man might ask out of what commonwealth Plato did banish them. In sooth, thence where he himself alloweth community of women.* So as* belike this banishment grew not for effeminate wantonness, since little should poetical sonnets be hurtful when a man might have what woman he listed. But I honour philosophical instructions, and bless the wits which bred them, so as they be not abused, which is likewise stretched to poetry. Saint Paul himself, who yet, for the credit of poets, allegeth twice two poets, and one of them by the name of a prophet, setteth a watchword upon philosophy,—indeed upon the abuse.* So doth Plato upon the abuse, not upon poetry. Plato found fault that the poets of his time filled the world with wrong opinions of the gods, making light tales of that unspotted essence,* and therefore would not have the youth depraved with

---

***Simonides, Pindar** : 둘 다 Syracuse의 폭군 Hiero the First의 환대를 받았다.

***Plato...a slave:** Plato 역시 Sicily의 Dionysius왕의 환대를 받았으나 곧 쫓겨나 적국의 포로가 되는 곤경을 당했고, 노예로 팔려가기까지 했었다는 이야기가 전해진다.

******Phaedrus* **or** ***Symposium*** **in Plato:** Plato의 두 저작에서 기발한 남녀관계를 말하고 있다.

***community of women:** *Republic*에서 Plato는 결혼제도를 반대하고, 여자를 공유하는 제도를 말하고 있다(5권, 449—62). 이런 "이상국"에서는 시인이 추방되어도 좋다는 뜻으로 Sidney는 말하고 있다.

***so as:** if.

***Saint Paul...upon the abuse;** 사도 바울은 실은 고대시인을 세번 인용했고 (사도행전 17장 28절, 디도서 1장 12절, 고린도 전서 15장 33절), 골로새서 2장 8절에서는 헛된 "철학"에 속지 말라고 경고를 했다(setteth a watchword on philosophy).

***that unspotted essence:** 신성.

such opinions. Herein may much be said; let this suffice: the poets did not induce such opinions, but did imitate those opinions already induced. For all the Greek stories can well testify that the very religion of that time stood upon many and many-fashioned gods; not taught so by the poets, but followed according to their nature of imitation. Who list may read in Plutarch the discourses of Isis and Osiris, of the cause why Oracles ceased, of the Divine Providence, and see whether the theology of that nation stood not upon such dreams, which the poets indeed superstitiously observed; and truly, (since they had not the light of Christ,) did much better in it than the philosophers, who, shaking off superstition, brought in atheism.

Plato therefore, (whose authority I had much rather justly construe than unjustly resist,) meant not in general of poets, in those words of which Julius Scaliger saith, *Qua authoritate barbari quidam atque hispidi abuti velint ad poetas e republica exigendos*;* but only meant to drive out those wrong opinions of the Deity, (whereof now, without further law, Christianity hath taken away all the hurtful belief,) perchance, (as he thought,) nourished by the then esteemed poets. And a man need go no further than to Plato himself to know his meaning; who, in his dialogue called *Ion*, giveth high and rightly divine commendation unto poetry. So as Plato, banishing the abuse, not the thing, not banishing it, but giving due honour unto it, shall be our patron and not our adversary.* For, indeed, I had much rather, (since truly I may do it,) show their mistaking of Plato, under whose lion's skin they would make an ass-like braying against poesy, than go about to overthrow his authority; whom, the wiser a man is, the more just cause he shall find to have in admiration; especially since he attributeth unto poesy more than myself do, namely to be a very inspiring of a divine force, far above man's wit as in the aforenamed dialogue is apparent.

Of the other side, who would show the honours have been

---

*'The rude and barbarous would abuse such an authority in order to drive the poets out of the state' (*Poetice*, 1, ii)

***So as Plato...adversary:** Plato는 시의 무자각성, 비합리성을 비꼰 것이다.

by the best sort of judgements granted them, a whole sea of examples would present themselves: Alexanders, Caesars, Scipios, all favourers of poets; Laelius,* called the Roman Socrates, himself a poet, so as part of *Heautontimoroumenos* in Terence was supposed to be made by him. And even the Greek Socrates, whom Apollo confirmed to be the only wise man, is said to have spent part of his old time in putting Aesop's Fables into verses; and therefore full evil should it become his scholar, Plato, to put such words in his master's mouth against poets. But what needs more? Aristotle writes the Art of Poesy; and why, if it should not be written? Plutarch teacheth the use to be gathered of them; and how, if they should not be read? And who reads Plutarch's either history or philosophy, shall find he trimmeth both their garments with guards* of poesy. But I list not to defend poesy with the help of her underling historiography. Let it suffice that it is a fit soil for praise to dwell upon; and what dispraise may set upon it, is either easily overcome, or transformed into just commendation.

So that, since the excellencies of it may be so easily and so justly confirmed, and the low-creeping objections so soon trodden down: it not being an art of lies, but of true doctrine; not of effeminateness, but of notable stirring of courage; not of abusing man's wit, but of strengthening man's wit; not banished, but honoured by Plato; let us rather plant more laurels for to engarland our poets' heads (which honour of being laureate, as besides them only triumphant captains were, is a sufficient authority to show the price they ought to be held in) than suffer the ill-savoured breath of such wrong speakers once to blow upon the clear springs of poesy.

But since I have run so long a career in this matter, me thinks, before I give my pen a full stop, it shall be but a little more lost time to inquire why England, the mother of excellent minds, should be grown so hard a stepmother to poets, who certainly

---

***Laelius:** B.C. 2세기경 로마의 철학자. Terence의 희곡 *Heautontimorumenos*(「고행하는 자」)의 일절을 지었다는 설이 있다.

***guards:** 「옷의 장식」.

in wit ought to pass all others, since all only proceedeth from their wit, being indeed makers of themselves, not takers of others. How can I but exclaim,

Musa, mihi causas memora, quo numine laeso?*

Sweet poesy! that hath anciently had kings, emperors, senators, great captains, such as, besides a thousand others, David, Adrian, Sophocles, Germanicus,* not only to favour poets, but to be poets; and of our nearer times can present for her patrons a Robert, King of Sicily; the great King Francis of France; King James of Scotland; such cardinals as Bembus and Bibbiena; such famous preachers and teachers as Beza and Melancthon; so learned philosophers as Fracastorius and Scaliger; so great orators as Pontanus and Muretus; so piercing wits as George Buchanan;* so grave counsellors as, besides many, but before all, that Hospital of France,* than whom, I think, that realm never brought forth a more accomplished judgement more firmly builded upon virtue; I say these, with numbers of others, not only to read others' poesies but to poetize for others' reading. That poesy, thus embraced in all other places, should only find in our time a hard welcome in England, I think the very earth lamenteth it, and therefore decketh our soil with fewer laurels than it was accustomed. For heretofore poets have in England also flourished; and, which is to be noted, even in those times when the trumpet of Mars did sound loudest. And now that an over-faint quietness should seem to strew the house for poets, they are almost in as good reputation as the mountebanks at Venice. Truly even that, as

---

*'Tell me, O Muse, in what way was her divinity being injured? (*Aeneid*, I, 8).

***David, ..., Germanicus:** 이들은 모두 군대 지휘관(captains)이면서 시인들이었다. 그러나 Sophocles는 장군의 지위에 있었던 적은 있으나 용맹을 떨친 일은 없다.

***Bembus,..., George Buchanan:** 아들은 모두 중세 말기, 르네상스 시대에 살았던 유럽의 저명인사들로서 시도 지었던 사람들이다.

***Hospital of France:** 프랑스의 16세기 정치가 Michael d'Hospital을 말한다.

of the one side it giveth great praise to poesy, which, like Venus (but to better purpose,) hath rather be troubled in the net with Mars, than enjoy the homely quiet of Vulcan*; so serves it for a piece of a reason why they are less grateful to idle England, which now can scarce endure the pain of a pen. Upon this necessarily followeth, that base men with servile wits undertake it, who think it enough if they can be rewarded of the printer. And so as Epaminondas* is said, with the honour of his virtue to have made an office, by his exercising it, which before was contemptible, to become highly respected; so these men, no more but setting their names to it, by their own disgracefulness disgrace the most graceful poesy. For now, without any commission, they do post over the banks of Helicon*, till they make the readers more weary than post-horses; while, in the mean time, they,

Queis meliore luto finxit praecordia Titan,*

are better content to suppress the outflowing of their wit than, by publishing them, to be accounted knights of the same order.

But I that, before ever I durst aspire unto the dignity, am admitted into the company of the paper-blurrers*, do find the very true cause of our wanting estimation is want of desert, taking upon us to be poets in despite of Pallas*. Now wherein we want desert were a thankworthy labour to express; but if I knew, I should have mended myself. But I, as I never desired the title, so have I neglected the means to come by it; only, overmastered by some thoughts, I yielded an inky tribute* unto

---

***which...Vulcan:** Venus 여신은 대장장이의 신인 Vulcan의 아내이나 군신 Mars와 밀회하다가 Vulcan이 던진 그물에 걸려 망신을 당한다.

***Empaminondas...an office:** Thebe의 Empaminondas는 미관말직을 맡아 잘 수행하여 그 직분을 유명하게 했다.

***Helicon:** 시의 원천이 된다는 산.

*'Whose hearts Titan has fashioned for finer clay' (*Satires*, XIV, 35).

***paper-blurrers:** 종이를 더럽히는 사. 즉, 글쓰는 자에 대한 냉소적 칭호.

***in despite of Pallas:** 지혜의 여신 Pallas(Minerva)의 허락도 없이, 즉 자격도 없이.

***inky tribute:** 「먹물의 공물」, 즉 시작품.

them. Marry, they that delight in poesy itself should seek to know what they do and how they do; and especially look themselves in an unflattering glass of reason, if they be inclinable unto it. For poesy must not be drawn by the ears, it must be gently led, or rather it must lead; which was partly the cause that made the ancient learned affirm it was a divine gift, and no human skill, since all other knowledges lie ready for any that hath strength of wit; a poet no industry can make if his own genius be not carried unto it. And therefore is it an old proverb: *Orator fit, poeta nascitur.** Yet confess I always that, as the fertilest ground must be manured, so must the highest-flying wit have a Daedalus to guide him. That Daedalus,* they say, both in this and in other, hath three wings to bear itself up into the air of due commendation: that is, art, imitation, and exercise. But these, neither artificial rules nor imitative patterns, we much cumber ourselves withal. Exercise indeed we do, but that very fore-backwardly,* for where we should exercise to know, we exercise as having known; and so is our brain delivered of much matter which never was begotten by knowledge.* For, there being two principal parts, matter to be expressed by words, and words to express the matter, in neither we use art or imitation rightly. Our matter is *quodlibet** indeed, though wrongly performing Ovid's verse,

Quicquid conabar dicere, versus erat;*

never marshalling it into any assured rank, that almost the readers cannot tell where to find themselves.

Chaucer, undoubtedly, did excellently in his *Troilus and Criseyde*; of whom, truly, I know not whether to marvel more,

---

*'The orator is made, the poet is born.'

***Daedalus:** 날개를 발명하여 하늘을 최초로 난 사람. 즉, 비행의 선구자.

***for-backwardly:** 「거꾸로」.

***and so...knowledge:** 진정한 지식으로 잉태된 것이 아닌 것들을 우리 머리가 쏟아놓는다.

****Quodlibet***: 'vague'.

*'Whatever I tried to say was verse' (*Tristia*, Ⅳ, 10, 25).

either that he in that misty time could see so clearly, or that we in this clear age walk so stumblingly after him. Yet had he great wants, fit to be forgiven in so reverend antiquity. I account the *Mirror for Magistrates** meetly furnished of beautiful parts; and in the Earl of Surrey's *Lyrics** many things tasting of a noble birth, and worthy of a noble mind. The *Shepheardes Calender** hath much poetry in his eclogues, indeed worthy the reading, if I be not deceived. That same framing of his style to an old rustic language I dare not allow, since neither Theocritus in Greek, Virgil in Latin, nor Sannazzaro in Italian did affect it. Besides these, I do not remember to have seen but few (to speak boldly) printed, that have poetical sinews in them; for proof whereof, let but most of the verses be put in prose, and then ask the meaning, and it will be found that one verse did but beget another, without ordering at the first what should be at the last; which becomes a confused mass of words, with a tinkling sound of rime, barely accompanied with reason.

Our tragedies and comedies not without cause cried out against, observing rules neither of honest civility nor of skilful poetry: excepting *Gorboduc*,* (again I say of those that I have seen,) which notwithstanding as it is full of stately speeches and well-sounding phrases, climbing to the height of Seneca's style, and as full of notable morality, which it doth most delightfully teach, and so obtain the very end of poesy; yet in truth it is very defectious in the circumstances; which grieveth me, because it might not remain as an exact model of all tragedies. For it is faulty both in place and time, the two necessary companions of all corporal actions. For where the stage should always represent but one place, and the uttermost time presupposed in it should be, both by Aristotle's precept and common reason, but one day, there is both many days and many

---

**Mirrour of Magistrates*: 16세기 중엽의 3류시인들이 비명에 간 영국의 왕이나 저명인사들의 전기를 운문으로 쓴 작품.

**Shepheard's Calendar*: Edmund Spenser의 출세작. 일부러 고어체와 방언을 사용해서 지은 전원시.

**Gorboduc*: Norton과 Sackville이 합작한 영국 최초의 비극의 하나.

places inartificially imagined.

But if it be so in *Gorboduc*, how much more in all the rest? where you shall have Asia of the one side, and Afric of the other, and so many other under-kingdoms,* that the player, when he cometh in, must ever begin with telling where he is, or else the tale will not be conceived. Now ye shall have three ladies walk to gather flowers, and then we must believe the stage to be a garden. By and by we hear news of shipwreck in the same place, and then we are to blame if we accept it not for a rock. Upon the back of that comes out a hideous monster with fire and smoke, and then the miserable beholders are bound to take it for a cave. While in the mean time two armies fly in, represented with four swords and bucklers, and then what hard heart will not receive it for a pitched field?

Now of time they are much more liberal. For ordinary it is that two young princes fall in love; after many traverses she is got with child, delivered of a fair boy, he is lost, groweth a man, falleth in love, and is ready to get another child, and all this in two hours' space; which how absurd it is in sense even sense may imagine, and art hath taught, and all ancient examples justified, and at this day the ordinary players in Italy will not err in. Yet will some bring in an example of Eunuchus in Terence, that containeth matter of two days, yet far short of twenty years. True it is, and so was it to be played in two days, and so fitted to the time it set forth. And though Plautus have in one place done amiss, let us hit with him, and not miss with him. But they will say, How then shall we set forth a story which containeth both many places and many times? And do they not know that a tragedy is tied to the laws of poesy, and not of history; not bound to follow the story, but having liberty either to feign a quite new matter, or to frame the history to the most tragical conveniency? Again, many things may be told which cannot be showed, if they know the difference betwixt reporting and representing. As for example I may speak, (though I am here,) of Peru, and in speech digress from

*under-kingdoms: 대국 사이에 있는 작은 여러 나라들.

that to the description of Calicut*; but in action I cannot represent it without Pacolet's horse.* And so was the manner the ancients took, by some *Nuntius** to recount things done in former time or other place.

Lastly, if they will represent an history, they must not, (as Horace saith,) begin *ab ovo*,* but they must come to the principal point of that one action which they will represent. By example this will be best expressed. I have a story of young Polydorus, delivered for safety's sake, with great riches, by his father Priamus to Polymnestor, King of Thrace, in the Trojan war time. He, after some years, hearing the overthrow of Priamus, for to make the treasure his own murdereth the child; the body of the child is taken up; Hecuba,* she, the same day, findeth a sleight* to be revenged most cruelly of the tyrant. Where now would one of our tragedy-writers begin, but with the delivery of the child? Then should he sail over into Thrace, and so spend I know not how many years, and travel numbers of places. But where doth Euripides? Even with the finding of the body, leaving the rest to be told by the spirit of Polydorus. This needs no further to be enlarged; the dullest wit may conceive it.

But, besides these gross absurdities, how all their plays be neither right tragedies nor right comedies, mingling kings and clowns, not because the matter so carrieth it, but thrust in the clown by head and shoulders* to play a part in majestical matters, with neither decency nor discretion; so as neither the admiration and commiseration, nor the right sportfulness, is by their mongrel tragi-comedy obtained. I know Apuleius* did

---

***Calicut:** 인도의 항구.
***Pacolet's horse:** 프랑스 옛이야기에 나오는 요술말.
***Nuncius:** Messenger.
****ab ovo*:** 'From the egg (or beginning)' 「처음부터」(*Art of poetry*, 1, 147).
***Polydorus, Priam, Polymnestor:** Euripides 의 *Hecuba* 에 나오는 인물들.
***slight:** 「계략」.
***by head and shoulders:** 「함부로, 닥치는 대로」.
***Apuleius:** 2세기 경의 문인. 여러 이야기를 뒤섞은 *Golden Ass* 라는 산문 이외에는 희곡 작품이 없음.

somewhat so, but that is a thing recounted with space of time, not represented in one moment; and I know the ancients have one or two examples of tragi-comedies, as Plautus hath *Amphitryo*.* But, if we mark them well, we shall find that they never, or very daintily, match hornpipes* and funerals. So falleth it out that, having indeed no right comedy in that comical part of our tragedy, we have nothing but scurrility, unworthy of any chaste ears, or some extreme show of doltishness, indeed fit to lift up a loud laughter, and nothing else; where the whole tract of a comedy should be full of delight, as the tragedy should be still maintained in a well-raised admiration.

But our comedians think there is no delight without laughter, which is very wrong; for though laughter may come with delight, yet cometh it not of delight, as though delight should be the cause of laughter; but well may one thing breed both together. Nay, rather in themselves they have, as it were, a kind of contrariety. For delight we scarcely do, but in things that have a conveniency to ourselves, or to the general nature; laughter almost ever cometh of things most disproportioned to ourselves and nature. Delight hath a joy in it either permanent or present; laughter hath only a scornful tickling. For example, we are ravished with delight to see a fair woman, and yet are far from being moved to laughter. We laugh at deformed creatures, wherein certainly we cannot delight. We delight in good chances, we laugh at mischances. We delight to hear the happiness of our friends and country, at which he were worthy to be laughed at that would laugh. We shall, contrarily, laugh sometimes to find a matter quite mistaken and go down the hill against the bias,* in the mouth of some such men, as for the respect of them one shall be heartily sorry, yet he cannot choose but laugh, and so is rather pained than delighted with laughter. Yet deny I not but that they may go well together. For as in Alexander's picture well set out we delight without laughter,

---

***Amphitrio*: 실제로는 comedy. 신이 등장하므로 약간 심각한 편일 뿐이다.

***hornpipes**: "merry tunes" of country folks.

***go down...bias**: 「엉뚱한 길로 접어들다(틀린 소리를 하다)」.

and in twenty mad antics we laugh without delight; so in Hercules,* painted, with his great beard and furious countenance, in woman's attire, spinning at Omphale's commandment, it breedeth both delight and laughter; for the representing of so strange a power in love procureth delight, and the scornfulness of the action stirreth laughter.

But I speak to this purpose, that all the end of the comical part be not upon such scornful matters as stir laughter only, but mixed with it that delightful teaching which is the end of poesy. And the great fault, even in that point of laughter, and forbidden plainly by Aristotle,* is that they stir laughter in sinful things, which are rather execrable than ridiculous; or in miserable, which are rather to be pitied than scorned. For what is it to make folks gape at a wretched beggar or a beggarly clown, or, against law of hospitality, to jest at strangers because they speak not English as well as we do? what do we learn? since it is certain:

> **Nil habet infelix paupertas durius in se,**
> **Quam quod ridiculos homines facit.***

But rather a busy loving courtier; a heartless threatening Thraso; a self-wise-seeming schoolmaster; a wry-transformed traveller: these if we saw walk in stage-names, which we play naturally, therein were delightful laughter and teaching delightfulness, as in the other, the tragedies of Buchanan* do justly bring forth a divine admiration.

But I have lavished out too many words of this play-matter. I do it, because, as they are excelling parts of poesy, so is there none so much used in England, and none can be more pitifully abused; which, like an unmannerly daughter, showing a bad education, causeth her mother Poesy's honesty to be called in

---

***Hercules...Omphale's commandment:** 영웅 Hercules는 Omphale라는 미인에게 반하여 그런 우스운 짓을 했다.

***the great fault...Aristotle:** *Poetics*, V.

*'Unhappy poverty has nothing worse than that it makes men ridiculous' (Juvenal, *Satires*, Ⅲ, 152—153)

***Buchanan, George:** 16세기 스콧틀랜드의 라틴어 시인.

question.

Other sorts of poetry almost have we none, but that lyrical kind of songs and sonnets, which, Lord, if he gave us so good minds, how well it might be employed, and with how heavenly fruit both private and public, in singing the praises of the immortal beauty, the immortal goodness of that God who giveth us hands to write, and wits to conceive!—of which we might well want words, but never matter; of which we could turn our eyes to nothing, but we should ever have new-budding occasions.

But truly, many of such writings as come under the banner of unresistible love, if I were a mistress would never persuade me they were in love; so coldly they apply fiery speeches, as men that had rather read lovers' writings, (and so caught up certain swelling phrases, which hang together like a man which once told me the wind was at north-west and by south, because he would be sure to name winds enough) than that in truth they feel those passions; which easily, as I think, may be bewrayed by that same forcibleness, or *energeia** (as the Greeks call it) of the writer. But let this be a sufficient, though short note, that we miss the right use of the material point of poesy.

Now for the outside of it, which is words, or (as I may term it) diction, it is even well worse; so is that honey-flowing matron, Eloquence, apparelled, or rather disguised, in a courtesan-like painted affection: one time with so far-fetched words, they may seem monsters, but must seem strangers, to any poor Englishman; another time with coursing of a letter,* as if they were bound to follow the method of a dictionary; another time with figures and flowers extremely winter-starved.*

But I would this fault were only peculiar to versifiers, and had not as large possession among prose-printers, and, (which is to be marvelled,) among many scholars, and, (which is to be

---

****Energeia***: 글의 힘. 감동력.

***coursing of a letter:** 시의 각 행의 첫 글자를 같은 글자로 시작하든가, 한 낱말을 이루게 하든가 하는 문자 유희. 때로는 alliteration을 가리키기도 했다.

***figures and flowers...starved:** 시의 행을 어떤 형상을 닮도록 배열하는 것. 이것이 Sidney에게는 매우 초라해 보였던 모양이다.

pitied,) among some preachers. Truly I could wish—if at least I might be so bold to wish in a thing beyond the reach of my capacity—the diligent imitators of Tully and Demosthenes (most worthy to be imitated) did not so much keep Nizolian paper-books* of their figures and phrases, as by attentive translation, as it were, devour them whole, and make them wholly theirs. For now they cast sugar and spice upon every dish that is served to the table; like those Indians, not content to wear ear-rings at the fit and natural place of the ears, but they will thrust jewels through their nose and lips, because they will be sure to be fine. Tully, when he was to drive out Catiline as it were with a thunderbolt of eloquence, often used that figure of repetition, as *Vivit. Vivit? Immo in senatum venit,** etc. Indeed, inflamed with a well-grounded rage, he would have his words, as it were, double out of his mouth; and so do that artificially, which we see men in choler do naturally. And we, having noted the grace of those words, hale them in sometime to a familiar epistle, when it were too much choler to be choleric. How well store of *similiter cadences* doth sound with the gravity of the pulpit, I would but invoke Demosthenes' soul to tell, who with a rare daintiness useth them. Truly they have made me think of the sophister that with too much subtlety would prove two eggs three, and though he might be counted a sophister, had none for his labour. So these men bringing in such a kind of eloquence, well may they obtain an opinion of a seeming fineness, but persuade few, which should be the end of their fineness.

Now for similitudes, in certain printed discourses, I think all herbarists, all stories of beasts, fowls, and fishes* are rifled up,

---

***Nizolian paper-book:** 16세기 Nizolius 란 사람이 Cicero의 명문에서 뽑은 좋은 표현들을 모아놓은 공책.

*'He lives. Lives?—He even comes into the senate.' (Cicero의 웅변으로 야심가 Catiline을 로마에서 추방함. 그러나 이런 문구를 아무데서나 함부로 쓰지 말라는 것).

***all stories...fishes:** 당시의 일부 문장가들은 글을 장식하기 위하여 식물학, 동물학 등 별별 책에서 기이한 사실들을 가져다가 비유로 사용하였다. 이런 경향은 형이상학파 시대에 더욱 현저했다.

that they may come in multitudes to wait upon any of our conceits, which certainly is as absurd a surfeit to the ears as is possible. For the force of a similitude not being to prove any thing to a contrary disputer, but only to explain to a willing hearer; when that is done, the rest is a most tedious prattling, rather overswaying the memory from the purpose whereto they were applied, than any whit informing the judgement, already either satisfied or by similitudes not to be satisfied.

For my part, I do not doubt, when Antonius and Crassus, the great forefathers of Cicero in eloquence, the one (as Cicero testifieth of them) pretended not to know art, the other not to set by it,* because with a plain sensibleness they might win credit of popular ears, which credit is the nearest step to persuasion, which persuasion is the chief mark of oratory,—I do not doubt, I say, but that they used these knacks very sparingly; which who doth generally use, any man may see doth dance to his own music, and so be noted by the audience more careful to speak curiously than to speak truly. Undoubtedly (at least to my opinion undoubtedly) I have found in divers small-learned courtiers a more sound style than in some professors of learning; of which I can guess no other cause, but that the courtier following that which by practice he findeth fittest to nature, therein, though he know it not, doth according to art, though not by art; where the other, using art to show art and not to hide art (as in these cases he should do) flieth from nature, and indeed abuseth art.*

But what! me thinks I deserve to be pounded for straying from poetry to oratory. But both have such an affinity in this wordish consideration, that I think this digression will make my meaning receive the fuller understanding: which is not to

---

***not to set by it:** (웅변을) 중요하게 여기지 않다. 여기 나오는 Antonius 는 Caesar 의 총신 Antonius 의 할아버지. Crassus 도 웅변 잘 하던 로마의 정치가.

*"말의 기술(Art)은 그것을 숨기는 데에 있다"는 옛 격언에 대한 언급. 자연스럽게 받아들여지도록 꾸민 말이 바로 그런 말이며, 조작적이라는 인상이 짙은 말은 자연스럽게 받아들여질 수가 없다는 것이다. 그래서 Sidney 는 학자들보다 courtier 가 더 낫다고 말하고 있다.

take upon me to teach poets how they should do, but only, finding myself sick among the rest, to show some one or two spots of the common infection grown among the most part of writers; that, acknowledging ourselves somewhat awry, we may bend to the right use both of matter and manner: whereto our language giveth us great occasion, being, indeed, capable of any excellent exercising of it.

I know some will say it is a mingled language. And why not so much the better, taking the best of both the other? Another will say it wanteth grammar. Nay, truly, it hath that praise that it wanteth not grammar: for grammar it might have, but it needs it not; being so easy in itself, and so void of those cumbersome differences of cases, genders, moods, and tenses, which, I think, was a piece of the Tower of Babylon's curse, that a man should be put to school to learn his mother-tongue. But for the uttering sweetly and properly the conceits of the mind, which is the end of speech, that hath it equally with any other tongue in the world; and is particularly happy in compositions of two or three words together,—near the Greek, far beyond the Latin, which is one of the greatest beauties can be in a language.

Now of versifying there are two sorts, the one ancient, the other modern. The ancient marked the quantity* of each syllable, and according to that framed his verse; the modern observing only number,* with some regard of the accent, the chief life of it standeth in that like sounding of the words, which we call rhyme. Whether of these be the more excellent would bear many speeches; the ancient no doubt more fit for music, both words and tune observing quantity; and more fit lively to express divers passions, by the low or lofty sound of the well-weighed syllable. The latter likewise with his rhyme striketh a certain music to the ear; and, in fine, since it doth delight, though by another way, it obtaineth the same purpose; there being in either, sweetness, and wanting in neither, majesty.

---

*the quantity: 여기서의 의미는 음절의 길고 짧음. 즉, 고전시의 운율의 기본.

*number: 음절의 수. 근대 유럽 시의 근본(물론 여기에 accent 가 첨가됨).

Truly the English, before any other vulgar language I know, is fit for both sorts. For, for the ancient, the Italian is so full of vowels that it must ever be cumbered with elisions; the Dutch so, of the other side, with consonants, that they cannot yield the sweet sliding fit for a verse. The French in his whole language hath not one word that hath his accent in the last syllable saving two, called antepenultima;* and little more hath the Spanish; and therefore very gracelessly may they use dactyls. The English is subject to none of these defects. Now for rhyme;* though we do not observe quantity, yet we observe the accent very precisely, which other languages either cannot do, or will not do so absolutely. That caesura, or breathing-place in the midst of the verse, neither Italian nor Spanish have, the French and we never almost fail of.

Lastly, even the very rhyme itself the Italian cannot put in the last syllable, by the French named the masculine rhyme, but still in the next to the last, which the French call the female,* or the next before that, which the Italians term *sdrucciola*.* The example of the former is *buono, suono*; of the *sdrucciola* is *femina, semina*. The French, of the other side, hath both the male as *bon, son*; and the female, as *plaise, taise*; but the *sdrucciola* he hath not. Where the English hath all three, as *due, true*; *father, rather*; *motion, potion*;* with much more which might be said, but that already I find the triflingness of this discourse is much too much enlarged.

So that since the ever praiseworthy poesy is full of virtue-breeding delightfulness, and void of no gift that ought to be in the noble name of learning; since the blames laid against it are

---

****Antepenultima*:** 끝에서 세번째 음절. 프랑스어에서는 끝에서 세번째 음절에 accent가 놓이는 낱말이 없다. 따라서 dactyl(강약약격)을 쓰기가 어렵다.

***rhyme:** 여기서는 rhythm이란 뜻.

***female:** 현대 용어로는 feminine(rhyme). rhyming word의 끝이 "강약(또는 장단)"으로 끝나는 것.

****sdracciola*:** "강약약"격(즉 dactyl)으로 끝나는 시의 행.

***motion**과 **potion**은 당시 영어에서는 대략 [móuʃiyɔn], [póuʃiyɔn], 즉 3음절(강약약)로 발음했다.

either false or feeble; since the cause why it is not esteemed in England is the fault of poet-apes;* not poets; since, lastly, our tongue is most fit to honour poesy, and to be honoured by poesy; I conjure you all that have had the evil luck to read this ink-wasting toy* of mine, even in the name of the Nine Muses, no more to scorn the sacred mysteries of poesy; no more to laugh at the name of Poets, as though they were next inheritors to Fools; no more to jest at the reverend title of 'a rhymer'; but to believe, with Aristotle,* that they were the ancient treasurers of the Grecians' divinity; to believe, with Bembus, that they were first bringers-in of all civility; to believe, with Scaliger, that no philosopher's precepts can sooner make you an honest man than the reading of Virgil; to believe, with Clauserus,* the translator of Cornutus, that it pleased the Heavenly Deity by Hesiod and Homer, under the veil of fables, to give us all knowledge, logic, rhetoric, philosophy natural and moral, and *quid non?** to believe, with me, that there are many mysteries contained in poetry which of purpose were written darkly, lest by profane wits it should be abused; to believe, with Landino,* that they are so beloved of the gods, that whatsoever they write proceeds of a divine fury; lastly, to believe themselves, when they tell you they will make you immortal by their verses.

Thus doing, your name shall flourish in the printers' shops. Thus doing, you shall be of kin to many a poetical preface. Thus doing, you shall be most fair, most rich, most wise, most all; you shall dwell upon superlatives. Thus doing, though you be *libertino patre natus*, you shall suddenly grow *Herculea proles.**

***poet-apes:** 시인이 아니면서 시인 흉내내는 사람. 가짜 시인.

***toy:** 하잘 것 없는 글.

*Aristotle은 실제로 이런 말을 한 적이 없다.

*16세기 스위스 학자 Clauserus가 A.D. 1세기의 그리이스어 시인 Cornutus를 번역하면서 그 서문에서 다음의 말을 했다.

****Quid non?*:** 'What not?'

***Landino:** 15세기 플로렌스의 인문학자.

*'the son of a former slave'...'Herculean offspring.'

Si quid mea carmina possunt.*

Thus doing, your soul shall be placed with Dante's Beatrice or Virgil's Anchises.*

But if—fie of such a but!*—you be born so near the dull-making cataract of Nilus,* that you cannot bear the planet-like music of poetry; if you have so earth-creeping a mind that it cannot lift itself up to look to the sky of poetry, or rather, by a certain rustical disdain, will become such a mome as to be a Momus of Poetry;* then, though I will not wish unto you the ass's ears of Midas,* nor to be driven by a poet's verses, as Bubonax* was, to hang himself; nor to be rhymed to death, as is said to be done in Ireland;* yet thus much curse I must send you in the behalf of all poets: that while you live, you live in love, and never get favour, for lacking skill of a sonnet; and when you die, your memory die from the earth, for want of an epitaph.

---

*'If my poems are able to do anything' (Virgil, *Aeneid*, 9, 446).

***your soul...Anchises:** 즉, 천국에 있게 될 것이다.

***fie...but:** 「but (그러나) 이란 소리는 집어치워라」.

***the dull-making...Nilus:** Nile강 폭포 근처에 살다가 귀가 먹은 족속에 대한 언급. 귀가 먹으면 천상의 음악 (planet-like music) 을 못듣는다.

***such a...poetry:** Mome은 바보, Momus는 비난자라는 뜻.

***the ass's ears of Midas:** Apollo의 음악이 나쁘다고 판단했던 Midas왕의 귀가 당나귀 귀로 변했다는 전설 (즉, 어리석은 판단에 대한 풍자).

***to be driven...hang himself:** 고대에 어떤 시인의 놀림을 받아 Bupalos (Bubonax는 잘못 쓰인 것임) 란 저명인사가 자살했다는 일화.

***to be rhymed...in Ireland:** 아일랜드의 음유시인 (Bard) 은 주문의 힘으로 쥐를 퇴치했다고 한다. 여기에서 rhyme a rat to death라는 속담이 생겨났다.

Francis Bacon

(1561—1626)

고급 관리의 아들로 태어나 케임브리지에서 수학하고 후에 법률 공부를 하여 정치에 발을 들여 놓아 57세 때에 드디어 대법관(Lord Chancellor)의 지위에까지 올랐다가 독직 사건으로 물러났다. 그러나 그는 혼자서 철학과 과학에 심취하여 아리스토텔레스의 철학과 중세적 철학을 배격하려는 의도에서 *The Advancement of Learning*(1605), *Novum Organum*(1620) 등 근대 철학사상의 이정표들을 저술하였다. 그의 *Essays*(1597-1625)는 너무나 잘 알려진 문장이다.

문학비평사에서 베이컨은 시가 상상의 산물임을 초보적인 심리학적 입장에서 주장한 까닭으로 기억되고 있다. 즉 역사는 기억, 시는 상상, 철학은 이성에 각각 연결되어 있다는 것이다. 상상의 산물인 시는 「꾸며낸 역사」(feigned history)의 형태를 취한다. 거짓 역사를 꾸미는 이유는 시드니도 말한 바와 같이 사람은 불완전한 진실보다 완전한 이상적 허구에 더 만족감을 느낄 수 있기 때문이다.

From Advancement of Learning (1607)

POESY is a part of learning in measure of words for the most part restrained, but in all other points extremely licensed, and doth truly refer to the imagination, which, being not tied to the laws of matter, may at pleasure join that which Nature hath severed, and sever that which Nature hath joined, and so make unlawful matches and divorces of things: *Pictoribus atque poetis etc. It is taken in two senses in respect of words or matter.* In the first sense it is but a character of style, and belongeth to arts of speech, and is not**

---

*'By painters and also poets, etc.' 자연에서 볼 수 없는 형상을 만드는 시의 능력을 말하고 있다.

***matter:** subject-matter.

pertinent for the present. In the later, it is, as hath been said,* one of the principal portions of learning, and is nothing else but feigned history, which may be styled as well in prose as in verse.

The use of this feigned history hath been to give some shadow of satisfaction to the mind of man in those points wherein the nature of things doth deny it, the world being in proportion inferior to the soul; by reason whereof there is agreeable to the spirit of man a more ample greatness, a more exact goodness, and a more absolute variety than can be found in the Nature of things. Therefore, because the acts or events of true history have not that magnitude which satisfieth the mind of man, poesy feigneth acts and events greater and more heroical; because true history propoundeth the successes and issues of actions not so agreeable to the merits of virtue and vice, therefore poesy feigns them more just in retribution and more according to revealed Providence; because true history representeth actions and events more ordinary and less interchanged, therefore poesy endueth them with more rareness and more unexpected and alternative variations: So as it appeareth that poesy serveth and conferreth to magnanimity, morality, and to delectation.* And therefore it was ever thought to have some participation of divineness, because it doth raise and erect the mind, by submitting the shows of things to the desires of the mind,* wherease reason doth buckle and bow the mind unto the Nature of things. And we see that by these insinuations and congruities with man's nature and pleasure, joined also with the agreement and consort it hath with music, it hath

***as hath...said:** 이 글의 앞부분에 다음과 같이 언급되어 있다. The parts of human learning have reference to the three parts of man's understanding, which is the seat of learning: history to his memory, poesy to his imagination, and philosophy to his reason.

***Therefore, because...so as...and to delectation:** 역사적 사실은 불만스럽다. 문학은 이같은 불만스러움을 해소시키도록 「창안된 역사」로서의 구실을 한다. 이러한 견해는 이미 Sidney에서 본 바이다.

***by submitting...mind:** 「사물의 현실적 모습을 마음의 욕구에 복종시킴으로써」.

had access and estimation in rude times and barbarous regions, where other learning stood* excluded.

The division of poesy which is aptest in the propriety thereof* (besides those divisions which are common unto it with history, as feigned epistles, feigned orations, and the rest) is into poesy narrative, representative, and allusive. The narrative is a mere* imitation of history with the excesses before remembered,* choosing for subject commonly wars and love, rarely state, and sometimes pleasure or mirth. Representative is as a visible history, and is an image of actions as if they were present, as history is of actions in nature as they are, that is past; allusive, or parabolical, is a narration applied only to express some special purpose or conceit: Which* later kind of parabolical wisdom was much more in use in the ancient times, as by the fables of Aesop, and the brief sentences of the seven;* and the use of hieroglyphics* may appear. And the cause was for that it was then of necessity to express and point of reason which was more sharp or subtle than the vulgar in that manner, because men in those times wanted both variety of examples and subtlety of conceit: And as hieroglyphics were before letters, so parables were before arguments: And nevertheless now and at all times they do retain much life and vigor, because reason cannot be so sensible, nor examples so fit.

But there remaineth yet another use of poesy parabolical opposite to that which we last mentioned; for that tendeth to demonstrate and illustrate that which is taught or delivered, and this other to retire* and obscure it: That is, when the secrets and mysteries of religion, policy, or philosophy, are involved in fables or parables. Of this in divine poesy we see the

---

***stood excluded:** remained excluded.

***The division...thereof:** 시의 성질상 가장 잘 어울리는 시의 구분.

***meer:** pure.

***before remembered:** above-mentioned.

***Which:** this (관계지시대명사)

***the seven:** the seven wise men of Greece.

***hieroglyphics:** 매우 애매하게 쓰인 상징적인 글

***retire:** 「뒤로 숨기다」.

use is authorized. In heathen poesy we see the exposition of fables doth fall out sometimes with great felicity, as in the fable that the giants being overthrown in their war against the gods, the Earth their mother in revenge thereof brought forth Fame:

> **Illam terra parens ira irritata deorum,**
> **Extremam, ut perhibent, Cœo enceladoque sororem**
> **Progenuit:***

expounded that when princes and monarchs have suppressed actual and open rebels, then the malignity of people, which is the mother of rebellion, doth bring forth libels and slanders, and taxations* of the states, which is of the same kind with rebellion, but more feminine: so in the fable that the rest of the gods having conspired to bind Jupiter, Pallas called Briareus with his hundred hands to his aid, expounded, that mornachies need not fear any curbing of their absoluteness by mighty subjects, as long as by wisdom they keep the hearts of the people, who will be sure to come in on their side: So in the fable that Achilles was brought up under Chiron the centaur,* who was part a man and part a beast, expounded ingenuously, but corruptly by Machiavelli, that it belongeth to the education and discipline of princes to know as well how to play the part of the lion in violence and the fox in guile, as of the man in virtue and justice. Nevertheless in many the like

---

*'In anger with the gods, it is said, Earth their mother brought forth [Fame], the last sister of Caeus and Enceladus' (Virgil, *Aeneid*, iv, 178). 그리이스 신화를 인간의 심리작용에 대한 parable로 해석하는 것은 중세, 르네상스의 전통의 하나였다. Earth의 자녀들인 Caeus와 Enceladus가 Jupiter와 기타 신들과 투쟁하다가 지게 되니까 Fame(유언비어)을 낳았다는 것이다.

***taxations:** 「비난」.

***So in the Fable...to his aid:** 또 다른 이야기에 따르면, 여러 신들이 Jupiter에게 반항하자 Pallas(지혜의 여신)는 팔이 백개나 되는 거인 Briarus의 도움으로 Jupiter를 구했다. 이는 왕이 지혜로우면 백성의 지지를 받는다는 진리의 parable로 해석한 것이다.

***Chiron the centaur:** 반인반마인 Chiron이 Achilles를 교육했다고 하는데, 이는 동물적 능력과 인간적 덕성을 다 갖춰야 한다는 뜻으로 해석(Macchiavelli가 왜곡했다는 것).

encounters*, I do rather think that the fable was first and the exposition devised than that the moral was first and thereupon the fable framed. For I find it was an ancient vanity in Chrisippus* that troubled himself with great contention to fasten the assertions of the stoics upon the fictions of the ancient poets. But yet that all the fables and fictions of the poets were but pleasure and not figure, I interpose no opinion. Surely of those poets which are not extant, even Homer himself (notwithstanding he was made a kind of scripture by the later schools of the Grecians)yet I should without any difficulty pronounce, that his fables had no such inwardness in his own meaning. But what they might have, upon a more original tradition, is not easy to affirm, for he was not the inventor of many of them. In this third part of learning which is poesy, I can report no deficience.* For being as a plant that cometh of the lust of the earth, without a formal seed, it hath sprung up and spread abroad, more than any other kind. But to ascribe unto it that which is due for the expressing of affections, passions, corruptions and customs, we are beholding to poets more than to the philosophers' works, and for wit and eloquence not much less than to orators' harangues. But it is not good to stay too long in the theater: let us now pass on to the judicial place or palace of the mind, which we are to approach and view, with more reverence and attention....

---

*encounter: style of address. 화법.

*like: similar.

*Chrisippus: 기원 3세기 그리이스의 stoic 철인. 신화를 우화적으로 해석했다.

*deficience: 「결함(을 말할 것이 없다)」.

Ben Jonson

(1574—1637)

목사의 유복자로 태어난 벤 죤슨은 고등학교격인 Westerminister School에서 당대 가장 이름 높던 학자요 교육가인 William Camden의 직접적 영향 하에 공부하여, 후일 대학 졸업자 못지 않는 고전에 대한 지식과 판단력을 갖게 되었다. 벽돌공, 군인에서 시작하여 배우가 되어 희곡을 창작하기에 이르러 1598년에 그의 첫 회심작인 *Everyman in His Humour*와 *Everyman out of His Humour*를 발표하여 극작가로 대성하였다. 궁정의 오락용 masque에도 대단한 솜씨를 보여 1616년에는 Poet Laureate이 되었다. 그의 여러 장르에 걸친 시도 일품이다.

*Timber: or Discoveries*는 1620년경에서 1635년경까지 고전문학론을 읽으면서 그가 발췌한 것과 해설한 것, 그의 경험담, 동료 작가들에 대한 비평 등을 특별한 체계없이 모아놓았던 것이다. 비록 잡기장에 지나지 않으나 직업적 문인으로서 문학의 일반적 이론, 원칙, 판단의 기준 등에 대하여 원만하고도 날카로운 견해를 보여주고 있다. 특히 그는 창작에 앞선 훈련과 연구를 강조하며, 창작에 임해서의 자제와 부단한 비판력의 발휘를 요청한다. I remember, the players have often mentioned it as an honour to Shakespeare that in his writing, (whatsoever he penned) he never blotted out a line. My answer has been, "Would he had blotted a thousand."란 그의 멋진 말 속에 그의 비판적 작가로서의 면모가 드러난다. 그러나 1623년 Shakespeare전집 서두에 붙인 추모시에서 그에 대한 최고의 사랑과 칭찬을 보낼 줄도 알았다. 그는 폭넓은 문인으로 과연 "The Tribe of Ben"을 인솔하는 literary lion 자격이 있었다.

From Timber: or Discoveries (1620–35)

[The Function of the Poet]

A POET is that which by the Greeks is called *exochen, o poietes,* a maker, or a feigner; his art, an art of imitation, of feigning, expressing the life of man in fit measure, numbers,* and harmony, according to Aristotle, from the word *poiein**, which signifies to make or feign. Hence he is called a poet, not he which writeth in measure only, but that feigneth and formeth a fable and writes things like the truth. For the fable and fiction is (as it were) the form and soul of any poetical work, or poem.

[A Poem as Distinct from Poesy]

A poem, as I have told you, is the work of the poet, the end and fruit of his labour and study. Poesy is his skill or craft of making, the very fiction itself, the reason or form of the work. And these three voices differ as the thing done, the doing, and the doer; the thing feigned, the feigning, and the feigner: so the poem, the poesy, and the poet. Now the poesy is the habit,* or the art; nay, rather the queen of arts, which had her original from heaven, received thence from the Hebrews, and had in prime estimation with the Greeks, transmitted to the Latins and all nations, that professed civility. The study of it (if we will trust Aristotle*) offers to mankind a certain rule and pattern of living well and happily, disposing us to all civil offices of society. If we will

---

***numbers:** 일정한 율격(measure)에 맞추어 쓴 싯귀. 운문.
*make란 뜻의 그리이스 낱말. *cf. Poetics,* I, 7.
***voices:** terms. 작품과 시와 시인을 구별하고 있다.
***habit:** settled practice. 「몸에 밴 기능」.
*Aristotle, *Politics* 제 8권 참조.

believe Tully,* it nourisheth and instructeth our youth, delights our age, adorns our prosperity, comforts our adversity, entertains us at home, keeps us company abroad, travels with us, watches, divides the times of our earnest* and sports, shares in our country recesses and recreations; insomuch as the wisest and best learned have thought her the absolute mistress of manners and nearest of kin to virtue. And whereas they entitle philosophy to be a rigid and austere poesy, they have (on the contrary) styled poesy a dulcet and gentle philosophy which leads on and guides us by the hand to action with a ravishing delight and incredible sweetness. But before we handle the kinds of poems with their special differences or make court to* the art itself as a mistress, I would lead you to the knowledge of our poet by a perfect information, what he is or should be by nature, by exercise, by imitation, by study; and so bring him down through the disciplines of grammar, logic, rhetoric and the ethics, adding somewhat* out of all peculiar to himself and worthy of your admittance or reception.

First, we require in our poet, or maker, (for that title our language affords him elegantly with the Greek) a goodness of natural wit. For whereas all other arts consist of doctrine and precepts, the poet must be able by nature and instinct to pour out the treasure of his mind; and as Seneca saith, *Aliquando secundum Anacreontem insanire jncundum esse:** by which he understands the poetical rapture. And according to that of Plato, *Frustra Poeticas fores sui compos pulsavit;* and of Aristotle, *Nullum magnum ingenium sine mixtura dementiae fuit. Nec potest grande aliquid, & supra caeteros loqui, nisi mota mens**. Then it riseth higher as by a divine instinct,

---

*Tully: 로마의 문장가 Marcus Tullius Cicero 를 가리킴. 그의 *Pro Archia Poeta*, 7 참조.

*earnest: 「진심」(명사).

*make court to: 「...에 사랑을 구하다」.

*somewhat: something.

*'Sometimes, like a second Anacreon, it is delightful to rave' (*De Tranquillitate Animi*, 15).

*'He who is his own master beats vainly at the gates of Poetry' (*Ion*).

when it contemns common and known conceptions. It utters somewhat above a mortal mouth. Then it gets aloft and flies away with his rider, whither, before, it was doubtful to ascent. This the poets understood by their Helicon, Pegasus, or Parnassus, and this made Ovid to boast:

> *Est Deus in nobis; agitante calescimus illo:*
> *Sedibus aethereis spiritus ille venit**.

And Lipsius* to affirm: *Scio, Poetam neminem praestantem fuisse, sine parte quadam uberiore divinae aurae.** And hence it is that the coming up of good poets (for I mind not mediocres, or *imos**) is so thin and rare among us; every beggarly corporation* affords the state a major or two bailiffs yearly: but, *solus Rex, aut Poeta non quotannis nascitur.* *

To this perfection of nature in our poet, we require exercise of those parts and frequent. If his wit will not arrive suddenly at the dignity of the ancients, let him not yet fall out with it, quarrel, or be over-hastily angry; offer* to turn it away from study in a humor, but come to it again upon better cogitation, try another time with labour. If then it succeed not, cast not away the quills yet, nor scratch the wainscot, beat not the poor desk, but bring all to the forge and file again, turn it anew. There is not statute law of the kingdom bids you be a poet against your will or the first quarter.* If it

---

*'There has been no great genius who has not been touched by madness, nor can you say anything great above other things unless the mind is excited' (*Poetics*, 17 장 1). Plato와 Aristotle의 글을 Seneca가 해설한 것을 옮겨온 것.

*'There is, in us, a god; by his urging, we grow warm; it is from the etherial regions that the spirit comes' (*Fasti*, vii, 5).

***Lipsius, Justus**: (1547-1606). Flemish scholar, authority on Roman literature.

*'I know that, without the divine breath or inspiration in abundance no poet has become illustrious.'

****mediocres* or *imos*:** mediocre or lowest (poets).

***Corporation:** 자치도시.

*'Only the King or the poet is not born every day.'

***offer:** try.

***the first Quarter:** 「꼭 해야 하는 일의 업무량」.

come in a year or two, it is well. The common rhymers pour forth verses such as they are, (*ex tempore) but there never come from them one sense worth the life of a day. A rhymer and a poet are two things. It is said of the incomparable Virgil that he brought forth his verses like a bear and after formed them with licking.* Scaliger the father* writes of him that he made a quantity of verses in the morning, which afore* night he reduced to a less number. But that which Valerius Maximus* hath left recorded of Euripides, the tragic poet, his answer to Alcestis*, another poet, is as memorable as modest; who, when it was told to Alcestis that Euripides had in three days brought forth but three verses and those with some difficulty and throes, Alcestis, glorying he could with ease have sent forth a hundred in the space. Euripides roundly replied like enough.* But here is the difference. Thy verses will not last those three days, mine will to all time. Which was as to tell him he could not write a verse. I have met many of these rattles that made a noise and buzzed. They had their hum and no more. Indeed, things wrote* with labour*deserve to be so read and will last their age.**

The third requisite in our poet or maker is imitation*, to

***it:** inspiration.

***ex tempore*:** 「즉흥적으로」.

***a bear:** 곰은 새끼를 낳으면 핥아서 곰의 꼴로 만든다는 전설이 있음.

***Scaliger, Julius Caesar:** (1484–1558). 프랑스에서 활약한 이탈리아의 인문학자. 수사학자였던 아들과 구별하기 위해 the father라고 함.

***of h.m:** about himeself.

***afore:** before.

***Valerius Maximus:** 1세기경의 일화수집가.

***Alcestis:** 그리이스의 극작가(?).

***like enough:** likely enough. 「그럴 듯하게」.

***wrote:** written.

***with labour:** Jonson은 이처럼 정성들여 작품을 쓰기를 강조했다. *cf.* I remember the players have often maintained it as a honor to Shakespeare that in his writing, (whatever he penned) he never blotted out a line. My answer hath been, would he had blotted a thousand. (On Shakeapeare, from *Timber, or Discoveries*).

******Imitation*:** 모범적 작품의 모방. 사숙. 자연의 모방에서 모범을 모방한다는 생각으로 옮겨온 것이 neo-classicism의 일단. *cf.* Pope, *Essay on Criticism.*

be able to convert the substance or riches of another poet to his own use. To make choice of one excellent man above the rest and so to follow him till he grow* very he, or so like him as the copy may be mistaken for the principal. Not as a creature that swallows what it takes in crude, raw, or indigested, but that feeds with an appetite and hath a stomach to concoct, divide, and turn all into nourishment. Not to imitate servily, as Horace saith*, and catch at vices for virtue, but to draw forth out of the best and choicest flowers with the bee and turn all into honey, work it into one relish and savour, make our imitation sweet, observe how the best writers have imitated, and follow them. How Virgil and Statius* have imitated Homer, how Horace, Archilochus*, how Alcaeus*, and the other lyrics, and so of the rest. But that which we especially require in him is an exactness of study and multiplicity of reading, which maketh a full man, not alone enabling him to know the history or argument of a poem and to report it, but so to master the matter and style as to show he knows how to handle, place, or dispose of either with elegancy when need shall be. And not think he can leap forth suddenly a poet by dreaming he hath been in Parnassus*, or having washed his lips (as they say) in Helicon*. There goes more to his making then so. For to nature, exercise, imitation and study, art must be added to make all these perfect. And though these challenge to themselves much in the making up of our maker, it is art only can lead him to perfection and leave him there in possession as planted by her hand. . . .

***grow:** turn into, become.

*Horace, *Art of Poetry*, 251—274..

***Statius:** 로마 시인.

***Archilochus, Alcaeus:** 고대 그리이스 시인들.

***Parnassus:** 그리이스의 산. 시 예술의 최고봉을 상징. 프랑스의 19세기 후반에 유행했던 「고답파」는 이 말에서 연유한다.

***Helicon:** Muse들이 거처하는 곳, 혹은 그 산에서 흐르는 시적 영감의 샘물.

John Dryden

(1631—1700)

청교도 평민의 집안에 태어나서 케임브리지를 졸업, 30세가 넘어 귀족 집안의 규수와 결혼하여 상류층에 본격적으로 발을 들여 놓았고, 상류층을 상대로 한 희곡을 창작함으로써 부와 명예를 다 얻었고, 1668년에 Poet Laureate이 되기에 이르렀다. 그를 출세시켜준 것은 희곡이지만 지금은 기껏 *All for Love*(1677)를 제외하고는 기억되는 바 없으며, 오히려 그가 현재의 명성을 얻게 한 것은 *Absalom and Achitophel*(1681) 등의 풍자시와 *The Hind and the Panther*(1687) 등의 논설적인 운문, 그리고 많은 분량의 비평이다.

Dr. Johnson은 드라이든을 가리켜 「원리 원칙에 의거하여 비평을 행한 영국 비평의 아버지」라 불렀는데, 그렇다고 해서 그가 비평 원론 같은 책을 지었다든지 한 적은 없다. 그의 비평은 엘리어트가 말한 소위 "작업실 비평"(workshop criticism)이라 할 수 있는 것으로서, 실제 창작에 임했을 때 당하는 비평적 문제를 체험자의 입장에서 깊고 날카롭게 파고드는 것이다. 드라이든의 모든 비평은 그의 창작 또는 번역서의 긴 서문으로 쓰인 것들이다.

단 하나의 예외가 바로 본서에 수록된 *An Essay of Dramatic Poesy*(1668)인데, 이 글은 다른 작품의 서문으로 쓰인 것이 아니고 단독적 비평문으로 쓰인 것이다.

영국이 네덜란드와의 해전에서 승리하던 날, 평민 직업 문인(드라이든 자신) 한 사람과, 당시의 상류 사회의 풍조를 좇아 문학, 특히 희곡에 관심이 크든가 직접 창작 경험이 있는 귀족 세 사람(가명 사용)이 템즈강에서 뱃놀이를 하면서 문학에 대한 논의를 벌인다.

네 사람은 당시 무슨 일이 일어나기만 하면 시구를 읊어대는 못난 시인들을 개탄한다. 그러다가 과거의 고전문학과 현대 문학의 상대적 우열에 관한 논쟁이 전개되고, 이어서 당시에 가장 총애받던 장르인 희곡을 놓고 판가름을 벌이기로 한다.

고전 희곡의 우수성을 주장하는 크라이티즈(Crites)는 당시 이탈리아와 프랑스의 보수적 문학 이론가들의 생각을 따라, 고전 작품들의 완전성을 강조하고 후세 작가들이 그것들을 모방해야 할 이유를 역설한다. 고전 작품들은 자연을 완전하게 모방하였으므로 후세 작가들은 그러한 고전을 충실히, 또한 능가하겠다는(emulate) 의지로 모방하기만 하면 저절로 자연을 재현하는 것이 된다는 것이다. 특히 고전 희곡 작가들은 시간과 장소와 행위(또는 인물)의 3일치(the three unities of time, place, action)의 법칙을 완성하여 그 완전한 실례를 보여주었으므로, 후세 작가들은 그 법칙을 지킴으로써만 고전적 희곡 작품의 제작에 성공할 수 있다는 말이다.

이에 대하여 유지니어스(Eugenius)는 현대 희곡이 고전의 모범을 통해서가 아니라 직접 자연을 모방할 수 있으며, 오히려 고전 희곡이 도달하지 못한 완전한 희곡의 형식을 성취하였으며, 같은 소재를 반복 사용한 고전 희곡과는 달리, 다양한 소재를 개발했고, 사랑과 같은 중요한 주제를 개발했으며, 권선징악에 있어서도 뚜렷한 주견을 보여 준다고 주장한다.

결국 고전 희곡의 옹호자가 판정패한 셈이다. 그러나 현대 희곡은 이탈리아와 프랑스의 대륙 계통의 작품과 영국의 작품으로 대별되는데, 그중 어느 것이 우세한가에 대해서 다시금 논쟁이 벌어진다. 리시데이어스(Lisideius)가 프랑스 희곡을 옹호하고 나선다.

그는 프랑스 희곡이 영국 희곡과 달리 3일치의 법칙을 엄격히 지킨다는 점을 강조한다. 프랑스 희곡은 영국 희곡과 달리 행위의 통일을 기하기 위하여 underplot(subplot)들을 사용하지 않으며, 또한 박진감(verisimilitude)을 조성하기 위하여 무대 위에서 전쟁 장면이나 죽음의 장면을 보이지 않으며, 또한 프랑스 희곡은 그 운문의 아름다움이 뛰어나다는 것이다.

드라이든 자신을 대변하는 니앤더(Neander)가 프랑스의 희곡에 비하여 영국 희곡의 우수함을 확인하는 책임을 맡게 된다. 그는 프랑스 희곡의 정확성이 자연의 생동감을 그대로 보여 주기에 오히려 장애가 되며, 고작 무생명한 조각, 즉 죽은 아름다움을 조성할 뿐이라고 본다. 문학의 생동감은 사람의 기질과 감정을 여실하게 보여 주는 데에서 생긴다는 것이다. 또한 영국 희곡은 슬픈 일과 기쁜 일을 섞음으로써 이른바 어울림(decorum)의 규칙을 깨뜨리지만, 그것이 오히려 관객에게 좋은 심리적 효과를 미치고 또한 다양성의 즐거움을 준다고 주장한다. 드라이든은 규칙을 준수하여 이른바 박진감을 조성한다는 정확한 작품보다, 실제의 관객에게 최대한의 흥미와 감동을 주는 작품을 옹호하고 그러한 바람직한 효과를 억압하는「정확한」작품의 가치를 의심하는 것이다.

이어서 그는 영국 극작가의 2대 거인인 셰익스피어와 벤 존슨을 비교한다. 이러한 비교 작가론은 영국 비평사상 시초에 속하는 것이다. 셰익스피어의 위대성은 자연을 있는 그대로 감동적으로 그려냄에 있다는 그의 짤막한 평은 그후 셰익스피어 비평의 기본처럼 되었다. 벤 존슨은 이른바 기질의 희극이라는 것을 창시하고 나름대로 정확한 작품의 모범을 보여 주었다는 점에서 칭찬받는다. 그의 *The Silent Woman*에 대한 분석 비평은 실제 비평의 효시에 속한다.

끝으로 그는 희곡에서 각운을 사용하는 문제를 논하는데, 자연을 모방한다는 희곡에서 각운은 부자연스럽다는 반대론에 대하여 희곡은 예술, 즉 인공의 산물이므로 어떤 형식을 사용하든지, 그것은 결코 자연 그대로일 수는 없으니, 각운이 있고 없고는 크게 문제될 것이 없고, 전 시대의 무운시(blank verse)는 너무 많이 사용되어 달리 창조적으로 쓸 여지가 없을 뿐 아니라, 각운은 자칫 방종하게 되기 쉬운 상상력을 창조적으로 정돈할 수도 있다고 주장한다. 이런 논의는 창작 실제에 관한 문제를 예리하게 다뤘다는 점에서 역시 비평사상 효시에 속한다.

이처럼 한 문제에 대해서 다각적인 견해를 제시하고, 창작과 독서(또는 관극)의 실제 경험에 중요성을 부여하는 태도는 영국 비평의 근본 태도를 굳히는 것이 되었다.

An Essay of Dramatic Poesy (1668)

It was that memorable day,* in the first summer of the late war, when our navy engaged the Dutch; a day wherein the two most mighty and best appointed fleets which any age had ever seen, disputed the command of the greater half of the globe, the commerce of nations, and the riches of the universe: while these vast floating bodies, on either side, moved against each other in parallel lines, and our countrymen, under the happy conduct of his Royal Highness, went breaking, by little and little, into the line of the enemies; the noise of the cannon from both navies reached our ears about the city;* so that all men being alarmed with it, and in a dreadful suspense of the event, which they knew was then deciding, every one went following the sound as his fancy led him; and leaving the town almost empty, some took towards the park, some cross the river, others down it; all seeking the noise in the depth of silence.

Among the rest, it was the fortune of Eugenius, Crites, Lisideius, and Neander,* to be in company together; three of them persons whom their wit and quality have made known to all the town; and whom I have chosen to hide under these borrowed names, that they may not suffer by so ill a relation as I am going to make of their discourse.*

Taking then a barge, which a servant of Lisideius had pro-

***memorable day:** 1665년 6월 3일을 가리킴. 영국과 네덜란드의 해전이 있었다.

***the city:** London.

***Eugenius, Charles Sackville, Lord Buckhurst:** (1638-1706), 궁정인, 시인.

***Crites, Sir Robert Howard:** (1626-98), 정치인, 극작가. Dryden의 처남.

***Lisideius, Sir Charles Sedly:** (1639-1701), 궁정인, 시인, 극작가.

***Neander:** 'the new man'이란 뜻으로, Dryden 자신이다.

***that they...discourse:** 그들이 논의한 바를 이제 내가 서툴게 전달함으로 말미암아 욕이 돌아가지 않도록. relation=report.

vided for them, they made haste to shoot* the bridge, and left behind them that great fall of waters* which hindered them from hearing what they desired: after which, having disengaged themselves from many vessels which rode at anchor in the Thames, and almost blocked up the passage towards Greenwich, they ordered the watermen to let fall their oars more gently; and then, every one favouring his own curiosity with a strict silence, it was not long ere they perceived the air to break about them like the noise of distant thunder, or of swallows in a chimney: those little undulations of sound, though almost vanishing before they reached them, yet still seeming to retain somewhat of their first horror, which they had betwixt the fleets. After they had attentively listened till such time as the sound by little and little went from them, Eugenius, lifting up his head, and taking notice of it, was the first who congratulated to the rest that happy omen of our nation's victory: adding, that we had but this* to desire in confirmation of it, that we might hear no more of that noise, which was now leaving the English coast. When the rest had concurred in the same opinion, Crites, a person of a sharp judgement, and somewhat too delicate a taste in wit, which the world have mistaken in him for ill-nature,* said, smiling to us, that if the concernment of this battle had not been so exceeding great, he could scarce have wished the victory at the price he knew he must pay for it, in being subject to the reading and hearing of so many ill verses as he was sure would be made on that subject. Adding, that no argument could scape* some of those eternal rhymers,*

***shoot:** move swiftly beyond.

***fall of waters:** 「배가 달릴 때 뒤에 생기는 물」.

***but this:** only this. this는 that 이하의 절을 가리킴.

***which...ill-nature:** 세상사람들로부터 못된 성미라고 오해받고 있는(그의 지나치게 섬세한 감수성).

***scape:** escape.

***eternal rhymers:** 근절되지 않는 시객들. 큰 사건만 생기면 그것을 전하는 글을 운문으로 지어서 파는 글쟁이들로, poets와 구별하여 rhymers라고 했다. Crites는 영국의 승전을 읊어댈 rhymers의 성화를 생각하고 그 승전의 값이 비싸다고 농담하고 있다.

who watch a battle with more diligence than the ravens and birds of prey; and the worst of them surest to be first in upon the quarry: while the better able, either out of modesty writ not at all, or set that* due value upon their poems, as to let them be often desired and long expected. 'There are some of those impertinent people of whom you speak,' answered Lisideius, 'who to my knowledge are already so provided, either way, that they can produce not only a panegyric* upon the victory, but, if need be, a funeral elegy on the duke;* wherein, after they have crowned his valour with many laurels, they will at last deplore the odds* under which he fell, concluding that his courage deserved a better destiny.' All the company smiled at the conceit* of Lisideius; but Crites, more eager than before, began to make particular exceptions* against some writers, and said, the public magistrate ought to send betimes to forbid them; and that it concerned the peace and quiet of all honest people, that ill poets should be as well silenced as seditious preachers. 'In my opinion,' replied Eugenius, 'you pursue your point too far; for as to my own particular, I am so great a lover of poesy, that I could wish them all rewarded, who attempt but to do well; at least, I would not have them worse used* than one of their brethren was by Sylla the Dictator:— *Quem in concione vidimus* (says Tully,) *cum ei libellum malus poeta de populo subjecisset, quod epigramma in eum fecisset tantummodo alternis versibus longiusculis, statim ex iis rebus quas tunc vendebat jubere ei praemium tribui, sub ea conditione ne quid postea scriberet.*'*

***that:** such 로 바꿀 것. 뒤의 as...절과 연결됨.

***panegyric:** 찬양시 (rhymers 는 찬양시와 장송곡을 미리 다 준비해 가지고 있다).

***the duke:** Duke of York. 앞에 나온 Royal Highness. 영국군 사령관.

***odds:** disadvantages.

***conceit:** 「기지」.

***exceptions:** 「비난」.

***used:** treated.

*'We have seen him at a public meeting, when a bad poet handed up from the crowd an epigram on him, written in rather unmetrical elegiacs. Sulla at once ordered him to be paid out of the sale of the booty, on the

'I could wish with all my heart,' replied Crites, 'that many whom we know were as bountifully thanked upon the same condition,—that they would never trouble us again. For amongst others, I have a mortal apprehension of two poets, whom this victory, with the help of both her wings, will never be able to escape.'* ''Tis easy to guess whom you intend,' said Lisideius; 'and without naming them, I ask you, if* one of them does not perpetually pay us with clenches* upon words,* and a certain clownish kind of raillery? if now and then he does not offer at a catachresis or Clevelandism;* wresting and torturing a word into another meaning: in fine;* if he be not one of those whom the French would call *un mauvais bouffon*;* one who is so much a well-willer* to the satire, that he intends at least to spare no man; and though he cannot strike a blow to hurt any, yet he ought to be punished for the malice of the action, as our witches are justly hanged, because they think themselves to be such; and suffer deservedly for believing they did mischief, because they meant it.' 'You have described him,' said Crites, 'so exactly, that I am afraid to come after you with my other extremity of poetry. He is one of those who, having had some advantage of education and converse, knows better than the other what a poet should be, but puts it into practice more unluckily than any man; his style and matter are everywhere alike: he is the most calm, peaceable writer you ever read: he never disquiets your passions with the least concernment, but

---

condition that he never write again (Cicero[=Tully], *Pro Archia*, X, 25). Sulla 는 로마의 장군으로 후에 독재자가 되었다.

***mortal apprehension:** great fear.

***her:** victory's.

***two poets:** 당시의 rhymer 들인 Robert Wild 와 Richard Flecknoe 를 가리킨다고 추정됨. 특히 후자에 대해 Dryden 은 몹시 비난조이다.

***if:** whether.

***clenches upon words:** puns.

***Clevelandism:** John Cleveland (1613-58)의 시풍. Metaphysical* Poetry 의 타락한 스타일을 쓴 시인.

***in fine:** 「짧게 말해서」.

****un mauvais buffon*:** a bad clown.

***well-willer:** 「(풍자시에) 뜻을 품고 있는 자」.

still leaves you in as even a temper as he found you;* he is a very Leveller* in poetry: he creeps along with ten little words in every line, and helps out* his numbers with ***For to***, and ***Unto***, and all the pretty expletives* he can find, till he drags them to the end of another line; while the sense is left tired half way behind it: he doubly starves all his verses, first for want of thought, and then of expression; his poetry neither has wit in it, nor seems to have it; like him in Martial:

Pauper videri *Cinna* vult, et est pauper.*

'He affects plainness, to cover his want of imagination: when he writes the serious way, the highest flight of his fancy is some miserable antithesis, or seeming contradiction; and in the comic he is still reaching at some thin conceit, the ghost of a jest,* and that too flies before him, never to be caught; these swallows which we see before us on the Thames are the just resemblance of his wit: you may observe how near the water they stoop, how many proffers* they make to dip, and yet how seldom they touch it; and when they do, it is but the surface: they skim over it but to catch a gnat, and then mount into the air and leave it.'

'Well, gentlemen,' said Eugenius, 'you may speak your pleasure of these authors; but though I and some few more about the town may give you a peaceable hearing, yet assure yourselves, there are multitudes who would think you malicious and them injured: especially him whom you first described; he is the very Withers* of the city: they have bought more

---

***as he found you:** 「독자가 처음 작품을 읽으려 할 때의 정신상태 그대로」 (작품의 효과가 전혀 없음을 비꼬고 있다).

***Leveller:** Cromwell 시대의 사회평등주의자. 여기서는 「시의 평형상태유지자」.

***help out:** 「빈틈을 메꾸다」.

***expletives:** 운율을 맞추기 위해 삽입시키는 do, dost, doth 따위.

*'Cinna wants to look poor, and so he is'(로마 시인 Martial의 *Epigrams*, viii, 19). 그 뜻은, 「가난한 척하지만, 실상은 정말로 가난하다」.

***ghost of a jest:** 농담을 해도 진짜는 못되고 「농담의 유령, 즉 헛 농담」에 불과하다.

***proffers:** 「...하려는 태세」.

***Withers, George:** (1588-1667), 선배 rhymer. Robert Wild가 바로 이 선배를 닮았다.

editions of his works than would serve to lay under all their pies at the Lord Mayor's Christmas.* When his famous poem first came out in the year 1660, I have seen them reading it in the midst of 'Change time;* nay so vehement they were at it, that they lost their bargain by the candles' ends;* but what will you say, if he has been received amongst great persons? I can assure you he is, this day, the envy of one who is lord in the art of quibbling; and who does not take it well,* that any man should intrude so far into his province.' 'All I would wish,' replied Crites, 'is, that they who love his writings, may still admire him, and his fellow poet: *Qui Bavium non odit*, &c.,* is curse sufficient.' 'And farther,' added Lisideius, 'I believe there is no man who writes well, but* would think he had hard measure, if their admirers should praise anything of his: *Nam quos contemnimus, eorum quoque laudes contemnimus*.'* 'There are so few who write well in this age,' says Crites, 'that methinks any praises should be welcome; they neither rise to the dignity of the last age, nor to any of the ancients: and we may cry out of* the writers of this time, with more reason than Petronius of his, *Pace vestra liceat dixisse, primi omnium eloquentium perdidistis*:* you have debauched the true old poetry so far, that Nature, which is the soul of it, is not in any of your writings.'

***they have bought...Lord Mayor's Christmas:** London 시장의 크리스마스 파티에 굉장한 수량의 파이를 굽는데, 그 받침으로 Wild의 시집 책장을 뜯어서 쓴다는 농담. Wild의 *Iter Boreale* (1660)은 무식한 평민 사이에서 인기가 높았다.

***'Change time:** Stock Exchange time. 「증권거래소의 영업 시간」.

***candle's end:** 촛불이 거의 다 타들어갔을 무렵에는 경매가가 아주 쌌다.

***does not...well:** 「...을 좋아하지 않는다」.

*'Who does not hate Bavius?' (Virgil, *Eclogues*, iii, 80), 「못난 자가 못난 시인을 좋아하라」는 뜻.

***but:** that...not. 「...하지 않을」(복합관계대명사)

*'We despise the praise of those we despise' (출처 미상). 「못난 이의 칭찬은 듣기 싫다」.

***of:** about, against.

*'Please, let me say that you have ruined eloquence more than anyone else' (로마의 풍자시인 Petronius의 *Satyricon*, 2).

'If your quarrel,' said Eugenius, 'to those who now write, be grounded only on your reverence to antiquity, there is no man more ready to adore those great Greeks and Romans than I am: but on the other side, I cannot think so contemptibly of the age in which I live, or so dishonourably of my own country, as not to judge we equal the ancients in most kinds of poesy, and in some surpass them; neither know I any reason why I may not be as zealous for the reputation of our age, as we find the ancients themselves were* in reference to those who lived before them. For you hear your Horace saying,

> Indignor quidquam reprehendi, non quia crasse
> Compositum, illepideve putetur, sed quia nuper.

And after:

> Si meliora dies, ut vina, poemata reddit,
> Scire velim, pretim chartis quotus arroget annus?*

'But I see I am engaging in a wide dispute, where the arguments are not like to reach close on either side; for poesy is of so large an extent, and so many both of the ancients and moderns have done well in all kinds of it, that in citing one against the other, we shall take up more time this evening than each man's occasions will allow him: therefore I would ask Crites to what part of poesy he would confine his arguments, and whether he would defend the general cause of the ancients against the moderns, or oppose any age of the moderns against this* of ours?'

Crites, a little while considering upon this demand, told Eugenius, that if he pleased, he would limit their dispute to Dramatic Poesy; in which he thought it not difficult to prove, either that the ancients were superior to the moderns, or the

*were: 다음에 zealous for the reputation of their age를 넣어 읽을 것.

*'I am displeased when any work is condemned, not because it is thought coarse or ungraceful, but because it is modern.'
'If time improves poems, as it does wine. I should like to know how many years must pass before writings become valuable?' (Horace, *Epistles*, II, i, 76 & 34).

*this: this age (of ours).

last age to this of ours.

Eugenius was somewhat surprised, when he heard Crites make choice of that subject. 'For ought I see,'* said he, 'I have undertaken a harder province than I imagined; for though I never judged the plays of the Greek or Roman poets comparable to ours, yet, on the other side, those we now see acted come short of many which were written in the last age: but my comfort is, if we are overcome, it will be only by our own countrymen: and if we yield to them in this one part of poesy, we more surpass them in all the other: for in the epic or lyric way, it will be hard for them to show us one such amongst them, as we have many now living, or who lately were: they can produce nothing so courtly writ, or which expresses so much the conversation of a gentleman, as Sir John Suckling*; nothing so even, sweet, and flowing, as Mr. Waller; nothing so majestic, so correct, as Sir John Denham; nothing so elevated, so copious, and full of spirit, as Mr. Cowley*; as for the Italian, French, and Spanish plays, I can make it evident, that those who now write surpass them; and that the drama is wholly ours.'

All of them were thus far of Eugenius's opinion, that the sweetness of English verse was never understood or practised by our fathers; even Crites himself did not much oppose it; and every one was willing to acknowledge how much our poesy is improved by the happiness* of some writers yet living; who first taught us to mould our thoughts into easy and significant words,—to retrench the superfluities of expression,—and to make our rhyme so properly a part of the verse, that it should never mislead the sense, but itself be led and governed by it.

Eugenius was going to continue this discourse, when Lisideius

---

***For ought I see:** 「아무리 보아도, 확실히」.

***Sir John Suckling** (1609–42), **Edmund Waller** (1606–87), **Sir John Denham** (1615–69): 이들은 모두 Metaphysical poetry의 유행에서 벗어나 잘 다듬은 시를 쓴 사람들로 대체로 왕당파에 속했다.

***Abraham Cowley** (1618–67): 이 사람도 왕당파이나, 모든 주제에 대하여 다양한 형식을 실험했던 시인이다.

***happiness:** appropriateness. 「잘 된 것」.

told him that it was necessary, before they proceeded further, to take a standing measure* of their controversy; for how was it possible to be decided who writ the best plays, before we know what a play should be? But, this once agreed on by both parties, each might have recourse to it, either to prove his own advantages, or to discover the failings of his adversary.

He had no sooner said this, but all desired the favour of him to give the definition of a play; and they were the more importunate, because neither Aristotle, nor Horace, nor any other, who had writ of that subject, had ever done it.

Lisideius, after some modest denials, at last confessed he had a rude notion of it; indeed, rather a description than a definition; but which served to guide him in his private thoughts, when he was to make a judgement of what others writ: that he conceived a play ought to be, *A just and lively image of human nature, representing its passions and humours, and the changes of fortune to which it is subject,* for the delight and instruction of mankind.*

This definition, though Crites raised a logical objection against it—that it was only *genere et fine*,* and so not altogether perfect, was yet well received by the rest; and after they had given order to the watermen to turn their barge, and row softly, that they might take the cool of the evening in their return, Crites, being desired by the company to begin, spoke on behalf of the ancients, in this manner:—

'If confidence presage a victory, Eugenius, in his own opinion, has already triumphed over the ancients: nothing seems more easy to him, than to overcome those whom it is our greatest praise to have imitated well; for we do not only build upon their foundations, but by their models. Dramatic Poesy had time enough, reckoning from Thespis* (who first invented it) to Aristophanes, to be born, to grow up, and to

***standing measure:** 「일정한 척도(를 택하다)」.

***changes...subject:** it, 즉 human nature가 겪어야 하는(subject to) 인간사의 흥망성쇠. 즉 인간의 제 행위.

***a logical objection:** 종류(genus)와 목적(finis)만 말하고 차이(differentia)는 말하지 않았다는 이의.

***Thespis:** 기원전 6세기경 그리이스 희곡의 창시자로 알려진 인물.

flourish in maturity. It has been observed of arts and sciences, that in one and the same century they have arrived to great perfection; and no wonder, since every age has a kind of universal genius, which inclines those that live in it to some particular studies: the work then, being pushed on by many hands, must of necessity go forward.

'Is it not evident, in these last hundred years, when the study of philosophy has been the business of all the Virtuosi in Christendom, that almost a new nature has been revealed to us? That more errors of the school* have been detected, more useful experiments in philosophy have been made, more noble secrets in optics, medicine, anatomy, astronomy, discovered, than in all those credulous and doting ages from Aristotle to us?—so true it is, that nothing spreads more fast than science, when rightly and generally cultivated.

'Add to this, the more than common emulation that was in those times of writing well; which though it be found in all ages and all persons that pretend to the same reputation, yet poesy, being then in more esteem than now it is, had greater honours decreed to the professors of it,* and consequently the rivalship was more high between them; they had judges ordained to decide their merit, and prizes to reward it; and historians have been diligent to record of Aeschylus, Euripides, Sophocles, Lycophron,* and the rest of them, both who they were that vanquished in these wars of the theatre, and how often they were crowned: while the Asian kings and Grecian commonwealths scarce afforded them a nobler subject than the unmanly luxuries of a debauched court, or giddy intrigues of a factious city:—*Alit aemulatio ingenia,* (says Paterculus,)* *et nunc invidia, nunc admiratio incitationem accendit*: Emulation is the spur of wit; and sometimes envy, sometimes admiration, quickens

---

***school:** 중세의 스콜라철학파.
***professors of it:** 「시를 천직으로 삼고 있는 사람, 즉 시인들」.
***Lycophron:** 기원전 3세기경 알렉산드리아의 비극 작가.
***Paterculus, Velleius:** 기원 전후의 로마 역사가. 텍스트에서 인용문 다음이 그 번역이다.

our endeavours.

'But now, since the rewards of honour are taken away, that virtuous emulation is turned into direct malice; yet so slothful, that it contents itself to condemn and cry down others, without attempting to do better: it is a reputation too unprofitable, to take the necessary pains for it; yet, wishing they had it, that desire is incitement enough to hinder others from it.* And this, in short, Eugenius, is the reason why you have now so few good poets, and so many severe judges. Certainly, to imitate the ancients well, much labour and long study is required; which pains, I have already shown, our poets would want encouragement to take, if yet they had ability to go through the work. Those ancients have been faithful imitators and wise observers of that nature which is so torn and ill represented in our plays; they have handed down to us a perfect resemblance of her; which we, like ill copiers, neglecting to look on, have rendered monstrous, and disfigured. But, that you may know how much you are indebted to those your masters, and be ashamed to have so ill requited them, I must remember* you, that all the rules by which we practise the drama at this day, (either such as relate to the justness and symmetry of the plot, or the episodical ornaments, such as descriptions, narrations, and other beauties, which are not essential to the play,) were delivered to us from the observations which Aristotle made, of those poets, who either lived before him, or were his contemporaries: we have added nothing of our own, except we have the confidence to say our wit is better; of which, none boast in this our age, but such as understand not theirs. Of that book which Aristotle has left us, *περὶ τῆς Ποιητικῆς*, Horace's *Art of Poetry* is an excellent comment, and, I believe, restores to us that Second Book of his concerning Comedy,* which is wanting

---

***that desire...it:** 명성에 대한 욕망으로 자극을 받아 남의 명성을 가로막는 것을 하게 되었다. 그래서 가혹한 비평가들이 많이 생겨났다는 의미이다.

***remember:** remind.

***Second Book of his concerning Comedy:** Aristotle의 희극론은 전해지지 않고 있다. Horace가 *The Art of Poetry*의 일부에서 희극에 관해 언급하고 있는데, 이것이 Aristotle의 희극론을 대신한다고 Dryden은 보고 있는 것이다. 앞의 그리이스어로 된 제목은 「시학」을 가리킴.

in him.

'Out of these two have been extracted the famous Rules,* which the French call *Des Trois Unités*, or, The Three Unities, which ought to be observed in every regular play; namely, of Time, Place, and Action.

'The unity of time they comprehend in twenty-four hours, the compass of a natural day, or as near as it can be contrived; and the reason of it is obvious to every one,—that the time of the feigned action, or fable of the play, should be proportioned as near as can be to the duration of that time in which it is represented: since therefore, all plays are acted on the theatre in the space of time much* within the compass of twenty-four hours, that play is to be thought the nearest imitation of nature, whose plot or action is confined within that time; and, by the same rule which concludes this general proportion of time, it follows, that all the parts of it are (as near as may be) to be equally subdivided; namely, that one act take not up the supposed time of half a day, which is out of proportion to the rest; since the other four are then to be straitened within the compass of the remaining half: for it is unnatural that one act, which being spoke or written is not longer than the rest, should be supposed longer by the audience; it is therefore the poet's duty, to take care that no act should be imagined to exceed the time in which it is represented on the stage; and that the intervals and inequalities of time be supposed to fall out between the acts.*

'This rule of time, how well it has been observed by the ancients, most of their plays will witness; you see them in their tragedies, (wherein to follow this rule, is certainly most diffi-

---

***the famous Rules:** 이른바 The Three Unities(삼일치의 법칙)은 Aristotle이 규정한 것이 아니고, 르네상스 시대 이탈리아의 학자 Castelvetro가 Aritstotle의 *Poetics*를 편찬하면서 삽입한 해설에서 온 것이다.

***in the space of time...hours:** 「24시간보다 훨씬 이내의 시간 범위에서」 (실제 상연은 보통 2~3시간 안에 이루어진다.)

*24시간 이내에 생긴 사건을 2~3시간 동안에 5막극으로 재현할 때는 반드시 사건을 5등분할 것이며, 막간에 나머지 시간이 흐른 것처럼 처리하라는 「시간의 통일」 법칙을 설명하고 있다.

cult,) from the very beginning of their plays, falling close into that part of the story which they intend for the action or principal object of it, leaving the former part to be delivered by narration: so that they set the audience, as it were, at the post where the race is to be concluded; and, saving them the tedious expectation of seeing the poet set out and ride the beginning of the course, they suffer you not to behold him, till he is in sight of the goal, and just upon you.*

'For the second unity, which is that of Place, the ancients meant by it, that the scene ought to be continued through the play, in the same place where it was laid in the beginning: for, the stage on which it is represented being but one and the same place, it is unnatural to conceive it many,*—and those far distant from one another. I will not deny but, by the variation of painted scenes, the fancy, which in these cases will contribute to its own deceit, may sometimes imagine it several places, with some appearance of probability; yet it still carries the greater likelihood of truth, if those places be supposed so near each other, as in the same town or city; which may all be comprehended under the larger denomination of one place; for a greater distance will bear no proportion to the shortness of time which is allotted, in the acting, to pass from one of them to another*; for the observation of this, next to the ancients, the French are to be most commended. They tie themselves so strictly to the unity of place, that you never see in any of their plays, a scene changed in the middle of an act: if the act begins in a garden, a street, or chamber, 'tis ended in the same place; and that you may know it to be the same, the stage is so supplied with persons, that it is never empty all the time: he who enters second, has business with him who was on before;

---

*긴 사건을 다룰 땐 그 사건의 마지막 부분(말하자면 goal line 부근)을 다루고, 그 전의 사건의 전말은 설명(narration)으로 처리하라는 것.

***conceive it many:** 하나의 장소(**stage**)를 다른 여러 장소로 생각하는 것.

*무대는 계속 한 장소를 나타내는 것이 좋되, 여의치 않을 경우에는 막간 사이에 옮겨갈 수 있는 한 도시 내의 장소로 그 범위를 한정시켜 변화를 가해야 한다는「장소의 통일」법칙을 설명하고 있다.

and before the second quits the stage, a third appears who has business with him. This Corneille calls *la liaison des scènes*,* the continuity or joining of the scenes; and 'tis a good mark of a well-contrived play, when all the persons are known to each other, and every one of them has some affairs with all the rest.

'As for the third unity, which is that of Action, the ancients meant no other by it than what the logicians do by their *finis*,* the end or scope of any action; that which is the first in intention, and last in execution: now the poet is to aim at one great and complete action, to the carrying on of which all things in his play, even the very obstacles, are to be subservient; and the reason of this is as evident as any of the former. For two actions, equally laboured and driven on by the writer, would destroy the unity of the poem; it would be no longer one play, but two: not but that there may be many actions in a play, as Ben Jonson has observed in his *Discoveries*;* but they must be all subservient to the great one, which our language happily expresses in the name of *under-plots*: such as in Terence's *Eunuch** is the difference and reconcilement of Thais and Phaedria, which is not the chief business of the play, but promotes the marriage of Chaerea and Chremes's sister, principally intended by the poet. There ought to be but one action, says Corneille, that is, one complete action, which leaves the mind of the audience in a full repose; but this cannot be brought to pass but by many other imperfect actions, which conduce to it, and hold the audience in a delightful suspense of what will be.

'If by these rules (to omit many other drawn from the pre-

***la liaison des scènes*: 「장면의 연속」. 막과 막은 연속이 끊기지만, 한 막 속에서의 장면들은 언제나 연속이 되도록 하는 수법. 프랑스의 극작가 Pierre Corneille (1606-84)가 완성한 기법으로 장소의 통일 법칙을 한층 더 강화시킨 것이다.

**finis*: 「목적, 끝」.

as Ben Jonson...his** ***Discoveries: 'One is considerable two ways, either as it is only separate and by itself, or as being composed of many parts, it begins to be one as those parts grow or are wrought together' (*Timber, or Discoveries*, Spingarn, p. 62).

**Eunuch*: 로마 극작가 Terence (195?-159 B.C.)의 희극작품.

cepts and practice of the ancients) we should judge our modern plays, 'tis probable that few of them would endure the trial: that which should be the business of a day, takes up in some of them an age; instead of one action, they are the epitomes of a man's life; and for one spot of ground, which the stage should represent, we are sometimes in more countries than the map can show us.

'But if we allow the Ancients to have contrived well, we must acknowledge them to have written better. Questionless we are deprived of a great stock of wit in the loss of Menander among the Greek poets, and of Caecilius, Afranius, and Varius, among the Romans*; we may guess at Menander's excellency by the plays of Terence, who translated some of his; and yet wanted so much of him, that he was called by C. Caesar the half-Menander; and may judge of Varius, by the testimonies of Horace, Martial, and Velleius Paterculus. 'Tis probable that these* could they be recovered, would decide the controversy; but so long as Aristophanes and Plautus are extant, while the tragedies of Euripides, Sophocles, and Seneca, are in our hands, I can never see one of those plays which are now written, but* it increases my admiration of the ancients. And yet I must acknowledge further, that to admire them as we ought, we should understand them better than we do. Doubtless many things appear flat to us, the wit of which depended on some custom or story, which never came to our knowledge; or perhaps on some criticism in their language, which being so long dead, and only remaining in their books, 'tis not possible they should make us understand perfectly. To read Macrobius* explaining the propriety and elegancy of many words in Virgil, which I had before passed over without consideration as common things, is enough to assure me that I ought to think the

*Caecilius, Afranius, Varius, Menander: 이들은 모두 고대의 극작가들로, 이름은 남아 있으나 전해오는 작품은 없다.

*these: the lost plays.

*but: unless.

*Macrobius: 기원 400년경에 활약한 로마 저술가. *Saturnalia*에서 Virgil을 논함.

same of Terence; and that in the purity of his style (which Tully so much valued that he ever carried his works about him) there is yet left in him great room for admiration, if I knew but where to place* it. In the mean time I must desire you to take notice, that the greatest man of the last age, Ben Jonson,* was willing to give place to them in all things: he was not only a professed imitator of Horace, but a learned plagiary of all the others; you track him everywhere in their snow:* if Horace, Lucan, Petronius Arbiter, Seneca, and Juvenal, had their own from him, there are few serious thoughts which are new in him: you will pardon me, therefore, if I presume he loved their fashion, when he wore their clothes. But since I have otherwise a great veneration for him, and you, Eugenius, prefer him above all other poets, I will use no further argument to you than his example: I will produce before you Father Ben,* dressed in all the ornaments and colours of the ancients; you will need no other guide to our party, if you follow him; and whether you consider the bad plays of our age, or regard the good plays of the last, both the best and worst of the modern poets will equally instruct you to admire the ancients.'

Crites had no sooner left speaking, but Eugenius, who had waited with some impatience for it, thus began:

'I have observed in your speech, that the former part of it is convincing as to what the moderns have profited by the rules of the ancients; but in the latter you are careful to conceal how much they have excelled them; we own all the helps we have from them, and want neither veneration nor gratitude, while we acknowledge that, to overcome them, we must make use of the advantages we have received from them: but to these assistances we have joined our own industry; for, had we sat

---

***place:** (좋은 점을) 「지적하다, 가려내다」.

***he was not...are new in him:** Ben Jonson 은 고전문학이라는 눈벌판에 자신의 자취를 남겼다. 즉, 고전을 섭렵하며 그속에서 많은 것을 훔쳐다 (plagiary) 이용했다. 그러므로 고전작가들이 Jonson 에게서 자기네 것들을 다시 찾아간다면 그에게 남아 있을 중요한 사상은 거의 없게 될 것이다.

***Father Ben:** 즉 Ben Jonson 을 말함. 그는 당시에 가장 존경받는 문인이어서 그런 칭호가 붙었다.

down with a dull imitation of them, we might then have lost somewhat of the old perfection, but never acquired any that was new. We draw not therefore after their lines, but those of nature;* and having the life before us, besides the experience of all they knew, it is no wonder if we hit some airs and features* which they have missed. I deny not what you urge of arts and sciences, that they have flourished in some ages more than others; but your instance in philosophy makes for me:* for if natural causes be more known now than in the time of Aristotle, because more studied, it follows that poesy and other arts may, with the same pains,* arrive still nearer to perfection; and, that granted,* it will rest for you to prove* that they wrought more perfect images of human life than we; which seeing in your discourse you have avoided to make good,* it shall now be my task to show you some part of their defects, and some few excellencies of the moderns. And I think there is none among us* can imagine I do it enviously, or with purpose to detract from them; for what interest of fame or profit can the living lose by the reputation of the dead? On the other side, it is a great truth which Velleius Paterculus affirms: *Audita visis libentius laudamus; et praesentia invidia praeterita admiratione prosequimur; et his nos obrui, illis instrui credimus: that praise or censure is certainly the**

***we draw not...of nature:** 고전작가들이 그은 선을 따라서 그리는 것이 아니라 자연 자체의 선을 따라 그린다. 이것은 고전작가의 모방을 자연의 모방 대신 내세웠던 신고전주의의 이론을 반박한 것이다. *cf.* Pope, *Essay on Criticism*, 135—140 행.

***airs and features:** 분위기 또는 인상과 겉모습. 고전문학이 발견하지 못했던 인생의 airs와 features를 현대문학이 우연히 발견(hit)할 수도 있으니까, 현대문학이 유리한 입장에 있다는 것.

***make for me:** support me.

***pains:** 「노력, 연구」.

***that granted:** 「그것을 인정하면」.

***it will...prove:** 「...을 당신이 증명할 책임이 있다」.

***to make good:** 「입증하다」. 현대영어에서는 making good이라 할 것이다.

***none...can:** none among us who can. There is someone who와 같은 구문에서 주격관계대명사 who는 생략되곤 했다.

*'We are more inclined to praise what we have heard than what has occurred before our eyes; we regard the present with envy, the past

most sincere, which unbribed posterity shall give us.

'Be pleased then in the first place to take notice, that the Greek poesy, which Crites has affirmed to have arrived to perfection in the reign of the old comedy,* was so far from it, that the distinction of it* into acts was not known to them; or if it were, it is yet so darkly delivered to us that we cannot make it out.

'All we know of it is, from the singing of their Chorus; and that too is so uncertain, that in some of their plays we have reason to conjecture they sung more than five times. Aristotle* indeed divides the integral parts of a play into four.* First, the *Protasis*, or entrance, which gives light only to the characters of the persons, and proceeds very little into any part of the action. Secondly, the *Epitasis*, or working up of the plot; where the play grows warmer;* the design or action of it is drawing on, and you see something promising that it will come to pass. Thirdly, the *Catastasis*, called by the Romans, *Status*, the height and full growth of the play: we may call it properly the counter-turn, which destroys that expectation, embroils the action in new difficulties, and leaves you far distant from that hope in which it found you;* as you may have observed in a violent stream resisted by a narrow passage,—it runs round to an eddy, and carries back the waters with more swiftness than it brought them on. Lastly, the *Catastrophe*, which the Grecians called λύσις, the French *le dénouement*, and we the discovery, or unravelling of the plot: there you see all things settling again upon their first foundations; and, the obstacles which hindered the design or action of the play once removed, it ends with that

---

with veneration, and believe that we are eclipsed by the former, but derive instruction from the latter' (*Historia Romana*, ii, 92).

***old comedy:** 기원전 5세기 이전의 그리이스의 희극. Aristophanes가 그 대표.

***it:** perfection.

***Aristotle...into four:** 사실은 르네상스 시대 이탈리아의 문학자 Scaliger의 구분이다.

***grows warmer:** 「열기가 더해간다」.

***that hope...you:** 「처음에 관객이 가졌던 희망」.

resemblance of truth and nature, that the audience are satisfied with the conduct of it. Thus this great man delivered to us the image of a play; and I must confess it is so lively, that from thence much light has been derived to the forming it more perfectly into acts and scenes: but what poet first limited to five the number of the acts, I know not; only we see it so firmly established in the time of Horace, that he gives it for a rule in comedy,—*Neu brevior quinto, neu sit productior actu.** So that you see the Grecians cannot be said to have consummated this art; writing rather by entrances, than by acts, and having rather a general indigested notion of a play, than knowing how and where to bestow the particular graces of it.

'But since the Spaniards at this day allow but three acts, which they call *Jornadas*, to a play, and the Italians in many of theirs follow them, when I condemn the ancients, I declare it is not altogether because they have not five acts to every play, but because they have not confined themselves to one certain number: it is building a house without a model; and when they succeeded in such undertakings, they ought to have sacrificed to Fortune, not to the Muses.*

'Next, for the plot, which Aristotle called τὸ μῦθος, and often τῶν πραγμάτων σύνθεσις,* and from him the Romans *Fabula*;* it has already been judiciously observed by a late writer, that in their tragedies it was only some tale derived from Thebes or Troy, or at least something that happened in those two ages; which was worn so threadbare by the pens of all the epic poets, and even by tradition* itself of the talkative Greeklings, (as Ben Jonson calls them,) that before it came upon the stage, it was already known to all the audience: and the people, so soon as ever they heard the name of Oedipus, knew

---

***Neu brevior...**: 'Let it be neither more nor less than five acts' (*Art of Poetry*). 이같은 주장 이후 유럽에서 5막극의 전통이 생겼다.

***when they...to the Muses:** 「고전작가들이 성공했다면, 그건 시신의 덕이 아니라 행운의 덕분이다」. Sacrifice: 「감사의 제사를 드리다」.

*'the plot', 'the arrangements of events' (*Poetics*, vi. 5)

****Fabula*:** 즉 fable. 당시에는 plot을 뜻했다. 그리이스어로는 myth.

***tradition:** 「구비문학」을 의미하고 있다.

as well as the poet, that he had killed his father by a mistake, and committed incest with his mother, before the play; that they were now to hear of a great plague, an oracle, and the ghost of Laius:* so that they sat with a yawning kind of expectation, till he was to come with his eyes pulled out, and speak a hundred or more verses in a tragic tone, in complaint of his misfortunes. But one Oedipus, Hercules, or Medea, had been tolerable: poor people, they escaped not so good cheap;* they had still the *chapon bouillé** set before them, till their appetites were cloyed with the same dish, and, the novelty being gone, the pleasure vanished; so that one main end of Dramatic Poesy in its definition, which was to cause delight, was of consequence destroyed.

'In their comedies, the Romans generally borrowed their plots from the Greek poets; and theirs was commonly a little girl stolen or wandered from her parents, brought back unknown to the city, there got with child by some lewd young fellow; who, by the help of his servant, cheats his father; and when her time comes to cry,—*Juno Lucina, fer opem*;*—one or other sees a little box or cabinet which was carried away with her, and so discovers her to her friends, if some god do not prevent it, by coming down in a machine;* and taking the thanks of it to himself.

'By the plot you may guess much of the characters of the persons. An old father, who would willingly, before he dies, see his son well married; his debauched son, kind in his nature to

---

***Laius:** Oedipus가 모르고 살해한 자신의 부친. 자신의 죄상이 밝혀지자 Oedipus는 자기의 두 눈을 뺀다.

***poor...cheap:** 「가련하게도 그리이스 사람들은 그렇게 쉽게 (같은 이야기를 반복해서 듣는 고통으로부터) 벗어날 수가 없었다」.

****Chapon bouillé*:** 「영계백숙」. 처음엔 맛있지만 늘 먹으면 싫증나는 음식.

****Juno*...:** 'Juno Lucina (Goddess of childbrith), give help to me'.

by coming...machine:** (희곡의 결말을 쉽게 맺기 위하여)「무대장치를 통해 신을 등장시킴으로써」. 신은 무슨 일이나 다 할 수 있으므로 해결이 잘 안 되는 인간사에 개입시키면 문제는 쉽게 풀리지만 흥미는 줄어든다. 따라서 우연에 의거하여 쉽게 해결하는 방법을 ***deus ex machina (a god out of a machine)이라 부르게 되었다.

his mistress, but miserably in want of money; a servant or slave, who has so much wit to strike in with* him, and help to dupe his father; a braggadocio captain, a parasite, and a lady of pleasure.

'As for the poor honest maid, on whom the story is built, and who ought to be one of the principal actors in the play, she is commonly a mute in it: she has the breeding of the old Elizabeth way, which was for maids to be seen and not to be heard; and it is enough you know she is willing to be married, when the fifth act requires it.

'These are plots built after the Italian mode of houses,—you see through them all at once: the characters are indeed the imitation of nature, but so narrow, as if they had imitated only an eye or a hand, and did not dare to venture on the lines of a face, or the proportion of a body.*

'But in how strait a compass soever they have bounded their plots and characters, we will pass it by, if they have regularly pursued them, and perfectly observed those three unities of time, place, and action; the knowledge of which you say is derived to us from them. But in the first place give me leave to tell you, that the unity of place, however it might be practised by them, was never any of their rules: we neither find it in Aristotle, Horace, or any who have written of it, till in our age the French poets first made it a precept of the stage. The unity of time, even Terence himself, who was the best and most regular of them, has neglected: his *Heautontimorumenos*, or Self-Punisher, takes up visibly two days, says Scaliger; the two first acts concluding the first day, the three last the day ensuing; and Euripides, in tying himself to one day, has committed an absurdity never to be forgiven him; for in one of his tragedies*

***strike in with...:** 「...와 뜻이 잘 맞다」.

***These are plots...:** 지금 전해지고 있는 로마의 희곡들은 소재가 다양하지 못할 뿐만 아니라, 인물들이나 plot이 모두 비슷비슷하다. 더우기 Horace는 희곡에서의 인물들은 다양하든가 특수해서는 안되고 금방 알아볼 수 있는 전형(type)이어야 한다고 했다.

***one of his tragedies:** 즉 Euripides의 *The Suppliants*를 말하며, 구성에 문제가 있는 작품이다.

he has made Theseus go from Athens to Thebes, which was about forty English miles, under the walls of it to give battle, and appear victorious in the next act; and yet, from the time of his departure to the return of the Nuntius, who gives the relation of his victory, Aethra and the Chorus have but thirty-six verses; which is not for every mile a verse.

'The like error is as evident in Terence's *Eunuch*, when Laches, the old man, enters by mistake into the house of Thais; where, betwixt his exit and the entrance of Pythias, who comes to give ample relation of the disorders he has raised within, Parmeno, who was left upon the stage, has not above five lines to speak. *C'est bien employer un temps si court*, says the French poet,* who furnished me with one of the observations: and almost all their tragedies will afford us examples of the like nature.

'It is true, they have kept the continuity, or, as you called it, *liaison des scènes*, somewhat better: two do not perpetually come in together, talk, and go out together; and other two succeed them, and do the same throughout the act, which the English call by the name of single scenes; but the reason is, because they have seldom above two or three scenes, properly so called, in every act; for it is to be accounted a new scene, not only every time the stage is empty; but every person who enters, though to others, makes it so;* because he introduces a new business. Now the plots of their plays being narrow, and the persons few, one of their acts was written in a less compass than one of our well-wrought scenes; and yet they are often deficient even in this. To go no farther than Terence; you find in the *Eunuch*, Antipho entering single in the midst of the third act, after Chremes and Pythias were gone off; in the same play you have likewise Dorias beginning the fourth act alone; and after she had made a relation of what was done at the Soldier's entertainment, (which by the way was very inartificial, because she

***French poet:** 즉 Corneille를 가리킨다. 바로 앞에 인용된 글의 뜻은 'It is well to employ a time so short'. 이 인용문이 담겨 있는 Corneille의 희곡 법칙에 관한 글(*Discours*)을 Dryden은 매우 탐독하였다.

***make it so:** make the scene a new one.

was presumed to speak directly to the audience, and to acquaint them with what was necessary to be known, but yet should have been so contrived by the poet as to have been told by persons of the drama to one another, and so by them to have come to the knowledge of the people,) she quits the stage, and Phaedria enters next, alone likewise: he also gives you an account of himself, and of his returning from the country, in monologue; to which unnatural way of narration Terence is subject in all his plays.* In his *Adelphi*, or Brothers, Syrus and Demea enter after the scene was broken by the departure of Sostrata, Geta, and Canthara; and indeed you can scarce look into any of his comedies, where you will not presently discover the same interruption.

'But as they have failed both in laying of their plots, and in the management, swerving from the rules of their own art by misrepresenting nature to us, in which they have ill satisfied one intention of a play, which was delight; so in the instructive part they have erred worse: instead of punishing vice and rewarding virtue, they have often shown a prosperous wickedness, and an unhappy piety: they have set before us a bloody image of revenge in Medea, and given her dragons to convey her safe from punishment; a Priam and Astyanax murdered, and Cassandra ravished, and the lust and murder ending in the victory of him who acted them:* in short, there is no indecorum in any of our modern plays, which if I would excuse, I could not shadow with some authority from the ancients.*

***to which...plays:** 「Terence는 그의 모든 희곡작품에서 그처럼 부자연스러운 이야기 방법을 따르고 있다」. 여기서 which는 관계지시대명사로 that의 뜻. be subject to: 「따르다, 복종하다」.

***a bloody image...in Medea:** 온갖 악행을 저지른 마녀 Medea는 용을 타고 탈주하고, Troy의 착한 임금 Priam과 그의 어린 손자 Astyanax는 무참히 살해당하고, 그의 딸 Cassandra는 겁탈당한다. 말하자면 도덕적으로 내려지는 벌과 상이 공평하지 않으므로, 교훈(instruction)이라는 문학의 중요 기능은 제구실을 못하는 것이라고 보는 것이다.

***there is...ancients:** 「현대극에서나 볼 수 있는 부도덕한 면을 보호하고자 한다면 고전극의 권위를 들어서 덮어버리지 못할 게 없다」는 뜻. shadow: 「허물을 감추다」.

'And one further note of them let me leave you: tragedies and comedies were not writ then as they are now, promiscuously, by the same person; but he who found his genius bending to the one, never attempted the other way. This is so plain, that I need not instance to you, that Aristophanes, Plautus, Terence; never any of them writ a tragedy; Aeschylus, Euripides, Sophocles, and Seneca, never meddled with comedy: the sock and buskin were not worn by the same poet.* Having then so much care to excel in one kind, very little is to be pardoned them, if they miscarried in it; and this would lead me to the consideration of their wit, had not Crites given me sufficient warning not to be too bold in my judgement of it; because, the languages being dead, and many of the customs and little accidents on which it depended lost to us,* we are not competent judges of it. But though I grant that here and there we may miss the application of a proverb or a custom, yet a thing well said will be wit in all languages; and though it may lose something in the translation, yet to him who reads it in the original, 'tis still the same: he has an idea of its excellency, though it cannot pass from his mind into any other expression or words than those in which he finds it. When Phaedria, in the *Eunuch*, had a command from his mistress to be absent two days, and, encouraging himself to go through with it,* said, *Tandem ego non illa caream, si sit opus, vel totum triduum*?*—Parmeno, to mock the softness of his master, lifting up his hands and eyes, cries out, as it were in admiration, *Hui! universum triduum!** the elegancy of which *universum*, though it cannot be rendered in our language, yet leaves an impression on our souls: but this happens seldom in him; in Plautus oftener, who is infinitely too bold in his

***sock and buskin:** sock는 희극배우가, buskin은 비극배우가 신던 신. 비유적으로 희극과 비극을 가리킨다.

***lost to us:** 「우리에게 전해지지 않은」.

***encouraging...with it:** 「그 명령을 따르겠다고 다짐하면서」.

* ***Tandem ego*...**: 'Shall I not do without her for even three days if necessary?'

****Hui!*...**: 'Alas, the total of three days!' (Phaedria, ***Eunuch***, Ⅱ, i).

metaphors and coining words, out of which* many times his wit is nothing; which questionless was one reason why Horace falls upon him so severely in those verses:

> Sed proavi nostri Plautinos et numeros et
> Laudavere sales, nimium patienter utrumque,
> Ne dicam stolide.*

For Horace himself was cautious to obtrude a new word on his readers, and makes custom and common use the best measure of receiving it into our writings:

> Multa renascentur quae nunc cecidere, cadentque
> Quae nunc sunt in honore vocabula, si volet usus,
> Quem penes arbitrium est, et jus, et norma loquendi.*

The not observing this rule is that which the world has blamed in our satirist, Cleveland: to express a thing hard and unnaturally, is his new way of elocution. 'Tis true, no poet but may sometimes use a catachresis: Virgil does it—

> Mistaque ridenti colocasia fundet acantho—*

in his eclogue of Pollio; and in his seventh *Aeneid*

> —mirantur et undae,
> Miratur nemus insuetum fulgentia longe
> Scuta virum fluvio pictasque innare carinas.*

And Ovid once so modestly, that he asks leave to do it:

> —quem, si verbo audacia detur,
> Haud metuam summi dixisse Palatia caeli:*

***out of which:** 「그것을 제외하면」.

****Sed proavi...***: 'But our ancestors praised the meter and wit of Plautus, admiring each of them tolerantly if not stupidly' (*Art of Poetry*, Ⅱ, 270—72).

****Multa...***: 'Many words now disused shall revive, and many now esteemed shall wither, if custom wills; for custom determines right usage in language' (*Ibid*, 70—72).

****Mistaque...***: 'The bean shall flower, joined with the laughing acanthus' (*Eclogues*, Ⅳ, 20)

****mirantur...***: 'Woods and the waters marvel at the shining shields and painted ship on the waves' (*Aeneid*, Ⅷ, 91).

calling the court of Jupiter by the name of Augustus's palace; though in another place he is more bold, where he says,—*et longas visent Capitolia pompas*.* But to do this always, and never be able to write a line without it, though it may be admired by some few pedants, will not pass upon those who know that wit is best conveyed to us in the most easy language; and is most to be admired when a great thought comes dressed in words so commonly received, that it is understood by the meanest apprehensions, as the best meat is the most easily digested: but we cannot read a verse of Cleveland's without making a face at it,* as if every word were a pill to swallow: he gives us many times a hard nut to break our teeth, without a kernel for our pains. So that there is this difference betwixt his Satires and doctor Donne's;* that the one gives us deep thoughts in common language, though rough cadence; the other gives us common thoughts in abstruse words: 'tis true, in some places his wit is independent of his words, as in that of the rebel Scot:

> Had Cain been Scot, God would have chang'd his doom;
> Not forc'd him wander, but confin'd him home.*

*Si sic omnia dixisset!** This is wit in all languages: it is like Mercury, never to be lost or killed:—and so that other—

**quem*...: 'If verbal license is allowed, I shall not fear to call it the imperial palace' (*Metamorphoses*, I, 175).

**et longas*...: 'The Capitol sees long processions' (*Ibid*, 561). 위에 인용된 예문들은 우스꽝스러운 비유를 사용한 파격문장(catachresis)이라고 Dryden은 보고 있다.

***make a face at...:** 「...을 보고 낯을 찡그리다」.

***Doctor Donne's:** 신학박사이자 설교가인 John Donne의 Satires는 매우 까다롭지만 깊은 사상을 담고 있다. 한국에서는 별로 읽혀지고 있지 않다. 다음의 the one은 Donne's.

***Had Cain been...:** *The Rebel Scot*, 63—64. 아벨을 죽인 벌로 추방당한 카인을 모형으로 해서, 한 스콧틀랜드의 방랑자가 사방을 돌아다니며 악행을 거듭하는 것을 그린 정치 풍자시. Dryden은 인용된 귀절만은 잘 되었다고 보고 있다.

**Si sic*...: 'If only he had spoken everything thus' (Juvenal, *Satires*, X, 123).

For beauty, like white powder,* makes no noise,
And yet the silent hypocrite destroys.*

You see the last line is highly metaphorical, but it is so soft and gentle, that it does not shock us as we read it.

'But, to return from whence I have digressed, to the consideration of the ancients' writing, and their wit (of which by this time you will grant us in some measure to be fit judges). Though I see many excellent thoughts in Seneca, yet he of them who had a genius most proper for the stage, was Ovid; he had a way of writing so fit to stir up a pleasing admiration and concernment,* which are the objects of a tragedy, and to show the various movements of a soul combating betwixt two different passions, that, had he lived in our age, or in his own could have writ with our advantages, no man but* must have yielded to him; and therefore I am confident the *Medea** is none of his: for, though I esteem it for the gravity and sententiousness of it, which he himself concludes to be suitable to a tragedy,—*Omne genus scripti gravitate tragaedia vincit*,*—yet it moves not my soul enough to judge that he, who in the epic way wrote things so near the drama as the story of Myrrha, of Caunus and Biblis, and the rest, should stir up no more concernment where he most endeavoured it. The master-piece of Seneca I hold to be that scene in the *Troades*, where Ulysses is seeking for Astyanax to kill him: there you see the tenderness of a mother so represented in Andromache,* that it raises compassion to a high degree in the reader, and bears the nearest resemblance

---

For beauty...**: Cleveland, ***Rupertismus, 39—40.

***white powder:** a gun powder supposed to explode without noise.

***admiration and concernment:** Aristotle 의 terror and pity 를 순화시킨 것.

***but:** that...not. there would have been 을 앞에 넣어 읽을 것.

****Medea*:** Seneca 의 작품이 Ovid 의 것으로 와전되어 왔었다. Dryden 의 판단이 옳다.

****Omne*...:** 'Tragedy exceeds every other kind of writing in gravity' (*Tristia*, Ⅱ, 381).

***Ulysses...Andromache:** Troy 의 영웅 Hector 왕자가 죽은 뒤 아내 Andromache 가 어린 아들 Astyanax 를 구하려고 애쓰다, 그리이스군의 Ulysses 장군에게 빼앗기고 그녀 자신은 성루에서 던져져 죽음을 당한다.

of any thing in the tragedies of the ancients to the excellent scenes of passion in Shakespeare, or in Fletcher:* for love-scenes, you will find few among them; their tragic poets dealt not with that soft passion, but with lust, cruelty, revenge, ambition, and those bloody actions they produced; which were more capable of raising horror than compassion in an audience: leaving love untouched, whose gentleness would have tempered them; which is the most frequent of all the passions, and which, being the private concernment of every person, is soothed by viewing its own image in a public entertainment.

'Among their comedies, we find a scene or two of tenderness, and that where you would least expect it, in Plautus; but to speak generally, their lovers say little, when they see each other, but *anima mea vita mea*; Ζωὴ καὶ ψυχή,* as the women in Juvenal's time used to cry out in the fury of their kindness. Any sudden gust of passion (as an ecstasy of love in an unexpected meeting) cannot better be expressed than in a word and a sigh, breaking one another. Nature is dumb on such occasions; and to make her speak, would be to represent her unlike herself. But there are a thousand other concernments of lovers, as jealousies, complaints, contrivances, and the like, where not to open their minds at large to each other, were to be wanting to their own love,* and to the expectation of the audience; who watch the movements of their minds, as much as the changes of their fortunes. For the imaging of the first is properly the work of a poet; the latter he borrows from the historian.'*

Eugenius was proceeding in that part of his discourse, when

***Fletcher, John** (1579-1625)는 **Francis Beaumont** (1584-1616)와 함께 여러 극작품을 합작하였고, 단독으로도 많은 작품을 썼는데, 당시에는 Shakespeare에 버금가는 명성을 누렸다.

**anima...*: 'My soul, my life' (Juvenal, *Satires*, VI, 195). 고전극은 사랑의 장면을 묘사하는 데 극히 미숙했었다.

***were...own love:** 「그들의 사랑에 미흡한 데가 있는 것이 될 것이다」.

***the latter...historian:** 「그들의 인간사는 역사가(또는 과거설화 집필자)에게서 빌려온다」. 시인은 주로 인간의 마음의 움직임을 상상하는 것이 직분이고 이야기 자체를 짓는 것은 아니다.

Crites interrupted him. 'I see,' said he, 'Eugenius and I are never like to have this question decided betwixt us; for he maintains, the moderns have acquired a new perfection in writing; I can only grant they have altered the mode of it. Homer described his heroes men of great appetites, lovers of beef broiled upon the coals, and good fellows; contrary to the practice of the French Romances, whose heroes neither eat, nor drink, nor sleep, for love. Virgil makes Aeneas a bold avower of his own virtues:

Sum pius Aeneas, fama super aethera notus;*

which, in the civility of our poets, is the character of a fanfaron or Hector: for with us the knight takes occasion to walk out, or sleep, to avoid the vanity of telling his own story, which the trusty 'squire is ever to perform for him. So in their love-scenes, of which Eugenius spoke last, the ancients were more hearty, we more talkative: they writ love as it was then the mode to make it; and I will grant thus much to Eugenius, that perhaps one of their poets, had he lived in our age, *si foret hoc nostrum fato delapsus in aevum*,* (as Horace says of Lucilius) he had altered many things;* not that they were not natural before, but that he might accommodate himself to the age in which he lived. Yet in the mean time, we are not to conclude any thing rashly against those great men, but preserve to them the dignity of masters, and give that honour to their memories, *quos Libitina sacravit*,* part of which we expect may be paid to us in future times.'

******Sum pius*...**: 'I am pious Aeneas, whose fame is known above the heaven' (*Aeneid*, I, 378—9). 자기 스스로 '나는 유명한 효자'라고 떠드는 사람은 오늘의 개화된 세계에서는 허풍장이 (fanfaron) 이거나 중세식 영웅 (Hector) 일 뿐이고, 현대의 영웅은 자신의 이야기를 스스로 하지 않고 그의 부하 (squire) 가 하도록 되어 있다.

***perhaps...many things:** perhaps if one of their poets had lived in our age, ..., he would have altered many things.

******si foret*...**: 'If he had been dropped into our age by fate' (*Satires*, I, 10, 68).

******quos Libitina*...**: 'Which the funeral goddess has consecrated' (Horace, *Epistles*, II, i, 49).

This moderation of Crites, as it was pleasing to all the company, so it put an end to that dispute; which Eugenius, who seemed to have the better of the argument, would urge no farther: but Lisideius, after he had acknowledged himself of Eugenius's opinion concerning the ancients, yet told him, he had forborne, till his discourse were ended, to ask him why he preferred the English plays above those of other nations? and whether we ought not to submit our stage to the exactness of our next neighbours?

'Though,' said Eugenius, 'I am at all times ready to defend the honour of my country against the French, and to maintain, we are as well able to vanquish them with our pens, as our ancestors have been with their swords; yet, if you please,' added he, looking upon Neander, 'I will commit this cause* to my friend's management; his opinion of our plays is the same with mine: and besides, there is no reason, that Crites and I, who have now left the stage, should re-enter so suddenly upon it; which is against the laws of comedy.'

'If the question had been stated,' replied Lisideius, 'who had writ best, the French or English, forty years ago, I should have been of your opinion, and adjudged the honour to our own nation; but since that time,' (said he, turning towards Neander,) 'we have been so long together bad Englishmen, that we had not leisure to be good poets. Beaumont, Fletcher, and Jonson, (who were only capable of bringing us to that degree of perfection which we have,) were just then leaving the world; as if in an age of so much horror,* wit and those milder studies of humanity, had no farther business among us. But the Muses, who ever follow peace, went to plant in another country: it was then, that the great Cardinal of Richelieu* began to take them into his protection; and that, by his encouragement,

***cause:** 「관철시키고자 하는 주장」.

***age:** 17세기 중엽 왕당파와 의회파 간에 내란이 벌어지고 청교도 혁명이 일어났던 시기를 말한다(1640-60).

***Cardinal, Duc de Richelieu:** (1585-1642). Louis XIII의 장관이 되어 전제정치를 펴는 한편, Académie Française를 창설하는 등 문화창달에 힘썼고, 그 일환으로 희곡의 3일치 법칙을 극작가들에게 강요했다.

Corneille, and some other Frenchmen, reformed their theatre (which before was as much below ours, as it now surpasses it and the rest of Europe). But because Crites in his discourse for the ancients has prevented me, by observing many rules of the stage which the moderns have borrowed from them, I shall only, in short, demand of you, whether you are not convinced that of all nations the French have best observed them? In the unity of time you find them so scrupulous, that it yet remains a dispute among their poets, whether the artificial day of twelve hours, more or less, be not meant by Aristotle, rather than the natural one of twenty-four; and consequently, whether all plays ought not to be reduced into that compass.* This I can testify, that in all their dramas writ within these last twenty years and upwards, I have not observed any that have extended the time to thirty hours: in the unity of place they are full* as scrupulous; for many of their critics limit it to that very spot of ground where the play is supposed to begin; none of them exceed the compass of the same town or city. The unity of action in all plays is yet more conspicuous; for they do not burden them with under-plots, as the English do: which is the reason why many scenes of our tragi-comedies carry on a design that is nothing of kin to the main plot; and that we see two distinct webs in a play, like those in ill-wrought stuffs;* and two actions, that is, two plays, carried on together, to the confounding of the audience; who, before they are warm in their concernments for one part, are diverted to another; and by that means espouse the interest of neither. From hence likewise it arises, that the one half of our actors are not known to the other. They keep their distances, as if they were Monta-

---

***In the Unity of Time...that compass:** Aristotle은 'Tragedy endeavors, as far as possible, to confine itself to a single revolution of the sun, or but slightly to exceed this limit' (*Poetics*, v, 4) 라고 했는데, 이를 하루 24시간으로 해석할 것이냐 아니면 동에서 서로 해가 운행하는 낮 12시간으로 해석할 것이냐의 논란이 생겼다. 프랑스 신고전주의자들은 시간의 통일을 강조한 나머지 그것을 12시간으로 더욱 줄여잡으려고 했다.

***full:** fully.

***stuffs:** 옷감.

gues and Capulets,* and seldom begin an acquaintance till the last scene of the fifth act, when they are all to meet upon the stage. There is no theatre in the world has anything so absurd as the English tragi-comedy; 'tis a drama of our own invention, and the fashion of it is enough to proclaim it so; here a course of mirth, there another of sadness and passion, and a third of honour and a duel: thus, in two hours and a half, we run through all the fits of Bedlam.* The French affords you as much variety on the same day, but they do it not so unseasonably, or *mal à propos*,* as we: our poets present you the play and the farce together; and our stages still retain somewhat of the original civility of the Red Bull:*

> Atque ursum et pugiles media inter carmina poscunt.*

The end of tragedies or serious plays, says Aristotle, is to beget admiration, compassion, or concernment; but are not mirth and compassion things incompatible? and is it not evident that the poet must of necessity destroy the former by intermingling of the latter? that is, he must ruin the sole end and object of his tragedy, to introduce somewhat that is forced into it, and is not of the body of it.* Would you not think that physician mad, who, having prescribed a purge, should immediately order you to take restringents?*

'But to leave our plays, and return to theirs. I have noted

***Montagues and Capulets:** Shakespeare의 *Romeo and Juliet*의 적대적인 두 집안. 이들이 서로 외면하고 지나는 것처럼, 한 연극 속에 두 이야기가 전개되어 서로 무관한 배우의 두 집단이 등장한다는 것.

***Bedlam:** Bethlehem의 약자로, London의 정신병자 수용소. 희극과 비극이 뒤섞여 있는 것은 광인 수용소 같다는 악평.

****mal à propos*:** 「적절하지 못하게」.

***Red Bull:** 아주 오래된 런던의 극장. 저질 쇼우까지 공연했다.

***Atque ursum...:** 'In the middle of plays they ask for a bear and boxers' (Horace, *Epistles*, Ⅱ, i, 185).

***to introduce...the body of it:** 억지로 집어넣은 것, 그러나 그 자체에 본래 속하지 않은 것을 도입하는 것(희비극). somewhat=something, of the body of: 「...과 한몸을 이룬」.

***purge:** 「설사제」.

***restringent:** 「지사제, 변비제」

one great advantage they have had in the plotting of their tragedies; that is, they are always grounded upon some known history: according to that of Horace, *Ex noto fictum carmen sequar*;* and in that they have so imitated the ancients, that they have surpassed them. For the ancients, as was observed before, took for the foundation of their plays some poetical fiction, such as under that consideration could move but little concernment in the audience, because they already knew the event of it. But the French goes farther:

> Atque ita mentitur, sic veris falsa remiscet,
> Primo ne medium, medio ne discrepet imum.*

He so interweaves truth with probable fiction, that he puts a pleasing fallacy upon us; mends the intrigues of fate, and dispenses with the severity of history, to reward that virtue which has been rendered to us there* unfortunate. Sometimes the story has left the success* so doubtful, that the writer is free, by the privilege of a poet, to take that which of two or more relations will best suit with his design: as for example, in the death of Cyrus, whom Justin and some others report to have perished in the Scythian war, but Xenophon affirms to have died in his bed of extreme old age.* Nay more, when the event is past dispute, even then we are willing to be deceived, and the poet, if he contrives it with appearance of truth, has all the audience of his party; at least during the time his play is acting: so naturally we are kind to virtue, when our own interest is not in question, that we take it up as the general concernment of mankind. On the other side, if you consider the historical

---

******Ex noto*...: 'I should write a poem from a well-known story' (*Art of Poetry*, 240).

***Atque ita mentitur...**: 'And he so lies, and mingles the true and the false, that you cannot tell the beginning, middle, or end apart' (*Ibid*, 151)

***there:** *ie.* in history. (역사는 반드시 도덕적인 것은 아니다).

***success:** 「뒷 이야기」.

***in the death...extreme old age:** Persia의 대왕 Cyrus (?–529 B.C.)에 관해서 3세기경의 로마인 Justin과 기원전 5세기 그리이스 저술가 Xenophon이 상반된 기록을 남겼다.

plays of Shakespeare, they are rather so many chronicles of kings, or the business many times of thirty or forty years, cramped into a representation of two hours and a half; which is not to imitate or paint nature, but rather to draw her in miniature, to take her in little; to look upon her through the wrong end of a perspective,* and receive her images not only much less, but infinitely more imperfect than the life: this, instead of making a play delightful, renders it ridiculous:

> Quodcunque ostendis mihi sic, incredulus odi.*

For the spirit of man cannot be satisfied but with truth, or at least verisimility; and a poem is to contain, if not *τὰ ἔτυμα*, yet *ἐτύμοισιν ὁμοῖα*;* as one of the Greek poets has expressed it.

'Another thing in which the French differ from us and from the Spaniards, is that they do not embarrass, or cumber themselves with too much plot; they only represent so much of a story as will constitute one whole and great action sufficient for a play; we, who undertake more, do but multiply adventures; which, not being produced from one another, as effects from causes, but barely following, constitute many actions in the drama, and consequently make it many plays.

'But by pursuing closely one argument, which is not cloyed with many turns, the French have gained more liberty for verse, in which they write; they have leisure to dwell on a subject which deserves it*; and to represent the passions, (which we have acknowledged to be the poet's work,) without being hurried from one thing to another, as we are in the plays of Calderon,* which we have seen lately upon our theatres, under

---

***to take her...of a perspective:** 「자연 (her) 을 축소시켜 보는 것, 즉 망원경을 거꾸로 해서 들여다보는 것」. (2,30 년 간에 벌어진 일을 2 시간 30분 동안의 연극으로 꾸미는 것).

***Quodcunque...:** 'Whatever you show me in that way I find unbelievable and disgusting' (Horace, *Art of Poetry*, 188)

*'True things', yet 'things like the truth'.

***subject...it:** 「자세히 다룰 만한 가치가 있는 주제」.

***Calderon, Pedro:** (1600-81). 스페인의 대 극작가로 120 여편의 희곡을 지었다.

the name of Spanish plots. I have taken notice but of one tragedy of ours, whose plot has that uniformity and unity of design in it, which I have commended in the French; and that is *Rollo*,* or rather, under the name of Rollo, the story of Bassianus and Geta in Herodian: there indeed the plot is neither large nor intricate, but just enough to fill the minds of the audience, not to cloy them. Besides, you see it founded upon the truth of history,—only the time of the action is not reducible to the strictness of the rules; and you see in some places a little farce mingled, which is below the dignity of the other parts; and in this all our poets are extremely peccant: even Ben Jonson himself, in *Sejanus* and *Catiline*,* has given us this olio* of a play, this unnatural mixture of comedy and tragedy; which to me sounds just as ridiculously as the history of David with the merry humours of Golias.* In *Sejanus* you may take notice of the scene betwixt Livia and the physician, which is a pleasant satire upon the artificial helps of beauty: in *Catiline* you may see the parliament of women; the little envies of them to one another; and all that passes betwixt Curio and Fulvia: scenes admirable in their kind, but of an ill mingle with the rest.

'But I return again to the French writers, who, as I have said, do not burden themselves too much with plot, which has been reproached to them by an ingenious person* of our nation as a fault; for, he says, they commonly make but one person considerable in a play; they dwell on him, and his concernments, while the rest of the persons are only subservient to set him off. If he intends this by it,—that there is one person in the play

---

***_Rollo_:** John Fletcher의 작품. 원명은 *The Bloody Brothers, or Rollo, Duke of Normandy*.

Sejanus**(1603), ***Catiline(1611): 둘 다 Ben Jonson이 로마의 역사를 소재로 하여 쓴 역사비극. 희극적 풍자적 요소를 가미했다.

***olio:** 「범벅」.

***the history...Golias:** 이 이야기는 중세의 연극에서 Golias[Goliath]에게 허풍장이역이 맡겨져서 웃음극으로 되었다.

***an ingenious person:** 영국 문화를 공격한 프랑스의 저술가에 대하여 반박문을 쓴 영국의 학사원 회원인 Thomas Sprat를 가리킨다. 그는 프랑스 희곡에서 한 인물만을 부각시키는 것을 비난했다.

who is of greater dignity than the rest, he must tax, not only theirs, but those of the ancients, and which he would be loth to do,* the best of ours; for it is impossible but that one person must be more conspicuous in it than any other, and consequently the greatest share in the action must devolve on him. We see it so in the management of all affairs; even in the most equal aristocracy, the balance cannot be so justly poised, but some one will be superior to the rest, either in parts, fortune, interest, or the consideration of some glorious exploit; which will reduce the greatest part of business into his hands.

'But, if he would have us to imagine, that in exalting one character the rest of them are neglected, and that all of them have not some share or other in the action of the play, I desire him to produce any of Corneille's tragedies, wherein every person, like so many servants in a well-governed family, has not some employment, and who is not necessary to the carrying on of the plot, or at least to your understanding it.

'There are indeed some protatic* persons in the ancients, whom they make use of in their plays, either to hear or give the relation: but the French avoid this with great address,* making their narrations only to, or by such, who are some way interested in the main design. And now I am speaking of relations, I cannot take a fitter opportunity to add this in favour of the French, that they often use them with better judgement and more *à propos** than the English do. Not that I commend narrations in general,—but there are two sorts of them. One, of those things which are antecedent to the play, and are related to make the conduct of it more clear to us. But 'tis a fault to choose such subjects for the stage as will force us on that rock,* because we see they are seldom listened to by the audi-

---

***which he would...to do:** 「그것은 그가 하고 싶지 않았을 텐데」. which는 the best of ours(영국의 극작가 중 가장 우수한 자)를 공격하는 것[tax]을 가리키는 관계대명사로 특이한 용법이다.

***protatic:** 연극의 첫 부분에만 등장하는.

***address:** 「수완」.

******à propos*:** 「적절하게」.

***as will...rock:** 「어려운 처지로 몰아넣을」(주제는 피하라).

ence, and that is many times the ruin of the play; for, being once let pass without attention, the audience can never recover themselves to understand the plot: and indeed it is somewhat unreasonable that they should be put to so much trouble, as that, to comprehend what passes in their sight, they must have recourse to what was done, perhaps, ten or twenty years ago.*

'But there is another sort of relations,* that is, of things happening in the action of the play, and supposed to be done behind the scenes; and this is many times both convenient and beautiful; for by it the French avoid the tumult to which we are subject in England, by representing duels, battles, and the like; which renders our stage too like the theatres where they fight prizes. For what is more ridiculous than to represent an army with a drum and five men behind it; all which the hero of the other side is to drive in before him; or to see a duel fought, and one slain with two or three thrusts of the foils, which we know are so blunted, that we might give a man an hour to kill another in good earnest* with them.

'I have observed that in all our tragedies, the audience cannot forbear laughing when the actors are to die; it is the most comic part of the whole play. All *passions* may be lively represented on the stage, if to the well-writing of them the actor supplies a good commanded voice, and limbs that move easily, and without stiffness; but there are many *actions* which can never be imitated to a just height: dying especially is a thing which none but a Roman gladiator could naturally perform on the stage, when he did not imitate or represent, but do it;* and therefore it is better to omit the representation of it.

'The words of a good writer, which describe it lively, will make a deeper impression of belief in us than all the actor can

---

*관객의 면전에서 전개되는 일을 이해하기 위해서 오래 전에 생겼던 일에 의존해야 한다는 것은 불합리하다.

***relations:** narrations. 연극에서 과거나 장외에서 생긴 일을 말하는 것.

***in good earnest:** 「진짜로」.

***do it:** die really. 죽는 장면은 정말로 죽는 것(검투사처럼) 이외에는 무대에서 연기가 불가능하다는 것.

insinuate into us, when he seems to fall dead before us; as a poet in the description of a beautiful garden, or a meadow, will please our imagination more than the place itself can please our sight. When we see death represented, we are convinced it is but fiction; but when we hear it related, our eyes, the strongest witnesses, are wanting,* which might have undeceived us; and we are all willing to favour the sleight, when the poet does not too grossly impose on us. They therefore who imagine these relations would make no concernment in the audience, are deceived, by confounding them with the other, which are of things antecedent to the play: those* are made often in cold blood, as I may say, to the audience; but these* are warmed with our concernments, which were before awakened in the play. What the philosophers say of motion, that, when it is once begun, it continues of itself, and will do so to eternity, without some stop put to it, is clearly true on this occasion: the soul, being already moved with the characters and fortunes of those imaginary persons, continues going of its own accord;* and we are no more weary to hear what becomes of them when they are not on the stage, than we are to listen to the news of an absent mistress. But it is objected, that if one part of the play may be related, then why not all? I answer, some parts of the action are more fit to be represented, some to be related. Corneille says judiciously, that the poet is not obliged to expose to view all particular actions which conduce to the principal: he ought to select such of them to be seen, which will appear with the greatest beauty, either by the magnificence of the show, or the vehemence of passions which they produce, or some other charm which they have in them; and let the rest arrive to the audience by narration. 'Tis a great mistake in us to believe the French present no part of the action on the stage; every alteration or crossing* of a design, every new-sprung

---

*wanting: absent. (보면 안 속아도 들으면 잘 속는다).

*those, these: those는 연극에서 이전의 일을 감정없이 (in cold blood) 알려준 것. these는 장외에서 벌어진 일을 알려준 것.

*of its own accord: 「스스로」.

*crossing: (계획의) 「어긋남」.

passion, and turn of it, is a part of the action, and much the noblest, except* we conceive nothing to be action till the players come to blows*; as if the painting of the hero's mind were not more properly the poet's work than the strength of his body. Nor does this anything contradict the opinion of Horace, where he tells us,

> Segnius irritant animos demissa per aurem,
> Quam quae sunt oculis subjecta fidelibus.

For he says immediately after,

> —Non tamen intus
> Digna geri promes in scenam; multaque tolles
> Ex oculis, quae mox narret facundia praesens.

Among which many he recounts some:

> Nec pueros coram populo Medea trucidet,
> Aut in avem Progne mutetur, Cadmus in anguem; &c.*

That is, those actions which by reason of their cruelty will cause aversion in us, or by reason of their impossibility, unbelief, ought either wholly to be avoided by a poet, or only delivered by narration. To which we may have leave to add, such as, to avoid tumult, (as was before hinted,) or to reduce the plot into a more reasonable compass of time, or for defect of beauty in them, are rather to be related than presented to the eye. Examples of all these kinds are frequent, not only among all the ancients, but in the best received* of our English poets. We find Ben Jonson using them in his *Magnetic Lady*,

---

***except:** unless.

***come to blow:** 「맞붙어 싸우다」.

*'What we hear through our ears stirs no less strongly than what we see through our eyes'.

'You should not bring onto the stage what should be done off it: many things should be kept out of sight and told instead with vivid readiness.'

'Medea should not cut up her children in front of the audience, Procne should not be changed into a bird there, nor Cadmus into a snake' (*Art of Poetry*, 180—87). 마녀 Medea는 아이들을 죽여서 요리했고, Procne는 제비로, Cadmus는 뱀으로 변했다고 한다. 무대에서 상연하기 곤란하다.

***the best received:** 가장 인기 있는 작가.

where one comes out from dinner, and relates the quarrels and disorders of it, to save the undecent appearance of them on the stage, and to abbreviate the story; and this in express imitation of Terence, who had done the same before him in his *Eunuch*, where Pythias makes the like relation of what had happened within at the Soldier's entertainment. The relations likewise of Sejanus's death, and the prodigies* before it, are remarkable; the one of which was hid from sight, to avoid the horror and tumult of the representation; the other, to shun the introducing of things impossible to be believed. In that excellent play, *The King and No King*, Fletcher goes yet farther; for the whole unravelling of the plot is done by narration in the fifth act, after the manner of the ancients; and it moves great concernment in the audience, though it be only a relation of what was done many years before the play. I could multiply other instances, but these are sufficient to prove that there is no error in choosing a subject which requires this sort of narrations; in the ill management of them, there may.

'But I find I have been too long in this discourse, since the French have many other excellences not common to us; as that you never see any of their plays end with a conversion, or simple change of will, which is the ordinary way which our poets use to end theirs. It shows little art in the conclusion of a dramatic poem, when they who have hindered the felicity during the four acts, desist from it in the fifth, without some powerful cause to take them off their design; and though I deny not but such reasons may be found, yet it is a path that is cautiously to be trod, and the poet is to be sure he convinces the audience that the motive is strong enough. As for example, the conversion of the Usurer in *The Scornful Lady*,* seems to me a little forced; for, being a Usurer, which implies a lover of money to the highest degree of covetousness,—and such the poet has represented him,—the account he gives for the sudden change

***progidies:** 「괴이한 사건들」.

* ***The Scornful Lady***: Beaumont and Fletcher 의 작품(1609). 고리대금업자가 사기를 당하고 마음을 고친다는 내용.

is, that he has been duped by the wild young fellow; which in reason might render him more wary another time, and make him punish himself with harder fare and coarser clothes, to get up again what he had lost: but that he should look on it as a judgement, and so repent, we may expect to hear in a sermon, but I should never endure it in a play.

'I pass by this; neither will I insist on the care they take, that no person after his first entrance shall ever appear, but the business which brings him upon the stage shall be evident; which rule, if observed, must needs render all the events in the play more natural; for there you see the probability of every accident, in the cause that produced it; and that which appears chance* in the play, will seem so reasonable to you, that you will there find it almost necessary: so that in the exit of the actor you have a clear account of his purpose and design in the next entrance; (though, if the scene be well wrought, the event* will commonly deceive you;) for there is nothing so absurd, says Corneille, as for an actor to leave the stage, only because he has no more to say.

'I should now speak of the beauty of their rhyme, and the just reason I have to prefer that way of writing in tragedies before ours in blank verse; but because it is partly received by us, and therefore not altogether peculiar to them, I will say no more of it in relation to their plays. For our own, I doubt not but it will exceedingly beautify them; and I can see but one reason why it should not generally obtain* that is, because our poets write so ill in it. This indeed may prove a more prevailing argument than all others which are used to destroy it, and therefore I am only troubled when great and judicious poets, and those who are acknowledged such, have writ or spoke against it: as for others, they are to be answered by that one sentence of an ancient author:—*Sed ut primo ad consequendos eos quos priores*

***that...chance:** 「우연으로 보이는 것」.
***event:** 「사건의 결말, 드러난 사실」.
***obtain:** (자동사) 「관습으로 성행하다」.
***Sed ut primo...:** 'But as we are inspired to follow those we consider most

*ducimus, accendimur, ita ubi aut proeteriri, aut aequari eos posse desperavimus, studium cum spe senescit: quod, scilicet, assequi non potest, sequi desinit; . . . praeteritoque eo in quo eminere non possumus, aliquid in quo nitamur, conquirimus.'**

Lisideius concluded in this manner; and Neander, after a little pause, thus answered him:

'I shall grant Lisideius, without much dispute, a great part of what he has urged against us; for I acknowledge that the French contrive their plots more regularly, and observe the laws of comedy, and decorum of the stage, (to speak generally,) with more exactness than the English. Further, I deny not but he has taxed us justly in some irregularities of ours, which he has mentioned; yet, after all, I am of opinion that neither our faults nor their virtues are considerable enough to place them above us.

'For the lively imitation of nature being in the definition of a play, those which best fulfil that law ought to be esteemed superior to the others. 'Tis true, those beauties of the French poesy are such as will raise perfection higher where it is;* but are not sufficient to give it where it is not: they are indeed the beauties of a statue, but not of a man, because not animated with the soul of poesy, which is imitation of humour and passions: and this Lisideius himself, or any other, however biassed to their party, cannot but acknowledge, if he will either compare the humours of our comedies, or the characters of our serious plays, with theirs. He who will look upon theirs which have been written till these last ten years, or thereabouts, will find it a hard matter to pick out two or three passable humours amongst them. Corneille himself, their arch-poet,* what has he

---

worthy, so—when we despair of excelling or equalling them—our enthusiasm and hope diminish. For what it cannot attain, it ceases to follow... When what we cannot excell is over, we look for something else for which to strive' (Villeius Paterculus, I, 17).

***such as...it is:** 「이미 완전한 것을 더 완전하게 만드는 것」(이 프랑스 극의 아름다움이다). 프랑스 극은 이미 다듬어져 있는 소재를 더 미화시킨 것이라는 생각.

***arch-poet:** 「대표 극작가」.

produced except *The Liar*,* and you know how it was cried up in France; but when it came upon the English stage, though well translated, and that part of Dorant acted to so much advantage as I am confident it never received in its own country, the most favourable to it would not put it in competition with many of Fletcher's or Ben Jonson's. In the rest of Corneille's comedies you have little humour; he tells you himself, his way is, first to show two lovers in good intelligence with each other; in the working up of the play to embroil them by some mistake, and in the latter end to clear it, and reconcile them.

'But of late years Molière, the younger Corneille,* Quinault,* and some others, have been imitating afar off the quick turns and graces of the English stage. They have mixed their serious plays with mirth, like our tragi-comedies, since the death of Cardinal Richelieu; which Lisideius and many others not observing, have commended that in them for a virtue which they themselves no longer practise. Most of their new plays are, like some of ours, derived from the Spanish novels. There is scarce one of them without a veil, and a trusty Diego, who drolls much after the rate of *The Adventures*.* But their humours, if I may grace them with that name, are so thin-sown, that never above one of them comes up in any play. I dare take upon me to find more variety of them in some one play of Ben Jonson's, than in all theirs together; as he who has seen *The Alchemist*, *The Silent Woman*, or *Bartholomew Fair*, cannot but acknowledge with me.

'I grant the French have performed what was possible on the

---

* ***The Liar***: Corneille의 작품(1642)으로 원명은 *Le Menteur*. 본 고장에서는 인기를 얻은 희극작품이나 영국에서는 일류배우 Charles Hart의 열연에도 불구하고 실패했던 모양이다.

***younger Corneille:** 형 Pierre Corneille의 명성에 눌려서 잘 알려지지 않았으나 이 Thomas Corneille(1625-1709)도 당대에는 작가 노릇을 했다.

***Quinault, Philippe:** (1635-88). 당시의 인기 극작가. 여기서 Dryden이 말하는 것처럼 영국 희극이 프랑스 희극에 영향을 끼친 적은 없다.

* ***The Adventures***: Sir Samuel Tuke의 작품 ***Adventures of Five Hours***(1663)을 가리킨다. 스패인 희곡작품을 본따서 지은 이 작품에 Diego라는 희극적 하인이 등장한다.

ground-work of the Spanish plays; what was pleasant before, they have made regular: but there is not above one good play to be writ on all those plots; they are too much alike to please often; which we need not the experience of our own stage to justify. As for their new way of mingling mirth with serious plot, I do not, with Lisideius, condemn the thing, though I cannot approve their manner of doing it. He tells us, we cannot so speedily recollect ourselves after a scene of great passion and concernment, as to pass to another* of mirth and humour, and to enjoy it with any relish: but why should he imagine the soul of man more heavy than his senses? Does not the eye pass from an unpleasant object to a pleasant in a much shorter time than is required to this? and does not the unpleasantness of the first commend the beauty of the latter? The old rule of logic might have convinced him, that contraries, when placed near, set off each other. A continued gravity keeps the spirit too much bent; we must refresh it sometimes, as we bait* in a journey that we may go on with greater ease. A scene of mirth, mixed with tragedy, has the same effect upon us which our music has betwixt the acts; which we find a relief to us from the best plots and language of the stage, if the discourses have been long. I must therefore have stronger arguments, ere I am convinced that compassion and mirth in the same subject destroy each other; and in the mean time cannot but conclude, to the honour of our nation, that we have invented, increased, and perfected a more pleasant way of writing for the stage, than was ever known to the ancients or moderns of any nation, which is tragi-comedy.

'And this leads me to wonder why Lisideius and many others should cry up the barrenness of the French plots, above the variety and copiousness of the English. Their plots are single; they carry on one design, which is pushed forward by all the actors, every scene in the play contributing and moving towards

---

***another:** another scene. 심각한 장면에서 희극적 장면으로 심리적으로 빨리 옮겨갈 수 없다는 이론을 반박하고 있다.

***bait:** (여행중에) 「쉬어 가다」.

it. Our plays, besides the main design, have under-plots or by-concernments, of less considerable persons and intrigues, which are carried on with the motion of the main plot: as they say the orb of the fixed stars, and those of the planets, though they have motions of their own, are whirled about by the motion of the *primum mobile*,* in which they are contained. That similitude expresses much of the English stage; for if contrary motions may be found in nature to agree; if a planet can go east and west at the same time;—one way by virtue of his own motion, the other by the force of the first mover;—it will not be difficult to imagine how the under-plot, which is only different, not contrary to the great design, may naturally be conducted along with it.

Eugenius has already shown us, from the confession of the French poets, that the unity of action is sufficiently preserved, if all the imperfect actions of the play are conducing to the main design; but when those petty intrigues of a play are so ill ordered, that they have no coherence with the other, I must grant that Lisideius has reason to tax that want of due connection; for co-ordination* in a play is as dangerous and unnatural as in a state. In the mean time he must acknowledge, our variety, if well ordered, will afford a greater pleasure to the audience.

'As for his other argument, that by pursuing one single theme they gain an advantage to express and work up* the passions, I wish any example he could bring from them would make it good;* for I confess their verses are to me the coldest I have ever read. Neither, indeed, is it possible for them, in the way they take, so to express passion, as that the effects of it should appear in the concernment of an audience, their speeches

---

primum mobile: 옛 천문학에서 별들의 운행에 동력을 보내는 근원. first mover.

***co-ordination:** 여기서는 equality of ranks, 즉 모든 인물들에게 동일한 중요성을 부여하는 것. 이런 <민주주의>는 오히려 무질서를 가져온다.

***work up:** (감정을) 「고조시키다」.

***make it good:** 「그 주장을 입증하다」.

being so many declamations, which tire us with the length; so that instead of persuading us to grieve for their imaginary heroes, we are concerned for our own trouble, as we are in tedious visits of bad company; we are in pain till they are gone. When the French stage came to be reformed by Cardinal Richelieu, those long harangues were introduced to comply with the gravity of a churchman. Look upon the *Cinna* and the *Pompey*; they are not so properly to be called plays, as long discourses of reason of state; and *Polyeucte** in matters of religion is as solemn as the long stops* upon our organs. Since that time it is grown into a custom, and their actors speak by the hour-glass, like our parsons; nay, they account it the grace of their parts, and think themselves disparaged by the poet, if they may not twice or thrice in a play entertain the audience with a speech of a hundred lines. I deny not but this may suit well enough with the French; for as we, who are a more sullen people, come to be diverted at our plays, so they, who are of an airy and gay temper, come thither to make themselves more serious: and this I conceive to be one reason why comedies are more pleasing to us, and tragedies to them. But to speak generally: it cannot be denied that short speeches and replies are more apt to move the passions and beget concernment in us, than the other; for it is unnatural for any one in a gust of passion to speak long together, or for another in the same condition to suffer* him, without interruption. Grief and passion are like floods raised in little brooks by a sudden rain; they are quickly up; and if the concernment be poured unexpectedly in upon us, it overflows us: but a long sober shower gives them leisure to run out as they came in, without troubling the ordinary current. As for comedy, repartee is one of its chiefest graces; the greatest pleasure of the audience is a chase of wit, kept up on both sides, and swiftly managed. And this our forefathers, if not we, have had in Fletcher's plays, to a much higher degree of perfection

---

***Cinna, Pompey, Polyeucte:** 세 작품 모두 Corneille의 작품이다.

***long stops:** (오르간의) 「저음 키」.

***suffer:** allow (him to speak long).

than the French poets can reasonably hope to reach.

'There is another part of Lisideius's discourse, in which he rather excused our neighbours, than commended them; that is, for aiming only to make one person considerable in their plays. 'Tis very true what he has urged, that one character in all plays, even without the poet's care, will have advantage of* all the others; and that the design of the whole drama will chiefly depend on it. But this hinders not that there may be more shining characters in the play: many persons of a second magnitude, nay, some so very near, so almost equal to the first, that greatness may be opposed to greatness, and all the persons be made considerable, not only by their quality, but their action. 'Tis evident that the more the persons are, the greater will be the variety of the plot. If then the parts are managed so regularly, that the beauty of the whole be kept entire, and that the variety become not a perplexed and confused mass of accidents, you will find it infinitely pleasing to be led in a labyrinth of design, where you see some of your way before you, yet discern not the end till you arrive at it. And that all this is practicable, I can produce for examples many of our English plays: as *The Maid's Tragedy*, *The Alchemist*, *The Silent Woman*: I was going to have named *The Fox*,* but that the unity of design seems not exactly observed in it; for there appear two actions in the play; the first naturally ending with the fourth act; the second forced from it in the fifth: which yet is the less to be condemned in him, because the disguise of Volpone, though it suited not with his character as a crafty or covetous person, agreed well enough with that of a voluptuary; and by it the poet gained the end at which he aimed, the punishment of vice, and the reward of virtue, both which that disguise produced. So that to judge equally of it, it was an excellent fifth act, but not so naturally proceeding from the former.

---

*of: over.

**The Maid's Tragedy*는 Beaumont and Fletcher의 작품(1619). *The Alchemist*와 *The Silent Woman*은 Ben Jonson의 작품. *The Fox*는 *Volpone, or the Fox*를 가리키는데 구성상의 문제가 있다고 보고 있다.

'But to leave this, and pass to the latter part of Lisideius's discourse, which concerns relations: I must acknowledge with him, that the French have reason to hide that part of the action which would occasion too much tumult on the stage, and to choose rather to have it made known by narration to the audience. Farther, I think it very convenient, for the reasons he has given, that all incredible actions were removed; but whether custom has so insinuated itself into our countrymen, or nature has so formed them to fierceness, I know not; but they will scarcely suffer* combats and other objects of horror to be taken from them. And indeed, the indecency of tumults is all which can be objected against fighting: for why may not our imagination as well suffer* itself to be deluded with the probability of it, as with any other thing in the play? For my part, I can with as great ease persuade myself that the blows are given in good earnest, as I can,* that they who strike them are kings or princes, or those persons which they represent. For objects of incredibility,—I would be satisfied* from Lisideius, whether we have any so removed from all appearance of truth, as are those of Corneille's *Andromède*; a play which has been frequented the most of any he has writ. If the Perseus, or the son of a heathen god, the Pegasus, and the Monster, were not capable to choke a strong belief, let him blame any representation of ours hereafter.* Those indeed were objects of delight; yet the reason is the same as to the probability: for he makes it not a Ballette* or masque, but a play, which is to resemble truth. But for death, that it ought not to be represented, I have, besides the arguments alleged by Lisideius, the authority of Ben Jonson, who has forborne it in his tragedies; for both the death of Sejanus and Catiline are related: though in the latter

---

***suffer:** 앞에 나온 주를 참조.

***I can:** 다음에 persuade myself 가 생략되어 있다.

***I would be satisfied:** 「해명을 듣고 싶다」.

*무대에서의 전쟁 장면이 사실로 믿기지 않는 거나, 신화적 인물이 사실로 믿기지 않는 거나 마찬가지라는 것. 즉 연극은 정확히 사실을 재현하는 것이 아니라 그럴 듯하게 꾸며 보이는 것이라는 주장.

***Ballette:** 무언극을 동반한 무대 무용. 현대 발레의 전신.

I cannot but observe one irregularity of that great poet; he has removed the scene in the same act from Rome to Catiline's army, and from thence again to Rome; and besides, has allowed a very inconsiderable time, after Catiline's speech, for the striking of the battle, and the return of Petreius, who is to relate the event of it to the senate: which I should not animadvert on him, who was otherwise a painful observer of *τὸ πρέπον*, or the *decorum* of the stage, if he had not used extreme severity in his judgement on the incomparable Shakespeare for the same fault.*—To conclude on this subject of relations; if we are to be blamed for showing too much of the action, the French are as faulty for discovering* too little of it: a mean betwixt both should be observed by every judicious writer, so as the audience may neither be left unsatisfied by not seeing what is beautiful, or shocked by beholding what is either incredible or undecent.

'I hope I have already proved in this discourse, that though we are not altogether so punctual as the French, in observing the laws of comedy, yet our errors are so few, and little, and those things wherein we excel them so considerable, that we ought of right* to be preferred before them. But what will Lisideius say, if they themselves acknowledge they are too strictly bounded by those laws, for breaking which he has blamed the English? I will allege Corneille's words, as I find them in the end of his Discourse of the three Unities:—*Il est facile aux spéculatifs d'être sévères, &c.* "'Tis easy for speculative persons to judge severely; but if they would produce to public view ten or twelve pieces of this nature, they would perhaps give more latitude to the rules than I have done, when by experience, they had known how much we are limited and constrained by them, and how many beauties of the stage they

---

***his judgement...the same fault:** Jonson 은 그의 희곡 *Everyman in His Humour* (1616) 의 prologue 에서, 시간과 장소의 통일을 안 지킨 Shakespeare 등의 역사극들을 비꼬는 말을 했다.

***discovering:** uncovering. 「알려줌」.

***of right:** 「당연히」.

banished from it."* To illustrate a little what he has said:— By their servile observations of the unities of time and place, and integrity of scenes, they have brought on themselves that dearth of plot, and narrowness of imagination, which may be observed in all their plays. How many beautiful accidents might naturally happen in two or three days, which cannot arrive with any probability in the compass of twenty-four hours? There is time to be allowed also for maturity of design, which, amongst great and prudent persons, such as are often represented in tragedy, cannot, with any likelihood of truth, be brought to pass at so short a warning.* Further; by tying themselves strictly to the unity of place, and unbroken scenes, they are forced many times to omit some beauties which cannot be shown where the act began; but might, if the scene were interrupted, and the stage cleared for the persons to enter in another place; and therefore the French poets are often forced upon absurdities; for if the act begins in a chamber, all the persons in the play must have some business or other to come thither, or else they are not to be shown that act; and sometimes their characters are very unfitting to appear there: as, suppose it were the king's bed-chamber; yet the meanest man in the tragedy must come and dispatch his business there, rather than in the lobby or courtyard, (which is fitter for him,) for fear the stage should be cleared, and the scenes broken. Many times they fall by it in a greater inconvenience; for they keep their scenes unbroken, and yet change the place; as in one of their newest plays, where the act begins in the street. There a gentleman is to meet his friend; he sees him with his man, coming out from his father's house; they talk together, and the first goes out: the second, who is a lover, has made an appointment with his mistress; she appears at the window, and then we are to imagine the scene lies under it. This gentleman is called away, and leaves his servant with his mistress; presently

---

*Thomas Corneille의 작품 *L'amour et la mode*(1651)을 가리킨다(제Ⅲ막 장면).

***at so short a warning:** 「그처럼 갑작스럽게」.

her father is heard from within; the young lady is afraid the servingman should be discovered, and thrusts him into a place of safety, which is supposed to be her closet. After this, the father enters to the daughter, and now the scene is in a house; for he is seeking from one room to another for this poor Philipin, or French Diego, who is heard from within, drolling and breaking many a miserable conceit on the subject of his sad condition. In this ridiculous manner the play goes forward, the stage being never empty all the while: so that the street, the window, the houses, and the closet, are made to walk about, and the persons to stand still. Now what, I beseech you, is more easy than to write a regular French play, or more difficult than to write an irregular English one, like those of Fletcher, or of Shakespeare?

'If they content themselves, as Corneille did, with some flat design, which, like an ill riddle, is found out ere it be half proposed, such plots we can make every way regular, as easily as they; but whenever they endeavour to rise to any quick turns and counterturns of plot, as some of them have attempted, since Corneille's plays have been less in vogue, you see they write as irregularly as we, though they cover it more speciously. Hence the reason is perspicuous, why no French plays, when translated, have, or ever can succeed on the English stage. For, if you consider the plots, our own are fuller of variety; if the writing, ours are more quick and fuller of spirit; and therefore 'tis a strange mistake in those who decry the way of writing plays in verse, as if the English therein imitated the French. We have borrowed nothing from them; our plots are weaved in English looms: we endeavour therein to follow the variety and greatness of characters which are derived to us from Shakespeare and Fletcher; the copiousness and well-knitting of the intrigues we have from Jonson; and for the verse itself we have English precedents of elder date than any of Corneille's plays. Not to name our old comedies before Shakespeare, which were all writ in verse of six feet, or Alexandrines, such as the French now use,*—I can show in Shakespeare, many scenes

*Dryden 의 헛된 애국심이 나타나 있다. 그 자신도 실은 프랑스 작품에서 따온 것이 많다.

of rhyme together, and the like in Ben Jonson's tragedies: in *Catiline* and *Sejanus* sometimes thirty or forty lines,—I mean besides the Chorus, or the monologues; which, by the way, showed Ben no enemy to this way of writing, especially if you read his *Sad Shepherd*, which goes sometimes on rhyme, sometimes on blank verse, like a horse who eases himself on trot and amble. You find him likewise commending Fletcher's pastoral of *The Faithful Shepherdess*, which is for the most part rhyme, though not refined to that purity to which it hath since been brought. And these examples are enough to clear us from a servile imitation of the French.

'But to return whence I have digressed: I dare boldly affirm these two things of the English drama;—First, that we have many plays of ours as regular as any of theirs, and which, besides, have more variety of plot and characters; and secondly, that in most of the irregular plays of Shakespeare or Fletcher, (for Ben Jonson's are for the most part regular,) there is a more masculine fancy and greater spirit in the writing, than there is in any of the French. I could produce, even in Shakespeare's and Fletcher's works, some plays which are almost exactly formed; as *The Merry Wives of Windsor*,* and *The Scornful Lady*: but because (generally speaking) Shakespeare, who writ first, did not perfectly observe the laws of comedy, and Fletcher, who came nearer to perfection, yet through carelessness made many faults; I will take the pattern of a perfect play from Ben Jonson, who was a careful and learned observer of the dramatic laws, and from all his comedies I shall select *The Silent Woman*; of which I will make a short examen, according to those rules which the French observe.'

As Neander was beginning to examine *The Silent Woman*, Eugenius, earnestly regarding him; 'I beseech you, Neander,' said he, 'gratify the company, and me in particular, so far, as before you speak of the play, to give us a character of the author; and tell us frankly your opinion, whether you do not

---

* ***The Merry Wives of Windsor:*** Shakespare의 작품. 시간이 약 2일 흐르는 것으로 되어 있다.

think all writers, both French and English, ought to give place to him.'

'I fear,' replied Neander, 'that in obeying your commands I shall draw some envy on myself. Besides, in performing them, it will be first necessary to speak somewhat of Shakespeare and Fletcher, his rivals in poesy; and one of them, in my opinion, at least his equal, perhaps his superior.

'To begin, then, with Shakespeare. He was the man who of all modern, and perhaps ancient poets, had the largest and most comprehensive soul. All the images of nature were still present to him, and he drew them, not laboriously, but luckily*; when he describes any thing, you more than see it, you feel it too. Those who accuse him to have wanted learning, give him the greater commendation: he was naturally learned; he needed not the spectacles of books to read nature; he looked inwards, and found her there*. I cannot say he is every where alike; were he so, I should do him injury to compare him with the greatest of mankind. He is many times flat, insipid; his comic wit degenerating into clenches, his serious swelling into bombast. But he is always great, when some great occasion is presented to him; no man can say he ever had a fit subject for his wit, and did not then raise himself as high above the rest of poets,

Quantum lenta solent inter viburna cupressi.*

The consideration of this made Mr. Hales* of Eton say, that there was no subject of which any poet ever writ, but he would produce* it much better done in Shakespeare; and however others are now generally preferred before him, yet the age

---

***luckily:** (자연의 모습들을 그리기만 하면) 「그냥 척척 들어맞게」.

*이 귀절은 그 후 Shakespeare 비평의 모범이 되었다.

***Quantum...:** 'As cypresses often do among bending osiers' (Virgil, *Eclogues*, I, 25)

***Hales, John:** (1584-1656). Eton College 의 fellow.

***produce:** 「제시하다, 내보이다」. 이 부근의 뜻은, 「다른 극작가의 무슨 주제든지 Shakespeare 의 작품에서 훨씬 잘 다루어져 있음을 보여줄 수 있다」.

wherein he lived, which had contemporaries with him Fletcher and Jonson, never equalled them to him in their esteem: and in the last king's court, when Ben's reputation was at highest, Sir John Suckling, and with him the greater part of the courtiers, set our Shakespeare far above him.

'Beaumont and Fletcher, of whom I am next to speak, had, with the advantage of Shakespeare's wit, which was their precedent, great natural gifts, improved by study: Beaumont especially being so accurate a judge of plays, that Ben Jonson, while he lived, submitted all his writings to his censure, and, 'tis thought, used his judgement in correcting, if not contriving, all his plots. What value he had for him, appears by the verses he writ to him: and therefore I need speak no further of it. The first play that brought Fletcher and him in esteem was their *Philaster*: for before that, they had written two or three very unsuccessfully, as the like is reported of Ben Jonson,* before he writ *Every Man in His Humour*. Their plots were generally more regular than Shakespeare's, especially those which were made before Beaumont's death; and they understood and imitated the conversation of gentlemen much better; whose wild debaucheries, and quickness of wit in repartees, no poet before them could paint as they have done. Humour, which Ben Jonson derived from particular persons, they made it not their business to describe: they represented all the passions very lively, but above all, love. I am apt to believe the English language in them arrived to its highest perfection: what words have since been taken in, are rather superfluous than ornamental. Their plays are now the most pleasant and frequent entertainments of the stage; two of theirs being acted through the year for one of Shakespeare's or Jonson's: the reason is, because there is a certain gaiety in their comedies, and pathos in their more serious plays, which suit generally with all men's humours. Shakespeare's language is likewise a little obsolete, and Ben Jonson's wit comes short of theirs.

***as the like...Jonson:** 「Ben Jonson에 관해서 그 비슷한 얘기가 전해지고 있듯이」.

'As for Jonson, to whose character I am now arrived, if we look upon him while he was himself, (for his last plays were but his dotages) I think him the most learned and judicious writer which any theatre ever had. He was a most severe judge of himself, as well as others. One cannot say he wanted wit, but rather that he was frugal of it. In his works you find little to retrench or alter. Wit, and language, and humour also in some measure, we had before him; but something of art was wanting to the drama, till he came. He managed his strength to more advantage than any who preceded him. You seldom find him making love in any of his scenes, or endeavouring to move the passions; his genius was too sullen and saturnine to do it gracefully, especially when he knew he came after those who had performed both to such a height. Humour was his proper sphere; and in that he delighted most to represent mechanic people. He was deeply conversant in the ancients, both Greek and Latin, and he borrowed boldly from them: there is scarce a poet or historian among the Roman authors of those times whom he has not translated* in *Sejanus* and *Catiline*. But he has done his robberies so openly, that one may see he fears not to be taxed by any law. He invades authors like a monarch; and what would be theft in other poets, is only victory in him. With the spoils of these writers he so represents old Rome to us, in its rites, ceremonies, and customs, that if one of their poets had written either of his tragedies, we had seen less of it than in him. If there was any fault in his language, 'twas that he weaved it too closely and laboriously, in his comedies especially: perhaps too, he did a little too much Romanize* our tongue, leaving the words which he translated almost as much Latin as he found them: wherein, though he learnedly followed their language, he did not enough comply with the idiom of ours. If I would compare him with Shakespeare, I must acknowledge him the more correct poet, but Shakespeare

---

***translate:** 「옮겨 놓다」. Ben Jonson 은 고전작가에게서 많은 것을 내놓고 빌려다 썼다.

***Romanize:** 「로마식으로, 즉 라틴식으로 만들다」.

the greater wit. Shakespeare was the Homer, or father of our dramatic poets; Jonson was the Virgil, the pattern of elaborate writing; I admire him, but I love Shakespeare. To conclude of him; as he has given us the most correct plays, so in the precepts which he has laid down in his *Discoveries*, we have as many and profitable rules for perfecting the stage, as any wherewith the French can furnish us.

'Having thus spoken of the author, I proceed to the examination of his comedy, *The Silent Woman.*

Examen of the Silent Woman

'To begin first with the length of the action; it is so far from exceeding the compass of a natural day, that it takes not up an artificial one.* 'Tis all included in the limits of three hours and a half, which is no more than is required for the presentment on the stage: a beauty perhaps not much observed; if it had,* we should not have looked on the Spanish translation of *Five Hours* with so much wonder. The scene of it is laid in London; the latitude of place is almost as little as you can imagine; for it lies all within the compass of two houses, and after the first act, in one. The continuity of scenes is observed more than in any of our plays, except his own *Fox* and *Alchemist.* They are not broken above twice or thrice at most in the whole comedy; and in the two best of Corneille's plays, the *Cid* and *Cinna,* they are interrupted once. The action of the play is entirely one; the end or aim of which is the settling Morose's estate on Dauphine. The intrigue of it is the greatest and most noble of any pure unmixed comedy in any language; you see in it many persons of various characters and humours, and all delightful. As first, Morose, or an old man, to whom all noise but his own talking is offensive. Some who would be thought critics, say this humour of his is forced: but to remove that objection, we may consider him first to be naturally of a delicate

---

***artificial one:** artificial day, 즉 12시간(예술적인 하루).

***if it had:** if the beauty had been observed.

***of a delicate hearing:** 「청각이 예민한」.

hearing,* as many are, to whom all sharp sounds are unpleasant; and secondly, we may attribute much of it to the peevishness of his age, or the wayward authority of an old man in his own house, where he may make himself obeyed; and to this the poet seems to allude in his name Morose.* Besides this, I am assured from divers persons, that Ben Jonson was actually acquainted with such a man, one altogether as ridiculous as he is here represented. Others say, it is not enough to find one man of such a humour; it must be common to more, and the more common the more natural. To prove this, they instance in the best of comical characters, Falstaff.* There are many men resembling him; old, fat, merry, cowardly, drunken, amorous, vain, and lying. But to convince these people, I need but tell them, that humour is the ridiculous extravagance of conversation, wherein one man differs from all others. If then it be common, or communicated to many, how differs it from other men's? or what indeed causes it to be ridiculous so much as the singularity of it? As for Falstaff, he is not properly one humour, but a miscellany of humours or images, drawn from so many several men: that wherein he is singular is his wit, or those things he says *praeter expectatum*,* unexpected by the audience; his quick evasions, when you imagine him surprised, which, as they are extremely diverting* of themselves, so receive a great addition from the person; for the very sight of such an unwieldy old debauched fellow is a comedy alone. And here, having a place so proper for it, I cannot but enlarge somewhat upon this subject of humour into which I am fallen. The ancients had little of it in their comedies; for the τὸ γελοῖον* of the old comedy, of which Aristophanes was chief, was

---

***Morose:** 「침울한」이란 뜻. Ben Jonson 은 인물의 특징적 기질 (humour) 을 가리키는 낱말로 그 인물의 이름을 삼았다. 이른바 comedy of humours 는 그의 창안이다.

***Falstaff:** Shakespeare 의 작품 *Henry* Ⅳ 의 1, 2 부, *Henry* Ⅴ, *Merry Wives of Windsor* 에 등장하는 가장 이름난 희극적 인물.

****praeter expectatum:*** 'beyond expectation'.

***diverting:** funny.

*'the laughable'

not so much to imitate a man, as to make the people laugh at some odd conceit, which had commonly somewhat of unnatural or obscene in it. Thus, when you see Socrates brought upon the stage, you are not to imagine him made ridiculous by the imitation of his actions, but rather by making him perform something very unlike himself; something so childish and absurd, as by comparing it with the gravity of the true Socrates, makes a ridiculous object for the spectators. In their new comedy* which succeeded, the poets sought indeed to express the *ἦθος*;* as in their tragedies the *πάθος** of mankind. But this *ἦθος* contained only the general characters of men and manners; as old men, lovers, serving-men, courtezans, parasites, and such other persons as we see in their comedies; all which they made alike: that is, one old man or father, one lover, one courtezan, so like another, as if the first of them had begot the rest of every sort: *Ex homine hunc natum dicas*.* The same custom they observed likewise in their tragedies. As for the French, though they have the word *humeur* among them, yet they have small use of it in their comedies or farces; they being but ill imitations of the *ridiculum*,* or that which stirred up laughter in the old comedy. But among the English 'tis otherwise: where by humour is meant some extravagant habit, passion, or affection, particular (as I said before) to some one person, by the oddness of which, he is immediately distinguished from the rest of men; which being lively and naturally represented, most frequently begets that malicious pleasure in the audience which is testified by laughter; as all things which are deviations from customs are ever the aptest to produce it:

---

new comedy: 336 B.C. 경에 시작된 그리이스의 희극형식. Menander가 그 대표적 작가였지만 지금은 작품이 전해지지 않고, 그것을 모방한 로마의 Plautus에서 그 대략적 모습을 짐작할 수 있다. 전형적 인물(type)을 등장시킨 것이 특징이다.

**ἦθος*: [ethos] character.

**πάθος*: [pathos] feeling, passion.

****Ex homine***...: 'You would say he was born from the other man' (Terence, *Eunuch*, 460).

****ridiculum:*** ridiculous.

though by the way this laughter is only accidental, as the person represented is fantastic or bizarre; but pleasure is essential to it, as the imitation of what is natural. The description of these humours, drawn from the knowledge and observation of particular persons, was the peculiar genius and talent of Ben Jonson; to whose play I now return.

'Besides Morose, there are at least nine or ten different characters and humours in *The Silent Woman*; all which persons have several concernments of their own, yet are all used by the poet, to the conducting of the main design to perfection. I shall not waste time in commending the writing of this play; but I will give you my opinion, that there is more wit and acuteness of fancy in it than in any of Ben Jonson's. Besides that he has here described the conversation of gentlemen in the persons of True-Wit, and his friends, with more gaiety, air, and freedom, than in the rest of his comedies. For the contrivance of the plot, 'tis extreme elaborate, and yet withal easy; for the λύσις,* or untying of it, 'tis so admirable, that when it is done, no one of the audience would think the poet could have missed it; and yet it was concealed so much before the last scene, that any other way would sooner have entered into your thoughts. But I dare not take upon me to commend the fabric of it, because it is altogether so full of art, that I must unravel every scene in it to commend it as I ought. And this excellent contrivance is still the more to be admired, because 'tis comedy, where the persons are only of common rank, and their business private, not elevated by passions or high concernments, as in serious plays. Here every one is a proper judge of all he sees, nothing is represented but that with which he daily converses: so that by consequence all faults lie open to discovery, and few are pardonable. 'Tis this which Horace has judiciously observed:

> Creditur, ex medio quia res arcessit, habere
> Sudoris minimum; sed habet Comedia tanto
> Plus oneris, quanto veniae minus.*

---

*λύσις: [lysis] unravelling. 「해결」.

But our poet who was not ignorant of these difficulties, has made use of all advantages; as he who designs a large leap takes his rise from the highest ground. One of these advantages is that which Corneille has laid down as the greatest which can arrive to any poem, and which he himself could never compass above thrice in all his plays; viz. the making choice of some signal and long-expected day, whereon the action of the play is to depend. This day was that designed by Dauphine for the settling of his uncle's estate upon him; which to compass,* he contrives to marry him. That the marriage had been plotted by him long beforehand, is made evident by what he tells True-wit in the second act, that in one moment he had destroyed what he had been raising many months.

'There is another artifice of the poet, which I cannot here omit, because by the frequent practice of it in his comedies he has left it to us almost as a rule; that is, when he has any character or humour wherein he would show a *coup de Maître*,* or his highest skill, he recommends it to your observation by a pleasant description of it before the person first appears. Thus, in *Bartholomew Fair* he gives you the pictures of Numps and Cokes, and in this those* of Daw, Lafoole, Morose, and the Collegiate Ladies; all which you hear described before you see them. So that before they come upon the stage, you have a longing expectation of them, which prepares you to receive them favourably; and when they are there, even from their first appearance you are so far acquainted with them, that nothing of their humour is lost to you.

'I will observe yet one thing further of this admirable plot; the business of it rises in every act. The second is greater than the first; the third than the second; and so forward to the fifth. There too you see, till the very last scene, new difficulties

---

*Creditur...: 'Comedy is thought to demand the least work; for it draws its subjects from ordinary life. But the less indulgence it has, the more work it requires' (*Epistles*, II, i).

***compass:** 「성취하다」.

***coup de Maitre:** master stroke. 「가장 멋진 수완」.

***in this:** in this play [*The Silent Woman*]. **those:** the persons.

arising to obstruct the action of the play; and when the audience is brought into despair that the business can naturally be effected, then, and not before, the discovery is made. But that the poet might entertain you with more variety all this while, he reserves some new characters to show you, which he opens not till the second and third act; in the second Morose, Daw, the Barber, and Otter; in the third the Collegiate Ladies: all which he moves afterwards in by-walks, or under-plots, as diversions to the main design, lest it should grow tedious, though they are still naturally joined with it, and somewhere or other subservient to it. Thus, like a skilful chess-player, by little and little he draws out his men, and makes his pawns*of use to his greater persons.

'If this comedy and some others of his, were translated into French prose, (which would now be no wonder to them, since Molière has lately given them plays out of verse, which have not displeased them,) I believe the controversy would soon be decided betwixt the two nations, even making them the judges. But we need not call our heroes to our aid. Be it spoken to the honour of the English, our nation can never want in any age such who are able to dispute the empire of wit with any people in the universe. And though the fury of a civil war, and power for twenty years together abandoned to a barbarous race of men, enemies of all good learning, had buried the muses under the ruins of monarchy; yet, with the restoration of our happiness, we see revived poesy lifting up its head, and already shaking off the rubbish which lay so heavy on it.* We have seen since his Majesty's return, many dramatic poems which yield not to those of any foreign nation, and which deserve all laurels but the English. I will set aside flattery and envy: it cannot be denied but we have had some little blemish either in the plot or writing of all those plays which have been made within

---

***pawns:** 서양 장기에서 졸에 해당하는 말들. 군소인물이란 뜻.

*청교도 혁명 당시에 극장은 부도덕한 것이라 하여 폐쇄됐었다(1642). 1660년 왕정복고 이후에 프랑스 희곡의 영향을 받은 작품이 다시 나오기 시작했다. 그러니 그 질은 아직 Dryden이 주장하는 만큼 높은 것이 못되었다.

these seven years; (and perhaps there is no nation in the world so quick to discern them, or so difficult to pardon them, as ours:) yet if we can persuade ourselves to use the candour of that poet, who, though the most severe of critics, has left us this caution by which to moderate our censures—

—ubi plura nitent in carmine, non ego paucis
Offendar maculis;—*

if, in consideration of their many and great beauties, we can wink at some slight and little imperfections, if we, I say, can be thus equal to ourselves, I ask no favour from the French. And if I do not venture upon any particular judgement of our late plays, 'tis out of the consideration which an ancient writer gives me: *vivorum, ut magna admiratio, ita censura difficilis*:* betwixt the extremes of admiration and malice, 'tis hard to judge uprightly of the living. Only I think it may be permitted me to say, that as it is no lessening to us to yield to some plays, and those not many, of our own nation in the last age, so can it be no addition to pronounce of our present poets, that they have far surpassed all the ancients, and the modern writers of other countries.'

This was the substance of what was then spoke on that occasion; and Lisideius, I think, was going to reply, when he was prevented thus by Crites: 'I am confident,' said he, 'that the most material things that can be said have been already urged on either side; if they have not, I must beg of Lisideius that he will defer his answer till another time: for I confess I have a joint quarrel to you both, because you have concluded, without any reason given for it, that rhyme is proper for the stage. I will not dispute how ancient it hath been among us to write this way; perhaps our ancestors knew no better till Shakespeare's time. I will grant it was not altogether left by him, and that Fletcher and Ben Jonson used it frequently

*ubi plura...: 'when many things shine in a poem, I shall not be offended at little faults' (Horace, *Ars Poetica*, 351).

**vivorum*...: 'as admiration for the living is great, so to criticise them is difficult' (Velleius Paterculus, *Historia Romona*, II, 36).

in their Pastorals,* and sometimes in other plays. Further,—I will not argue whether we received it originally from our own countrymen, or from the French; for that is an inquiry of as little benefit, as theirs who, in the midst of the great plague,* were not so solicitous to provide against it, as to know whether we had it from the malignity of our own air, or by transportation from Holland. I have therefore only to affirm, that it is not allowable in serious plays; for comedies, I find you already concluding with me. To prove this, I might satisfy myself to tell you, how much in vain it is for you to strive against the stream of the people's inclination; the greatest part of which are prepossessed so much with those excellent plays of Shakespeare, Fletcher, and Ben Jonson, which have been written out of rhyme, that except you could bring them such as were written better in it, and those too by persons of equal reputation with them, it will be impossible for you to gain your cause with them,* who will still be judges. This it is to which, in fine, all your reasons must submit. The unanimous consent of an audience is so powerful, that even Julius Caesar (as Macrobius reports of him,) when he was perpetual dictator, was not able to balance it on the other side; but when Laberius, a Roman Knight, at his request contended in the *Mime* with another poet, he was forced to cry out, *Etiam favente me victus es, Laberi.** But I will not on this occasion take the advantage of the greater number, but only urge such reasons against rhyme, as I find in the writings of those who have argued for the other way. First then, I am of opinion, that rhyme is unnatural in a play, because dialogue there is presented as the effect of sudden thought: for a play is the imitation of nature; and since no man, without premeditation, speaks in rhyme, neither ought he to do it on the stage. This hinders not but the fancy may be

---

***Pastorals:** 17세기 초에 유행한 전원극.

***plague:** 당시의 무서운 전염병인 흑사병.

***to gain your cause with them:** 「일반대중에게 당신의 주장을 설득시키려면」.

****Etiam*...:** 'You are beaten, Laberius' (Macrobius, *Saturnalia Convivia*, Ⅱ, 7).

there elevated to a higher pitch of thought than it is in ordinary discourse; for there is a probability that men of excellent and quick parts may speak noble things *extempore*:* but those thoughts are never fettered with the numbers or sound of verse without study, and therefore it cannot be but unnatural to present the most free way of speaking in that which is the most constrained. For this reason, says Aristotle, 'tis best to write tragedy in that kind of verse which is the least such,* or which is nearest prose: and this amongst the ancients was the Iambic, and with us is blank verse, or the measure of verse kept exactly without rhyme. These numbers therefore are fittest for a play; the others for a paper of verses, or a poem; blank verse being as much below them, as rhyme is improper for the drama. And if it be objected that neither are blank verses made *extempore*, yet, as nearest nature, they are still to be preferred.—But there are two particular exceptions,* which many besides myself have had to verse; by which it will appear yet more plainly how improper it is in plays. And the first of them is grounded on that very reason for which some have commended rhyme; they say, the quickness of repartees in argumentative scenes receives an ornament from verse. Now what is more unreasonable than to imagine that a man should not only light upon the wit, but the rhyme too, upon the sudden? This nicking* of him who spoke before both in sound and measure, is so great a happiness, that you must at least suppose the persons of your play to be born poets: *Arcades omnes, et cantare pares, et respondere parati*: they must have arrived to the degree of *quicquid conabar dicere*;*— to make verses almost whether they will or no. If they are any thing below this, it will look rather like the design of

---

***extempore:** 「즉흥적으로」.
***such:** verse. 가장 운문다운 성질이 적은 운문. *Poetics*, Ⅳ, 14에서 iambic 이 가장 구어체를 닮았으므로 비극에 적합하다는 말을 하고 있다.
***exception:** 「반대」. *cf*. have exception to...: 「...에 반대하다」.
***nicking:** matching precisely.
******Arcades*...; ...*quicquid*...: 'Both Arcadians, prepared to sing on equal terms and to reply' (Virgil, *Eclogues*, Ⅶ, 4); 'Whatever I tried to say [would be verse]' (Ovid).

two, than the answer of one: it will appear that your actors hold intelligence together*; that they perform their tricks like fortune-tellers, by confederacy. The hand of art will be too visible in it, against that maxim of all professions—*Ars est celare artem**; that it is the greatest perfection of art to keep itself undiscovered. Nor will it serve you to object, that however you manage it, 'tis still known to be a play; and, consequently, the dialogue of two persons understood to be the labour of one poet. For a play is still an imitation of nature; we know we are to be deceived, and we desire to be so; but no man ever was deceived but with a probability of truth; for who will suffer a gross lie to be fastened on him? Thus we sufficiently understand, that the scenes which represent cities and countries to us are not really such, but only painted on boards and canvas; but shall that excuse the ill painture or designment of them? Nay, rather ought they not be laboured with so much the more diligence and exactness, to help the imagination? since the mind of man does naturally tend to truth; and therefore the nearer any thing comes to the imitation of it, the more it pleases.

'Thus, you see, your rhyme is incapable of expressing the greatest thoughts naturally, and the lowest it cannot with any grace: for what is more unbefitting the majesty of verse, than to call a servant, or bid a door be shut in rhyme? and yet you are often forced on this miserable necessity. But verse, you say, circumscribes a quick and luxuriant fancy, which would extend itself too far on every subject, did not the labour* which is required to well-turned and polished rhyme, set bounds to it. Yet this argument, if granted, would only prove that we may write better in verse, but not more naturally. Neither is it able to evince that; for he who wants judgement to confine his fancy in blank verse, may want it as much in rhyme: and he who has it will avoid errors in both kinds. Latin verse was as

---

***hold...together:** 「서로 내통하다」.

***Ars...:** 'Art is to conceal art' (잘 알려진 격언이다).

***did not the labour:** if the labour did not...

great a confinement to the imagination of those poets, as rhyme to ours; and yet you find Ovid saying too much on every subject. *Nescivit* (says Seneca) *quod bene cessit relinquere:** of which he gives you one famous instance in his description of the deluge:

> Omnia pontus erat, deerant quoque litora ponto.
> Now all was sea, nor had that sea a shore.*

Thus Ovid's fancy was not limited by verse, and Virgil needed not verse to have bounded his.

'In our own language we see Ben Jonson confining himself to what ought to be said, even in the liberty of blank verse; and yet Corneille, the most judicious of the French poets, is still varying the same sense a hundred ways, and dwelling eternally on the same subject, though confined by rhyme. Some other exceptions I have to verse; but since these I have named are for the most part already public, I conceive it reasonable they should first be answered.'

'It concerns me less than any,' said Neander, (seeing he had ended,) 'to reply to this discourse; because when I should have proved that verse may be natural in plays, yet I should always be ready to confess, that those which I have written in this kind come short of that perfection which is required. Yet since you are pleased I should undertake this province, I will do it, though with all imaginable respect and deference, both to that person from whom you have borrowed your strongest arguments, and to whose judgement, when I have said all, I finally submit. But before I proceed to answer your objections, I must first remember* you, that I exclude all comedy from my defence; and next that I deny not but blank verse may be also used; and content myself only to assert, that in serious plays where the subject and characters are great, and the plot unmixed with

---

**Nescivit*...: 'He did not know to end when he had better stop' (Marcus Seneca, *Controversiae*, ix, 5).

*Ovid, *Metamorphoses*, i. 292.

*remember: remind.

mirth, which might allay or divert these concernments which are produced, rhyme is there as natural and more effectual than blank verse.

'And now having laid down this as a foundation,—to begin with Crites,—I must crave leave to tell him, that some of his arguments against rhyme reach no farther than, from the faults or defects of ill rhyme, to conclude against the use of it in general. May not I conclude against blank verse by the same reason? If the words of some poets who write in it, are either ill chosen, or ill placed, which makes not only rhyme, but all kind of verse in any language unnatural, shall I, for their vicious affectation, condemn those excellent lines of Fletcher, which are written in that kind? Is there any thing in rhyme more constrained than this line in blank verse?—*I heaven invoke, and strong resistance make*; where you see both the clauses are placed unnaturally, that is, contrary to the common way of speaking, and that without the excuse of a rhyme to cause it: yet you would think me very ridiculous, if I should accuse the stubbornness of blank verse for this, and not rather the stiffness of the poet. Therefore, Crites, you must either prove that words, though well chosen, and duly placed, yet render not rhyme natural in itself; or that, however natural and easy the rhyme may be, yet it is not proper for a play. If you insist on the former part, I would ask you, what other conditions are required to make rhyme natural in itself, besides an election of apt words, and a right disposition of them? For the due choice of your words expresses your sense naturally, and the due placing them adapts the rhyme to it. If you object that one verse may be made for the sake of another, though both the words and rhyme be apt, I answer, it cannot possibly so fall out; for either there is a dependence of sense betwixt the first line and the second, or there is none: if there be that connection, then in the natural position of the words the latter line must of necessity flow from the former; if there be no dependence, yet still the due ordering of words makes the last line as natural in itself as the other: so that the necessity of a rhyme never forces any but bad or lazy writers to say what they would not otherwise. 'Tis true, there is both care and art required to write in verse. A good poet never establishes the first line, till he has sought out such a rhyme as may fit the sense, already prepared to heighten the second: many times the close of the sense falls into the middle of the next verse, or farther off, and he may often prevail* himself of the same advantages in English which Virgil had in Latin,—he may break off in the hemistich,* and begin another line. Indeed, the not observing these two last things, makes plays which are writ in verse, so tedious: for though, most commonly, the sense is to be confined to the couplet, yet nothing that does *perpetuo tenore fluere*,* run in the same channel, can please always. 'Tis like the murmuring of a stream, which not varying in the fall, causes at first attention, at last drowsiness. Variety of cadences is the best rule; the greatest help to the actors, and refreshment to the audience.

'If then verse may be made natural in itself, how becomes it unnatural in a play? You say the stage is the representation of nature, and no man in ordinary conversation speaks in rhyme. But you foresaw when you said this, that it might be answered—neither does any man speak in blank verse, or in measure without rhyme. Therefore you concluded, that which is nearest nature is still to be preferred. But you took no notice that rhyme might be made as natural as blank verse, by the well placing of the words, &c. All the difference between them, when they are both correct, is, the sound in one, which the other wants; and if so, the sweetness of it, and all the advantage resulting from it, which are handled in the Preface to *The Rival Ladies*,* will yet stand good. As for that place of Aristotle, where he says, plays should be writ in that kind of verse which is nearest prose, it makes little for you; blank verse being properly

---

*prevail: avail. *cf*. avail oneself of...: 「...을 이용하다」.

*hemistich: 시의 한 행의 절반.

**perpetuo*...: 'flow in the same channel' (Cicero, *De Oratore*, vi, 21).

**The Rival Ladies*: Dryden의 1664년 작품. 이 희곡에서 rhymed verse의 사용을 주장하는 서문을 실었다.

but measured prose. Now measure alone, in any modern language, does not constitute verse; those of the ancients in Greek and Latin consisted in quantity of words,* and a determinate number of feet. But when, by the inundation of the Goths and Vandals into Italy, new languages were introduced, and barbarously mingled with the Latin, of which the Italian, Spanish, French, and ours, (made out of them and the Teutonic,) are dialects, a new way of poesy was practised; new, I say, in those countries, for in all probability it was that of the conquerors in their own nations: at least we are able to prove, that the eastern people have used it from all antiquity.* *Vide* Daniel's *Defence of Rhyme*.* This new way consisted in measure or number of feet, and rhyme; the sweetness of rhyme, and observation of accent, supplying the place of quantity in words, which could neither exactly be observed by those barbarians, who knew not the rules of it, neither was it suitable to their tongues, as it had been to the Greek and Latin. No man is tied in modern poesy to observe any further rule in the feet of his verse, but that they be dissyllables*; whether Spondee, Trochee, or Iambic, it matters not; only he is obliged to rhyme: neither do the Spanish, French, Italian, or Germans, acknowledge at all, or very rarely, any such kind of poesy as blank verse amongst them. Therefore, at most 'tis but a poetic prose, a *sermo pedestris; and as such, most fit for comedies, where I acknowledge rhyme to be improper.—Further; as to that quotation of Aristotle, our couplet verses may be rendered as near prose as blank verse itself, by using those advantages I lately named,—as breaks in a hemistich, or running the sense into**

***quantity of words:** 「낱말의 소리의 장단(음량)」. 그리이스와 로마의 시는 이러한 소리의 장단에 기초하여 운문을 만들었다.

Rhyme 은 동방 및 북방의 야만족이 유럽에 가져온 것이라는 생각이 유행했으나, 사실의 여부는 분명하지 않다. rhymed verse 는 서유럽에서는 중세 이후에 유행하기 시작함. 또 운율도 quantity 아닌 quality, 즉 accent 의 강약에 의존함.** ***Defence of Rhyme : 시인 Samuel Daniel(1562-1619)의 각운을 옹호하는 평론(1602).

***dissyllables: 2음절 foot. 즉 강약이든 약강이든 한 단위를 이루고 있다.**

****sermo pedestris*:** 'pedestrian discourse'. 「산문적인 글」.

another line,—thereby making art and order appear as loose and free as nature: or not tying ourselves to couplets strictly, we may use the benefit of the Pindaric way* practised in *The Siege of Rhodes**; where the numbers vary, and the rhyme is disposed carelessly, and far from often chiming. Neither is that other advantage of the ancients to be despised, of changing the kind of verse when they please, with the change of the scene, or some new entrance; for they confine not themselves always to iambics, but extend their liberty to all lyric numbers, and sometimes even to hexameter. But I need not go so far to prove that rhyme, as it succeeds to all other offices* of Greek and Latin verse, so especially to this of plays, since the custom of nations at this day confirms it; the French, Italian, and Spanish tragedies are generally writ in it; and sure the universal consent of the most civilized parts of the world, ought in this, as it doth in other customs, to include the rest.

'But perhaps you may tell me, I have proposed such a way to make rhyme natural, and consequently proper to plays, as is unpracticable; and that I shall scarce find six or eight lines together in any play, where the words are so placed and chosen as is required to make it natural. I answer, no poet need constrain himself at all times to it. It is enough he makes it his general rule; for I deny not but sometimes there may be a greatness in placing the words otherwise; and sometimes they may sound better; sometimes also the variety itself is excuse enough. But if, for the most part, the words be placed as they are in the negligence of prose, it is sufficient to denominate the way practicable; for we esteem that to be such, which in the trial oftener succeeds than misses. And thus far you may find the practice made good in many plays: where you do not, remember still, that if you cannot find six natural rhymes together, it will be as hard for you to produce as many lines in

---

***Pindaric way:** 그리이스 서정시인 Pindar의 일정치 않은 길이의 시행을 흉내낸 시형.

****The Siege of Rhodes*:** William Davenant (1606-68)의 영웅극 오페라(1656).

***offices:** 「일거리, 기능」.

blank verse, even among the greatest of our poets, against which I cannot make some reasonable exception.

'And this, Sir, calls to my remembrance the beginning of your discourse, where you told us we should never find the audience favourable to this kind of writing, till we could produce as good plays in rhyme, as Ben Jonson, Fletcher, and Shakespeare, had writ out of it. But it is to raise envy to the living, to compare them with the dead. They are honoured, and almost adored by us, as they deserve; neither do I know any so presumptuous of themselves as to contend with them. Yet give me leave to say thus much, without injury to their ashes; that not only we shall never equal them but they could never equal themselves, were they to rise and write again. We acknowledge them our fathers in wit; but they have ruined their estates themselves, before they came to their children's hands. There is scarce a humour, a character, or any kind of plot, which they have not used. All comes sullied or wasted to us: and were they to entertain this age, they could not now make so plenteous treatments out of such decayed fortunes. This therefore will be a good argument to us, either not to write at all, or to attempt some other way. There is no bays to be expected in their walks: *tentanda via est, qua me quoque possum tollere humo.**

'This way of writing in verse they have only left free to us; our age is arrived to a perfection in it, which they never knew; and which (if we may guess by what of theirs we have seen in verse, as *The Faithful Shepherdess*, and *Sad Shepherd*)* 'tis probable they never could have reached. For the genius of every age is different; and though ours excel in this, I deny not but to imitate nature in that perfection which they did in

****tentanda via est***...'I must explore to find out a way by which I can raise myself' (Virgil, *Georgics*, Ⅲ, 8—9). 찬란한 전통의 중압에 따른 후대 시인들의 고민은 문제가 된다. 이른바 The Burdens of the Past [W. J. Bate 의 저서명]라는 것이다.

****The Faithful Shepherdess*** 는 Ben Jonson 의 미완성 전원희극으로 부분적으로 압운되어 있고, ***Sad Shepherd*** 는 Fletcher 의 처녀작이다. 이들 선배작가들의 압운 극은 미숙한 상태였다.

prose,* is a greater commendation than to write in verse exactly. As for what you have added—that the people are not generally inclined to like this way,—if it were true, it would be no wonder, that betwixt the shaking off an old habit, and the introducing of a new, there should be difficulty. Do we not see them stick to Hopkins' and Sternhold's psalms, and forsake those of David, I mean Sandys' translation of them?* If by the people you understand the multitude, the οἱ πολλοί,* 'tis no matter what they think; they are sometimes in the right, sometimes in the wrong: their judgement is a mere lottery. *Est ubi plebs recte putat, est ubi peccat. Horace says it of the vulgar, judging poesy. But if you mean the mixed audience of the populace and the noblesse, I dare confidently affirm that a great part of the latter sort are already favourable to verse; and that no serious plays written since the King's return have been more kindly received by them, than *The Siege of Rhodes*, the *Mustapha*, *The Indian Queen*, and *Indian Emperor*.***

'But I come now to the inference of your first argument. You said that the dialogue of plays is presented as the effect of sudden thought, but no man speaks suddenly, or *extempore*, in rhyme; and you inferred from thence, that rhyme, which you acknowledge to be proper to epic poesy, cannot equally be proper to dramatic, unless we could suppose all men born so much more than poets, that verses should be made in them, not by them.*

***prose:** 옛 희곡작가들은 blank verse로 썼는데 이를 prose라 한 것은 과장된 표현이다.

*구약 중 David왕의 시편 (Psalms)을 John Hopkins와 Thomas Sternhold가 운문으로 번역, 1549년에 출판했었는데, 그보다 번역이 잘 된 George Sandys의 번역본보다 훨씬 인기가 있어서 19세기까지 애독되었다.

*〔oi polloi〕. 「대중」.

****Est ubi*...:** 'It is where common people think they are right that they are wrong' (Horace, *Epistles*, Ⅱ, i. 63).

****Mustapha***는 Roger Boyle, Earl of Orrery(1621-79)의 작품(1664)이고, ***The Indian Queen***은 Dryden과 Howard (이 대화의 Crites)의 공동작(1664)이며, ***Indian Emperor***는 그 후편으로 Dryden이 1665년에 지은 것. 모두 영웅극(heroic drama)이다.

***verses...by them:** 운문은 시인에 의해 만들어지는 게 아니라 사람들 마음

'It has been formerly urged by you, and confessed by me, that since no man spoke any kind of verse *extempore*, that which was nearest nature was to be preferred. I answer you, therefore, by distinguishing betwixt what is nearest to the nature of comedy, which is the imitation of common persons and ordinary speaking, and what is nearest the nature of a serious play: this last is indeed the representation of nature, but 'tis nature wrought up to a higher pitch. The plot, the characters, the wit, the passions, the descriptions, are all exalted above the level of common converse, as high as the imagination of the poet can carry them, with proportion to verisimility. Tragedy, we know, is wont to image to us the minds and fortunes of noble persons, and to portray these exactly; heroic rhyme is nearest nature, as being the noblest kind of modern verse.

> Indignatur enim privatis et prope socco
> Dignis carminibus narrari cena Thyestae—*

says Horace: and in another place,

> Effutire leves indigna tragoedia versus—*.

Blank verse is acknowledged to be too low for a poem, nay more, for a paper of verses;* but if too low for an ordinary sonnet, how much more for tragedy, which is by Aristotle, in the dispute betwixt the epic poesy and the dramatic, for many reasons he there alleges, ranked above it?

'But setting this defence aside, your argument is almost as strong against the use of rhyme in poems as in plays; for the epic way is every where interlaced with dialogue, or discoursive scenes; and therefore you must either grant rhyme to be improper there, which is contrary to your assertion, or admit it

---

속에 이미 만들어져 있다는 것, 즉 시는 만드는 것이 아니라 타고난다는 것. Dryden은 이에 반대했다.

**Indignatur*...: 'For Thyestes' supper scorns to be treated in the language of common life, language unworthy of the tragic style' (Horace, *Ars Poetica*, 90—1).

**Effutire*...: ' Tragedy thinks it unworthy to chatter in silly verses' (*Ibid* 231).

***a paper of verses:** 운문 신문 (broad-side ballad).

into plays by the same title which you have given it to poems. For though tragedy be justly preferred above the other, yet there is a great affinity between them, as may easily be discovered in that definition of a play which Lisideius gave us. The *genus* of them is the same,—a just and lively image of human nature, in its actions, passions, and traverses of fortune: so is the end,—namely, for the delight and benefit of mankind. The characters and persons are still the same, viz. the greatest of both sorts; only the manner of acquainting us with those actions, passions, and fortunes, is different. Tragedy performs it *viva voce*,* or by action, in dialogue; wherein it excels the epic poem, which does it chiefly by narration, and therefore is not so lively an image of human nature. However, the agreement betwixt them is such, that if rhyme be proper for one, it must be for the other. Verse, 'tis true, is not the effect of sudden thought; but this hinders not that sudden thought may be represented in verse, since those thoughts are such as must be higher than nature can raise them without premeditation, especially to a continuance of them, even out of verse; and consequently you cannot imagine them to have been sudden either in the poet or in the actors. A play, as I have said, to be like nature, is to be set above it; as statues which are placed on high are made greater than the life, that they may descend to the sight in their just proportion.

'Perhaps I have insisted too long on this objection; but the clearing of it will make my stay shorter on the rest.* You tell us, Crites, that rhyme appears most unnatural in repartees, or short replies: when he who answers, (it being presumed he knew not what the other would say, yet) makes up that part of the verse which was left incomplete, and supplies both the sound and measure of it. This, you say, looks rather like the confederacy of two, than the answer of one.

'This, I confess, is an objection which is in every man's

**viva voce*: 'with live voice.'

***the clearing...the rest:** 「반대론을 분명히 하는 것이 나머지 부분에 대한 나의 논의를 단축시킬 것이다」.

mouth, who loves not rhyme: but suppose, I beseech you, the repartee were made only in blank verse, might not part of the same argument be turned against you? for the measure is as often supplied there, as it is in rhyme*; the latter half of the hemistich as commonly made up, or a second line subjoined as a reply to the former; which any one leaf in Jonson's plays will sufficiently clear to you. You will often find in the Greek tragedians, and in Seneca, that when a scene grows up into the warmth of repartees, which is the close fighting of it, the latter part of the trimeter* is supplied by him who answers; and yet it was never observed as a fault in them by any of the ancient or modern critics. The case is the same in our verse, as it was in theirs; rhyme to us being in lieu of quantity to them. But if no latitude is to be allowed a poet, you take from him not only his licence of *quidlibet audendi*,* but you tie him up in a straiter compass than you would a philosopher. This is indeed *Musas colere severiores*.* You would have him follow nature, but he must follow her on foot: you have dismounted him from his Pegasus. But you tell us, this supplying the last half of a verse, or adjoining a whole second to the former, looks more like the design of two, than the answer of one. Suppose we acknowledge it: how comes this confederacy to be more displeasing to you, than in a dance which is well contrived? You see there the united design of many persons to make up one figure: after they have separated themselves in many petty divisions, they rejoin one by one into a gross: the confederacy is plain amongst them, for chance could never produce any thing so beautiful; and yet there is nothing in it, that shocks your sight. I acknowledge the hand of art appears in repartee, as of necessity it must in all kind of verse. But there is also the quick and poignant brevity of it (which is a high imitation of

---

*Blank verse에서도 foot의 수를 맞추기 위해서는 꾸며서 자리를 메꾸는 수 밖에 없으니까 artificial 하기는 마찬가지다.

***trimeter:** three-foot line에서 마지막 1 foot는 상대방이 말하는 것으로 되어 있는 것. 운문극에서 흔히 사용되는 방식이다.

****quidlibet audendi*:** 'daring anything' (Horace, *Ars Poetica*, 10).

****Musas*...:** 'to cultivate the stricter muses' (Martial, *Epigrams*, IX, xi, 17).

nature in those sudden gusts of passion) to mingle with it; and this, joined with the cadency and sweetness of the rhyme, leaves nothing in the soul of the hearer to desire. 'Tis an art which appears; but it appears only like the shadowings of painture, which being to cause the rounding of it, cannot be absent; but while that is considered, they are lost:* so while we attend to the other beauties of the matter, the care and labour of the rhyme is carried from us, or at least drowned in its own sweetness, as bees are sometimes buried in their honey. When a poet has found the repartee, the last perfection he can add to it, is to put it into verse. However good the thought may be, however apt the words in which 'tis couched, yet he finds himself at a little unrest, while rhyme is wanting: he cannot leave it till that comes naturally, and then is at ease, and sits down contented.

'From replies, which are the most elevated thoughts of verse, you pass to those which are most mean, and which are common with the lowest of household conversation. In these, you say, the majesty of verse suffers. You instance in the calling of a servant, or commanding a door to be shut, in rhyme. This, Crites, is a good observation of yours, but no argument: for it proves no more but that such thoughts should be waived, as often as may be, by the address of the poet. But suppose they are necessary in the places where he uses them, yet there is no need to put them into rhyme. He may place them in the beginning of a verse, and break it off, as unfit, when so debased, for any other use; or granting the worst,—that they require more room than the hemistich will allow, yet still there is a choice to be made of the best words, and least vulgar, (provided they be apt,) to express such thoughts. Many have blamed rhyme in general, for this fault, when the poet with a little care might have redressed it. But they do it with no more justice, than if English poesy should be made ridiculous for

*그림의 명암법 (shadowings)은 입체감 (rounding)을 주기 위한 것인데, 거기에 지나치게 주의를 기울이면 명암효과가 사라지고 말듯이, 희곡에서 rhyme에 지나치게 주의를 보내면 희곡의 흐름의 자연스러움이 사라진다는 것.

the sake of the Water-poet's rhymes.* Our language is noble, full, and significant; and I know not why he who is master of it may not clothe ordinary things in it as decently as the Latin, if he use the same diligence in his choice of words: *delectus verborum origo est eloquentiae.** It was the saying of Julius Caesar, one so curious in his,* that none of them can be changed but for a worse. One would think, *unlock the door*, was a thing as vulgar as could be spoken; and yet Seneca could make it sound high and lofty in his Latin:

Reserate clusos regii postes laris.
Set wide the palace gates.*

'But I turn from this exception, both because it happens not above twice or thrice in any play that those vulgar thoughts are used; and then too, (were there no other apology to be made, yet,) the necessity of them, which is alike in all kind of writing, may excuse them. For if they are little and mean in rhyme, they are of consequence such* in blank verse. Besides that the great eagerness and precipitation with which they are spoken, makes us rather mind the substance than the dress; that for which they are spoken, rather than what is spoke. For they are always the effect of some hasty concernment, and something of consequence depends on them.

'Thus, Crites, I have endeavoured to answer your objections; it remains only that I should vindicate an argument for verse, which you have gone about to overthrow. It had formerly been said, that the easiness of blank verse renders the poet too luxuriant, but that the labour of rhyme bounds and circumscribes an over-fruitful fancy; the sense there being commonly confined to the couplet, and the words so ordered that the rhyme naturally follows them, not they the rhyme. To this

---

***Water-poet's rhymes:** 템즈강의 사공이었던 John Taylor (1580-1653) 의 대중적 인기를 끌었던 시.

***delectus...:** 'the source of eloquence is choice in words' (Cicero, *Brutus*, 72)

***one...in his:** [Caesar,] a person so careful in his choice of words.

******Hyppolytus*, 860.

***such:** little and mean.

you answered, that it was no argument to the question in hand; for the dispute was not which way a man may write best, but which is most proper for the subject on which he writes.

'First, give me leave, Sir, to remember you, that the argument against which you raised this objection, was only secondary: it was built on this hypothesis,—that to write in verse was proper for serious plays. Which supposition being granted, (as it was briefly made out in that discourse, by showing how verse might be made natural,) it asserted, that this way of writing was a help to the poet's judgement, by putting bounds to a wild overflowing fancy. I think, therefore, it will not be hard for me to make good what it was to prove on that supposition. But you add, that were this let pass, yet he who wants judgement in the liberty of his fancy, may as well show the defect of it when he is confined to verse; for he who has judgement will avoid errors, and he who has it not, will commit them in all kinds of writing.

'This argument, as you have taken it from a most acute person, so I confess it carries much weight in it: but by using the word judgement here indefinitely, you seem to have put a fallacy upon us. I grant, he who has judgement, that is, so profound, so strong, or rather so infallible a judgement, that he needs no helps to keep it always poised and upright, will commit no faults either in rhyme or out of it. And on the other extreme, he who has a judgement so weak and crazed that no helps can correct or amend it, shall write scurvily out of rhyme, and worse in it. But the first of these judgements is no where to be found, and the latter is not fit to write at all. To speak therefore of judgement as it is in the best poets; they who have the greatest proportion of it, want other helps than from it, within. As for example, you would be loth to say, that he who is endued with a sound judgement has no need of history, geography, or moral philosophy, to write correctly. Judgement is indeed the master-workman in a play; but he requires many subordinate hands, many tools to his assistance. And verse I affirm to be one of these; 'tis a rule* and line by which he keeps

*rule: 줄 치는 자.

his building compact and even, which otherwise lawless imagination would raise either irregularly or loosely; at least, if the poet commits errors with this help, he would make greater and more without it:—'tis, in short, a slow and painful, but the surest kind of working. Ovid, whom you accuse for luxuriancy in verse, had perhaps been farther guilty of it, had he writ in prose. And for your instance of Ben Jonson, who, you say, writ exactly without the help of rhyme; you are to remember, 'tis only an aid to a luxuriant fancy, which his was not: as he did not want imagination, so none ever said he had much to spare.* Neither was verse then refined so much, to be a help to that age, as it is to ours. Thus then the second thoughts being usually the best, as receiving the maturest digestion from judgement, and the last and most mature product of those thoughts being artful and laboured verse, it may well be inferred, that verse is a great help to a luxuriant fancy; and this is what that argument which you opposed was to evince.'

Neander was pursuing this discourse so eagerly, that Eugenius had called to him twice or thrice, ere he took notice that the barge stood still, and that they were at the foot of Somerset-stairs,* where they had appointed it to land. The company were all sorry to separate so soon, though a great part of the evening was already spent; and stood a-while looking back on the water, upon which the moon-beams played, and made it appear like floating quicksilver: at last they went up through a crowd of French people, who were merrily dancing in the open air, and nothing* concerned for the noise of guns which had alarmed the town that afternoon. Walking thence together to the Piazze,* they parted there; Eugenius and Lisideius to some pleasant appoinment they had made, and Crites and Neander to their several lodgings.

***as he did...to spare:** 「상상력이 모자랐던 것은 아니나, 남아돌 만큼 많지도 않았다」.

***Somerset-stairs:** 템즈강변의 선착장(현재는 폐쇄됨).

***nothing:** (부사) not at all.

***Piazze:** 당시 런던의 유흥가. Covent Garden 근처에 있었다.

Joseph Addison

(1672—1719)

목사의 아들로 태어나 옥스포드를 마치고, 목사가 되려던 뜻을 버리고 외교관, 정치가로 훈련을 쌓아 국무차관을 지내고, 죽을 때까지 국회의원 노릇을 했다. 그러는 동안 당시의 취미에 맞는 수필, 평론을 써서 그의 대학 친구인 Richard Steele과 함께 편집한 잡지 *The Tatler*와 *The Spectator*에 발표하였다.

그의 평론은 주로 *The Spectator*(1711-12)에 실렸던 것으로, 밀튼의 〈실락원〉에 대한 선구적 평론 18편과 "The Pleasures of Imagination"이라는 제하에 쓴 11편의 문학론은 중요하다.

애디슨은 신고전주의 시대에 속하나 문학의 심리적 효과라는 다분히 개인적이고 경험주의적인 문제에 관심을 보인다. 즉 그는 매우 영국적이다.

상상의 즐거움은 우선 시각에서 온다. 시각적 즐거움은 대상을 직접 보는 것과 기억 속에서 시각적 경험을 되살리는 것에서 온다. 이 두 가지 경험에서 얻는 즐거움은 대상의 웅장함, 신기함, 아름다움(부분과 전체의 조화)에서 연유한다. 웅장함, 즉 숭엄미(the sublime)는 그가 롱기누스의 "낭만적" 사상에 공감했음을 말한다. 또한 경험의 회상 속에서 형상과 사상들이 서로 결합하여 새로운 형상을 만든다는 생각은 홉즈에서 코울리지로 이어지는 맥락을 말해준다.

여기 수록한 글은 *Spectator* 제 416 호(1712년 6월 27일자)에 실렸던 글이다. 사물을 직접 보는 것이 아니고 사물을 모방, 묘사, 표현한 것(예술 작품)을 볼 때에 느끼는 상상의 즐거움을 논하고 있다. 또한 "취미"(relish)에 따라 즐거움의 정도가 달라짐, 즉 감상의 주관성을 말하고 있다.

From The Pleasures of the Imagination (1712)

I at first divided the Pleasures of the Imagination, into such as arise from Objects that are actually before our Eyes, or that once entered in at our Eyes, and are afterwards called up into the Mind either barely by its own Operations, or on occasion of something without us, as Statues, or Descriptions.* We have already considered the first Division, and shall therefore enter on the other, which, for Distinction sake, I have called the Secondary Pleasures of the Imagination. When I say the Ideas we receive from Statues, Descriptions, or such like Occasions, are the same that were once actually in our View, it must not be understood that we had once seen the very Place, Action, or Person which are carved or described. It is sufficient, that we have seen Places, Persons, or Actions in general, which bear a Resemblance, or at least some remote Analogy with what we find represented. Since it is in the Power of the Imagination, when it is once stocked with particular Ideas, to enlarge, compound, and vary them at her* own Pleasure.

Among the different Kinds of Representation, *Statuary* is the most natural, and shews us something likest* the Object that is represented. To make use of a common Instance, let

---

***I at first...as Statues, or Descriptions:** Addison은 *Spectator* 412호(1712년 6월 23일자)에서 이미 'those pleasures of the imagination which arise from the actual view and survey of outward objects"를 말한 바 있다. 또한 그런 즐거움이 "the subject of what is great, uncommon, or beautiful"에서 온다고도 하였다. 그가 말하는 "great"란 "sublime"과 비슷한 개념이고, "uncommon"은 신기함(new, novel)을 뜻한다. 사물을 직접 볼 때 상상이 자극되어 느끼는 즐거움을 primary pleasures라 할 수 있다.

***her:** imagination을 받는다. 상상은 그리이스 신화의 여신이다.

***likest:** most like.

one who is born Blind take an Image* in his Hands, and trace out with his Fingers the different Furrows and Impressions of the Chisel, and he will easily conceive how the Shape of a Man, or Beast, may be represented by it; but should he draw his Hand over a *Picture,* where all is smooth and uniform, he would never be able to imagine how the several* Prominencies and Depressions* of a human Body could be shewn on a plain Piece of Canvas, that has in it no Unevenness or Irregularity. *Description* runs yet further from the things it represents than Painting; for a Picture bears a real Resemblance to its Original, which Letters and Syllables are wholly void of. Colours speak all Languages, but Words are understood only by such a People or Nation. For this reason, tho' Men's Necessities quickly put them on finding out Speech,* Writing is probably of a later Invention than Painting; particularly we are told, that in *America* when the *Spaniards* first arrived there, Expresses* were sent to the Emperor of *Mexico* in Paint, and the News of his Country delineated by the Strokes of a Pencil, which was a more natural Way than that of Writing, tho' at the same time much more imperfect, because it is impossible to draw the little connexions of Speech, or to give the Picture of a Conjunction or an Adverb. It would be yet more strange, to represent visible Objects by Sounds that have no Ideas annexed to them, and to make something like Description in *Musick.* Yet it is certain, there may be confused, imperfect Notions of this Nature raised in the Imagination by an Artificial Composition of Notes;* and we find that great Masters in the Art are able, sometimes to set their Hearers in the heat and hurry of a Battle, to overcast their Minds with melancholy Scenes and Apprehensions of Deaths and Funerals, or to lull them into pleasing Dreams of Groves and Elisiums.

---

*Image: (인물의) 「조각」.
*several: 「각각의」.
*depressions: 「움푹 들어간 곳」.
*Men's necessities...speech: 사람의 필요가 곧 언어를 발명하게 했다.
*Expresses: 「속보. 급한 전갈문」.
*Notes: 「악보」.

In all these Instances, this Secondary Pleasure of the Imagination proceeds from that Action of the Mind, which compares the Ideas arising from the Original Objects, with the Ideas we receive from the Statue, Picture, Description, or Sound that represents them. It is impossible for us to give the necessary Reason, why this Operation of the Mind is attended* with so much Pleasure, as I have before observed on the same Occasion; but we find a great variety of Entertainments derived from this single Principle: For it is this that not only gives us a relish of Statuary, Painting and Description, but makes us delight in all the Actions and Arts of Mimickry.* It is this that makes the several kinds of Wit pleasant, which consists, as I have formerly shewn, in the Affinity of Ideas: And we may add, it is this also that raises the little Satisfaction we sometimes find in the different Sorts of false Wit;* whether it consist in the Affinity of Letters, as an Anagram, Acrostick; or of Syllables, as in Doggerel Rhimes, Echos; or of Words, as in Puns, Quibbles; or of a whole Sentence or Poem, to Wings, and Altars. The *final Cause*, probably, of annexing Pleasure to this Operation of the Mind, was to quicken and encourage us in our Searches after Truth, since the distingushing one thing from another, and the right discerning betwixt our Ideas, depends wholly upon our comparing them together, and observing the Congruity or Disagreement that appears among the several Works of Nature.

But I shall here confine my self to those Pleasures of the Imagination, which proceed from Ideas raised by *Words*, because most of the Observations that agree with Descriptions, are equally Applicable to Painting and Statuary.

Words, when well chosen, have so great a Force in them, that a Description often gives us more lively Ideas than the Sight of Things themselves. The Reader finds a Scene drawn

---

*attended: accompanied.

*Mimickry: imitation.

*false wit: 말의 소리라든가, 글자의 형태, 낱말의 배열 형식(날개 모양 또는 제단 모양) 등으로 특별한 효과를 내는 것을 Addison은 false wit라 부르고 있다. 이런 효과도 미미하게나마 즐거움을 더해준다는 것이다.

in Stronger Colours, and painted more to the Life in his Imagination, by the help of Words, than by an actual Survey of the Scene which they describe. In this Case the Poet seems to get the better of Nature; he takes, indeed, the Landskip after her, but gives it more vigorous Touches, heightens its Beauty, and so enlivens the whole Piece, that the Images which flow from the Objects themselves appear weak and faint, in Comparison of those that come from the Expressions. The Reason, probably, may be, because in the Survey of any Object, we have only so much of it painted on the Imagination, as comes in at the Eye;* but in its Description, the Poet gives us as free a View of it as he pleases, and discovers to us several Parts, that either we did not attend to, or that lay out of our Sight when we first beheld it. As we look on any Object, our Idea of it is, perhaps, made up of two or three simple Ideas; but when the Poet represents it, he may either give us a more complex Idea of it, or only raise in us such Ideas as are most apt to affect the Imagination.

It may be here worth our while to examine, how it comes to pass* that several Readers, who are all acquainted with the same Language, and know the Meaning of the Words they read, should nevertheless have a different Relish of the same Descriptions. We find one transported* with a Passage, which another runs over with Coldness and Indifference, or finding the Representation extremely natural, where another can perceive nothing of Likeness and Conformity. This different Taste must proceed either from the *Perfection of Imagination* in one more than in another, or from the *different Ideas* that several Readers affix to the same Words. For, to have a true Relish, and form a right Judgment of a Description, a Man should be born with a good Imagination, and must have well weighed the Force and Energy that lye in the several Words of a Language, so as to be able to distinguish which are most significant and expressive of their proper Ideas, and what additional Strength and Beauty they are capable of receiving

---

*as comes...eye: 「눈에 들어오는 만큼의」(외부의 인상). 앞의 so와 연결.
*come to pass: happen.
*transported: 「황홀한」.

from Conjunction with others. The Fancy must be warm, to retain the Print of those Images it hath received from outward Objects; and the Judgment discerning, to know what Expressions are most proper to cloath and adorn them to the best Advantage. A Man who is deficient in either of these Respects, tho' he may receive the general Notion of a Description, can never see distinctly all its particular Beauties: As a Person with a weak Sight may have the confused Prospect of a Place that lyes before him, without entering into its several Parts, or discerning the variety of its Colours in their full Glory and Perfection.

Edward Young

(1683—1765)

옥스포드를 졸업하고 평생을 목사로 지내면서 유럽 전체에 "명상의 시"를 유행시킨 유명한 장시 *Night Thoughts on Life, Death, and Immortality*(1742-45)를 발표했고, 또 비평사에서 중요한 위치를 차지하고 있는 논문 *Conjectures on Original Composition*(1719)을 썼다.

이 논문은 18세기 중엽, 영국 지성인 사이에 자주 논의되던 천재성, 독창성, 개인적 취미 등 다분히 경험주의적이고도 주관주의적인 화제들의 핵심을 다루고 있다. 더욱 직접적으로는 보수적인 신고전주의에 대한 적극적인 반발의 한 표현이다. 문학적 모방은 곧 고전에 대한 모방이어야 한다는 신고전주의의 처방에 대항하여, 문학적 모방은 자연을 직접 모방하는 것이어야 한다고 주장하는 것이다. 개인이 자연을 직접 모방한 것을 "독창적" 작품이라 할 수 있는데, 에드워드 영은 이 "독창적"(original)이란 말이 개인에 대한 찬사가 된다는, 즉 독창성은 가치가 있다는 새로운 주장을 펴고 있는 것이다.

오늘날 남과 다른 일을 혼자 해낸다는 의미의 "독창성"은 높은 가치가 인정되나, 신고전주의 시대에 그것은 이단설이었다. 존슨은 고전의 모방을 거부하고, 개인의 독특함 아닌 보편성을 옹호했다. 그러나 에드워드 영은 고전의 모방뿐 아니라, 개인의 독창성까지 옹호하고 있다.

물론 이것은 고전의 거부를 뜻하지 않는다. 자연을 직접 모방함으로써 고전과 같은 작품을 만들 수 있고, 고전의 정신과 동궤에 놓일 수 있다고 하는 것이다. 그리고 영은 개인의 독창성의 발휘가 반드시 기괴하여 남들이 못 알아볼 정도가 되리라고는 걱정하지 않고, 오히려 더 많은 사람들의 편견없는 공감을 자아낼 수 있으리라 믿었다. 이 믿음은 존슨의 것도 될 수 있고, 또한 더 의미 깊게는, 워즈워드의 것도 될 수 있을 것이다.

From Conjectures on Original Composition (1759)

I BEGIN with *original* composition,* and the more willingly as it seems an original subject to me, who have seen nothing hitherto written on it. But first, a few thoughts on composition in general. Some are of opinion that its growth at present is too luxuriant, and that the press is overcharged.* Overcharged, I think, it could never be if none were admitted but such as brought their imprimatur* from *sound understanding* and the *public good.* Wit, indeed, however brilliant, should not be permitted to gaze self-enamored on its useless charms in that fountain of fame (if so I may call the press), if beauty is all that it has to boast; but, like the first Brutus,* it should sacrifice its most darling offspring to the sacred interests of virtue and real service of mankind.

This restriction allowed, the more composition the better. To men of letters and leisure, it is not a noble amusement but a sweet refuge; it improves their parts,* and promotes their peace. It opens a back door out of the bustle of this busy and idle world into a delicious garden of moral and intellectual fruits and flowers, the key of which is denied to the rest of

---

*Samuel Richardson의 소설 *Sir Charles Grandison*을 읽고 감명받은 나머지 독창적인 현대적 genre인 소설은 고전문학을 본따지 않은 original composition이라고 선언하고 있다. 고전을 지나치게 숭상하면 독창성이 없어진다는 생각에서 진일보하여, 독창성 그 자체의 가치를 높이는 선구적 의견을 제시한다.

***original composition:** Young은 *original* composition(독창적 저술) 이외에 *moral* composition을 또 쓰려고 했으나, 하지 못하였다.

***overcharge:** overcrowd.

***imprimature:** 「출판허가」.

***Brutus:** 기원전 5, 6세기 경의 로마의 법치주의 지도자. 자기의 아들들이 범법했다 하여 사형을 선고했다.

***parts:** 「타고난 저마다의 능력」.

mankind. When stung with idle anxieties, or teased with fruitless impertinence, or yawning over insipid diversions, then we perceive the blessing of a lettered recess.* With what a gust* do we retire to our disinterested and immortal friends in our closet, and find our minds, when applied to some favorite theme, as naturally and as easily quieted and refreshed as a peevish child (and peevish children are we all till we fall asleep) when laid to the breast? Our happiness no longer lives on charity, nor bids fair* for a fall by leaning on that most precarious and thorny pillow, another's pleasure, for our repose.* How independent of the world is he who can daily find new acquaintance that at once entertain and improve him, in the little world, the minute but fruitful creation of his own mind? . . .

The mind of a man of genius is a fertile and pleasant field, pleasant as Elysium and fertile as Tempe;* it enjoys a perpetual spring. Of that spring, *originals* are the fairest flowers: *imitations* are of quicker growth but fainter bloom. Imitations are of two kinds, one of nature, one of authors. The first we call *originals,* and confine the term *imitation* to the second. I shall not enter into the curious inquiry of what is or is not, strictly speaking, original, content with what all must allow, that some compositions are more so than others; and the more they are so, I say, the better. Originals are, and ought to be, great favorites, for they are great benefactors; they extend the republic of letters and add a new province to its dominion. Imitators only give us a sort of duplicates of what we had, possibly much better before, increasing the mere drug* of books, while all that makes them valuable, *knowledge* and *genius,* are at a stand. The pen of an original writer, like Armida's wand,* out of a barren waste calls a

---

***lettered recess:** 「글과 더불어 취하는 휴식」.

***gust:** gusto. 「즐김, 신이 남」.

***nor bids...for our repose:** (우리가 홀로 글을 지을 때) 우리는 남의 즐거움이라는 불안한 베개(즉 남이 지은 책)에 우리의 휴식을 얻으려고 기대다가 넘어질 위험이 있지도 않다. bid fair for: ...하기 쉽다.

***Elysium** 은 천국, **Tempe** 는 이상향. (그리이스 신화)

***drug:** 「팔리지 않는 물건, 쓸 데 없는 물건」.

***Armida's wand:** 마녀의 요술 지팡이 (Tasso 의 *Jerusalemme Liberata* 에

blooming spring. Out of that blooming spring an imitator is a transplanter of laurels, which sometimes die on removal, always languish in a foreign soil . . . .

Still farther: an imitator shares his crown, if he has one, with the chosen object of his imitation; an original enjoys an undivided applause. An original may be said to be of a *vegetable* nature; it rises spontaneously from the vital root of genius; it *grows,* it is not *made. Imitations are often a sort of *manufacture,* wrought up by those *mechanics, art* and *labor,* out of pre-existent materials not their own.**

Again: we read imitation with somewhat of his languor who listens to a twice-told tale. Our spirits rouse at an original; that is a perfect stranger, and all throng to learn what news from a foreign land. And though it comes like an Indian prince, adorned with feathers only, having little of weight, yet of our attention it will rob the more solid, if not equally new. Thus every telescope is lifted at a new-discovered star; it makes a hundred astronomers in a moment, and denies equal notice to the sun. But if an original, by being as excellent as new, adds admiration to surprise, then are we at the writer's mercy;* on the strong wing of his imagination we are snatched from Britain to Italy, from climate to climate, from pleasure to pleasure; we have no home, no thought, of our own till the magician drops his pen. And then, falling down into ourselves, we awake to flat realities, lamenting the change, like the beggar who dreamt himself a prince.

It is with thoughts as it is with words, and with both as with men:* they may grow old and die. Words tarnished by passing through the mouths of the vulgar are laid aside as inelegant and obsolete. So thoughts, when become too common, should lose their currency, and we should send new metal to the mint, that is, new meaning to the press. . . .

But why are originals so few? Not because the writer's

***An original...not *made*:** 독창성은 식물성이라 생장하는 것이라고 생각하는 입장은 이른바 낭만적 유기론(organicism)의 근본강령이다.

***are we...mercy:** 「작가는 우리를 마음대로 끌고 다닐 수 있다」.

***It is...with men:** 「생각은 말과 같고, 생각과 말은 사람과 같다」.

harvest is over, the great reapers of antiquity having left nothing to be gleaned after them; nor because the human mind's teeming time is past, or because it is incapable of putting forth unprecedented births; but because illustrious examples *engross, prejudice,* and *intimidate.* They *engross* our attention, and so prevent a due inspection of ourselves; they *prejudice* our judgment in favor of their abilities, and so lessen the sense of our own; and they *intimidate* us with the splendor of their renown, and thus under diffidence bury our strength. Nature's impossibilities and those of diffidence lie wide asunder.

Let it not be suspected that I would weakly insinuate anything in favor of the moderns as compared with ancient authors; no, I am lamenting their great inferiority. But I think it is no necessary inferiority, that it is not from divine destination, but from some cause far beneath the moon.* I think that human souls, through all periods, are equal. . . .

After all, the first ancients had no merit in being originals. They could *not* be imitators. Modern writers have a *choice* to make, and therefore have a merit in their power. They may soar in the regions of *liberty* or move in the soft fetters of easy *imitation;* and imitation has as many plausible reasons to urge as Pleasure had to offer to Hercules. Hercules made the choice of a hero, and *so* became immortal.*

Yet let not assertors of classic excellence imagine that I deny the tribute it so well deserves. He that admires not ancient authors betrays a secret he would conceal, and tells the world that he does not understand them. Let us be as far from neglecting* as from copying their admirable compositions. Sacred be their rights, and inviolable their fame. Let our understanding feed on theirs; they afford the noblest nourishment. But let them nourish, not annihilate, our own. When we read, let our imagination kindle at their charms; when we

---

***far beneath the moon:** 「이 세상에 속한, 즉 운명적인 것이 아닌」.

***Hercules made...became immortal:** Hercules는 덕행(virtue)과 쾌락(pleasure) 중 어느 것을 택하겠느냐는 신의 질문에 덕행을 택하여 고된 영웅의 생을 마쳤다. 독창성은 힘들고 모방은 쉽다는 비유이다.

***neglecting:** 다음에 their admirable compositions를 넣어 읽을 것.

write, let our judgment shut them out of our thoughts; treat even Homer himself as his royal admirer was treated by the cynic:* bid him stand aside, nor shade our composition from the beams of our own genius; for nothing original can rise, nothing immortal can ripen, in any other sun.

Must we then, you say, not imitate ancient authors? Imitate them, by all means, but imitate aright. He that imitates the divine *Iliad* does not imitate Homer, but he who takes the same method which Homer took for arriving at a capacity of accomplishing a work so great. Tread in his steps to the sole fountain of immortality; drink where he drank, at the true Helicon,* that is, at the breast of nature. Imitate, but imitate not the *composition,* but the *man.* For may not this paradox pass into a maxim? viz. "The less we copy the renowned ancients, we shall resemble them the more."

But possibly you may reply, that you must either imitate Homer or depart from nature. Not so. For suppose you was to change place in time with Homer; then, if you write naturally, you might as well charge Homer with an imitation of you. Can you be said to imitate Homer for writing *so,* as you would have written if Homer had never been? As far as a regard to nature and sound sense will permit a departure from your predecessors, so far, ambitiously, depart from them; the farther from them in *similitude,* the nearer are you to them in *excellence;* you rise by it into an original, become a noble collateral, not a humble descendant from them. Let us build our compositions with the spirit and in the taste of the ancients, but not with their materials. Thus will they resemble the structures of Pericles at Athens, which Plutarch commends* for having had an air of antiquity as soon as they were built. All eminence and distinction lies out of the beaten road;* excursion and deviation are necessary to find it; and the more

---

***as his royal...cynic:** 여기서 royal admirer는 Alexander 대왕, the cynic은 Diogenes. 대왕이 무얼 해 줄 수 있는가 하고 물으니 Diogenes는 해를 가리지 않도록 비켜서 달라고만 했다.

***Helicon:** (그리이스 신화) 시의 영감을 나타내는 산, 또 그 산의 샘물.

***Plutarch commends:** Plutarch의 *Life of Pericles*에 나오는 말. 건물을 새로 지었는데도 오래된 건축 같게 지었다는 것.

***beaten road:** 「사람이 많이 다닌 길」.

remote your path from the highway, the more reputable, if like poor Gulliver (of whom anon*) you fall not into a ditch* in your way to glory.

What glory to come near, what glory to reach, what glory (presumptuous thought) to surpass, our predecessors? And is that then, in nature, absolutely impossible? Or is it not, rather, contrary to nature to fail in it? Nature herself sets the ladder; all wanting is our ambition to climb. For by the bounty of nature we are as strong as our predecessors, and by the favor of time (which is but another round* in nature's scale), we stand on higher ground. As to the first, were *they* more than men? or are *we* less? Are not our minds cast in the same mold with those before the Flood?* The Flood affected matter; mind escaped. As to the second, though we are moderns, the world is an ancient, more ancient far than when they whom we most admire filled it with their fame. . . . It is by a sort of noble contagion, a general familiarity with their writings, and not by any particular sordid theft, that we can be the better for those who went before us. . . .

A *genius* differs from a *good understanding* as a magician from a good architect; that raises his structure by means invisible; this by the skillful use of common tools. Hence genius has ever been supposed to partake of something divine. *Nemo unquam vir magnus fuit, sine aliquo afflatu divino.* *

***Learning,* destitute of this superior aid, is fond and proud of what has cost it much pains, is a great lover of rules, and boaster of famed examples. As beauties less perfect who owe half their charms to cautious art, learning inveighs against natural unstudied graces and small harmless inaccuracies, and sets rigid bounds to that liberty to which genius owes its supreme glory, but the no-genius its frequent ruin. For unprescribed beauties and unexampled excellence, which are**

***like poor Gulliver...into a ditch:** Gulliver가 끝에 가서 심한 염세주의에 빠진 것을 말함. **of whom anon:** 「그에 관해서는 곧 언급할 터이다」.

***round:** 「사다리의 한 층」.

***the Flood:** 「노아의 홍수」. 노아와 그의 가족을 통해 인간정신은 그대로 살아났음.

******Nemo*...: 'No one was ever a great man without some divine inspiration' (Cicero. *De Natura Deorum*, Ⅱ, lvi, 167).

characteristics of *genius,* lie without* the pale of *learning's* authorities and laws; which pale, genius must leap to come at them.* But by that leap, if genius is wanting, we break our necks; we lose that little credit which possibly we might have enjoyed before. For rules, like crutches, are a needful aid to the lame, though an impediment to the strong. A Homer casts them away, and like his Achilles,

*Jura negat sibi nata, nihil non arrogat,**

by native force of mind. There is something in poetry beyond prose-reason; there are mysteries in it not to be explained, but admired, which render mere prose-men infidels to their divinity. . . .

Of genius there are two species, an earlier and a later, or call them *infantine* and *adult.* An adult genius comes out of nature's hand, as Pallas out of Jove's head, at full growth and mature: Shakespeare's genius was of this kind. On the contrary, Swift stumbled at the threshold and set out for distinction on feeble knees. His was an infantine genius, a genius which, like other infants, must be nursed and educated, or it will come to nought. Learning is its nurse and tutor; but this nurse may overlay with an indigested load, which smothers common sense; and this tutor may mislead with pedantic prejudice, which vitiates the best understanding. As too great admirers of the fathers of the church have sometimes set up their authority against the true sense of Scripture; so too great admirers of the classical fathers have sometimes set up their authority or example against reason. . . .

***without:** outside.「(울타리) 밖에」.

***them:** unprescribed beauties and unexampled excellence.(규정되지 않은 아름다움과 선례가 없는 훌륭함. 즉 독창성).

***Jura negat...:** 'denies that laws were made for him; nothing he does not arrogate to himself' (Horace, *Ars Poetica*, 122).

Alexander Pope

(1688—1744)

국법에 의하여 대학에 진학할 수 없는 가톨릭 집안의 불구자 아들인 포우프는 가정교사와 자습의 덕으로 남부럽지 않은 고전 지식을 쌓았을 뿐 아니라, 일찍부터 시적 천재를 발휘하여, 놀랍게도 여기 수록된 *An Essay on Criticism*을 21세에 창작하기에 이르렀다. 이러한 시적 천재의 덕분으로 그는 자기보다 나이도 많고 지위도 높은 사람들과 교유할 수 있었고, 경제적 자립도 할 수 있었다. 그의 *Iliad* 번역은 일품이며, 철학적 논술의 시 *Essay on Man*과 *Moral Essays*도 놀라운 작품이나, 그의 최대작은 풍자시 *The Dunciad*일 것이다.

포우프는 물론 비평가는 아니나, 그의 날카로운 풍자적 성향이 암시하듯, 언제나 「비평적」인 시인이었다. *An Essay on Criticism*은 멀리 로마의 호라티우스의 *Ars Poetica*, 르네상스 시대 이탈리아의 비다(Vida)의 *De arte poetica*, 프랑스의 브왈로(Boileau)의 *L'Art poétique* 같은, 운문으로 쓴 시론의 장르에 속하는 것으로 포우프는 그런 작품들을 면밀히 공부하고 그 방법을 완전히 터득한 후 그들을 능가할 야심에서 지은 것이다. 그의 야심은 적중하여 이 작품은 동 계열의 작품 중 최고봉을 이룬다는 평을 받는다.

그가 공부한 것은 주로 대륙의 신고전주의 문학관이었으므로 이 작품의 근본 사상은 보수적 정통적 신고전주의 문학관일 수 밖에 없다.

3부분으로 되어 있는 이 재기발랄한 글의 첫 부분은 비평의 일반적 자질을 다룬다. 비평가는 우선 자신의 한계를 알아야 하며, 객관적인 자연을 알아야 한다. 자연은 모든 가치의 대원천이다. 그런데 자연은 고전이 완벽하게 모방하였으므로, 후세인은 겸허하게 고전을 따라야 한다. 고전의 규칙은 자연을 방법화한 것이므로 반드시 지켜야 한다. 그러나 단지 흉내를 내라는 것이 아니라 그 정신을 함께 본받으라는 것이다. 규칙을 벗어나는 득의의 순간도 있지만, 아무나 도달할 수 있는 것은 아니다.

제 2 부에서도 비평가가 겸허해져야 함을 강조한다. 비평가는 사소한 흠을 찾아내려고 하지 말고 작품을 전체로 보는 안목이 필요하다. 오직 규칙만, 언어만, 또는 운율만 보는 것은 매우 해롭다. 비평가에게는 인간다운 관용이 필요하다. 새로운 것에 집착하든가 개인적 취향에 좌우되지 않아야 한다.

제 3 부는 이상적인 비평가의 모습을 다룬다. 좋은 비평가는 정직, 겸손, 유연함, 용기가 있다. 고전적 비평가들을 일별함으로써 그들을 모범으로 제시한다.

An Essay on Criticism 은 당시 신고전주의의 문학관을 기억하기 좋은 경구의 형식으로 간단 명료하게 요약할 뿐 아니라, 실제 비평에 있어서 기피할 사항도 풍자와 재치로 제시하고 있다. 특히 자연과 고전과 법칙의 관계, 전체성에 대한 강조, 고전적 인품을 가진 비평가의 관용적 태도, 창작 실제의 문제, 롱기누스의 것과 같은 이질적 사상의 소화 등에 우리의 흥미가 쏠린다.

An Essay on Criticism (1711)

'Tɪs hard to say, if greater want of skill
Appear in writing or in judging ill;*
But, of the two, less dang'rous is th' offence
To tire our patience, than mislead our sense.*
Some few in that, but numbers err in this,
Ten censure wrong for one who writes amiss;*

1—2. 「못난 창작과 못난 비평 중 어느 것이 더 재주없는 것인지 말하기가 힘들다」. ill=(adv.) badly. in writing ill or in judging ill 로 읽을 것.

3—4. 「참을성을 기진하게 만드는 것(즉, 창작)이 우리의 지각을 오도하는 것(즉, 비평)보다는 덜 위험스럽다」.

6. 「못난 창작 하나에 그릇된 비평이 열 편이나 생기는 판이다」.

A fool might once himself alone expose,
Now one in verse makes many more in prose.*
'Tis with our judgments as our watches, none
Go just alike, yet each believes his own.
In Poets as true genius is but rare,
True Taste* as seldom is the Critic's share;
Both must alike from Heav'n derive their light,
These born to judge, as well as those to write.
Let such teach others who themselves excel,
And censure freely who have written well.
Authors are partial to their wit, 'tis true,
But are not Critics to their judgment too?
Yet if we look more closely, we shall find
Most have the seeds of judgment in their mind:
Nature affords at least a glimm'ring light;
The lines, tho' touch'd but faintly, are drawn right.*
But as the slightest sketch, if justly trac'd,
Is by ill-colouring but the more disgrac'd,
So by false learning is good sense defac'd:
Some are bewilder'd in the maze of schools,
And some made* coxcombs Nature meant but fools.
In search of wit these lose their common sense,
And then turn* Critics in their own defence:
Each burns alike, who can, or cannot write,
Or with a Rival's, or an Eunuch's spite.*

---

8. 「한 사람의 운문바보(즉 못난 시인)가 더 많은 산문바보(즉 못난 비평가)를 만든다」.

12. **Taste:** 미세한 차이를 판별해내는 능력. 즉 감식력(비평가가 꼭 가져야 하는 것).

21—25. 「자연은 모든 사람에게 옳은 지각(sense)를 조금씩 부여했다. 마치 희미하게 그은 선도 바로 그은 선인 것처럼. 그러나 색칠을 잘못 해서 그림 전체를 버리는 것처럼 잘못 배운 지식으로 말미암아 타고난 지각마저 버리게 된다」.

27. **made:** 앞에 are를 삽입. 「본래 바보로 태어난 자가 배웠답시고 아는 체하는 자가 되기도 한다」.

29. **turn**=become

30—31. 「글을 쓸 줄 아는 자든 모르는 자든 간에 꼭같이 경쟁자나 무능자의 앙심을 품고 속이 탄다」.

All fools have still an itching to deride,
And fain would be upon the laughing side.
If Maevius scribble in Apollo's spite,*
There are who judge still worse than he can write.
Some have at first for Wits, then Poets pass'd,*
Turn'd Critics next, and prov'd plain fools at last.
Some neither can for Wits nor Critics pass,
As heavy mules are neither horse nor ass.
Those half-learn'd witlings, num'rous in our isle,
As half-form'd insects on the banks of Nile;
Unfinish'd things, one knows not what to call,
Their generation's*so equivocal:
To tell 'em, would a hundred tongues require,
Or one vain wit's, that might a hundred tire.
But you who seek to give and merit fame,
And justly bear a Critic's noble name,
Be sure yourself and your own reach to know,
How far your genius, taste, and learning go;
Launch not beyond your depth, but be discreet,
And mark that point where sense and dulness meet.
Nature to all things fix'd the limits fit,
And wisely curb'd proud man's pretending wit.
As on the land while here the ocean gains,
In other parts it leaves wide sandy plains;*
Thus in the soul while memory prevails,
The solid pow'r of understanding fails;
Where beams of warm imagination play,
The memory's soft figures melt away.
One science only will one genius fit;

---

34. 「Apollo(시신)의 영감이 없음에도 불구하고 Maevius(로마의 3류시인)가 시를 써대기는 하지만」(그보다도 더 못 쓰는 비평가가 있다).

36. **pass'd:** passed. 「...으로 통하다, ...으로 알려지다(...for)」.

43. **generation's:** generation is. 「그들의 출생 경위는」.

54—55. 당시의 지리학에서는 바다가 육지의 한 쪽을 침식하여 다른 쪽에다 뱉아놓는다고 생각했다. 그와 마찬가지로 사람의 정신능력도 한 쪽이 잘 났으면 다른 한 쪽은 못날 수 있다는 것. 그래서 각자는 자신의 장단점을 알아야 한다. 즉 자신의 한계를 아는 것이 중요하다.

So vast is art, so narrow human wit:
Not only bounded to peculiar arts,
But oft in those* confin'd to single parts.
Like kings we lose the conquests gain'd before,
By vain ambition still to make them more;
Each might his sev'ral* province well command,
Would all but stoop* to what they understand.
  First follow Nature, and your judgment frame
By her just standard, which is still* the same:
Unerring NATURE, still divinely bright,
One clear, unchang'd, and universal light,
Life, force, and beauty, must to all impart,
At once the source, and end, and test of Art.*
Art from that fund* each just supply provides,
Works without show, and without pomp presides:
In some fair body thus th' informing soul
With spirits feeds, with vigour fills the whole,
Each motion guides, and ev'ry nerve sustains;
Itself unseen, but in th' effects, remains.*
Some, to whom Heav'n in wit has been profuse,
Want as much more, to turn it to its use;
For wit and judgment often are at strife,
Tho' meant each other's aid, like man and wife.
'Tis more to guide, than spur the Muse's steed;
Restrain his fury, than provoke his speed;
The winged courser,* like a gen'rous horse,

---

63. **those:** arts. 「자기의 기능 중에도 또 특수분야가 있다」.

65. **sev'ral:** several=respective. 「각자의」.

67. **Would...:** If all only would....

68—73. 자연은 모두에게 예술의 원천이며, 목적이며, 기준을 제공한다는 신고전주의의 기본 강령. 예술은 자연에서 나오는 것이며(원천), 자연을 모방하는 것이며(목적), 자연스러워야 하는 것(기준)이 예술의 판단기준(test)이 된다.

74. **that fund:** Nature.

76—79. *cf.* "Art is to hide art".

84. **the Muse's steed:** 「시신의 말」. 즉 Pegasus. 시적 영감을 상징하는 날개 돋힌 말. 이 말에다 박차를 가하는 것보다는 오히려 잘 이끄는 것이 좋다.

Shows most true mettle when you check his course.
  Those RULES of old discovered, not devis'd,
Are Nature still, but Nature methodiz'd;
Nature, like liberty, is but restrain'd
By the same laws which first herself ordain'd.
  Hear how learn'd Greece her useful rules indites,
When to repress, and when indulge our flights:
High on Parnassus' top her sons she show'd,*
And pointed out those arduous paths they trod;
Held from afar, aloft, th' immortal prize,
And urg'd the rest by equal steps to rise.
Just precepts thus from great examples giv'n,
She drew from them what they deriv'd from Heav'n.
The gen'rous Critic fann'd the Poet's fire,
And taught the world with reason to admire.
Then Criticism the Muse's handmaid prov'd,*
To dress her charms, and make her more belov'd:
But following wits* from that intention stray'd,
Who could not win the mistress, woo'd the maid;
Against the Poets their own arms they turn'd,
Sure to hate most the men from whom they learn'd.
So modern 'Pothecaries,* taught the art
By Doctor's bills* to play the Doctor's part,

---

86. 문학의 법칙들은 함부로 꾸며낸 것이 아니라 자연을 사람이 이용하기 쉽게 방법화 시킨 것이라는 생각은 신고전주의의 강령이다. *cf.* 'If the rules be well considered, we shall find them to be made only to reduce Nature into method" (Dryden, preface to "Troilus and Cressida").

94. **Parnassus** 는 시신들이 거처하는 높은 산. 「그리이스가 Parnassus 산정에 도착한 모범적인 시인들(her sons)을 세상에 보였주었다」. 산정으로 오르는 길은 험하다. 그 모범들로부터 문학의 법칙(precepts, rules)이 추출된 것이다. 그리고 모범들 자신은 하늘로부터 문학의 방법을 배웠다. 즉 그들은 절대적 시원이고 그 이후는 그 뒤를 모방에 의하여 따르는 것일 뿐이다. 다음 Virgil의 예를 보라.

102. **prov'd**=become. 「비평은 창작(Muse)의 시녀」.

104. **following wits:** 「그 뒤를 이온 시인들」(온 시 자체는 버려두고 비평과 한 패가 되었다).

108. **Pothecaries:** apothecaries. 「약제사」.

109. **Doctor's bills:** 「의사의 처방전」.

Bold in the practice of mistaken rules,
Prescribe, apply, and call their masters fools.
Some on the leaves of ancient authors prey;*
Nor time nor moths e'er spoil'd so much as they.
Some drily plain, without invention's*aid,
Write dull receipts how poems may be made.
These leave the sense, their learning to display,
And those explain the meaning quite away:*
You then whose judgment the right course would steer,
Know well each ANCIENT's proper character;
His fable, subject, scope in ev'ry page;
Religion, Country, genius of his Age:
Without all these at once before your eyes,
Cavil you may, but never criticize.
Be Homer's works your study and delight,
Read them by day, and meditate by night;
Thence form your judgment, thence your maxims bring,
And trace the Muses upward to their spring.
Still with itself compar'd, his text peruse;
And let your comment be the Mantuan Muse:*
When first young Maro in his boundless mind
A work t'outlast immortal Rome design'd,
Perhaps he seem'd above the critic's law,
And but from Nature's fountains scorn'd to draw:*

---

112. 옛 문헌이라면 덮어놓고 깊이 연구하는 것을 책좀벌레라고 풍자하고 있다. **leaves:** pages.

114. **invention:** 수사학 용어로, 「좋은 생각을 해냄」의 뜻.

116—117. **these:** 저자, 즉 문헌연구자. **those:** 우둔한 문학 교사.

129. **Mantuan Muse:** Mantua에서 태어난 Virgil을 가리킨다. 그의 full name은 Publius Vergilius Maro. 다음 행에서는 Maro로 불리고 있다. 여기서 comment는 「결론」의 뜻.

133. 「자연」 자체의 근원에서만 불후의 작품을 추출해내려고 했다. 여기서 but=except. 자연을 최고도로 모방한 Homer이니까 Homer가 곧 「자연」이고, 따라서 후배인 그가 Homer를 모방하는 것이 곧 「자연」을 모방하는 것이다. 최대 시인의 하나인 Virgil이 그랬거늘 후세의 모든 시인도 과거의 모범을 모방하는 도리 밖에 없다는 것이 보수적 신고전주의의 문학관이다.

But when t'examine ev'ry part he came,
Nature and Homer were, he found, the same.
Convinc'd, amaz'd, he checks the bold design;
And rules as strict his labour'd work confine,
As if the Stagirite* o'erlook'd each line.
Learn hence for ancient rules a just esteem;
To copy nature is to copy them.
Some beauties yet no Precepts can declare,
For there's a happiness as well as care*
Music resembles Poetry, in each
Are nameless graces which no methods teach,
And which a master-hand alone can reach.
If, where the rules not far enough extend,
(Since rules were made but to promote their end)
Some lucky Licence answer to the full
Th' intent propos'd, that Licence is a rule.
Thus Pegasus, a nearer way to take,
May boldly deviate from the common track;
From vulgar bounds with brave disorder part,
And snatch a grace beyond the reach of art,
Which without passing thro' the judgment, gains
The heart, and all its end at once attains.*
In prospects thus, some objects please our eyes,
Which out of nature's common order rise,
The shapeless rock, or hanging precipice.

---

138. **Stagirite:** Stagira에서 태어난 Aristotle을 가리킨다. 그가 문학의 법칙의 최고권위이다.

142. **care**는 문학법칙을 따라 열심히 작업하는 것. **happiness**는 법칙과 관계없이「운좋게」적절한 표현, 또는 제작을 하게 되는 것. 신고전주의의 편협해지기 쉬운 법칙주의에 열린 틈을 인정하고 있다. 그러나 그 틈은 아무에게나 언제든지 열려 있는 것은 아니라는 주의가 주어진다(161행 이하).

146—155. 비평적 판단(또는 법칙)과 무관하게 독자의 심중에 직접 도달하는 작품을 lucky licence, brave disorder, beyond the reach of art 등으로 표현하고 있는 바, 이러한 미를 숭엄미(the sublime)라 하여 그 황홀함(extasy)의 효과를 기리게 된 것은 Longinus의 *The Sublime*이란 저서가 17세기 유럽에 소개된 이후부터이다. 깎아지른 절벽, 기괴한 바위 등 '거대한 무질서'의 미가 곧 숭엄미이다.

Great wits sometimes may gloriously offend,
And rise to faults true Critics dare not mend.
But tho' the Ancients thus their rules invade,
(As Kings dispense with laws themselves have made)
Moderns, beware! or if you must offend
Against the precept, ne'er transgress its End;
Let it be seldom, and compell'd by need;
And have, at least, their precedent to plead.
The Critic else proceeds without remorse,
Seizes your fame, and puts his laws in force.
I know there are*; to whose presumptuous thoughts
Those freer beauties, ev'n in them, seem faults.
Some figures monstrous and mis-shap'd appear,
Consider'd singly, or beheld too near,
Which, but proportion'd to their light, or place,
Due distance reconciles to form and grace.*
A prudent chief* not always must display
His pow'rs in equal ranks, and fair array.
But with th' occasion and the place comply,
Conceal his force, nay seem sometimes to fly.
Those oft are stratagems which error seem,
Nor is it Homer nods, but we that dream.
Still green with bays each ancient Altar stands,
Above the reach of sacrilegious hands;
Secure from Flames, from Envy's fiercer rage,
Destructive War, and all-involving Age:*
See, from each clime the learn'd their incense bring!
Hear, in all tongues consenting* Paeans ring!

---

169. **are** 다음에 **some people**을 넣을 것.

174. 작품의 실수로 보이는 것 중에는, 대국적 견지에서 작품내 요소들의 상호관련성을 주의해 볼 때, 균형을 이루는 것도 있으므로 비평가는 조심해야 한다. Homer에서 흠을 찾기 전에 우리가 엉뚱한 데를 짚고 있지 않은가 반성하라는 것이다.

175. **chief:** 「군대의 사령관」. 후퇴를 가장하는 것도 실은 좋은 작전으로, 작품에서 실수한 체하는 것과 같다.

184. **all-involving age:** 「모든 것을 묻어버리는 시간」.

186. **consenting:** 「찬양하는」. (고전의 절대적 권위를 모든 나라가 찬양한다는 것).

In praise so just let ev'ry voice be join'd,
And fill the gen'ral chorus of mankind.
Hail, Bards triumphant! born in happier days;
Immortal heirs of universal praise!
Whose honours with increase of ages grow,
As streams roll down, enlarging as they flow;
Nations unborn* your mighty names shall sound,
And worlds applaud that must not yet be found!*
Oh may some spark of your celestial fire,
The last, the meanest of your sons inspire,
(That on weak wings, from far, pursues your flights;
Glows while he reads, but trembles as he writes)
To teach vain Wits a science little known,
T' admire superior sense, and doubt their own!*

Of all the Causes which conspire to blind
Man's erring judgment, and misguide the mind,
What the weak head with strongest bias rules,
Is *Pride*, the never-failing vice of fools.*
Whatever nature has in worth denied,
She gives in large recruits of needful pride;
For as in bodies, thus in souls, we find
What wants in blood and spirits, swell'd with wind:
Pride, where wit fails, steps in to our defence,
And fills up all the mighty Void of sense.

---

193. **Nations unborn:** 「앞으로 태어날 만백성, 후세대」.

194. 「아직 발견되지 않은 세상들까지도 고전 시인들을 찬양하게 될 것이다」.

200. **their own:** their own sense. 「자신의 판단은 의심하고, 더 훌륭한 판단은 숭상하도록」.

204. ***Pride:*** 현대의 사실적 윤리에서 pride는 하나의 미덕으로 되어 있으나 기독교사상에서는 죄악 중의 죄악으로 규정된 것이다. 중세의 7대악(seven deadly Sins)의 첫째가 그것이었다. Pride는 여기서도 "swelled with wind" (208행)라고 표현되어 있는데, 중세 르네상스 시대에도 '허풍선이', '잔뜩 거대하지만 공기와 물과 흙으로 빚어진 거인' 등으로 형상화하곤 했다. 또한 살갗이 부어오른 것을 'proud wound(바람이 들었다)'라고 했다. wit나 sense가 모자랄 때 그 자리를 메우는 것이 헛바람같은 pride이다.

If once right reason drives that cloud away,
Truth breaks upon us with resistless day.
Trust not yourself; but your defects to know,
Make use of ev'ry friend—and ev'ry foe.
  A *little learning* is a dang'rous thing;
Drink deep, or taste not the Pierian spring:*
There shallow draughts intoxicate the brain,
And drinking largely* sobers us again.
Fir'd at first sight with what the Muse imparts,
In fearless youth we tempt the heights of Arts,
While from the bounded level of our mind
Short views we take, nor see the lengths behind;
But more advanc'd, behold with strange surprise
New distant scenes of endless science* rise!
So pleas'd at first the tow'ring Alps we try,
Mount o'er the vales, and seem to tread the sky,
Th' eternal snows appear already past,
And the first clouds and mountains seem the last;
But, those attain'd, we tremble to survey
The growing labours of the lengthen'd way,
Th' increasing prospect tires our wand'ring eyes,
Hills peep o'er hills, and Alps on Alps arise!
  A perfect Judge will read each work of Wit
With the same spirit that its author writ:
Survey the WHOLE, nor seek slight faults to find
Where nature moves, and rapture warms the mind;
Nor lose, for that malignant dull delight,*
The gen'rous pleasure to be charm'd with Wit.
But in such lays as neither ebb, nor flow,

---

216. **Pierian spring:** (Muses의 또다른 이름인) 「Pierides의 샘」, 즉 시적 영감의 샘. 「깊이 마시지 않으려거든 아예 맛도 보지 말아라」는 것은 시를 조금만 아는 것 가지고는 오히려 위험하다는 뜻.

218. **largely:** much. 「조금 마시면 취할 뿐이고, 많이 마시면 제정신이 다시 든다」.

224. **science:** 「일반적인 지식, 앎, 깨달음」의 뜻.

237. **malignant dull delight:** 전체의 미를 못 보고 작은 결함을 찾아내는 「악의에 찬 우둔한 재미」.

Correctly cold, and regularly low,
That shunning faults, one quiet tenor keep;
We cannot blame indeed—but we may sleep.*
In wit, as nature, what affects our hearts
Is not th' exactness of peculiar parts;
'Tis not a lip, or eye, we beauty call,
But the joint force and full result of all.
Thus when we view some well-proportion'd dome,
(The world's just wonder, and ev'n thine, O Rome!)
No single parts unequally surprise,
All comes united to th' admiring eyes;
No monstrous height, or breadth, or length appear;
The Whole at once is bold, and regular.
  Whoever thinks a faultless piece to see,
Thinks what ne'er was, nor is, nor e'er shall be.
In every work regard the writer's End,*
Since none can compass more than they intend;
And if the means be just, the conduct true,
Applause, in spite of trivial faults, is due;
As men of breeding, sometimes men of wit,
T' avoid great errors, must the less* commit:
Neglect the rules each verbal Critic* lays,
For not to know some trifles, is a praise.
Most Critics, fond of some subservient art,
Still make the Whole depend upon a Part:
They talk of principles, but notions prize;*
And all to one lov'd Folly sacrifice.*

239—242. "틀린 것 없으나 열정이 없고, 법칙은 잘 지켰으나 저조한 작품"은 비난할 수는 없다. 다만 독자가 너무 심심해서 졸게 된다(매우 이름난 귀절이다).

255. 작가의 목적을 중시하라는 이 말은 오늘날의 intentional fallacy의 이론과 비교해 볼 만하다. 여기서는 부분에 집착하지 말고 전체의 구도를 보라는 뜻에서 주로 이 말을 하고 있다.

260. **the less:** the less errors.「큰 실수를 피하려고 작은 실수를 저지름」.

261. **verbal critic:**「규칙의 조항에 얽매인 비평가」.

265. **notions:**「단순한 개념」(원칙과는 다름). **prize:**「중요하게 여기다」.

266. **sacrifice:** dedicate.

Once on a time, La Mancha's Knight,* they say,
A certain bard encount'ring on the way,
Discours'd in terms as just, with looks as sage,
As e'er could Dennis* of the Grecian stage;
Concluding all were desp'rate sots and fools,
Who durst depart from Aristotle's rules.
Our Author, happy in a judge so nice,*
Produc'd his Play, and begg'd the Knight's advice;
Made him observe the subject, and the plot,
The manners, passions, unities; what not?
All which, exact to rule, were brought about,
Were but* a Combat in the lists left out.
'What! leave the Combat out?' exclaims the Knight;
Yes, or we must renounce the Stagirite.
'Not so by Heav'n' (he answers in a rage),
'Knights, squires, and steeds, must enter on the stage.'
So vast a throng the stage can ne'er contain.
'Then build a new, or act it in a plain.'
Thus Critics, of less judgment than caprice,
Curious not knowing, not exact but nice,
Form short Ideas; and offend in arts
(As most in manners) by a love to parts.
Some to *Conceit* alone their taste confine,
And glitt'ring thoughts struck out at ev'ry line;
Pleas'd with a work where nothing's just or fit;
One glaring Chaos and wild heap of wit.
Poets like painters, thus, unskill'd to trace
The naked nature and the living grace,
With gold and jewels cover ev'ry part,
And hide with ornaments their want of art.

---

267. **La Mancha's Knight:** Don Quixote.

270. **Dennis, John:** (1657-1734). 당대의 이름난 비평가로, Pope에 의해 자주 공격을 받음. 그리이스의 희곡을 논하는 Dennis를 Pope는 Don Quixote에 비하고 있다.

273. **happy...nice:** 「그처럼 까다로운(nice) 비평가를 만나 반가와서」.

278. **Were but:** If only...were.

True Wit is Nature to advantage dress'd,*
What oft was thought, but ne'er so well express'd;
Something, whose truth convinc'd at sight we find,
That gives us back the image of our mind.
As shades more sweetly recommend the light,
So modest plainness sets off sprightly wit.
For works may have more wit than does 'em good,
As bodies perish thro' excess of blood.
Others for *Language* all their care express,
And value books, as women men, for Dress:*
Their praise is still,—the Style is excellent:
The Sense, they humbly take upon content:*
Words are like leaves; and where they most abound,
Much fruit of sense beneath is rarely found,
False Eloquence, like the prismatic glass,*
Its gaudy colours spreads on ev'ry place;
The face of Nature we no more survey,
All glares alike, without distinction gay:*
But true expression, like th' unchanging Sun,
Clears and improves whate'er it shines upon,
It gilds all objects, but it alters none.
Expression is the dress of thought, and still
Appears more decent, as more suitable;*
A vile conceit in pompous words express'd,
Is like a clown in regal purple dress'd:
For diff'rent styles with diff'rent subjects sort,

---

297. wit에 대한 이름난 정의. 형이상학파 시의 conceit에 대한 반발이 엿보인다.

306. **as women...dress:** 「여자가 남자를 옷차림 때문에 높이 평가하듯」(여성에 대한 풍자가 곁들여져 있음). 언어는 "dress of thoughts"라는 신고전주의 사상.

308. **take upon content:** 「자세히 검토하지도 않고 받아들이다」.

311. **prismatic glass:** 「프리즘」. 바로 전 세대에 Newton이 프리즘을 이용하여 광학의 기초를 다졌다.

314. **without...gay:** gay without distinction. 구별 없이 찬란할 뿐인 것도 역시 무질서이다.

318—9. **still...suitable:** 「더 잘 어울릴수록 더욱 적절해 보인다」.

As several*garbs with country, town, and court.
Some by old words to fame have made pretence;*
Ancients in phrase, mere moderns in their sense;
Such labour'd nothings, in so strange a style,
Amaze th' unlearn'd, and make the learned smile.
Unlucky, as Fungoso in the play,*
These sparks*with awkward vanity display
What the fine gentleman wore yesterday;
And but so mimic ancient wits at best,
As apes our grandsires,* in their doublets drest.
In words, as fashions, the same rule will hold;
Alike fantastic,* if too new, or old:
Be not the first by whom the new are try'd,
Nor yet the last to lay the old aside.
　But most by Numbers*judge a Poet's song;
And smooth or rough, with them is right or wrong:
In the bright Muse though thousand charms conspire,
Her voice is all these tuneful fools admire;
Who haunt Parnassus but to please their ear,
Not mend their minds; as some to Church repair,
Not for the doctrine, but the music there.*
These* equal syllables alone require,
Tho' oft the ear the open vowels tire;

---

323. **several:** respective.

324. **make pretence to:** 「…의 자격, 권리가 있다고 자처하다 · 주장하다」. 이 행의 뜻은 「옛 낱말을 써서 유명해지려고 하였다」.

328. **Fungoso:** Ben Jonson 의 *Every Man out of his Humour* 에 나오는 인물(못난 학생).

329. **these sparks:** 옛 글을 흉내내어 아는 체하는 자들.

332. **As apes** 다음에 mimic 을 넣어 읽을 것. 「원숭이가 저고리를 입고 노인을 흉내내듯」.

334. **fantastic:** 「기괴한, 안 어울리는」. 「너무 새로와도, 너무 낡아도 안되는 유행처럼」.

337. **Numbers:** versification 운율. 이하에서 Pope 자신이 내용에 꼭 어울리는 운율의 솜씨를 보여주고 있다(특히 345, 346, 347, 348—51 행).

339—343. 시의 소리 효과에만 주의를 기울이는 태도를 비판하고 있다. 즉 마음을 고치는 게 중요하다는 것이다.

344. **These:** 시의 음향효과만 좋아하는 자들.

While expletives their feeble aid do join;
And ten low words oft creep in one dull line:
While they ring round the same unvary'd chimes,
With sure returns of still expected rhymes;
Where-e'er you find 'the cooling western breeze,'
In the next line, it 'whispers through the trees';
If crystal streams 'with pleasing murmurs creep,'
The reader's threaten'd (not in vain) with 'sleep':*
Then, at the last and only couplet fraught
With some unmeaning thing they call a thought,
A needless Alexandrine* ends the song
That, like a wounded snake, drags its slow length along.
Leave such to tune their own dull rhymes, and know
What's roundly smooth or languishingly slow;
And praise the easy vigour of a line,
Where Denham's strength, and Waller's sweetness* join.
True ease in writing comes from art, not chance,
As those move easiest who have learn'd to dance.
'Tis not enough no harshness gives offence,
The sound must seem an Echo to the sense:*
Soft is the strain when Zephyr gently blows,
And the smooth stream in smoother numbers flows;
But when loud surges lash the sounding shore,
The hoarse, rough verse should like the torrent roar:
When Ajax* strives some rock's vast weight to throw,
The line too labours, and the words move slow;

352—353. Crystal streams 'with pleasing murmurs creep'이라는 판에 박은 구절이 나오면 독자는 으레 십십해져서 졸음(sleep)이 오게 되어 있다.

356. **Alexandrine:** a hexameter line. 즉 12음절의 시행. 보통 긴 stanza를 내용적(사상적)으로 마무리할 때 쓰이나, 별로 마무리할 것도 없는데 멋으로 사용하는 예를 비꼬고 있다. (357행이 바로 그 예).

361. **Denham, Waller:** 두 사람 다 영시에 세련미를 가져다준 선구자들.

366. 이 행은 과연 부드러운 봄바람 같은 음향효과를 갖고 있는데, 이하 373행까지는 소리가 뜻에 반향(echo)처럼 들리는 예를 실제로 보여주고 있다.

370. **Ajax:** *Iliad*에 나오는 그리이스의 영웅. 지혜는 모자라나 끈질기고 힘센 용사(그를 묘사한 부분 자체가 음성적으로 그의 특성을 나타내고 있는 듯하다).

Not so, when swift Camilla* scours the plain,
Flies o'er th' unbending corn, and skims along the main.
Hear how Timotheus'* varied lays surprise,
And bid alternate passions fall and rise!
While, at each change, the son of Libyan Jove*
Now burns with glory, and then melts with love,
Now his fierce eyes with sparkling fury glow,
Now sighs steal out, and tears begin to flow:
Persians and Greeks like turns of nature found,
And the world's victor stood subdu'd by Sound!
The pow'r of Music all our hearts allow,
And what Timotheus was, is DRYDEN* now.
Avoid Extremes; and shun the fault of such,
Who still are pleas'd too little or too much.
At ev'ry trifle scorn to take offence;*
That* always shows great pride, or little sense;
Those heads, as stomachs, are not sure* the best,
Which nauseate* all, and nothing can digest.
Yet let not each gay Turn* thy rapture move;
For fools admire, but men of sense approve:
As things seem large which we thro' mists descry,
Dulness is ever apt to magnify.
Some foreign writers, some our own despise;*

---

372. **Camilla:** Virgil의 *Aeneid*에 등장하는 재빠른 여걸. Aeneas의 적수.
374. **Timotheus:** (447-357 B.C.). 그리이스의 서정시인. 그의 시와 음악으로 Alexander 대왕의 감정을 슬펐다 기뻤다 하게 하였다고 함.
376. **Libyan Jove:** Alexander 대왕이 Libya의 Zeus 신전에 갔을 때 Zeus (Jove)의 아들이라는 신탁을 받았다.
383. Pope는 당시 Dryden의 Ode인 "Alexander's Feasts" (Timotheus의 고사를 노래한 시)의 음악적 효과를 매우 높이 기렸다.
386. 이 시행의 올바른 어순은, Scorn to take offence at every trifle. 「사소한 흠을 볼 때마다 언짢아하는 습성을 대범하게 버려라」.
387. **that:** to take offence.
388. **sure:** surely.
389. **nauseate:** (무엇이든 다) 「역겨워하다, 싫어하다」.
390. **Turn:** 「말투. 표현」.
394. 이 행을 풀이하면, Some (people) despise foreign authors, some (others) despise our own authors. 다음 행도 같은 생략구문.

The Ancients only, or the Moderns prize.
Thus Wit, like Faith, by each man is apply'd
To one small sect, and all are damn'd beside.
Meanly they seek the blessing to confine,
And force that sun but on a part to shine,
Which not alone the southern wit* sublimes,
But ripens spirits in cold northern climes;
Which from the first has shone on ages past,
Enlights the present, and shall warm the last;
Tho' each may feel increases and decays,
And see now clearer and now darker days.
Regard not then if Wit be old or new,
But blame the false, and value still the true.
Some ne'er advance a Judgment of their own,
But catch the spreading notion of the Town;
They reason and conclude by precedent,
And own stale nonsense which they ne'er invent.
Some judge of authors' names, not works, and then
Nor praise nor blame the writings, but the men.
Of all this servile herd the worst is he
That in proud dulness joins with Quality.*
A constant Critic at the great man's board,
To fetch and carry nonsense for my Lord.
What woful stuff this madrigal would be,
In some starv'd hackney sonneteer, or me?
But let a Lord once own the happy lines,
How the wit brightens! how the style refines!*
Before his sacred name flies ev'ry fault,

---

400. **southern wit:** 남유럽의 문학. 즉 고전과 근대 이탈리아의 문학. 문학의 남북관계를 언급하고 있다. **sublime:** (동사) 「높이다, 고양하다」.

415. **Quality:** 지체높은 양반(다음 행의 great man). 문학의 patron에게는 식객노릇이나 하면서 아는 체하는 우둔한 자(proud dulness)를 비꼬고 있다.

417—421. 이 연가가 굶주린 3류시인이나 나(Pope)의 작품인 경우 얼마나 못나 보일까? 그러나 양반 나으리가 그 싯귀를 자기 것이라고 일단 말하기만 하면 그 시는 대번에 빛난다. (시 아닌 작자를 보고 칭찬하는 짓— 이른바 intentional fallacy 임).

And each exalted stanza teems with thought!
The Vulgar thus through Imitation err;
As oft the Learn'd* by being singular;
So much they scorn the crowd, that if the throng
By chance go right, they purposely go wrong;
So Schismatics the plain believers quit,
And are but damn'd for having too much wit.
Some praise at morning what they blame at night;
But always think the last opinion right.
A Muse by these is like a mistress us'd,
This hour she's idoliz'd, the next abus'd;
While their weak heads like towns unfortify'd,
'Twixt sense and nonsense daily change their side.
Ask them the cause; they're wiser still, they say;
And still to-morrow's wiser than to-day.
We think our fathers fools, so wise we grow,
Our wiser sons, no doubt, will think us so.
Once School-divines* this zealous isle o'er-spread;
Who knew most Sentences,* was deepest read;
Faith, Gospel, all, seem'd made to be disputed,
And none had sense enough to be confuted:
Scotists and Thomists;* now, in peace remain,
Amidst their kindred cobwebs in Duck-lane:*
If Faith itself has different dresses worn,
What wonder modes in Wit should take their turn?
Oft, leaving what is natural and fit,
The current folly proves the ready wit;*

---

425. **Learn'd:** 다음에 ear를 넣어 읽을 것. 「식자는 독특한 이론을 내세우다가 틀린다」.

440. **School-divines:** 중세의 스콜라 신학자들.

441. **Sentences:** Peter Lombardi의 책 *The Book of Sentences*. 고전 신학자들의 명언집으로 논쟁방법의 교본 구실을 함.

444. **Scotists**는 중세의 Duns Scotus를, **Thomists**는 Thomas Aquinas를 따르는 학파.

445. **Duck-lane:** 중고서적상들이 있는 런던의 거리. 르네상스와 신고전주의 시대에 중세의 학문은 가장 천하게 대접받았다.

449. 유행하는 엉터리 문학이 임기응변의 재치로 통하고 있다.

And authors think their reputation safe,
Which lives as long as fools are pleas'd to laugh.*
 Some valuing those of their own side or mind,
Still make themselves the measure of mankind:
Fondly we think we honour merit then,
When we but praise ourselves in other men.
Parties in Wit attend on those* of State,
And public faction doubles private hate.
Pride, Malice, Folly, against Dryden rose,
In various shapes of Parsons, Critics, Beaux;*
But sense surviv'd, when merry jests were past;
For rising merit will buoy up at last.
Might he return, and bless once more our eyes,
New Blackmores and new Milbourns* must arise:
Nay should great Homer lift his awful head,
Zoilus* again would start up from the dead.
Envy will* merit, as its shade, pursue;
But like a shadow, proves the substance true;
For envy'd Wit, like Sol* eclips'd, makes known
Th' opposing body's grossness, not its own,
When first that sun too pow'rful beams displays,
It draws up vapours which obscure its rays;
But ev'n those clouds at last adorn its way,
Reflect new glories, and augment the day.
 Be thou the first true merit to befriend;
His praise is lost, who stays;* till all commend.

---

451. 바보들이 멋지다고 웃는 동안만 지속되는 명성.

456. 문학 파벌과 정치 파벌이 서로 어울린다는 것. 특히 영국에서 Whigs와 Tories는 정치뿐 아니라 문학적 파벌도 되었다.

459. 당시 Dryden을 공격한 사람들 중에는 목사, 평론가, 똑똑한 체하는 신사(귀족)들이 있었다.

453. Sir Richard Blackmore와 Luke Milbourn 목사는 Dryden을 공격한 인물들.

465. **Zoilus:** Homer를 공격한 그리이스의 문법가(3, 4세기 B.C.).

466. **will** 다음에 purse.

468. **Sol:** sun.

475. **stay:** remain silent.

Short is the date, alas, of modern rhymes,
And 'tis but just to let them live betimes.
No longer now that golden age appears,
When Patriarch-wits surviv'd a thousand years:
Now length of Fame (our second life) is lost,
And bare threescore is all ev'n that can boast;
Our sons their fathers' failing language see,
And such as Chaucer is, shall Dryden be.*
So when the faithful pencil has design'd
Some bright Idea of the master's mind,
Where a new world leaps out at his command,
And ready Nature waits upon his hand;
When the ripe colours soften and unite,
And sweetly melt into just shade and light;
When mellowing years their full perfection give,
And each bold figure just begins to live,
The treach'rous colours the fair art betray,
And all the bright creation fades away!
Unhappy Wit,* like most mistaken things,
Atones not for that envy which it brings.
In youth alone its empty praise we boast,
But soon the short-liv'd vanity is lost:
Like some fair flow'r the early spring supplies,
That gaily blooms, but ev'n in blooming dies.
What is this Wit, which must our cares employ?
The owner's wife, that other men enjoy;
Then most our trouble still when most admir'd,
And still the more we give, the more requir'd;
Whose fame with pains we guard, but lose with ease,
Sure some to vex, but never all to please;
'Tis what the vicious fear, the virtuous shun,
By ſools 'tis hated, and by knaves undone!*

---

483. Chaucer의 영어를 알지 못하듯 Dryden의 문학도 이해되지 못하리라. 당시에 근대 작가의 명성이 오래 가지 못함은 언어의 변천에 있다고 보는 견해가 강했다. 그림에 있어서 색체가 오래 가지 못함과 같은 것이다.

494. **Unhappy wit:** 질투심만 불러일으키고 그 보상은 주지 못하므로 시적 재질은 불행하다는 것이다.

  If Wit so much from Ign'rance undergo,
Ah let not Learning too commence*its foe!
Of old,* those met rewards who could excel,
And such were prais'd who but endeavour'd well:
Tho' triumphs were to gen'rals only due,
Crowns were reserv'd to grace the soldiers too.
Now, they who reach Parnassus' lofty crown,
Employ their pains to spurn some others down;
And while self-love each jealous writer rules,
Contending wits become the sport of fools:
But still the worst with most regret commend,
For each ill Author is as bad a Friend.
To what base ends, and by what abject ways,
Are mortals urg'd thro' sacred*lust of praise!
Ah ne'er so dire a thirst of glory boast,
Nor in the Critic let the Man be lost.
Good-nature and good-sense must ever join;
To err is human, to forgive, divine.
  But if in noble minds some dregs remain
Not yet purg'd off, of spleen and sour disdain;
Discharge that rage on more provoking crimes,
Nor fear a dearth in these flagitious times:*
No pardon vile Obscenity should find,
Tho' wit and art conspire to move your mind;
But Dulness with Obscenity must prove
As shameful sure as Impotence in love.
In the fat age of pleasure, wealth and ease,
Sprung the rank weed, and thriv'd with large increase:

500—507. 시인은 언제나 고민해야 하고, 그의 시를 즐기는 것은 남들이다. 악한 자는 두려워하고(풍자시에 등장할까봐), 선한 자는 피하며(선한 자는 시인이 아니라 도덕군자가 된다), 바보들은 미워하며(시를 지을 수 없으니까), 악당들에게 해를 당한다.

509. **commence:** come to be. 「학문까지 시의 원수가 되지 말거라」.

510. **of old:** 「옛적에는」.

521. **sacred:** 여기서는 cursed.

529. 남을 욕하려거든 요즈음(Charles Ⅱ 당시)의 악한 세대에 욕해도 부족(dearth)할 걱정이 없으니 그런 것이나 욕하라. **fear:** 「걱정하다」(반어적).

When love was all an easy Monarch's*care;
Seldom at council, never in a war:
Jilts*rul'd the state, and statesmen farces writ;
Nay wits had pensions, and young Lords had wit:
The Fair sate panting at a Courtier's play,*
And not a Mask went unimprov'd away:*
The modest fan was lifted up no more,
And Virgins smil'd at what they blush'd before.
The following licence of a Foreign reign*
Did all the dregs of bold Socinus drain;
Then unbelieving priests reform'd the nation,
And taught more pleasant methods of salvation;
Where Heav'n's free subjects might their rights dispute,
Lest God himself should seem too absolute:
Pulpits their sacred satire learn'd to spare,
And Vice admir'd to find a flatt'rer there!
Encourag'd thus, Wit's Titans*brav'd the skies,
And the press groan'd with licens'd blasphemies.
These monsters, Critics! with your darts engage,
Here point your thunder, and exhaust your rage!
Yet shun their fault, who, scandalously nice,*
Will needs mistake an author into vice;*
All seems infected that th' infected spy,
As all looks yellow to the jaundic'd eye.

---

536. **easy Monarch:** Charles Ⅱ를 가리킨다. 명예혁명으로 쫓겨난 방탕한 왕.
538. **Jilts:** 왕의 정부들.
540—543. 당시 상류층 여인들의 풍기문란함에 대한 풍자. **the Fair**=women.
541. 귀부인들은 극장에서 mask를 쓰고 교제를 즐겼다. 「마스크를 쓴 여자마다 연극을 보고 나서 더 좋은 사람이 되어서 갔다」(비꼬는 말).
544. **Foreign reign:** Charles Ⅱ를 몰아내고 왕이 된 화란 출신의 William Ⅲ를 가리킨다. 종교의 자유를 허용했는데, 삼위일체설를 부인한 16세기 이탈리아의 이단적 신학자 Laelus Socinus의 찌꺼기까지 다 마셔버렸다는 것은 당시의 종교의 자유로 각종 이단설이 난무했음을 말한다. 그 중에는 신의 절대권력을 부인하는 Whig 계열의 목사들도 있었다.
552. **Wit's Titans:** 당시 신의 권위를 깎아내린 이신주의자들(deists).
556. **nice:** 「까다로운, 따지기를 잘 하는」.
557. 「으레 (needs) 한 저자의 글을 악의로 곡해하려고 하는」.

LEARN then what MORALS Critics ought to show,
For 'tis but half a Judge's task, to know.
'Tis not enough, taste, judgment, learning, join;
In all you speak, let truth and candour shine:
That not alone what to your sense is due
All may allow; but seek your friendship too.
Be silent always when you doubt your sense;
And speak, tho' sure, with seeming diffidence:
Some positive, persisting fops we know,
Who, if once wrong, will needs be always so;
But you, with pleasure own* your errors past,
And make each day a Critic on the last.
'Tis not enough, your counsel still be true;
Blunt truths more mischief than nice falsehoods do;
Men must be taught as if you taught them not,
And things unknown* propos'd as things forgot.
Without Good Breeding, truth is disapprov'd;
That only makes superior sense belov'd.
Be niggards of advice on no pretence;
For the worst avarice is that of sense.
With mean complacence ne'er betray your trust,
Nor be so civil as to prove unjust.
Fear not the anger of the wise to raise;
Those best can bear reproof, who merit praise.
'Twere well might critics* still this freedom take,
But Appius* reddens at each word you speak,
And stares, tremendous, with a threat'ning eye,
Like some fierce tyrant in old tapestry.
Fear* most to tax an Honourable fool,
Whose right it is, uncensur'd, to be dull;
Such, without wit, are Poets when they please,

570. **own:** 「시인하다」.
575. **unknown:** 다음에 must be를 넣을 것.
584. **'Twere well might critics::** It would be well, if critics might....
585. **Appius:** John Dennis를 가리킨다.
586. **Fear:** 「조심하라」.

As without learning they can take Degrees:*
Leave dang'rous truths to unsuccessful Satires;*
And flattery to fulsome Dedicators;*
Whom, when they praise, the world believes no more,
Than when they promise to give scribbling o'er.*
'Tis best sometimes your censure to restrain,
And charitably let the dull be vain:
Your silence there is better than your spite,
For who can rail so long as they can write?
Still humming on, their drowsy course they keep,
And lash'd so long, like tops, are lash'd asleep.
False steps but help them to renew the race,
As, after stumbling, Jades will mend their pace.
What crowds of these, impenitently bold,
In sounds and jingling syllables grown old,
Still run on* Poets, in a raging vein,
Ev'n to the dregs and squeezings of the brain,
Strain out the last dull droppings of their sense,
And rhyme with all the rage of Impotence.
Such shameless Bards we have; and yet 'tis true,
There are as mad abandon'd Critics too.
The bookful blockhead, ignorantly read,
With loads of learned lumber in his head,
With his own tongue still edifies his ears,
And always list'ning to himself appears.
All books he reads, and all he reads assails,
From Dryden's Fables down to Durfey's Tales.*

590—591. 학문이 없는데도 학위를 타는 사람들에게 시적 능력이 없이 시인으로 자처하는 자들을 비기고 있다. 그 때에는 정부각료들에게 학위를 주었다.

592. 못난 풍자시일수록 중대한(위험한) 진리를 담고 있는 척한다.

593. **Dedicators:** patron을 구하기 위하여 자기의 저서에다 귀족 아무개에게 바친다(dedicated to Lord ——)는 아부의 글을 붙이는 자들.

595. **give...o'er:** give up scribbling. 「글 쓰기를 포기하다」.

606. **run on:** persist in being.

617. Dryden은 *Fables, Acient and Modern*이라는 명작을 썼지만, Durfey는 잡문을 쓴 3류 문인.

With him, most authors steal their works, or buy;*
Garth did not write his own Dispensary.*
Name a new Play, and he's the Poet's friend,*
Nay show'd his faults—but when would Poets mend?
No place so sacred from such fops is barr'd,
Nor is Paul's church more safe than Paul's churchyard:*
Nay, fly to Altars; there they'll talk you dead:
For Fools rush in where Angels fear to tread.
Distrustful sense with modest caution speaks,
It still looks home, and short excursions makes;*
But rattling nonsense in full volleys breaks,
And never shock'd, and never turn'd aside,
Bursts out, resistless, with a thund'ring tide.
  But where's the man, who counsel can bestow,
Still pleas'd to teach, and yet not proud to know?
Unbiass'd, or by favour, or by spite;*
Not dully prepossess'd, nor blindly right;
Tho' learn'd, well-bred; and tho' well-bred, sincere,
Modestly bold, and humanly severe:
Who to a friend his faults can freely show,
And gladly praise the merit of a foe?
Blest with a taste exact, yet unconfin'd;
A knowledge both of books and human kind:
Gen'rous converse; a soul exempt from pride;
And love to praise, with reason on his side?

---

618. 책만 잔뜩 읽은 자에 의하면, 대개의 저자들은 남의 글을 표절하든가 사든가 한다고. 즉, 유식한 체하는 자일수록 남의 글의 원천에 대해서 말이 많다.

619. Sir Samuel Garth는 의사로서 *The Dispensary*라는 풍자시를 썼다. Pope가 칭찬한 문사.

620. 새 희곡 이름만 나오면 자기는 그 작가의 친구로서 결함을 지적했는데, 시인들은 충고를 받고도 고치는 법이 없다고 bookful blockhead는 말하고 있다.

623. **Paul's church:** 런던 중심부에 있는 St. Paul's cathedral. 당시 상인들이 근처에서 상담을 벌였고, 시정의 무뢰배들도 모여들었다.

627. 조심스런 판단의 소유자는 항상 출발점(home)을 벗어나지 않으며 멀리 나가지도 않는다.

633. **or...or:** either...or....

Such once were Critics; such the happy few,
Athens and Rome in better ages knew.
The mighty Stagirite first left the shore,
Spread all his sails, and durst the deeps explore:
He steer'd securely, and discover'd far,
Led by the light of the Maeonian Star.*
Poets, a race long unconfin'd, and free,
Still fond and proud of savage liberty,
Receiv'd his laws; and stood convinc'd 'twas fit,
Who conquer'd Nature, should preside o'er Wit.
Horace still charms with graceful negligence,*
And without method talks us into sense,
Will, like a friend, familiarly convey
The truest notions in the easiest way.
He, who supreme in judgment, as in wit,
Might boldly censure, as he boldly writ,
Yet judg'd with coolness, tho' he sung with fire;
His Precepts teach but what his works inspire.
Our Critics take a contrary extreme,
They judge with fury, but they write with phlegm:
Nor suffers Horace more in wrong Translations
By Wits, than Critics in as wrong Quotations.*
See Dionysius* Homer's thoughts refine,
And call new beauties forth from ev'ry line!
Fancy and art in gay Petronius* please,
The scholar's learning, with the courtier's ease.
In grave Quintilian's* copious work, we find
The justest rules, and clearest method join'd:
Thus useful arms in magazines we place,

---

648. **Maeonian Star:** Homer를 가리킨다. Maeonia는 Homer의 출생지인 Lydia의 별명.

653. **graceful negligence:** 냉혹하든가 경색되지 아니한 유연함. 자연스러움.

663—664. Horace나 고대의 비평가들이 꼭같이 잘못 번역되고, 잘못 인용되고 있다.

665. **Dionysius:** 기원전 1세기경의 그리이스의 수사학자.

667. **Petronius:** 기원 1세기경의 로마의 평론가, 풍자가.

669. **Quintilian:** 기원 1세기의 로마의 수사학자. 고전 수사법의 집대성자.

All rang'd in order, and dispos'd with grace,
But less to please the eye, than arm the hand,
Still fit for use, and ready at command.
  Thee, bold Longinus! all the Nine* inspire,
And bless their Critic* with a Poet's fire.
An ardent Judge, who zealous in his trust,
With warmth gives sentence, yet is always just;
Whose own example strengthens all his laws;
And is himself that great Sublime he draws.
  Thus long succeeding Critics justly reign'd,
Licence repress'd, and useful laws ordain'd.
Learning and Rome alike in empire grew;
And Arts still follow'd where her Eagles flew;*
From the same foes, at last, both felt their doom,
And the same age saw Learning fall, and Rome.
With Tyranny, then Superstition join'd,
As that the body, this enslav'd the mind;*
Much was believ'd, but little understood,
And to be dull was constru'd to be good;
A second deluge Learning thus o'er-run,
And the Monks finish'd what the Goths begun.*
  At length Erasmus, that great injur'd name,
(The glory of the Priesthood, and the shame!)*
Stemm'd the wild torrent of a barb'rous age,
And drove those holy Vandals* off the stage.
  But see! each Muse, in LEO's* golden days,

---

675. **all the Nine:** the Nine Muses.

676. **their Critic:** the Muses' Critic. 즉 Longinus. 따라서 675—6의 뜻은, 「시에 대한 그의 평론 자체가 매우 고양된 시적 영감을 불러일으킨다」.

684. **Eagles flew:** 로마군의 군기.

688. As Tyranny enslaved the bcdy, Superstition enslaved the mind.

692. Goth족이 시작한 암흑시대를 Monk들이 완성했다는 생각은 르네상스, 신고전주의 시대의 공통된 편견.

693—694. Erasmus는 카톨릭 교회의 신부이면서도 인문학자로서 개신교에 영향을 주었으므로, glory이며 동시에 shame이라는 애매한 평가를 받았다.

696. **holy Vandals:** 중세의 성직자들을 비꼬아 일컫는 말.

**Starts from her trance, and trims her wither'd bays,
Rome's ancient Genius, o'er its ruins spread,
Shakes off the dust, and rears his rev'rend head.
Then Sculpture and her sister-arts revive;
Stones leap'd to form, and rocks began to live;
With sweeter notes each rising Temple rung;
A Raphael painted, and a Vida* sung.
Immortal Vida: on whose honour'd brow
The Poet's bays and Critic's ivy grow:
Cremona now shall ever boast thy name,
As next in place to Mantua, next in fame!
But soon by impious arms from Latium* chas'd,
Their ancient bounds the banish'd Muses pass'd;
Thence Arts o'er all the northern world advance,
But Critic-learning flourish'd most in France:
The rules a nation, born to serve, obeys;
And Boileau* still in right of Horace sways.
But we, brave Britons, foreign laws despis'd,
And kept unconquer'd, and unciviliz'd;
Fierce for the liberties of wit, and bold,
We still defy'd the Romans, as of old.*
Yet some there were, among the sounder few
Of those who less presum'd, and better knew,
Who durst assert the juster ancient cause,
And here restor'd Wit's fundamental laws.
Such was the Muse, whose rules and practice tell,
'Nature's chief Master-piece is writing well.'**

---

697. **Leo:** Leo X 법왕. 1513년에 법왕이 되자, 인문학자들은 문예부흥의 시작으로 환호하였다.

704. **Vida, Marco Girolamo:** (1490?-1566). 이탈리아의 인문학자. 시론 *Poetica*를 저술함. Cremona 출신.

709. **Latium:** 즉 Rome. Bourbon 공의 Rome 약탈로 이탈리아는 분란을 겪음.

714. **Boileau, Nicolas:** (1636–1711). 프랑스의 시인, 비평가. 그의 *Art poétique*는 Pope의 *Essay on Criticism*의 모델이 되었다.

715—718. 대륙문화를 거부함으로써 자유를 지킴과 동시에 미개상태를 고수한다는 부작용도 있음을 말한다. 예전 Briton들은 로마군에 대항해 싸웠는데, 로마군대를 순순히 받아들였던 프랑스는 먼저 문명화되었다.

Such was Roscommon,* not more learn'd than good,
With manners gen'rous as his noble blood;
To him the wit of Greece and Rome was known,
And ev'ry author's merit, but his own.*
Such late was Walsh*—the Muse's judge and friend,
Who justly knew to blame or to commend;
To failings mild, but zealous for desert;
The clearest head, and the sincerest heart.
This humble praise, lamented shade! receive,
This praise at least a grateful Muse* may give:
The Muse, whose early voice you taught to sing,
Prescrib'd her heights, and prun'd her tender wing,
(Her guide now lost) no more attempts to rise,
But in low numbers short excursions tries:
Content, if hence th' unlearn'd their wants may view,
The learn'd reflect on what before they knew:
Careless of censure, nor too fond of fame;
Still pleas'd to praise, yet not afraid to blame,
Averse alike to flatter, or offend;
Not free from faults, nor yet too vain to mend.

---

725. **Roscommon, Earl of, Wentworth Dillon:** (1633–85). Horace의 *Art of Poetry*를 번역. *An Essay on Translated Verse*에서 처음으로 Milton을 찬양.

728. **but his own:** except his own merit. 남의 장점은 다 알되 자기、장점은 모르는 겸손한 사람.

729. **Walsh, William:** 어린 Pope에게 "correct poet"가 되라는 충고를 해준 무명시인. Pope가 *Essay on Criticism*을 쓰기 조금 전에 사망. 그래서 Pope는 그를 이 글 말미에서 조상하고 있다(lamented shade!: 「내가 애도하는 망령이시어!」).

734. **Muse:** Pope 자신의 시적 자아를 가리킨다.

Samuel Johnson

(1709—1784)

서적상의 아들로 태어나 옥스포드를 잠시 다니고 교사 노릇을 하다가 1737년 런던에서 가난한 문필 생활에 뛰어들었다. 산문, 운문 등 닥치는 대로 집필하는 도중에 상당한 수준의 시를 쓰기도 했고, 1750년에 *The Rambler*라는 잡지(주 2회 간행)를 2년간 편집하면서 평론가로서의 명성을 확립했고, 1755년에는 유명한 영어 사전을 출간하기에 이르렀다. 1760년대에는 James Boswell, Reynolds, Burke 등의 문필가들을 거느린 "Literary Club"의 주재자로 활약했으며, 셰익스피어 전집 편찬과 *Lives of the Poets*(1779-81)같은 대기획물에 손을 대기도 했다. 보즈웰의 유명한 평전이 아니었다면 그가 현재 누리는 명성은 많이 삭감됐을 터이지만, 그의 비평의 가치는 결코 줄어들지 않을 것이다.

Preface to *The Plays of William Shakespeare*(1765)는 10여년이나 걸려서 편찬 완료한 셰익스피어 전집의 서설로 쓰인 글이다. 현대 비평가 Kermode는 존슨의 이 글이 아직도 최고의 셰익스피어 비평이라고 주장할 만큼 이 글은 셰익스피어 문학의 정곡을 찌르고 있고, 그 비평의 태도가 건실하고 탁월한 식견을 보이고 있다.

존슨은 고전주의의 문학관을 체득한 비평가였지만, 편협한 교조주의에 대해서 가장 크게 저항한 사람이었다. 그의 관후한 태도에서 우리는 고전주의의 이념과 프랑스·이탈리아의 신고전주의의 처방이 얼마나 서로 거리가 먼가를 짐작할 수 있다.

존슨은 우선 문학의 가치는 과학적 논술과는 달리 사람들이 얼마나 오래 지속적으로 존중하느냐에 의해 정해진다고 주장한다. 그런데 한 사물에 대한 평가는 그와 같은 종류의 사물들과의 비교를 통하지 않고는 이루어질 수 없다. 다시 말하면 오랫동안 지속적으로 존중되는 것은 그 동안 그 비슷한 다른 것들과 거듭 비교해서 우월하다는 다수의 의견을 낳은 까닭이다. 즉 가치 판단에 있어서 집단의 지속적 경험은 절대적으로 필요하다. 보편적 가치란 바로 그렇게 하여 성립된다.

많은 사람을 오래도록 즐겁게 해 줄 수 있는 것은 오직 보편적인 인간 본성(general nature)을 올바르게 나타낸 것뿐이라고 존슨은 주장한다. 이것이 그의 고전주의 문학관의 요체이다.

세익스피어는 존슨 당시에 이미 백오륙십 년 동안 존중되어 왔으므로 충분히 고전적 지위를 확보했다. 그것은 곧 그가 보편적 인간성을 정확하게 보여주었다는 것을 입증한다. 그가 창조한 인물은 어디서나 만날 수 있는, 개체 아닌 전형(species)들이다. 그는 「영웅(주인공)」을 내세우지 않고 사람을 내세운다. 그에게는 편벽됨, 기이함, 기발함이 없다. 따라서 영웅과 천박한 부류를 엄격히 구별해야 한다는 신고전주의의 어울림(decorum)의 규칙은 깨어질 수밖에 없다. 희극과 비극을 뒤섞지 말라는 규칙 역시 인간의 실제를 그대로 보여주려는 그의 더 큰 예술적 의도에서 깨어질 수밖에 없다.

존슨은 세익스피어가 비극에서는 다소 무리를 하는데 반하여 희극에서는 완전히 자연스럽다는 견해를 피력한다. 이는 인간성의 보편성을 강조하는 그의 문학관의 소치이며 어쩌면 그 문학관의 한계를 암시하는지도 모른다.

존슨은 세익스피어의 결점을 눈감아주는 맹목적 예찬자는 아니다. 그는 세익스피어의 도덕관념이 때로는 편의주의적임을 꼬집고 있다. 모든 글은 사람을 가르치는 것이 목적인 바, 문학은 즐겁게 함으로써 가르친다고 믿는 그의 고전주의적 입장에서 볼 때 그 점에 있어서 세익스피어의 결점이 돋보이지 않을 수 없었다.

그러나 볼테르 같은 프랑스 비평가나, Thomas Rymer 같은 영국 비평가들이 공격하듯, 세익스피어가 어울림의 법칙, 삼일치의 법칙, 순수 장르의 법칙 등을 지키지 않는 데 대해서는 절대로 유감을 표명치 않는다. 그는 무대의 박진감은 결코 실생활과 동질의 것이 아님을 실제 경험에 호소하며 강조하고, 관객의 상상력이 얼마나 쉽게, 능동적으로 무대 위의 진행 상황을 흡수하는지를 지적한다. 또한 인생의 여러 양상을 되도록 많이 보여주는 셰익스피어의 연극이 다양성에서 오는 생동미와 폭넓은 교훈을 줄 수 있음을 설파한다.

모친의 장례 비용을 마련키 위해 단숨에 집필했다는 *Rasselas* (1759)는 요즈음 각광받는 이른바 "교양 소설"의 선구로서, 제10장은 왕자 Rasselas의 스승 Imlac의 문학론으로 되어 있어 이채롭다. 존슨은 임락의 말을 통하여, 신고전주의 기본 강령의 하나인 "고전의 모방" 이론을 거부하고 실제의 경험을 강조하며, 그렇다고 해서 독특하고 개별적이고 특이한 경험을 귀중히 여기지 않고, 모든 사람에게 알려질 수 있는 보편적 경험이 문학적으로 가치있다고 강조한다. 시인은 책을 통해서가 아니라 넓은 경험을 통해서 무엇을 쓸지를 배워야 한다는 이 생각은 경험주의적인 영국 기질을 암시하는 바 있다. 이는 "셰익스피어 서설"에서 더욱 뚜렷하게 제창되는 문학관이다.

*The Lives of the Poets*의 한 부분인 "The Life of Cowley"는 형이상학파 시의 특징을 약간 보인 Abraham Cowley를 다룬 평전인데, 이 글에서 존슨은 형이상학파 시인들이 "가장 이질적인 생각들을 폭력적으로 서로 연결시켰다"는 유명한 말을 하고 있다. 17세기의 일단의 시인들을 Metaphysical하다는 평을 한 것은 드라이든이었으나, 이 명칭을 유명하게 만든 것은 존슨의 이 글인 것이다. 존슨은 그들의 박학다식과 놀라운 기상을 업신여기지는 않지만, 문학의 보편성을 강조하는 그가 그들에 대하여 유감을 표명하지 않을 수 없다. 그의 생각은 오늘날 부정되고 있지만, 한편 존슨의 비판의 근거가 박약하다고 할 사람은 하나도 없다.

From Rasselas* (1759)

A DISSERTATION UPON POETRY

WHEREVER I went, I found that poetry was considered as the highest learning, and regarded with a veneration somewhat approaching to that which man would pay to the Angelic Nature.* And yet it fills me with wonder, that, in almost all countries, the most ancient poets are considered as the best: whether it be that every other kind of knowledge is an acquisition gradually attained, and poetry is a gift conferred at once; or that the first poetry of every nation surprised them as a novelty, and retained the credit by consent which it received by accident at first: or whether, as the province of poetry is to describe Nature and Passion, which are always the same, the first writers took possession of the most striking objects for description, and the most probable occurrences for fiction, and left nothing to those that followed them, but transcription of the same events, and new combinations of the same images. Whatever be the reason, it is commonly observed that the early writers are in possession of nature, and their followers* of art: that the first excel in strength and invention, and the latter in elegance and refinement.*

"I was desirous to add my name to this illustrious fraternity.* I read all the poets of Persia and Arabia, and was able to repeat by memory the volumes that are suspended* in the

---

*이 도덕소설의 주인공 Rasselas는 Abyssinia의 왕자로, 스승 Imlac와 함께 애급으로 여행하며 많은 경험을 겪고 좋은 이야기를 듣는다.

***Angelic Nature:** 「초인간적 능력」.

*시와 기타 학술의 차이를 말하고 있다. 기타 학술은 점진적 발전의 결과이므로 근대로 올수록 그 성취가 훌륭해지나, 시는 고대에 이미 개화하여 자연의 모든 양상을 다 표현했고 그래서 그 후세대는 기교만 발전시킨다는 사상이다. followers 다음에 are in possession을 넣어서 읽을 것.

***this illustrious fraternity:** 「이 저명한 집단」. 즉 시인의 무리.

***suspended:** 책이나 두루마리 등을 공중에 「매달아」 진열했다고 함.

mosque of Mecca. But I soon found that no man was ever great by imitation. My desire of excellence impelled me to transfer my attention to nature and to life. Nature was to be my subject, and men to be my auditors: I could never describe what I had not seen: I could not hope to move those with delight or terror, whose interests and opinions I did not understand.

"Being now resolved to be a poet, I saw every thing with a new purpose; my sphere of attention was suddenly magnified: no kind of knowledge was to be overlooked. I ranged mountains and deserts for images and resemblances, and pictured upon my mind every tree of the forest and flower of the valley. I observed with equal care the crags of the rock and the pinnacles of the palace. Sometimes I wandered along the mazes of the rivulet, and sometimes watched the changes of the summer clouds. To a poet nothing can be useless. Whatever is beautiful, and whatever is dreadful, must be familiar to his imagination: he must be conversant with all that is awfully vast or elegantly little. The plants of the garden, the animals of the wood, the minerals of the earth, and meteors of the sky, must all concur to store his mind with inexhaustible variety: for every idea is useful for the enforcement or decoration of moral or religious truth; and he, who knows most, will have most power of diversifying his scenes, and of gratifying his reader with remote allusions and unexpected instruction.

"All the appearances of nature I was therefore careful to study, and every country which I have surveyed has contributed something to my poetical powers."

"In so wide a survey," said the prince, "you must surely have left much unobserved. I have lived, till now, within the circuit of these mountains, and yet cannot walk abroad without the sight of something which I had never beheld before, or never heeded."

"The business of a poet," said Imlac, "is to examine, not the individual, but the species;* to remark general properties

---

***not the individual but the species:** 「개체가 아니라 종(種)」. 이순신은 개체이나, 장군, 이씨 성을 가진 남자는 종류이다. 많은 사람들이 다 알 수 있는 사실, 즉 보편을 추구하라는 의미.

and large appearances; he does not number the streaks of the tulip, or describe the different shades in the verdure of the forest. He is to exhibit in his portraits of nature such prominent and striking features, as recall the original to every mind; and must neglect the minuter discriminations, which one may have remarked, and another have neglected, for* those characteristics which are alike obvious to vigilance and carelessness.

"But the knowledge of nature is only half the task of a poet; he must be acquainted likewise with all the modes of life. His character requires that he estimate the happiness and misery of every condition; observe the power of all the passions in all their combinations, and trace the changes of the human mind as they are modified by various institutions and accidental influences of climate or custom, from the sprightliness of infancy to the despondence of decrepitude. He must divest himself of the prejudices of his age or country; he must consider right and wrong in their abstracted and invariable state; he must disregard present laws and opinions, and rise to general and transcendental truths, which will always be the same: he must therefore content himself with the slow progress of his name;* contemn the applause of his own time, and commit his claims to the justice of posterity. He must write as the interpreter of nature, and the legislator of mankind, and consider himself as presiding over the thoughts and manners of future generations; as a being superior to time and place.

"His labour is not yet at an end: he must know many languages and many sciences; and, that his style may be worthy of his thoughts, must, by incessant practice, familiarize to himself every delicacy of speech and grace of harmony."

***for:** 앞의 neglect에 연결된다. neglect something for...: 「어떤 것을 주의해 보지 않고 ...을 주시하다」.

***the slow progress of his name:** 「명성이 느리게 얻어지는 것」.

From Preface to Shakespeare (1765)

THAT praises are without reason lavished on the dead, and that the honours due only to excellence are paid to antiquity, is a complaint likely to be always continued by those, who, being able to add nothing to truth, hope for eminence from the heresies of paradox; or those, who, being forced by disappointment upon consolatory expedients,* are willing to hope from posterity what the present age refuses, and flatter themselves that the regard which is yet denied by envy, will be at last bestowed by time.

Antiquity, like every other quality that attracts the notice of mankind, has undoubtedly votaries that reverence it, not from reason, but from prejudice. Some seem to admire indiscriminately whatever has been long preserved, without considering that time has sometimes co-operated with chance;* all perhaps are more willing to honour past than present excellence; and the mind contemplates genius through the shades of age, as the eye surveys the sun through artificial opacity.* The great contention of criticism is to find the faults of the moderns, and the beauties of the ancients. While an author is yet living we estimate his powers by his worst performance, and when he is dead, we rate them by his best.

To works, however, of which the excellence is not absolute and definite, but gradual and comparative; to works not raised

---

***being forced...expedients:** 「실망으로 인하여 손쉬운 위안을 구할 수 밖에 없어서」. (옛것에 대해서는 그 가치를 따지지 않고 우선 찬양부터 보낸다는 불평은 궤변으로 이름을 날리려는 사람의 말이든지, 아니면 오늘날은 당장 칭찬을 못 받아도 미래에 가서는 칭찬을 받게 되리라고 믿는 사람의 말이든지 둘 중의 하나이다.)

***without...chance:** 「오랜 세월이 흘렀을 뿐만 아니라 우연이 개입되는 경우도 있다는 사실을 잊고서」.

***artificial opacity:** 「채색유리 같은 것」(을 통하여 태양을 보듯, 오랜 세월이라는 그림자를 통하여 빛나는 천재의 모습을 살핀다).

upon principles demonstrative and scientific, but appealing wholly to observation and experience, no other test can be applied than length of duration and continuance of esteem. What mankind have long possessed they have often examined and compared; and if they persist to value the possession, it is because frequent comparisons have confirmed opinion in its favour.* As among the works of nature no man can properly call a river deep, or a mountain high, without the knowledge of many mountains, and many rivers; so in the productions of genius, nothing can be styled excellent till it has been compared with other works of the same kind.* Demonstration* immediately displays its power, and has nothing to hope or fear from the flux of years; but works tentative and experimental must be estimated by their proportion to the general and collective ability of man, as it is discovered in a long succession of endeavours. Of the first building that was raised, it might be with certainty determined that it was round or square; but whether it was spacious or lofty must have been referred to time. The Pythagorean scale of numbers was at once discovered to be perfect; but the poems of *Homer** we yet know not to transcend the common limits of human intelligence, but* by remarking, that nation after nation, and century after century, has been able to do little more than transpose his incidents, new-name his characters, and paraphrase his sentiments.

The reverence due to writings that have long subsisted arises therefore not from any credulous confidence in the superior wisdom of past ages, or gloomy persuasion of the degeneracy of

---

***in its favour:** 「그것이 좋다고 하는」(생각을 굳혔다). its는 the possession.

***nothing can...the same kind:** 같은 종류끼리의 비교에서 가치를 확인한다는 사상은 신고전주의의 법칙주의와는 상당한 차이가 있는 것이다. 같은 genre 안에서만 비교가 가능하다는 생각은 현대적 이론이다.

***Demonstration:** 「수학이나 과학의 증명」(진리냐 허위냐 하는 사실이 당장에 판명된다).

***the poems of Homer:** 다음의 know의 목적어.

***but:** except. 이 근처의 뜻은, 「Homer의 위대성〔transcend the common limit...〕에 대해서는 모든 후세대가 그의 모방에 그쳤다는 사실을 상기〔remarking〕하는 것 밖에는 달리 알 도리가 없다」.

mankind, but is the consequence of acknowledged and indubitable positions, that what has been longest known has been most considered, and what is most considered is best understood.

The Poet, of whose works I have undertaken the revision*, may now begin to assume the dignity of an ancient, and claim the privilege of established fame and prescriptive* veneration. He has long outlived his century, the term commonly fixed as the test of literary merit.* Whatever advantages he might once derive from personal allusions, local customs, or temporary opinions, have for many years been lost; and every topic of merriment, or motive of sorrow, which the modes of artificial life afforded him, now only obscure the scenes which they once illuminated. The effects of favour and competition are at an end; the tradition of his friendships and his enmities has perished; his works support no opinion with arguments, nor supply any faction with invectives; they can neither indulge vanity nor gratify malignity; but are read without any other reason than the desire of pleasure, and are therefore praised only as pleasure is obtained; yet, thus unassisted by interest or passion,* they have passed through variations of taste and changes of manners, and, as they devolved from one generation to another, have received new honours at every transmission.

But because human judgement, though it be gradually gaining upon certainty, never becomes infallible; and approbation, though long continued, may yet be only the approbation of prejudice or fashion; it is proper to inquire, by what peculiarities of excellence *Shakespeare* has gained and kept the favour of his countrymen.

Nothing can please many, and please long, but just represen-

***revision:** 「편찬」.

***prescriptive:** 「마땅한」.

***He has long outlived...literary merit:** 보통 사후 1세기가 지나도 명성이 죽지 않으면 위대한 작가라는 평가가 내려진 것이라는 생각. term: 「기간」(그 동안에 일시적인 요소는 다 사라진다).

***interest or passion:** 「사사로운 이해관계나 감정」(이것은 문학 작품의 진가를 알아보는 데 장애가 된다. *cf.* disinterestedness, impersonality).

tations of general nature. Particular manners can be known to few, and therefore few only can judge how nearly they are copied. The irregular combinations of fanciful invention may delight awhile, by that novelty of which the common satiety* of life sends us all in quest; but the pleasures of sudden wonder are soon exhausted, and the mind can only repose on the stability of truth.

Shakespeare is above all writers, at least above all modern writers, the poet of nature; the poet that holds up to his readers a faithful mirror of manners and of life. His characters are not modified by the customs of particular places, unpractised by the rest of the world; by the peculiarities of studies or professions, which can operate but upon small numbers; or by the accidents of transient fashions or temporary opinions: they are the genuine progeny of common humanity, such as the world will always supply, and observation will always find. His persons act and speak by the influence of those general passions and principles by which all minds are agitated, and the whole system of life is continued in motion. In the writings of other poets a character is too often an individual; in those of *Shakespeare* it is commonly a species.

It is from this wide extension of design that so much instruction is derived. It is this which fills the plays of *Shakespeare* with practical axioms and domestic wisdom. It was said of *Euripides*, that every verse was a precept; and it may be said of *Shakespeare*, that from his works may be collected a system of civil and economical prudence. Yet his real power is not shown in the splendour of particular passages, but by the progress of his fable, and the tenor of his dialogue; and he that tries to recommend him by select quotations, will succeed like the pedant in *Hierocles*,* who, when he offered his house to sale, carried a brick in his pocket as a specimen.

It will not easily be imagined how much *Shakespeare* excels in

---

*satiety: 「무미건조함」(인생의 무미건조함 때문에 우리는 신기한 것〔novelty〕을 찾게 되는데, 그런 기발한 것은 잠시 즐거울 뿐이다).

*Hierocles: 5세기 경의 Alexandria의 신플라톤주의자.

accommodating his sentiments to real life, but* by comparing him with other authors. It was observed of the ancient schools of declamation,* that the more diligently they were frequented, the more was the student disqualified for the world, because he found nothing there which he should ever meet in any other place. The same remark may be applied to every stage but that of *Shakespeare*. The theatre, when it is under any other direction, is peopled by such characters as were never seen, conversing in a language which was never heard, upon topics which will never arise in the commerce* of mankind. But the dialogue of this author is often so evidently determined by the incident which produces it, and is pursued with so much ease and simplicity, that it seems scarcely to claim the merit of fiction,* but to have been gleaned by diligent selection out of common conversation, and common occurrences.

Upon every other stage the universal agent is love, by whose power all good and evil is distributed, and every action quickened or retarded. To bring a lover, a lady and a rival into the fable; to entangle them in contradictory obligations, perplex them with oppositions of interest, and harass them with violence of desires inconsistent with each other; to make them meet in rapture and part in agony; to fill their mouths with hyperbolical joy and outrageous sorrow; to distress them as nothing human ever was distressed; to deliver them as nothing human ever was delivered; is the business of a modern dramatist. For this probability is violated, life is misrepresented, and language is depraved.* But love is only one of many passions;

***but:** except.

***schools of declamation:** 「웅변 학교」(이 학교에서는 괴상한 말투를 가르쳤기 때문에 학생이 그곳에 열심히 다닐수록 세상의 말씨와 멀어졌다는 것).

***commerce:** 사회관계.

***it seems...fiction:** 「허구가 잘 꾸며진 덕분에 작품이 잘 되었다고 보이지 않고」.

***upon every other stage...:** 근대문학의 고질적 특징은 사랑의 문제를 지나치게 많이 취급하는 것이라는 비판. 인생은 문학이 보여주는 것만큼 사랑의 문제로 가득찬 것이 아니므로 개연성〔probability〕이 파괴되며, 따라서 인생 자체도 그릇되게 표현되어진다는 것이다.

and as it has no great influence upon the sum of life, it has little operation in the dramas of a poet,* who caught his ideas from the living world, and exhibited only what he saw before him. He knew, that any other passion, as* it was regular or exorbitant, was a cause of happiness or calamity.

Characters thus ample and general were not easily discriminated and preserved, yet perhaps no poet ever kept his personages more distinct from each other. I will not say with *Pope*,* that every speech may be assigned to the proper speaker, because many speeches there are which have nothing characteristical; but perhaps, though some may be equally adapted to every person, it will be difficult to find any that can be properly transferred from the present possessor to another claimant. The choice is right, when there is reason for choice.

Other dramatists can only gain attention by hyperbolical or aggravated* characters, by fabulous and unexampled excellence or depravity, as the writers of barbarous romances invigorated* the reader by a giant and a dwarf; and he that should form his expectations of human affairs from the play, or from the tale, would be equally deceived. *Shakespeare* has no heroes; his scenes are occupied only by men, who act and speak as the reader thinks that he should himself have spoken or acted on the same occasion: Even where the agency is supernatural the dialogue is level with life. Other writers disguise the most natural passions and most frequent incidents; so that he who contemplates them in the book will not know them in the world: *Shakespeare* approximates the remote, and familiarizes the wonderful; the event which he represents will not happen, but if it were possible, its effects would probably be such as he

---

***a poet:** Shakespeare 자신.

***as:** according as.

***with *Pope*:** Pope가 편찬한 Shakespeare 전집(1725)의 서문. 이 글에서 Pope은 Shakespeare의 완전성을 믿은 나머지, 조금이라도 실수한 데가 있으면 그것을 원고나 인쇄의 잘못으로 돌리든가, 배우의 불완전한 기억 또는 다른 사람의 가필 때문에 생겨난 오류라고 단정하곤 했다.

***aggravated:** 「보통 이상으로 악한」.

***invigorate:** 「신나게 하다」.

has assigned*; and it may be said, that he has not only shown human nature as it acts in real exigencies, but as it would be found in trials, to which it cannot be exposed.*

This therefore is the praise of *Shakespeare*, that his drama is the mirror of life; that he who has mazed his imagination, in following the phantoms which other writers raise up before him, may here be cured of his delirious ecstasies, by reading human sentiments in human language, by scenes from which a hermit may estimate the transactions of the world,* and a confessor* predict the progress of the passions.

His adherence to general nature has exposed him to the censure of critics, who form their judgements upon narrower principles. *Dennis* and *Rhymer* think his *Romans* not sufficiently *Roman*; and *Voltaire* censures his kings as not completely royal. *Dennis* is offended, that *Menenius*, a senator of *Rome*, should play the buffoon; and *Voltaire* perhaps thinks decency violated when the *Danish* Usurper is represented as a drunkard.* But *Shakespeare* always makes nature predominate over accident; and if he preserves the essential character, is not very careful of distinctions superinduced and adventitious. His story requires Romans or kings, but he thinks only on men. He knew that

---

***assign:** attribute.

***he has not...cannot be exposed:** 「실제의 긴박한 상황에서 행동하는 대로의 인간성을 보여주었을 뿐만 아니라, 인간성이 실제로 겪을 수 없는 가상적 시련에 처했을 때의 개연적인 모습도 보여주었다」. 여기서 개연적인 모습을 "probability"라고 한다.

***by reading...of the world:** Shakespeare가 하도 세상사를 여실히 그려주고 있기 때문에, 세상사를 모르는 은둔자〔hermit〕조차 그를 읽으면 세상사를 알 수 있을 정도이다.

***confessor:** 카톨릭 교회의 고해를 듣는 신부, 즉 세속적 욕정을 모르는 사람.

***Dennis and Rymer...as a drunkard:** Thomas Rymer는 *A Short View of Tragedy*(1693)에서, John Dennis는 *An Essay on the Genius and Writings of Shakespeare* (1712)에서, 또한 Voltaire는 "L'Appel à toutes les Nations de l'Europe" (1761) 등에서, 주로 Shakespeare가 decorum을 지키지 않았다는 이유로 공격. 특히 Johnson은 Voltaire와 서로 논쟁을 벌였다. Menenius는 *Coriolanus*에 등장하는 인물이고, the Danish Usurper는 *Hamlet*에 등장하는 Claudius를 말한다.

Rome, like every other city, had men of all dispositions; and wanting a buffoon, he went into the senate-house for that which the senate-house would certainly have afforded him. He was inclined to show a usurper and a murderer not only odious but despicable, he therefore added drunkenness to his other qualities, knowing that kings love wine like other men, and that wine exerts its natural power upon kings. These are the petty cavils of petty minds; a poet overlooks the casual distinction of country and condition, as a painter, satisfied with the figure, neglects the drapery.

The censure which he has incurred by mixing comic and tragic scenes, as it extends to all his works, deserves more consideration. Let the fact be first stated, and then examined.

Shakespeare's plays are not in the rigorous and critical sense either tragedies or comedies, but compositions of a distinct kind; exhibiting the real state of sublunary nature, which partakes of good and evil, joy and sorrow, mingled with endless variety of proportion and innumerable modes of combination; and expressing the course of the world, in which the loss of one is the gain of another; in which, at the same time, the reveller is hasting to his wine, and the mourner burying his friend; in which the malignity of one is sometimes defeated by the frolic of another; and many mischiefs and many benefits are done and hindered without design.

Out of this chaos of mingled purposes and casualties, the ancient poets, according to the laws which custom had prescribed, selected some the crimes of men, and some their absurdities; some* the momentous vicissitudes of life, and some the lighter occurrences; some the terrors of distress, and some the gaieties of prosperity. Thus rose the two modes of imitation, known by the names of *tragedy* and *comedy*, compositions intended to promote different ends by contrary means, and considered as so little allied,* that I do not recollect among the *Greeks* or *Romans* a single writer who attempted both.

---

*some: 「고대시인〔ancient poets〕 중 어떤 이는」.
*allied: related.

Shakespeare has united the powers of exciting laughter and sorrow not only in one mind, but in one composition. Almost all his plays are divided between serious and ludicrous characters, and, in the successive evolutions of the design, sometimes produce seriousness and sorrow, and sometimes levity and laughter.

That this is a practice contrary to the rules of criticism* will be readily allowed; but there is always an appeal open from criticism to nature. The end of writing is to instruct; the end of poetry is to instruct by pleasing. That the mingled drama may convey all the instruction of tragedy or comedy cannot be denied, because it includes both in its alternations of exhibition and approaches nearer than either to the appearance of life, by showing how great machinations and slender designs may promote or obviate one another, and the high and the low co-operate in the general system by unavoidable concatenation.

It is objected, that by this change of scenes the passions are interrupted in their progression, and that the principal event, being not advanced by a due gradation of preparatory incidents, wants* at last the power to move, which constitutes the perfection of dramatic poetry. This reasoning is so specious,* that it is received as true even by those who in daily experience feel it to be false. The interchanges of mingled scenes seldom fail to produce the intended vicissitudes of passion. Fiction cannot move so much, but that the attention may be easily transferred; and though it must be allowed that* pleasing melancholy be sometimes interrupted by unwelcome levity, yet let it be considered likewise, that melancholy is often not pleasing, and that the disturbance of one man may be the relief

---

***rules of criticism:** decorum의 법칙을 말한다(Shakespeare가 이 법칙을 위반한 것을 대번에 시안할 수 있다).

***want:** 「모자라다」. 희극과 비극이 교차되면 단일한 감정이 점차적으로 전개되는 것을 막아 감동력이 적어진다는 설에 대하여 Johnson이 답변하고 있다.

***specious:** 「겉으로 보기엔 그럴 듯하나 거짓인」.

***but that:** unless. 독자의 주의가 여러 곳으로 옮겨갈 수 있어야만 허구는 재미가 있다.

of another; that different auditors have different habitudes; and that, upon the whole, all pleasure consists in variety.

The players,* who in their edition divided our author's works into comedies, histories, and tragedies,* seem not to have distinguished the three kinds by any very exact or definite ideas.

An action which ended happily to the principal persons, however serious or distressful through its intermediate incidents, in their opinion, constituted a comedy. This idea of a comedy continued long amongst us; and plays were written, which, by changing the catastrophe, were tragedies today, and comedies tomorrow.

Tragedy was not in those times a poem of more general dignity or elevation than comedy; it required only a calamitous conclusion, with which the common criticism of that age was satisfied, whatever lighter pleasure it afforded in its progress.

History was a series of actions, with no other than chronological succession, independent on* each other, and without any tendency to introduce or regulate the conclusion. It is not always very nicely distinguished from tragedy. There is not much nearer approach to unity of action in the tragedy of *Antony and Cleopatra*, than in the history of *Richard the Second*. But a history might be continued through many plays; as it had no plan, it had no limits.

Through all these denominations of the drama, *Shakespeare's* mode of composition is the same; an interchange of seriousness and merriment, by which the mind is softened at one time, and exhilarated at another. But whatever be his purpose, whether to gladden or depress, or to conduct the story, without vehemence or emotion, through tracts of easy and familiar dialogue, he never fails to attain his purpose; as he commands us, we laugh or mourn, or sit silent with quiet expectation, in tran-

---

***the players:** Shakespeare의 친구 배우였던 John Heminges와 Henry Condell. 이들은 1623년에 First Folio를 내면서 Shakespeare의 작품들을 희극, 사극, 비극으로 구분했다.

***on:** of.

quillity without indifference.

When *Shakespeare's* plan is understood, most of the criticisms of *Rhymer* and *Voltaire* vanish away. The play of *Hamlet* is opened, without impropriety, by two sentinels; *Iago* bellows at *Brabantio's* window, without injury to the scheme of the play, though in terms which a modern audience would not easily endure; the character of *Polonius* is seasonable and useful; and the Grave-diggers themselves may be heard with applause.

Shakespeare engaged in dramatic poetry with the world open before him; the rules of the ancients were yet known to few; the public judgement was unformed; he had no example of such fame as might force him upon* imitation, nor critics of such authority as might restrain his extravagance: He therefore indulged his natural disposition, and his disposition, as *Rhymer* has remarked, led him to comedy. In tragedy he often writes, with great appearance of toil and study, what is written at last with little felicity; but in his comic scenes, he seems to produce without labour, what no labour can improve.* In tragedy he is always struggling after some occasion to be comic; but in comedy he seems to repose, or to luxuriate, as in a mode of thinking congenial to his nature. In his tragic scenes there is always something wanting, but his comedy often surpasses expectation or desire. His comedy pleases by the thoughts and the language, and his tragedy for the greater part by incident and action. His tragedy seems to be skill, his comedy to be instinct.

The force of his comic scenes has suffered little diminution from the changes made by a century and a half, in manners or in words. As his personages act upon principles arising from genuine passion, very little modified by particular forms, their pleasures and vexations are communicable to all times and to all places; they are natural, and therefore durable; the adventitious peculiarities of personal habits are only superficial dyes, bright and pleasing for a little while, yet soon fading to a dim tinct, without any remains of former lustre: but the discrimina-

---

***upon:** to. 모방을 강요할 만한 유명한 모범 작가도 없었다.

***what...improve:** 「공들여 개선할 필요가 없는 것, 즉 완전한 것」.

tions of true passion are the colours of nature; they pervade the whole mass, and can only perish with the body that exhibits them. The accidental compositions of heterogeneous modes are dissolved by the chance which combined them; but the uniform simplicity of primitive qualities neither admits increase, nor suffers decay. The sand heaped by one flood is scattered by another, but the rock always continues in its place. The stream of time, which is continually washing the dissoluble fabrics of other poets, passes without injury by the adamant of *Shakespeare*.

If there be, what I believe there is, in every nation, a style which never becomes obsolete, a certain mode of phraseology so consonant and congenial to the analogy and principles of its respective language as to remain settled and unaltered; this style is probably to be sought in the common intercourse of life, among those who speak only to be understood, without ambition of elegance. The polite are always catching modish innovations, and the learned depart from established forms of speech, in hope of finding or making better; those who wish for distinction forsake the vulgar,* when the vulgar is right; but there is a conversation above grossness and below refinement, where propriety resides, and where this poet seems to have gathered his comic dialogue. He is therefore more agreeable to the ears of the present age any than other author equally remote, and among his other excellencies deserves to be studied as one of the original masters of our language.

These observations are to be considered not as unexceptionably constant, but as containing general and predominant truth. *Shakespeare's* familiar dialogue is affirmed to be smooth and clear, yet not wholly without ruggedness or difficulty; as a country may be eminently fruitful, though it has spots unfit for cultivation: His characters are praised as natural, though their sentiments are sometimes forced, and their actions improbable; as the earth upon the whole is spherical, though its surface is

---

***vulgar:** 도덕적 의미가 없이 단지 「일반인」을 뜻함. 언제나 변함없는 「일반인」의 언어에 비하여 상류층, 식자층의 언어는 유행적일 뿐이다.

varied with protuberances and cavities.

Shakespeare* with his excellences has likewise faults, and faults sufficient to obscure and overwhelm any other merit. I shall show them in the proportion in which they appear to me, without envious malignity or superstitious veneration. No question can be more innocently discussed than a dead poet's pretensions* to renown; and little regard is due to that bigotry which sets candour higher than truth.

His first defect is that to which may be imputed most of the evil in books or in men. He sacrifices virtue to convenience, and is so much more careful to please than to instruct, that he seems to write without any moral purpose. From his writings indeed a system of social duty may be selected, for he that thinks reasonably must think morally; but his precepts and axioms drop casually from him; he makes no just distribution of good or evil, nor is always careful to show in the virtuous a disapprobation of the wicked; he carries his persons indifferently through right and wrong, and at the close dismisses them without further care, and leaves their examples to operate by chance. This fault the barbarity of his age cannot extenuate; for it is always a writer's duty to make the world better, and justice is a virtue independent on time or place.*

The plots are often so loosely formed, that a very slight consideration may improve them, and so carelessly pursued, that he seems not always fully to comprehend his own design. He omits opportunities of instructing or delighting which the train of his story seems to force upon him, and apparently rejects those exhibitions which would be more affecting, for the sake of those which are more easy.

***pretensions:** (…의 자격이 있다는) 「주장」.

***little regard…than truth:** 객관적 진실보다도 주관적 (개인적) 솔직성을 더 높이 보는 고집스런 태도에는 주의를 별로 보낼 필요가 없다.

***His first defect…:** 고전주의 시대에는 poetic justice에 대한 요청이 컸는데, 이는 철저한 권선징악, 도덕적 논공행상을 강조한 것이다. 그러나 Shakespeare는 그와 같은 인위적 도덕율을 강권하지 않았는데, Johnson은 그것을 Shakespeare의 결점이라고 말하고 있다.

It may be observed, that in many of his plays the latter part is evidently neglected. When he found himself near the end of his work, and in view of his reward, he shortened the labour to snatch the profit. He therefore remits his efforts where he should most vigorously exert them, and his catastrophe is improbably produced or imperfectly represented.

He had no regard to distinction of time or place, but gives to one age or nation, without scruple, the customs, institutions, and opinions of another, at the expense not only of likelihood, but of possibility. These faults *Pope** has endeavoured, with more zeal than judgement, to transfer to his imagined interpolators. We need not wonder to find *Hector* quoting *Aristotle*,* when we see the loves of *Theseus* and *Hippolyta* combined with the *Gothic* mythology of fairies.* *Shakespeare*, indeed, was not the only violator of chronology, for in the same age *Sidney*, who wanted not the advantages of learning, has, in his *Arcadia*, confounded the pastoral with the feudal times, the days of innocence, quiet and security, with those of turbulence, violence, and adventure.

In his comic scenes he is seldom very successful when he engages his characters in reciprocations of smartness and contests of sarcasm; their jests are commonly gross, and their pleasantry licentious; neither his gentlemen nor his ladies have much delicacy, nor are sufficiently distinguished from his clowns by any appearance of refined manners. Whether he represented the real conversation of his time is not easy to determine; the reign of *Elizabeth* is commonly supposed to have been a time of stateliness, formality and reserve; yet perhaps the relaxations of that severity were not very elegant. There must, however, have been always some modes of gaiety preferable to others, and a writer ought to choose the best.

****Pope***: the preface to Pope's edition of *The Works of Shakespeare* (1725).

****Hector* quoting *Aristotle***: *Troilus and Cressida*, Ⅱ, ii, 166.

***the loves of…of fairies:** 말하자면 고대 그리이스의 신화와 중세 게르만의 신화가 결합된 모습을 볼 수 있다는 것으로, 이 대목은 *A Midsummer Night's Dream* 을 지칭하고 있다.

In tragedy his performance seems constantly to be worse, as his labour is more. The effusions of passion which exigence forces out are for the most part striking and energetic; but whenever he solicits his invention, or strains his faculties, the offspring of his throes is tumour, meanness, tediousness, and obscurity.

In narration he affects a disproportionate pomp of diction, and a wearisome train of circumlocution, and tells the incident imperfectly in many words, which might have been more plainly delivered in few. Narration in dramatic poetry is naturally tedious, as it is unanimated and inactive, and obstructs the progress of the action; it should therefore always be rapid, and enlivened by frequent interruption. *Shakespeare* found it an encumbrance, and instead of lightening it by brevity, endeavoured to recommend it by dignity and splendour.

His declamations or set speeches are commonly cold and weak, for his power was the power of nature; when he endeavoured, like other tragic writers, to catch opportunities of amplification,* and instead of inquiring what the occasion demanded, to show how much his stores of knowledge could supply, he seldom escapes without the pity or resentment of his reader.

It is incident* to him to be now and then entangled with an unwieldy sentiment, which he cannot well express, and will not reject; he struggles with it a while, and if it continues stubborn, comprises it in words such as occur,* and leaves it to be disentangled and evolved by those* who have more leisure to bestow upon it.

Not that always where the language is intricate the thought is subtle, or the image always great where the line is bulky; the equality* of words to things is very often neglected, and trivial

---

***amplification:** 수사법의 하나로 말을 길게 확충, 부연함.
***incident to...:** 「...에 흔히 있는」.
***occur:** 「우연히 생각나다」.
***those:** 즉 Shakespeare 주석자.
***equality:** 여기서는 「일치」.

sentiments and vulgar ideas disappoint the attention, to which they are* recommended by sonorous epithets and swelling figures.

But the admirers of this great poet have never less reason to indulge their hopes of supreme excellence, than when he seems fully resolved to sink them in dejection, and mollify them with tender emotions by the fall of greatness, the danger of innocence, or the crosses* of love. He is not long soft and pathetic without some idle conceit, or contemptible equivocation. He no sooner begins to move, than he counteracts himself; and terror and pity, as they are rising in the mind, are checked and blasted by sudden frigidity.

A quibble is to *Shakespeare*, what luminous vapours* are to the traveller; he follows it at all adventures; it is sure to lead him out of his way, and sure to engulf him in the mire. It has some malignant power over his mind, and its fascinations are irresistible. Whatever be the dignity or profundity of his disquisition, whether he be enlarging knowledge or exalting affection, whether he be amusing attention with incidents, or enchaining it in suspense, let but a quibble spring up before him, and he leaves his work unfinished. A quibble is the golden apple for which he will always turn aside from his career, or stoop from his elevation. A quibble, poor and barren as it is, gave him such delight, that he was content to purchase it, by the sacrifice of reason, propriety and truth. A quibble was to him the fatal *Cleopatra** for which he lost the world, and was content to lose it.

It will be thought strange, that, in enumerating the defects of this writer, I have not yet mentioned his neglect of the unities; his violation of those laws which have been instituted and established by the joint authority of poets and of critics.

***they:** 의미상 the attention을 가리키니까, it이어야 한다.

***the crosses of love:** 「사랑의 어긋남, 실패」.

***luminous vapour:** 길손을 유혹하는 도깨비불. Shakespeare의 말장난 (quibble)은 천박할 때가 많다.

***A quibble...to lost it:** 희대의 영웅 Antony가 요부 Cleopatra에게 혹하여 모든 야망을 버린 고사. Shakespeare 자신이 그 내용을 희곡으로 썼다.

For his other deviations from the art of writing I resign him to critical justice, without making any other demand in his favour, than that which must be indulged* to all human excellence: that his virtues be rated with his failings: But, from the censure which this irregularity may bring upon him, I shall, with due reverence to that learning* which I must oppose, adventure to try how I can defend him.

His histories, being neither tragedies nor comedies, are not subject to any of their laws; nothing more is necessary to all the praise which they expect, than that the changes of action be so prepared as to be understood, that the incidents be various and affecting, and the characters consistent, natural, and distinct. No other unity is intended, and therefore none is to be sought.

In his other works he has well enough preserved the unity of action. He has not, indeed, an intrigue regularly perplexed and regularly unravelled: he does not endeavour to hide his design only to discover it, for this is seldom the order of real events, and *Shakespeare* is the poet of nature.* But his plan has commonly what *Aristotle* requires, a beginning, a middle, and an end; one event is concatenated with another, and the conclusion follows by easy consequence. There are perhaps some incidents that might be spared,* as in other poets there is much talk that only fills up time upon the stage; but the general system makes gradual advances, and the end of the play is the end of expectation.

To the unities of time and place he has shown no regard; and perhaps a nearer view of the principles on which they stand will

---

***indulge:** 「허용하다」(모든 사람의 우수성에 반드시 따르기 마련이라는 사실을 인정해야 한다는 요청을 할 뿐이다).

***learning:** 「유식한 이론」. 즉, 3일치의 법칙 등의 희곡이론.

***In his other works...the poet of nature:** Shakespeare를 칭찬하면서 당시 프랑스 희곡의 인위성과 조작성을 비꼬고 있다. 규칙적으로 얽어놓았다가 규칙적으로 풀어놓고, 계략을 꾸민 척했다가 빤히 들여다보이는 방법으로 드러내는 것은 인생의 진면목(order of real events)이 아니라는 것이다.

***that...spared**: 「없어도 될」(사건들). Shakespeare의 작품 속에는 생략해도 무방한 부분이 있지만, 그러나 대체로 action의 통일성을 기하고 있다.

diminish their value, and withdraw* from them the veneration which, from the time of *Corneille*, they have very generally received, by discovering* that they have given more trouble to the poet, than pleasure to the auditor.

The necessity of observing the unities of time and place arises from the supposed necessity of making the drama credible. The critics hold it impossible, that an action of months or years can be possibly believed to pass in three hours; or that the spectator can suppose himself to sit in the theatre, while ambassadors go and return between distant kings, while armies are levied and towns besieged, while an exile wanders and returns, or till he whom they saw courting his mistress, shall lament the untimely fall of his son. The mind revolts from evident falsehood, and fiction loses its force when it departs from the resemblance of reality.

From the narrow limitation of time necessarily arises the contraction of place. The spectator, who knows that he saw the first act at *Alexandria*, cannot suppose that he sees the next at *Rome*, at a distance to which not the dragons of *Medea** could, in so short a time, have transported him; he knows with certainty that he has not changed his place, and he knows that place cannot change itself; that what was a house cannot become a plain; that what was *Thebes* can never be *Persepolis**.

Such is the triumphant language with which a critic exults over the misery of an irregular poet,* and exults commonly without resistance or reply.* It is time therefore to tell him by the authority of *Shakespeare*, that he assumes, as an unquestionable principle, a position,* which, while his breath is forming it

---

***withdraw:** 「제거하다」. 즉, 시간과 장소의 통일에다 주어지는·존중심을 제거하다.

***by discovering:** (법칙들이 청중에게 즐거움을 더해 주는 것보다는 작가에게 어려움을 더 많이 주었다는 것을) 「드러냄으로써」.

***dragons of Medea:** (그리이스 신화) 요부 Medea를 태우고 달아나는 용.

***Persepolis:** Persia의 고대 도시.

***Such is...or reply:** 비평가가 규칙을 안 지킨〔irregular〕 불쌍한 작가들을 꼼짝 못하게 공박하며 신나서 떠드는 소리〔triumphant language〕가 바로 이렇다. Johnson의 비꼬는 말.

***position:** 「전제」(말은 그렇게 하지만 잘 이해하여 보면 가짜인).

into words, his understanding pronounces to be false. It is false, that any representation is mistaken for reality; that any dramatic fable in its materiality* was ever credible, or, for a single moment, was ever credited.

The objection arising from the impossibility of passing the first hour at *Alexandria*, and the next at *Rome*, supposes,* that when the play opens, the spectator really imagines himself at *Alexandria*, and believes that his walk to the theatre has been a voyage to Egypt, and that he lives in the days of *Antony* and *Cleopatra*. Surely he that imagines this may imagine more. He that can take the stage at one time* for the palace of the *Ptolemies*,* may take it in half an hour for the promontory of *Actium*.* Delusion, if delusion be admitted, has no certain limitation; if the spectator can be once persuaded, that his old acquaintance are *Alexander* and *Caesar*, that a room illuminated with candles is the plain of *Pharsalia*,* or the bank of *Granicus*,* he is in a state of elevation above the reach of reason, or of truth, and from the heights of empyrean poetry, may despise the circumscriptions of terrestrial nature. There is no reason why a mind thus wandering in ecstasy should count the clock, or why an hour should not be a century in that calenture* of the brains that can make the stage a field.

The truth is, that the spectators are always in their senses, and know, from the first act to the last, that the stage is only a stage, and that the players are only players. They came to hear a certain number of lines recited with just gesture and elegant

---

*in its materiality: 「액면 그대로의」(희곡 이야기).
*suppose: 「전제하다」.
*at one time: 「일단」(=once).
*Ptolemies: Egypt의 왕가. Cleopatra도 이 왕가에 속해 있었다.
*Actium: 그리이스 서북방의 곶. Cleopatra와 Antony의 군대가 로마군에게 패한 곳.
*Pharsalia: 그리이스 동북방의 지역. Caesar가 Pompey를 무찌른 곳.
*Granicus: 터어키에 있는 강 이름. Alexander 대왕이 Persia 대군을 쳐부수고, 후에 로마 장군 Lucullus가 Pontus의 왕 Mithridates의 군대를 쳐부순 곳.
*calenture: 「일사병」. 심한 흥분 상태.

modulation. The lines relate to some action, and an action must be in some place; but the different actions that complete a story may be in places very remote from each other; and where is the absurdity* of allowing that space to represent first *Athens*, and then *Sicily*, which was always known to be neither *Sicily* nor *Athens*, but a modern theatre?

By supposition, as place is introduced, time may be extended; the time required by the fable elapses for the most part between the acts; for, of so much of the action as is represented, the real and poetical duration is the same. If, in the first act, preparations for war against *Mithridates* are represented to be made in *Rome*, the event of the war may, without absurdity, be represented, in the catastrophe, as happening in *Pontus*; we know that there is neither war, nor preparation for war; we know that we are neither in *Rome* nor *Pontus*; that neither *Mithridates* nor *Lucullus* are before us. The drama exhibits successive imitations of successive actions; and why may not the second imitation represent an action that happened years after the first, if it be so connected with it, that nothing but time can be supposed to intervene? Time is, of all modes of existence, most obsequious to the imagination; a lapse of years is as easily conceived as a passage of hours. In contemplation we easily contract the time of real actions, and therefore willingly permit it to be contracted when we only see their imitation.

It will be asked, how the drama moves, if it is not credited. It is credited with all the credit due to a drama. It is credited, whenever it moves, as a just picture of a real original; as representing to the auditor what he would himself feel, if he were to do or suffer what is there feigned to be suffered or to be done. The reflection that strikes the heart is not, that the evils before us are real evils, but that they are evils to which we ourselves may be exposed. If there be any fallacy, it is not that we fancy the players,* but that we fancy ourselves unhappy for a moment;

***where is the absurdity:** 「무슨 이상할 데가 있느냐」. 즉, 이상할 것 없다.
***Rome nor Pontus…Mithridates nor Lucullus:** 앞에 나온 Granicus 강에 대한 주를 보라.
***players:** 다음에 unhappy를 넣어서 읽을 것.

but we rather lament the possibility than suppose the presence of misery, as a mother weeps over her babe, when she remembers that death may take it from her. The delight of tragedy proceeds from our consciousness of fiction; if we thought murders and treasons real, they would please no more.

Imitations produce pain or pleasure, not because they are mistaken for realities, but because they bring realities to mind. When the imagination is recreated by a painted landscape, the trees are not supposed capable to give us shade, or the fountains coolness; but we consider, how we should be pleased with such fountains playing beside us, and such woods waving over us. We are agitated in reading the history of *Henry* the Fifth, yet no man takes his book for the field of *Agincourt.** A dramatic exhibition is a book recited with concomitants that increase or diminish its effect. Familiar comedy is often more powerful on the theatre, than in the page; imperial tragedy is always less. The humour of *Petruchio** may be heightened by grimace; but what voice or what gesture can hope to add dignity or force to the soliloquy of *Cato.**

A play read, affects the mind like a play acted. It is therefore evident, that the action is not supposed to be real; and it follows, that between the acts a longer or shorter time may be allowed to pass, and that no more account of space or duration is to be taken by the auditor of a drama, than by the reader of a narrative, before whom may pass in an hour the life of a hero, or the revolutions of an empire.

Whether *Shakespeare* knew the unities, and rejected them by design, or deviated from them by happy ignorance, it is, I think, impossible to decide, and useless to inquire. We may reasonably suppose, that, when he rose to notice,* he did not

---

***Agincourt:** 프랑스 북부에 있는 도시. 1415년 영국의 Henry V가 승전한 곳.

***Petruchio:** Shakespeare의 *Taming of the Shrew*에 나오는 희극적 인물.

***Cato:** Addison의 고전적 비극 *Cato*의 주인공. Johnson은 비극보다는 희극이 더 무대 상연에 알맞다고 본다. Shakespeare의 비극에 대해서도 그렇게 보았다.

***when he rose to notice:** 「유명해졌을 때」.

want* the counsels and admonitions of scholars and critics, and that he at last deliberately persisted in a practice, which he might have begun by chance. As nothing is essential to the fable, but unity of action, and as the unities of time and place arise evidently from false assumptions, and, by circumscribing the extent of the drama, lessen its variety, I cannot think it much to be lamented, that they were not known by him, or not observed: Nor, if such another poet could arise, should I very vehemently reproach him, that his first act passed at *Venice*, and his next in *Cyprus*. Such violations of rules merely positive,* become* the comprehensive genius of *Shakespeare*, and such censures are suitable to the minute and slender criticism of *Voltaire*:

> Non usque adeo permiscuit imis
> Longus summa dies, ut non, si voce Metelli
> Serventur leges, malint a Caesare tolli.*

Yet when I speak thus slightly of dramatic rules, I cannot but recollect how much wit and learning may be produced against me; before such authorities I am afraid to stand, not that I think the present question one of those that are to be decided by mere authority, but because it is to be suspected, that these precepts* have not been so easily received but for better reasons than I have yet been able to find. The result of my inquiries, in which it would be ludicrous to boast of impartiality, is, that the unities of time and place are not essential to a just drama, that though they may sometimes conduce to pleasure, they are always to be sacrificed to the nobler beauties of variety and instruction; and that a play, written with nice observation of critical rules, is to be con-

---

***want:** 원하다의 뜻이 아니라, 「모자라다, 없다」의 뜻.
***positive:** artificial
***become:** 「~에 어울리다, 알맞다」.
******Non usque*...: 'The course of time has not wrought such confusion that the laws would not rather be trampled on by Caesar than saved by Metellus' (Lucan, *The Civil War*, Ⅲ, 138).
***precepts:** 다음에 would를 넣어 읽을 것 (would not have been).

templated as an elaborate curiosity, as the product of superfluous and ostentatious art, by which is shown, rather what is possible, than what is necessary.

He that, without diminution of any other excellence, shall preserve all the unities unbroken, deserves the like* applause with the architect, who shall display all the orders of architecture in a citadel, without any deduction from its strength; but the principal beauty of a citadel is to exclude the enemy; and the greatest graces of a play, are to copy nature and instruct life.

Perhaps, what I have here not dogmatically but deliberately written, may recall the principles of the drama to a new examination. I am almost frighted at my own temerity; and when I estimate the fame and the strength of those that maintain the contrary opinion, am ready to sink down in reverential silence; as *Aeneas* withdrew from the defence of *Troy*, when he saw *Neptune* shaking the wall, and *Juno* heading the besiegers.*

Those whom my arguments cannot persuade to give their approbation to the judgement of *Shakespeare*, will easily, if they consider the condition of his life, make some allowance for his ignorance.

Every man's performances, to be rightly estimated, must be compared with the state of the age in which he lived, and with his own particular opportunities; and though to the reader a book be not worse or better for the circumstances of the author, yet as there is always a silent reference of human works to human abilities, and as the inquiry, how far man may extend his designs, or how high he may rate his native force, is of far greater dignity than in what rank we shall place any particular performance, curiosity is always busy to discover the instruments, as well as to survey the workmanship, to know how much is to be ascribed to original powers, and how much to casual and adventitious help. The palaces of *Peru* or *Mexico* were certainly mean and incommodious habitations, if com-

---

*like: same. citadel은 방어용이니까 화려한 장식은 실상 필요없는 것. 마찬가지로 장소, 시간의 통일은 재치를 보인 장식에 불과하다는 것.

*as Aeneas...the besiegers: Virgil, *Aeneid*, II, 610—14.

pared to the houses of *European* monarchs; yet who could forbear to view them with astonishment, who remembered that they were built without the use of iron?*

The *English* nation, in the time of *Shakespeare*, was yet struggling to emerge from barbarity. The philology*of *Italy* had been transplanted hither in the reign of *Henry* the Eighth; and the learned languages had been successfully cultivated by *Lily*, *Linacre*, and *More*; by *Pole*, *Cheke*, and *Gardiner*; and afterwards by *Smith*, *Clerk*, *Haddon*, and *Ascham*.* Greek was now taught to boys in the principal schools; and those who united elegance with learning, read, with great diligence, the *Italian* and *Spanish* poets. But literature was yet confined to professed scholars, or to men and women of high rank. The public was gross and dark; and to be able to read and write, was an accomplishment still valued for its rarity.

Nations, like individuals, have their infancy. A people newly awakened to literary curiosity, being yet unacquainted with the true state of things, knows not how to judge of that which is proposed as its resemblance. Whatever is remote from common appearances is always welcome to vulgar, as to childish credulity; and of a country unenlightened by learning, the whole people is the vulgar. The study of those who then aspired to plebeian learning was laid out upon adventures, giants, dragons, and enchantments. *The Death of Arthur**was the favourite volume.

The mind, which has feasted on the luxurious wonders of fiction, has no taste of the insipidity of truth. A play which imitated only the common occurrences of the world, would, upon the admirers of *Palmerin* and *Guy* of *Warwick*,* have made

---

***Every man's performance...:** 절대적 비평 원칙을 적용하지 않고 역사적 상대성을 인정하는 비평 태도는 당시로서는 상당히 새로운 것이었다.

***philology:** 문헌연구.

***Lilly, Linaucre,...Ascham:** 이들은 모두 영국의 15세기 초반에 활약한 인문학자들.

****The Death of Arthur*:** Sir Thomas Malory의 중세 문학작품. 신고전주의자들은 모두 중세의 문학을 무식의 소치로 경멸하였다.

****Palmerin, Guy of Warwick*:** 모두 중세의 로망스.

little impression; he that wrote for such an audience was under the necessity of looking round for strange events and fabulous transactions, and that incredibility, by which maturer knowledge is offended, was the chief recommendation of writings, to unskilful curiosity.

Our author's plots are generally borrowed from novels, and it is reasonable to suppose, that he chose the most popular, such as were read by many, and related by more; for his audience could not have followed him through the intricacies of the drama, had they not held the thread of the story in their hands.

The stories, which we now find only in remoter authors, were in his time accessible and familiar. The fable of *As You Like It*, which is supposed to be copied from *Chaucer's* Gamelyn,* was a little pamphlet of those times; and old Mr. *Cibber** remembered the tale of *Hamlet* in plain *English* prose, which the critics have now to seek in *Saxo Grammaticus*.*

His *English* histories he took from *English* chronicles and *English* ballads; and as the ancient writers were made known to his countrymen by versions, they supplied him with new subjects; he dilated some of *Plutarch's* lives into plays, when they had been translated by *North*.*

His plots, whether historical or fabulous, are always crowded with incidents, by which the attention of a rude people was more easily caught than by sentiment or argumentation; and such is the power of the marvellous even over those who despise it, that every man finds his mind more strongly seized by the tragedies of *Shakespeare* than of any other writer; others please us by particular speeches, but he always makes us anxious for the event, and has perhaps excelled all but *Homer* in securing the first purpose of a writer, by exciting restless and unquench-

---

***Gamelyn:** *The Tale of Gamelyn*은 Johnson 시대까지도 Chaucer의 작품으로 알려져 왔었으나, 작자 미상의 작품으로 밝혀졌음.

***Cibber, Colley:** (1671-1757). 배우, 극작가.

***Saxo Grammaticus:** 12세기의 역사가. 그가 쓴 〈덴마크의 역사〉에 Hamlet 이야기가 나온다.

***Plutarch's Lives...by North:** Sir Thomas North가 1579년에 Plutarch의 *Lives*(영웅전)을 번역했다.

able curiosity and compelling him that reads his work to read it through.

The shows and bustle with which his plays abound have the same original. As knowledge advances, pleasure passes from the eye to the ear, but returns, as it declines, from the ear to the eye. Those to whom our author's labours were exhibited had more skill in pomps or processions than in poetical language, and perhaps wanted some visible and discriminated events, as comments on the dialogue. He knew how he should most please; and whether his practice is more agreeable to nature, or whether his example has prejudiced the nation, we still find that on our stage something must be done as well as said, and inactive declamation is very coldly heard, however musical or elegant, passionate or sublime.

*Voltaire** expresses his wonder, that our author's extravagances are endured by a nation, which has seen the tragedy of *Cato*. Let him be answered, that *Addison* speaks the language of poets, and *Shakespeare*, of men. We find in *Cato* innumerable beauties which enamour us of its author, but we see nothing that acquaints us with human sentiments or human actions; we place it with the fairest and the noblest progeny which judgement propagates by conjunction with learning, but *Othello* is the vigorous and vivacious offspring of observation impregnated by genius. *Cato* affords a splendid exhibition of artificial and fictitious manners, and delivers just and noble sentiments, in diction easy, elevated and harmonious, but its hopes and fears communicate no vibration to the heart; the composition refers us only to the writer; we pronounce the name of *Cato*, but we think on *Addison*......

****Voltaire*...**: 여기에 나온 Voltaire의 언급은, *Lettres sur les Anglais* (1734), XVIII에 나온다.

From Life of Cowley* (1779-81)

COWLEY, like other poets who have written with narrow views, and, instead of tracing intellectual pleasures in the mind of man, paid their court to temporary prejudices, has been at one time too much praised, and too much neglected at another.

Wit, like all other things subject by their nature to the choice of man, has its changes and fashions, and at different times takes different forms. About the beginning of the seventeenth century appeared a race of writers that may be termed the *metaphysical poets,* of whom, in a criticism on the works of Cowley, it is not improper to give some account.

The metaphysical poets were men of learning, and to show their learning was their whole endeavour; but, unluckily resolving to show it in rhyme, instead of writing poetry they only wrote verses, and very often such verses as stood the trial of the finger better than of the ear;* for the modulation was so imperfect, that they were only found to be verses by counting the syllables.

If the father of criticism* has rightly denominated poetry *an imitative art,* these writers will, without great wrong, lose their right to the name of poets, for they cannot be said to have imitated anything; they neither copied nature nor life, neither painted the forms of matter, nor represented the operations of intellect.

---

*본 비평문은 *Lives of English poets* (1779-81) 중 *Life of Cowley*에서 뽑은 것임. 근본에 있어 Abraham Cowley (1618-67)는 "metaphysical poet"라 할 수 없으나, Johnson은 Cowley의 시의 특징을 논하는 가운데 metaphysical poetry에 대한 이론을 폈는데, 현대의 이론이 이에서 출발하고 있을 만큼 중요한 비평이라 하겠다.

***such verses...of the ear:** 그 리듬은 귀로 들어서 파악할 수 있는 것이 아니라, 손가락으로 음절의 수를 세어서 파악할 수 있다는 견해. 그러나 metaphysical poetry의 리듬은 특수한 효과를 노린 것이었음이 지금은 잘 밝혀져 있다.

***the father of criticism:** 즉, Aristotle.

Those, however, who deny them to be poets, allow them to be wits. Dryden confesses of* himself and his contemporaries, that they fall below Donne in wit, but maintains that they surpass him in poetry.

If wit be well described by Pope, as being "that which has been often thought, but was never before so well expressed," they certainly never attained, nor ever sought it; for they endeavoured to be singular in their thoughts, and were careless of their diction. But Pope's account of wit is undoubtedly erroneous: he depresses it below its natural dignity, and reduces it from strength of thought to happiness of language.*

If by a more noble and more adequate conception that be considered as wit which is at once natural and new, that which, though not obvious, is, upon its first production, acknowledged to be just; if it be that* which he that never found it wonders how he missed, to wit of this kind the metaphysical poets have seldom risen. Their thoughts are often new, but seldom natural; they are not obvious, but neither are they just; and the reader, far from wondering that he missed them, wonders more frequently by what perverseness of industry they were ever found.

But wit, abstracted from its effects upon the hearer, may be more rigorously and philosophically considered as a kind of *discordia concors;* a combination of dissimilar images, or discovery of occult resemblances in things apparently unlike. Of wit, thus defined, they have more than enough. The most hetrogeneous ideas are yoked by violence together; nature and art are ransacked for illustrations, comparisons, and allusions; their learning instructs, and their subtlety surprises; but the reader commonly thinks his improvement dearly bought, and, though he sometimes admires, is seldom pleased.*

***of:** about.

***If wit be well...happiness of language:** Pope, *Essay on Criticism*, 297—8 행을 볼 것.

***that:** 다음에 오는 which 이하의 선행사.

****discordia concors*:** 'harmonious discord'.

From this account of their compositions it will be readily inferred that they were not successful in representing or moving the affections. As they were wholly employed on something unexpected and surprising, they had no regard to that uniformity of sentiment which enables us to conceive and to excite the pains and the pleasure of other minds: they never inquired what, on any occasion, they should have said or done, but wrote rather as beholders than partakers of human nature; as beings looking upon good and evil, impassive and at leisure; as Epicurean deities,* making remarks on the actions of men, and the vicissitudes of life, without interest and without emotion. Their courtship was void of fondness, and their lamentation of sorrow.* Their wish was only to say what they hoped had been never said before.

Nor was the sublime more within their reach than the pathetic; for they never attempted that comprehension and expanse of thought which at once fills the whole mind, and of which the first effect is sudden astonishment, and the second rational admiration. Sublimity is produced by aggregation, and littleness by dispersion. Great thoughts are always general, and consist in positions not limited by exceptions, and in descriptions not descending to minuteness. It is with great propriety that subtlety, which in its original import means exility* of particles, is taken in its metaphorical meaning for nicety of distinction. Those writers who lay on the watch for* novelty could have little hope of greatness; for great things cannot have escaped former observation. Their attempts were always analytic; they broke every image into fragment; and could no more represent, by their slender con-

---

***the reader...seldom pleased:** 독자는 자기가 그 wit에서 배운 바(improvement)가 값비싼 댓가를 치른 것으로 느낀다(배운 내용은 별로 없이 이해하는 데 힘만 들였다).

***Epicurean deities:** 「쾌락주의자적 신들」. (신이 쾌락주의자가 된다면 인간사에 대하여 구경만 하고 있을 것이다).

***Their courtship...sorrow:** 「그들의 연애는 애정적 탐닉도, 한탄의 슬픔도 없다」.

***exility:** smallness.

***lay on the watch for...:** 「...을 노리다」.

ceits and laboured particularities, the prospects of nature, or the scenes of life, than he who dissects a sunbeam with a prism can exhibit the wide effulgence of a summer noon.

What they wanted* however of the sublime, they endeavoured to supply by hyperbole; their amplification had no limits; they left not only reason but fancy behind them; and produced combinations of confused magnificence, that not only could not be credited, but could not be imagined.

Yet great labour, directed by great abilities, is never wholly lost: if they frequently threw away their wit upon false conceits, they likewise sometimes struck out unexpected truth; if their conceits were far-fetched, they were often worth the carriage.* To write on their plan, it was at least necessary to read and think. No man could be born a metaphysical poet, nor assume the dignity of a writer, by descriptions copied from descriptions, by imitations borrowed from imitations, by traditional imagery, and hereditary similes, by readiness of rhyme, and volubility of syllables.

In perusing the works of this race of authors, the mind is exercised either by recollection or inquiry; either something already learned is to be retrieved, or something new is to be examined. If their greatness seldom elevates, their acuteness often surprises; if the imagination is not always gratified, at least the powers of reflection and comparison are employed; and in the mass of materials which ingenious absurdity has thrown together, genuine wit and useful knowledge may be sometimes found buried perhaps in grossness of expression, but useful to those who know their value; and such as, when they are expanded to perspicuity, and polished to elegance, may give lustre to works which have more propriety though less copiousness of sentiment.

***want:** 「부족하다」 (...of).

***if their conceits...the carriage:** conceits가 far-fetched였다면 그걸 멀리서 가져온 보람은 있었다.

Sir Joshua Reynolds

(1723—1792)

목사의 아들로 태어나 이탈리아에서 미술 공부를 한 당대 최고의 초상화가로, Royal Academy of Arts의 초대 회장을 지냈다. 존슨의 클럽의 일원으로 있으면서 그로부터 폭넓은 고전적 보편주의 예술관을 터득했고, 1769-1790년 간 미술학도들에게 행한 15회의 *Discourses*에 그의 예술관이 잘 표현되어 있다.

그는 인간성의 계발, 보편성의 제시 등 고전주의의 이념을 그의 예술론의 요체로 삼고 있으면서도, 개인의 상상력과 감수성에 궁극적 강조점을 둠으로써, 그의 경험주의적이고도 자유로운 태도를 보이고 있다. 그는 18세기 말, 신고전주의의 교조적 경향이 설득력을 잃어가던 시기에, 새로운 예술관의 태동을 느끼고 있었던 듯싶다. 자연에의 복속이 아닌, 자연으로부터의 벗어남(deviation), 또는 자연을 능가함을 예술의 힘으로 상정한다는 것은 이상주의 예술관, 곧 시드니가 가졌던 것같은 신플라톤 사상의 회복을 암시하며 또한 낭만주의의 이념을 내다보는 것이기도 한다.

레놀즈의 초기 *Discourses*와 비교해볼 때, 여기 실린 후기의 것이 얼마나 더 "낭만적"으로 되어 있는가를 쉽게 알아보게 된다. 그 자신이 젊은 시절보다 훨씬 더 자유주의자가 된 것이다. 예술관의 급격한 변화를 볼 수 있다.

Discourse XIII (1786)

Delivered to the Students of the Royal Academy, on the Distribution of the Prizes, December 11, 1786

Art not merely Imitation, but under the Direction of the Imagination. In what Manner Poetry, Painting, Acting, Gardening, and Architecture depart from Nature

GENTLEMEN,

To discover beauties, or to point out faults, in the works of celebrated masters, and to compare the conduct of one artist with another, is certainly no mean or inconsiderable part of criticism; but this is still no more than to know the art through the artist. This test of investigation must have two capital defects; it must be narrow, and it must be uncertain. To enlarge the boundaries of the art of painting, as well as to fix its principles, it will be necessary, that *that* art and *those* principles* should be considered in their correspondence with the principles of the other arts which, like this, address themselves primarily and principally to the imagination* When those connected and kindred principles are brought together to be compared, another comparison will grow out of this; that is, the comparison of them all with those of human nature, from whence arts derive the materials upon which they are to produce their effects.

When this comparison of art with art, and of all arts with the nature of man, is once made with success, our guiding lines are as well ascertained and established, as they can be in matters of this description.*

This, as it is the highest style of criticism, is at the same time the soundest; for it refers to the eternal and immutable nature of things.

You are not to imagine that I mean to open to you at large, or to recommend to your research, the whole of this vast field of science. It is certainly much above my faculties to reach it; and though it may not be above yours to comprehend it fully, if it were fully and properly brought before you, yet perhaps the most perfect criticism requires habits of speculation and abstraction, not very consistent with the employment which ought to occupy and the habits of mind which

---

***that art and those principles:** 뒤에 나오는 which의 선행사.

***address themselves...to** (the imagination): (상상과) 직접 관련을 맺다.

***description:** 「종류」. Reynolds는 현대적 aesthetics의 형성을 상정하고 있다.

ought to prevail in a practical artist. I only point out to you these things, that when you do criticise (as all who work on a plan will criticise more or less), your criticism may be built on the foundation of true principles; and that though you may not always travel a great way, the way that you do travel may be the right road.

I observe, as a fundamental ground, common to all the arts with which we have any concern in this discourse, that they address themselves only to two faculties of the mind, its imagination and its sensibility.

All theories which attempt to direct or to control the art, upon any principles falsely called rational, which we form to ourselves upon a supposition of what ought in reason to be the end or means of art, independent of the known first effect produced by objects on the imagination, must be false and delusive. For though it may appear bold to say it, the imagination is here the residence of truth. If the imagination be affected, the conclusion is fairly drawn; if it be not affected, the reasoning is erroneous, because the end is not obtained; the effect itself being the test, and the only test, of the truth and efficacy of the means.

There is in the commerce of life, as in art, a sagacity which is far from being contradictory to right reason, and is superior to any occasional exercise of that faculty;* which supersedes it; and does not wait for the slow progress of deduction, but goes at once, by what appears a kind of intuition, to the conclusion. A man endowed with this faculty feels and acknowledges the truth, though it is not always in his power, perhaps, to give a reason for it; because he cannot recollect and bring before him all the materials that gave birth to his opinion; for very many and very intricate considerations may unite to form the principle, even of small and minute parts, involved in, or dependent on, a great system of things: though these in process of time are forgotten, the right impression still remains fixed in his mind.

***that faculty:** right reason. 빠른 직관을 느린 reason(이성)보다 우위에 두고 있다.

This impression is the result of the accumulated experience of our whole life, and has been collected, we do not always know how, or when. But this mass of collective observation, however acquired, ought to prevail over that reason, which, however powerfully exerted on any particular occasion, will probably comprehend but a partial view of the subject; and our conduct in life as well as in the arts is, or ought to be, generally governed by this habitual reason; it is our happiness that we are enabled to draw on such funds.* If we were obliged to enter into a theoretical deliberation on every occasion, before we act, life would be at a stand, and art would be impracticable.

It appears to me, therefore, that our first thoughts, that is, the effect which anything produces on our minds, on its first appearance, is never to be forgotten; and it demands for that reason, because it is the first, to be laid up with care.* If this be not done, the artist may happen to impose on himself by* partial reasoning; by a cold consideraton of those animated thoughts which proceed, not perhaps from caprice or rashness (as he may afterwards conceit), but from the fulness of his mind, enriched with the copious stores of all the various inventions which he had ever seen, or had ever passed in his mind. These ideas are infused into his design, without any conscious effort; but if he be not on his guard, he may reconsider and correct them, till the whole matter is reduced to a commonplace invention.

This is sometimes the effect of what I mean to caution you against; that is to say, an unfounded distrust of the imagination and feeling, in favour of narrow, partial, confined, argumentative theories; and of principles that seem to apply to the design in hand; without considering those general impressions on the fancy in which real principles of *sound reason,* and of much more weight and importance, are involved, and, as it were, lie hid, under the appearance of a sort of vulgar sentiment.

***draw...funds:** 「이런 밑천(기본 능력)의 힘을 빌리다」.
***be laid...care:** 「조심스레 간직하다」.
***impose on himself by...:** 「...으로 속다」.

Reason, without doubt, must ultimately determine everything; at this minute it is required to inform us when that very reason is to give way to feeling.

Though I have often spoken of that mean conception of our art which confines it to mere imitation, I must add, that it may be narrowed to such a mere matter of experiment, as to exclude from it the application of science, which alone gives dignity and compass to any art. But to find proper foundations for science is neither to narrow nor to vulgarise it; and this is sufficiently exemplified in the success of experimental philosophy. It is the false system of reasoning, grounded on a partial view of things, against which I would most earnestly guard you. And I do it the rather,* because those narrow theories, so coincident with* the poorest and most miserable practice, and which are adopted to give it countenance,* have not had their origin in the poorest minds, but in the mistakes, or possibly in the mistaken interpretations, of great and commanding authorities. We are not therefore in this case misled by feeling, but by false speculation.

When such a man as Plato speaks of painting as only an imitative art,* and that our pleasure proceeds from observing and acknowledging the truth of the imitation, I think he misleads us by a partial theory. It is in this poor, partial, and so far false view of the art, that Cardinal Bembo* has chosen to distinguish even Raffaelle himself, whom our enthusiasm honours with the name of Divine. The same sentiment is adopted by Pope in his epitaph on Sir Godfey Kneller;* and he turns the panegyric solely on imitation, as it is a sort of deception.

***I do it the rather, because...**: 「내가 경고하고자 하는 더 큰 이유는…」.
***coincident with...**: 「...과 함께 붙어다니는, 수반하는」.
***give countenance:** 「...을 지지해 주다」.
***such a man...the imitation:** Plato, *Republic*, X.(그림, 문학에 대한 공격).
***Cardinal Bembo:** 르네상스 시대 이탈리아의 승려, 학자. 그의 Raffaelle 묘비명에서 그런 말을 했다.
***The same sentiment...Kneller:** Alexander Pope는 초상화가 Kneller의 묘비명에서 Bembo의 묘비명을 거의 번역하다시피 했다.

I shall not think my time misemployed, if by any means I may contribute to confirm your opinion of what ought to be the object of your pursuit; because, though the best critics must always have exploded* this strange idea, yet I know that there is a disposition towards a perpetual recurrence to it, on account of its simplicity and superficial plausibility. For this reason I shall beg leave to lay before you a few thoughts on this subject; to throw out some hints that may lead your minds to an opinion (which I take to be the truth), that painting is not only to be considered as an imitation, operating by deception, but that it is, and ought to be, in many points of view, and strictly speaking, no imitation at all of external nature. Perhaps it ought to be as far removed from the vulgar idea of imitation, as the refined civilised state in which we live is removed from a gross state of nature; and those who have not cultivated their imaginations, which the majority of mankind certainly have not, may be said, in regard to arts, to continue in this state of nature. Such men will always prefer imitation to that excellence which is addressed to another faculty that they do not possess; but these are not the persons to whom a painter is to look, any more than a judge of morals and manners ought to refer controverted points* upon those subjects to the opinions of people taken from the banks of the Ohio, or from New Holland.*

It is the lowest style only of arts, whether of painting, poetry, or music, that may be said, in the vulgar sense, to be naturally pleasing. The higher efforts of those arts, we know by experience, do not affect minds wholly uncultivated. This refined taste is the consequence of education and habit; we are born only with a capacity of entertaining this refinement, as we are born with a disponsition to receive and obey all the rules and regulations of society; and so far it may be said to be natural to us, and no further.

What has been said, may show the artist how necessary it

***explode:** 「허위임을 드러내다」.

***controverted point:** 「논란이 있는 문제점」.

***the bank of Ohio, New Holland:** 두 곳 모두 그 당시에는 미개지역이었다. New Holland는 New York의 옛 이름.

is, when he looks about him for the advice and criticism of his friends, to make some distinction of the character, taste, experience, and observation in this art of those from whom it is received. An ignorant uneducated man may, like Apelles's critic,* be a competent judge of the truth of the representation of a sandal; or to go somewhat higher, like Molière's old woman,* may decide upon what is nature, in regard to comic humour; but a critic in the higher style of art ought to possess the same refined taste, which directed the artist in his work.

To illustrate this principle by a comparison with other arts, I shall now produce some instances to show, that they, as well as our own art, renounce the narrow idea of nature, and the narrow theories derived from that mistaken principle, and apply to that reason only which informs us not what imitation is, — a natural representation of a given object, — but what it is natural for the imagination to be delighted with. And perhaps there is no better way of acquiring this knowledge, than by this kind of analogy: each art will corroborate and mutually reflect the truth on the other. Such a kind of juxtaposition may likewise have this use, that whilst the artist is amusing himself in the contemplation of other arts, he may habitually transfer the principles of those arts to that which he professes;* which ought to be always present in his mind, and to which everything is to be referred.

So far is art from being derived from, or having any immediate intercourse with, particular nature as its model, that there are many arts that set out with a professed deviation

---

***Apelles's critic:** 로마의 학자 Pliny의 *Natural History*(xxxv, 85)에, 제화공이 Apelles의 조각의 샌달에 대하여 비평했다 한다. 그리이스 예술은 그러한 닮음(imitation)의 기준을 가장 강조했다는 설을 Pliny가 퍼뜨렸다.

***Molière's old woman:** Boileau(1636–1711; 프랑스의 시인, 비평가)에 의하면, Molière는 늙은 하녀에게 작품을 먼저 읽어 주고 정말 희극적인가를 알아냈다고 한다. 이러한 naturally pleasing art를 Reynolds는 비판하고, refined taste가 고급 예술의 비평에 필요하다고 주장한다.

***the artist is...he professes:** 미술, 음악, 문학 등 각 예술의 원칙들을 각각의 예술가가 잘 알고 있을 필요가 있다는 것. 즉 음악가는 시의 원칙에 대해서도 알고 있는 것이 필요하다는 주장.

from it.

This is certainly not so exactly true in regard to painting and sculpture. Our elements are laid in gross common nature, — an exact imitation of what is before us: but when we advance to the higher state, we consider this power of imitation, though first in the order of acquisition, as by no means the highest in the scale of perfection.

Poetry addresses itself to the same faculties and the same dispositions as painting, though by different means. The object of both is to accommodate itself to all the natural propensities and inclinations of the mind. The very existence of poetry depends on the licence it assumes of deviating from actual nature, in order to gratify natural propensities by other means, which are found by experience full* as capable of affording such gratification. It sets out* with a language in the highest degree artificial, a construction of measured words, such as never is, nor ever was used by man. Let this measure be what it may, whether hexameter or any other metre used in Latin or Greek — or rhyme, or blank verse varied with pauses and accents, in modern languages, — they are all equally removed from nature, and equally a violation of common speech. When this artificial mode has been established as the vehicle of sentiment, there is another principle in the human mind, to which the work must be referred, which still renders it more artificial, carries it still further from common nature, and deviates only to render it more perfect. That principle is the sense of congruity coherence, and consistency, which is a real existing principle in man; and it must be gratified. Therefore having once adopted a style and a measure not found in common discourse, it is required that the sentiments also should be in the same proportion elevated above common nature, from the necessity of there being an agreement of the parts among themselves, that one uniform whole may be produced.

To correspond therefore with this general system of devia-

*full: fully.
*set out: 「장식하다」. a construction이 목적어.

tion from nature, the manner in which poetry is offered to the ear, the tone in which it is recited, should be as far removed from the tone of conversation, as the words of which that poetry is composed. This naturally suggests the idea of modulating the voice by art, which I suppose may be considered as accomplished to the highest degree of excellence in the recitative of the Italian Opera; as we may conjecture it was in the chorus that attended the ancient drama. And though the most violent passions, the highest distress, even death itself, are expressed in singing or recitative, I would not admit as sound criticism the condemnation of such exhibitions on account of their being unnatural.

If it is natural for our senses, and our imaginations, to be delighted with singing, with instrumental music, with poetry, and with graceful action, taken separately (none of them being in the vulgar sense natural, even in that separate state); it is conformable to experience, and therefore agreeable to reason as connected with and referred to experience, that we should also be delighted with this union of music, poetry, and graceful action, joined to every circumstance of pomp and magnificence calculated to strike the senses of the spectator. Shall reason stand in the way, and tell us that we ought not to like what we know we do like, and prevent us from feeling the full effect of this complicated exertion of art? This is what I would understand by poets and painters being allowed to dare everything; for what can be more daring, than accomplishing of means, none of which have their archetypes in actual nature?

So far therefore is servile imitation from being necessary, that whatever is familiar, or in any way reminds us of what we see and hear every day, perhaps does not belong to the higher provinces of art, either in poetry or painting. The mind is to be transported, as Shakspeare expresses it, *beyond the ignorant present** to ages past. Another and a higher order of beings is supposed; and to those beings everything which is introduced into the work must correspond. Of this conduct,

*beyond the ignorant present: *Macbeth*, I, v, 57.

under these circumstances, the Roman and Florentine schools afford sufficient examples. Their style by this means is raised and elevated above all others; and by the same means the compass of art itself is enlarged.

We often see grave and great subjects attempted by artists of another school; who, though excellent in the lower class of art, proceeding on the principles which regulate that class, and not recollecting, or not knowing, that they were to address themselves to another faculty of the mind, have become perfectly ridiculous.

The picture which I have at present in my thoughts is a sacrifice of Iphigenia, painted by Jan Steen, a painter of whom I have formerly had occasion to speak with the highest approbation; and even in this picture, the subject of which is by no means adapted to his genius, there is nature and expression; but it is such expression, and the countenances are so familiar, and consequently so vulgar, and the whole accompanied with such finery of silks and velvets, that one would be almost tempted to doubt, whether the artist did not purposely intend to burlesque his subject.

Instances of the same kind we frequently see in poetry. Parts of Hobbes's translation of Homer are remembered and repeated merely for the familiarity and meanness of their phraseology, so ill corresponding with the ideas which ought to have been expressed, and, as I conceive, with the style of the original.

We may proceed in the same manner through the comparatively inferior branches of art. There are in works of that class, the same distinction of a higher and a lower style; and they take their rank and degree in proportion as the artist departs more, or less, from common nature, and makes it an object of his attention to strike the imagination of the spectator by ways belonging specially to art, — unobserved and untaught out of the school of its practice.

If our judgments are to be directed by narrow, vulgar, untaught, or rather ill-taught reason, we must prefer a portrait by Denner or any other high finisher, to those of Titian or Vandyck; and a landscape of Vanderheyden to those of Titian or Rubens; for they are certainly more exact representations of nature.

If we suppose a view of nature represented with all the truth of the *camera obscura,* and the same scene represented by a great artist, how little and mean will the one appear in comparison of the other, where no superiority is supposed from the choice of the subject. The scene shall be the same, the difference only will be in the manner in which it is presented to the eye. With what additional superiority then will the same artist appear when he has the power of selecting his materials, as well as elevating his style? Like Nicolas Poussin, he transports us to the environs of ancient Rome, with all the objects which a literary education makes so precious and interesting to man: or, like Sebastian Bourdon, he leads us to the dark antiquity of the Pyramids of Egypt; or, like Claude Lorrain, he conducts us to the tranquillity of arcadian scenes and fairyland.

Like the history-painter, a painter of landscapes in this style and with this conduct sends the imagination back into antiquity; and, like the poet, he makes the elements sympathise with his subject; whethe the clouds roll in volumes, like those of Titian or Salvator Rosa, or, like those of Claude, are gilded with the setting sun; whether the mountains have sudden and bold projections, or are gently sloped; whether the branches of his trees shoot out abruptly in right angles from their trunks, or follow each other with only a gentle inclination. All these circumstances contribute to the general character of the work, whether it be of the elegant, or of the more sublime kind. If we add to this the powerful materials of lightness and darkness, over which the artist has complete dominion, to vary and dispose them as he pleases; to diminish, or increase them, as will best suit his purpose, and correspond to the general idea of his work; a landscape thus conducted, under the influence of a poetical mind, will have the same superiority over the more ordinary and common views, as Milton's *Allegro* and *Penseroso* have over a cold prosaic narration or description; and such a picture would make a more forcible impression on the mind than the real scenes, were they presented before us.

If we look abroad to other arts, we may observe the same distinction, the same division into two classes; each of them acting under the influence of two different principles, in which the one follows nature, the other varies it, and sometimes departs from it.

The theatre, which is said *to hold the mirror up to nature,** comprehends both those sides. The lower kind of comedy or farce, like the inferior style of painting, the more naturally it is represented, the better; but the higher appears to me to aim no more at imitation, so far as it belongs to anything like deception, or to expect that the spectators should think that the events there represented are really passing before them, than Raffaelle in his cartoons, or Poussin in his sacraments,* expected it to be believed, even for a moment, that what they exhibited were real figures.

For want of this distinction, the world is filled with false criticism. Raffaelle is praised for naturalness and deception,* which he certainly has not accomplished, and as certainly never intended; and our late great actor, Garrick,* has been as ignorantly praised by his friend Fielding; who doubtless imagined he had hit upon an ingenious device, by introducing in one of his novels (otherwise a work of the highest merit) an ignorant man, mistaking Garrick's representation of a scene in Hamlet for reality. A very little reflection will convince us, that there is not one circumstance in the whole scene that is of the nature of deception. The merit and excellence of Shakspeare, and of Garrick,* when they were engaged in such scenes, is of a different and much higher kind. But what adds to the falsity of this intended compliment is that the best stage-representation appears even more unnatural to a person of such a character,* who is supposed never to have seen a play before, than it does to those who have had a habit of allowing

---

*to hold the mirror up to nature. *Hamlet*, Ⅲ, ii, 24.

*Poussin in his sacraments: 프랑스 고전파 화가의 거두 Nicolas Poussin이 그린 환상적 성례전 그림들.

*deception: 사실인 것처럼 속이는 기법.

*David Garrick: (1717-79). Johnson의 제자. 당대 최고의 배우.

for those necessary deviations from nature which the art requires.

In theatric representation, great allowances must always be made for the place in which the exhibition is represented; for the surrounding company, the lighted candles, the scenes visibly shifted in your sight, and the language of blank verse, so different from common English; which merely as English must appear surprising in the mouths of Hamlet, and all the court and natives of Denmark. These allowances are made; but their being made puts an end to all manner of deception:* and further, we know that the more low, illiterate, and vulgar any person is, the less he will be disposed to make these allowances, and of course to be deceived by any imitation; the things in which the trespass against nature and common probability is made in favour of the theatre being quite within the sphere of such uninformed men.

Though I have no intention of entering into all the circumstances of unnaturalness in theatrical representations, I must observe, that even the expression of violent passion is not always the most excellent in proportion as it is the most natural; so great terror and such disagreeable sensations may be communicated to the audience, that the balance may be destroyed by which pleasure is preserved, and holds its predominance in the mind: violent distortion of action, harsh screamings of the voice, however great the occasion, or however natural on such occasion, are therefore not admissible in the theatric art. Many of these allowed deviations from nature arise from the necessity which there is, that everything should be raised and enlarged beyond its natural state; that the full effect may come home to the spectator, which otherwise would be lost in the comparatively extensive space of the theatre. Hence the deliberate and stately step, the studied

---

***a person of such a character:** Fielding의 *Tom Jones*, XVI, v에 나오는 Partridge란 인물.

***These allowances...all manner of deception:** 이런 것들을 으레 있는 일로 인정해 준다. 그러나 그렇게 으레 있는 일로 인정해 준다는 사실이 그것이 사실인 줄로 착각하지 않도록 해 준다. their=allowances. make allowance: 「용인하다」.

grace of action, which seems to enlarge the dimensions of the actor, and alone to fill the stage. All this unnaturalness, though right and proper in its place, would appear affected and ridiculous in a private room; *quid enim deformius, quam scenam in vitam transferre?**

And here I must observe, and I believe it may be considered as a general rule, that no art can be engrafted with success on another art. For though they all profess the same origin, and to proceed from the same stock, yet each has it own peculiar modes both of imitating nature, and of deviating from it, each for the accomplishment of its own particular purpose. These deviations, more especially, will not bear transplantation to another soil.

If a painter should endeavour to copy the theatrical pomp and parade of dress and attitude, instead of that simplicity, which is not a greater beauty in life than it is in painting, we should condemn such pictures, as painted in the meanest style.

So also gardening, as far as gardening is an art, or entitled to that appellation, is a deviation from nature; for if the true taste consists, as many hold, in banishing every appearance of art, or any traces of the footsteps of man, it would then be no longer a garden. Even though we define it "Nature to advantage dress'd,"* and in some sense is such, and much more beautiful and commodious for the recreation of man; it is, however, when so dressed, no longer a subject for the pencil of a landscape-painter, as all landscape-painters know, who love to have recourse to nature herself, and to dress her according to the principles of their own art; which are far different from those of gardening, even when conducted according to the most approved principles; and such as a landscape-painter himself would adopt in the disposition of his own grounds, for his own private satisfaction.

I have brought together as many instances as appear necessary to make out the several points which I wished to

---

quid enim...: 'For what [would be] more disgraceful to carry over the stage into real life?' (Bacon, *Advancement of Learning*).

***Nature to advantage dress'd:** Pope, *Essay on Criticism*, 297 행.

suggest to your consideration in this discourse, that your own thoughts may lead you further in the use that may be made of the analogy of the arts, and of the restraint which a full understanding of the diversity of many of their principles ought to impose on the employment of that analogy.

The great end of all those arts is, to make an impression on the imagination and the feeling. The imitation of nature frequently does this. Sometimes it fails, and something else succeeds. I think therefore the true test of all the arts is not solely whether the production is a true copy of nature, but whether it answers the end of art, which is to produce a pleasing effect upon the mind.

It remains only to speak a few words of architecture, which does not come under the denomination of an imitative art. It applies itself, like music (and I believe we may add poetry), directly to the imagination, without the intervention of any kind of imitation.

There is in architecture, as in painting, an inferior branch of art, in which the imagination appears to have no concern. It does not, however, acquire the name of a polite and liberal art, from its usefulness, or administering to our wants or necessities, but from some higher principle: we are sure that in the hands of a man of genius it is capable of inspiring sentiment, and of filling the mind with great and sublime ideas.

It may be worth the attention of artists to consider what materials are in their hands, that may contribute to this end; and whether this art has it not in its power to address itself to the imagination with effect, by more ways than are generally employed by architects.

To pass over the effect produced by that general symmetry and proportion, by which the eye is delighted, as the ear is with music, architecture certainly possesses many principles in common with poetry and painting. Among those which may be reckoned as the first is that of affecting the imagination by means of association of ideas. Thus, for instance, as we have naturally a veneration for antiquity, whatever building brings to our remembrance ancient customs and manners, such as the castles of the barons of ancient chivalry, is sure to give this delight. Hence it is that *towers and battlements* are so often selected by the painter and the poet, to make a part of the composition of their ideal landscape; and it is from hence in a great degree, that in the buildings of Vanbrugh,* who was a poet as well as an architect, there is a greater display of imagination than we shall find perhaps in any other, and this is the ground of the effect we feel in many of his works, notwithstanding the faults with which many of them are justly charged. For this purpose, Vanbrugh appears to have had recourse to some of the principles of the Gothic architecture; which, though not so ancient as the Grecian, is more so to our imagination, with which the artist is more concerned than with absolute truth.

The barbaric splendour of those Asiatic buildings, which are now publishing by a member of this Academy,* may possibly, in the same manner, furnish an architect, not with models to copy, but with hints of composition and general effect, which would not otherwise have occurred.

It is, I know, a delicate and hazardous thing (and as such* I have already pointed it out), to carry the principles of one art to another, or even to reconcile in one object the various modes of the same art, when they proceed on different principles. The sound rules of the Grecian architecture are not to be lightly sacrificed. A deviation from them, or even an addition to them, is like a deviation or addition to, or from, the rules of other arts, — fit only for a great master, who is thoroughly conversant in the nature of man, as well as all combinations in his own art.

It may not be amiss for the architect to take advantage *sometimes* of that to which I am sure the painter ought always to have his eyes open, I mean the use of accidents; to follow when they lead, and to improve them, rather than always to trust to a regular plan. It often happens that additions have been made to houses, at various times, for use or pleasure. As

---

***Sir John Vanbrugh:** (1664-1726). 극작가, 바로크 건축가.

***a member of this Academy:** 즉, William Hodges를 말함. 인도의 건축물을 소개했다.

***as such:** as hazardous thing.

such buildings depart from regularity, they now and then acquire something of scenery by this accident, which I should think might not unsuccessfully be adopted by an architect, in an original plan, if it does not too much interfere with convenience. Variety and intricacy is a beauty and excelllence in every other of the arts which address the imagination; and why not in architecture?

The forms and turnings of the streets of London, and other old towns, are produced by accident, without any original plan or design; but they are not always the less pleasant to the walker or spectator, on that account. On the contrary, if the city had been built on the regular plan of Sir Christopher Wren, the effect might have been, as we know it is in some new parts of the town, rather unpleasing; the uniformity might have produced weariness, and a slight degree of disgust.

I can pretend to no skill in the detail of architecture. I judge now of the art, merely as a painter. When I speak of Vanbrugh, I mean to speak of him in the language of our art. To speak then of Vanbrugh in the language of a painter, he had originality of invention, he understood light and shadow, and had great skill in composition. To support his principal object he produced his second and third groups or masses; he perfectly understood in his art what is the most difficult in ours, the conduct of the background, by which the design and invention is set off to the greatest advantage. What the background is in painting, in architecture is the real ground on which the building is erected; and no architect took greater care than he that his work should not appear crude and hard: that is, it did not abruptly start out of the ground without expectation or preparation.

This is a tribute which a painter owes to an architect who composed like a painter; and was defrauded of the due reward of his merit by the wits of his time, who did not understand the principles of composition in poetry better than he; and who knew little or nothing of what he understood perfectly, the general ruling principles of architecture and painting. His fate was that of the great Perrault; both were the object of the petulant sarcasms of factious men of letters; and both have left some of the fairest ornaments which to this day decorate their several countries; the façade of the Louvre, Blenheim, and Castle Howard.

Upon the whole, it seems to me, that the object and intention of all the arts is to supply the natural imperfection of things, and often to gratify the mind by realising and embodying what never existed but in the imagination.

It is allowed on all hands, that facts and events, however they may bind the historian, have no dominion over the poet or the painter. With us, history is made to bend and conform to this great idea of art. And why? Because these arts, in their highest province, are not addressed to the gross senses, but to the desires of the mind, to that spark of divinity which we have within, impatient of being circumscribed and pent up by the world which is about us. Just so much as our art has of this, just so much of dignity, I had almost said of divinity, it exhibits; and those of our artists who possessed this mark of distinction in the highest degree acquired from thence the glorious appellation of Divine.

William Wordsworth

(1770—1850)

영국 서북부 Cumberland 지방의 변호사의 아들로 태어나, 좋은 자연 환경 속에서 소년기를 보내고(그러나 14세 때에 부친을 여읨), 케임브리지에 진학, 별로 뛰어나지 못한 학업을 마치고, 혁명 중의 프랑스로 여행, 진보주의 정치에 공감하는 한편 프랑스 여인과 연애하다가 귀국, 매우 심란한 상태에서 누이 동생 Dorothy의 격려를 받아 시에 정진하기 시작, 이웃이 된 코울리지와의 교유로 문학에 대한 이해를 더욱 깊이 하고, 그와 합작으로 영시사에 획기적인 작품집 *Lyrical Ballads* (1798)을 내기에 이르렀다.

1800년에 *Lyrical Ballads*의 재판을 내면서 붙인 서문이 영미 비평사상 가장 유명한 문헌의 하나가 되었다는 것은 놀랄만한 일이다. 워즈워드는 결코 비평가는 아니었고, 문학에 대하여 해박한 지식이나 이론적인 사고에 능한 사람도 아니었다. 단지 그는 과거의 문학에 대한 강한 반발과 자기가 새로 개발한 주제와 문제에 대한 열렬한 신념을 가진 시인이었다.

워즈워드는, 일상적인 생활에서 사건이나 상황을 선택하여, 사람들이 실제로 사용하는 말에서 골라 이를 묘사하되, 그 위에 상상의 색채를 입혀 평범한 사실이 비상하게 보이도록 하며, 또한 그런 사건과 정황 속에서 인간 본성의 근본 법칙을 추적함으로써 흥미를 자아내는 것이 그의 시의 목적이라고 하였다. 그는 일상적 상황 중에서도 농촌의 생활을 택하였는데, 그 까닭은, 농촌 생활이야 말로 변함 없고 아름다운 자연과 연결되어 있어 인간 본성의 모습이 그대로 드러나기 때문이며, 따라서 농촌의 말씨도 가장 좋은 상태의 언어를 보존하고 있기 때문에 잘 정리하여 쓰면 그대로 시가 될 수 있다고 했다.

그러나 이러한 좋은 소재와 문체가 주어져 있다고 해도 시인 자신이 적절한 준비가 되어 있지 않으면 소용이 없다. 진정한 시는 강렬한 감정의 자발적 유출인 까닭에, 시인은 우선 강렬한 감정을 가진 자라야 한다. 그는 보통 이상의 유기적 감수성을 지닌 사람으로 자연의 아름다움을 민감하게 느낄 줄 알 뿐 아니라 또한 그러한 느낌들을 토대로 하여 스스로 깊이 생각할 줄 알아야 하며, 이처럼 스스로 생각함으로 말미암아 스스로 흥분하고 기뻐할 줄 알아야 한다. 외부의 자극 없이도 스스로의 회상으로, 생각으로, 상상으로 감흥을 느낄 수 있는 능력을 워즈워드는 매우 귀중하게 여겼고, 그런 능력을 키워주는 것이 시의 가장 중요한 효용가치라고 보았다. 강렬한 감정의 자발적 유출은, 당장의 외부적 자극 때문에 발생하는 것이 아니라, 고요함 속에서 느꼈던 정서를 회상할 때에 발생하는 것이다.

이러한 자질을 구비한 시인이 농촌에 관한 소재를 농촌의 말씨로 표현한 시는 18세기에 문학적 규칙에 따라서 "시어"(poetic diction)로 쓴 운문과는 판이한 시가 될 것임은 분명하다. 워즈워드는 인위적인 운문의 규칙을 제거하고 쓴 시는 감정을 잘 표현한 산문과 별로 다름이 없다고 주장한다. 시의 본질은 운문이나 수사법이나 시어에서 찾을 것이 아니라 "직접적인 즐거움"(immediate pleasure)을 주는 능력에서 찾아야 한다고 그는 주장한다. 고전주의 문학관에서는 즐거움과 교훈, 또는 즐거움을 통한 교훈을 주는 것이 시라고 하였는데, 워즈워드는 교훈이라는 말을 제거하고 대신 "즐거움"의 개념을 확대하고 있다. 시가 주는 즐거움은 사람과 자연이 서로 교감하는 데서 오는 것이다. 시를 통하여 자연은 무생명, 무표정한 것이 아니고 사람과 친근한 상대가 된다. 자아와 타자 사이에 친화감을 느끼는 것은 무슨 도덕적 교훈이나 지식에 앞서 즐거움인 것이다.

시와 산문이 서로 본질적 차이가 없다고 하였지만, 워즈워드는, 시의 즐거움을 더하기 위하여 운율과 각운을 부가하는 것(superadd)을 마다하지 않는다. 그러나 그런 말재간이 시의 본질을 구성하지 않는다는 것을 그는 재삼 확인한다. 따라서 그의 시는 주로 운율법, 시어, 수사법의 기교를 발휘한 시와는 본질적으로 다른, 진정으로 자연스럽게 즐거운 시가 될 것이라는 확신이 서 있다.

Preface to Lyrical Ballads (1800)

THE first Volume of these Poems has already been submitted to general perusal.* It was published, as an experiment, which, I hoped, might be of some use to ascertain, how far, by fitting to metrical arrangement a selection of the real language of men in a state of vivid sensation, that sort of pleasure and that quantity of pleasure may be imparted, which a Poet may rationally endeavour to impart.

I had formed no very inaccurate estimate of the probable effect of those Poems: I flattered myself that they who should be pleased with them would read them with more than common pleasure: and, on the other hand, I was well aware, that by those who should dislike them, they would be read with more than common dislike. The result has differed from my expectation in this only, that a greater number have been pleased than I ventured to hope I should please.

* * * * *

Several of my Friends are anxious for the success of these Poems, from a belief, that, if the views with which they were composed were indeed realised, a class of Poetry would be produced, well adapted to interest mankind permanently, and not unimportant in the quality, and in the multiplicity of its moral relations: and on this account they have advised me to prefix a systematic defence of the theory upon which the Poems were written. But I was unwilling to undertake the task, knowing that on this occasion the Reader would look coldly upon my arguments, since I might be suspected of having been principally influenced by the selfish and foolish hope of *reasoning* him into an approbation of these particular Poems: and I was

---

*1798 년에 초판이 나왔었다.

still more unwilling to undertake the task, because, adequately to display the opinions, and fully to enforce the arguments, would require a space wholly disproportionate to a preface. For, to treat the subject with the clearness and coherence of which it is susceptible,* it would be necessary to give a full account of the present state of the public taste in this country, and to determine how far this taste is healthy or depraved; which, again, could not be determined, without pointing out in what manner language and the human mind act and re-act on each other, and without retracing the revolutions, not of literature alone, but likewise of society itself. I have therefore altogether declined to enter regularly upon this defence; yet I am sensible, that there would be something like impropriety in abruptly obtruding* upon the Public, without a few words of introduction, Poems so materially different from those upon which general approbation is at present bestowed.

It is supposed, that by the act of writing in verse an Author makes a formal engagement that he will gratify certain known habits of association;* that he not only thus apprises the Reader that certain classes of ideas and expressions will be found in his book, but that others will be carefully excluded. This exponent or symbol held forth by metrical language must in different eras of literature have excited very different expectations: for example, in the age of Catullus, Terence, and Lucretius, and that of Statius or Claudian;* and in our own country, in the age of Shakespeare and Beaumont and Fletcher, and that of Donne and Cowley, or Dryden, or Pope. I will not take upon me* to determine the exact import of the promise which, by the act of writing in verse, an Author, in the present day makes to his

---

***susceptible:** 「...이 가능한, ...를 허용하는(of)」. 이 구문의 뜻은, 「그 주제는 명백하고 일관성 있는 취급이 가능한 성질의 것이므로, 그렇게 취급하기 위해서는」.

***obtrude:** 「불쑥 내밀다」. 목적어는 poems.

***association:** 「연상」. ("시"하면 독자들의 머리에 연상되는 효과가 정해져 있다는 것).

***Catullus...Claudian:** 이들은 모두 Rome의 시인들.

***take upon...:** 「...의 일을 맡다, 담당하다」.

reader: but it will undoubtedly appear to many persons that I have not fulfilled the terms of an engagement thus voluntarily contracted. They who have been accustomed to the gaudiness and inane phraseology of many modern writers, if they persist in reading this book to its conclusion, will, no doubt, frequently have to struggle with feelings of strangeness and awkwardness: they will look round for poetry, and will be induced to inquire by what species of courtesy* these attempts can be permitted to assume that title. I hope therefore the reader will not censure me for attempting to state what I have proposed to myself to perform; and also (as far as the limits of a preface will permit) to explain some of the chief reasons which have determined me in the choice of my purpose: that at least he may be spared any unpleasant feeling of disappointment, and that I myself may be protected from one of the most dishonourable accusations which can be brought against an Author; namely, that of an indolence which prevents him from endeavouring to ascertain what is his duty, or, when his duty is ascertained, prevents him from performing it.

The principal object, then, proposed in these Poems was to choose incidents and situations from common life, and to relate or describe them, throughout, as far as was possible in a selection of language really used by men, and, at the same time, to throw over them a certain colouring of imagination, whereby ordinary things should be presented to the mind in an unusual aspect; and, further, and above all, to make these incidents and situations interesting by tracing in them, truly though not ostentatiously, the primary laws of our nature: chiefly, as far as regards the manner in which we associate ideas in a state of excitement. Humble and rustic life was generally chosen, because, in that condition, the essential passions of the heart find a better soil in which they can attain their maturity, are less under restraint, and speak a plainer and more emphatic language; because in that condition of life our elementary feelings co-exist in a state of greater simplicity, and, conse-

---

*courtesy: 「특별난 취급, 호의」.

quently, may be more accurately contemplated, and more forcibly communicated; because the manners of rural life germinate from those elementary feelings, and, from the necessary character of rural occupations, are more easily comprehended, and are more durable; and, lastly, because in that condition the passions of men are incorporated with the beautiful and permanent forms of nature. The language, too, of these men has been adopted (purified indeed from what appear to be its real defects, from all lasting and rational causes of dislike or disgust) because such men hourly communicate with the best objects from which the best part of language is originally derived; and because, from their rank in society and the sameness and narrow circle of their intercourse, being less under the influence of social vanity, they convey their feelings and notions in simple and unelaborated expressions. Accordingly, such a language, arising out of repeated experience and regular feelings, is a more permanent, and a far more philosophical language, than that which is frequently substituted for it by Poets, who think that they are conferring honour upon themselves and their art, in proportion as they separate themselves from the sympathies of men, and indulge in arbitrary and capricious habits of expression, in order to furnish food for fickle tastes, and fickle appetites, of their own creation.

I cannot, however, be insensible to the present outcry against the triviality and meanness, both of thought and language, which some of my contemporaries have occasionally introduced into their metrical compositions; and I acknowledge that this defect, where it exists, is more dishonourable to the Writer's own character than false refinement or arbitrary innovation, though I should contend at the same time, that it is far less pernicious in the sum of its consequences. From such verses the Poems in these volumes will be found distinguished at least by one mark of difference, that each of them has a worthy *purpose*. Not that I always began to write with a distinct purpose formally conceived; but habits of meditation have, I trust, so prompted and regulated my feelings, that my descriptions of such objects as strongly excite those feelings, will be found to carry along with them a *purpose*. If this opinion be erroneous, I can have little right to the name of a Poet. For all good poetry is the spontaneous overflow of powerful feelings: and though this be true, Poems to which any value can be attached were never produced on any variety of subjects but by a man who, being possessed of more than usual organic sensibility, had also thought long and deeply. For our continued influxes of feeling are modified and directed by our thoughts, which are indeed the representatives of all our past feelings*; and, as by contemplating the relation of these general representatives to each other, we discover what is really important to men, so, by the repetition and continuance of this act, our feelings will be connected with important subjects, till at length, if we be originally possessed of much sensibility, such habits of mind will be produced, that, by obeying blindly and mechanically the impulses of those habits, we shall describe objects, and utter sentiments, of such a nature, and in such connection with each other, that the understanding of the Reader must necessarily be in some degree enlightened, and his affections strengthened and purified.*

It has been said that each of these poems has a purpose. Another circumstance must be mentioned which distinguishes these Poems from the popular Poetry of the day; it is this, that the feeling therein developed gives importance to the action and situation, and not the action and situation to the feeling.*

---

*For...feelings: Thought 은 feeling 의 representative(대표)이고, feeling 은 sense perception 의 잔재라는 영국의 전통적 경험주의 철학의 일단.

*Feeling 은 thought 과 직결되므로 훌륭한 감성을 소유한 사람은 으레 좋은 생각을 나타내게 되니까, 그의 시는 독자가 공감할 만한 좋은 사상을 담게 된다는 것.

*그의 시에 전개되는 feeling 이 시골생활에 중요성을 부여하는 것이지, 시골생활이 그 feeling 을 중요하게 하는 것은 아니다. 따라서 중심적 역할을 하는 것은 Wordsworth 자신의 feeling—thought—이다. 즉 subject 는 Wordsworth 의 feeling—thought 이다.

A sense of false modesty shall not prevent me from asserting,* that the Reader's attention is pointed to this mark of distinction, far less for the sake of these particular Poems than from the general importance of the subject. The subject is indeed important! For the human mind is capable of being excited without the application of gross and violent stimulants; and he must have a very faint perception of its* beauty and dignity who does not know this, and who does not further know, that one being is elevated above another, in proportion as he possesses this capability.* It has therefore appeared to me, that to endeavour to produce or enlarge this capability is one of the best services in which, at any period, a Writer can be engaged; but this service, excellent at all times, is especially so at the present day. For a multitude of causes, unknown to former times, are now acting with a combined force to blunt the discriminating powers of the mind, and, unfitting it for all voluntary exertion, to reduce it to a state of almost savage torpor. The most effective of these causes are the great national events which are daily taking place, and the increasing accumulation of men in cities, where the uniformity of their occupations produces a craving for extraordinary incident, which the rapid communication of intelligence* hourly gratifies. To this tendency of life and manners the literature and theatrical exhibitions of the country have conformed themselves.* The invaluable works of our elder writers, I had almost said the works of Shakespeare and Milton, are driven into neglect by frantic novels,* sickly and stupid German Tragedies,* and deluges of idle and extravagant

---

***A sense...asserting:** 「헛된 겸손 때문에 (…한) 주장을 삼갈 생각은 없다」.
***its:** of human mind.
***this capability:** 외부의 자극 없이도 스스로 흥분할 수 있는 능력. 이 능력이 크면 클수록 그 사람은 훌륭한 사람이다. 시는 이 능력을 길러준다. 그리고 이 능력은 공감력, 동정심 등의 근원이다.
***intelligence:** 「정보」(신문보도 따위).
***conform oneself to...:** 「...에 자신을 일치시키다」.
***frantic novels:** 주로 당시의 선정적인 Gothic novels를 가리킴. Ann Radcliff의 *Mysteries of Udolpho* (1794) 등.
***German Tragedies:** Schiller나 Goethe의 초기작품들. 번역되어 상연되었다.

stories in verse.—When I think upon this degrading thirst after outrageous stimulation, I am almost ashamed to have spoken of the feeble endeavour made in these volumes to counteract it; and, reflecting upon the magnitude of the general evil, I should be oppressed with no dishonourable melancholy, had I not a deep impression of certain inherent and indestructible qualities of the human mind, and likewise of certain powers in the great and permanent objects that act upon it, which are equally inherent and indestructible; and were there not added to this impression a belief, that the time is approaching when the evil will be systematically opposed, by men of greater powers, and with far more distinguished success.

Having dwelt thus long on the subjects and aim of these Poems, I shall request the Reader's permission to apprise him of* a few circumstances relating to their *style*, in order, among other reasons, that he may not censure me for not having performed what I never attempted. The Reader will find that personifications of abstract ideas rarely occur in these volumes; and are utterly rejected, as an ordinary device to elevate the style, and raise it above prose. My purpose was to imitate, and, as far as is possible, to adopt the very language of men; and assuredly such personifications* do not make any natural or regular part of that language. They are, indeed, a figure of speech occasionally prompted by passion, and I have made use of them as such; but have endeavoured utterly to reject them as a mechanical device of style, or as a family language* which Writers in metre seem to lay claim to* by prescription. I have wished to keep the Reader in the company of flesh and blood, persuaded that by so doing I shall interest him. Others who pursue a different track will interest him likewise; I do not interfere with their claim, but wish to prefer a claim of my own.

---

*apprise someone of...: 「...에게 ...을 알려주다」.

*such personification: 추상명사를 의인화하여 사용함.

*a family language: 「가족 언어」. 즉 운문작가들이 으레 (by prescription) 쓰기로 되어 있는 언어.

*lay claim to...: 「...에 대하여 권리를 주장하다」.

There will also be found in these volumes little of what is usually called poetic diction*; as much pains has been taken to avoid it as is ordinarily taken to produce it; this has been done for the reason already alleged, to bring my language near to the language of men; and further, because the pleasure which I have proposed to myself to impart, is of a kind very different from that which is supposed by many persons to be the proper object of poetry. Without being culpably particular, I do not know how to give my Reader a more exact notion of the style in which it was my wish and intention to write, than by informing him that I have at all times endeavoured to look steadily at my subject; consequently, there is I hope in these Poems little falsehood of description, and my ideas are expressed in language fitted to their respective importance. Something must have been gained by this practice, as it is friendly to one property of all good poetry, namely, good sense: but it has necessarily cut me off from a large portion of phrases and figures of speech which from father to son have long been regarded as the common inheritance of Poets. I have also thought it expedient to restrict myself still further, having abstained from the use of many expressions, in themselves proper and beautiful, but which have been foolishly repeated by bad Poets, till such feelings of disgust are connected with them as it is scarcely possible by any art of association to overpower.

If in a poem there should be found a series of lines, or even a single line, in which the language, though naturally arranged, and according to the strict laws of metre, does not differ from that of prose, there is a numerous class of critics, who, when they stumble upon these prosaisms, as they call them, imagine that they have made a notable discovery, and exult over the Poet as over a man ignorant of his own profession. Now these men would establish a canon of criticism which the Reader will conclude he must utterly reject, if he wishes to be pleased with

---

***poetic diction:** 18세기에 특히 발달했던 매우 인위적인 시적 말투. 예컨대 다음에 나오는 Thomas Gray의 시에서 태양을 reddening Phoebus라 한 것은 그 예이다.

these volumes. And it would be a most easy task to prove to him, that not only the langnage of a large portion of every good poem, even ot tne most elevated character, must necessarily, except with reference to the metre, in no respect differ from that of good prose, but likewise that some of the most interesting parts of the best poems will be found to be strictly the language of prose when prose is well written. The truth of this assertion might be demonstrated by innumerable passages from almost all the poetical writings, even of Milton himself. To illustrate the subject in a general manner, I will here adduce a short composition of Gray, who was at the head of those who, by their reasonings, have attempted to widen the space of separation betwixt Prose and Metrical composition, and was more than any other man curiously elaborate in the structure of his own poetic diction.

> 'In vain to me the smiling mornings shine,
> And reddening Phoebus lifts his golden fire:
> The birds in vain their amorous descant join,
> Or cheerful fields resume their green attire.
> These ears, alas! for other notes repine;
> *A different object do these eyes require;*
> *My lonely anguish melts no heart but mine;*
> *And in my breast the imperfect joys expire;*
> Yet morning smiles the busy race to cheer,
> And new-born pleasure brings to happier men;
> The fields to all their wonted tribute bear;
> To warm their little loves the birds complain.
> *I fruitless mourn to him that cannot hear,*
> *And weep the more because I weep in vain.*'*

It will easily be perceived, that the only part of this Sonnet which is of any value is the lines printed in Italics; it is equally obvious, that, except in the rhyme, and in the use of the single word 'fruitless' for fruitlessly, which is so far a defect, the language of these lines does in no respect differ from that of prose.

By the foregoing quotation it has been shown that the

*"Sonnet on the Death of Mr. Richard West".

language of Prose may yet be well adapted to Poetry; and it was previously asserted, that a large portion of the language of every good poem can in no respect differ from that of good Prose. We will go further. It may be safely affirmed, that there neither is, nor can be, any *essential* difference between the language of prose and metrical composition. We are fond of tracing the resemblance between Poetry and Painting, and, accordingly, we call them Sisters: but where shall we find bonds of connection sufficiently strict to typify the affinity betwixt metrical and prose composition? They both speak by and to the same organs; the bodies in which both of them are clothed may be said to be of the same substance, their affections are kindred, and almost identical, not necessarily differing even in degree; Poetry sheds no tears 'such as Angels weep,' but natural and human tears; she can boast of no celestial ichor that distinguishes her vital juices from those of prose; the same human blood circulates through the veins of them both.

If it be affirmed that rhyme and metrical arrangement of themselves constitute a distinction which overturns what has just been said on the strict affinity of metrical language with that of prose, and paves the way for other artificial distinctions which the mind voluntarily admits, I answer that the language of such Poetry as is here recommended is, as far as is possible, a selection of the language really spoken by men; that this selection, wherever it is made with true taste and feeling, will of itself form a distinction far greater than would at first be imagined, and will entirely separate the composition from the vulgarity and meanness of ordinary life; and, if metre be superadded thereto, I believe that a dissimilitude will be produced altogether sufficient for the gratification of a rational mind. What other distinction would we have? Whence is it to come? And where is it to exist? Not, surely, where the Poet speaks through the mouths of his characters: it cannot be necessary here, either for elevation of style, or any of its supposed ornaments: for, if the Poet's subject be judiciously chosen, it will naturally, and upon fit occasion, lead him to passions the language of which, if selected truly and judiciously, must necessarily be dignified and variegated, and alive* with metaphors and figures. I forbear to speak of an incongruity which would shock the intelligent Reader, should the Poet interweave any foreign* splendour of his own with that which the passion naturally suggests: it is sufficient to say that such addition is unnecessary. And, surely, it is more probable that those passages, which with propriety* abound with metaphors and figures, will have their due effect, if, upon other occasions where the passions are of a milder character, the style also be subdued and temperate.

But, as the pleasure which I hope to give by the Poems now presented to the Reader must depend entirely on just notions upon this subject, and, as it is in itself of high importance to our taste and moral feelings, I cannot content myself with these detached remarks. And if, in what I am about to say, it shall appear to some that my labour is unnecessary, and that I am like a man fighting a battle without enemies, such persons may be reminded, that, whatever be the language outwardly holden* by men, a practical faith in the opinions which I am wishing to establish is almost unknown. If my conclusions are admitted, and carried as far as they must be carried if admitted at all, our judgements concerning the works of the greatest Poets both ancient and modern will be far different from what they are at present, both when we praise, and when we censure: and our moral feelings influencing and influenced by these judgments will, I believe, be corrected and purified.

Taking up the subject, then, upon general grounds, let me ask, what is meant by the word Poet? What is a Poet? To whom does he address himself? And what language is to be expected from him?—He is a man speaking to men: a man,

---

*alive with: 「...으로써 생생한 인상을 주는」.
*foreign: 「어울리지 않는」.
*with propriety: 「적절하게」.
*holden: held(=thought of).

it is true, endowed with more lively sensibility, more enthusiasm and tenderness, who has a greater knowledge of human nature, and a more comprehensive soul, than are supposed to be common among mankind; a man pleased with his own passions and volitions, and who rejoices more than other men in the spirit of life that is in him; delighting to contemplate similar volitions and passions as manifested in the goings-on* of the Universe, and habitually impelled to create them where he does not find them. To these qualities he has added a disposition to be affected more than other men by absent things as if they were present; an ability of conjuring up in himself passions, which are indeed far from being the same as those produced by real events, yet (especially in those parts of the general sympathy which are pleasing and delightful) do more nearly resemble the passions produced by real events, than anything which, from the motions of their own minds merely, other men are accustomed to feel in themselves:—whence, and from practice, he has acquired a greater readiness and power in expressing what he thinks and feels, and especially those thoughts and feelings which, by his own choice, or from the structure of his own mind, arise in him without immediate external excitement.*

But whatever portion of this faculty we may suppose even the greatest Poet to possess, there cannot be a doubt that the language which it will suggest to him, must often, in liveliness and truth, fall short of* that which is uttered by men in real life, under the actual pressure of those passions, certain shadows of which the Poet thus produces, or feels to be produced, in himself.

However exalted a notion we would wish to cherish of* the character of a Poet, it is obvious, that while he describes and

---

*goings-on: 「여러 양상」. 우주의 양상 속에서 시인 자신의 마음의 양상과 닮은 것을 본다는 생각. 자아와 우주의 공감, 교감을 믿은 것이다.

*실재하지 않는 사물에 대해서도 스스로 감흥을 느낄 수 있는 능력, 외부의 자극 없이도 흥분할 수 있는 자율적이고 자발적인 능력을 그는 중요시했다.

*fall short of...: 「...에 뒤지다, ...보다 모자라다」.

*cherish of...: conceive about 「...에 대하여 ...한 생각을 가지다」.

imitates passions, his employment is in some degree mechanical, compared with the freedom and power of real and substantial action and suffering. So that it will be the wish of the Poet to bring his feelings near to those of the persons whose feelings he describes, nay, for short spaces of time, perhaps, to let himself slip into an entire delusion, and even confound and identify his own feelings with theirs; modifying only the language which is thus suggested to him by a consideration that he describes for a particular purpose, that of giving pleasure. Here, then, he will apply the principle of selection which has been already insisted upon. He will depend upon this for removing what would otherwise be painful or disgusting in the passion; he will feel that there is no necessity to trick out* or to elevate nature: and, the more industriously he applies this principle, the deeper will be his faith that no words, which *his* fancy or imagination can suggest, will be to be compared with those which are the emanations of reality and truth.

But it may be said by those who do not object to the general spirit of these remarks, that, as it is impossible for the Poet to produce upon all occasions language as exquisitely fitted for the passion as that which the real passion itself suggests, it is proper that he should consider himself as in the situation of a translator, who does not scruple to substitute excellences of another kind for those which are unattainable by him; and endeavours occasionally to surpass his original, in order to make some amends for the general inferiority to which he feels that he must submit. But this would be to encourage idleness and unmanly despair. Further, it is the language of men who speak of what they do not understand; who talk of Poetry as of a matter of amusement and idle pleasure; who will converse with us as gravely about a *taste** for Poetry, as they express it, as

---

*trick out: 「걸치레를 하다」. 실제의 언어는 잘 선택하기만 하면 더 다른 꾸밈이 필요없다는 것.

*18세기 비평에서 taste란 말이 많이 쓰였는데, Wordsworth는 이 말의 함축적 의미를 싫어한다. '술맛'에 대한 취미를 연상시킨다고 보았기 때문이다.

if it were a thing as indifferent as a taste for rope-dancing, or Frontiniac or Sherry. Aristotle, I have been told, has said, that Poetry is the most philosophic of all writing*: it is so: its object is truth, not individual and local, but general, and operative; not standing upon external testimony, but carried alive into the heart by passion; truth which is its own testimony, which gives competence and confidence to the tribunal to which it appeals, and receives them from the same tribunal. Poetry is the image of man and nature. The obstacles which stand in the way of the fidelity of the Biographer and Historian, and of their consequent utility, are incalculably greater than those which are to be encountered by the Poet who comprehends the dignity of his art. The Poet writes under one restriction only, namely, the necessity of giving immediate pleasure to a human Being possessed of that information which may be expected from him, not as a lawyer, a physician, a mariner, an astronomer, or a natural philosopher, but as a Man. Except this one restriction, there is no object standing between the Poet and the image of things; between this, and the Biographer and Historian, there are a thousand.

Nor let this necessity of producing immediate pleasure be considered as a degradation of the Poet's art. It is far otherwise. It is an acknowledgement of the beauty of the universe, an acknowledgement the more sincere, because not formal,* but indirect; it is a task light and easy to him who looks at the world in the spirit of love: further, it is a homage paid to the native and naked dignity of man, to the grand elementary principle of pleasure, by which he knows, and feels, and lives, and moves. We have no sympathy but what is propagated by pleasure: I would not be misunderstood; but wherever we sympathise with pain, it will be found that the sympathy is produced and carried on by subtle combinations with pleasure. We have no knowledge, that is, no general principles drawn

---

***Poetry is...all writing:** Aristotle은 '시는 역사보다 더 철학적이다'라고 했지 이렇게 말하지는 않았다.

***formal:** public의 뜻.

from the contemplation of particular facts, but* what has been built up by pleasure, and exists in us by pleasure alone. The Man of science, the Chemist and Mathematician, whatever difficulties and disgusts they may have had to struggle with, know and feel this. However painful may be the objects with which the Anatomist's knowledge is connected, he feels that his knowledge is pleasure; and where he has no pleasure he has no knowledge. What then does the Poet? He considers man and the objects that surround him as acting and re-acting upon each other, so as to produce an infinite complexity of pain and pleasure; he considers man in his own nature and in his ordinary life as contemplating this with a certain quantity of immediate knowledge, with certain convictions, intuitions, and deductions, which from habit acquire the quality of intuitions; he considers him as looking upon this complex scene of ideas and sensations, and finding every where objects that immediately excite in him sympathies which, from the necessities of his nature, are accompanied by an overbalance of enjoyment.

To this knowledge which all men carry about with them, and to these sympathies in which, without any other discipline than that of our daily life, we are fitted to take delight, the Poet principally directs his attention. He considers man and nature as essentially adapted to each other, and the mind of man as naturally the mirror of the fairest and most interesting properties of nature. And thus the Poet, prompted by this feeling of pleasure, which accompanies him through the whole course of his studies, converses with general nature, with affections akin to those, which, through labour and length of time, the Man of science has raised up in himself, by conversing with those particular parts of nature which are the objects of his studies. The knowledge both of the Poet and the Man of science is pleasure; but the knowledge of the one cleaves to us as a necessary part of our existence, our natural and unalienable inheritance; the other is a personal and individual acquisition, slow to come to us, and by no habitual and direct

*but: except for.

sympathy connecting us with our fellow-beings. The Man of science seeks truth as a remote and unknown benefactor; he cherishes and loves it in his solitude: the Poet, singing a song in which all human beings join with him, rejoices in the presence of truth as our visible friend and hourly companion. Poetry is the breath and finer spirit of all knowledge; it is the impassioned expression which is in the countenance of all Science. Emphatically may it be said of the Poet, as Shakespeare hath said of man, 'that he looks before and after.'* He is the rock of defence for human nature; an upholder and preserver, carrying everywhere with him relationship and love. In spite of difference of soil and climate; of language and manners, of laws and customs: in spite of things silently gone out of mind, and things violently destroyed; the Poet binds together by passion and knowledge the vast empire of human society, as it is spread over the whole earth, and over all time. The objects of the Poet's thoughts are every where; though the eyes and senses of man are, it is true, his favourite guides, yet he will follow wheresoever he can find an atmosphere of sensation in which to move his wings. Poetry is the first and last of all knowledge—it is as immortal as the heart of man. If the labours of Men of science should ever create any material revolution, direct or indirect, in our condition, and in the impressions which we habitually receive, the Poet will sleep then no more than at present; he will be ready to follow the steps of the Man of science, not only in those general indirect effects, but he will be at his side, carrying sensation into the midst of the objects of the science itself. The remotest discoveries of the Chemist, the Botanist, or Mineralogist, will be as proper objects of the Poet's art as any upon which it can be employed, if the time should ever come when these things shall be familiar to us, and the relations under which they are contemplated by the followers of these respective sciences shall be manifestly and palpably material to us as enjoying and suffering beings. If the time should ever come when what is now called science, thus

*_Hamlet_, IV, iv, 37.

familiarised to men, shall be ready to put on, as it were, a form of flesh and blood, the Poet will lend his divine spirit to aid the transfiguration, and will welcome the Being thus produced, as a dear and genuine inmate of the household of man.—It is not, then, to be supposed that any one, who holds that sublime notion of Poetry which I have attempted to convey, will break in upon* the sanctity and truth of his pictures by transitory and accidental ornaments, and endeavour to excite admiration of himself by arts,* the necessity of which must manifestly depend upon the assumed meanness of his subject.

What has been thus far said applies to Poetry in general; but especially to those parts of composition where the Poet speaks through the mouths of his characters; and upon this point it appears to authorise the conclusion that there are few persons of good sense, who would not allow that the dramatic parts of composition* are defective, in proportion as they deviate from the real language of nature, and are coloured by a diction of the Poet's own, either peculiar to him as an individual Poet or belonging simply to Poets in general; to a body of men who, from the circumstance of their compositions being in metre, it is expected will employ a particular language.

It is not, then, in the dramatic parts of composition that we look for this distinction of language; but still it may be proper and necessary where the Poet speaks to us in his own person and character. To this I answer by referring the Reader to the description before given of a Poet. Among the qualities there enumerated as principally conducing to form a Poet, is implied nothing differing in kind from other men, but only in degree. The sum of what was said is, that the Poet is chiefly distinguished from other men by a greater promptness to think and feel without immediate external excitement, and a greater power in expressing such thoughts and feelings as are produced

---

***break in upon:** 「침해하다」.
***arts:** (겉치레의) 「기교」. 즉, 다루는 주제가 저급인 까닭에 필요한 기교.
***the dramatic parts of composition:** 작중인물들이 발언하는 대목(실제로 사용하는 언어를 모방한 것).

in him in that manner. But these passions and thoughts and feelings are the general passions and thoughts and feelings of men. And with what are they connected? Undoubtedly with our moral sentiments and animal* sensations, and with the causes which excite these; with the operations of the elements, and the appearances of the visible universe; with storm and sunshine, with the revolutions of the seasons, with cold and heat, with loss of friends and kindred, with injuries and resentments, gratitude and hope, with fear and sorrow. These, and the like, are the sensations and objects which the Poet describes, as they are the sensations of other men, and the objects which interest them. The Poet thinks and feels in the spirit of human passions. How, then, can his language differ in any material degree from that of all other men who feel vividly and see clearly? It might be *proved* that it is impossible. But supposing that this were not the case, the Poet might then be allowed to use a peculiar language when expressing his feelings for his own gratification, or that of men like himself. But Poets do not write for Poets alone, but for men. Unless therefore we are advocates for that admiration which subsists upon ignorance, and that pleasure which arises from hearing what we do not understand, the Poet must descend from this supposed height; and, in order to excite rational sympathy, he must express himself as other men express themselves. To this it may be added, that while he is only selecting from the real language of men, or, which amounts to the same thing* composing accurately in the spirit of such selection, he is treading upon safe ground, and we know what we are to expect from him. Our feelings are the same with respect to metre; for, as it may be proper to remind the Reader, the distinction of metre is regular and uniform, and not, like that which is produced by what is usually called POETIC DICTION, arbitrary, and subject to infinite caprices upon which no calculation whatever can be made. In the one case, the Reader is utterly at the mercy of the Poet,

---

***animal:** 「살아있는, 활동적인」.
***which...thing:** 「결국 같은 말이지만」.

respecting what imagery or diction he may choose to connect with the passion; whereas, in the other, the metre obeys certain laws, to which the Poet and Reader both willingly submit because they are certain, and because no interference is made by them with the passion* but such as the concurring testimony of ages has shown to heighten and improve the pleasure which co-exists with it.

It will now be proper to answer an obvious question, namely, Why, professing these opinions, have I written in verse? To this, in addition to such answer as is included in what has been already said, I reply, in the first place, Because, however I may have restricted myself, there is still left open to me what confessedly constitutes the most valuable object of all writing, whether in prose or verse; the great and universal passions of men, the most general and interesting of their occupations, and the entire world of nature before me—to supply endless combinations of forms and imagery. Now, supposing for a moment that whatever is interesting in these objects may be as vividly described in prose, why should I be condemned for attempting to superadd to such description, the charm which, by the consent of all nations, is acknowledged to exist in metrical language?* To this, by such as are yet unconvinced, it may be answered that a very small part of the pleasure given by Poetry depends upon the metre, and that it is injudicious to write in metre, unless it be accompanied with the other artificial distinctions of style with which metre is usually accompanied, and that, by such deviation, more will be lost from the shock which will thereby be given to the Reader's associations than will be counterbalanced by any pleasure which he can derive

---

*no interference...passion: they do not interfere with the passion.

*Wordsworth 는 운문과 산문이 본질상 동일하다고 했지만, 하필 운문으로 썼느냐는 질문에 대하여, 이왕 좋은 글을 쓰려는 차에 운문의 아름다움까지 덧붙이면 (superadd) 금상첨화가 될 것이니 왜 마다하겠느냐고 강조한다. 또한 운문을 일단 쓰면 다른 시적 방법(실제 언어와는 다른)도 자연 쓰게 마련이라는 주장에 대하여 'naked and simple poetry'가 가능하다고 답하고 있다.

from the general power of numbers. In answer to those who still contend for the necessity of accompanying metre with certain appropriate colours of style in order to the accomplishment of its appropriate end, and who also, in my opinion, greatly under-rate the power of metre in itself, it might, perhaps, as far as relates to these Volumes, have been almost sufficient to observe, that poems are extant, written upon more humble subjects, and in a still more naked and simple style, which have continued to give pleasure from generation to generation. Now, if nakedness and simplicity be a defect, the fact here mentioned affords a strong presumption that poems somewhat less naked and simple are capable of affording pleasure at the present dav; and, what I wished *chiefly* to attempt, at present, was to justify myself for having written under the impression of this belief.*

But various causes might be pointed out why, when the style is manly, and the subject of some importance, words metrically arranged will long continue to impart such a pleasure to mankind as he who proves the extent of that pleasure will be desirous to impart.* The end of Poetry is to produce excitement in co-existence with* an overbalance of pleasure; but, by the supposition, excitement is an unusual and irregular state of the mind; ideas and feelings do not, in that state, succeed each other in accustomed order. If the words, however, by which this excitement is produced be in themselves powerful, or the images and feelings have an undue proportion of pain connected with them, there is some danger that the excitement may be carried beyond its proper bounds. Now the co-presence of something

---

***this belief:** that poems somewhat less naked and simple are capable of affording pleasure. Wordsworth는 시에다 약간의 장식을 허용하는 것이다.

***as he...to impart:** 「운문이 주는 쾌감이 얼마나 큰지를 입증하는 자(시인)가 주고자 하는」.

***excitement in co-existence with an overbalance of pleasure:** 「넘치는 쾌감과 동시에 존재하는 흥분」. co-existence는 뒤에 나오는 co-presence와 비슷한 뜻. 감정에는 괴로움과 쾌감이 있는데, 쾌감이 더 커야(overbalance) 한다고 주장하는 것이다. 또한 운율은 생경한 괴로움을 길들이는 효과가 있다.

regular, something to which the mind has been accustomed in various moods and in a less excited state, cannot but have great efficacy in tempering and restraining the passion by an intertexture* of ordinary feeling, and of feeling not strictly and necessarily connected with the passion. This is unquestionably true; and hence, though the opinion will at first appear paradoxical, from the tendency of metre to divest language, in a certain degree, of its reality, and thus to throw a sort of half-consciousness of unsubstantial existence over the whole composition, there can be little doubt but that more pathetic situations and sentiments, that is, those which have a greater proportion of pain connected with them, may be endured in metrical composition, especially in rhyme, than in prose. The metre of the old ballads is very artless; yet they contain many passages which would illustrate this opinion; and, I hope, if the following Poems be attentively perused, similar instances will be found in them. This opinion may be further illustrated by appealing to the Reader's own experience of the reluctance with which he comes to the re-perusal of the distressful parts of *Clarissa Harlowe*, or *The Gamester*;* while Shakespeare's writings, in the most pathetic scenes, never act upon us, as pathetic, beyond the bounds of pleasure—an effect which, in a much greater degree than might at first be imagined, is to be ascribed to small, but continual and regular impulses of pleasurable surprise from the metrical arrangement.—On the other hand (what it must be allowed will much more frequently happen) if the Poet's words should be incommensurate with the passion, and inadequate to raise the Reader to a height of desirable excitement, then, (unless the Poet's choice of his metre has been grossly injudicious) in the feelings of pleasure which the Reader has been accustomed to connect with metre in general, and in

---

***intertexture:** 「뒤섞임」(일상적 감정과 예술적으로 조성된 감정을 뒤섞는 것).

****Clarissa Harlowe*** 는 Samuel Richardson 의 소설(1748). ***The Gamester*** 는 Edward Moore 의 비극(1753). 두 작품 다 읽기에 심히 괴로운 부분들이 있다.

the feeling, whether cheerful or melancholy, which he has been accustomed to connect with that particular movement of metre, there will be found something which will greatly contribute to impart passion to the words, and to effect the complex end which the Poet proposes to himself.

If I had undertaken a SYSTEMATIC defence of the theory here maintained, it would have been my duty to develop the various causes upon which the pleasure received from metrical language depends. Among the chief of these causes is to be reckoned a principle which must be well known to those who have made any of the Arts the object of accurate reflection: namely, the pleasure which the mind derives from the perception of similitude in dissimilitude.* This principle is the great spring of the activity of our minds, and their chief feeder. From this principle the direction of the sexual appetite, and all the passions connected with it, take their origin: it is the life of our ordinary conversation; and upon the accuracy with which similitude in dissimilitude, and dissimilitude in similitude are perceived, depend our taste and our moral feelings. It would not be a useless employment to apply this principle to the consideration of metre, and to show that metre is hence enabled to afford much pleasure, and to point out in what manner that pleasure is produced. But my limits will not permit me to enter upon this subject, and I must content myself with a general summary.

I have said that poetry is the spontaneous overflow of powerful feelings: it takes its origin from emotion recollected in tranquillity: the emotion is contemplated till, by a species of re-action, the tranquillity gradually disappears, and an emotion, kindred to that which was before the subject of contemplation, is gradually produced, and does itself actually exist in the mind. In this mood successful composition generally begins,

---

***similitude in dissimilitude:** 서로 다른 것들 중에서 비슷한 것을 발견함 (또는 그 반대). Coleridge는 이를 unity in multeity라고 했다. 운율의 즐거움은 바로 이 원칙에서 온다는 것뿐만 아니라 모든 즐거움이 거기서 온다는 것이다.

and in a mood similar to this it is carried on;* but the emotion, of whatever kind, and in whatever degree, from various causes, is qualified by various pleasures, so that in describing any passions whatsoever, which are voluntarily described, the mind will, upon the whole, be in a state of enjoyment. If Nature be thus cautious to preserve in a state of enjoyment a being so employed, the Poet ought to profit by the lesson held forth to him, and ought especially to take care, that, whatever passions he communicates to his Reader, those passions, if his Reader's mind be sound and vigorous, should always be accompanied with an overbalance of pleasure. Now the music of harmonious metrical language, the sense of difficulty overcome, and the blind association of pleasure which has been previously received from works of rhyme or metre of the same or similar construction, an indistinct perception perpetually renewed of language closely resembling that of real life, and yet, in the circumstance of metre, differing from it so widely—all these imperceptibly make up a complex feeling of delight, which is of the most important use in tempering the painful feeling always found intermingled with powerful descriptions of the deeper passions. This effect is always produced in pathetic and impassioned poetry; while, in lighter compositions, the ease and gracefulness with which the Poet manages his numbers are themselves confessedly a principal source of the gratification of the Reader. All that it is *necessary* to say, however, upon this subject, may be effected by affirming, what few persons will deny, that, of two descriptions, either of passions, manners, or characters, each of them equally well executed, the one in prose and the other in verse, the verse will be read a hundred times where the prose is read once.*

***in a mood...carried on:** 「이런 기분과 비슷한 기분 속에서 작품 제작은 진행된다」. 시는 감정이 저절로 넘치는 것이지만, 실제적 경험의 순간에 넘치는 것이 아니라 고요한 회상의 결과로 다시금 생기는 흥분 상태에서 생긴다는 것. 이 흥분 상태는 즐거움이 더 크다는 것. (슬픈 경험을 다루는 경우라도). 이 즐거움을 조성하는 방법의 하나가 운율이다.

***the verse will be read...the prose is read once:** 이러한 그의 주장은 적

Having thus explained a few of my reasons for writing in verse, and why I have chosen subjects from common life, and endeavoured to bring my language near to the real language of men, if I have been too minute in pleading my own cause,* I have at the same time been treating a subject of general interest; and for this reason a few words shall be added with reference solely to these particular poems, and to some defects which will probably be found in them. I am sensible that my associations must have sometimes been particular instead of general, and that, consequently, giving to things a false importance, I may have sometimes written upon unworthy subjects; but I am less apprehensive on this account, than that my language may frequently have suffered from those arbitrary connections of feelings and ideas with particular words and phrases, from which no man can altogether protect himself. Hence I have no doubt, that, in some instances, feelings, even of the ludicrous, may be given to my Readers by expressions which appeared to me tender and pathetic.* Such faulty expressions, were I convinced they were faulty at present, and that they must necessarily continue to be so,* I would willingly take all reasonable pains to correct. But it is dangerous to make these alterations on the simple authority of a few individuals, or even of certain classes of men; for where the understanding of an Author is not convinced, or his feelings altered, this* cannot be done without great injury to himself: for his own feelings are his stay and support; and, if he set them aside in

---

중하지 못했다. 당시 그는 산문의 발전을 예견하지 못했던 모양이다. 그는 산문과 운문이 본질적으로 꼭 같다고 믿고, 운문은 산문이 하는 일을 그대로 하면서 운율이라는 즐거운 요소를 더 갖고 있기 때문에 선호될 것이라고 본 것이다.

***plead one's own cause:** 「자기의 입장을 변호하다」.

*낱말의 어감은 사람에 따라 다를 수 있으므로, **Wordsworth** 자신에게 좋게 보이는 낱말도 다른 사람에게는 우스꽝스러운 것일 수 있다는 게 큰 문제이다.

***so:** faulty.

***this:** correction. (저자가 표현이 잘못 되었음을 깨닫든지 감정이 변하지 않는 경우에는, 수정한다는 것은 저자에게 큰 해를 가하는 것이다).

one instance, he may be induced to repeat this act till his mind shall lose all confidence in itself, and become utterly debilitated. To this it may be added, that the critic ought never to forget that he is himself exposed to the same errors as the Poet, and, perhaps, in a much greater degree: for there can be no presumption in saying of most readers, that it is not probable they will be so well acquainted with the various stages of meaning through which words have passed, or with the fickleness or stability of the relations of particular ideas to each other; and, above all, since they are so much less interested in the subject, they may decide lightly and carelessly.

Long as the Reader has been detained, I hope he will permit me to caution him against a mode of false criticism which has been applied to Poetry, in which the language closely resembles that of life and nature. Such verses have been triumphed over in parodies, of which Dr. Johnson's stanza is a fair specimen:—

'I put my hat upon my head
And walked into the Strand,
And there I met another man
Whose hat was in his hand.'*

Immediately under these lines let us place one of the most justly-admired stanzas of the 'Babes in the Wood.'

'These pretty Babes with hand in hand
Went wandering up and down;
But never more they saw the Man
Approaching from the Town.'*

In both these stanzas the words, and the order of the words, in no respect differ from the most unimpassioned conversation. There are words in both, for example, 'the Strand,' and 'the Town,' connected with none but the most familiar ideas; yet

*Johnson이 지나치게 단순한 민요를 놀리느라고 지은 nonsense verse (parody).

*옛 민요의 일절로, 과연 이 싯귀는 Johnson의 것보다 특별히 시적인지 따져볼 만하다.

the one stanza we admit as admirable, and the other as a fair example of the superlatively contemptible. Whence arises this difference? Not from the metre, not from the language, not from the order of the words; but the *matter* expressed in Dr. Johnson's stanza is contemptible. The proper method of treating trivial and simple verses, to which Dr. Johnson's stanza would be a fair parallelism, is not to say, this is a bad kind of poetry, or, this is not poetry; but, this wants sense; it is neither interesting in itself, nor can *lead* to any thing interesting; the images neither originate in that sane state of feeling which arises out of thought, nor can excite thought or feeling in the Reader. This is the only sensible manner of dealing with such verses. Why trouble yourself about the species till you have previously decided upon the genus? Why take pains to prove that an ape is not a Newton, when it is self-evident that he is not a man?

One request I must make of my reader, which is, that in judging these Poems he would decide by his own feelings genuinely, and not by reflection upon what will probably be the judgement of others. How common is it to hear a person say, I myself do not object to this style of composition, or this or that expression, but, to such and such classes of people it will appear mean or ludicrous! This mode of criticism, so destructive of all sound unadulterated judgement, is almost universal: let the Reader then abide, independently, by his own feelings, and, if he finds himself affected, let him not suffer such conjectures to interfere with his pleasure.

If an Author, by any single composition, has impressed us with respect for his talents, it is useful to consider this as affording a presumption, that on other occasions where we have been displeased, he, nevertheless, may not have written ill or absurdly; and further, to give him so much credit for this one composition as may induce us to review what has displeased us, with more care than we should otherwise have bestowed upon it.* This is not only an act of justice, but, in our decisions upon

*지금까지 대수롭지 않게 여겨지던 작가가 좋은 작품을 쓰면, 그의 앞 작품들도 다시 살펴 볼 아량이 있어야 한다는 것.

poetry especially, may conduce, in a high degree, to the improvement of our own taste; for an *accurate* taste in poetry, and in all the other arts, as Sir Joshua Reynolds has observed, is an *acquired* talent, which can only be produced by thought and a long-continued intercourse with the best models of composition. This is mentioned, not with so ridiculous a purpose as to prevent the most inexperienced Reader from judging for himself, (I have already said that I wish him to judge for himself;) but merely to temper the rashness of decision, and to suggest, that, if Poetry be a subject on which much time has not been bestowed, the judgement may be erroneous; and that, in many cases, it necessarily will be so.

Nothing would, I know, have so effectually contributed to further the end which I have in view, as to have shown of what kind the pleasure is, and how that pleasure is produced, which is confessedly produced by metrical composition essentially different from that which I have here endeavoured to recommend: for the Reader will say that he has been pleased by such composition; and what more can be done for him? The power of any art is limited; and he will suspect, that, if it be proposed to furnish him with new friends, that can be only upon condition of his abandoning his old friends. Besides, as I have said, the Reader is himself conscious of the pleasure which he has received from such composition, composition to which he has peculiarly attached the endearing name of Poetry; and all men feel an habitual gratitude, and something of an honourable bigotry, for the objects which have long continued to please them: we not only wish to be pleased, but to be pleased in the particular way in which we have been accustomed to be pleased. There is in these feelings enough to resist a host of arguments; and I should be the less able to combat them successfully, as I am willing to allow, that, in order entirely to enjoy the Poetry which I am recommending, it would be necessary to give up much of what is ordinarily enjoyed. But, would my limits have permitted me to point out how this pleasure is produced, many obstacles might have been removed, and the Reader* assisted in perceiving that the powers of language are not so limited as he may suppose; and that it is possible for poetry to give other enjoyments, of a purer, more lasting, and more exquisite nature. This part of the subject has not been altogether neglected, but it has not been so much my present aim to prove, that the interest excited by some other kinds of poetry is less vivid, and less worthy of the nobler powers of the mind, as to offer reasons for presuming, that if my purpose were fulfilled, a species of poetry would be produced, which is genuine poetry; in its nature well adapted to interest mankind permanently, and likewise important in the multiplicity and quality of its moral relations.*

From what has been said, and from a perusal of the Poems, the Reader will be able clearly to perceive the object which I had in view: he will determine how far it has been attained; and, what is a much more important question, whether it be worth attaining: and upon the decision of these two questions will rest my claim to the approbation of the Public.

Appendix

Perhaps, as I have no right to expect that attentive perusal, without which, confined, as I have been, to the narrow limits of a preface, my meaning cannot be thoroughly understood, I am anxious to give an exact notion of the sense in which the phrase poetic diction has been used; and for this purpose, a few words shall here be added, concerning the origin and characteristics of the phraseology, which I have condemned under that name.

The earliest poets of all nations generally wrote from passion excited by real events; they wrote naturally, and as men: feeling powerfully as they did, their language was daring, and figurative. In succeeding times, Poets, and Men ambitious of the

---

*Reader 다음에 might have been을 넣어서 읽을 것.

*Wordsworth는 종래의 시와는 다른 종류의 시, 그가 믿기로는 더 진실된 시를 제시하려고 하는데, 그것이 받아들여지기 위해서는 독자의 시에 대한 taste가 바뀔 필요가 있음을 암시한다.

fame of Poets, perceiving the influence of such language, and desirous of producing the same effect without being animated by the same passion, set themselves to a mechanical adoption of these figures of speech, and made use of them, sometimes with propriety, but much more frequently applied them to feelings and thoughts with which they had no natural connection whatsoever. A language was thus insensibly produced, differing materially from the real language of men in *any situation*. The Reader or Hearer of this distorted language found himself in a perturbed and unusual state of mind: when affected by the genuine language of passion he had been in a perturbed and unusual state of mind also: in both cases he was willing that his common judgement and understanding should be laid asleep, and he had no instinctive and infallible perception of the true to make him reject the false; the one served as a passport for the other. The emotion was in both cases delightful, and no wonder if he confounded the one with the other, and believed them both to be produced by the same, or similar causes. Besides, the Poet spoke to him in the character of a man to be looked up to, a man of genius and authority. Thus, and from a variety of other causes, this distorted language was received with admiration; and Poets, it is probable, who had before contented themselves for the most part with misapplying only expressions which at first had been dictated by real passion, carried the abuse still further, and introduced phrases composed apparently in the spirit of the original figurative language of passion, yet altogether of their own invention, and characterised by various degrees of wanton deviation from good sense and nature.

It is indeed true, that the language of the earliest Poets was felt to differ materially from ordinary language, because it was the language of extraordinary occasions; but it was really spoken by men, language which the Poet himself had uttered when he had been affected by the events which he described, or which he had heard uttered by those around him. To this language it is probable that metre of some sort or other was early superadded. This separated the genuine language of Poetry still further from common life, so that whoever read or heard the poems of these earliest Poets felt himself moved in a way in which he had not been accustomed to be moved in real life, and by causes manifestly different from those which acted upon him in real life. This was the great temptation to all the corruptions which have followed: under the protection of this feeling succeeding Poets constructed a phraseology which had one thing, it is true, in common with the genuine language of poetry, namely, that it was not heard in ordinary conversation; that it was unusual. But the first Poets, as I have said, spoke a language which, though unusual, was still the language of men. This circumstance, however, was disregarded by their successors; they found that they could please by easier means: they became proud of modes of expression which they themselves had invented, and which were uttered only by themselves. In process of time metre became a symbol or promise of this unusual language, and whoever took upon him to write in metre, according as he possessed more or less of true poetic genius, introduced less or more of this adulterated phraseology into his compositions, and the true and the false were inseparably interwoven until, the taste of men becoming gradually perverted, this language was received as a natural language: and at length, by the influence of books upon men, did to a certain degree really become so. Abuses of this kind were imported from one nation to another, and with the progress of refinement this diction became daily more and more corrupt, thrusting out of sight the plain humanities of nature by a motley masquerade of tricks, quaintnesses, hieroglyphics, and enigmas.

It would not be uninteresting to point out the causes of the pleasure given by this extravagant and absurd diction. It depends upon a great variety of causes, but upon none, perhaps, more than its influence in impressing a notion of the peculiarity and exaltation of the Poet's character, and in flattering the Reader's self-love by bringing him nearer to a sympathy with that character; an effect which is accomplished by unsettling ordinary habits of thinking, and thus assisting the Reader to approach to that perturbed and dizzy state of mind in which if he does not find himself, he imagines that he is *balked* of a peculiar enjoyment which poetry can and ought to bestow.

The sonnet quoted from Gray, in the Preface, except the lines printed in Italics, consists of little else but this diction, though not of the worst kind; and indeed, if one may be permitted to say so, it is far too common in the best writers both ancient and modern. Perhaps in no way, by positive example, could more easily be given a notion of what I mean by the phrase *poetic diction* than by referring to a comparison between the metrical paraphrases which we have of passages in the Old and New Testament, and those passages as they exist in our common Translation. See Pope's 'Messiah' throughout; Prior's 'Did sweeter sounds adorn my flowing tongue,' &c. &c. 'Though I speak with the tongues of men and of angels,' &c. &c. 1st Corinthians, chap. xiii. By way of immediate example, take the following of Dr. Johnson:

> 'Turn on the prudent Ant thy heedless eyes,
> Observe her labours, Sluggard, and be wise;
> No stern command, no monitory voice,
> Prescribes her duties, or directs her choice;
> Yet, timely provident, she hastes away
> To snatch the blessings of a plenteous day;
> When fruitful Summer loads the teeming plain,
> She crops the harvest, and she stores the grain.
> How long shall sloth usurp thy useless hours,
> Unnerve thy vigour, and enchain thy powers?
> While artful shades thy downy couch enclose,
> And soft solicitation courts repose,
> Amidst the drowsy charms of dull delight,
> Year chases year with unremitted flight,
> Till Want now following, fraudulent and slow,
> Shall spring to seize thee, like an ambush'd foe.'

From this hubbub of words pass to the original. 'Go to the Ant, thou Sluggard, consider her ways, and be wise: which having no guide, overseer, or ruler, provideth her meat in the summer, and gathereth her food in the harvest. How long wilt thou sleep, O Sluggard? when wilt thou arise out of thy sleep? Yet a little sleep, a little slumber, a little folding of the hands to sleep. So shall thy poverty come as one that travelleth, and thy want as an armed man.' Proverbs, chap. vi.

One more quotation, and I have done. It is from Cowper's Verses supposed to be written by Alexander Selkirk:—

'Religion! what treasure untold
Resides in that heavenly word!
More precious than silver and gold,
Or all that this earth can afford.
But the sound of the church-going bell
These valleys and rocks never heard,
Ne'er sighed at the sound of a knell,
Or smiled when a sabbath appeared.

Ye winds, that have made me your sport,
Convey to this desolate shore
Some cordial endearing report
Of a land I must visit no more.
My Friends, do they now and then send
A wish or a thought after me?
O tell me I yet have a friend,
Though a friend I am never to see.'

This passage is quoted as an instance of three different styles of composition. The first four lines are poorly expressed; some Critics would call the language prosaic; the fact is, it would be bad prose, so bad, that it is scarcely worse in metre. The epithet 'church-going' applied to a bell, and that by so chaste a writer as Cowper, is an instance of the strange abuses which Poets have introduced into their language, till they and their Readers take them as matters of course, if they do not single them out expressly as objects of admiration. The two lines 'Ne'er sighed at the sound,' &c., are, in my opinion, an instance of the language of passion wrested from its proper use, and, from the mere circumstance of the composition being in metre, applied upon an occasion that does not justify such violent expressions; and I should condemn the passage, though perhaps few Readers will agree with me, as vicious poetic diction. The last stanza is throughout admirably expressed: it would be equally good whether in prose or verse, except that the Reader has an exquisite pleasure in seeing such natural language so naturally connected with metre. The beauty of this stanza tempts me to conclude with a principle which ought never to be lost sight of, and which has been my chief guide in all I have said,—namely, that in works *of imagination and sentiment*, for of these only have I been treating, in proportion as ideas and feelings are valuable, whether the composition be in prose or in verse, they require and exact one and the same language. Metre is but adventitious to composition, and the phraseology for which that passport is necessary, even where it may be graceful at all, will be little valued by the judicious.

Samuel Taylor Coleridge

(1772—1834)

시골 교회의 목사였던 부친을 일찍 여의어, 자선 학생으로 런던의 고등학교를 다니고 케임브리지에 진학하였으나 얼떨결에 경기병으로 입대, 친지들의 주선으로 군대에서 나와 케임브리지에 복학하였으나 중퇴하여 평생 후회할 성급한 결혼을 했다. 정치, 종교에 관한 강연을 하는 한편 시와 산문을 발표하였다. 1797년에 전부터 안면이 있는 워즈워드의 이웃이 되어 이듬해에 *Lyrical Ballads*를 합작 발표한 사실은 너무나 유명하다.

잡지 편집, 시와 산문의 집필, 종교, 문학, 철학, 정치에 관한 강연으로 가난하고 병약한 생애를 바쁘게 산 코울리지는 그의 사상을 집약한 단행본으로서는 *Biographia Literaria*만을 남겼을 뿐이고, 많은 시 작품을 미완성으로, 더 많은 논문을 초고 형태의 흩어진 파편으로 남겼다. 그의 문학 사상은 후세에 끼친 영향이 굉장했음에도 불구하고 아직도 완전히 정리되지 못하고 있다. 그만큼 그의 사상은 다양하고 폭넓으며 서로 충돌하는 요소들을 내포하고 있기도 하다.

Biographia Literaria(1817)는 자신의 생애의 중반기까지의 그의 사상의 형성 과정을 기술한 자서전이다. 책 전체가 그의 문학관을 이해하는 데에 필수적이나, 특히 그의 상상 이론을 간략하게 정리한 제 13장 말미, *Lyrical Ballads*의 서문에 나타나는 워즈워드의 시론에 대한 비평과 그의 유기적 형식 이론을 피력한 제 14장과 17장, 운율 이론을 다룬 18장 등은 중요하다. 독일의 관념철학의 영향, 특히 Schelling의 영향을 받았다는 유기적 형식 이론은 "Shakespeare's Judgement Equal to His Genius"(1818?)와 "On Poesy or Art"(1818)에 집약되어 있다. 이 마지막 논문은 Friedrich Schelling의 「예술과 자연의 관계에 대하여」라는 논문에 많이 의존하고 있는 것으로 알려져 있다.

Biographia Literaria 제 14장에서 코울리지는 워즈워드와 더불어 세련된 도시생활이나 고전을 모방한 풍자시, 사회시와는

달리 자연에 충실함으로써 일반 독자의 공감을 불러일으킬 시를 쓸 수 있으리라는 결론에 도달, 워즈워드는 사실적 소재를, 코울리지 자신은 초자연적 소재를 취급하기로 하였다는 말을 하고 있는데, 이것이 바로 영국 낭만주의의 태동이었던 것이다.

워즈워드는 시집 서문에서 시와 산문이 서로 본질적 차이가 없다는 주장을 하였는 바, 코울리지는 이의 이론적 모순을 지적한다. 시와 산문이 서로 같은 요소를 공유하고 있다면, 그 차이는 그 요소들을 서로 다르게 배합한 까닭이고, 배합이 다른 것은 글의 목적이 다른 까닭이라고 말한다. 시의 운율은 산문에다 그냥 갖다 붙인 것이 아니라, 시의 다른 요소들과 뗄 수 없이 결합된 것이다. 즉 모든 요소들은 각각의 특성을 가진 채로 하나의 전체를 이루도록 화합한다. 요소들의 특성이 없다면 그것들이 모인 덩어리는 단지 한 덩어리일 뿐이고 부분과 전체의 긴장과 화합의 관계는 생길 수 없다. 좋은 시는 독자로 하여금 결말에 도달하고자 서둘러 읽어 나가지 않고 처음부터 끝까지 그 각 부분에서 즐거움을 얻고 그 즐거움들이 화합하여 전체를 이루고, 또한 그 전체에 속하여 있음으로 말미암아 부분들이 살아나는 모습을 즐기게 한다.

근본에 있어 다양하고, 서로 다르며, 서로 상충하는 부분들을 하나의 전체로 통일, 융합, 화해시키는 정신의 능력은 바로 상상력이다. 코울리지의 상상의 개념 중 특이한 것은 상상과 공상을 명확히 구분한다는 것이다. *Biographia Literaria* 제 4장과 13장의 짤막한 부분은 어떤 긴 이론적 논문보다도 상상과 공상의 구분을 명확히 해주고 있다. 상상은 다시 1차적 상상과 2차적 상상으로 구분되는데, 1차적 상상은 외부의 형상을 파악하는 주체의 기본적 능력을 말하고, 2차적 상상은 예술적 창조의 실제에 그 능력이 구체적으로 쓰인 양상을 말한다. 이러한 상상과는 달리 공상은 논리적 연결성을 벗어난 기억의 유희같은 것이다. 17세기의 홉즈 같은 이론가들이 상정했던 상상이란 실은 공상에 가까운 것이었다고 할 수 있다.

제 18 장에서는 좀 더 본격적으로 워즈워드의 시어의 개념을 비판한다. 워즈워드가 농촌의 언어를 거의 그대로 옮겨서 시를 썼다고 주장했으나, 코울리지는, 농촌의 언어 중에서 「골라서」 운율에 맞추어 재배합을 한 것이 천재적 시인인 워즈워드인 만큼, 그 시는 이미 농촌의 언어가 아니라 농촌의 언어를 재료로 하여 창조된 워즈워드의 시라고 명쾌하게 지적한다.

"Shakespeare's Judgement Equal to His Genius"에서는, 셰익스피어가 후천적으로는 판단력, 즉 비평적 안목이 보잘 것 없는 인물이지만 오직 놀라운 천부적 능력으로 기적 같은 작품을 생산했다는 끈질긴 이단설에 대하여, 타고난 그대로의 천재가 모든 사람이 감탄할 예술 작품이 되기 위하여서는 적절한 형식을 취하지 않을 수 없는 바, 바로 그 형식은 판단력, 비평적 안목에 의하여 주어지는 것이라고 주장한다. 자연이 예술 작품으로 구체화되기 위해서는 반드시 형식이 필요하다. 그러나 천재의 경우에 있어 그 형식은 외부로부터 처방에 의하여 주어지는 것이 아니라 내부의 자연이 외부로 향하여 성장하면서 동시에 취하는 모습인 것이다. 마치 나무의 생명이 씨가 싹이 터서 자람에 따라 스스로를 그 나무 껍질의 굴레 속에서 구현하는 것과도 같다. 이것이 바로 유기적 형식(organic form)이라는 것이며, 이는 생명과 그 형식의 불가분의 관계와도 같고, 내용에서 구분될 수 있는 기계적 형식과는 전혀 다른 것이다. 시인이 있기 전에 미리 마련된 시의 규칙이나 형식적 제약은 기계적 형식인 것이다.

"유기적 형식"의 개념은 "On Poesy or Art"에서 더욱 깊고 넓게 개진된다. 그는 예술은 자연의 모방이라는 고전적인 사상을 재해석한다. 모방은 모사(copy)가 아님을 그는 역설하고, 모방은 자연을 있는 그대로 옮겨 놓는 것이 아니라 같은 것과 다른 것을 동시에 포함하되 그 두 상극을 자체 내에서 화합시킨다고 한다. 모방의 대상은 자연의 아름다움으로서, 아름다움은 다양 속의 통일에서 온다. 그러나 이 통일, 이 형식은 살아 있는 다양성에서 스스로 우러나는 양상이어야 하고 기성의 제약의 결과에서 생겨난 것이어서는 안된다.

그러나 외부의 자연은 무한히, 무의미하게 다양할 뿐, 통일된 형식을 이루어서 보여주지는 않는다. 형식까지도 자연이 보여준다고 한 고전주의 이론가와는 달리, 코울리지는 시인이 자연의 다양함을 경험하고 나서 자신의 내부로 침잠하였다가 다시 자연의 다양성과 접할 때 그 다양성을 화합할 통일적 형식을 창조하게 된다고 주장한다. 이런 의미에서 예술은 자연과 인간을 화합시켜 주는 중재자인 것이다. 궁극적으로 예술은 인간으로 하여금 자연 속에서 인간답게 살 수 있게 해 준다고 믿은 것이다. 이런 사상은 오늘날의 미학 및 인식론으로 이어지고 있다.

On Imagination

REPEATED meditations led me first to suspect, (and a more intimate analysis of the human faculties, their appropriate marks, functions, and effects matured my conjecture into full conviction,) that fancy and imagination were two distinct and widely different faculties, instead of being, according to the general belief, either two names with one meaning, or, at furthest, the lower and higher degree of one and the same power. It is not, I own, easy to conceive a more opposite translation of the Greek *Phantasia* than the Latin Imagination;* but it is equally true that in all societies there exists an instinct of growth, a certain collective, unconscious good

*그리이스어의 **Phantasia** 란 말을 라틴어로 **Imaginatio** 라고 번역했는데, 그 후 phantasia 는 다시 fantasy (fancy) 로 그대로 음역하여 사용되기 시작했다. 그러니까 두 단어는 애초에는 동의어였다가 후에 오면서 서로 뜻이 전혀 달라진 것이다.

sense working progressively to desynonymize* those words originally of the same meaning, which the conflux* of dialects had supplied to the more homogeneous languages, as the Greek and German: and which the same cause, joined with accidents of translation from original works of different countries, occasion in mixt languages like our own. The first and most important point to be proved is, that two conceptions perfectly distinct are confused under one and the same word, and (this done) to appropriate that word exclusively to one meaning, and the synonyme (should there be one) to the other. But if (as will be often the case in the arts and sciences) no synonyme exists, we must either invent or borrow a word. In the present instance the appropriation has already begun, and been legitimated in the derivative adjective: Milton had a highly *imaginative*, Cowley, a very *fanciful* mind. If therefore I should succeed in establishing the actual existences of two faculties generally different, the nomenclature would be at once determined. To the faculty by which I had characterized Milton, we should confine the term *imagination;* while the other would be contradistinguished as *fancy*. Now were it once fully ascertained, that this division is no less grounded in nature, than that of delirum from mania*, or Otway's

Lutes, lobsters, seas of milk, and ship of amber*,

from Shakespeare's

What! have his daughters brought him to this pass?*

or from the preceding apostrophe to the elements; the theory of the fine arts, and of poetry in particular, could not,

---

***desynonymize:** 「뜻을 다르게 만들다」.

***conflux:** confluence. 「여러가지가 뒤섞임」. 영어는 그리이스어나 독일어보다 '뒤섞임'이 많은 언어이다. 그래서 동의어인 phantasia와 imaginatio를 동의어가 아닌 다른 뜻의 두 단어로 받아들인 것이다.

*delirium과 mania가 구별되듯 fancy와 imagination로 구별되는 것은 억지가 아니라 자연적 사실에 근거를 두고 있다.

*극작가 Thomas Otway (1652-82)의 *Venice Preserved*, V, ii, 151. fancy의 예.

*Shakespeare의 *Lear*, Ⅲ, iv, 63. imagination의 예.

I thought, but derive some addition and important light. It would in its immediate effects furnish a torch of guidance to the philosophical critic;* and ultimately to the poet himself. In energetic minds, truth soon changes by domestication into power; and from directing in the discrimination and appraisal of the product, becomes influencive* in the production. To admire on principle, is the only way to imitate without loss of originality.

The IMAGINATION then, I consider either as primary, or secondary. The primary IMAGINATION I hold to be the living Power and prime Agent of all human Perception, and as a repetition* in the finite mind of the eternal act of creation in the infinite I AM.* The secondary Imagination I consider as an echo of the former, coexisting with the conscious will, yet still as identical with the primary in the *kind* of its agency, and differing only in *degree*, and in the *mode* of its operation. It dissolves, diffuses, dissipates, in order to recreate; or where this process is rendered impossible, yet still at all events it struggles to idealize and to unify. It is essentially *vital*, even as all objects (*as* objects) are essentially fixed and dead.

FANCY, on the contrary, has no other counters* to play with, but fixities and definites. The Fancy is indeed no other than a mode of Memory emancipated from the order of time and space; while it is blended with, and modified by that empirical phenomenon of the will, which we express by the word CHOICE. But equally with the ordinary memory the Fancy must receive all its materials ready made from the law of association.

***philosophical critic:** 이론비평가, 문학이론가.

***influencive:** influential.

***repetition:** 뒤의 of the eternal act...에 연결됨. 「반복」이라기보다는 「반영」이라는 뜻.

***the infinite I AM:** 영원한 주체적 존재, 즉 하나님. 구약성서에서 하나님은 "I am that I am"으로 자칭한다.

***counter:** 「맞수, 놀이상대」.

From Biographia Literaria (1817)

CHAPTER XIV

Occasion of the Lyrical Ballads, and the objects originally proposed —Preface to the second edition—The ensuing controversy, its causes and acrimony—Philosophic definitions of a poem and poetry with scholia.

DURING the first year* that Mr. Wordsworth and I were neighbours, our conversations turned frequently on the two cardinal points of poetry, the power of exciting the sympathy of the reader by a faithful adherence to the truth of nature, and the power of giving the interest of novelty by the modifying colours of imagination.* The sudden charm, which accidents of light and shade, which moon-light or sun-set diffused over a known and familiar landscape, appeared to represent the practicability of combining both. These are the poetry of nature. The thought suggested itself (to which of us I do not recollect) that a series of poems might be composed of two sorts. In the one, the incidents and agents were to be, in part at least, supernatural; and the excellence aimed at was to consist in the interesting of the affections* by the dramatic truth of such emotions, as would naturally accompany such situations, supposing them real. And real in *this* sense* they have been to every human being who, from whatever source of delusion, has at any time believed himself under supernatural agency. For the second class, subjects were to be chosen from ordinary life; the charac-

---

*1797 년.

***the two cardinal...of imagination:** 사실적 문학과 상상적 문학의 두 영역을 말한다. 이 둘은 결합할 수도 있다.

***the interesting of the affections:** 「감정에게 자극을 유발시키는 것」.

***real in *this* sense:** 환상적인 소재도 정서적 진실성을 획득할 수 있으므로, '이런' 의미에서 사실적인 것이다. 다음에 오는 they 는 such (supernatural) situations.

ters and incidents were to be such, as will be found in every village and its vicinity, where there is a meditative and feeling mind to seek after them, or to notice them, when they present themselves.

In this idea originated the plan of the *Lyrical Ballads*; in which it was agreed, that my endeavours should be directed to persons and characters supernatural, or at least romantic; yet so as to transfer from our inward nature a human interest and a semblance of truth sufficient to procure for these shadows of imagination* that willing suspension of disbelief for the moment, which constitutes poetic faith.* Mr. Wordsworth, on the other hand, was to propose to himself* as his object, to give the charm of novelty to things of every day, and to excite a feeling analogous to the supernatural, by awakening the mind's attention from the lethargy of custom, and directing it to the loveliness and the wonders of the world before us; an inexhaustible treasure, but for which, in consequence of the film of familiarity and selfish solicitude, we have eyes, yet see not, ears that hear not, and hearts that neither feel nor understand.*

With this view I wrote 'The Ancient Mariner,' and was preparing among other poems, 'The Dark Ladie,' and the 'Christabel,' in which I should have more nearly realized my ideal, than I had done in my first attempt. But Mr. Wordsworth's industry had proved so much more successful, and the number of his poems so much greater, that my compositions, instead of forming a balance, appeared rather an interpolation of heterogeneous matter. Mr. Wordsworth added two or three

---

***shadows of imagination:** 즉 persons and characters supernatural, or at least romantic. 이런 가상적 인물에게도 인간적 진실의 면모를 부여해야 한다는 것.

***willing suspension of disbelief:** 「불신의 자발적 중단」. (매우 유명한 비평 개념).

***propose to oneself:** 「…을 하기로 정하다, …을 책임지다」. (목적어는 to give the charm...).

*평범한 사물이라 해도 놀라운 면이 있건만 친숙의 막이 덮여서 우리가 보지 못하고 있는데, 이를 다시금 보여주는 시를 Wordsworth 가 쓰기로 했다는 것.

poems written in his own character, in the impassioned, lofty, and sustained diction, which is characteristic of his genius. In this form the 'Lyrical Ballads' were published; and were presented by him, as an *experiment*,* whether subjects, which from their nature rejected the usual ornaments and extra-colloquial style of poems in general, might not be so managed in the language of ordinary life as to produce the pleasurable interest, which it is the peculiar business of poetry to impart. To the second edition he added a preface of considerable length; in which, notwithstanding some passages of apparently a contrary import, he was understood to contend for the extension of this style to poetry of all kinds, and to reject as vicious and indefensible all phrases and forms of style that were not included in what he (unfortunately, I think, adopting an equivocal expression) called the language of *real* life. From this preface, prefixed to poems in which it was impossible to deny the presence of original genius, however mistaken its direction might be deemed, arose the whole long-continued controversy. For from the conjunction of perceived power with supposed heresy I explain the inveteracy* and in some instances, I grieve to say, the acrimonious passions, with which the controversy has been conducted by the assailants.

Had Mr. Wordsworth's poems been the silly, the childish things, which they were for a long time described as being; had they been really distinguished from the compositions of other poets merely by meanness of language and inanity of thought; had they indeed contained nothing more than what is found in the parodies and pretended imitations of them; they must have sunk at once, a dead weight, into the slough of oblivion, and have dragged the preface along with them. But

---

*experiment: 오늘날에는 예술의 '실험'이 당연한 것으로 여겨지지만, 당시로서는 아마 처음으로 이 개념을 사용했을 것이다. 그만큼 *Lyrical Ballads* 는 의도적으로 혁명적이었다.

*inveteracy: 「고질, 끈덕짐」. Wordsworth 의 주장이 유력하다는 것을 인식함과 동시에 그것이 이단적 사설이라는 생각이 한데 어울리는 바람에 공격자들의 논란이 끈질겼고, 때에 따라서는 유감스럽게도 통열하기도 하였다고 생각한다.

year after year increased the number of Mr. Wordsworth's admirers. They were found too not in the lower classes of the reading public, but chiefly among young men of strong sensibility and meditative minds; and their admiration (inflamed perhaps in some degree by opposition) was distinguished by its intensity, I might almost say, by its *religious* fervour. These facts, and the intellectual energy of the author, which was more or less consciously felt, where it was outwardly and even boisterously denied,* meeting with sentiments of aversion to his opinions, and of alarm at their consequences, produced an eddy of criticism, which would of itself have borne up the poems by the violence with which it whirled them round and round. With many parts of this preface, in the sense attributed to them, and which the words undoubtedly seem to authorize, I never concurred;* but on the contrary objected to them as erroneous in principle, and as contradictory (in appearance at least) both to other parts of the same preface, and to the author's own practice in the greater number of the poems themselves. Mr. Wordsworth in his recent collection has, I find, degraded this prefatory disquisition to the end of his second volume, to be read or not at the reader's choice. But he has not, as far as I can discover, announced any change in his poetic creed. At all events, considering it as the source of a controversy, in which I have been honoured more than I deserve by the frequent conjunction of my name with his, I think it expedient to declare once for all, in what points I coincide with his opinions, and in what points I altogether differ. But in order to render myself intelligible I must previously, in as few words as possible, explain my ideas, first, of a POEM; and secondly, of POETRY itself, in *kind*, and in *essence*.

The office of philosophical *disquisition* consists in just *distinction*; while it is the privilege of the philosopher to preserve himself constantly aware, that distinction is not division. In

---

*Wordsworth의 일견 '무식한' 시 때문에 그는 지성적이지 못하다는 설이 강력했고, 지금도 그런 편견은 다소 남아 있다.

*concurred: 앞에 나온 with이하와 연결됨. concur with...: 「...에 동의하다」.

order to obtain adequate notions of any truth, we must intellectually separate its distinguishable parts; and this is the technical *process* of philosophy. But having so done, we must then restore them in our conceptions to the unity, in which they actually co-exist; and this is the *result* of philosophy. A poem contains the same elements as a prose composition; the difference therefore must consist in a different combination of them, in consequence of a different object being proposed.* According to the difference of the object will be the difference of the combination. It is possible, that the object may be merely to facilitate the recollection of any given facts or observations by artificial arrangement; and the composition will be a poem, merely because it is distinguished from prose by metre, or by rhyme, or by both conjointly. In this, the lowest sense, a man might attribute the name of a poem to the well-known enumeration of the days in the several months;

> 'Thirty days hath September,
> April, June, and November,' &c.

and others of the same class and purpose. And as a particular pleasure is found in anticipating the recurrence of sounds and quantities, all compositions that have this charm superadded, whatever be their contents, *may* be entitled poems.

So much for the superficial *form*. A difference of object and contents supplies an additional ground of distinction. The immediate purpose may be the communication of truths; either of truth absolute and demonstrable, as in works of science; or of facts experienced and recorded, as in history. Pleasure, and that of the highest and most permanent kind, may *result* from the *attainment* of the end; but it is not itself the immediate end. In other works the communication of pleasure may be the immediate purpose*; and though truth, either moral or intellectual, ought to be the *ultimate* end, yet this will distinguish

---

***in consequence...proposed:** 「다른 목적을 꾀하는 까닭에, 목적이 다른 까닭에」.

***immediate purpose of pleasure:** (Wordsworth 는 Coleridge에게서 이 개념

the character of the author, not the class to which the work belongs.* Blest indeed is that state of society, in which the immediate purpose would be baffled by the perversion of the proper ultimate end; in which no charm of diction or imagery could exempt the Bathyllus even of an Anacreon, or the Alexis of Virgil, from disgust and aversion!*

But the communication of pleasure may be the immediate object of a work not metrically composed; and that object may have been in a high degree attained, as in novels and romances. Would then the mere superaddition of metre, with or without rhyme, entitle *these* to the name of poems?* The answer is, that nothing can permanently please, which does not contain in itself the reason why it is so, and not otherwise. If metre be superadded, all other parts must be made consonant with it. They must be such, as to justify the perpetual and distinct attention to each part, which an exact correspondent recurrence of accent and sound are calculated to excite. The final definition then, so deduced, may be thus worded. A poem is that species of composition, which is opposed to works of science, by proposing for its *immediate* object pleasure,* not truth; and from all other species (having *this* object in common with it) it is dis-

---

을 배웠을 것이다). *cf.* The common essence of all [art] consists in the excitement of emotion for the ***immediate purpose of pleasure*** through the medium of beauty; herein contra-distinguishing poetry from science, the immediate object and primary purpose of which is truth and possible utility. (The sciences indeed may and will give a high and pure pleasure; and the Fine Arts may lead to important truth, in being in various ways useful in the ordinary meaning of the word; but these are not the directed characteristic ends. ...). "On the Principles of Genial Criticism concerning the Fine Arts" (1814).

***Bathylus** 는 pantomine 의 대가. **Alexis** 는 comedy 의 대가로서, Anacreon 과 Virgil 같은 심오한 진리의 시인들과는 반대로 통속작가들. 심각한 시를 통속화하면 아무리 아름답게 꾸몄더라도 혐오감을 자아내는 사회는 수준 높은 사회라는 것.

*Wordsworth 는 산문과 운문의 본질적 차이가 없다면서 meter 는 단지 superadded 한 것이라고 했는데, Coleridge 가 이의 오류를 명쾌히 지적하고 있다.

***by proposing...pleasure:** 여기서 pleasure 는 동명사 proposing 의 목적어.

criminated by proposing to itself such delight from the *whole*, as is compatible with a distinct gratification from each component *part*.*

Controversy is not seldom excited in consequence of the disputants attaching each a different meaning to the same word; and in few instances has this been more striking, than in disputes concerning the present subject. If a man chooses to call every composition a poem, which is rhyme, or measure, or both, I must leave his opinion uncontroverted. The distinction is at least competent to characterize the writer's intention. If it were subjoined, that the whole is likewise entertaining or affecting, as a tale, or as a series of interesting reflections, I of course admit this as another fit ingredient of a poem, and an additional merit. But if the definition sought for be that of a *legitimate* poem, I answer, it must be one, the parts of which mutually support and explain each other; all in their proportion harmonizing with, and supporting the purpose and known influences of metrical arrangement. The philosophic critics of all ages coincide with the ultimate judgement of all countries, in equally denying the praises of a just poem, on the one hand, to a series of striking lines or distiches, each of which, absorbing the whole attention of the reader to itself, disjoins it from its context, and makes it a separate whole, instead of a harmonizing part; and on the other hand, to an unsustained composition, from which the reader collects rapidly the general result, unattracted by the component parts. The reader should be carried forward, not merely or chiefly by the mechanical impulse of curiosity, or by a restless desire to arrive at the final solution; but by the pleasurable activity of mind excited by the attractions of the journey itself. Like the motion of a serpent, which the Egyptians made the emblem of intellectual power; or like the path of sound through the air; at every step he

**whole*과 *part*의 상호관련성. part들은 각각 독자적 즐거움(distinct gratification)이 있고, 이들은 또한 전체가 주는 즐거움(delight from the whole)과 화합한다. 부분과 전체의 어울림, 의존적 상호관계에 관한 유기체설을 논하고 있다. 다음의 legitimate poem에 대한 정의를 참조.

pauses and half recedes, and from the retrogressive movement collects the force which again carries him onward. 'Praecipitandus est *liber* spiritus,'* says Petronius Arbiter most happily.* The epithet, *liber*, here balances the preceding verb; and it is not easy to conceive more meaning condensed in fewer words.

But if this should be admitted as a satisfactory character of a poem, we have still to seek for a definition of poetry. The writings of PLATO, and Bishop TAYLOR, and the 'Theoria Sacra' of BURNET,* furnish undeniable proofs that poetry of the highest kind may exist without metre, and even without the contra-distinguishing objects of a poem. The first chapter of Isaiah (indeed a very large portion of the whole book) is poetry in the most emphatic sense; yet it would be not less irrational than strange to assert, that pleasure, and not truth, was the immediate object of the prophet. In short, whatever *specific* import we attach to the word, poetry, there will be found involved in it, as a necessary consequence, that a poem of any length neither can be, nor ought to be, all poetry. Yet if a harmonious whole is to be produced, the remaining parts must be preserved *in keeping* with the poetry; and this can be no otherwise effected than by such a studied selection and artificial arrangement, as will partake of *one*,* though not a *peculiar* property of poetry. And this again can be no other than the property of exciting a more continuous and equal attention than the language of prose aims at, whether colloquial or written.

My own conclusions on the nature of poetry, in the strict use

---

***praecipitandus...spiritus:** 'The free sprit should be urged on'(로마의 문필가 Petronius Arbiter의 *Satyricon*의 일절).

***most happily:** 「가장 적절하게」.

*시를 반대한 Plato, 17세기 대설교가 Jeremy Taylor, 역시 17세기 *Theoria Sacra*(=*Sacred Theory of the Earth*)의 저자인 Thomas Burnet의 산문들은 운율이 없으나 매우 리드미컬하고 시적이다. 그러나 그들의 immediate purpose는 truth이니까 시는 아니다. 운문은 산문과 달리 모든 부분에(운율의 최소 단위에) 흥미가 골고루 가게 한다.

***studied:** 「세심한」.

***one:** 즉 one property of poetry. (시에만 있는 특징은 아니나 시의 한 중요 특징을 가질 세심한 선택과 배열).

of the word, have been in part anticipated in the preceding disquisition on the fancy and imagination. What is poetry? is so nearly the same question with, what is a poet? that the answer to the one is involved in the solution of the other. For it is a distinction resulting from the poetic genius itself, which sustains and modifies the images, thoughts, and emotions of the poet's own mind.

The poet, described in *ideal* perfection, brings the whole soul of man into activity, with the subordination of its faculties to each other, according to their relative worth and dignity.* He diffuses a tone and spirit of unity, that blends, and (as it were) *fuses*, each into each, by that synthetic and magical power, to which we have exclusively appropriated the name of imagination. This power, first put in action by the will and understanding, and retained under their irremissive, though gentle and unnoticed, control (*laxis effertur habenis*)* reveals itself in the balance or reconciliation of opposite or discordant qualities: of sameness, with difference*; of the general, with the concrete; the idea, with the image; the individual, with the representative; the sense of novelty and freshness, with old and familiar objects; a more than usual state of emotion, with more than usual order; judgment ever awake and steady self-possession, with enthusiasm and feeling profound or vehement; and while it blends and harmonizes the natural and the artificial, still subordinates art to nature; the manner to the matter; and our admiration of the poet to our sympathy with the poetry.* 'Doubtless,' as Sir John Davies observes of the soul (and his words may with slight alteration be applied, and even more

---

*시는 사람의 온 영혼을 작동시키되, 무질서하게 흥분시키는 것이 아니라 영혼의 여러 기능들의 높고 낮음에 따라서 상하서열의 질서를 지킨다.

***laxis...*: 'Is carried along with loose reins.'

***of sameness, with difference:** 즉 balance or reconciliation of sameness with difference. 이하 같은 구문. 「서로 상반되는 것끼리의 균형 또는 화합」.

***our admiration...with the poetry:** 「시인에 대한 우리의 예찬을 시에 대한 우리의 공감에 부차적인 것으로 만든다」. 즉, 시인보다 시가 우리의 관심을 끈다.

appropriately, to the poetic IMAGINATION)

'Doubtless this could not be, but that she turns
Bodies to spirit by sublimation strange,
As fire converts to fire the things it burns,
As we our food into our nature change.

From their gross matter she abstracts their forms,
And draws a kind of quintessence from things;
Which to her proper nature she transforms,
To bear them light on her celestial wings.
Thus does she, when from individual states
She doth abstract the universal kinds;
Which then re-clothed in divers names and fates
Steal access through our senses to our minds.'

Finally, GOOD SENSE is the BODY of poetic genius, FANCY its DRAPERY, MOTION its LIFE, and IMAGINATION the SOUL that is everywhere, and in each; and forms all into one graceful and intelligent whole.

CHAPTER XVII

Examination of the tenets peculiar to Mr. Wordsworth—Rustic life (above all, *low* and rustic life) especially unfavourable to the formation of a human diction—The *best* parts of language the product of philosophers, not of clowns or shepherds—Poetry essentially ideal and generic—The language of Milton as much the language of *real* life, yea, incomparably more so than that of the cottager.

As far then as Mr. Wordsworth in his preface contended, and most ably contended, for a reformation in our poetic diction, as far as he has evinced* the truth of passion, and the *dramatic*

*철학적 시인 Sir John Davies(1569-1626)의 장시 *Nosce Teipsum* (Know Thyself)의 일절. Soul에 관한 것이지만 imagination에 관한 것으로도 해석할 수 있다고 Coleridge는 주장하고 있다. 시 속에 있는 she는 soul을 가리킨다.

***evince:** 여기서는 「폭로하다」의 뜻.

propriety of those figures and metaphors in the original poets, which, stripped of their justifying reasons, and converted into mere artifices of connection or ornament, constitute the characteristic falsity in the poetic style of the moderns;* and as far as he has, with equal acuteness and clearness, pointed out the process by which this change was effected, and the resemblances between that state into which the reader's mind is thrown by the pleasurable confusion of thought from an unaccustomed train of words and images;* and that state which is induced by the natural language of impassioned feeling; he undertook a useful task, and deserves all praise, both for the attempt and for the execution. The provocations* to this remonstrance in behalf of truth and nature were still of perpetual recurrence before and after the publication of this preface. I cannot likewise but add, that the comparison of such poems of merit, as have been given to the public within the last ten or twelve years, with the majority of those produced previously to the appearance of that preface, leave no doubt on my mind, that Mr. Wordsworth is fully justified in believing his efforts to have been by no means ineffectual. Not only in the verses of those who have professed their admiration of his genius, but even of those who have distinguished themselves by hostility to his theory, and depreciation of his writings, are the impressions of his principles plainly visible. It is possible, that with these principles others may have been blended, which are not equally evident; and some which are unsteady and subvertible from the narrowness or imperfection of their basis. But it is more than possible, that these errors of defect or exaggeration, by kindling and feeding the controversy, may have conduced not only to the wider propagation of the accompanying truths, but that, by their

---

***moderns:** 18세기 말에서 19세기 초까지의 poetic diction에 의존하던 시인들.

*실생활에서 들어보지 못한 이상한 시어를 읽으면서 저도 모르게 (기분좋게) 생각이 혼란되는 상태. (이에 비하여 Wordsworth는 평범한 말을 사용할 것을 주장한 것이다).

***provocations:** Wordsworth의 반론을 자극하는 보수적인 시와 비평들.

frequent presentation to the mind in an excited state, they may have won for them a more permanent and practical result. A man will borrow a part from his opponent the more easily, if he feels himself justified in continuing to reject a part. While there remain important points in which he can still feel himself in the right, in which he still finds firm footing for continued resistance, he will gradually adopt those opinions, which were the least remote from his own convictions, as not less congruous with his own theory than with that which he reprobates. In like manner with a kind of instinctive prudence, he will abandon by little and little his weakest posts, till at length he seems to forget that they had ever belonged to him, or affects to consider them at most as accidental and 'petty annexments,' the removal of which leaves the citadel unhurt and unendangered.

My own differences from certain supposed parts of Mr. Wordsworth's theory ground themselves on the assumption, that his words had been rightly interpreted, as purporting that the proper diction for poetry in general consists altogether in a language taken, with due exceptions, from the mouths of men in real life, a language which actually constitutes the natural conversation of men under the influence of natural feelings. My objection is, first, that in *any* sense this rule is applicable only to *certain* classes of poetry; secondly, that even to these classes it is not applicable, except in such a sense, as hath never by any one (as far as I know or have read) been denied or doubted; and lastly, that as far as, and in that degree in which it is *practicable*, yet as a *rule* it is useless, if not injurious, and therefore either need not, or ought not to be practised. The poet informs his reader, that he had generally chosen *low and rustic* life; but not *as* low and rustic, or in order to repeat that pleasure of doubtful moral effect,* which persons of elevated rank and of superior refinement oftentimes derive from

*실제 언어의 모방은 재미있지만, 도덕적 효용은 적은 듯하다는 것. 그러나 식자들이 하층민의 언어를 흉내내어 얻는 효과는 다음에 열거된 세 가지이다.

a happy *imitation* of the rude unpolished manners and discourse of their inferiors. For the pleasure so derived may be traced to three exciting causes. The first is the naturalness, in *fact*, of the things represented. The second is the apparent naturalness of the *representation*, as raised and qualified by an imperceptible infusion of the author's own knowledge and talent, which infusion does, indeed, constitute it an *imitation* as distinguished from a mere *copy*.* The third cause may be found in the reader's conscious feeling of his superiority awakened by the contrast presented to him; even as for the same purpose the kings and great barons of yore retained sometimes *actual* clowns and fools, but more frequently shrewd and witty fellows in that *character*.* These, however, were not Mr. Wordsworth's objects. *He* chose low and rustic life, 'because in that condition the essential passions of the heart find a better soil, in which they can attain their maturity, are less under restraint, and speak a plainer and more emphatic language; because in that condition of life our elementary feelings coexist in a state of greater simplicity, and consequently may be more accurately contemplated, and more forcibly communicated; because the manners of rural life germinate from those elementary feelings; and from the necessary character of rural occupations are more easily comprehended, and are more durable; and lastly, because in that condition the passions of men are incorporated with the beautiful and permanent forms of nature.'

Now it is clear to me, that in the most interesting of the poems, in which the author is more or less dramatic, as 'the Brothers,' 'Michael,' 'Ruth,' 'the Mad Mother,' &c., the persons introduced are by no means taken *from low or rustic life* in the common acceptation of those words; and it is not less clear, that the sentiments and language, as far as they can be conceived to have been really transferred from the minds and

---

***imitation, copy:** 이론가들이 늘 다루는 두 개념이다. 녹음기에 의한 기록은 copy가 될 것이고, 소설가의 재구성은 imitation이 될 것이다. Imitation은 저자의 내밀한 간섭 (imperceptible infusion)의 결과이다.

***in that charater:** fool이나 clown이라는 역할.

conversation of such persons, are attributable to causes and circumstances not necessarily connected with 'their occupations and abode.' The thoughts, feelings, language, and manners of the shepherd-farmers in the vales of Cumberland and Westmoreland,* as far as they are actually adopted in those poems, may be accounted for from causes, which will and do produce the same results in *every* state of life, whether in town or country.* As the two principal* I rank that INDEPENDENCE, which raises a man above servitude, or daily toil for the profit of others, yet not above the necessity of industry and a frugal simplicity of domestic life; and the accompanying unambitious, but solid and religious, EDUCATION, which has rendered few books familiar, but the Bible, and the liturgy or hymn book. To this latter cause, indeed, which is so far *accidental*, that it is the blessing of particular countries and a particular age, not the product of particular places or employments, the poet owes the show of probability, that his personages might really feel, think, and talk with any tolerable resemblance to his representation. It is an excellent remark of Dr. Henry More's,* (*Enthusiasmus Triumphatus*; Sec. XXXV.), that 'a man of confined education, but of good parts, by constant reading of the Bible will naturally form a more winning and commanding rhetoric than those that are learned; the intermixture of tongues and of artificial phrases debasing *their* style.'

It is, moreover, to be considered that to the formation of healthy feelings, and a reflecting mind, *negations* involve impediments not less formidable than sophistication and vicious

---

*Cumberland, Westmoreland: 이 두 지역은 Wordsworth의 시의 배경이 되는 영국 서북부지방.

*Wordsworth가 작품에 사용한 대로의 언어는 영국 서북부의 시골말이라기보다는 어디에서나 들을 수 있는 보편적인 언어라는 것. 이 견해는 매우 중요한 지적인데, Wordsworth는 copy 아닌 imitation을 제시한 것이다. from: by.

*principal: principal causes. Wordsworth가 사용한 언어의 효과의 두 원인, 즉 independence와 education. 영국의 평민은 당시 유럽에서 가장 수준이 높았음.

*Henry More: 17세기 Cambridge 대학의 Platonists의 거두.

intermixture. I am convinced, that for the human soul to prosper in rustic life a certain vantage-ground is pre-requisite. It is not every man that is likely to be improved by a country life or by country labours. Education, or original sensibility, or both, must pre-exist, if the changes, forms, and incidents of nature are to prove a sufficient stimulant.* And where these are not sufficient, the mind contracts and hardens by want of stimulants: and the man becomes selfish, sensual, gross, and hard-hearted. Let the management of the POOR LAWS* in Liverpool, Manchester, or Bristol be compared with the ordinary dispensation of the poor rates in agricultural villages, where the *farmers* are the overseers and guardians of the poor. If my own experience have not been particularly unfortunate, as well as that of the many respectable country clergymen with whom I have conversed on the subject, the result would engender more than scepticism concerning the desirable influences of low and rustic life in and for itself. Whatever may be concluded on the other side, from the stronger local attachments and enterprising spirit of the Swiss, and other mountaineers, applies to a particular mode of pastoral life, under forms of property that permit and beget manners truly republican, not to rustic life in general, or to the absence of artificial cultivation. On the contrary the mountaineers, whose manners have been so often eulogized, are in general better educated and greater readers than men of equal rank elsewhere. But where this is not the case, as among the peasantry of North Wales, the ancient mountains, with all their terrors and all their glories, are pictures to the blind, and music to the deaf.*

I should not have entered so much into detail upon this passage, but here seems to be the point, to which all the lines

---

*단순히 농촌에 산다고 해서 좋은 사람이 된다는 보장이 없다는 이 생각은 Wordsworth 나 Rousseau 의 단순한 자연회귀사상의 오류를 예리하게 지적하고 있다.

***the poor laws:** 「빈민구제법」. 요즘의 사회복지법의 선구. 이 법에 따라 수용소가 설치됨.

*교육이 없는 산간 주민들에게는 소경의 경치요 귀머거리의 음악인 셈이다.

of difference converge as to their source and centre. (I mean, as far as, and in whatever respect, my poetic creed *does* differ from the doctrines promulged in this preface.) I adopt with full faith the principle of Aristotle, that poetry as poetry is essentially *ideal*, that it avoids and excludes all *accident*; that its apparent individualities of rank, character, or occupation must be *representative* of a class; and that the *persons* of poetry must be clothed with *generic* attributes, with the *common* attributes of the class: not with such as one gifted individual might *possibly* possess, but such as from his situation it is most probable beforehand that he *would* possess.* If my premises are right and my deductions legitimate, it follows that there can be no *poetic* medium between the swains of Theocritus and those of an imaginary golden age.*

The characters of the vicar and the shepherd-mariner in the poem of 'THE BROTHERS,' that of the shepherd of Greenhead Ghyll in the 'MICHAEL,'* have all the verisimilitude and representative quality, that the purposes of poetry can require. They are persons of a known and abiding class, and their manners and sentiments the natural product of circumstances common to the class. Take 'MICHAEL' for instance:

> 'An old man stout of heart, and strong of limb:
> His bodily frame had been from youth to age
> Of an unusual strength: his mind was keen,
> Intense, and frugal, apt for all affairs,
> And in his shepherd's calling he was prompt
> And watchful more than ordinary men.
> Hence he had learnt the meaning of all winds,
> Of blasts of every tone; and oftentimes
> When others heeded not, he heard the South*

---

cf. Poetics, IX. 아무리 사실적인 인물을 모델로 했더라도 작가가 문학적으로 취급하면 사실적인 데 머물지 않고 보편적 (generic, ideal)으로 된다는 것.

*그리이스의 전원시인 Theocritus의 인물들은 모두 사실적 인물에서 따온 것이나, 시 속에서의 그들의 말씨는 시골사람의 것이 아니라 시적인 것이다.

***"The Brothers"**와 **"Michael"**은 Wordsworth의 시의 방법이 잘 구현된 작품들.

***the South:** south wind.

Make subterraneous music, like the noise
Of bagpipers on distant Highland hills.
The shepherd, at such warning, of his flock
Bethought him,* and he to himself would say,
The winds are now devising work for me!
And truly at all times the storm, that drives
The traveller to a shelter, summon'd him
Up to the mountains. He had been alone
Amid the heart of many thousand mists,
That came to him and left him on the heights.
So liv'd he, till his eightieth year was pass'd.
And grossly that man errs, who should suppose
That the green valleys, and the streams and rocks,
Were things indifferent to the shepherd's thoughts.
Fields, where with cheerful spirits he had breath'd
The common air; the hills, which he so oft
Had climb'd with vigorous steps; which had impress'd
So many incidents upon his mind
Of hardship, skill or courage, joy or fear;
Which, like a book, preserved the memory
Of the dumb animals, whom he had sav'd,
Had fed or shelter'd, linking to such acts,
So grateful in themselves, the certainty
Of honourable gain; these fields, these hills
Which were his living being, even more
Than his own blood—what could they less? had laid
Strong hold on his affections, were to him
A pleasurable feeling of blind love,
The pleasure which there is in life itself.'

On the other hand, in the poems which are pitched at a lower note, as the 'HARRY GILL,' 'IDIOT BOY,' the *feelings* are those of human nature in general; though the poet has judiciously laid the *scene* in the country, in order to place *himself* in the vicinity of interesting images, without the necessity of ascribing a sentimental perception of their beauty to the persons of his drama. In the 'Idiot Boy,'* indeed, the mother's character is not so

*Bethought him: Bethought him of his flock. 「자기 양떼를 기억했다」. bethink는 재귀동사로 현재는 쓰이지 않음.

*"The Idiot Boy"의 주인공인 백치아들은 어머니의 긴급한 심부름을 가면

much a real and native product of a 'situation where the essential passions of the heart find a better soil, in which they can attain their maturity and speak a plainer and more emphatic language,' as it is an impersonation of an instinct abandoned by judgement. Hence the two following charges seem to me not wholly groundless: at least, they are the only plausible objections, which I have heard to that fine poem. The one is, that the author has not, in the poem itself, taken sufficient care to preclude from the reader's fancy the disgusting images of *ordinary morbid idiocy*, which yet it was by no means his intention to represent. He has even by the 'burr, burr, burr,' uncounteracted by any preceding description of the boy's beauty, assisted in recalling them. The other is, that the idiocy of the *boy* is so evenly balanced by the folly of the *mother*, as to present to the general reader rather a laughable burlesque on the blindness of anile dotage, than an analytic display of maternal affection in its ordinary workings.

In the "Thorn"* the poet himself acknowledges in a note the necessity of an introductory poem, in which he should have portrayed the character of the person from whom the words of the poem are supposed to proceed: a superstitious man moderately imaginative, of slow faculties and deep feelings, 'a captain of a small trading vessel, for example, who, being past the middle age of life, had retired upon an annuity, or small independent income, to some village or country town of which he was not a native, or in which he had not been accustomed to live. Such men having nothing to do become credulous and talkative from indolence.' But in a poem, still more in a lyric poem (and the NURSE in Shakespeare's *Romeo and Juliet* alone prevents me from extending the remark even to dramatic *poetry*, if indeed the Nurse itself can be deemed alto-

---

서 "burr, burr"라고 중얼거린다. 백치에 관한 유치한 글이 아닌가 하는 의심이 들 정도로 이 시는 괴이하다. 어머니의 모성애라는 보편적 주제가 잘 드러나 있지 못하다.

* "**The Thorn**"도 역시 실패작. 서정시에 말이 많은 화자의 말을 그대로 인용하는 것은 무리가 있다는 것. 오히려 시인 자신이 하는 말이 좋았으리라는 것이다.

gether a case in point) it is not possible to imitate truly a dull and garrulous discourser, without repeating the effects of dullness and garrulity. However this may be, I dare assert, that the parts (and these form the far larger portion of the whole) which might as well or still better have proceeded from the poet's own imagination, and have been spoken in his own character, are those which have given, and which will continue to give, universal delight; and that the passages exclusively appropriate to the supposed narrator, such as the last couplet of the third stanza; the seven last lines of the tenth; and the five following stanzas, with the exception of the four admirable lines at the commencement of the fourteenth, are felt by many unprejudiced and unsophisticated hearts, as sudden and unpleasant sinkings from the height to which the poet had previously lifted them, and to which he again re-elevates both himself and his reader.

If then I am compelled to doubt the theory, by which the choice of *characters* was to be directed, not only *a priori*, from grounds of reason, but both from the few instances in which the poet himself *need* be supposed to have been governed by it, and from the comparative inferiority of those instances; still more must I hesitate in my assent to the sentence which immediately follows the former citation; and which I can neither admit as particular fact, or as general rule. 'The language too of these men is adopted (purified indeed from what appear to be its real defects, from all lasting and rational causes of dislike or disgust) because such men hourly communicate with the best objects from which the best part of language is originally derived; and because, from their rank in society and the sameness and narrow circle of their intercourse, being less under the action of social vanity, they convey their feelings and notions in simple and unelaborated expressions.' To this I reply; that a rustic's language, purified from all provincialism and grossness, and so far reconstructed as to be made consistent with the rules of grammar (which are in essence no other than the laws of universal logic, applied to psychological materials) will not differ from the language of any other man of common sense, however learned or refined he may be, except as far as the notions, which the rustic has to convey, are fewer and more indiscriminate. This will become still clearer, if we add the consideration (equally important though less obvious) that the rustic, from the more imperfect development of his faculties, and from the lower state of their cultivation, aims almost solely to convey *insulated facts*, either those of his scanty experience or his traditional belief; while the educated man chiefly seeks to discover and express those *connections* of things, or those relative *bearings* of fact to fact, from which some more or less general law is deducible. For *facts* are valuable to a wise man, chiefly as they lead to the discovery of the indwelling *law*, which is the true *being* of things, the sole solution of their modes of existence, and in the knowledge of which consists our dignity and our power.

As little can I agree with the assertion, that from the objects with which the rustic hourly communicates the best part of language is formed. For first, if to communicate with an object implies such an acquaintance with it, as renders it capable of being discriminately reflected on; the distinct knowledge of an uneducated rustic would furnish a very scanty vocabulary. The few things, and modes of action, requisite for his bodily conveniences, would alone be individualized; while all the rest of nature would be expressed by a small number of confused general terms. Secondly, I deny that the words and combinations of words derived from the objects, with which the rustic is familiar, whether with distinct or confused knowledge, can be justly said to form the *best* part of language. It is more than probable, that many classes of the brute creation* possess discriminating sounds, by which they can convey to each other notices of such objects as concern their food, shelter, or safety. Yet we hesitate to call the aggregate of such sounds a language, otherwise than metaphorically. The best part of human language, properly so called, is derived from reflection

*brute creation: 「야생동물」.

on the acts of the mind itself. It is formed by a voluntary appropriation of fixed symbols to internal acts, to processes and results of imagination, the greater part of which have no place in the consciousness of uneducated man; though in civilized society, by imitation and passive remembrance of what they hear from their religious instructors and other superiors, the most uneducated share in the harvest* which they neither sowed or reaped. If the history of the phrases in hourly currency* among our peasants were traced, a person not previously aware of the fact would be surprised at finding so large a number, which three or four centuries ago were the exclusive property of the universities and the schools; and, at the commencement of the Reformation, had been transferred from the school to the pulpit, and thus gradually passed into common life. The extreme difficulty, and often the impossibility, of finding words for the simplest moral and intellectual processes of the languages of uncivilized tribes has proved perhaps the weightiest obstacle to the progress of our most zealous and adroit missionaries. Yet these tribes are surrounded by the same nature as our peasants are; but in still more impressive forms; and they are, moreover, obliged to *particularize* many more of them. When, therefore, Mr. Wordsworth adds, 'accordingly, such a language' (meaning, as before, the language of rustic life purified from provincialism) 'arising out of repeated experience and regular feelings, is a more permanent, and a far more philosophical language, than that which is frequently substituted for it by poets, who think they are conferring honour upon themselves and their art in proportion as they indulge in arbitrary and capricious habits of expression:' it may be answered, that the language, which he has in view, can be attributed to rustics with no greater right, than the style of Hooker or Bacon to Tom Brown or Sir Roger

---

***harvest:** 「문화적 노력으로 생긴 성과, 즉 지식」. 이 지식은 무식한 사람들이 노력에 의하지 않고서도, 설교 등을 통해 상당한 정도로 알게 된다는 것.

***hourly currency:** 「늘 통용되고 있는 것」.

L'Estrange.* Doubtless, if what is peculiar to each were omitted in each, the result must needs be the same. Further, that* the poet, who uses an illogical diction, or a style fitted to excite only the low and changeable pleasure of wonder by means of groundless novelty, substitutes a language of *folly* and *vanity*, not for that of the *rustic*, but for that of *good sense* and *natural feeling*.

Here let me be permitted to remind the reader, that the positions, which I controvert, are contained in the sentences—'*a selection of the* REAL *language of men;*'—'*the language of these men*' (i.e. men in low and rustic life) *has been adopted.*' '*I propose to myself to imitate, and, as far as is possible, to adopt the very language of men.*' '*Between the language of prose and that of metrical composition, there neither is, nor can be any essential difference.*' It is against these exclusively that my opposition is directed.

I object, in the very first instance, to an equivocation in the use of the word 'real'. Every man's language varies, according to the extent of his knowledge, the activity of his faculties, and the depth or quickness of his feelings. Every man's language has, first, its *individualities*; secondly, the common properties of the *class* to which he belongs; and thirdly, words and phrases of *universal* use. The language of Hooker, Bacon, Bishop Taylor, and Burke* differs from the common language of the learned class only by the superior number and novelty of the thoughts and relations which they had to convey. The language of Algernon Sidney* differs not at all from that, which every well-educated gentleman would wish to write, and (with due allowances for the undeliberateness, and less connected train, of thinking natural and proper to conversation) such as he would wish to talk. Neither one nor the other differ half so much

---

***Tom Brown** 과 **L'Estrange** 는 17세기 후반에서 18세기 초에 활약한 2류 저널리스트. 그들의 문장은 16세기 최대 산문가인 Richard Hooker나 Bacon에 결코 미칠 수 없다.

***that:** 훨씬 앞에 나온 it may be answered에 의미상 연결된다.

***Bishop Jeremy Taylor** 는 17세기 중엽의 대 설교가. **Edmund Burke** 는 18세기 후반 에이레 출신의 문장가.

***Algernon Sidney:** 17세기의 혁신 정치가, 문장가. Wordsworth 가 칭찬함.

from the general language of cultivated society, as the language of Mr. Wordsworth's homeliest composition differs from that of a common peasant. For 'real' therefore, we must substitute *ordinary*, or *lingua communis*.* And this, we have proved, is no more to be found in the phraseology of low and rustic life than in that of any other class. Omit the peculiarities of each, and the result of course must be common to all. And assuredly the omissions and changes to be made in the language of rustics, before it could be transferred to any species of poem, except the drama or other professed imitation, are at least as numerous and weighty, as would be required in adapting to the same purpose the ordinary language of tradesmen and manufacturers. Not to mention, that the language so highly extolled by Mr. Wordsworth varies in every county, nay in every village, according to the accidental character of the clergyman, the existence or non-existence of schools; or even, perhaps, as the exciseman, publican, or barber, happen to be, or not to be, zealous politicians, and readers of the weekly newspaper *pro bono publico*.* Anterior to cultivation, the *lingua communis* of every country, as Dante has well observed,* exists everywhere in parts, and no where as a whole.

Neither is the case rendered* at all more tenable by the addition of the words, *in a state of excitement*. For the nature of a man's words, where he is strongly affected by joy, grief, or anger, must necessarily depend on the number and quality of the general truths, conceptions and images, and of the words expressing them, with which his mind had been previously stored. For the property of passion is not to *create*; but to set in increased activity. At least, whatever new connections of thoughts or images, or (which is equally, if not more than

---

******lingua communis***:** 'common language' 「공용어」. **Wordsworth**가 real language라고 한 것은 한 집단의 공용어란 의미 이외에 다른 것을 뜻하지 않는 것이라는 것. 실제 언어는 다 그런 성질의 것이다.

******pro bono publico***:** 'for the public good'.

***Dante**는 그의 *De Vulgari Eloquentia*에서 이탈리아의 전국적 공용어를 찾을 수 없음을 개탄했다.

***rendered:** made.

equally, the appropriate effect of strong excitement), whatever generalizations of truth or experience, the heat of passion may produce; yet the terms of their conveyance must have pre-existed in his former conversations, and are only collected and crowded together by the unusual stimulation.* It is indeed very possible to adopt in a poem the unmeaning repetitions, habitual phrases, and other blank counters,* which an unfurnished or confused understanding interposes at short intervals, in order to keep hold of his subject, which is still slipping from him, and to give him time for recollection; or in mere aid of vacancy, as in the scanty companies of a country stage the same player pops backwards and forwards, in order to prevent the appearance of empty spaces, in the procession of Macbeth, or Henry VIIIth. But what assistance to the poet, or ornament to the poem, these can supply, I am at a loss to conjecture. Nothing assuredly can differ either in origin or in mode more widely from the *apparent* tautologies of intense and turbulent feeling, in which the passion is greater and of longer endurance than to be exhausted or satisfied by a single representation of the image or incident exciting it. Such repetitions I admit to be a beauty of the highest kind; as illustrated by Mr. Wordsworth himself from the song of Deborah. '*At her feet he bowed, he fell, he lay down; at her feet he bowed, he fell; where he bowed, there he fell down dead.*'*

---

*흥분상태의 시골사람의 말을 그대로 사용했다는 Wordsworth의 주장에 대하여 흥분(passion)은 언어사용을 자극할 수는 있으되 언어를 창조하지는 못한다는 것이다. 즉, 미리 알고 있는 말이 있어야 흥분상태에서 사용할 수 있다는 것.

***blank counters:** 「무의미한 어귀」. (우리말의 '거시기' 같은 것).

*구약 「판관기」 5장 27절. 여기의 반복은 상투적 어귀의 반복과는 다른 예술적 차원의 것이다.

Shakespeare's Judgment Equal to His Genius (1818?)

THUS, then, Shakespeare appears, from his *Venus and Adonis* and *Rape of Lucrece* alone, apart from all his great works, to have possessed all the conditions of the true poet. Let me now proceed to destroy, as far as may be in my power, the popular notion that he was a great dramatist by mere instinct, that he grew immortal in his own despite, and sank below men of second or third-rate power when he attempted aught beside the drama — even as bees construct their cells and manufacture their honey to admirable perfection; but would in vain attempt to build a nest. Now this mode of reconciling a compelled sense of inferiority with a feeling of pride began in a few pedants, who, having read that Sophocles was the great model of tragedy, and Aristotle the infallible dictator of its rules, and finding that the *Lear, Hamlet, Othello,* and other masterpieces were neither in imitation of Sophocles nor in obedience to Aristotle — and, not having (with one or two exceptions) the courage to affirm, that the delight which their country received from generation to generation, in defiance of the alterations of circumstances and habits, was wholly groundless — took upon them, as a happy medium and refuge, to talk of Shakespeare as a sort of beautiful *lusus naturae,** a delightful monster, wild, indeed, and without taste or judgment, but like the inspired idiots so much venerated in the East,* uttering, amid the strangest follies, the sublimest truths. In nine places out of ten in which I find

---

***in his own despite:** 「자기 자신도 뜻하지 않게」.

****lusus naturae*:** 'funny thing of nature.' Shakespeare가 고전을 모방하지도, 법칙을 따르지도 않았으면서 (즉 무식한 사람이면서) 놀라운 작품을 썼으니, '자연'에 의하여 만들어진 즐겁고 놀라운 현상이라는 것. Voltaire 등도 이같은 견해를 보였다.

*동양의 어느 종파에서는 무식한 사람의 말 속에 진실이 들어있다고 믿음.

his awful name mentioned, it is with some epithet of "wild," "irregular," "pure child of nature," etc. If all this be true, we must submit to it; though to a thinking mind it cannot but be painful to find any excellence, merely human, thrown out of all human analogy,* and thereby leaving us neither rules for imitation, nor motives to imitate; but, if false, it is a dangerous falsehood; for it affords a refuge to secret self-conceit, enables a vain man at once to escape his reader's indignation by general* swollen panegyrics, and merely by his *ipse dixit** to treat as contemptible what he has not intellect enough to comprehend, or soul to feel, without assigning any reason, or referring his opinion to any demonstrative principle; thus leaving Shakespeare as a sort of Grand Lama,* adored indeed, and his very excrements prized as relics, but with no authority or real influence. I grieve that every late voluminous edition of his works would enable me to substantiate the present charge* with a variety of facts, one-tenth of which would of themselves exhaust the time allotted to me. Every critic, who has or has not made a collection of black letter books — in itself a useful and respectable amusement — puts on the seven-league boots of self-opinion,* and strides at once from an illustrator* into a supreme judge, and blind and deaf, fills his three-ounce phial at the waters of Niagara;* and determines positively the greatness of the

---

***thrown out...analogy:** 모든 인간과의 공통요소가 없는 것으로 치부되어 제외되는 것.

***general:** 「근거없이 막연한」.

****ipse dixit*:** 'he said' 「그 분은 말씀하셨다」(권위자의 이름을 들먹이는 말투).

***Grand Lama:** 티베트 종교의 절대적 지도자. 그의 일거일동, 언행 일체가 신성시된다.

***charge:** 「비난」. Coleridge가 당시의 Shakespeare 예찬이 전혀 허황된 것임을 비난하는 것.

***seven-league...self-opinion:** 「굉장히 큰 자만심」. (seven-league boots는 동화에 나오는 요술신발로, 한꺼번에 7 leagues나 갈 수 있다고) 기껏 black letter books를 모은 무식한 평론가를 야유한다.

***illustrator:** 「삽화가」. 즉 남의 책을 읽고 흉내내는 차.

***the water of Niagara:** 즉 Shakespeare를 가리킨다. 겨우 3oz 들어갈 정도의 병으로 그 엄청난 양의 물을 담으려 하는 못난 평론가들의 판단력을 비꼬고 있다.

cataract to be neither more nor less than his three-ounce phial has been able to receive.

I think this a very serious subject. It is my earnest desire — my passionate endeavour — to enforce at various times and by various argunments and instances the close and reciprocal connection of just taste with pure morality. Without that acquaintance with the heart of man, or that docility and childlike gladness to be made acquainted with it, which those only can have, who dare look at their own hearts — and that with a steadiness which religion only has the power of reconciling with sincere humility; without this, and the modesty produced by it, I am deeply convinced that no man, however wide his erudition, however patient his antiquarian researches, can possibly understand, or be worthy of understanding, the writings of Shakespeare.

Assuredly, that criticism of Shakespeare will alone be genial which is reverential. The Englishman, who without reverence, a proud and affectionate reverence, can utter the name of William Shakespeare, stands disqualified for the office of critic. He wants one at least of the very senses, the language of which he is to employ,* and will discourse, at best but as a blind man, while the whole harmonious creation of light and shade with all its subtle interchange of deepening and dissolving colours rises in silence to the silent *fiat** of the uprising Apollo. However inferior in ability I may be to some who have followed me, I own I am proud that I was the first in time who publicly demonstrated to the full extent of the position, that the supposed irregularity and extravagancies of Shakespeare were the mere dreams of a pedantry that arraigned the eagle because it had not the dimensions of the swan.* In all the successive courses of lectures delivered by me, since

---

***He wants...employ:** Shakepeare에 대한 존경심이 없는 비평가는 그가 사용할 언어의 의미 중의 적어도 한 가지는 모른다.

***fiat:** 「명령, 분부」. 다음의 Apollo는 태양, 비유적으로 Shakespeare를 가리킨다.

*eagle이 swan과 다르다고 해서 비난한 현학의 풍조. Shakespeare는 swan처럼 조용한 grace와는 전혀 다른 기개 즉 eagle 같은 비상하는 용기를 가졌다는 비유.

my first attempt at the Royal Institution, it has been, and it still remains, my object, to prove that in all points from the most important to the most minute, the judgment of Shakespeare is commensurate with his genius, nay, that his genius reveals itself in his judgment, as in its most exalted form. And the more gladly do I recur to this subject from the clear conviction, that to judge aright, and with distinct consciousness of the grounds of our judgment, concerning the works of Shakespeare, implies the power and the means of judging rightly of all other works of intellect, those of abstract science alone excepted.

It is a painful truth that not only individuals, but even whole nations, are ofttimes so enslaved to the habits of their education and immediate circumstances, as not to judge disinterestedly even on those subjects, the very pleasure arising from which consists in its distinterestedness, namely, on subjects of taste and polite literature.* Instead of deciding concerning their own modes and customs by any rule of reason, nothing appears rational, becoming, or beautiful to them, but what coincides with the peculiarities of their education. In this narrow circle, individuals may attain to exquisite discrimination, as the French critics have done in their own literature; but a true critic can no more be such* without placing himself on some central point, from which he may command the whole, that is, some general rule, which, founded in reason, or the faculties common to all men, must therefore apply to each, than an astronomer can explain the movements of the solar system without taking his stand in the sun. And let me remark, that this will not tend to produce despotism, but, on the contrary, true tolerance, in the critic. He will, indeed, require, as the spirit and substance of a work, something true in human nature itself, and independent of all circumstances; but in the mode of applying it, he will estimate genius and judgment according to the felicity* with which the imperishable soul of intellect shall have

***polite literature:** 「문학」. (literature는 문헌, 글 일체를 가리킨다).
***such:** a true critic.
***felicity:** 「적절함, 잘 어울림」.

adapted itself to the age, the place, and the existing manners. The error he will expose lies in reversing this, and holding up the mere circumstances as perpetual, to the utter neglect of the power which can alone animate them. For art cannot exist without, or apart from, nature; and what has man of his own* to give to his fellow-man, but his own thoughts and feelings, and his observations so far as they are modified by his own thoughts or feelings?

Let me, then, once more submit this question to minds emancipated alike from national, or party, or sectarian prejudice. Are the plays of Shakespeare works of rude uncultivated genius, in which the splendour of the parts compensates, if aught can compensate, for the barbarous shapelessness and irregularity of the whole? Or is the form equally admirable with the matter, and the judgment of the great poet not less deserving our wonder than his genius? Or, again, to repeat the question in other words: Is Shakespeare a great dramatic poet on account only of those beauties and excellencies which he possesses in common with the ancients, but with diminished claims to our love and honour to the full extent of his differences from them? Or are these very differences additional proofs of poetic wisdom, at once results and symbols of living power as contrasted with lifeless mechanism — of free and rival originality as contradistiguished from servile imitation, or, more accurately, a blind copying of effects, instead of a true imitation of the essential principles? Imagine not that I am about to oppose genius to rules. No! the comparative value of these rules is the very cause to be tried.* The spirit of poetry, like all other living powers, must of necessity circumscribe itself by rules, were it only to unite power with beauty. It must embody in order to reveal itself; but a living body is of necessity an organized one; and what is organization but the connection of parts in and for a whole, so that each part is at once end and means? This is the discovery of criticism; it is a necessity of the human mind; and

---

***of his own:** what에 걸림. 「(사람은) 자기 자신의 (어떤 것을)…」.

***the comparative...to be tried:** 「문학의 법칙들이 상대적인 가치를 가졌다는 것은 그들을 실제로 실험해 보아야 할 이유가 된다」.

all nations have felt and obeyed it, in the ınvention of metre, and measured sounds, as the vehicle and *involucrum** of poetry, itself a fellow-growth from the same life, even as the bark is to the tree!

No work of true genius dares want its appropriate form, neither indeed is there any danger of this. As it must not, so genius cannot, be lawless; for it is even this that constitutes its genius — the power of acting creatively under laws of its own origination. How then comes it that not only single *Zoili*,* but whole nations have combined in unhesitating condemnation of our great dramatist, as a sort of African nature, rich in beautiful monsters, as a wild heath where islands of fertility look the greener from the surrounding waste, where the loveliest plants now shine out among unsightly weeds, and now are choked by their parasitic growth, so intertwined that we cannot disentangle the weed without snapping the flower? In this statement I have had no reference to the vulgar abuse of Voltaire, save as far as his charges are coincident with the decisions of Shakespeare's own commentators and (so they would tell you) almost idolatrous admirers. The true ground of the mistake lies in the confounding mechanical regularity with organic form. The form is mechanic, when on any given material we impress a pre-determined form, not necessarily arising out of the properties of the material; as when to a mass of wet clay we give whatever shape we wish it to retain when hardened. The organic form, on the other hand, is innate; it shapes, as it developes, itself from within, and the fulness of its development is one and the same with the perfection of its outward form. Such as the life is, such is the form. Nature, the prime genial artist, inexhaustible in diverse powers, is equally inexhaustrible in forms, each exterior is the physiognomy of the being within its true image reflected and

---

***involucrum:** 「껍질」. 이 근처의 뜻은, 시의 운율은 나무의 껍질과 나무가 동시에 자라는 것처럼 시 자체와 동시에 성장하는 것이지 단순히 덧붙인 게 아니다. 운율, 즉 시의 형식적 제약(법칙)은 시의 성장에 불가결한 요소인 것이다.

***Zoili:** Zoilus 들. Zoilus 는 예전에 Homer 를 악평했다는 비평가로, 악평의 전형.

thrown out from the concave mirror:* and even such is the appropriate excellence of her chosen poet, of our own Shakespeare, himself a nature humanized, a genial understanding, directing self-consciously a power and an implicit wisdom deeper even than our consciousness.

I greatly dislike beauties and selections* in general; but as proof positive of his unrivalled excellence, I should like to try Shakespeare by this criterion. Make out your amplest catalogue of all the human faculties, as reason or the moral law, the will, the feeling of the coincidence of the two (a feeling *sui generis et demonstratio demonstrationum**) called the conscience, the understanding, or prudence, wit, fancy, imagination, judgment, and then of the objects on which these are to be employed, as the beauties, the terrors, and the seeming caprices of nature, the capabilities, that is, the actual and the ideal, of the human mind, conceived as an individual or as a social being, as in innocence or in guilt, in a play-paradise or in a war-field of temptation; and then compare with Shakespeare under each of these heads all or any of the writers in prose and verse that have ever lived! Who, that is competent to judge, doubts the result? And ask your own hearts, ask your own commonsense to conceive the possibility of this man being — I say not, the drunken savage of that wretched sciolist,* whom Frenchmen, to their shame, have honoured before their elder and better worthies — but the anomalous, the wild, the irregular, genius of our daily criticism! What! are we to have miracles in sport? — Or, I speak reverently, does God choose idiots by whom to convey divine truths to man?

***concave mirror:** 「오목렌즈거울」. 작품의 외면은 내면의 모습을 집약하여 보여준다는 것.

***beauties and selections:** 이른바 purple patches. 한 작품에서 좋은 부분만 골라낸 것.

*양심 (conscience) 은 reason (moral law) 과 will 의 화합상태로서, unique and self-evident 한 것이다.

***sciolist:** 천박한 지식의 소유자. Voltaire 를 가리킨다. 그는 Shakespeare 를 'inspired savage'라고 했다. Coleridge 는 Voltaire 보다도 Shakespeare 를 단순한 '자연의 아들'이라고 찬양하는 현대 비평가들을 더 idiot 라고 꾸짖고 있다.

On Poesy or Art (1818)

MAN communicates by articulation of sounds, and paramountly by the memory in the ear; nature by the impression of bounds and surfaces on the eye, and through the eye it gives significance and appropriation, and thus the conditions of memory, or the capability of being remembered, to* sounds, smells, &c. Now Art, used collectively for painting, sculpture, architecture and music, is the mediatress between, and reconciler of, nature and man. It is, therefore, the power of humanizing nature, of infusing the thoughts and passions of man into everything which is the object of his contemplation; color, form, motion, and sound, are the elements which it combines, and it stamps them into unity in the mould of a moral idea.

The primary art is writing; — primary, if we regard the purpose abstracted from the different modes of realizing it, those steps of progression of which the instances are still visible in the lower degrees of civilization. First, there is mere gesticulation; then rosaries or *wampum;** then picture-language; then hieroglyphics, and finally alphabetic letters. These all consist of a translation of man into nature, of a substitution of the visible for the audible.

The so called music of savage tribes as little deserves the name of art for the understanding, as the ear warrants it for music. Its lowest state is a mere expression of passion by the sounds which the passion itself necessitates; — the highest amounts to no more than a voluntary reproduction of these sounds in the absence of the occasioning causes,* so as to give

---

***to:** 앞의 gives에 연결됨. 사람끼리는 소리(말)로, 자연과 사람은 눈(시각)으로 의사소통을 한다는 것. 그리고 예술은 자연과 사람 사이의 중개자(mediatress)로서 청각과 시각을 통하여 의사소통한다.

***wampum:** 「조개껍질 이은 것」(일종의 rosary). 미국 원주민의 돈. Coleridge는 이를 의사소통의 도구로 생각했던 모양이다.

***a voluntary...causes:** 외부의 자극(원인)이 없이도 스스로 소리를 내는 것, 이것이 곧 음악예술의 시이다.

the pleasure of contrast, — for example, by the various outcries of battle in the song of security and triumph. Poetry also is purely human; for all its materials are from the mind, and all its products are for the mind. But it is the apotheosis of the former state,* in which by excitement of the associative power passion itself imitates order, and the order resulting produces a pleasureable passion, and thus it elevates the mind by making its feelings the object of its reflexion. So likewise, whilst it recalls the sights and sounds that had accompanied the occasions of the original passions, poetry impregnates them with an interest not their own by means of the passions, and yet tempers the passion by the calming power which all distinct images exert on the human soul. In this way poetry is the preparation for art, inasmuch as it avails itself of the forms of nature to recall, to express, and to modify the thoughts and feelings of the mind. Still, however, poetry can only act through the intervention of articulate speech, which is so peculiarly human, that in all languages it constitutes the ordinary phrase by which man and nature are contradistinguished. It is the original force of the word "brute," and even "mute" and "dumb" do not convey the absence of sound, but the absence of articulated sounds.

As soon as the human mind is intelligibly addressed by an outward image exclusively of articulate speech, so soon does art commence. But please to observe that I have laid particular stress on the words "human mind," — meaning to exclude thereby all results common to man and all other sentient creatures, and consequently confining myself to the effect produced by the congruity of the animal* impression with the reflective powers of the mind; so that not the thing presented, but that which is re-presented by the thing, shall be the source of the pleasure. In this sense nature itself is to a religious observer the art of God; and for the same cause art

---

*시는 정신에서 나오는 것, 그러나 정신 그 자체에 대한 최대의 예찬(신격화)이다.

***animal:** 여기서는 「생리적」이란 뜻. 단순한 생리적 감각과 정신기능의 화합을 논하고 있다. 사물의 생리적 감각(presentation)에 대하여 정신적 반응으로 파악한 양상은 사물의 representation인 것이다.

itself might be defined as of a middle quality between a thought and a thing, or, as I said before, the union and reconciliation of that which is nature with that which is exclusively human. It is the figured language of thought, and is distinguished from nature by the unity of all the parts in one thought or idea. Hence nature itself would give us the impression of a work of art, if we could see the thought which is present at once in the whole and every part; and a work of art will be just in proportion as it adequately conveys the thought, and rich in proportion to the variety of parts which it holds in unity.

If, therefore, the term "mute" be taken as opposed not to sound but to articulate speech, the old definition of painting will in fact be the true and best definition of the Fine Arts in general, that is, *muta poesis, mute poesy, and so of course poesy. And, as all languages perfect themselves by a gradual process of desynonymizing words originally equivalent, I have cherished the wish to use the word "poesy" as the generic or common term, and to distinguish that species of poesy which is not *muta poesis* by its usual name "poetry"; while of all the other species which collectively form the Fine Arts, there would remain this as the common definition, — that they all, like poetry, are to express intellectual purposes, thoughts, conceptions, and sentiments which have their origin in the human mind, — not, however, as poetry does, by means of articulate speech, but as nature or the divine art does, by form, color, magnitude, proportion, or by sound, that is, silently or musically.**

Well! it may be said — but who has ever thought otherwise? We all know that art is the imitatress* of nature. And, doubtless, the truths which I hope to convey would be barren truisms, if all men meant the same by the words "imitate" and "nature." But it would be flattering mankind at large, to

---

*__*muta poesis*:__ 'mute poesy'. "시는 말하는 그림이요 그림은 말없는 시"라는 명언은 고대 그리이스의 Simonides가 한 말로 전해지고 있다. 어쨌든 그림도 poesy라는 생각이다.

***imitatress:** art를 여성으로 본 것. 그래서 imitator의 여성형을 쓰고 있다. 앞에 나온 mediatress와 같은 용법.

presume that such is the fact. First, to imitate. The impression on the wax is not an imitation, but a copy, of the seal; the seal itself is an imitation. But, further, in order to form a philosophic conception, we must seek for the kind, as the heat in ice, invisible light, &c., whilst, for practical purposes, we must have reference to the degree.* It is sufficient that philosophically we understand that in all imitation two elements must coexist, and not only coexist, but must be perceived as coexisting. These two constitutent elements are likeness and unlikeness, or sameness and difference, and in all genuine creations of art there must be a union of these disparates. The artist may take his point of view where he pleases, provided that the desired effect be perceptibly produced, — that there be likeness in the difference, difference in the likeness, and a reconcilement of both in one. If there be likeness to nature without any check of difference, the result is disgusting, and the more complete the delusion, the more loathsome the effect. Why are such simulations of nature, as wax-work figures of men and women, so disagreeable? Because, not finding the motion and the life which we expected, we are shocked as by a falsehood, every circumstance of detail, which before induced us to be interested, making the distance from truth more palpable. You set out with a supposed reality and are disappointed and disgusted with the deception; whilst, in respect to a work of genuine imitation, you begin with an acknowledged total difference, and then every touch of nature gives you the pleasure of an approximation to truth. The fundamental principle of all this is undoubtedly the horror of falsehood and the love of truth inherent in the human breast. The Greek tragic dance rested on these principles, and I can deeply sympathize in imagination with the Greeks in this favorite part of their theatrical exhibitions, when I call to mind the pleasure I felt in beholding the combat of the Horatii and Curiatii most ex-

*사물에서 종류가 다른 것과 정도가 다른 것은 전혀 별개이지만 우리는 자주 혼동하고 있다. 예컨대 얼음과 끓는 물은 종류가 다른 것이 아니라 온도의 차이만이 있을 뿐이다. 어둠과 밝음도 마찬가지.

quisitely danced in Italy to the music of Cimarosa.*

Secondly, as to nature. We must imitate nature! yes, but what in nature, — all and every thing? No, the beautiful in nature. And what then is the beautiful? What is beauty? It is, in the abstract, the unity of the manifold, the coalescence of the diverse; in the concrete, it is the union of the shapely (*formosum*) with the vital. In the dead organic it depends on regularity of form, the first and lowest species of which is the triangle with all its modifications, as in crystals, architecture, &c.; in the living organic it is not mere regularity of form, which would produce a sense of formality; neither is it subservient to any thing beside itself. It may be present in a disagreeable object, in which the proportion of the parts constitutes a whole; it does not arise from association, as the agreeable does, but sometimes lies in the rupture of association; it is not different to different invididuals and nations, as has been said, nor is it connected with the ideas of the good, or the fit, or the useful. The sense of beauty is intuitive, and beauty itself is all that inspires without, and aloof from, and even contrarily to, interest.

If the artist copies the mere nature, the *natura naturata,** what idle rivalry! If he proceeds only from a given form, which is supposed to answer to the notion of beauty, what an emptiness, what an unreality there always is in his productions, as in Cipriani's* pictures! Believe me, you must master the essence, the *natura naturans,** which presupposes a bond between nature in the higher sense and the soul of man.

The wisdom in nature is distinguished from that in man by the co-instantaneity* of the plan and the execution; the thought and the product are one, or are given at once; but there is no reflex act, and hence there is no moral responsibility. In man there is reflexion, freedom, and choice; he is,

---

*고대 이탈리아의 패권을 결정짓기 위하여 Horatii 가의 3형제와 Curiatii 가의 3형제가 결투한 비극적 전설이 있음. Cimarosa는 17세기 이탈리아의 작곡가로 위의 전설을 무용곡으로 다루었다.

***Cipriani:** 18세기 영국에서 활약한 이탈리아 화가.

****natura naturata*** 피조물로서의 자연. ***natura naturans*** 창조자로서의 자연.

***co-instantaneity:** 「동시성, 같이 일어남」.

therefore, the head of the visible creation. In the objects of nature are presented, as in a mirror, all the possible elements, steps, and processes of intellect antecedent to consciousness, and therefore to the full development of the intelligential act; and man's mind is the very focus of all the rays of intellect which are scattered throughout the images of nature. *Now* so to place these images, totalized, and fitted to the limits of the human mind, as to elicit from, and to superinduce upon, the forms themselves the moral reflexions to which they approximate, to make the external internal, the internal external, to make nature thought, and thought nature, — this is the mystery of genius in the Fine Arts. Dare I add that the genius must act on the feeling, that body is but a striving to become mind, — that it is mind in its essence!

In every work of art there is a reconcilement of the external with the internal; the conscious is so impressed on the unconscious as to appear in it; as compare mere letters inscribed on a tomb with figures themselves constituting the tomb. He who combines the two is the man of genius; and for that reason he must partake of both. Hence there is in genius itself an unconscious activity; nay, that is the genius in the man of genius. And this is the true exposition of the rule that the artist must first eloign himself from nature in order to return to her with full effect. Why this? Because if he were to begin by mere painful copying, he would produce masks only, not forms breathing life. He must out of his own mind create forms according to the severe laws of the intellect, in order to generate in himself that co-ordination of freedom and law, that involution of obedience in the prescript, and of the prescript in the impulse to obey, which assimilates him to nature, and enables him to understand her. He merely absents himself for a season from her, that his own spirit, which has the same ground with nature, may learn her unspoken language in its main radicals, before he approaches to her endless compositions of them. Yes, not to acquire cold notions — lifeless technical rules — but living and life-producing ideas, which shall contain their own evidence, the certainty that they are essentially one with the germinal

causes in nature, — his consciousness being the focus and mirror of both, — for this does the artist for a time abandon the external real in order to return to it with a complete sympathy with its internal and actual. For of all we see, hear, feel and touch the substance is and must be in ourselves; and therefore there is no alternative in reason between the dreary (and thank heaven! almost impossible) belief that every thing around us is but a phantom, or that the life which is in us is in them* likewise; and that to know is to resemble, when we speak of objects out of ourselves, even as within ourselves to learn is, according to Plato,* only to recollect; — the only effective answer to which, that I have been fortunate to meet with, is that which Pope has consecrated for future use in the line —

And coxcombs vanquish Berkeley with a grain!*

The artist must imitate that which is within the thing, that which is active through form and figure, and discourses to us by symbols — the *Natur-geist, or spirit of nature, as we unconsciously imitate those whom we love; for so only can he hope to produce any work truly natural in the object and truly human in the effect. The idea which puts the form together cannot itself be the form. It is above form, and is its essence, the universal in the individual, or the individuality itself, the glance and the exponent of the indwelling power.**

Each thing that lives has its moment of self-exposition, and so has each period of each thing, if we remove the disturbing forces of accident. To do this is the business of ideal art, whether in images of childhood, youth, or age, in

---

***them:** 의미상 every thing을 가리킴.「사물」.

*Plato에 의하면 배운다는 것은 형상, 즉 관념을 얻는다는것인데, 그런 관념은 이미 우리 의식 속에 자리잡고 있다가 능동적으로 표면화된다는 것이다. 즉 외부 사물에 대한 진정한 지식은 내가 이미 타고난 것을 다시 기억해내는 것이나 마찬가지다.

*이것은 Pope이 아니라 John Brown의 "Essay on Satire" Ⅱ의 일절이다. 그 뜻은, 철학자 George Berkeley의 주관주의적 인식론을 유식한 체하는 자들이 상식에 근거하여 비웃는다는 것이다.

***Natur-geist*:** spirit of Nature. 독일의 관념철학자들, 특히 Schelling이 주장한 우주자연과 인간 속에 내재하는 근본정신.

man or in woman. Hence a good portrait is the abstract of the personal; it is not the likeness for actual comparison, but for recollection. This explains why the likeness of a very good portrait is not always recognized; because some persons never abstract, and amongst these are especially to be numbered the near relations and friends of the subject, in consequence of the constant pressure and check exercised on their minds by the actual presence of the original. And each thing that only appears to live has also its possible position of relation to life, as nature herself testifies, who where she cannot be, prophesies her being in the crystallized metal, or the inhaling plant.

The charm, the indispensable requisite, of sculpture is the unity of effect. But painting rests in a material remoter from nature, and its compass is therefore greater. Light and shade give external, as well as internal, being even with all its accidents, whilst sculpture is confined to the latter. And here I may observe that the subjects chosen for works of art, whether in sculpture or painting, should be such as really are capable of being expressed and conveyed within the limits of those arts. Moreover they ought to be such as will affect the spectator by their truth, their beauty, or their sublimity, and therefore they may be addressed to the judgement, the senses, or the reason. The peculiarity of the impression which they may make, may be derived either from color and form, or from proportion and fitness, or from the excitement of the moral feelings; or all these may be combined. Such works as do combine these sources of effect must have the preference in dignity.

Imitation of the antique may be too exclusive, and may produce an injurious effect on modern sculpture; — 1st, generally, because such an imitation cannot fail to have a tendency to keep the attenion fixed on externals rather than on the thought within; — 2ndly, because, accordingly, it leads the artist to rest satisfied with that which is always imperfect, namely, bodily form, and circumscribes his views of mental expression to the ideas of power and grandeur only; — 3rdly, because it induces an effort to combine together two incongruous things, that is to say, modern feelings in antique forms; — 4thly, because it speaks in a language, as it were, learned and dead, the tones of which, being unfamiliar, leave the common spectator cold and unimpressed; — and lastly, because it necessarily causes a neglect of thoughts, emotions and images of profounder interest and more exalted dignity, as motherly, sisterly, and brotherly love, piety, devotion, the divine become human, — the Virgin, the Apostle, the Christ. The artist's principle in the statue of a great man should be the illustration of departed* merit; and I cannot but think that a skilful adoption of modern habiliments would, in many instances, give a variety and force of effect which a bigoted adherence to Greek or Roman costume precludes. It is, I believe, from artists finding Greek models unfit for several important modern purposes, that we see so many allegorical figures on monuments and elsewhere. Painting was, as it were, a new art, and being unshackled by old models it chose its own subjects, and took an eagle's flight. And a new field seems opened for modern sculpture in the symbolical expression of the ends of life, as in Guy's monument, Chantrey's children in Worcester Cathedral, &c.*

Architecture exhibits the greatest extent of the difference from nature which may exist in works of art. It involves all the powers of design, and is sculpture and painting inclusively. It shews the greatness of man, and should at the same time teach him humility.

Music is the most entirely human of the fine arts, and has the fewest *analoga** in nature. Its first delightfulness is simple accordance with the ear; but it is an associated thing, and recalls the deep emotions of the past with an intellectual sense of proportion. Every human feeling is greater and larger than the exciting cause, — a proof, I think, that man is designed

---

*위인의 조상을 만들려면 그 위인의 사라져 보이지 않는(departed) 장점을 예시하는 것이 예술가의 원칙이다.

*17—18세기 자선사업가 Thomas Guy의 조상, 그리고 Coleridge 당시의 조각가 Sir Francis Chantrey의 조각작품 "Sleeping Children"을 칭찬하고 있다.

****analoga*:** 「유사한 것」.

for a higher state of existence; and this is deeply implied in music, in which there is always something more and beyond the immediate impression.

With regard to works in all the branches of the fine arts, I may remark that the pleasure arising from novelty must of course be allowed its due place and weight. This pleasure consists in the identity of two opposite elements, that is to say — sameness and variety. If in the midst of the variety there be not some fixed object for the attention, the unceasing succession of the variety will prevent the mind from observing the difference of the individual objects; and the only thing remaining will be the succession, which will then produce precisely the same effect as sameness. This we experience when we let the trees or hedges pass before the fixed eye during a rapid movement in a carriage, or, on the other hand, when we suffer a file of soldiers or ranks of men in procession to go on before us without resting the eye on any one in particular. In order to derive pleasure from the occupation of the mind, the principle of unity must always be present, so that in the midst of the multeity the centripetal force be never suspended, nor the sense be fatigued by the predominance of the centrifugal force.* This unity in multeity I have elsewhere stated as the principle of beauty. It is equally the source of pleasure in variety, and in fact a higher term including both. What is the seclusive or distinguishing term between them?

Remember that there is a difference between form as proceeding, and shape as superinduced; — the latter is either the death or the imprisonment of the thing; — the former is its self-witnessing and self-effected sphere of agency. Art would or should be the abridgment of nature. Now the fulness of nature is without character, as water is purest when without taste, smell, or color; but this is the highest, the apex only, — it is not the whole. The object of art is to give the whole *ad hominem;** hence each step of nature hath its ideal, and hence the possibility of a climax up to the perfect form of

---

*구심력은 말하자면 통일성에의 의지이고, 원심력은 다양성에의 의지이다. 이들이 균형을 이루어야 한다. 'unity in multeity'라는 미의 원칙.

****ad hominem*:** 'to men.'

a harmonized chaos.

To the idea of life victory or strife is necessary; as virtue consists not simply in the absence of vices, but in the overcoming of them. So it is in beauty. The sight of what is subordinated and conquered heightens the strength and the pleasure; and this should be exhibited by the artist either inclusively in his figure, or else out of it, and beside it to act by way of supplement and contrast. And with a view to this, remark the seeming identity of body and mind in infants, and thence the loveliness of the former; the commencing separation in boyhood, and the struggle of equilibrium in youth: thence onward the body is first simply indifferent; then demanding the translucency of the mind not to be worse than indifferent; and finally all that presents the body as body becoming almost of an excremental nature.

William Hazlitt

(1778—1830)

자유주의 교단의 목사의 아들로 태어나 정규 교육을 받지 못했으나, 화가가 되려던 애초의 목적을 바꾸어 문필가가 된 해즐릿은 Charles Lamb과 더불어 당대의 수필의 대가로 군림하게 되었고, 또한 *Characters of Shakespeare's Plays*(1817-18), *Lectures on the English Poets*(1818-19), *English Comic Writers*(1819), *The Spirit of the Age*(1825) 등 일련의 비평집을 발표한 정력적인 비평가가 되었다.

영국의 낭만주의의 경향이 그렇듯, 해즐릿도 인간의 정서와 예술의 관계를 중시하며, 자연에 대한 정서적 반응 자체를 시적이라고 믿으며, 예술의 궁극적 도덕성을 믿고 있다. 나 아닌 남에 대한 정서적 반응 중에서 예술은 특히 공감적 동일화(sympathetic identification)를 이루어 주며, 바로 이런 능력이야말로 상상의 능력이라고 보았다. 즉 상상은 공감 능력, 다시 말하면 화합의 능력인 것이다. 바로 이러한 화합의 능력 때문에 상상, 또 상상의 표현인 예술이 높은 도덕성을 띤다는 것이다. 셰익스피어는 상상적 화합의 능력을 최대 한도로 발휘한 만큼 또한 최고의 도덕가이기도 하다.

해즐릿은 정서 또는 상상의 활동적인 상태를 강조한다. 즉 상상은 가만히 앉아서 관조하는 능력이 아니라 스스로 생동하며 또한 생동하는 사물에 강한 흥미를 느끼는 것이다. 이를 그는 "gusto"라 했다.

"On Poetry in General"은 *Lectures on the English Poets*의 제1장으로서, 모든 생동하는 자연 속에, 움직이는 인성 속에 시가 배태되어 있다는 그의 근본 사상이 표현되어 있다. 이처럼 모든 생동하는 생의 양상의 표현이 시이므로 시는 보편성을 가질 수가 있다. 다른 평론들에서 해즐릿은 특이한 현상에 대한 독특한 반응을 보인다는 이유로 루소나 워즈워드를 비난한 바 있다.

From On Poetry in General (1818)

The best general notion which I can give of poetry is, that it is the natural impression of any object or event, by its vividness exciting an involuntary movement of imagination and passion, and producing, by sympathy, a certain modulation of the voice, or sounds, expressing it.

In treating of poetry, I shall speak first of the subject-matter of it, next of the forms of expression to which it gives birth, and afterwards of its connexion with harmony of sound.

Poetry is the language of the imagination and the passions. It relates to whatever gives immediate pleasure or pain to the human mind. It comes home to the bosoms and businesses of men; for nothing but what so comes home to them in the most general and intelligible shape, can be a subject for poetry. Poetry is the universal language which the heart holds with nature and itself. He who has a contempt for poetry, cannot have much respect for himself, or for anything else. It is not a mere frivolous accomplishment (as some persons have been led to imagine), the trifling amusement of a few idle readers or leisure hours — it has been the study and delight of mankind in all ages. Many people suppose that poetry is something to be found only in books, contained in lines of ten syllables, with like endings: but wherever there is a sense of beauty, or power, or harmony, as in the motion of a wave of the sea, in the growth of a flower that "spreads its sweet leaves to the air, and dedicates its beauty to the sun," —*there* is poetry, in its birth. If history is a grave study, poetry may be said to be a graver: its materials lie deeper, and are spread wider. History treats, for the most part, of the cumbrous and unwieldy masses of things, the empty cases in which the affairs of the world are packed, under the heads of intrigue or war, in different states, and from century to century: but there is no thought or feeling that can have entered into the mind of man, which he would be eager to communicate to others, or which they would listen to with delight, that is not a fit subject for poetry. It is not a branch of authorship: it is "the stuff of which our life is made." The rest is "mere oblivion," a dead letter: for all that is worth remembering in life, is the poetry of it. Fear is poetry, hope is poetry, love is poetry, hatred is poetry; contempt, jealousy, remorse, admiration, wonder, pity, despair, or madness, are all poetry. Poetry is that fine particle within us, that expands, rarefies, refines, raises our whole being: without it "man's life is poor as beast's." Man is a poetical animal: and those of us who do not study the principles of poetry, act upon them all our lives, like Molière's *Bourgeois Gentilhomme,** who had always spoken prose without knowing it. The child is a poet in fact, when he first plays at hide-and-seek, or repeats the story of Jack the Giant-killer; the shepherd-boy is a poet, when he first crowns his mistress with a garland of flowers; the countryman, when he stops to look at the rainbow; the city-apprentice, when he gazes after the Lord Mayor's show; the miser, when he hugs his gold; the courtier, who builds his hopes upon a smile; the savage, who paints his idol with blood; the slave, who worships a tyrant, or the tyrant, who fancies himself a god; — the vain, the ambitious, the proud, the choleric man, the hero and the coward, the beggar and the old, all live in a world of their own making; and the poet does no more than describe what all the others think and act. . . .

Poetry then is an imitation of nature, but the imagination and the passions are a part of man's nature. We shape things according to our wishes and fancies, without poetry; but poetry is the most emphatical language that can be found for those creations of the mind "which ecstasy is very cunning

*Molière의 작품 *Bourgeois Gentilhomme*(1670)의 주인공 Jourdain은 자기가 평상시 하는 말이 '산문'이라는 얘기를 듣고 신기해 한다. 이처럼 사람은 자신도 모르게 시적 원칙에 따라 사는 「잠재적 시인」, 즉 시적 동물(a poetical animal)인 것이다.

in."* Neither a mere description of natural objects, nor a mere delineation of natural feelings, however distinct or forcible, constitutes the ultimate end and aim of poetry, without the heightenings of the imagination. The light of poetry is not only a direct but also a reflected light, that while it shows us the object, throws a sparkling radiance on all around it: the flame of the passions, communicated to the imagination, reveals to us, as with a flash of lightning, the inmost recesses of thought, and penetrates our whole being. Poetry represents forms chiefly as they suggest other forms; feelings, as they suggest forms or other feelings. Poetry puts a spirit of life and motion into the universe. It describes the flowing, not the fixed. It does not define the limits of sense, or analyse the distinctions of the understanding, but signifies the excess of the imagination beyond the actual or ordinary impression of any object or feeling. The poetical impression of any object is that uneasy, exquisite sense of beauty or power that cannot be contained within itself; that is impatient of all limit; that (as flame bends to flame) strives to link itself to some other image of kindred beauty or grandeur; to enshrine itself, as it were, in the highest forms of fancy, and to relieve the aching sense of pleasure by expressing it in the boldest manner, and by the most striking examples of the same quality in other instances. Poetry, according to Lord Bacon, for this reason, "has something divine in it, because it raises the mind and hurries it into sublimity, by conforming the shows of things to the desires of the soul, instead of subjecting the soul to external things, as reason and history do."* It is strictly the language of the imagination; and the imagination is that faculty which represents objects, not as they are in themselves, but as they are moulded by other thoughts and feelings, into an infinite variety of shapes and combinations of power. This language is not the less true to nature, because it is false in point of fact; but so much the more true and natural, if it conveys the

---

***which ecstasy is very cunning in**: for which strong emotional states are favorable. 여기에서 cunning=capable, able.

**Advancement of Learning*, I, iv.

impression which the object under the influence of passion makes on the mind. Let an object, for instance, be presented to the senses in a state of agitation or fear — and the imagination will distort or magnify the object, and convert it into the likeness of whatever is most proper to encourage the fear. "Our eyes are made the fools" of our other faculties. This is the universal law of the imagination . . . We compare a man of gigantic stature to a tower: not that he is anything like so large, but because the excess of his size beyond what we are accustomed to expect, or the usual size of things of the same class, produces by contrast a greater feeling of magnitude and ponderous strength than another object of ten times the same dimensions. The intensity of the feeling makes up for the disproportion of the objects.* Things are equal to the imagination, which have the power of affecting the mind with an equal degree of terror, admiration, delight, or love. When Lear calls upon the heavens to avenge his cause, "for they are old like him,"* there is nothing extravagant or impious in this sublime identification of his age with theirs; for there is no other image which could do justice to the agonizing sense of his wrongs and his despair!

Poetry is the high-wrought* enthusiasm of fancy and feeling. As in describing natural objects, it impregnates sensible impressions with the forms of fancy, so it describes the feelings of pleasure or pain, by blending them with the strongest movements of passion, and the most striking forms of nature. Tragic poetry, which is the most impassioned species of it, strives to carry on the feeling to the utmost point of sublimity or pathos, by all the force of comparison or contrast; loses the sense of present suffering in the imaginary exaggeration of it; exhausts the terror or pity by an unlimited indulgence of it; grapples with impossibilities in its desperate impatience of restraint; throws us back upon the past, forward into the

---

***The intensity...object:** 「감정의 격렬함이 대상의 불균형을 보충해준다」. 실제의 대상이 작아도 감정이 크면 그 만큼 대상도 크게 확대된다는 것.

******Lear*, Ⅱ, iv, 193.

***high-wrought:** 「고양된, 고조된」.

future; brings every moment of our being or object of nature in startling review before us; and in the rapid whirl of events, lifts us from the depths of woe to the highest contemplations on human life. When Lear says of Edgar, "Nothing but his unkind daughters could have brought him to this";* what a bewildered amazement, what a wrench of the imagination, that cannot be brought to conceive of any other cause of misery than that which has bowed it down, and absorbs all other sorrow in its own! His sorrow, like a flood, supplies the sources of all other sorrow. Again, when he exclaims in the mad scene, "The little dogs and all, Tray, Blanche, and Sweetheart, see, they bark at me! it is passion lending occasion to imagination to make every creature in league against him, conjuring up ingratitude and insult in their least looked-for and most galling shapes, searching every thread and fibre of his heart, and finding out the last remaining image of respect or attachment in the bottom of his breast, only to torture and kill it! . . .

One mode in which the dramatic exhibition of passion excites our sympathy without raising our disgust is, that in proportion as it sharpens the edge of calamity and disappointment, it strengthens the desire of good. It enhances our consciousness of the blessing, by making us sensible of the magnitude of the loss. The storm of passion lays bare and shows us the rich depths of the human soul: the whole of our existence, the sum total of our passions and pursuits, of that which we desire and that which we dread, is brought before us by contrast; the action and reaction are equal; the keenness of immediate suffering only gives us a more intense aspiration after, and a more intimate paricipation with the antagonist world of good; makes us drink deeper of the cup of human life; tugs at the heartstrings; loosens the pressure about them; and calls the springs of thought and feeling into play with tenfold force.

Impassioned poetry is an emanation of the moral and in-

**Lear*, III, iv, 72—73. "Nothing could have subdued nature / To such a lowness but his unkind daughters."

tellectual part of our nature, as well as of the sensitive — of the desire to know, the will to act, and the power to feel; and ought to appeal to these different parts of our constitution, in order to be perfect. The domestic or prose tragedy,* which is thought to be the most natural, is in this sense the least so, because it appeals almost exclusively to one of these faculties, our sensibility. The tragedies of Moore and Lillo,* for this reason, however affecting at the time, oppress and lie like a dead weight upon the mind, a load of misery which it is unable to throw off: the tragedy of Shakespeare, which is true poetry, stirs our inmost affections; abstracts evil from itself by combining it with all the forms of imagination, and with the deepest workings of the heart, and rouses the whole man within us.

The pleasure, however, derived from tragic poetry, is not anything peculiar to it as poetry, as a fictitious and fanciful thing. It is not an anomaly of the imagination. It has its source and groundwork in the common love of strong excitement. As Mr. Burke observes, people flock to see a tragedy;* but if there were a public execution in the next street, the theatre would very soon be empty. It is not then the difference between fiction and reality that solves the difficulty. Children are satisfied with the stories of ghosts and witches in plain prose: nor do the hawkers* of full, true, and particular accounts of murders and executions about the streets, find it necessary to have them turned into penny ballads, before they can dispose of these interesting and authentic documents. The grave politician drives a thriving trade of abuse and calumnies poured out against those whom he makes his

---

***The domestic or prose tragedy:** 일상생활을 다루는 산문비극. 매우 감상적이었고, 아직은 큰 성공을 거두지 못했다.

***George Lillo** (1693–1739)는 *The London Merchant* (1731)이라는 domestic tragedy in prose의 최초의 작품을 썼고, 그의 후계자 **Edward Moore** (1712–57)는 *The Gamester* (1753)를 썼다.

*Edmund Burke, *A Philosophical Inquiry into the Sublime and the Beautiful*, I, 15.

***hawkers:** 중대 사건, 특히 엽기적 사건을 운문(ballad)으로 써서 길거리에서 팔던 사람들.

enemies for no other end than that he may live by them. The popular preacher makes less frequent mention of heaven than of hell. Oaths and nicknames are only a more vulgar sort of poetry or rhetoric. We are as fond of indulging our violent passions as of reading a description of those of others. We are as prone to make a torment of our fears, as to luxuriate in our hopes of good. If it be asked, Why we do so? the best answer will be, Because we cannot help it. The sense of power is as strong a principle in the mind as the love of pleasure. Objects of terror and pity exercise the same despotic control over it as those of love or beauty. It is as natural to hate as to love, to despise as to admire, to express our hatred or contempt, as our love or admiration.

> Masterless passion sways us to the mood
> Of what it likes or loathes.

Not that we like what we loathe; but we like to indulge our hatred and scorn of it; to dwell upon it, to exasperate our idea of it by every refinement of ingenuity and extravagance of illustration; to make it a bugbear to ourselves, to point it out to others in all the splendour of deformity, to embody it to the senses, to stigmatize it by name, to grapple with it in thought, in action, to sharpen our intellect, to arm our will against it, to know the worst we have to contend with, and to contend with it to the utmost. Poetry is only the highest eloquence of passion, the most vivid form of expression that can be given to our conception of anything, whether pleasurable or painful, mean or dignified, delightful or distressing. It is the perfect coincidence of the image and the words with the feeling we have, and of which we cannot get rid in any other way, that gives an instant "satisfaction to the thought." This is equally the orgin of wit and fancy, of comedy and tragedy, of the sublime and pathetic. When Pope says of the Lord Mayor's shows, —

> Now night descending, the proud scene is o'er,
> But lives in Settle's numbers one day more!*

* *Dunciad*, I, 89—90. Lord Mayor의 우스꽝스런 신년기념식을 못난 시인 Elkanah Settle이 다음날 읊은 것을 비꼼.

— when Collins* makes Danger, "with limbs of giant mould,"

> — Throw him on the steep
> Of some loss hanging rock asleep:

when Lear calls out ine extreme anguish,

> Ingratitude, thou marble-hearted fiend,
> How much more hideous shew'st in a child
> Than the sea-monster!

— the passion of contempt in the one case, of terror in the other, and of indignation in the last, is perfectly satisfied. We see the thing ourselves, and show it to others as we feel it to exist, and as, in spite of ourselves, we are compelled to think of it. The imagination, by thus embodying and turning them to shape, gives an obvious relief to the indistinct and importunate cravings of the will. — We do not wish the thing to be so; but we wish it to appear such as it is. For knowledge is conscious power; and the mind is no longer, in this case, the dupe, though it may be the victim of vice or folly. . . .

***Collins, William:** (1721-59). 고전풍의 서정시(ode)에 능했던 시인.

Percy Bysshe Shelley

(1792—1822)

부유한 귀족 집안에 태어나 옥스포드에 진학했으나 급진사상의 영향을 받아 무신론을 표방하자 퇴학 당했고, 이어 성급히 결혼한 아내를 얼마 후 버리고 Mary Godwin 이란 여자와 사랑의 도피행을 하자 아내가 자살하여 둘은 결혼했으나 사회적 평판이 나빠 주로 이탈리아에 체재하며 시인으로, 사상가로 원숙하게 되어가다가 29세 때 원인 모르게 바다에서 익사했다.

A Defence of Poetry(1821)는 당돌한 급진주의자에서 보다 원숙한 신플라톤 사상가로 입지하여 가던 셸리의 모습을 보여주는 명문으로서, 그의 친구이자 풍자문인인 Thomas Love Peacock 의 농담기를 섞어서 쓴 시의 무용론에 대한 진지한 답변으로 쓴 것이다.

셸리는 인간의 정신 작용을 상상과 이성으로 나누고 이성을 분석, 계량의 도구로, 상상을 종합, 가치 파악의 능력으로 상정한다. 시는 바로 이러한 상상의 표현이다.

시드니처럼 셸리도 시를 인간의 시작과 더불어 같이 시작되었다고 주장한다. 시는 자연과 인간, 인간과 인간 사이의 관계를 파악하는 순간, 즉 인간이 자연 속에서 사회를 이루어 살기 시작한 이래 자연히 생길 수밖에 없다는 것이다. 시는 반드시 문자로 기록된 것만을 뜻하기 이전에, 인간과 자연, 인간과 인간 사이에 친화를 가져온 모든 문화적 창조를 뜻한다. 인간을 위하여 자연을 이용하는 발명가도, 사회의 질서를 가져온 법률가도, 음악가도, 건축가도 모두 시인인 것이다. 궁극에 있어 시는 모든 진선미의 근본인 신의 마음의 표현인 셈이다.

시의 현실적 효용 가치는 세속적인 도덕률을 가르침에 있지 않고 나 자신으로부터 밖으로 나가서 남과 공감, 화합할 수 있는 능력, 즉 사랑을 가지도록 우리의 상상력을 확충해 주는 데 있다고 주장한다.

신플라톤 사상의 신비적 영향을 받은 셸리는 특이한 시의 영감설을 믿는다. 시는 거룩한 정신이 인간을 순간적으로 관통하고 지나간 흔적이라고 본 것이다. 시인은 자의대로 시를 지을 수 있는 것이 아니다. 시인은 마치 나팔처럼 그 정신이 그를 휩쓸고 지나갈 때 자기도 다 알 수 없는 굉장한 소리를 내게 되는 것이다. 그 소리로 말미암아 세상은 더 나은 세계로 발전하므로 시인은 가위 "공인되지 않은 세계의 입법자"라 할 수 있는 것이다.

A Defence of Poetry (1840)

ACCORDING to one mode of regarding those two classes of mental action, which are called reason and imagination, the former may be considered as mind contemplating the relations borne by one thought to another, however produced;* and the latter, as mind acting upon those thoughts so as to colour them with its own light, and composing from them, as from elements, other thoughts, each containing within itself the principle of its own integrity. The one is the *τὸ ποιεῖν*,* or the principle of synthesis, and has for its object those forms which are common to universal nature and existence itself; the other is the *τὸ λογίζειν*,* or principle of analysis, and its action regards the relations of things, simply as relations; considering thoughts, not in their integral unity, but as the algebraical representations which conduct to certain general results. Reason is the enumeration of quantities already known; imagination is the perception of the value of those quantities, both separately and as a whole. Reason respects the differences, and imagination the similitudes of things. Reason is to imagination as the instrument to the agent, as the body to the spirit, as the shadow to the substance.

---

*however produced: 생각들 자체가 어떻게 생성되었는지는 관계하지 않고.

*to make.

*to reason.

Poetry, in a general sense, may be defined to be 'the expression of the imagination': and poetry is connate with the origin of man. Man is an instrument over which a series of external and internal impressions are driven, like the alternations of an ever-changing wind over an Aeolian lyre,* which move it by their motion to ever-changing melody. But there is a principle within the human being, and perhaps within all sentient beings, which acts otherwise than in a lyre, and produces not melody alone, but harmony, by an internal adjustment of the sounds and motions thus excited to the impressions which excite them. It is as if the lyre could accommodate its chords to the motions of that which strikes them, in a determined proportion of sound; even as the musician can accommodate his voice to the sound of the lyre. A child at play by itself will express its delight by its voice and motions; and every inflection of tone and every gesture will bear exact relation to a corresponding antitype* in the pleasurable impressions which awakened it; it will be the reflected image of that impression; and as the lyre trembles and sounds after the wind has died away, so the child seeks, by prolonging in its voice and motions the duration of the effect, to prolong also a consciousness of the cause. In relation to the objects which delight a child, these expressions are what poetry is to higher objects.* The savage (for the savage is to ages what the child is to years) expresses the emotions produced in him by surrounding objects in a similar manner; and language and gesture, together with plastic or pictorial imitation, become the image of the combined effect of those objects and his apprehension of them. Man in society, with all his passions and his pleasures, next becomes the object of the passions and pleasures

---

***Aeolian lyre:** 또는 Aeolian harp. 바람이 잘 통하는 곳에 놔누면 저절로 소리가 나게 되어 있는 악기. Aeolus: 바람의 신. 사람은 그런 악기처럼 외부로부터 무수한 인상을 받아 "소리"를 내는 동시에 자기 자신의 내부로부터의 응답의 "소리"를 합쳐 화음을 낸다는 것이다. 인상과 반응(표현)의 심리적 메카니즘을 낭만적으로 설명한 것.

***antitype:** 대상. 표현은 인상(자극)과 서로 상응한다는 것.

*어린이를 즐겁게 해 주는 사물과 그러한 표현의 관계는 더 고등한 사물과 시의 관계와 같다. (그 다음 괄호 속의 구문도 같은 구문).

of man; an additional class of emotions produces an augmented treasure of expression; and language, gesture, and the imitative arts, become at once the representation and the medium, the pencil and the picture, the chisel and the statue, the chord and the harmony. The social sympathies, or those laws from which, as from its elements, society results, begin to develop themselves from the moment that two human beings co-exist; the future is contained within the present as the plant within the seed; and equality, diversity, unity, contrast, mutual dependence, become the principles alone capable of affording the motives according to which the will of a social being is determined to action, inasmuch as he is social; and constitute pleasure in sensation, virtue in sentiment, beauty in art, truth in reasoning, and love in the intercourse of kind. Hence men, even in the infancy of society, observe a certain order of their words and actions, distinct from that of the objects and the impressions represented by them, all expression being subject to the laws of that from which it proceeds. But let us dismiss those more general considerations which might involve an inquiry into the principles of society itself, and restrict our view to the manner in which the imagination is expressed upon its forms.

In the youth of the world, men dance and sing and imitate natural objects, observing in these actions, as in all others, a certain rhythm or order. And, although all men observe a similar, they observe not the same order in the motions of the dance, in the melody of the song, in the combinations of language, in the series of their imitations of natural objects. For there is a certain order or rhythm belonging to each of these classes of mimetic representation, from which the hearer and the spectator receive an intenser and purer pleasure than from any other: the sense of an approximation to this order has been called taste by modern writers. Every man in the infancy of art, observes an order which approximates more or less closely to that from which this highest delight results: but the diversity is not sufficiently marked,* as that its gradations should be

*그 질서의 다양함은 그 상호간의 차이점들을 알 수 있을 만큼 충분히 인식

sensible, except in those instances where the predominance of this faculty of approximation to the beautiful (for so we may be permitted to name the relation between this highest pleasure and its cause) is very great. Those in whom it exists to excess are poets, in the most universal sense of the word; and the pleasure resulting from the manner in which they express the influence of society or nature upon their own minds, communicates itself to others, and gathers a sort of reduplication from the community. Their language is vitally metaphorical; that is, it marks the before unapprehended relations of things and perpetuates their apprehension, until words, which represent them, become, through time, signs for portions or classes of thoughts instead of pictures of integral thoughts; and then, if no new poets should arise to create afresh the associations which have been thus disorganized, language will be dead to all the nobler purposes of human intercourse. These similitudes or relations are finely said by Lord Bacon to be 'the same footsteps of nature impressed upon the various subjects of the world'*—and he considers the faculty which perceives them as the storehouse of axioms common to all knowledge. In the infancy of society every author is necessarily a poet, because language itself is poetry; and to be a poet is to apprehend the true and the beautiful, in a word, the good which exists in the relation, subsisting, first between existence and perception, and secondly between perception and expression. Every original language near to its source is in itself the chaos of a cyclic poem: the copiousness of lexicography and the distinctions of grammar are the works of a later age, and are merely the catalogue and the form of the creations of poetry.

But poets, or those who imagine and express this indestructible order, are not only the authors of language and of music, of the dance, and architecture, and statuary, and painting; they are the institutors of laws, and the founders of civil society, and

---

되지 못하고 있다. (우주의 무한한, 미묘한 다양성의 조화는 시인만이 안다는 것).

**Advancement of Learning*, Ⅱ. 정확한 인용은 아니다.

the inventors of the arts of life,* and the teachers, who draw* into a certain propinquity with the beautiful and the true, that partial apprehension of the agencies of the invisible world which is called religion. Hence all original religions are allegorical, or susceptible of allegory, and, like Janus, have a double face of false and true.* Poets, according to the circumstances of the age and nation in which they appeared, were called, in the earlier epochs of the world, legislators or prophets: a poet essentially comprises and unites both these characters. For he not only beholds intensely the present as it is, and discovers those laws according to which present things ought to be ordered, but he beholds the future in the present, and his thoughts are the germs of the flower and the fruit of latest time. Not that I assert poets to be prophets in the gross sense of the word, or that they can foretell the form as surely as they foreknow the spirit of events: such is the pretence of superstition, which would make poetry an attribute of prophecy, rather than prophecy an attribute of poetry. A poet participates in the eternal, the infinite, and the one; as far as relates to his conceptions, time and place and number are not.* The grammatical forms which express the moods of time, and the difference of persons, and the distinction of place, are convertible with respect to the highest poetry without injuring it as poetry; and the choruses of Aeschylus, and the *Book of Job*, and Dante's *Paradise*, would afford, more than any other writings, examples of this fact, if the limits of this essay did not forbid citation. The creations of sculpture, painting, and music, are illustrations still more decisive.

Language, colour, form, and religious and civil habits of action, are all the instruments and materials of poetry; they may be called poetry by that figure of speech which considers

---

***inventors...of life:** 「삶의 방법을 창안한 자」. 즉 철인과 종교인.

***draw** 의 목적격은 that partial 이하.

*종교는 모두 allegory 로 표현되는 바, allegory 는 진실을 담은 꾸민 이야기인 것이다.

***as far as...are not:** 「그의 관념에서는 시간, 장소, 수는 존재하지 않는다」.

the effect as a synonym of the cause.* But poetry in a more restricted sense expresses those arrangements of language, and especially metrical language, which are created by that imperial faculty, whose throne is curtained within the invisible nature of man. And this springs from the nature itself of language, which is a more direct representation of the actions and passions of our internal being, and is susceptible of more various and delicate combinations, than colour, form, or motion, and is more plastic and obedient to the control of that faculty of which it is the creation. For language is arbitrarily produced by the imagination, and has relation to thoughts alone; but all other materials, instruments, and conditions of art, have relations among each other, which limit and interpose between conception and expression. The former is as a mirror which reflects, the latter as a cloud which enfeebles, the light of which both are mediums of communication. Hence the fame of sculptors, painters, and musicians, although the intrinsic powers of the great masters of these arts may yield in no degree to that of those who have employed language as the hieroglyphic of their thoughts, has never equalled that of poets in the restricted sense of the term; as two performers of equal skill will produce unequal effects from a guitar and a harp. The fame of legislators and founders of religions, so long as their institutions last, alone seems to exceed that of poets in the restricted sense; but it can scarcely be a question, whether, if we deduct the celebrity which their flattery of the gross opinions of the vulgar usually conciliates, together with that which belonged to them in their higher character of poets, any excess will remain.

We have thus circumscribed the word poetry within the limits of that art which is the most familiar and the most perfect expression of the faculty itself. It is necessary, however, to make the circle still narrower, and to determine the distinc-

*이런 비유를 metonymy 라고 한다. 언어, 색깔, 형식 등은 시의 영향으로 생긴 것인데, 그들을 시라고 하면 바로 metonymy. 영향을 원인으로 바꾸어 말한 것이다.

tion between measured and unmeasured language; for the popular division into prose and verse is inadmissible in accurate philosophy.

Sounds as well as thoughts have relation both between each other and towards that which they represent, and a perception of the order of those relations has always been found connected with a perception of the order of the relations of thoughts. Hence the language of poets has ever affected a sort of uniform and harmonious recurrence of sound, without which it were not poetry, and which is scarcely less indispensable to the communication of its influence, than the words themselves, without reference to that peculiar order. Hence the vanity of translation; it were as wise to cast a violet into a crucible that you might discover the formal principles of its colour and odour, as seek to transfuse from one language into another the creations of a poet. The plant must spring again from its seed, or it will bear no flower—and this is the burthen of the curse of Babel.*

An observation of the regular mode of the recurrence of harmony in the language of poetical minds, together with its relation to music, produced metre, or a certain system of traditional forms of harmony and language. Yet it is by no means essential that a poet should accommodate his language to this traditional form, so that the harmony, which is its spirit, be observed. The practice is indeed convenient and popular, and to be preferred, especially in such composition as includes much action: but every great poet must inevitably innovate upon the example of his predecessors in the exact structure of his peculiar versification. The distinction between poets and prose writers is a vulgar error. The distinction between philosophers and poets has been anticipated. Plato was essentially a poet—the truth and splendour of his imagery, and the melody of his language, are the most intense that it is possible to conceive. He

---

*Babel 탑을 쌓으려고 모여들었던 사람들의 언어를 신이 각자 다르게 만듦으로써 탑의 건조가 중단되고 방언이 생겼다는 구약 「창세기」의 이야기. 시를 외국어로 번역할 수 없는 것은 시의 음성적 요소를 「번역」할 수 없기 때문이다.

rejected the harmony of the epic, dramatic, and lyrical forms, because he sought to kindle a harmony in thoughts divested of shape and action, and he forbore to invent any regular plan of rhythm which would include, under determinate forms, the varied pauses of his style. Cicero sought to imitate the cadence of his periods;* but with little success. Lord Bacon was a poet. His language has a sweet and majestic rhythm, which satisfies the sense, no less than the almost superhuman wisdom of his philosophy satisfies the intellect; it is a strain which distends, and then bursts the circumference of the reader's mind, and pours itself forth together with it into the universal element with which it has perpetual sympathy. All the authors of revolutions in opinion are not only necessarily poets as they are inventors, nor even as their words unveil the permanent analogy of things by images which participate in the life of truth; but as their periods are harmonious and rhythmical, and contain in themselves the elements of verse; being the echo of the eternal music. Nor are those supreme poets, who have employed traditional forms of rhythm on account of the form and action of their subjects, less capable of perceiving and teaching the truth of things, than those who have omitted that form. Shakespeare, Dante, and Milton (to confine ourselves to modern writers) are philosophers of the very loftiest power.*

A poem is the very image of life expressed in its eternal truth. There is this difference between a story* and a poem, that a story is a catalogue of detached facts, which have no other connection than time, place, circumstance, cause and effect; the other is the creation of actions according to the unchangeable forms of human nature, as existing in the mind of the Creator, which is itself the image of all other minds. The one is partial, and applies only to a definite period of time, and a certain combination of events which can never again recur;

---

*period: 여러 절로 되어 있고, 가장 중요한 부분이 끝에 놓인 문장.

*좋은 문장을 쓴 철인들도 시인일 뿐 아니라, 전통적 운율을 사용한 시인들도 철인이라는 주장.

*story: 여기서는 history 의 뜻.

the other is universal, and contains within itself the germ of a relation to whatever motives or actions have place in the possible varieties of human nature. Time, which destroys the beauty and the use of the story of particular facts, stripped of the poetry which should invest them, augments that of poetry, and for ever develops new and wonderful applications of the eternal truth which it contains. Hence epitomes have been called the moths of just history; they eat out the poetry of it. A story of particular facts is as a mirror which obscures and distorts that which should be beautiful: poetry is a mirror which makes beautiful that which is distorted.

The parts of a composition may be poetical, without the composition as a whole being a poem. A single sentence may be considered as a whole, though it may be found in the midst of a series of unassimilated portions; a single word even may be a spark of inextinguishable thought. And thus all the great historians, Herodotus, Plutarch, Livy, were poets; and although the plan of these writers, especially that of Livy, restrained them from developing this faculty in its highest degree, they made copious and ample amends for their subjection, by filling all the interstices of their subjects with living images.

Having determined what is poetry, and who are poets, let us proceed to estimate its effects upon society.

Poetry is ever accompanied with pleasure: all spirits on which it falls open themselves to receive the wisdom which is mingled with its delight. In the infancy of the world, neither poets themselves nor their auditors are fully aware of the excellence of poetry: for it acts in a divine and unapprehended manner, beyond and above consciousness; and it is reserved for future generations to contemplate and measure the mighty cause and effect in all the strength and splendour of their union. Even in modern times, no living poet ever arrived at the fulness of his fame; the jury which sits in judgement upon a poet, belonging as he does to all time, must be composed of his peers: it must be impanelled by Time from the selectest of the wise of many generations. A poet is a nightingale, who sits in darkness and sings to cheer its own solitude with sweet sounds; his auditors are as men entranced by the melody of an unseen musician, who feel that they are moved and softened, yet know not whence or why. The poems of Homer and his contemporaries were the delight of infant Greece; they were the elements of that social system which is the column upon which all succeeding civilization has reposed. Homer embodied the ideal perfection of his age in human character; nor can we doubt that those who read his verses were awakened to an ambition of becoming like to Achilles, Hector, and Ulysses: the truth and beauty of friendship, patriotism, and persevering devotion to an object, were unveiled to their depths in these immortal creations: the sentiments of the auditors must have been refined and enlarged by a sympathy with such great and lovely impersonations, until from admiring they imitated, and from imitation they identified themselves with the objects of their admiration. Nor let it be objected, that these characters are remote from moral perfection, and that they are by no means to be considered as edifying patterns for general imitation. Every epoch, under names more or less specious, has deified its peculiar errors; Revenge is the naked idol of the worship of a semi-barbarous age; and Self-deceit is the veiled image of unknown evil, before which luxury and satiety lie prostrate. But a poet considers the vices of his contemporaries as the temporary dress in which his creations must be arrayed, and which cover without concealing the eternal proportions of their beauty. An epic or dramatic personage is understood to wear them around his soul, as he may the ancient armour or modern uniform around his body; whilst it is easy to conceive a dress more graceful than either. The beauty of the internal nature cannot be so far concealed by its accidental vesture, but that the spirit of its form shall communicate itself to the very disguise, and indicate the shape it hides from the manner in which it is worn. A majestic form and graceful motions will express themselves through the most barbarous and tasteless costume. Few poets of the highest class have chosen to exhibit the beauty of their conceptions in its naked truth and splendour;

and it is doubtful whether the alloy of costume, habit, &c., be not necessary to temper this planetary music for mortal ears.

The whole objection, however, of the immorality of poetry rests upon a misconception of the manner in which poetry acts to produce the moral improvement of man. Ethical science arranges the elements which poetry has created, and propounds schemes and proposes examples of civil and domestic life: nor is it for want of admirable doctrines that men hate, and despise, and censure, and deceive, and subjugate one another. But poetry acts in another and diviner manner. It awakens and enlarges the mind itself by rendering* it the receptacle of a thousand unapprehended combinations of thought. Poetry lifts the veil from the hidden beauty of the world, and makes familiar objects be as if they were not familiar; it reproduces all that it represents, and the impersonations clothed in its Elysian light stand thenceforward in the minds of those who have once contemplated them, as memorials of that gentle and exalted content which extends itself over all thoughts and actions with which it co-exists. The great secret of morals is love; or a going out of our own nature,* and an identification of ourselves with the beautiful which exists in thought, action, or person, not our own. A man, to be greatly good, must imagine intensely and comprehensively; he must put himself in the place of another and of many others; the pains and pleasures of his species must become his own. The great instrument of moral good is the imagination; and poetry administers to the effect* by acting upon the cause.* Poetry enlarges the circumference of the imagination by replenishing it with thoughts of ever new delight, which have the power of attracting and assimilating to their own nature all other thoughts, and which form new intervals and interstices whose void for ever craves fresh food. Poetry strengthens the faculty which is the organ of the moral

---

***rendering:** making.

***our own nature:** 우리들 자신의 사사로운 생각, 성격 등.

***the effect:** moral good, **the cause:** imagination. 즉 시는 imagination에 작용하여 moral good를 낳게 한다.

nature of man, in the same manner as exercise strengthens a limb. A poet therefore would do ill to embody his own conceptions of right and wrong, which are usually those of his place and time, in his poetical creations, which participate in neither.* By this assumption of the inferior office of interpreting the effect, in which perhaps after all he might acquit himself* but imperfectly, he would resign a glory in the participation of the cause. There was little danger that Homer, or any of the eternal poets, should have so far misunderstood themselves as to have abdicated this throne of their widest dominion. Those in whom the poetical faculty, though great, is less intense, as Euripides, Lucan, Tasso, Spenser, have frequently affected a moral aim, and the effect of their poetry is diminished in exact proportion to the degree in which they compel us to advert to this purpose.

Homer and the cyclic poets* were followed at a certain interval by the dramatic and lyrical poets of Athens, who flourished contemporaneously with all that is most perfect in the kindred expressions of the poetical faculty; architecture, painting, music, the dance, sculpture, philosophy, and we may add, the forms of civil life. For although the scheme of Athenian society was deformed by many imperfections which the poetry existing in chivalry and Christianity has erased from the habits and institutions of modern Europe; yet never at any other period has so much energy, beauty, and virtue been developed; never was blind strength and stubborn form so disciplined and rendered subject to the will of man, or that will less repugnant to the dictates of the beautiful and the true, as during the century which preceded the death of Socrates. Of no other epoch in the history of our species have we records and fragments

---

***neither:** 즉 nor his place and time. 시인은 자기 시대와 장소의 시시비비의 관념을 구현하려고 하면 안된다. 즉, 당장의 도덕적 효과(effect)를 노려서는 안된다.

***acquit oneself:** 「임무를 수행하다」. 당장의 도덕적 효과보다는 도덕의 근원(cause), 즉 imagination에 참여하는 영광을 갖도록 하라는 것이다.

***cyclic poets:** Homer가 다루지 않은 Trojan War의 episodes를 다룬 그리이스의 서사시인들.

stamped so visibly with the image of the divinity in man. But it is poetry alone, in form, in action, and in language, which has rendered this epoch memorable above all others, and the storehouse of examples to everlasting time. For written poetry existed at that epoch simultaneously with the other arts, and it is an idle inquiry to demand which gave and which received the light, which all, as from a common focus, have scattered over the darkest periods of succeeding time. We know no more of cause and effect than a constant conjunction of events: poetry is ever found to co-exist with whatever other arts contribute to the happiness and perfection of man. I appeal to what has already been established to distinguish between the cause and the effect.

It was at the period here adverted to, that the drama had its birth; and however a succeeding writer may have equalled or surpassed those few great specimens of the Athenian drama which have been preserved to us, it is indisputable that the art itself never was understood or practised according to the true philosophy of it, as at Athens. For the Athenians employed language, action, music, painting, the dance, and religious institutions, to produce a common effect in the representation of the highest idealisms of passion and of power; each division in the art was made perfect in its kind by artists of the most consummate skill, and was disciplined into a beautiful proportion and unity one towards the other. On the modern stage a few only of the elements capable of expressing the image of the poet's conception are employed at once. We have tragedy without music and dancing; and music and dancing without the highest impersonations of which they are the fit accompaniment, and both without religion and solemnity. Religious institution has indeed been usually banished from the stage. Our system of divesting the actor's face of a mask, on which the many expressions appropriated to his dramatic character might be moulded into one permanent and unchanging expression, is favourable only to a partial and inharmonious effect; it is fit for nothing but a monologue, where all the attention may be directed to some great master of ideal mimicry. The modern practice of blending comedy with tragedy, though liable to great abuse in point of practice, is undoubtedly an extension of the dramatic circle*; but the comedy should be as in *King Lear*, universal, ideal, and sublime. It is perhaps the intervention of this principle which determines the balance in favour of *King Lear* against the *Oedipus Tyrannus* or the *Agamemnon*, or, if you will, the trilogies with which they are connected; unless the intense power of the choral poetry, especially that of the latter, should be considered as restoring the equilibrium. *King Lear*, if it can sustain this comparison, may be judged to be the most perfect specimen of the dramatic art existing in the world; in spite of the narrow conditions to which the poet was subjected by the ignorance of the philosophy of the drama which has prevailed in modern Europe. Calderon,* in his religious Autos,* has attempted to fulfil some of the high conditions of dramatic representation neglected by Shakespeare; such as the establishing a relation between the drama and religion, and the accommodating them to music and dancing; but he omits the observation of conditions still more important, and more is lost than gained by the substitution of the rigidly-defined and ever-repeated idealisms of a distorted superstition for the living impersonations of the truth of human passion.

But I digress.—The connection of scenic exhibitions* with the improvement or corruption of the manners of men has been universally recognised: in other words, the presence or absence of poetry in its most perfect and universal form, has been found to be connected with good and evil in conduct or habit. The corruption which has been imputed to the drama as an effect, begins, when the poetry employed in its constitution ends: I appeal to the history of manners whether the periods of the

---

*그리이스의 비극작가 Aeschylus에 이르기까지 그리이스 비극은 3부작으로 되어 있었다.

***Calderon:** Spain 최대의 르네상스 극작가(1600-81). **Autos**=plays

***scenic exhibitions:** 즉 무대예술. Shelley는 종합예술로서의 연극(특히 고전 스타일의 연극)을 시의 최고봉(poetry in its most perfect form)으로 보고 있다.

growth of the one* and the decline of the other* have not corresponded with an exactness equal to any example of moral cause and effect.

The drama at Athens, or wheresoever else it may have approached to its perfection, ever co-existed with the moral and intellectual greatness of the age. The tragedies of the Athenian poets are as mirrors in which the spectator beholds himself, under a thin disguise of circumstance, stripped of all but that ideal perfection and energy which every one feels to be the internal type of all that he loves, admires, and would become. The imagination is enlarged by a sympathy with pains and passions so mighty, that they distend in their conception the capacity of that by which they are conceived; the good affections are strengthened by pity, indignation, terror and sorrow; and an exalted calm is prolonged from the satiety of this high exercise of them into the tumult of familiar life: even crime is disarmed of half its horror and all its contagion by being represented as the fatal consequence of the unfathomable agencies of nature; error is thus divested of its wilfulness; men can no longer cherish it as the creation of their choice. In the drama of the highest order there is little food for censure or hatred; it teaches rather self-knowledge and self-respect. Neither the eye nor the mind can see itself, unless reflected upon that which it resembles. The drama, so long as it continues to express poetry, is a prismatic and many-sided mirror, which collects the brightest rays of human nature and divides and reproduces them from the simplicity of their elementary forms, and touches them with majesty and beauty, and multiplies all that it reflects, and endows it with the power of propagating its like* wherever it may fall.

But in periods of the decay of social life, the drama sympathizes with that decay. Tragedy becomes a cold imitation of the form of the great masterpieces of antiquity, divested of all harmonious accompaniment of the kindred arts; and often the

---

***the one:** corruption, **the other:** poetry

***its like:** 「그와 비슷한 것」.

very form misunderstood, or a weak attempt to teach certain doctrines, which the writer considers as moral truths; and which are usually no more than specious flatteries of some gross vice or weakness, with which the author, in common with his auditors, are infected. Hence what has been called the classical and domestic drama. Addison's *Cato** is a specimen of the one*; and would* it were not superfluous to cite examples of the other! To such purposes poetry cannot be made subservient. Poetry is a sword of lightning, ever unsheathed, which consumes the scabbard that would contain it. And thus we observe that all dramatic writings of this nature are unimaginative in a singular degree; they affect* sentiment and passion, which, divested of imagination, are other names for caprice and appetite. The period in our own history of the grossest degradation of the drama is the reign of Charles II, when all forms in which poetry had been accustomed to be expressed became hymns to the triumph of kingly power over liberty and virtue. Milton stood alone illuminating an age unworthy of him. At such periods the calculating principle pervades all the forms of dramatic exhibition, and poetry ceases to be expressed upon them. Comedy loses its ideal universality: wit succeeds to humour; we laugh from self-complacency and triumph, instead of pleasure; malignity, sarcasm, and contempt, succeed to sympathetic merriment; we hardly laugh, but we smile. Obscenity, which is ever blasphemy against the divine beauty in life, becomes, from the very veil which it assumes, more active if less disgusting: it is a monster for which the corruption of society for ever brings forth new food, which it devours in secret.

The drama being that form under which a greater number of modes of expression of poetry are susceptible of being combined than any other, the connection of poetry and social good is more observable in the drama than in whatever other form. And it is indisputable that the highest perfection of human

---

***the one:** classical drama. Addison의 *Cato*는 고전극을 모방한 것.

***would:** I wish.

***affect:** 「...을 가장하다, ...인 척하다」.

society has ever corresponded with the highest dramatic excellence; and that the corruption or the extinction of the drama in a nation where it has once flourished, is a mark of a corruption of manners, and an extinction of the energies which sustain the soul of social life. But, as Machiavelli says of political institutions, that life may be preserved and renewed, if men should arise capable of bringing back the drama to its principles. And this is true with respect to poetry in its most extended sense: all language, institution and form, require not only to be produced but to be sustained: the office and character of a poet participates in the divine nature as regards providence, no less than as regards creation.

Civil war, the spoils of Asia, and the fatal predominance first of the Macedonian, and then of the Roman arms, were so many symbols of the extinction or suspension of the creative faculty in Greece. The bucolic writers,* who found patronage under the lettered tyrants of Sicily and Egypt, were the latest representatives of its most glorious reign. Their poetry is intensely melodious; like the odour of the tuberose, it overcomes and sickens the spirit with excess ot sweetness; whilst the poetry of the preceding age was as a meadow-gale of June, which mingles the fragrance of all the flowers of the field, and adds a quickening and harmonizing spirit of its own which endows the sense with a power of sustaining its extreme delight. The bucolic and erotic delicacy in written poetry is correlative with that softness in statuary, music, and the kindred arts, and even in manners and institutions, which distinguished the epoch to which I now refer. Nor is it the poetical faculty itself, or any misapplication of it, to which this want of harmony is to be imputed. An equal sensibility to the influence of the senses and the affections is to be found in the writings of Homer and Sophocles: the former,

*bucolic writers: 전원시인들. 즉 Theocritus, Bion, Moschus 등. 이들은 그리이스가 마케도니아에게 망한 뒤, 이른바 hellenism 문명 시대에 감미로운 전원시와 연애시를 써서 유행시켰다. 그들의 온갖 기술적 재치와 감미로움에도 불구하고 "정신"이 결여된 까닭에 최고의 문학이 되지 못한다. Shelley는 그들의 감미로움 자체를 낮하지 않는다.

especially, has clothed sensual and pathetic images with irresistible attractions. Their superiority over these succeeding writers consists in the presence of those thoughts which belong to the inner faculties of our nature, not in the absence of those which are connected with the external: their incomparable perfection consists in a harmony of the union of all. It is not what the erotic poets have, but what they have not, in which their imperfection consists. It is not inasmuch as they were poets, but inasmuch as they were not poets, that they can be considered with any plausibility as connected with the corruption of their age. Had that corruption availed so as to extinguish in them the sensibility to pleasure, passion, and natural scenery, which is imputed to them as an imperfection, the last triumph of evil would have been achieved. For the end of social corruption is to destroy all sensibility to pleasure; and, therefore, it is corruption. It begins at the imagination and the intellect as at the core, and distributes itself thence as a paralysing venom, through the affections into the very appetites, until all become a torpid mass in which hardly sense survives. At the approach of such a period, poetry ever addresses itself to those faculties which are the last to be destroyed, and its voice is heard, like the footsteps of Astraea,* departing from the world. Poetry ever communicates all the pleasure which men are capable of receiving: it is ever still the light of life; the source of whatever of beautiful or generous or true can have place in an evil time. It will readily be confessed that those among the luxurious citizens of Syracuse and Alexandria, who were delighted with the poems of Theocritus, were less cold, cruel, and sensual than the remnant of their tribe. But corruption must utterly have destroyed the fabric of human society before poetry can ever cease. The sacred links of that chain have never been entirely disjoined, which descending through the minds of many men is attached to those great minds, whence as from a magnet the invisible effluence is sent forth, which at once connects, animates, and

*Astraea: Justice의 여신. 지상이 낙원이었을 때에는 인간과 함께 살다가 하늘로 올라가 버렸다고 한다.

sustains the life of all. It is the faculty which contains within itself the seeds at once of its own and of social renovation. And let us not circumscribe the effects of the bucolic and erotic poetry within the limits of the sensibility of those to whom it was addressed. They may have perceived the beauty of those immortal compositions, simply as fragments and isolated portions: those who are more finely organized, or born in a happier age, may recognise them as episodes to that great poem, which all poets, like the co-operating thoughts of one great mind, have built up since the beginning of the world.

The same revolution within a narrower sphere had place in ancient Rome; but the actions and forms of its social life never seem to have been perfectly saturated with the poetical element. The Romans appear to have considered the Greeks as the selectest treasuries of the selectest forms of manners and of nature, and to have abstained from creating in measured language, sculpture, music, or architecture, anything which might bear a particular relation to their own condition, whilst it should bear a general one to the universal constitution of the world. But we judge from partial evidence, and we judge perhaps partially. Ennius, Varro, Pacuvius, and Accius,* all great poets, have been lost. Lucretius is in the highest, and Virgil in a very high sense, a creator. The chosen delicacy of expressions of the latter, are as a mist of light which conceal from us the intense and exceeding truth of his conceptions of nature.

Livy is instinct with poetry. Yet Horace, Catullus, Ovid, and generally the other great writers of the Virgilian age, saw man and nature in the mirror of Greece. The institutions also, and the religion of Rome, were less poetical than those of Greece, as the shadow is less vivid than the substance. Hence poetry in Rome seemed to follow, rather than accompany, the perfection of political and domestic society. The true poetry of Rome lived in its institutions;* for whatever of beautiful, true

*이들 고대 로마의 시인들의 작품은 전해지지 않는다.

*Shelley 는 로마제국의 "시"는 문학과 예술에서가 아니라, 제도, 법률, 행정, 군사조직에서 가장 잘 나타났다고 본다. 이들 인간질서의 방법은 모두 "시"인 것이다.

and majestic, they contained, could have sprung only from the faculty which creates the order in which they consist. The life of Camillus,* the death of Regulus;* the expectation of the senators,* in their godlike state, of the victorious Gauls; the refusal of the republic to make peace with Hannibal, after the battle of Cannae,* were not the consequences of a refined calculation of the probable personal advantage to result from such a rhythm and order in the shows of life, to those who were at once the poets and the actors of these immortal dramas. The imagination beholding the beauty of this order, created it out of itself according to its own idea; the consequence was empire, and the reward everlasting fame. These things are not the less poetry *quia carent vate sacro*.* They are the episodes of that cyclic poem written by Time upon the memories of men. The Past, like an inspired rhapsodist, fills the theatre of everlasting generations with their harmony.

At length the ancient system of religion and manners had fulfilled the circle of its evolutions. And the world would have fallen into utter anarchy and darkness, but that there were found poets among the authors of the Christian and chivalric systems of manners and religion, who created forms of opinion and action never before conceived; which, copied into the imaginations of men, became as generals to the bewildered armies of their thoughts. It is foreign to the present purpose to touch upon the evil produced by these systems: except that we protest, on the ground of the principles already established, that no portion of it can be attributed to the poetry they contain.

It is probable that the poetry of Moses, Job, David, Solomon, and Isaiah, had produced a great effect upon the mind of Jesus and his disciples. The scattered fragments preserved to us by the biographers of this extraordinary person, are all instinct

---

*__Camillus:__ Gaul 족속을 물리친 장군. **Regulus:** 자신의 목숨을 희생한 애국자. **senators:** 이들은 Gaul 족이 쳐들어 왔을 때 자신들을 희생제물로 바치기 위하여 기다리고 있었다. Shelley 는 이같은 영웅적 행위 자체를 "시"로 본 것이다.

*Carthage 의 Hannibal 이 Cannae 에서 로마군을 무찔렀다 (216 B.C.).

**quia*...: 'Because they lack the divine poet' (Horace, *Odes*, IV, ix, 28).

with the most vivid poetry. But his doctrines seem to have been quickly distorted. At a certain period after the prevalence of a system of opinions founded upon those promulgated by him, the three forms*into which Plato had distributed the faculties of mind underwent a sort of apotheosis, and became the object of the worship of the civilized world. Here it is to be confessed that 'Light' seems to 'thicken',*

> **And the crow makes wing to the rooky wood;**
> **Good things of day begin to droop and drowse,**
> **Whiles night's black agents to their preys do rouse.***

But mark how beautiful an order has sprung from the dust and blood of this fierce chaos! how the world, as from a resurrection, balancing itself on the golden wings of knowledge and of hope, has reassumed its yet unwearied flight into the heaven of time. Listen to the music, unheard by outward ears, which is as a ceaseless and invisible wind, nourishing its everlasting course with strength and swiftness.

The poetry in the doctrines of Jesus Christ, and the mythology and institutions of the Celtic* conquerors of the Roman empire, outlived the darkness and the convulsions connected with their growth and victory, and blended themselves in a new fabric of manners and opinion. It is an error to impute the ignorance of the dark ages to the Christian doctrines or the predominance of the Celtic nations. Whatever of evil their agencies may have contained sprang from the extinction of the poetical principle, connected with the progress of despotism and superstition. Men, from causes too intricate to be here discussed, had become insensible and selfish: their own will had become feeble, and yet they were its slaves, and thence the

---

***the three forms:** Plato가 *Timaeus*에서 구분한 정신의 3영역. 즉, the immortal soul, or reason; the higher mortal soul, or affections of the heart; and the lower mortal soul, or appetites. 유럽 윤리 사상의 근간의 하나. 기독교 철학과 결합됨.

*이른바 중세 암흑기를 말하고 있다. 그 아래 인용된 *Macbeth*, Ⅱ, ii, 50에서도 어둠이 짙어옴을 나타내고 있다.

***Celtic:** 틀린 말. Teutonic 또는 Germanic이라고 해야 옳다. 로마는 이들에게 패망.

slaves of the will of others: lust, fear, avarice, cruelty, and fraud, characterized a race amongst whom no one was to be found capable of *creating* in form, language, or institution. The moral anomalies of such a state of society are not justly to be charged upon any class of events immediately connected with them, and those events are most entitled to our approbation which could dissolve it most expeditiously. It is unfortunate for those who cannot distinguish words from thoughts, that many of these anomalies have been incorporated into our popular religion.

It was not until the eleventh century that the effects of the poetry of the Christian and chivalric systems began to manifest themselves. The principle of equality had been discovered and applied by Plato in his *Republic*,* as the theoretical rule of the mode in which the materials of pleasure and of power produced by the common skill and labour of human beings ought to be distributed among them. The limitations of this rule were asserted by him to be determined only by the sensibility of each, or the utility to result to all. Plato, following the doctrines of Timaeus and Pythagoras, taught also a moral and intellectual system of doctrine, comprehending at once the past, the present, and the future condition of man. Jesus Christ divulged the sacred and eternal truths contained in these views to mankind, and Christianity, in its abstract purity, became the exoteric expression of the esoteric doctrines of the poetry and wisdom of antiquity. The incorporation of the Celtic nations with the exhausted population of the south, impressed upon it the figure of the poetry existing in their mythology and institutions. The result was a sum of the action and reaction of all the causes included in it; for it may be assumed as a maxim that no nation or religion can supersede any other without incorporating into itself a portion of that which it supersedes. The abolition of personal and domestic slavery, and the emancipation of women from a great part of the degrading restraints of

*기독교가 Plato 사상의 영향을 받았다는 설. Hellenism의 영향은 다소 있으나, 거의 관련이 없다.

antiquity, were among the consequences of these events.

The abolition of personal slavery is the basis of the highest political hope that it can enter into the mind of man to conceive. The freedom of women produced the poetry of sexual love. Love became a religion, the idols of whose worship were ever present.* It was as if the statues of Apollo and the Muses had been endowed with life and motion, and had walked forth among their worshippers; so that earth became peopled by the inhabitants of a diviner world. The familiar appearances and proceedings of life became wonderful and heavenly, and a paradise was created as out of the wrecks of Eden. And as this creation itself is poetry, so its creators were poets; and language was the instrument of their art: 'Galeotto fù il libro, e chi lo scrisse.'* The Provençal Trouveurs,* or inventors, preceded Petrarch, whose verses are as spells which unseal the inmost enchanted fountains of the delight which is in the grief of love. It is impossible to feel them without becoming a portion of that beauty which we contemplate: it were superfluous to explain how the gentleness and elevation of mind connected with these sacred emotions can render men more amiable, more generous and wise, and lift them out of the dull vapours of the little world of self. Dante understood the secret things of love even more than Petrarch. His *Vita Nuova* is an inexhaustible fountain of purity of sentiment and language: it is the idealized history of that period and those intervals of his life which were dedicated to love. His apotheosis of Beatrice in Paradise, and the gradations of his own love and her loveliness, by which as by steps he feigns himself to have ascended to the throne of the Supreme Cause,* is the most glorious imagination of modern poetry. The acutest critics have justly reversed the

---

*낭만적 연애문학이 생긴 것은 기독교의 영향으로 12, 13세기 남유럽에서였다.

Galeotto...:** 'the book, and he who wrote it, was a Galeotto.' Dante, ***Inferno, V, 137에서 금지된 사랑 때문에 죽은 Francesca가 하는 말. Galeotto의 연애담을 연인 Paolo와 함께 읽다가 서로 사랑하게 되었었다.

***The Provençal Trouveurs:** 남프랑스(프로방스)의 음유시인들(troubadours).

***Supreme Cause:** God.

judgement of the vulgar, and the order of the great acts of the *Divina Commedia*, in the measure of the admiration which they accord to the Hell, Purgatory, and Paradise. The latter is a perpetual hymn of everlasting love. Love, which found a worthy poet in Plato* alone of all the ancients, has been celebrated by a chorus of the greatest writers of the renovated world; and the music has penetrated the caverns of society, and its echoes still drown the dissonance of arms and superstition. At successive intervals, Ariosto, Tasso, Shakespeare, Spenser, Calderon, Rousseau, and the great writers of our own age, have celebrated the dominion of love, planting as it were trophies in the human mind of that sublimest victory over sensuality and force. The true relation borne to each other by the sexes into which human kind is distributed has become less misunderstood; and if the error which confounded diversity with inequality of the powers of the two sexes has been partially recognised in the opinions and institutions of modern Europe, we owe this great benefit to the worship of which chivalry was the law, and poets the prophets.

The poetry of Dante may be considered as the bridge thrown over the stream of time, which unites the modern and ancient world. The distorted notions of invisible things which Dante and his rival Milton have idealized, are merely the mask and the mantle in which these great poets walk through eternity enveloped and disguised. It is a difficult question to determine how far they were conscious of the distinction which must have subsisted in their minds between their own creeds and that of the people. Dante at least appears to wish to mark the full extent of it by placing Riphaeus,* whom Virgil calls *justissimus unus*, in Paradise, and observing a most heretical caprice in his distribution of rewards and punishments. And Milton's poem contains within itself a philosophical refuta-

*Plato, *Symposium* 에서 "everyone becomes a poet as soon as he is touched by a poet."

***Riphaeus:** Virgil 이 *Aeneid*, Ⅱ, 426 에서 "foremost in justice"라고 칭찬한 사람. 이교도지만 Dante는 기독교의 천국에 들어갔다고 했다.

tion of that system* of which, by a strange and natural antithesis, it has been a chief popular support. Nothing can exceed the energy and magnificence of the character of Satan as expressed in *Paradise Lost.* It is a mistake to suppose that he could ever have been intended for the popular personification of evil. Implacable hate, patient cunning, and a sleepless refinement of device to inflict the extremest anguish on an enemy, these things are evil; and, although venial in a slave, are not to be forgiven in a tyrant; although redeemed by much that ennobles his defeat in one subdued, are marked by all that dishonours his conquest in the victor. Milton's Devil as a moral being is as far superior to his God, as one who perseveres in some purpose which he has conceived to be excellent, in spite of adversity and torture, is to one who in the cold security of undoubted triumph inflicts the most horrible revenge upon his enemy, not from any mistaken notion of inducing him to repent of a perseverence in enmity, but with the alleged design of exasperating him to deserve new torments. Milton has so far violated the popular creed (if this shall be judged to be a violation) as to have alleged no superiority of moral virtue to his God over his Devil. And this bold neglect of a direct moral purpose is the most decisive proof of the supremacy of Milton's genius. He mingled as it were the elements of human nature as colours upon a single pallet, and arranged them in the composition of his great picture according to the laws of epic truth, that is, according to the laws of that principle by which a series of actions of the external universe and of intelligent and ethical beings is calculated to excite the sympathy of succeeding generations of mankind. The *Divina Commedia* and *Paradise Lost* have conferred upon modern mythology a systematic form; and when change and time shall have added one more superstition to the mass of those which have arisen and decayed upon the

---

***that system:** 기독교의 교리. Dante와 Milton은 기독교를 신봉했으나, 일반 교인들과는 엄청나게 다른 시적 해석을 하고 있었다고 Shelley는 믿는다. Dante는 이교도를 천국에 넣었고, Milton은 God보다 오히려 Satan 편이었다는 것이다(이 해석은 오늘날 부정되고 있다).

earth, commentators will be learnedly employed in elucidating the religion of ancestral Europe, only not utterly forgotten because it will have been stamped with the eternity of genius.

Homer was the first and Dante the second epic poet: that is, the second poet, the series of whose creations bore a defined and intelligible relation to the knowledge and sentiment and religion of the age in which he lived, and of the ages which followed it: developing itself in correspondence with their development. For Lucretius had limed* the wings of his swift spirit in the dregs of the sensible world; and Virgil, with a modesty that ill became his genius, had affected the fame of an imitator, even whilst he created anew all that he copied; and none among the flock of mock-birds, though their notes are sweet, Apollonius Rhodius, Quintus (Calaber) Smyrnaeus, Nonnus, Lucan, Statius, or Claudian, have sought even to fulfil a single condition of epic truth. Milton was the third epic poet. For if the title of epic in its highest sense be refused to the *Aeneid*, still less can it be conceded to the *Orlando Furioso*, the *Gerusalemme Liberata*, the *Lusiad*, or the *Faerie Queene*.*

Dante and Milton were both deeply penetrated with the ancient religion of the civilized world; and its spirit exists in their poetry probably in the same proportion as its forms survived in the unreformed worship of modern Europe. The one preceded and the other followed the Reformation at almost equal intervals. Dante was the first religious reformer, and Luther surpassed him rather in the rudeness and acrimony, than in the boldness of his censures of papal usurpation. Dante was the first awakener of entranced Europe; he created a language, in itself music and persuasion, out of a chaos of inharmonious barbarisms. He was the congregator of those great spirits who presided over the resurrection of learning; the

---

***lime:** 「끈끈이칠을 하다, 새를 잡을 때 날개에다 끈끈이를 묻히다」. Lucretius는 굉장한 시인이었으나, Materialism을 믿어 물질을 노래했으므로 비상하지 못했다. 즉 그의 시의 날개엔 끈끈이가 묻은 셈이었다.

*르네상스 유럽 시인들의 서사시. Shelley는 이들을 진정한 epic으로 보지 않는다.

Lucifer of that starry flock which in the thirteenth century shone forth from republican Italy, as from a heaven, into the darkness of the benighted world. His very words are instinct with spirit; each is as a spark, a burning atom of inextinguishable thought; and many yet lie covered in the ashes of their birth, and pregnant with a lightning which has yet found no conductor. All high poetry is infinite; it is as the first acorn, which contained all oaks potentially. Veil after veil may be undrawn, and the inmost naked beauty of the meaning never exposed. A great poem is a fountain for ever overflowing with the waters of wisdom and delight; and after one person and one age has exhausted all its divine effluence which their peculiar relations enable them to share, another and yet another succeeds, and new relations are ever developed, the source of an unforeseen and an unconceived delight.

The age immediately succeeding to that of Dante, Petrarch, and Boccaccio, was characterized by a revival of painting, sculpture, and architecture. Chaucer caught the sacred inspiration, and the superstructure of English literature is based upon the materials of Italian invention.

But let us not be betrayed from a defence into a critical history of poetry and its influence on society. Be it enough to have pointed out the effects of poets, in the large and true sense of the word, upon their own and all succeeding times.

But poets have been challenged to resign the civic crown* to reasoners and mechanists, on another plea. It is admitted that the exercise of the imagination is most delightful, but it is alleged that that of reason is more useful. Let us examine, as the grounds of this distinction, what is here meant by utility. Pleasure or good, in a general sense, is that which the consciousness of a sensitive and intelligent being seeks, and in which, when found, it acquiesces. There are two kinds of pleasure, one durable, universal, and permanent; the other transitory and particular. Utility may either express the means of producing the former or the latter. In the former sense, whatever strengthens

*civic crown: 실제 사회의 최고의 지위.

and purifies the affections, enlarges the imagination, and adds spirit to sense, is useful. But a narrower meaning may be assigned to the word utility, confining it to express that which banishes the importunity of the wants of our animal nature, the surrounding men with security of life, the dispersing the grosser delusions of superstition, and the conciliating such a degree of mutual forbearance among men as may consist with the motives of personal advantage.

Undoubtedly the promoters of utility, in this limited sense, have their appointed office in society. They follow the footsteps of poets, and copy the sketches of their creations into the book of common life. They make space and give time. Their exertions are of the highest value, so long as they confine their administration of the concerns of the inferior powers of our nature within the limits due to the superior ones. But whilst the sceptic destroys gross superstitions, let him spare to deface, as some of the French writers have defaced, the eternal truths charactered* upon the imaginations of men. Whilst the mechanist abridges, and the political economist combines labour, let them beware that their speculations, for want of correspondence with those first principles which belong to the imagination, do not tend, as they have in modern England, to exasperate at once the extremes of luxury and of want. They have exemplified the saying, 'To him that hath, more shall be given; and from him that hath not, the little that he hath shall be taken away.'* The rich have become richer, and the poor have become poorer; and the vessel of the state is driven between the Scylla and Charybdis of anarchy and despotism. Such are the effects which must ever flow from an unmitigated exercise of the calculating faculty.

It is difficult to define pleasure in its highest sense; the definition involving a number of apparent paradoxes. For, from an inexplicable defect of harmony in the constitution of human nature, the pain of the inferior is frequently connected with the

---

*character: 「새기다」.

*신약 「마태복음」 25장 14—30절 참조. 그리스도의 말씀은 물론 다른 뜻에서 한 것임.

pleasures of the superior portions of our being. Sorrow, terror, anguish, despair itself, are often the chosen expressions of an approximation to the highest good. Our sympathy in tragic fiction depends on this principle; tragedy delights by affording a shadow of that pleasure which exists in pain. This is the source also of the melancholy which is inseparable from the sweetest melody. The pleasure that is in sorrow is sweeter than the pleasure of pleasure itself. And hence the saying, 'It is better to go to the house of mourning than to the house of mirth.'* Not that this highest species of pleasure is necessarily linked with pain. The delight of love and friendship, the ecstasy of the admiration of nature, the joy of the perception and still more of the creation of poetry, is often wholly unalloyed.

The production and assurance of pleasure in this highest sense is true utility. Those who produce and preserve this pleasure are poets or poetical philosophers.

The exertions of Locke, Hume, Gibbon, Voltaire, Rousseau, and their disciples, in favour of oppressed and deluded humanity, are entitled to the gratitude of mankind. Yet it is easy to calculate the degree of moral and intellectual improvement which the world would have exhibited, had they never lived. A little more nonsense would have been talked for a century or two; and perhaps a few more men, women, and children, burnt as heretics. We might not at this moment have been congratulating each other on the abolition of the Inquisition in Spain. But it exceeds all imagination to conceive what would have been the moral condition of the world if neither Dante, Petrarch, Boccaccio, Chaucer, Shakespeare, Calderon, Lord Bacon, nor Milton, had ever existed; if Raphael and Michael Angelo had never been born; if the Hebrew poetry had never been translated; if a revival of the study of Greek literature had never taken place; if no monuments of ancient sculpture had been handed down to us; and if the poetry of the religion of the ancient world had been extinguished together with its belief. The human mind could never, except by the intervention of

*구약 「잠언」 7장 2절.

these excitements, have been awakened to the invention of the grosser sciences, and that application of analytical reasoning to the aberrations of society which it is now attempted to exalt over the direct expression of the inventive and creative faculty itself.

We have more moral, political, and historical wisdom than we know how to reduce into practice; we have more scientific and economical knowledge than can be accommodated to the just distribution of the produce which it multiplies. The poetry in these systems of thought is concealed by the accumulation of facts and calculating processes. There is no want of knowledge respecting what is wisest and best in morals, government, and political economy, or at least what is wiser and better than what men now practise and endure. But we let *'*I dare not* wait upon *I would*,* like the poor cat in the adage.'* We want* the creative faculty to imagine that which we know; we want the generous impulse to act that which we imagine; we want the poetry of life: our calculations have outrun conception; we have eaten more than we can digest. The cultivation of those sciences which have enlarged the limits of the empire of man over the external world, has, for want of the poetical faculty, proportionally circumscribed those of the internal world; and man, having enslaved the elements, remains himself a slave. To what but a cultivation of the mechanical arts in a degree disproportioned to the presence of the creative faculty, which is the basis of all knowledge, is to be attributed the abuse of all invention for abridging and combining labour, to the exasperation of the inequality of mankind? From what other cause has it arisen that the discoveries which should have lightened, have added a weight to the curse imposed on Adam?* Poetry, and the principle of Self of which money is the visible incarnation, are

*__*I dare not*__: 우유부단, __*I would*__: 의지. 즉 하려고 하는 의지에 우유부단이 늘상 따라다니게 한다는 것.

***like...adage:** 「우유부단한 고양이처럼」이라는 뜻의 격언. 여기서 adage는 구체적으로 "Care killed the cat" (걱정근심만 하다가 고양이는 죽었다) 라는 격언을 말함.

***want:** lack.

***the curse...Adam:** 인류의 조상 Adam에게 내린 저주. 즉 노동.

the God and Mammon* of the world.

The functions of the poetical faculty are twofold; by one it creates new materials of knowledge, and power, and pleasure; by the other it engenders in the mind a desire to reproduce and arrange them according to a certain rhythm and order which may be called the beautiful and the good. The cultivation of poetry is never more to be desired than at periods when, from an excess of the selfish and calculating principle, the accumulation of the materials of external life exceed the quantity of the power of assimilating them to the internal laws of human nature. The body has then become too unwieldy for that which animates it.

Poetry is indeed something divine. It is at once the centre and circumference of knowledge; it is that which comprehends all science, and that to which all science must be referred. It is at the same time the root and blossom of all other systems of thought; it is that from which all spring, and that which adorns all; and that which, if blighted, denies the fruit and the seed, and withholds from the barren world the nourishment and the succession of the scions of the tree of life. It is the perfect and consummate surface and bloom of all things; it is as the odour and the colour of the rose to the texture of the elements which compose it, as the form and splendour of unfaded beauty to the secrets of anatomy and corruption.* What were virtue, love, patriotism, friendship—what were the scenery of this beautiful universe which we inhabit; what were our consolations on this side of the grave—and what were our aspirations beyond it, if poetry did not ascend to bring light and fire from those eternal regions where the owl-winged* faculty of calculation dare not ever soar? Poetry is not like reasoning, a power

---

***God and Mammon:** 신약 「마태복음」 6 장 24 절, "Ye cannot serve God and Mammon'.

*It is as A to B, as C to D의 구문. 「A와 B의 관계는 C와 D의 관계와 같다」.

***owl-winged:** 높이도, 멀리도, 환한 낮에도 날지 못하는 부엉이(에다 인간의 계산적 기능, 즉 이성을 비유하고 있다).

to be exerted acording to the determination of the will. A man cannot say, 'I will compose poetry.' The greatest poet even cannot say it; for the mind in creation is as a fading coal, which some invisible influence, like an inconstant wind, awakens to transitory brightness; this power arises from within, like the colour of a flower which fades and changes as it is developed, and the conscious portions of our natures* are unprophetic either of its approach or its departure. Could this influence be durable in its original purity and force, it is impossible to predict the greatness of the results; but when composition begins, inspiration is already on the decline, and the most glorious poetry that has ever been communicated to the world is probably a feeble shadow of the original conceptions of the poet. I appeal to the greatest poets of the present day, whether it is not an error to assert that the finest passages of poetry are produced by labour and study. The toil and the delay recommended by critics, can be justly interpreted to mean no more than a careful observation of the inspired moments, and an artificial connexion of the spaces between their* suggestions by the intertexture of conventional expressions; a necessity only imposed by the limitedness of the poetical faculty itself; for Milton conceived the *Paradise Lost* as a whole before he executed it in portions. We have his own authority also for the muse having 'dictated' to him the 'unpremeditated song.'* And let this be an answer to those who would allege the fifty-six various readings of the first line of the *Orlando Furioso*.* Compositions so produced are to poetry what mosaic is to painting. The instinct and intuition of the poetical faculty is still more ob-

---

***the conscious portions of our natures:** 우리 정신의 의식계. 시는 무의식과 관계 있다는 설의 반향. 아무리 좋은 시작품이라도 무의식적 영감(시상) 그 자체보다는 못하다는 것.

***their:** of the inspired moments.

***dictated...song:** *Paradise Lost*, IX, 23-4.

**Orlando Furioso*: Ariosto는 이 작품을 1503년경에 시작하여 그가 죽던 1533년까지 개작을 거듭했다. Shelley는 이처럼 의식적으로 만든 작품을 mosaic에 지나지 않는다고 보며, 시는 무의식적 · 무의지적 성장 과정이라고 보는 것이다.

servable in the plastic and pictorial arts: a great statue or picture grows under the power of the artist as a child in the mother's womb; and the very mind which directs the hands in formation, is incapable of accounting to itself for the origin, the gradations, or the media of the process.

Poetry is the record of the best and happiest moments of the happiest and best minds. We are aware of evanescent visitations of thought and feeling, sometimes associated with place or person, sometimes regarding our own mind alone, and always arising unforeseen and departing unbidden, but elevating and delightful beyond all expression: so that even in the desire and the regret they leave, there cannot but be pleasure, participating as it does in the nature of its object. It is as it were the interpenetration of a diviner nature through our own; but its footsteps are like those of a wind over the sea, which the morning calm erases, and whose traces remain only, as on the wrinkled sand which paves it. These and corresponding conditions of being are experienced principally by those of the most delicate sensibility and the most enlarged imagination; and the state of mind produced by them is at war with every base desire. The enthusiasm of virtue, love, patriotism, and friendship is essentially linked with such emotions; and whilst they last, self appears as what it is, an atom to a universe. Poets are not only subject to these experiences as spirits of the most refined organization, but they can colour all that they combine with the evanescent hues of this ethereal world; a word, a trait in the representation of a scene or a passion will touch the enchanted chord, and reanimate, in those who have ever experienced these emotions, the sleeping, the cold, the buried image of the past. Poetry thus makes immortal all that is best and most beautiful in the world; it arrests the vanishing apparitions which haunt the interlunations of life,* and veiling them or* in language or in form, sends them forth among mankind, bearing

---

***interlunations of life:** 인생에 있어서 특별히 「빛나는 순간들」. Shelley 의 신조어.

***or:** either.

sweet news of kindred joy to those with whom their sisters* abide —abide, because there is no portal of expression from the caverns of the spirit which they inhabit into the universe of things. Poetry redeems from decay the visitations of the divinity in man.

Poetry turns all things to loveliness; it exalts the beauty of that which is most beautiful, and it adds beauty to that which is most deformed; it marries exultation and horror, grief and pleasure, eternity and change; it subdues to union under its light yoke all irreconcilable things. It transmutes all that it touches, and every form moving within the radiance of its presence is changed by wondrous sympathy to an incarnation of the spirit which it breathes: its secret alchemy turns to potable gold* the poisonous waters which flow from death through life; it strips the veil of familiarity from the world, and lays bare the naked and sleeping beauty which is the spirit of its forms.

All things exist as they are perceived; at least in relation to the percipient. 'The mind is its own place, and in itself can make a Heaven of Hell, a Hell of Heaven.'* But poetry defeats the curse which binds us to be subjected to the accident of surrounding impressions. And whether it spreads its own figured curtain, or withdraws life's dark veil from before the scene of things, it equally creates for us a being within our being. It makes us the inhabitant of a world to which the familiar world is a chaos. It reproduces the common universe of which we are portions and percipients, and it purges from our inward sight the film of familiarity which obscures from us the wonder of our being. It compels us to feel that which we perceive, and to imagine that which we know. It creates anew the universe, after it has been annihilated in our minds by the recurrence of impressions blunted by reiteration. It justifies the bold and true word of Tasso: *Non merita nome di creatore, se non Iddio ed il Poeta.**

***their sisters:** 시인이 곱게 꾸며서 보내준 형상들(apparitions)과 닮은 형상들(sisters). 시인이 아닌 보통 사람들(those)의 마음 속에 거하므로 표현의 출구(portal)가 없었다.

***potable gold:** 액체 황금. 중세 연금술에서 만병통치의 영약(elixir).

**Paradise Lost*, I, 245—5.

A poet, as he is the author to others of the highest wisdom, pleasure, virtue, and glory, so he ought personally to be the happiest, the best, the wisest, and the most illustrious of men. As to his glory, let time be challenged to declare whether the fame of any other institutor of human life be comparable to that of a poet. That he is the wisest, the happiest, and the best, inasmuch as he is a poet, is equally incontrovertible: the greatest poets have been men of the most spotless virtue, of the most consummate prudence, and, if we would look into the interior of their lives, the most fortunate of men: and the exceptions, as they regard those who possessed the poetic faculty in a high yet inferior degree, will be found on consideration* to confirm rather than destroy the rule. Let us for a moment stoop to the arbitration of popular breath,* and usurping and uniting in our own persons the incompatible characters of accuser, witness, judge, and executioner, let us decide without trial, testimony, or form, that certain motives of those who are 'there sitting where we dare not soar,'* are reprehensible. Let us assume that Homer was a drunkard, that Virgil was a flatterer, that Horace was a coward, that Tasso was a madman, that Lord Bacon was a peculator, that Raphael was a libertine, that Spenser was a poet laureate.* It is inconsistent with this division* of our subject to cite living poets, but posterity has done ample justice to the great names now referred to. Their errors have been weighed and found to have been dust in the balance; if their sins 'were as scarlet, they are now white as snow'*: they have been washed in the blood of the mediator and redeemer,

---

***Non...**: 'None but God and the poet deserves the name of creator.' Tasso 의 말로 전해짐.

***on consideration:** 「잘 생각해 보면」.

***Let us...breath:** 「항간에 떠도는 무책임한 소리에 짐짓 귀를 기울여보자」.

***who are...not soar':** 즉 시인. *Paradise Lost*, Ⅳ, 829.

***Spenser...laureate:** Spenser 는 실제로는 계관시인이 아니었으나, 항간에는 그가 그 일을 했었다고 알려져 있다. Shelley 당시에는 계관시인이 될 경우 권력층에 아부하는 자로 간주되기도 했다.

***divison:** part(논의의 이 부분 : 이것이 first part 가 될 예정이었다).

*구약 「이사야서」 1 장 18 절.

Time. Observe in what a ludicrous chaos the imputations of real or fictitious crime have been confused in the contemporary calumnies against poetry and poets; consider how little is, as it appears—or appears, as it is; look to your own motives, and judge not, lest ye be judged.

Poetry, as has been said, differs in this respect from logic, that it is not subject to the control of the active powers of the mind, and that its birth and recurrence have no necessary connection with the consciousness or will. It is presumptuous to determine that these* are the necessary conditions of all mental causation, when mental effects are experienced insusceptible of being referred to them. The frequent recurrence of the poetical power, it is obvious to suppose, may produce in the mind a habit of order and harmony correlative with its own nature and with its effects upon other minds. But in the intervals of inspiration, and they may be frequent without being durable, a poet becomes a man* and is abandoned to the sudden reflux of the influences under which others habitually live.* But as he is more delicately organized than other men, and sensible to pain and pleasure, both his own and that of others, in a degree unknown to them, he will avoid the one and pursue the other with an ardour proportioned to this difference. And he renders himself obnoxious to calumny when he neglects to observe the circumstances under which these objects of universal pursuit and flight* have disguised themselves in one another's garments.

But there is nothing necessarily evil in this error, and thus cruelty, envy, revenge, avarice, and the passions purely evil, have never formed any portion of the popular imputations on

---

***these:** consciousness and will. 뒤의 them 도 마찬가지. 정신작용에 이들이 반드시 필요하다고 단정하는 것은 옳지 않다는 것.

*시인은 영감이 떠오르지 않는 경우(intervals), 보통사람과 같은 생활을 한다.

***these objects...flight:** 「만인이 다 추구하든가 피하는 대상」. 즉 쾌락과 고통. 이런 쾌락과 고통의 여러 양상들이 나타나는 실제 생활(circumstances)을 따르지 않으면 사람들에게 욕을 먹는다. 시인들에 대한 부도덕의 비난은 통상적인 생활방식에 어긋나기 때문이지, 흉악한 범죄를 저지르기 때문은 아니다.

the lives of poets.

I have thought it most favourable to the cause of truth to set down these remarks according to the order in which they were suggested to my mind, by a consideration of the subject itself, instead of observing the formality of a polemical reply; but if the view which they contain be just, they will be found to involve a refutation of the arguers against poetry, so far at least as regards the first division of the subject. I can readily conjecture what should have moved the gall of some learned and intelligent writers who quarrel with certain versifiers; I, like them, confess myself unwilling to be stunned by the Theseids of the hoarse Codri*of the day. Bavius and Maevius* undoubtedly are, as they ever were, insufferable persons. But it belongs to a philosophical critic to distinguish rather than confound.

The first part of these remarks has related to poetry in its elements and principles; and it has been shown, as well as the narrow limits assigned them would permit, that what is called poetry in a restricted sense, has a common source with all other forms of order and of beauty, according to which the materials of human life are susceptible of being arranged, and which is poetry in a universal sense.

The second part*will have for its object an application of these principles to the present state of the cultivation of poetry, and a defence of the attempt to idealize the modern forms of manners and opinions, and compel them into a subordination to the imaginative and creative faculty. For the literature of England, an energetic development of which has ever preceded or accompanied a great and free development of the national will, has arisen as it were from a new birth. In spite of the low-thoughted envy which would undervalue contemporary merit, our own will be a memorable age in intellectual achievements,

---

*로마의 풍자시인 Juvenal의 *Satires*에 나오는 못난 시인 Cordus의 *Theseid* 같은 졸작.

***Bavius and Maevius:** 역시 못난 시인들.

*the second part와 the third part는 쓰지 못했다.

and we live among such philosophers and poets as surpass beyond comparison any who have appeared since the last national struggle for civil and religious liberty.* The most unfailing herald, companion, and follower of the awakening of a great people to work a beneficial change in opinion or institution, is poetry. At such periods there is an accumulation of the power of communicating and receiving intense and impassioned conceptions respecting man and nature. The persons in whom this power resides, may often, as far as regards many portions of their nature, have little apparent correspondence with that spirit of good of which they are the ministers. But even whilst they deny and abjure, they are yet compelled to serve the power which is seated on the throne of their own soul. It is impossible to read the compositions of the most celebrated writers of the present day without being startled with the electric life which burns within their words. They measure the circumference and sound the depths of human nature with a comprehensive and all-penetrating spirit, and they are themselves perhaps the most sincerely astonished at its manifestations; for it is less their spirit than the spirit of the age. Poets are the hierophants of an unapprehended inspiration; the mirrors of the gigantic shadows which futurity casts upon the present; the words which express what they understand not; the trumpets which sing to battle and feel not what they inspire; the influence which is moved not, but moves. Poets are the unacknowledged legislators of the world.

*즉 1642-8년간의 Puritan Revolution을 말함.

John Keats

(1795—1821)

전세마차 영업을 하던 집안의 여러 형제 중 맏이로 태어나 일찌기 부모를 여의고 고등학교를 졸업하자 의사의 조수가 되었으나, 시인이 되기로 결심, 가난과 질병(폐결핵)에도 불구하고 약 5년 간에 영국 대표적 시인의 한 사람으로 급성장하였다. 25세에 친구들의 도움으로 요양차 이탈리아에 여행하던 중 객사하였다.

키이츠는 물론 비평가는 아니었지만, 자기의 예술에 대하여 면밀하게 생각하고 남의 작품에 대하여서도 비상한 관심을 가진 "양심적" 시인이었다. 그는 다른 산문은 남기지 않았지만 약 5년 간에 걸쳐 친척과 친구들에게 쓴 많은 편지 중 약 300여통이 남아 있다. 이 중 시에 관하여 쓴 몇 통이 시의 이론상 매우 중요한 개념들을 담고 있어, 영미 비평사에서 고임을 받고 있는 것이다.

"아름다움은 참이요, 참은 아름다움"이라고 키이츠는 그의 유명한 시에서 선언한 바 있는데, 그의 편지에서도 순수한 감각의 삶에서 상상으로 파악한 아름다움이 곧 참이 되는 "절대상상"의 세계를 그리워한다. 이성의 차가운 눈길이 발견하는 차가운 참이 아니라, 상상이 발견하는 온기 있는 참의 세계를 동경한 것이다.

이러한 절대적 상상의 세계를 구축하기 위하여 시인은 일관된 도덕적 인격이나 명징한 논리를 추구하는 합리적 태도가 필요한 것이 아니라, 정반대로 "소극적 수용력"(negative capability)이 필요하다. 인격이나 합리적 태도는 사물에 대한 적극성을 말한다. 그러나 시인은 모든 경험을 주어지는 그대로 다 받아들이는 수용성이 필요하다. 따라서 시인은 성격이나 자기의식(identity)이 없을수록 바람직하다. 바로 이러한 이유에서 그는 시인이 자기의 독특한 정서나 경험을 내세우는 것(예컨대 워즈워드)을 반대하며, 시는 모름지기 나무에서 잎새가 피듯 저절로 피어나야 한다고 주장한 것이다. 워즈워드의 태도를 "자기중심적 숭엄미"(egotistical sublime)라고 한 것은 기막힌 평이다.

From The Letters

From Letter to Benjamin Bailey, 22 November 1817:

I AM certain of nothing but of the holiness of the Heart's affections and the truth of Imagination. What the imagination seizes as Beauty must be truth—whether it existed before or not—for I have the same Idea of all our Passions as of Love: they are all, in their sublime,* creative of essential Beauty. In a word, you may know my favourite speculation by my first Book* and the little song* I sent in my last—which is a representation from* the fancy of the probable mode of operating in these Matters. The Imagination may be compared to Adam's dream,—he awoke and found it truth.* I am the more zealous in this affair, because I have never yet been able to perceive how any thing can be known for truth by consecutive reasoning—and yet it must be. Can it be that even the greatest Philosopher ever arrived at his goal without putting aside numerous objections? However it may be, O for a life of Sensations* rather than of Thoughts! It is 'a Vision in the form of Youth', a Shadow of reality to come—and this consideration has further convinced me, for it has come as auxiliary to another favourite speculation of mine—that we shall enjoy ourselves hereafter by having what we called happiness on Earth repeated in a finer tone and so repeated. And yet such a fate can only befall

---

***in their sublime:** 「숭고한 경지에 있어서」. sublime=sublimity.

***first Book:** *Endymion* 의 Book I 을 말함.

***little song:** "O Sorrow" (*Endymion*, IV, 146 행 이하)를 가리킨다.

***from:** 「...으로 부터 생겨나온」.

***Adam's dream:** Adam 이 잠들었다가 깨어보니 Eve 가 창조되어 있었음. *Paradise Lost*, VIII. 460 에 Adam 이 꿈 속에서 Eve 를 본 것으로 되어 있음.

***Sensations:** "intuitive perception through the sense"란 뜻으로 해석됨. Reason 이나 Thought 가 아닌 감각에 의한 세계의 인식을 Keats 는 갈망하였다.

those who delight in Sensation, rather than hunger as you do after Truth. Adam's dream will do here, and seems to be a conviction that Imagination and its empyreal reflection is the same as human Life and its Spiritual repetition. But as I was saying—the simple imaginative Mind may have its rewards in the repetition of its own silent Working coming continually on the Spirit with a fine Suddenness—to compare great things with small, have you never by being surprised with an old Melody, in a delicious place, by a delicious voice, felt over again your very speculations and surmises at the time it first operated on your soul?—do you not remember forming to yourself the singer's face more beautiful than it was possible, and yet with the elevation of the Moment you did not think so? —even then you were mounted on the Wings of Imagination so high—that the Prototype must be hereafter—that delicious face you will see.* What a time! I am continually running away from the subject—sure this cannot be exactly the case with a complex Mind—one that is imaginative and at the same time careful of its fruits—who would exist partly on Sensation, partly on thought—to whom it is necessary that years should bring the philosophic Mind?—Such a one I consider yours, and therefore it is necessary to your eternal Happiness that you not only drink this old Wine of Heaven, which I shall call the redigestion of our most ethereal Musings on Earth, but also increase in knowledge and know all things.

From Letter to George and Thomas Keats, 21 December 1817:

I had not a dispute but a disquisition with Dilke,* on various subjects; several things dovetailed in my mind, and at once it struck me what quality went to form a Man of Achievement, especially in Literature, and which Shakespeare possessed so

*다소 난삽하게 쓰인 이 부분의 뜻은, 보이지 않는 성악가의 상상적인 모습은 실제보다 훨씬 더 아름다운데, 바로 그 아름다운 얼굴(Prototype: 이상적인 모습)은 내세(life to come)에서나 만날 수 있다는 것. 즉 상상은 현실을 뛰어넘어 더 아름다운 미래의 세계를 예감한다는 것.

***Dilke:** Keats의 친구.

enormously—I mean *Negative Capability*, that is, when man is capable of being in uncertainties, mysteries, doubts, without any irritable reaching after* fact and reason.—Coleridge, for instance, would let go by* a fine isolated verisimilitude caught from the Penetralium* of mystery, from being incapable of remaining content with half-knowledge. This pursued through volumes would perhaps take us no further than this, that with a great poet the sense of Beauty overcomes every other consideration, or rather obliterates all consideration.

From Letter to John Hamilton Reynolds, 3 February 1818:

We hate poetry that has a palpable design upon us—and, if we do not agree, seems to put its hand in its breeches pocket.* Poetry should be great and unobtrusive, a thing which enters into one's soul, and does not startle it or amaze it with itself, but with its subject.—How beautiful are the retired flowers! How would they lose their beauty were they to throng into the highway crying out, 'Admire me, I am a violet!—Dote upon me, I am a primrose!"

From Letter to John Taylor, 27 February 1818:

In Poetry I have a few axioms, and you will see how far I am from their centre. First, I think Poetry should surprise by a fine excess* and not by singularity—it should strike the reader as a wording of his own highest thoughts, and appear almost a remembrance. Second, its touches of Beauty should never be half-way, thereby making the reader breathless instead of content: the rise, the progress, the setting of imagery should,

---

***irritable reaching after...:** 「...에 대한 초조한 추구」(이성적 진리에 대한 조급한 태도).

***let go by:** 「지나쳐버리다」.

***Penetralium:** 내면의 세계. 이 부분은, Coleridge가 만년에 철학에 심취하여, 하나의 멋진 image를 발견할 때에도 철학적 논리성이 없다 하여 버리게 되었음을 비꼬고 있다.

***put its...pocket:** 「주머니에 손을 찔러넣고는 상종하려 하지 않다」. 자기의 의도만을 고집하는 시인의 시를 비꼼.

***fine excess:** 「그윽히 넘쳐남」. singularity(눈에 돋보이는 독특함)의 반대.

like the sun, come natural to him—shine over him, and set soberly although in magnificence, leaving him in the luxury of twilight. But it is easier to think what Poetry should be than to write it—and this leads me on to another axiom. That if Poetry comes not as naturally as the leaves to a tree, it had better not come at all.

From Letter to Richard Woodhouse, 27 October 1818:

As to the poetical Character itself (I mean that sort of which, if I am anything, I am a member; that sort distinguished from the Wordsworthian or egotistical sublime;* which is a thing *per se* and stands alone), it is not itself—it has no self—it is every thing and nothing.—It has no character—it enjoys light and shade; it lives in gusto, be it foul or fair, high or low, rich or poor, mean or elevated.—It has as much delight in conceiving an Iago as an Imogen.* What shocks the virtuous philosopher, delights the chameleon Poet. It does no harm from its relish of the dark side of things any more than from its taste for the bright one, because they both end in speculation.* A Poet is the most unpoetical of any thing in existence, because he has no Identity—he is continually in for*—and filling some other body.—The sun, the moon, the sea, and men and women who are creatures of impulse, are poetical and have about them an unchangeable attribute.—The poet has none, no identity—he is certainly the most unpoetical of all God's creatures. If then he has no self, and if I am a Poet, where is the wonder that I should say I would write no more? Might I not at that very instant have been cogitating on the Characters of Saturn and

---

***Wordsworthian or egotistical sublime:** Keats는 Wordsworth를 존경하면서도, 지나치게 자기중심적인 위압감을 가지고 군림한다고 보았다. 그는 Wordsworth가 이름 없는 들꽃을 보고 혼자 감격한 나머지 다른 사람들도 그처럼 감격하기를 위압적으로 요청한다고 느낀 것이다. 그래서 Keats는 Wordsworth의 시를 독불장군의 그것(a thing *per se*)이라 보았고, 자기는 그런 유파에 속하지 않는다고 말한다.

***Imogen:** Shakespeare의 *Cymbeline*에 나오는 착한 여주인공.

***speculation:** "disinterested contemplation"이란 뜻일 듯.

***in for:** informing의 탈자인 듯.

Ops?* It is a wretched thing to confess, but is a very fact, that not one word I ever utter can be taken for granted as an opinion growing out of my identical nature—how can it, when I have no nature? When I am in a room with people, if I ever am free from speculating on creations of my own brain, then not myself goes home to myself: but the identity of every one in the room begins so to press upon me that I am in a very little time annihilated—not only among men; it would be the same in a nursery of children.

From Letter to Percy Bysshe Shelley, 16 August 1820:

I received a copy of the *Cenci*,* as from yourself, from Hunt.* There is only one part of it I am judge of: the Poetry, and dramatic effect, which by many spirits nowadays is considered the Mammon.* A modern work, it is said, must have a purpose, which may be the God. *An artist* must serve Mammon—he must have 'self concentration', selfishness perhaps. You, I am sure, will forgive me for sincerely remarking that you might curb your magnanimity and be more of an artist, and 'load every rift'* of your subject with ore. The thought of such discipline must fall like cold chains upon you, who perhaps never sat with your wings furled for six months together. And is not this extraordinary talk for the writer of *Endymion*! whose mind was like a pack of scattered cards.—I am picked up and sorted to a pip.* My Imagination is a Monastery and I am its Monk. . . .

***Saturn and Ops:** Keats 가 *Hyperion* 에서 다룬 Zeus 이전의 신들.

******Cenci*:** Shelley 의 희곡.

***Hunt, Leigh:** (1784-1859). 비평가. Shelley 와 Keats 의 친구.

***Mammon:** 돈의 신. 이기심의 신. 여기서는 작가의 단일한 목적에 집착함을 뜻함.

***'load every rift':** Spenser, *Faerie Queene*, Ⅱ, vii, 28. 구석구석마다 시의 황금으로 채워넣을 일이자(즉 시인 노릇이나 잘 할 일이지), 시 이외의 사실에 너무 참견하는 Shelley 를 은근히 비꼬고 있다. 시인은 예술에 있어서 "이기적" (serve Mammon) 이어야 한다는 것.

***I am picked...to a pip:** 트럼프카드들 같은 내 마음은 한데 모아져서 별로 점수가 없는 껍데기들의 덩어리가 된다. Keats 는 자기 자신의 identity 가 없으을 여기서도 간주하고 있다 sort: 「카드를 치다」.

John Ruskin

(1819—1900)

런던의 부유한 주류 상인과 신앙심 깊은 모친 사이에서 태어나 가정교사에게 교육을 받고 옥스포드를 졸업했다. 유복한 환경 덕분에 일찍부터 유럽 여행을 하여 유럽의 미술을 깊이 감상하고, 그것을 토대로 미술 비평사의 큰 업적으로 인정되는 *Modern Painters*(전 5권, 1843-60)와 건축 비평인 *The Stones of Venice*(전 3권, 1851-3)을 저술했다. 예술의 사회적 책임에 깊은 관심을 가졌던 그는 칼라일의 영향으로 종교적·도덕적 사회주의를 주장하는 *Unto This Last*(1860-62) 등의 저서를 쓰기도 했다.

러스킨은 주로 미술과 사회에 관하여 방대한 저작을 남겼으나, 거의 모든 글에 문학에 대한 언급이 들어 있고, 또 그의 예술 및 사회 비평은 문학 비평으로 쉽게 원용될 수 있다. 그의 예술은 신플라톤주의의 영향을 받아, 아름다움은 무한의 한 현시라고 보았으며, 삼라만상은 이데아의 상징이라 믿었다. 코울리지로부터는 상상의 개념에 있어서 영향을 받아서, 상상은 인간과 신(자연)을 연결시켜 주며, 상상에 의하여 자연의 재료에서 선택하고 배합하여 질서와 미를 창조한다고 하였다.

"Of the Pathetic Fallacy" (1856)는 *Modern Painters*의 제3권 제4부의 일부로서, 자연에 대한 인간의 정서적 반응과 표현방식의 건전성을 강조하는 이름난 글이다. 자연을 볼 때 아무런 느낌이 없는 자, 강하게 느끼되 무비판적인 자, 강하게 느끼고 강하게 생각하는 자, 보이는 것에 구애받지 않고 더 높은 것을 생각하는 자 중에서 세번째 사람이 진정한 시인이고, 맨 나중 사람은 종교적 예언자이다. 자연에 대하여 강하게 느끼되 제대로 판단하지 못하는 것을「감상적 허위」라 이름하고, 이는 아류 시인들의 전형적 결함이라고 말한다.

Of the Pathetic Fallacy (1856)

§ 1. GERMAN dulness, and English affectation, have of late much multiplied among us the use of two of the most objectionable words that were ever coined by the troublesomeness of metaphysicians — namely, 'Objective' and 'Subjective'.

No words can be more exquisitely, and in all points, useless; and I merely speak of them that I may, at once and for ever, get them out of my way, and out of my reader's. But to get that done, they must be explained.

The word 'Blue', say certain philosophers, means the sensation of colour which the human eye receives in looking at the open sky, or at a bell gentian.

Now, say they farther, as this sensation can only be felt when the eye is turned to the object, and as, therefore, no such sensation is produced by the object when nobody looks at it, therefore the thing, when it is not looked at, is not blue; and thus (say they) there are many qualities of things which depend as much on something else as on themselves. To be sweet, a thing must have a taster; it is only sweet while it is being tasted, and if the tongue had not the capacity of taste, then the sugar would not have the quality of sweetness.

And then they agree that the qualities of things which thus depend upon our perception of them, and upon our human nature as affected by them, shall be called Subjective; and the qualities of things which they always have, irrespective of any other nature, as roundness or squareness, shall be called Objective.

From these ingenious views the step is very easy to a farther opinion, that it does not much matter what things are in themselves, but only what they are to us; and that the only real truth of them is their appearance to, or effect upon, us. From which position, with a hearty desire for mystification, and much egotism, selfishness, shallowness, and impertinence, a philosopher may easily go so far as to believe, and say, that everything in the world depends upon his seeing or thinking of it, and that nothing, therefore, exists, but what he sees or thinks of.

§ 2. Now, to get rid of all these ambiguities and troublesome words at once, be it observed that the word 'Blue' does *not* mean the *sensation* caused by a gentian on the human eye; but it means the *power* of producing that sensation; and this power is always there, in the thing, whether we are there to experience it or not, and would remain there though there were not left a man on the face of the earth. Precisely in the same way gunpowder has a power of exploding. It will not explode if you put no match to it. But it has always the power of so exploding, and is therefore called an explosive compound, which it very positively and assuredly is, whatever philosophy may say to the contrary.*

In like manner, a gentian does not produce the sensation of blueness if you don't look at it. But it has always the power of doing so; its particles being everlastingly so arranged by its Maker. And, therefore, the gentian and the sky are always verily blue, whatever philosophy may say to the contrary; and if you do not see them blue when you look at them, it is not their fault but yours.

§ 3. Hence I would say to these philosophers: If, instead of using the sonorous phrase, 'It is objectively so,' you will use the plain old phrase, 'It *is* so;' and if instead of the sonorous phrase, 'It is subjectively so,' you will say, in plain old English, 'It does so,' or 'It seems so to me;' you will, on the whole, be more intelligible to your fellow-creatures: and besides, if you find that a thing which generally 'does so' to other people (as a gentian looks blue to most men), does *not* so to you, on any particular occasion, you will not fall into the impertinence of saying, that the thing is not so, or did not so, but you will say simply (what you will be all the better for speedily finding

---

***to the contrary:** 「그에 반대로」.

out*), that something is the matter with you. If you find that you cannot explode the gunpowder, you will not declare that all gunpowder is subjective, and all explosion imaginary, but you will simply suspect and declare yourself to be an ill-made match. Which, on the whole, though there may be a distant chance of a mistake about it, is, nevertheless, the wisest conclusion you can come to until farther experiment.

§ 4. Now, therefore, putting these tiresome and absurd words quite out of our way, we may go on at our ease to examine the point in question — namely, the difference between the ordinary, proper, and true appearances of things to us; and the extraordinary, or false appearances, when we are under the influence of emotion, or contemplative fancy; false appearances, I say, as being entirely unconnected with any real power or character in the object, and only imputed to it by us.

For instance —

> The spendthrift crocus, bursting through the mould
> Naked and shivering, with his cup of gold.

This is very beautiful, and yet very untrue. The crocus is not a spendthrift, but a hardy plant; its yellow is not gold, but saffron. How is it that we enjoy so much the having it put into our heads* that it is anything else than a plain crocus?

It is an important question. For, throughout our past reasonings about art, we have always found that nothing could be good, or useful, or ultimately pleasurable, which was untrue. But here is something pleasurable in written poetry which is nevertheless *un*true. And what is more, if we think over our favourite poetry, we shall find it full of this kind of fallacy, and that we like it all the more for being so.

§ 5. It will appear also, on consideration of the matter, that this fallacy is of two principal kinds. Either, as in this

---

***what you will...finding out:** 「당신이 빨리 발견할수록 좋을 텐데」.

*미국 시인 Oliver Wendell Holmes의 시, *Astraea*의 일절.

***the having...our heads...:** 우리 머리속에 that 이하의 생각이 들어와 박히게 하는 것.

case of the crocus, it is the fallacy of wilful fancy, which involves no real expectation that it will be believed; or else it is a fallacy caused by an excited state of the feelings, making us, for the time, more or less irrational. Of the cheating of the fancy we shall have to speak presently; but, in this chapter, I want to examine the nature of the other error, that which the mind admits when affected strongly by emotion. Thus, for instance, in *Alton Locke* —

They rowed her in across the rolling foam —
The cruel, crawling foam.*

The foam is not cruel, neither does it crawl. The state of mind which attributes to it these characters of a living creature is one in which the reason is unhinged by grief. All violent feelings have the same effect. They produce in us a falseness in all our impressions of external things, which I would generally characterize as the 'Pathetic Fallacy'.

§ 6. Now we are in the habit of considering this fallacy as eminently a character of poetical description, and the temper of mind in which we allow it as one eminently poetical, because passionate. But, I believe, if we look well into the matter, that we shall find the greatest poets do not often admit this kind of falseness — that it is only the second order of poets who much delight in it.

Thus, when Dante describes the spirits falling from the bank of Acheron* 'as dead leaves flutter from a bough,* he gives the most perfect image possible of their utter lightness, feebleness, passiveness, and scattering agony of despair, without, however, for an instant losing his own clear perception that *these* are souls, and *those* are leaves; he makes no confusion of one with the other. But when Coleridge speaks of

The one red leaf, the last of its clan,

*영국 시인 Charles Kingsley의 시, *Alton Locke*의 일절.
***Acheron:** 「지옥의 강」.
***'as dead...a bough'** Dante, *Inferno*, Ⅲ, 112—14.

That dances as often as dance it can.*

he has a morbid, that is to say, a so far false, idea about the leaf: he fancies a life in it, and will, which there are not; confuses its powerlessness with choice,* its fading death with merriment, and the wind that shakes it with music. Here, however, there is some beauty, even in the morbid passage; but take an instance in Homer and Pope. Without the knowledge of Ulysses, Elpenor, his youngest follower, has fallen from an upper chamber in the Circean palace, and has been left dead, unmissed by his leader, or companions, in the haste of their departure.* They cross the sea to the Cimmerian land; and Ulysses summons the shades from Tartarus.* The first which appears is that of the lost Elpenor. Ulysses, amazed, and in exactly the spirit of bitter and terrified lightness which is seen in Hamlet,* addresses the spirit with the simple, startled words: —

Elpenor! How camest thou under the shadowy darkness?
Hast thou come faster on foot than I in my black ship?

Which Pope renders thus: —

O, say, what angry power Elpenor led
To glide in shades, and wander with the dead?
How could thy soul, by realms and seas disjoined,
Outfly the nimble sail, and leave the lagging wind?

I sincerely hope the reader finds no pleasure here, either in the nimbleness of the sail, or the laziness of the wind! And yet how is it that these conceits are so painful now, when they have been pleasant to us in the other instances?

**Christabel*, I, 49—50.

***confuses...with music:** 시든 잎새는 기운이 없는데, 그것을 스스로(with choice) 춤추는 것으로 혼동했다.

**Odyssey*, XI, 56—7. 율리시즈가 죽은 혼령들이 모여 있는 지옥(Cimmerian Land)에 가니까 Elpenor의 혼백〔shade〕이 나타난다.

*"Well said, old mole! can'st work i' the ground so fast?" (Hamlet이 죽은 부친의 혼령에게 하는 말. *Hamlet*, I, v, 162).

*Pope가 번안한 Homer. 당시에는 최고의 인기를 끌었다.

§ 7. For a very simple reason. They are not a *pathetic* fallacy at all, for they are put into the mouth of the wrong passion — a passion which never could possibly have spoken them — agonized curiosity. Ulysses wants to know the facts of the matter; and the very last thing his mind could do at the moment would be to pause, or suggest in anywise what was *not* a fact. The delay in the first three lines, and conceit in the last, jar upon us instantly, like the most frightful discord in music. No poet of true imaginative power could possibly have written the passage.

Therefore, we see that the spirit of truth must guide us in some sort, even in our enjoyment of fallacy. Coleridge's fallacy has no discord in it, but Pope's has set our teeth on edge.* Without farther questioning, I will endeavour to state the main bearings of this matter.

§ 8. The temperament which admits the pathetic fallacy, is, as I said above, that of a mind and body in some sort too weak to deal fully with what is before them or upon them; borne away,* or overclouded, or over-dazzled by emotion; and it is a more or less noble state, according to the force of the emotion which has induced it. For it is no credit to a man that he is not morbid or inaccurate in his perceptions, when he has no strength of feeling to warp them; and it is in general a sign of higher capacity and stand in the ranks of being, that the emotions should be strong enough to vanquish, partly, the intellect, and make it believe what they choose. But it is still a grander condition when the intellect also rises, till it is strong enough to assert its rule against, or together with, the utmost efforts of the passions; and the whole man stands in an iron glow, white hot, perhaps, but still strong, and in no wise* evaporating; even if he melts, losing none of his weight.

So, then, we have the three ranks: the man who perceives rightly, because he does not feel, and to whom the primrose is very accurately the primrose, because he does not love it. Then, secondly, the man who perceives wrongly, because he

---

***set...on edge:** 「이가 시리게 하다, 심한 부조화를 느끼게 하다」.
***borne away:** 「도취되어서」(=overborne, carried away).
***in no wise:** never.

feels, and to whom the primrose is anything else than a primrose: a star, or a sun, or a fairy's shield, or a forsaken maiden. And then, lastly, there is the man who perceives rightly in spite of his feelings, and to whom the primrose is for ever nothing else than itself — a little flower, apprehended in the very plain and leafy fact of it, whatever and how many soever the associations and passions may be, that crowd around it. And, in general, these three classes may be rated in comparative order, as the men who are not poets at all, and the poets of the second order, and the poets of the first; only however great a man may be, there·are always some subjects which *ought* to throw him off his balance; some, by which his poor human capacity of thought should be conquered, and brought into the inaccurate and vague state of perception, so that the language of the highest inspiration becomes broken, obscure, and wild in metaphor, resembling that of the weaker man, overborne by weaker things.*

§ 9. And thus, in full, there are four classes: the men who feel nothing, and therefore see truly; the men who feel strongly, think weakly, and see untruly (second order of poets); the men who feel strongly, think strongly, and see truly (first order of poets); and the men who, strong as human creatures can be, are yet submitted to influences stronger than they, and see in a sort untruly, because what they see is inconceivably above them. This last is the usual condition of prophetic inspiration.

§ 10. I separate these classes, in order that their character may be clearly understood; but of course they are united each to the other by imperceptible transitions, and the same mind, according to the influences to which it is subjected, passes at different times into the various states. Still, the difference between the great and less man is, on the whole, chiefly in this point of *alterability*.* That is to say, the one knows too much,

*아무리 위대한 인간이라도 지성과 감성의 균형이 깨지는 순간은 있어야 한다는 것(이런 부류의 인간이 예언자이다).

***alterability:** 한 사람이 위에 언급된 네 부류의 반응을 다 보일 수도 있다. 즉 경우에 따라 그처럼 반응이 변할 수 있음(alterability)도 위대성의 표시이다.

and perceives and feels too much of the past and future, and of all things beside and around that which immediately affects him, to be in anywise shaken by it. His mind is made up; his thoughts have an accustomed current; his ways are steadfast; it is not this or that new sight which will at once unbalance him. He is tender to impression at the surface, like a rock with deep moss upon it; but there is too much mass of him to be moved. The smaller man, with the same degree of sensibility, is at once carried off his feet; he wants to do something he did not want to do before; he views all the universe in a new light through his tears; he is gay or enthusiastic, melancholy or passionate, as things come and go to him. Therefore the high creative poet might even be thought, to a great extent, impassive (as shallow people think Dante stern), receiving indeed all feelings to the full, but having a great centre of reflection and knowledge in which he stands serene, and watches the feeling, as it were, from far off.

Dante, in his most intense moods, has entire command of himself, and can look around calmly, at all moments, for the image or the word that will best tell what he sees to the upper or lower world. But Keats and Tennyson, and the poets of the second order, are generally themselves subdued by the feelings under which they write, or, at least, write as choosing to be so,* and therefore admit certain expressions and modes of thought which are in some sort diseased or false.

§ 11. Now so long as we see that the *feeling* is true, we pardon, or are even pleased by, the confessed fallacy of sight which it induces: we are pleased, for instance, with those lines of Kingsley's, above quoted, not because they fallaciously describe foam, but because they faithfully describe sorrow. But the moment the mind of the speaker becomes cold, that moment every such expression becomes untrue, as being for ever untrue in the external facts. And there is no greater baseness in literature than the habit of using these metaphorical expressions in cold blood. An inspired writer, in full impetuosity of passion, may speak wisely and truly of

***as choosing to be so:** 「감정에 지배되는 것을 원하는 듯이」.

'raging waves of the sea, foaming out their own shame'*; but it is only the basest writer who cannot speak of the sea without talking of 'raging waves', 'remorseless floods', 'ravenous billows', &c.; and it is one of the signs of the highest power in a writer to check all such habits of thought, and to keep his eyes fixed firmly on the *pure fact*, out of which if any feeling comes to him or his reader, he knows it must be a true one.

To keep to the waves, I forget who it is who represents a man in despair, desiring that his body may be cast into the sea,

> *Whose changing mound, and foam that passed away,*
> Might mock the eye that questioned where I lay.*

Observe, there is not a single false, or even overcharged, expression. 'Mound' of the sea wave is perfectly simple and true; 'changing' is as familiar as may be; 'foam that passed away', strictly literal; and the whole line descriptive of the reality with a degree of accuracy which I know not any other verse, in the range of poetry, that altogether equals. For most people have not a distinct idea of the clumisiness and massiveness of a large wave. The word 'wave' is used too generally of ripples and breakers, and bendings in light drapery or grass: it does not by itself convey a perfect image. But the word 'mound' is heavy, large, dark, definite; there is no mistaking the kind of wave meant, nor missing the sight of it. Then the term 'changing' has a peculiar force also. Most people think of waves as rising and falling. But if they look at the sea carefully, they will perceive that the waves do not rise and fall. They change. Change both place and form, but they do not fall; one wave goes on, and on, and still on; now lower, now higher, now tossing its mane like a horse, now building itself together like a wall, now shaking, now steady, but still the same wave, till at last it seems struck by something, and changes, one knows not how, — becomes another wave.

The close of the line insists on this image, and paints it

---

*신약 유다서, 13절.

*작자 미상.

still more perfectly, — 'foam that passed away'. Not merely melting, disappearing, but passing on, out of sight, on the career of the wave. Then, having put the absolute ocean fact as far as he may before our eyes, the poet leaves us to feel about it as we may, and to trace for ourselves the opposite fact, — the image of the green mounds that do not change, and the white and written stones that do not pass away; and thence to follow out* also the associated images of the calm life with the quiet grave, and the despairing life with the fading foam:

> Let no man move his bones.
> As for Samaria, her king is cut off like the foam upon the water.*

But nothing of this is actually told or pointed out, and the expressions, as they stand, are perfecly severe and accurate, utterly uninfluenced by the firmly governed emotion of the writer. Even the word 'mock' is hardly an exception, as it may stand merely for 'deceive' or 'defeat', without implying any impersonation of the waves.

§ 12. It may be well, perhaps, to give one or two more instances to show the peculiar dignity possessed by all passages which thus limit their expression to the pure fact, and leave the hearer to gather what he can from it. Here is a notable one from the Iliad. Helen, looking from the Scaean gate of Troy over the Grecian host, and telling Priam the names of its captains, says at last:

> I see all the other dark-eyed Greeks; but two I cannot see, — Castor and Pollux, — whom one mother bore with me. Have they not followed from fair Lacedaemon, or have they indeed come in their sea-wandering ships, but now will not enter into the battle of men, fearing the shame and the scorn that is in Me?

Then Homer:

> So she spoke. But them, already, the life-giving earth possessed,

---

*follow out: 「끝까지 추적하다」.

*구약 열왕기 하, 23 : 18 및 호세아 10 : 7.

there in Lacedaemon, in the dear fatherland.*

Note, here, the high poetical truth carried to the extreme. The poet has to speak of the earth in sadness, but he will not let that sadness affect or change his thoughts of it. No; though Castor and Pollux be dead, yet the earth is our mother still, fruitful, life-giving. These are the facts of the thing. I see nothing else than these. Make what you will of them....*

§ 14. Now in this there is the exact type of the consummate poetical temperament. For, be it clearly and constantly remembered, that the greatness of a poet depends upon the two faculties, acuteness of feeling, and command of it. A poet is great, first in proportion to the strength of his passion, and then, that strength being granted, in proportion to his government of it; there being, however, always a point beyond which it would be inhuman and monstrous if he pushed this government, and, therefore, a point at which all feverish and wild fancy becomes just and true. Thus the destruction of the kingdom of Assyria cannot be contemplated firmly by a prophet of Israel. The fact is too great, too wonderful. It overthrows him, dashes him into a confused element of dreams. All the world is, to his stunned thought, full of strange voices. 'Yea, the fir-trees rejoice at thee, and the cedars of Lebanon, saying, "Since thou art gone down to the grave, no feller is come up against us."'* So, still more, the thought of the presence of Deity cannot be borne without this great astonishment. 'The mountains and the hills shall break forth before you into singing, and all the trees of the field shall clap their hands.'*

**Iliad*, Ⅲ, 243. Helen 은 그리이스의 Lacedaemon 출신으로 Castor 와 Pollux 란 두 오빠가 있었다. Troy 에 와 있는 Helen 은 그리이스 군 지도자 중에서 두 오빠를 볼 수가 없는데, 그들은 이미 고국에서 죽었던 것이다.

*이 다음에 이어지는 글(§ 13)은 프랑스의 긴 민요를 인용, 해설하는 부분인데, 생략한다.

*구약, 이사야, 14 : 8.

*구약, 이사야, 55 : 12. 북방의 앗수르(Assyria)는 이스라엘의 최대 적국이었다.

§ 15. But by how much this feeling is noble when it is justified by the strength of its cause, by so much it is ignoble when there is not cause enough for it; and beyond all other ignobleness is the mere affectation of it, in hardness of heart. Simply bad writing may almost always, as above noticed, be known by its adoption of these fanciful metaphorical expressions, as a sort of current coin,* yet there is even a worse, at least a more harmful, condition of writing than this, in which such expressions are not ignorantly and feelinglessly caught up, but, by some master, skilful in handling, yet insincere, deliberately wrought out with chill and studied* fancy; as if we should try to make an old lava stream look red-hot again, by covering it with dead leaves, or white-hot, with hoarfrost.

When Young is lost in veneration, as he dwells on the character of a truly good and holy man, he permits himself for a moment to be overborne by the feeling so far as to exclaim:

> **Where shall I find him? angels, tell me where.**
> **You know him; he is near you; point him out.**
> **Shall I see glories beaming from his brow,**
> **Or trace his footsteps by the rising flowers?***

This emotion has a worthy cause, and is thus true and right. But now hear the cold-hearted Pope say to a shepherd girl:

> **Where'er you walk, cool gales shall fan the glade;**
> **Trees, where you sit, shall crowd into a shade;**
> **Your praise the birds shall chant in every grove,**
> **And winds shall waft it to the powers above.**
> **But would you sing, and rival Orpheus' strain,**
> **The wondering forests soon should dance again;**
> **The moving mountains hear the powerful call,**
> **And headlong streams hang, listening, in their fall.***

This is not, nor could it for a moment be mistaken for, the

***current coin:** 아무나 쓸 수 있는 동전같은 비유. 즉, 닳아빠진 표현법.
***studied:** 「억지로 꾸민」.
*Edward Young의 *Night Thcughts*, Ⅱ, 345.
*"Pastoral: Summer."

language of passion. It is simple falsehood, uttered by hypocrisy; definite absurdity, rooted in affectation, and coldly asserted in the teeth of* nature and fact. Passion will indeed go far in deceiving itself; but it must be a strong passion, not the simple wish of a lover to tempt his mistress to sing. Compare a very closely parallel passage in Wordsworth, in which the lover has lost his mistress:

Three years had Barbara in her grave been laid,
When thus his moan he made: —

'Oh move, thou cottage, from behind yon oak,
    Or let the ancient tree uprooted lie,
That in some other way yon smoke
    May mount into the sky.
If still behind yon pine-tree's ragged bough,
    Headlong, the waterfall must come,
    Oh, let it, then, be dumb —
Be anything, sweet stream, but that which thou art now.'*

Here is a cottage to be moved, if not a mountain, and a waterfall to be silent, if it is not to hang listening: but with what different relation to the mind that contemplates them! Here, in the extremity of its agony, the soul cries out wildly for relief, which at the same moment it partly knows to be impossible, but partly believes possible, in a vague impression that a miracle *might* be wrought to give relief even to a less sore distress, — that nature is kind, and God is kind, and that grief is strong: it knows not well what *is* possible to such grief. To silence a stream, to move a cottage wall, — one might think it could do as much as that!

§ 16. I believe these instances are enough to illustrate the main point I insist upon respecting the pathetic fallacy, — that so far as it *is* a fallacy, it is always the sign of a morbid state of mind, and comparatively of a weak one. Even in the most inspired prophet it is a sign of the incapacity of his human sight or thought to bear what has been revealed to it. In ordinary poetry, if it is found in the thoughts of the poet

---

*in the teeth of...: 「...에도 불구하고, ...과 정반대로」.

**"'Tis said that some have died for love."

himself, it is at once a sign of his belonging to the inferior school; if in the thoughts of the characters imagined by him, it is right or wrong according to the genuinenss of the emotion from which it springs; always, however, implying necessarily *some* degree of weakness in the character.

Take two most exquisite instances from master hands. The Jessy of Shenstone, and the Ellen of Wordsworth, have both been betrayed and deserted. Jessy, in the course of her most touching complaint, says:

> If through the garden's flowery tribes I stray,
> Where bloom the jasmines that could once allure,
> 'Hope not to find delight in us,' they say.
> 'For we are spotless, Jessy; we are pure.*

Compare with this some of the words of Ellen:

> 'Ah, why,' said Ellen, sighing to herself,
> 'Why do not words, and kiss, and solemn pledge,
> And nature, that is kind in woman's breast,
> And reason, that in man is wise and good,
> And fear of Him who is a righteous Judge, —
> Why do not these prevail for human life,
> To keep two hearts together, that began
> Their springtime with one love, and that have need
> Of mutual pity and forgiveness, sweet
> To grant, or be received; — while that poor bird —
> O, come and hear him! Thou who hast to me
> Been faithless, hear him; — though a lowly creature,
> One of God's simple children, that yet know not
> The Universal Parent, *how* he sings!
> As if he wished the firmament of heaven
> Should listen, and give back to him the voice
> Of his triumphant constancy and love.
> The proclamation that he makes, how far
> His darkness doth transcend our fickle light.'*

The perfection of both these passages, as far as regards truth and tenderness of imagination in the two poets, is quite

*William Shenstone (1714—63),

*Wordsworth,

insuperable. But, of the two characters imagined, Jessy is weaker than Ellen, exactly in so far as something appears to her to be in nature which is not. The flowers do not really reproach her. God meant them to comfort her, not to taunt her; they would do so if she saw them rightly.

Ellen, on the other hand, is quite above the slightest erring emotion. There is not the barest film of fallacy in all her thoughts. She reasons as calmly as if she did not feel. And, although the singing of the bird suggests to her the idea of its desiring to be heard in heaven, she does not for an instant admit any veracity in the thought. 'As if,' she says, — 'I know he means nothing of the kind; but it does verily seem as if.' The reader will find, by examining the rest of the poem, that Ellen's character is throughout consistent in this clear though passionate strength.

It is, I hope, now made clear to the reader in all respects that the pathetic fallacy is powerful only so far as it is pathetic, feeble so far as it is fallacious, and, therefore, that the dominion of Truth is entire, over this, as over every other natural and just state of the human mind.

Matthew Arnold

(1822—1888)

유명한 교육자의 아들로 태어나 옥스포드에서 수학, 30세 이후 타계할 때까지 장학관 노릇을 하였다. 처음 시인으로 시작하였으나, 35세 이후에는 거의 산문만 썼다. 문학, 문화, 종교, 교육 등 다양한 주제에 대하여 많은 산문을 발표하였는데, *Culture and Anarchy*(1869)는 대표적 문화평론집이고, 두 권의 *Essays in Criticism* (1st series, 1865; 2nd series, 1888)은 대표적 문학평론집이다.

문학과 인간의 본성 또는 문학과 개인의 관계에서 문학의 가치를 논한 과거의 문학 효용론자들과는 달리, 아놀드는 현실사회에 대한, 진정으로 좋은 문학의 효용가치를 역설하였다. 그의 문학관은 「교양」(culture)이라는 것에 집약되는데, 그가 말한 「교양」은 과거로부터 사람이 생각한 최고 최선의 것을 체득한 정신적 상태를 말하는 것으로, 그것에 의하지 않고서는 현대사회의 무비판적 이기주의와 물질주의를 이길 수 없다고 믿었다. 최고의 교양은 위대한 문학, 즉 고전에서만 얻어질 수 있다는 것이 그의 문학인다운 판단이었다. 종교나 철학마저도 그 교리나 주장보다는 그것들이 내포한 문학성 때문에 인류사회에 가치가 있다고 생각했다.

"The Function of Criticism at the Present Time"(1864)은 비평을 경멸하고 창작만을 숭상하는 당대의 영국적 풍조를 비판함으로써 시작한다. 창작은 물론 숭상받을 만한 작업이지만, 그것이 이루어지기 위해서는 훌륭한 사상들이 활발히 교류되어야 하는데, 비평이야말로 바로 그러한 사상의 교류를 형성해준다. 비평이 형성해 주는 사상의 배경 없이 참다운 창작은 없다. 영국 문학이 초기의 낭만주의 시대가 가자 침체한 것은 물질주의, 실용주의 및 배타적 국민주의로 말미암아 비평 정신이 위축되었기 때문이다.

비평은 「호기심」에서 시작되는데, 이는 다름 아니라 「세상에 알려지고 생각된 최선의 것」을 알고자 하는 본능인 것이다. 비평적 정신은 단지 알고자 하는 「자유로운 활동」을 벌이므로,

당연히 「이기심을 초탈한 정신 상태」(disinterestedness)이다. 이기심이란, 단지 자기 자신의 욕심을 채우려는 심보뿐만 아니라, 자기가 속한 집단, 계급, 민족, 자기가 하는 사업의 이익을 앞세우는 까닭에 객관적 비평정신이 미약해진 상태이다. 따라서 소박한 사회참여는 참다운 비평정신을 위배하는 것이다. 민족문학에만 집착하는 태도는 애국적이지만 역시 비평정신을 해친다. 따라서 비평가는 다른 나라의 문학을 잘 알아야 한다.

이처럼 창작의 전제조건으로서의 비평을 내세운 아놀드는 후기에 이르러서는 아예 시를 「인생의 비평」(criticism of life)라고 규정하였다. 즉 가장 좋은 인생을 살기 위한, 사심 없는 심사숙고가 바로 인생의 비평이며, 이를 기록한 것이 시라고 본 것이다.

"The Study of Poetry"(1880)는 만년의 아놀드의 비평 사상을 집약하는 대표적 논문이다. 그는 제도화되고 교리화된 종교와 사소한 논리에만 집착하는 철학은 실용주의적이고 과학만능적인 현대사회에서 더 이상 인생을 해석하고 사람을 위로하고 희망을 줄 수 없다고 단정하고, 그 일은 진정으로 훌륭한 시만이 할 수 있다고 주장한다.

그러나 그러한 막중한 사명을 감당하기 위한 시는 진정한 의미의 높은 수준의 인생 비평이어야 한다. 따라서 높은 수준의 시를 선별하기 위한 「사심 없는」 비평 안목을 잃지 말아야 한다. 이러한 비평 안목을 위협하는 두 요소는 역사적 평가와 개인적 평가라는 것이다. 역사적 평가는 어떤 글이 단지 오래 묵은 것이라는 이유로 문학적 가치를 부여하는 것을 말하고, 개인적 평가는 개별 독자 자신에게 좋게 느껴지기 때문에 높은 가치를 부여하는 것을 말한다. 이 두 가지 평가는 당시의 낭만주의적 개인주의의 경향과, 고대 및 중세의 기록을 다루던 역사문헌학의 발흥에서 생긴 것이었다.

「시금석」(touchstone)의 이론은 아놀드가 종교를 대신하여 인류의 지주가 될 만큼 「진실되고 심각한」 문학을 선별하는 방법으로 제시한 논란이 많은 이론이다. 시금석이란 금의 순도를 알아내기 위해 금을 문질러 보던 돌로서, 한 문학 작품의 「순도」를 알아보기 위해서는 잘 알려진 위대한 문학 작품의 대표적인 구절과 나란히 놓고 비교해 보는 것이 상책이라는 것이다. 호머나 단테나 셰익스피어나 밀튼 등 위대한 시인의 위대한 명구들을 마음속에 준비했다가 새로 만나는 작품과 비교하여 별로 손색이 없으면 진정한 인생의 비평다운 시로 간주해도 좋다는 것이다.

중세 영국의 초오서는 아름다움과 진실을 내포함에도 불구하고 「시금석」에 비교해 본 결과 충분한 「고도의 심각성」을 갖고 있지 못하다고 그는 말한다. 드라이든과 포우프는 시의 대가가 아니라 산문의 대가들이다. 즉 시인이 아니다. 그레이는 고전정신의 약간을 흉내냈고, 번즈는 아름다움을 내포하고 있지만 역시 심각성, 성실성이 모자란다. 「개인적 평가」가 주어지기 쉬운 19세기 시인들에 대해서는 이 논문 말고 다른 논문들에서 다룬다.

아놀드의 비평은 오늘날에 크게 위세를 떨치고 있는 사회·문화적 비평의 선구로서 큰 의의가 있다. 문화 사회의 중심 세력으로서의 문학적 교양을 최고의 가치로 강조한 그의 태도는 처음에는 미국의 Irving Babbit을 필두로 한 이른바 Neo-humanism 비평가들에게 영향을 주었고 후에는 Lionel Trilling 같은 자유주의자에게도 영향을 미쳤다. 문학의 사회윤리적 가치, 폭넓은 비평정신을 믿는 오늘날의 비평 태도는 조금씩은 아놀드의 영향을 받았다고 할 수 있다.

또한 유럽의 고대, 중세, 근대 문학을 두루 섭렵하고 사회 문화 전반에 걸쳐 비평정신을 발휘한 아놀드는 코울리지 이후 자국의 문학을 주로 논란하던 당시 비평에 전기를 마련하였고, 이러한 「비교문학적」, 「세계문학적」, 「문화비평적」 관점은 오늘날에 널리 이어지고 있다.

The Function of Criticism at the Present Time (1864)

MANY objections have been made to a proposition which, in some remarks of mine on translating Homer,* I ventured to put forth; a proposition about criticism, and its importance at the present day. I said: "Of the literature of France and Germany, as of the intellect of Europe in general, the main effort, for now many years, has been a critical effort; the endeavour, in all branches of knowledge, theology, philosophy, history, art, science, to see the object as in itself it really is." I added, that owing to the operation in English literature of certain causes, "almost the last thing for which one would come to English literature is just that very thing which now Europe most desires, — criticism"; and that the power and value of English literature was thereby impaired. More than one rejoinder declared that the importance I here assigned to criticism was excessive, and asserted the inherent superiority of the creative effort of the human spirit over its critical effort. And the other day, having been led by a Mr. Shairp's* excellent notice of Wordsworth* to turn again to his biography, I found, in the words of this great man, whom I, for one, must always listen to with the profoundest respect, a sentence passed on the critic's business, which seems to justify every possible disparagement of it. Wordsworth says in one of his letters:

"The writers in these publications" (the Reviews), "while they prosecute their inglorious employment, cannot be supposed to be in a state of mind very favourable for being af-

---

*"On Translating Homer" (1861) 란 평론.

*스코트랜드의 비평가 J. C. Shairp 의 "Essay on Wordsworth"는 *North British Review* (Aug. 1864)에 실려 있다.

fected by the finer influences of a thing so pure as genuine poetry."*

And a trustworthy reporter of his conversation quotes a more elaborate judgment to the same effect:

"Wordsworth holds the critical power very low, infinitely lower than the inventive; and he said to-day that if the quantity of time consumed in writing critiques on the works of others were given to original composition, of whatever kind it might be, it would be much better employed; it would make a man find out sooner his own level, and it would do infinitely less mischief. A false or malicious criticism may do much injury to the minds of others; a stupid invention, either in prose or verse, is quite harmless."*

It is almost too much to expect of poor human nature, that a man capable of producing some effect in one line* of literature, should, for the greater good of society, voluntarily doom himself to impotence and obscurity in another. Still less is this to be expected from men addicted to the composition of the "false or malicious criticism" of which Wordsworth speaks. However, everybody would admit that a false or malicious criticism had better never have been written. Everybody, too, would be willing to admit, as a general proposition, that the critical faculty is lower than the inventive. But is it true that criticism is really, in itself, a baneful and injurious employment; is it true that all time given to writing critiques on the works of others would be much better employed if it were given to original composition, of whatever kind this may be? Is it true that Johnson had better have gone on producing more *Irenes:** instead of writing his *Lives of the Poets;* is it certain that Wordsworth himself was better employed in making his Ecclesiastical Sonnets* than when he

---

***"The writers...poetry"**: To Bernard Barton (Christopher Wordsworth, *Memoirs*[1856], Ⅱ, 53).

***"Wordsworth holds...harmless"**: In W. Knight, *Life of Wordsworth* Ⅲ, 438.

***line:** kind(즉 비평).

****Irenes*** Johnson의 비극작품(1749). 실패작.

***Ecclesiastical Sonnets:** Wordsworth의 졸작으로 알려진 1821년의 종교 sonnet들.

made his celebrated Preface so full of criticism, and criticism of the works of others? Wordsworth was himself a great critic, and it is to be sincerely regretted that he has not left us more criticism; Goethe was one of the greatest of critics, and we may sincerely congratulate ourselves that he has left us so much criticism. Without wasting time over the exaggeration which Wordsworth's judgment on criticism clearly contains, or over an attempt to trace the causes, — not difficult, I think, to be traced, — which may have led Wordsworth to this exaggeration, a critic may with advantage seize an occasion for trying his own conscience, and for asking himself of what real service, at any given moment, the practice of criticism either is or may be made to his own mind and spirit, and to the minds and spirits of others.

The critical power is of lower rank than the creative. True; but in assenting to this proposition, one or two things are to be kept in mind. It is undeniable that the exercise of a creative power, that a free creative activity, is the highest function of man; it is proved to be so by man's finding in it his true happiness. But it is undeniable, also, that men may have the sense of exercising this free creative activity in other ways than in producing great works of literature or art; if it were not so, all but a very few men would be shut out from the true happiness of all men. They may have it in well-doing, they may have it in learning, they may have it even in criticising. This is one thing to be kept in mind. Another is, that the exercise of the creative power in the production of great works of literature or art, however high this exercise of it may rank, is not at all epochs and under all conditions possible; and that therefore labour may be vainly spent in attempting it, which might with more fruit be used in preparing for it, in rendering it possible. This creative power works with elements, with materials; what if it has not those materials, those elements, ready for its use? In that case it must surely wait till they are ready. Now, in literature, — I will limit myself to literature, for it is about literature that the question arises, — the elements with which the creative power works are ideas; the best ideas on every matter which literature touches, current at the time. At any rate we may lay it down as certain* that in modern literature no manifestation of the creative power not working with these can be very important or fruitful. And I say *current* at the time, not merely accessible at the time; for creative literary genius does not principally show itself in discovering new ideas,* that is rather the business of the philosopher. The grand work of literary genius is a work of synthesis and exposition, not of analysis and discovery; its gift lies in the faculty of being happily inspired by a certain intellectual and spiritual atmosphere, by a certain order of ideas, when it finds itself in them; of dealing divinely with these ideas, presenting them in the most effective and attractive combinations, — making beautiful works with them, in short. But it must have the atmosphere, it must find itself amidst the order of ideas, in order to work freely; and these it is not so easy to command. This is why great creative epochs in literature are so rare, this is why there is so much that is unsatisfactory in the productions of many men of real genius; because, for the creation of a master-work of literature two powers must concur, the power of the man and the power of the moment, and the man is not enough without the moment; the creative power has, for its happy exercise, appointed elements, and those elements are not in its own control.

Nay, they are more within the control of the critical power. It is the business of the critical power, as I said in the words already quoted, "in all branches of knowledge, theology, philosophy, history, art, science, to see the object as in itself it really is." Thus it tends, at last, to make an intellectual situation of which the creative power can profitably avail itself. It tends to establish an order of ideas, if not absolutely true, yet true by comparison with that which it displaces; to make the best ideas prevail. Presently these new ideas reach society, the touch of truth is the touch of life, and there is a stir and growth everywhere; out of this stir and growth come

---

***lay it down as certain:** 「분명하다고 단언하다」.

***creative...new ideas:** 창작적 천재는 주로 새로운 사상을 발견하는 일에만 두각을 나타내는 건 아니다.

the creative epochs of literature.

Or, to narrow our range, and quit these considerations of the general march of genius and of society, — considerations which are apt to become too abstract and impalpable, — every one can see that a poet, for instance, ought to know life and the world before dealing with them in poetry; and life and the world being in modern times very complex things, the creation of a modern poet, to be worth much, implies a great critical effort behind it; else it must be a comparatively poor, barren, and short-lived affair. This is why Byron's poetry had so little endurance in it, and Goethe's so much; both Byron and Goethe had a great productive power, but Goethe's was nourished by a great critical effort providing the true materials for it, and Byron's was not; Goethe knew life and the world, the poet's necessary subjects, much more comprehensively and thoroughly than Byron. He knew a great deal more of them, and he knew them much more as they really are.

It has long seemed to me that the burst of creative activity in our literature, through the first quarter of this century, had about it in fact something premature;* and that from this cause its productions are doomed, most of them, in spite of the sanguine hopes which accompanied and do still accompany them, to prove hardly more lasting than the productions of far less splendid epochs. And this prematureness comes from its having proceeded without having its proper data, without sufficient materials to work with. In other words, the English poetry of the first quarter of this century, with plenty of energy, plenty of creative force, did not know enough. This makes Byron so empty of matter, Shelley so incoherent, Wordsworth even, profound as he is, yet so wanting in completeness and variety. Wordsworth cared little for books, and disparaged Goethe. I admire Wordsworth, as he is, so much that I cannot wish him different; and it is vain, no doubt, to imagine such a man different from what he is, to suppose that he *could* have been different. But surely the one thing want-

***had about...premature:** 「실상 어딘가 미숙한 데가 있었다」.

ing to make Wordsworth an even greater poet than he is, — his thought richer, and his influence of wider application, — was that he should have read more books, among them, no doubt, those of that Goethe whom he disparaged without reading him.

But to speak of books and reading may easily lead to a misunderstanding here. It was not really books and reading that lacked to our poetry at this epoch: Shelley had plenty of reading, Coleridge had immense reading. Pindar and Sophocles, — as we all say so glibly, and often with so little discernment of the real import of what we are saying, — had not many books; Shakespeare was no deep reader. True; but in the Greece of Pindar and Sophocles, in the England of Shakespeare, the poet lived in a current of ideas in the highest degree animating and nourishing to the creative power; society was, in the fullest measure, permeated by fresh thought, intelligent and alive. And this state of things is the true basis for the creative power's exercise, in this it finds its data, its materials, truly ready for its hand; all the books and reading in the world are only valuable as they are helps to this. Even when this does not actually exist, books and reading may enable a man to construct a kind of semblance of it in his own mind, a world of knowledge and intelligence in which he may live and work. This is by no means an equivalent to the artist for the nationally diffused* life and thought of the epochs of Sophocles or Shakespeare; but, besides that it may be a means of preparation for such epochs, it does really constitute, if many share in it, a quickening and sustaining atmosphere of great value. Such an atmosphere the many-sided learning and the long and widely combined critical effort of Germany formed for Goethe, when he lived and worked. There was no national glow of life and thought there as in the Athens of Pericles or the England of Elizabeth. That was the poet's weakness. But there was a sort of equivalent for it in the complete culture and unfettered thinking of a large body of Germans. That was his strength. In the England of the first

---

***nationally diffused:** (신선한 사상들이) 「널리 퍼져있는」.

quarter of this century there was neither a national glow of life and thought, such as we had in the age of Elizabeth, nor yet a culture and a force of learning and criticism such as were to be found in Germany. Therefore the creative power of peotry wanted, for success in the highest sense, materials and a basis; a thorough interpretation of the world was necessarily denied to it.

At first sight it seems strange that out of the immense stir of the French Revolution and its age should not have come a crop of works of genius equal to that which came out of the stir of the great productive time of Greece, or out of that of the Renascence, with its powerful episode the Reformation. But the truth is that the stir of the French Revolution took a character which essentially distinguished it from such movements as these. These were, in the main, disinterestedly intellectual and spiritual movements; movements in which the human spirit looked for its satisfaction in itself and in the increased play of its own activity. The French Revolution took a political, practical character. The movement, which went on in France under the old *régime*, from 1700 to 1789, was far more really akin than that of the Revolution itself to the movement of the Renascence; the France of Voltaire and Rousseau told far more powerfully upon the mind of Europe than the France of the Revolution. Goethe reproached this last expressly with having "thrown quiet culture back." Nay, and the true key to how much in our Byron, even in our Wordsworth, is this!* — that they had their source in a great movement of feeling, not in a great movement of mind. The French Revolution, however, — that object of so much blind love and so much blind hatred, — found undoubtedly its motive-power in the intelligence of men, and not in their practical sense; this is what distinguishes it from the English Revolution of Charles the First's time.* This is what makes it

*Goethe 가 프랑스혁명을 비난한 이유가 Byron 과 Wordsworth 에 대해서도 시사하는 바가 크다.

***the English Revolution of Charles the First's time:** 이른바 Puritan Revolution.

a more spiritual event than our Revolution, an event of much more powerful and world-wide interest, though practically less successful; it appeals to an order of ideas which are universal, certain, permanent. 1789 asked of a thing, Is it rational? 1642 asked of a thing, Is it legal? or, when it went furthest, Is it according to conscience? This is the English fashion, a fashion to be treated, within its own sphere, with the highest respect; for its success, within its own sphere, has been prodigious. But what is law in one place is not law in another; what is law here to-day is not law even here to-morrow; and as for conscience, what is binding on one man's conscience is not binding on another's. The old woman who threw her stool at the head of the surpliced minister in St. Giles's Church at Edinburgh* obeyed an impulse to which millions of the human race may be permitted to remain strangers. But the prescriptions of reason are absolute, unchanging, of universal validity; *to count by tens* is the easiest way of counting*—that is a proposition of which every one, from here to the Antipodes, feels the force; at least I should say so if we did not live in a country where it is not impossible that any morning we may find a letter in the *Times* declaring that a decimal coinage is an absurdity.* That a whole nation should have been penetrated with an enthusiasm for pure reason, and with an ardent zeal for making its presciptions triumph, is a very remarkable thing, when we consider how little of mind, or anything so worthy and quickening as mind, comes into the motives which alone, in general, impel great masses of men. In spite of the extravagant direction given to this enthusiasm, in spite of the crimes and follies in which it lost itself, the French Revolution derives from the force,

---

***the old woman...at Edinburgh:** 당시 실제로 있었던 일로, 종파적 양심의 발로였다. 이 행위에 대해 다른 많은 사람들은 전혀 무관심(stranger)했다는 것.

***tens:** 「십진법」.

***any morning...is an absurdity:** 영국의 화폐는 얼마 전까지도 12진법, 20진법 등 복잡했는데, 이를 비난하자, 그에 대하여 영국인들이 매일 신문지상에 독자투고를 보내어 오히려 10진법 화폐를 비난했다는 것을 비꼬고 있다.

truth, and universality of the ideas which it took for its law, and from the passion with which it could inspire a multitude for these ideas, a unique and still living power; it is, — it will probably long remain, — the greatest, the most animating event in history. And as no sincere passion for the things of the mind, even though it turn out in many respects an unfortunate passion, is ever quite thrown away and quite barren of good, France has reaped from hers one fruit — the natural and legitimate fruit though not precisely the grand fruit she expected; she is the country in Europe where *the people* is most alive.

But the mania for giving an immediate political and practical application to all these fine ideas of the reason was fatal. Here an Englishman is in his element:* on this theme we can all go on for hours. And all we are in the habit of saying on it has undoubtedly a great deal of truth. Ideas cannot be too much prized in and for themselves, cannot be too much lived with; but to transport them abruptly into the world of politics and practice, violently to revolutionise this world to their bidding, — that is quite another thing. There is the world of ideas and there is the world of practice; the French are often for suppressing the one and the English the other; but neither is to be suppressed. A member of the House of Commons said to me the other day: "That a thing is an anomaly, I consider to be no objection to it whatever."* I venture to think he was wrong; that a thing is an anomaly *is* an objection to it, but absolutely and in the sphere of ideas: it is not necessarily, under such and such circumstances, or at such and such a moment, an objection to it in the sphere of politics and practice. Joubert* has said beautifully: "*C'est la force et le droit qui règlent toutes choses dans le monde; la force en attendant le droit.*" (Force and right are the governors of this world; force till right is ready.) *Force till right is ready;* and till right is

---

***in his element:** 「활동하기에 꼭 알맞은 환경에 처한」.

***That a thing...it whatever:** 「한 사실이 괴상망칙하다고 해도 그 자체에는 문제가 되지 않는다」.

***Joubert, Joseph:** (1754-1824). 프랑스의 2류 문필가. Arnold는 "Joubert"라는 평론을 쓸 만큼 좋아했다.

ready, force, the existing order of things, is justified, is the legitimate ruler. But right is something moral, and implies inward recognition, free assent of the will; we are not ready for right, — *right*, so far as we are concerned, *is not ready*, — until we have attained this sense of seeing it and willing it. The way in which for us it may change and transform force, the existing order of things, and become, in its turn, the legitimate ruler of the world, should depend on the way in which, when our time comes, we see it and will it. Therefore for other people enamoured of their own newly discerned right, to attempt to impose it upon us as ours, and violently to substitute their right for our force, is an act of tyranny, and to be resisted. It sets at nought the second great half of our maxim, *force till right is ready*. This was the grand error of the French Revolution; and its movement of ideas, by quitting the intelletual sphere and rushing furiously into the political sphere, ran, indeed, a prodigious and memorable course, but produced no such intellectual fruit as the movement of ideas of the Renascence, and created, in opposition to itself, what I may call an *epoch of concentration*. The great force of that epoch of concentration was England; and the great voice of that epoch of concentration was Burke.* It is the fashion to treat Burke's writings on the French Revolution as superannuated and conquered by the event; as the eloquent but unphilosophical tirades of bigotry and prejudice. I will not deny that they are often disfigured by the violence and passion of the moment, and that in some directions Burke's view was bounded, and his observation therefore at fault. But on the whole, and for those who can make the needful corrections, what distinguishes these writings is their profound, permanent, fruitful, philosophical truth. They contain the true philosophy of an epoch of concentration, dissipate the heavy atmosphere which its own nature is apt to engender round it, and make its resistance rational instead of mechanical.

***Burke, Edmund:** (1729-97). 에이레 출신의 대 문장가요 웅변가. "Reflections on the Revolution in France" **(1790)**에서 프랑스혁명의 파괴성향을 비난.

But Burke is so great because, almost alone in England, he brings thought to bear upon politics, he saturates politics with thought. It is his accident that his ideas were at the service of an epoch of concentration, not of an epoch or expansion; it is his characteristic that he so lived by ideas, and had such a source of them welling up within him, that he could float even an epoch of concentration and English Tory politics with them. It does not hurt him that Dr. Price* and the Liberals were enraged with him; it does not even hurt him that George the Third* and the Tories were enchanted with him. His greatness is that he lived in a world which neither English Liberalism nor English Toryism is apt to enter; — the world of ideas, not the world of catchwords and party habits. So far is it from being really true of him that he "to party gave up what was meant for mankind," that at the very end of his fierce struggle with the French Revolution, after all his invectives against its false pretensions, hollowness, and madness, with his sincere convictions of its mischievousness, he can close a memorandum on the best means of combating it, some of the last pages he ever wrote, — the *Thoughts on French Affairs*, in December 1791, — with these striking words: —

"The evil is stated, in my opinion, as it exists. The remedy must be where power, wisdom, and information, I hope, are more united with good intentions than they can be with me. I have done with this subject, I believe, for ever. It has given me many anxious moments for the last two years. *If a great change is to be made in human affairs, the minds of men will be fitted to it; the general opinions and feelings will draw that way. Every fear, every hope will forward it; and then they who persist in opposing this mighty current in human affairs, will appear rather to resist the decrees of Providence itself, than the mere designs of men. They will not be resolute and firm, but perverse and obstinate.*"

That return of Burke upon himself* has always seemed to

***Price, Richard:** Burke 당시의 급진파 목사. 프랑스혁명을 찬동했다.

***George the Third:** 당시의 영국 국왕.

***That return of Burke upon himself:** Burke가 자신을 반성하는 자세로 돌아옴.

me one of the finest things in English literature, or indeed in any literature. That is what I call living by ideas: when one side of a question has long had your earnest support, when all your feelings are engaged, when you hear all round you no language but one, when your party talks this language like a steam engine and can imagine no other, — still to be able to think, still to be irresistibly carried, if so it be, by the current of thought to the opposite side of the question, and, like Balaam,* to be unable to speak anything *but what the Lord has put in your mouth.* I know nothing more striking, and I must add that I know nothing more un-English.

For the Englishman in general is like my friend the Member of Parliament, and believes, point-blank, that for a thing to be an anomaly is absolutely no objection to it whatever. He is like the Lord Auckland* of Burke's day, who, in a memorandum on the French Revolution, talks of certain "miscreants, assuming the name of philosophers, who have presumed themselves capable of establishing a new system of society." The Englishman has been called a political animal, and he values what is political and practical so much that ideas easily become objects of dislike in his eyes, and thinkers, "miscreants," because ideas and thinkers have rashly meddled with politics and practice. This would be all very well if the dislike and neglect confined themselves to ideas transported out of their own sphere, and meddling rashly with practice; but they are inevitably extended to ideas as such, and to the whole life of intelligence; practice is everything, a free play of the mind is nothing. The notion of the free play of the mind upon all subjects being a pleasure in itself, being an object of desire, being an essential provider of elements without which a nation's spirit, whatever compensations it may have for them, must, in the long run, die of inanition, hardly enters into an Englishman's thoughts. It is noticeable that the word *curiosity,* which in other languages is used in a good sense; to

---

***Balaam:** 히브리인들을 저주하려고 했으나 하나님이 반대로 축복의 말을 하도록 시킨 가짜 예언자. 즉, 울며 겨자 먹기로 옳은 말을 한 사람. 구약 민수기, 22—24.

***Lord Auckland, William Eden:** (1744-1814). 문필가, 외교관.

mean, as a high and fine quality of man's nature, just this disinterested love of a free play of the mind on all subjects, for its own sake, — it is noticeable, I say, that this word has in our language no sense of the kind, no sense but a rather bad and disparaging one. But criticism, real criticism, is essentially the exercise of this very quality. It obeys an instinct prompting it to try to know the best that is known and thought in the world, irrespectively of practice, politics, and everything of the kind; and to value knowledge and thought as they approach this best, without the intrusion of any other considerations whatever. This is an instinct for which there is, I think, little original sympathy in the practical English nature, and what there was of it has undergone a long benumbing period of blight and suppression in the epoch of concentration which followed the French Revolution.

But epochs of concentration cannot well endure for ever; epochs of expansion, in the due course of things, follow them. Such an epoch of expansion seems to be opening in this country. In the first place all danger of a hostile forcible pressure of foreign ideas upon our practice has long disappeared; like the traveller in the fable, therefore, we begin to wear our cloak a little more loosely. Then, with a long peace, the ideas of Europe steal gradually and amicably in, and mingle, though in infinitesimally small quantities at a time, with our own notions. Then, too, in spite of all that is said about the absorbing and brutalising influence of our passionate material progress, it seems to me indisputable that this progress is likely, though not certain, to lead in the end to an apparition* of intellectual life; and that man, after he has made himself perfectly comforatable and has now to determine what to do with himself next, may begin to remember that he has a mind, and that the mind may be made the source of great pleasure. I grant it is mainly the privilege of faith, at present, to discern this end to our railways, our business, and our fortune-making; but we shall see if, here as elsewhere, faith is not in the end the true prophet.* Our ease, our travelling,

***apparition:** 「출현」의 뜻으로 쓰임.

*Arnold는 **mind**와 **faith**를 대비시키고 있다. mind는 free한 반면에 faith

and our unbounded liberty to hold just as hard and securely as we please to the practice to which our notions have given birth, all tend to beget an inclination to deal a little more freely with these notions themselves, to canvass them a little, to penetrate a little into their real nature. Flutterings of curiosity, in the foreign sense of the word, appear amongst us, and it is in these that criticism must look to find its account. Criticism first; a time of true creative activity, perhaps, — which, as I have said, must inevitably be preceded amongst us by a time of criticism, — hereafter, when criticism has done its work.

It is of the last importance that English criticism should clearly discern what rule for its course, in order to avail itself of the field now opening to it, and to produce fruit for the future, it ought to take. The rule may be summed up in one word, — *disinterestedness.* And how is criticism to show disinterestedness? By keeping aloof from what is called "the practical view of things"; by resolutely following the law of its own nature, which is to be a free play of the mind on all subjects which it touches. By steadily refusing to lend itself to any of those ulterior, political, practical considerations about ideas, which plenty of people will be sure to attach to them, which perhaps ought often to be attached to them, which in this country at any rate are certain to be attached to them quite sufficiently, but which criticism has really nothing to do with.* Its business is, as I have said, simply to know the best that is known and thought in the world, and by in its turn making this known, to create a current of true and fresh ideas. Its business is to do this with inflexible honesty, with due ability; but its business is to do no more, and to leave alone all questions of practical consequences and applications, questions which will never fail to have due prominence given to them. Else criticism, besides being really false to its

---

는 한 목표에 집착한다. 영국의 실질적 활동의 항목을 파악하는 것은 faith이지만, faith가 궁극적으로 모든 것을 다 말해주리라 믿기는 어렵다고 보는 것이다. 이 주제는 "Sweetness and Light"에서 잘 전개되고 있다.

*ideas의 실천적인 면은 얼마든지 고려할 사람이 많고 또 그래야 당연하나, 비평의 일은 아니다.

own nature, merely continues in the old rut which it has hitherto followed in this country, and will certainly miss the chance now given to it. For what is at present the bane of criticism in this country? It is that practical considerations cling to it and stifle it. It subserves interests not its own. Our organs of criticism are organs of men and parties having practical ends to serve, and with them those practical ends are the first thing and the play of mind the second; so much play of mind as is compatible with the prosecution of those practical ends is all that is wanted. An organ like the *Revue des Deux Mondes.** having for its main function to understand and utter the best that is known and thought in the world, existing, it may be said, as just an organ for a free play of the mind, we have not. But we have the *Edinburgh Review,* existing as an organ of the old Whigs, and for as much play of mind as may suit its being that;* we have the *Quarterly Review,* existing as an organ of the Tories, and for as much play of mind as may suit its being that; we have the *British Quarterly Review,* existing as an organ of the political Dissenters, and for as much play of mind as may suit its being that; we have the *Times,* existing as an organ of the common, satisfied, well-to-do Englishman, and for as much play of mind as may suit its being that. And so on through all the various fractions, political and religious, of our society; every fraction has, as such, its organ of criticism, but the notion of combining all fractions in the common pleasure of a free disinterested play of mind meets with no favour. Directly* this play of mind wants to have more scope, and to forget the pressure of practical considerations a little, it is checked, it is made to feel the chain. We saw this the other day in the extinction, so much to be regretted, of the *Home and Foreign Review.* Perhaps in no organ of criticism in this country was there so much knowledge, so much play of mind; but these could not save it. The *Dubin Review* subordinates play of

---

***Revue des Deux Mondes*:** 현재까지 간행되고 있는 프랑스의 평론지.
***as much play...being that:** 「진보당의 기구라는 사실에 알맞을 만큼」.
*이들 잡지들은 Arnold의 말대로 특정 정파를 옹호하는 입장을 취했다.
***Directly:** As soon as.

mind to the practical business of English and Irish Catholicism, and lives. It must needs be that men should act in sects and parties, that each of these sects and parties should have its organ, and should make this organ subserve the interests of its action; but it would be well, too, that there should be criticism, not the minister of these interests, not their enemy, but absolutely and entirely independent of them. No other criticism will ever attain any real authority or make any real way towards its end, — the creating a current of true and fresh ideas.

It is because criticism has so little kept in the pure intellectual sphere, has so little detached itself from practice, has been so directly polemical and controversial, that it has so ill accomplished, in this country, its best spiritual work; which is to keep man from a self-satisfaction which is retarding and vulgarising, to lead him towards perfection, by making his mind dwell upon what is excellent in itself, and the absolute beauty and fitness of things. A polemical practical criticism makes men blind even to the ideal imperfection of their practice, makes them willingly assert its ideal perfection, in order the better to secure it against attack; and clearly this is narrowing and baneful for them. If they were reassured on the practical side, speculative considerations of ideal perfection they might be brought to entertain, and their spiritual horizon would thus gradually widen. Sir Charles Adderley* says to the Warwickshire farmers:

"Talk of the improvement of breed!* Why, the race we ourselves represent, the men and women, the old Anglo-Saxon race, are the best breed in the whole world. . . . The absence of a too enervating climate, too unclouded skies, and a too luxurious nature, has produced so vigorous a race of people, and has rendered us so superior to all the world."

Mr. Roebuck says to the Sheffield cutlers:

"I look around me and ask what is the state of England? Is not property safe? Is not every man able to say what he likes?

***Addeley** 는 보수파, 뒤에 나오는 **John Arthur Roebuck** 는 개혁파였으나, Arnold 는 둘 다 비꼬고 있다.

***Talk of...of breed!:** 「영국 인종의 개선을 운운하다니！」.

Can you not walk from one end of England to the other in perfect security? I ask you whether, the world over or in past history, there is anything like it? Nothing. I pray that our unrivalled happiness may last."

Now obviously there is a peril for poor human nature in words and thoughts of such exuberant self-satisfaction, until we find ourselves safe in the streets of the Celestial City.*

Das wenige verschwindet leicht dem Blicke
*Der vorwärts sieht, wie viel noch übrig bleibt**

says Goethe; "the little that is done seems nothing when we look forward and see how much we have yet to do." Clearly this is a better line of reflection for weak humanity, so long as it remains on this earthly field of labour and trial.

But neither Sir Charles Adderley nor Mr. Roebuck is by nature inaccessible to considerations of this sort. They only lose sight of them owing to the controversial life we all lead, and the practical form which all speculation takes with us. They have in view opponents whose aim is not ideal, but practical; and in their zeal to uphold their own practice against these innovators, they go so far as even to attribute to this practice an ideal perfection. Somebody has been wanting to introduce a six-pound franchise,* or to abolish church-rates,* or to collect agricultural statistics by force, or to diminish local self-government. How natural, in reply to such proposals, very likely improper or ill-timed, to go a little beyond the mark and to say stoutly, "Such a race of people as we stand, so superior to all the world! The old Anglo-Saxon race, the best breed in the whole world! I pray that our unrivalled happiness may last! I ask you whether, the world over or in past history, there is anything like it?" And so long as criticism answers this dithyramb* by insisting that the old Anglo-Saxon race would be still more superior to all others if

---

***the Celestial City:** 「천국」.
**Iphigenie auf Tauris*, I, ii. 91—92.
***Somebody...franchise:** 1년에 재산수입이 6파운드 이상 되는 시민은 두표권을 갖게 하자는 의견.
***church-rates:** 영국 교회가 부과하는 세금
***dithyramb:** 「열광적 찬양」.

it had no church-rates, or that our unrivalled happiness would last yet longer with a six-pound franchise, so long will the strain, "The best breed in the whole world!" swell louder and louder, everything ideal and refining will be lost out of sight, and both the assailed and their critics will remain in a sphere, to say the truth, perfectly unvital, a sphere in which spiritual progression is impossible. But let criticism leave church-rates and the franchise alone, and in the most candid spirit, without a single lurking thought of practical innovation, confront with our dithyramb this paragraph on which I stumbled in a newspaper immediately after reading Mr. Roebuck:

"A shocking child murder has just been committed at Nottingham. A girl named Wragg left the workhouse there on Saturday morning with her young illegitimate child. The child was soon afterwards found dead on Mapperly Hills, having been strangled. Wragg is in custody."

Nothing but that; but, in juxtaposition with the absolute eulogies of Sir Charles Adderley and Mr. Roebuck, how eloquent, how suggestive are those few lines! "Our old Anglo-Saxon breed, the best in the whole world!" — how much that is harsh and ill-favoured there is in this best! *Wragg!* If we are to talk of ideal perfection, of "the best in the whole world," has any one reflected what a touch of grossness in our race, what an original short-coming in the more delicate spiritual perceptions, is shown by the natural growth amongst us of such hideous names, — Higginbottom, Stiggins, Bugg!* In Ionia and Attica they were luckier in this respect than "the best race in the world"; by the Ilissus* there was no Wragg, poor thing! And "our unrivalled happiness"; — what an element of grimness, bareness, and hideousness mixes with it and blurs it; the workhouse, the dismal Mapperly Hills, — how dismal those who have seen them will remember; — the gloom, the smoke, the cold, the strangled illegitimate child! "I ask you whether, the world over or in past history,

*g 음이 들어있는 이름은 어감상 나쁘게 들리는 모양이다.

***Illisus:** 아테네 근처에 있는 강 이름.

there is anything like it?" Perhaps not, one is inclined to answer; but at any rate, in that case, the world is very much to be pitied. And the final touch, — short, bleak and inhuman: *Wragg is in custody*. The sex lost in the confusion of our unrivalled happiness; or (shall I say?) the superfluous Christian name lopped off by the straightforward vigour of our old Anglo-Saxon breed! There is profit for the spirit in such contrasts as this; criticism serves the cause of perfection by establishing them. By eluding sterile conflict, by refusing to remain in the sphere where alone narrow and relative conceptions have any worth and validity, criticism may diminish its momentary importance, but only in this way has it a chance of gaining admittance for those wider and more perfect conceptions to which all its duty is really owed. Mr. Roebuck will have a poor opinion of an adversary who replies to his defiant songs of triumph only by murmuring under his breath, *Wragg is in custody;* but in no other way will these songs of triumph be induced gradually to moderate themselves, to get rid of what in them is excessive and offensive, and to fall into a softer and truer key.

It will be said that it is a very subtle and indirect action which I am thus prescribing for criticism, and that, by embracing in this manner the Indian virtue of detachment and abandoning the sphere of practical life, it condemns itself to a slow and obscure work. Slow and obscure it may be, but it is the only proper work of criticism. The mass of mankind will never have any ardent zeal for seeing things as they are; very inadequate ideas will always satisfy them. On these inadequate ideas reposes, and must repose, the general practice of the world. That is as much as saying that whoever sets himself to see things as they are will find himself one of a very small circle; but it is only by this small circle resolutely doing its own work that adequate ideas will ever get current at all. The rush and roar of practical life will always have a dizzying and attracting effect upon the most collected* spectator, and tend to draw him into its

***collected:** 「침착한, 정신을 바로 차리고 있는」.

vortex; most of all will this be the case where that life is so powerful as it is in England. But it is only by remaining collected, and refusing to lend himself to the point of view of the practical man, that the critic can do the practical man any service; and it is only by the greatest sincerity in pursuing his own course, and by at last convincing even the practical man of his sincerity, that he can escape misunderstandings which perpetually threaten him.

For the practical man is not apt for fine distinctions, and yet in these distinctions truth and the highest culture greatly find their account. But it is not easy to lead a practical man, — unless you reassure him as to your practical intentions, you have no chance of leading him, — to see that a thing which he has always been used to look at from one side only, which he greatly values, and which, looked at from that side, quite deserves, perhaps, all the prizing and admiring which he bestows upon it, — that this thing, looked at from another side, may appear much less beneficent and beautiful, and yet retain all its claims to our practical allegiance. Where shall we find language innocent enough, how shall we make the spotless purity of our intentions evident enough, to enable us to say to the political Englishman that the British Constitution itself, which, seen from the practical side, looks such a magnificent organ of progress and virtue, seen from the speculative side, — with its compromises, its love of facts, its horror of theory, its studied avoidance of clear thoughts, — that, seen from this side, our august Constitution sometimes looks, — forgive me, shade of Lord Somers!* — a colossal machine for the manufacture of Philistines?* How is Cobbett* to say this and not be misunderstood, blackened as he is with the smoke of a lifelong conflict in the field of political practice? how is Mr. Carlyle* to say it and not be

---

***Lord Somers, John:** (1651-1716). 영국의 헌법학자로 대법관을 지냄.

***Philistines:** 돈벌이에만 급급한 중산계급인에게 Arnold가 붙인 이름. 본래는 히브리인을 괴롭힌 족속. 블레셋 사람.

***Cobbett, William:** (1762-1835). 영국의 정치평론가.

***Carlyle**과 **Ruskin**은 비평가였지만, 실제 정치·경제 문제에 대하여 당파적 입장에서 개입하여 많은 논설을 썼다. Carlyle의 *Latter-day Pamphlets*

misunderstood, after his furious raid into this field with his *Latter-day Pamphlets?* how is Mr. Ruskin, after his pugnacious political economy? I say, the critic must keep out of the region of immediate practice in the political, social, humanitarian sphere if he wants to make a beginning for that more free speculative treatment of things, which may perhaps one day make its benefits felt even in this sphere, but in a natural and thence irresistible manner.

Do what he will, however, the critic will still remain exposed to frequent misunderstandings, and nowhere so much as in this country. For here people are particularly indisposed even to comprehend that without this free disinterested treatment of things, truth and the highest culture are out of the question. So immersed are they in practical life, so accustomed to take all their notions from this life and its processes, that they are apt to think that truth and culture themselves can be reached by the processes of this life, and that it is an impertient singularity to think of reaching them in any other. "We are all *terrae filii,*"* cries their eloquent advocate; "all Philistines together. Away with the notion of proceeding by any other course than the course dear to the Philistines; let us have a social movement, let us organise and combine a party to pursue truth and new thought, let us call it *the liberal party,* and let us all stick to each other, and back each other up. Let us have no nonsense about independent criticism, and intellectual delicacy, and the few and the many. Don't let us trouble ourselves about foreign thought; we shall invent the whole thing for ourselves as we go along. If one of us speaks well, applaud him; if one of us speaks ill, applaud him too; we are all in the same movement, we are all liberals, we are all in pursuit of truth." In this way the pursuit of truth becomes really a social, practical, pleasurable affair, almost requiring a chairman, a secretary, and advertisements; with the excitement of an occasional scandal, with a little resistance to give the happy sense of difficulty overcome;

(1850)은 "선의의 독재자"의 정치를 옹호하는 글이며, Ruskin의 *Unto this Last* (1862)는 사회개혁을 강조한 글이다.

***terrae filii**: 'sons of the earth'.

but, in general, plenty of bustle and very little thought. To act is so easy, as Goethe says; to think is so hard! It is true that the critic has many temptations to go with the stream, to make one of the party movement one of these *terrae filii;* it seems ungracious to refuse to be a *terrae filius* when so many excellent people are; but the critic's duty is to refuse, or, if resistance is vain, at least to cry with Obermann: *Périssons en résistant.**

How serious a matter it is to try and resist, I had ample opportunity of experiencing when I ventured some time ago to criticise the celebrated first volume of Bishop Colenso.* The echoes of the storm which was then raised I still, from time to time, hear grumbling round me. That storm arose out of a misunderstanding almost inevitable. It is a result of no little culture to attain to a clear perception that science and religion are two wholly different things. The multitude will for ever confuse them; but happily that is of no great real importance, for while the multitude imagines itself to live by its false science, it does really live by its true religon. Dr. Colenso,* however, in his first volume did all he could to strengthen the confusion, and to make it dangerous. He did this with the best intentions, I freely admit, and with the most candid ignorance that this was the natural effect of what he

---

Périssons en résistant*: 'Let us perish while resisting'. 프랑스의 문인 E. P. de Sénancourt (1770-1846)의 소설 *Obermann* (1804)의 주인공 Obermann이 하는 말. 이 소설은 Arnold가 애독했던 책이다.

*[원주] So sincere is my dislike to all personal attack and controversy, that I abstain from reprinting, at this distance of time from the occasion which called them forth; I feel bound, however, after all that has passed, to make here a final declaration, of my sincere impenitence for having published them. Nay, I cannot forbear repeating yet once more, for his benefit and that of his readers, this sentence from my original remarks upon him. *There is truth of science and truth of religion; truth of science does not become truth of religion till it is made religious.* And I will add: Let us have all the science there is from the men of science; from the men of religion let us have religion.

*Arnold는 **John William Colenso, Bishop of Natal**의 성서에 대한 직역격 해석 태도를 비판했다. ("The Bishop and the Philosopher", *Macmillan's Magazin*, Jan. 1863).

was doing; but, says Joubert, "Ignorance, which in matters of morals extenuates the crime, is itself, intellectual matters, a crime of the first order." I criticised Bishop Colenso's speculative confusion. Immediately there was a cry raised: "What is this? here is a liberal attacking a liberal. Do not you belong to the movement? are you not a friend of truth? Is not Bishop Colenso in pursuit of truth? then speak with proper respect of his book. Dr. Stanley* is another friend of truth, and you speak with proper respect of his book; why make these invidious differences? both books are excellent, admirable, liberal; Bishop Colenso's perhaps the most so, because it is the boldest, and will have the best practical consequences for the liberal cause. Do you want to encourage to the attack of a brother liberal his, and your, and our implacable enemies, the *Church and State Review* or the *Record,* — the High Church rhinoceros and the Evangelical hyaena?* Be silent, therefore; or rather speak, speak as loud as ever you can! and go into ecstasies over the eighty and odd pigeons."

But criticism cannot follow this coarse and indiscriminate method. It is unfortunately possible for a man in pursuit of truth to write a book which reposes upon a false conception. Even the practical consequences of a book are to genuine criticism no recommendation of it, if the book is, in the highest sense, blundering.* I see that a lady* who herself, too, is in pursuit of truth, and who writes with great ability, but a little too much, perhaps, under the influence of the practical spirit of the English liberal movement, classes Bishop Colenso's book and M. Renan's* together, in her

---

***Arthur P. Stanley** 의 저서를 Arnold 는 Colenso 의 저서와 비교했었다.

*the ***Church and State Review*** 는 보수적인 국교회의 기관지, the ***Record*** 는 복음주의 교단의 기관지. Colenso 나 Stanley 는 그 둘에 다 반대 입장이었다.

***Even the practical...blundering:** 「책이 오류를 범하고 있으면, 그 책이 실제로 좋은 결과를 낳는다 해도 진정한 비평이 보기에는 하등의 칭찬할 것이 없다」.

a lady:** Frances Cobbe 를 가리키며, 여기서 언급된 저서는 그녀의 ***Broken Lights (1864).

***Renan, Ernest:** (1823-1892). 프랑스의 사상가로, 그의 〈예수의생애 (*La Vie de Jésus*)〉(1863) 는 명저.

survey of the religious state of Europe, as facts of the same order, works, both of them, of "great importance"; "great ability, power, and skill"; Bishop Colenso's, perhaps, the most powerful; at least, Miss Cobbe gives special expression to her gratitude that to Bishop Colenso "has been given the strength to grasp, and the courage to teach, truths of such deep import." In the same way, more than one popular writer has compared him to Luther. Now it is just this kind of false estimate which the critical spirit is, it seems to me, bound to resist. It is really the strongest possible proof of the low ebb at which, in England, the critical spirit is, that while the critical hit in the religious literature of Germany is Dr. Strauss's* book, in that of France M. Renan's book, the book of Bishop Colenso is the critical hit in the religious literature of England. Bishop Colenso's book reposes on a total misconception of the essential elements of the religious problem, as that problem is now presented for solution. To criticism, therefore, which seeks to have the best that is known and thought on this problem, it is, however well meant, of no importance whatever. M. Renan's book attempts a new synthesis of the elements furnished to us by the Four Gospels. It attempts, in my opinon, a synthesis, perhaps premature, perhaps impossible, certainly not successful. Up to the present time, at any rate, we must acquiesce in Fleury's sentence on such recastings of the Gospel story: *Quiconque s'imagine la pouvoir mieux écrire, ne l'entend pas.** M. Renan had himself passed by anticipation a like sentence of his own work,* when he said: "If a new presentation of the character of Jesus were offered to me, I would not have it; its very clearness would be, in my opinion, the best proof of its insufficiency." His friends may with perfect justice rejoin that at the sight of the Holy Land and of the actual scene of the

*__David Friedrich Strauss__의 〈예수전〉(1835)은 소설가 George Eliot에 의해 영역됨(1846). Renan, Strauss, Colenso는 모두 복음서를 과학적, 역사적, 현대적으로 해석한 사람들.

**Quiconque...*: 'Whoever imagines he can write it better does not understand it.' 복음서를 자기 주장대로 뜯어맞추고 가감하는 자유주의 신학사상에 대한 비판.

Gospel story, all the current of M. Renan's thoughts may have naturally changed, and a new casting of that story irresistibly suggested itself to him; and that this is just a case for applying Cicero's maxim: Change of mind is not inconsistency — *nemo doctus unquam mutationem consilii inconstantiam dixit esse.** Nevertheless, for criticism, M. Renan's first thought must still be the truer one, as long as his new casting so fails more fully to commend itself, more fully (to use Coleridge's happy phrase about the Bible) to *find* us.* Still M. Renan's attempt is, for criticism, of the most real interest and importance, since, with all its difficulty, a fresh synthesis of the New Testament *data* — not a making war on them, in Voltaire's fashion, not a leaving them out of mind, in the world's fashion, but the putting a new construction upon them, the taking them from under the old, traditional, conventional point of view and placing them under a new one, — is the very essence of the religious problem, as now presented; and only by efforts in this direction can it receive a solution.

Again, in the same spirit in which she judges Bishop Colenso, Miss Cobbe, like so many earnest liberals of our practical race, both here and in America, herself sets vigorously about a positive reconstruction of religion, about making a religion of the future out of hand,* or at least setting about* making it. We must not rest, she and they are always thinking and saying, in negative criticism, we must be creative and constructive; hence we have such works as her recent *Religious Duty,* and works still more considerable, perhaps, by others, which will be in every one's mind. These works often have much ability; they often spring out of sincere convictions, and a sincere wish to do good; and they sometimes,

---

***M. Renan...own work:** 「르낭 씨도 자기 저술에 대하여 이미 그 비슷한 판결을 내렸었다」. pass a sentence on: 「...에게 판결을 내리다」.

****nemo doctus...***: 'No learned man has said that it is inconsistent to change one's mind.'

****find* us:** 「우리 마음에 들다」라는 뜻이나, 기독교 사상에서 우리가 신을 발견하는 것이 아니라 신이 우리를 찾으신다는 신조를 나타내는 표현.

***out of hand:** 「즉흥적으로」.

***set about:** 「착수하다」.

perhaps, do good. Their fault is (if I may be permitted to say so) one which they have in common with the British College of Health, in the New Road. Every one knows the British College of Health; it is that building with the lion and the statue of the Goddess Hygeia* before it; at least I am sure about the lion, though I am not absolutely certain about the Goddess Hygeia. This building does credit, perhaps, to the resources of Dr. Morrison* and his disciples; but it falls a good deal short of one's idea of what a British College of Health ought to be. In England, where we hate public interference and love individual enterprise, we have a whole crop of places like the British College of Health; the grand name without the grand thing. Unluckily, creditable to individual enterprise as they are, they tend to impair our taste by making us forget what more grandiose, noble, or beautiful character properly belongs to a public institution. The same may be said of the religions of the future of Miss Cobbe and others. Creditable, like the British College of Health, to the resources of their authors, they yet tend to make us forget what more grandiose, noble, or beautiful character properly belongs to religious constructions. The historic religions, with all their faults, have had this; it certainly belongs to the religious sentiment, when it truly flowers, to have this; and we impoverish our spirit if we allow a religion of the future without it. What then is the duty of criticism here? To take the practical point of view, to applaud the liberal movement and all its works, — its New Road religions* of the future into the bargain, — for their general utility's sake? By no means; but to be perpetually dissatisfied with these works, while they perpetually fall short of a high and perfect ideal.

For criticism, these are elementary laws; but they never

***Goddess Hygeia:** 위생의 여신.

***James Morison** 은 "Morison's Pills"를 만병통치약으로 팔았다. 그는 자신을 "Hygeist"라 칭하면서, British College of Health 란 이름 좋은 간판을 내세워 못난 장사를 했다.

***New Road religions:** Morison 의 "College of Health"가 있던 New Road 란 지역 이름에 빗대어 이름만 그럴싸하게 좋은 「New Road식 종교」란 뜻. 종교의 종교성을 빼놓은 것을 비판.

can be popular, and in this country they have been very little followed, and one meets with immense obstacles in following them. That is a reason for asserting them again and again. Criticism must maintain its independence of the practical spirit and its aims. Even with well-meant efforts of the practical spirit it must express dissatisfaction, if in the sphere of the ideal they seem improverishing and limiting. It must not hurry on to the goal because of its practical importance. It must be patient, and know how to wait; and flexible, and know how to attach itself to things and how to withdraw from them. It must be apt to study and praise elements that for the fulness of spiritual perfection are wanted, even though they belong to a power which in the practical sphere may be maleficent. It must be apt to discern the spiritual shortcomings or illusions of powers that in the practical sphere may be beneficent. And this without any notion of favouring or injuring, in the practical sphere, one power or the other; without any notion of playing off,* in this sphere, one power against the other. When one looks, for instance, at the English Divorce Court, — an institution which perhaps has its practical conveniences, but which in the ideal sphere is so hideous; an institution which neither makes divorce impossible nor makes it decent, which allows a man to get rid of his wife, or a wife of her husband, but makes them drag one another first, for the public edification, through a mire of unutterable infamy, — when one looks at this charming institution, I say, with its crowded trials, its newspaper reports, and its money compensations, this institution in which the gross unregenerate British Philistine has indeed stamped an image of himself, — one may be permitted to find the marriage theory of Catholicism refreshing and elevating.* Or when Protestantism, in virtue of its supposed rational and intellectual origin, gives the law to criticism too magisterially, crtiticism may and must remind it that its pretensions, in this respect, are illusive and do it harm; that the Reformation was a moral rather than an intellectual event; that Luther's

***play off...against...:** 「...과 ...을 충돌시키다, 싸움붙이다」.

*Catholicism 은 이혼을 허락하지 않는다.

theory of grace no more exactly reflects the mind of the spirit than Bossuet's philosophy of history reflects it;* and that there is no more antecedent probability of the Bishop of Durham's stock of ideas being agreeable to perfect reason than of Pope Pius the Ninth's.* But criticism will not on that account forget the achievements of Protestantism in the practical and moral sphere; nor that, even in the intellectual sphere, Protestantism, though in a blind and stumbling manner, carried forward the Renascence, while Catholicism threw itself violently across its path.

I lately heard a man of thought and energy contrasting the want of ardour and movement which he now found amongst young men in this country with what he remembered in his own youth, twenty years ago. "What reformers we were then!" he exclaimed; "What a zeal we had! how we canvassed every institution in Church and State, and were prepared to remodel them all on first principles!" He was inclined to regret, as a spiritual flagging, the lull which he saw. I am disposed rather to regard it as a pause in which the turn to a new mode of spiritual progress is being accomplished. Everything was long seen, by the young and ardent amongst us, in inseparable connection with politics and practical life. We have pretty well exhausted the benefits of seeing things in this connection, we have got all that can be got by so seeing them. Let us try a more disinterested mode of seeing them; let us betake ourselves more to the serener life of the mind and spirit. This life, too, may have its excesses and dangers; but they are not for us at present. Let us think of quietly enlarging our stock of true and fresh ideas, and not, as soon as we get an idea or half an idea, be running out with it into the street, and trying to make it rule there. Our ideas will, in the end, shape the world all the better for maturing a

---

***Luther** 는 믿음을 통해서만 신의 은총이 내린다고 하였다(행위와는 무관). 17세기 프랑스의 사제 Jacques Bossuet 는 모든 역사적 사실들은 신의 지도로 Catholic 교회를 이롭게 하기 위하여 생기는 것이라 주장했다. 두 사상 모두 지성적 판단과는 거리가 멀다.

***Bishop of Durham** 의 개신교 사상이나 법왕 Pius 9세의 카톨릭 사상이나 똑같이 지성적 판단(비평)과는 무관하다는 것.

little.* Perhaps in fifty years' time it will in the English House of Commons be an objection to an institution that it is an anomaly, and my friend the Member of Parliament will shudder in his grave. But let us in the meanwhile rather endeavour that in twenty years' time it may, in English literature, be an objection to a proposition that it is absurd. That will be a change so vast, that the imagination almost fails to grasp it. *Ab integro saeclorum nascitur ordo.* *

If I have insisted so much on the course which criticism must take where politics and religion are concerned, it is because, where these burning matters are in question, it is most likely to go astray. I have wished, above all, to insist on the attitude which criticism should adopt towards things in general; on its right tone and temper of mind. But then comes another question as to the subject-matter which literary criticisms should most seek. Here, in general, its course is determined for it by the idea which is the law of its being; the idea of a disinterested endeavour to learn and propagate the best that is known and thought in the world, and thus to establish a current of fresh and true ideas. By the very nature of things, as England is not all the world, much of the best that is known and thought in the world cannot be of English growth, must be foreign; by the nature of things, again, it is just this that we are least likely to know, while English thought is streaming in upon us from all sides, and takes excellent care that we shall not be ignorant of its existence. The English critic of literature, therefore, must dwell much on foreign thought, and with particular heed on any part of it, which, while significant and fruitful in itself, is for any reason specially likely to escape him. Again, judging is often spoken of as the critic's one business, and so in some sense it is; but the judgment which almost insensibly forms itself in a fair and clear mind, along with fresh knowledge, is the valuable one; and thus knowledge, and ever fresh

---

***Our ideas will...a little:** 「우리의 사상은 어느 정도 성숙함으로 말미암아 궁극적으로 세상을 보다 더 훌륭하게 형성할 것이다」.

**Ab integro...*: 'Order is born from the renewal of generations'.

knowledge, must be the critic's great concern for himself. And it is by communicating fresh knowledge, and letting his own judgment pass along with it, — but insensibly, and in the second place, not the first, as a sort of companion and clue, not as an abstract lawgiver, — that the critic will generally do most good to his readers. Sometimes, no doubt, for the sake of establishing an author's place in literature, and his relation to a central standard (and if this is not done, how are we to get at our *best in the world?*) criticism may have to deal with a subject-matter so familiar that fresh knowledge is out of the question, and then it must be all judgment; an enunciation and detailed application of principles. Here the great safeguard is never to let oneself become abstract, always to retain an intimate and lively consciousness of the truth of what one is saying, and, the moment this fails us, to be sure that something is wrong. Still under all circumstances, this mere judgment and application of principles is, in itself, not the most satisfactory work to the critic; like mathematics, it is tautological, and cannot well give us, like fresh learning, the sense of creative activity.

But stop, some one will say; all this talk is of no practical use to us whatever; this criticism of yours is not what we have in our minds when we speak of criticism; when we speak of critics and criticism, we mean critics and criticism of the current English literature of the day; when you offer to tell criticism its function, it is to this criticism that we expect you to address yourself. I am sorry for it, for I am afraid I must disappoint these expectations. I am bound by my own definition of criticism: *a disinterested endeavour to learn and propagate the best that is known and thought in the world.* How much of current English literature comes into this "best that is known and thought in the world"? Not very much I fear; certainly less, at this moment, than of the current literature of France or Germany. Well, then, am I to alter my definition of criticism, in order to meet the requirements of a number of practising English critics, who, after all, are free in their choice of a business? That would be making criticism lend itself just to one of those alien practical considerations, which, I have said, are so fatal to it. One may say, indeed, to those who have to deal with the mass — so much better disregarded — of current English literature, that they may at all event endeavour, in dealing with this to try it, so far as they can, by the standard of the best that is known and thought in the world; one may say, that to get anywhere near this standard, every critic should try and possess one great literature, at least, besides his own; and the more unlike his own, the better. But, after all, the criticism I am really concerned with, — the criticism which alone can much help us for the future, the criticism which, throughout Europe, is at the present day meant, when so much stress is laid on the importance of criticism and the critical spirit, — is a criticism which regards Europe as being, for intellectual and spiritual purposes, one great confederation, bound to a joint action and working to a common result; and whose members have, for their proper outfit, a knowledge of Greek, Roman, and Eastern antiquity, and of one another. Special, local, and temporary advantages being put out of account,* that modern nation will in the intellectual and spiritual sphere make most progress, which most thoroughly carries out this program. And what is that but saying that we too, all of us, as individuals, the more thoroughly we carry it out, shall make the more progress?

There is so much inviting us! — what are we to take? what will nourish us in growth towards perfection? That is the question which, with the immense field of life and of literature lying before him, the critic has to answer; for himself first, and afterwards for others. In this idea of the critic's business the essays brought together in the following pages have had their origin; in this idea, widely different as are their subjects, they have, perhaps, their unity.

I conclude with what I said at the beginning: to have the sense of creative activity is the great happiness and the great proof of being alive, and it is not denied to criticism to have it; but then criticism must be sincere, simple, flexible, ar-

---

***being...account:** 「...는 논외로 하고」.

dent, ever widening its knowledge. Then it may have, in no contemptible measure, a joyful sense of creative activity; a sense which a man of insight and conscience will prefer to what he might derive from a poor, starved, fragmentary, inadequate creation. And at some epochs no other creation is possible.

Still, in full measure, the sense of creative activity belongs only to genuine creation; in literature we must never forget that. But what true man of letters ever can forget it? It is no such common matter for a gifted nature to come into possession of a current of true and living ideas, and to produce amidst the inspiration of them, that we are likely to underrate it. The epochs of Aeschylus and Shakespeare make us feel their pre-eminence. In an epoch like those is, no doubt, the true life of literature; there is the promised land, towards which criticism can only beckon. That promised land it will not be ours to enter, and we shall die in the wilderness: but to have desired to enter it, to have saluted it from afar, is already, perhaps, the best distinction among contemporaries; it will certainly be the best title* to esteem with posterity.

*title: (후세에까지 존경받을) 「자격」.

The Study of Poetry (1880)

'THE future of poetry is immense, because in poetry, where it is worthy of its high destinies, our race, as time goes on, will find an ever surer and surer stay.* There is not a creed which is not shaken, not an accredited dogma which is not shown to be questionable, not a received tradition which does not threaten to dissolve. Our religion has materialised itself in the fact, in the supposed fact; it has attached its emotion to the fact, and now the fact is failing it. But for poetry the idea is everything; the rest is a world of illusion, of divine illusion. Poetry attaches its emotion to the idea; the idea *is* the fact.* The strongest part of our religion to-day is its unconscious poetry.'*

Let me be permitted to quote these words of my own, as uttering the thought which should, in my opinion, go with us and govern us in all our study of poetry. In the present work it is the course of one great contributory stream to the world-river of poetry that we are invited to follow. We are here invited to trace the stream of English poetry. But whether we set ourselves, as here, to follow only one of the several streams that make the mighty river of poetry, or whether we seek to know them all, our governing thought should be the same. We should conceive of poetry worthily, and more highly than it has been the custom to conceive of it. We should conceive of it as capable of higher uses, and called to higher destinies, than those which in general men have assigned to it hitherto. More and more mankind will

---

*이 평론은 T. H. Ward가 편찬한 *The English Poets* 라는 방대한 전집의 서문으로 쓴 글인데, 글 중에 이 전집에 대한 언급이 자주 나온다.

***stay:** 「지탱」.

***Our religion has...the idea is the fact:** 종교는 역사적 물리적 사실에 근거를 두었었는데, 그런 사실들이 과학에 의하여 와해되고 있는데 반하여, 시(문학)는 idea에 근거를 두고 있는 까닭에 존속할 수 있다는 것.

*서두에 인용된 글은 Arnold 자신의 Introduction to *The Hundred Greatest Men* (1880)에 실려 있다.

discover that we have to turn to poetry to interpret life for us, to console us, to sustain us. Without poetry, our science will appear incomplete; and most of what now passes with us* for religion and philosophy will be replaced by poetry. Science, I say, will appear incomplete without it. For finely and truly does Wordsworth call poetry 'the impassioned expression which is in the countenance of all science'; and what is a countenance without its expression? Again, Wordsworth finely and truly calls poetry 'the breath and finer spirit of all knowledge': our religion, parading evidences such as those on which the popular mind relies now; our philosophy, pluming itself on* its reasonings about causation and finite and infinite being; what are they but the shadows and dreams and false shows of knowledge? The day will come when we shall wonder at ourselves for having trusted to them, for having taken them seriously; and the more we perceive their hollowness, the more we shall prize 'the breath and finer spirit of knowledge' offered to us by poetry.

But if we conceive thus highly of the destinies of poetry, we must also set our standard for poetry high, since poetry, to be capable of fulfilling such high destinies, must be poetry of a high order of excellence. We must accustom ourselves to a high standard and to a strict judgement. Sainte-Beuve relates* that Napoleon one day said, when somebody was spoken of in his presence as a charlatan: 'Charlatan as much as you please; but where is there *not* charlatanism?'—'Yes,' answers Sainte-Beuve, 'in politics, in the art of governing mankind, that is perhaps true. But in the order of thought, in art, the glory, the eternal honour is that charlatanism shall find no entrance; herein lies the inviolableness of that noble portion of man's being.' It is admirably said, and let us hold fast to it. In poetry, which is thought and art in one, it is the glory, the eternal honour, that charlatanism shall find no entrance; that this

---

***what...with us:** 「지금 우리들 사이에서 (철학과 종교로) 통하고 있는 것」.
***plume oneself on...:** 「...을 자랑하다」.
***Sainte-Beuve relates...:** 프랑스의 비평가 Charles Augustin Sainte-Beuve (1804-69)의 *Les Cahiers*에서 인용.

noble sphere be kept inviolate and inviolable. Charlatanism is for confusing or obliterating the distinctions between excellent and inferior, sound and unsound or only half-sound, true and untrue or only half-true. It is charlatanism, conscious or unconscious, whenever we confuse or obliterate these. And in poetry, more than anywhere else, it is unpermissible to confuse or obliterate them. For in poetry the distinction between excellent and inferior, sound and unsound or only half-sound, true and untrue or only half-true, is of paramount importance. It is of paramount importance because of the high destinies of poetry. In poetry, as a criticism of life under the conditions fixed for such a criticism by the laws of poetic truth and poetic beauty, the spirit of our race will find, we have said, as time goes on and as other helps fail, its consolation and stay. But the consolation and stay will be of power in proportion to the power of the criticism of life. And the criticism of life will be of power in proportion as the poetry conveying it is excellent rather than inferior, sound rather than unsound or half-sound, true rather than untrue or half-true.

The best poetry is what we want; the best poetry will be found to have a power of forming, sustaining, and delighting us, as nothing else can. A clearer, deeper sense of the best in poetry, and of the strength and joy to be drawn from it, is the most precious benefit which we can gather from a poetical collection such as the present. And yet in the very nature and conduct of such a collection there is inevitably something which tends to obscure in us the consciousness of what our benefit should be, and to distract us from the pursuit of it. We should therefore steadily set it before our minds at the outset, and should compel ourselves to revert constantly to the thought of it as we proceed.

Yes; constantly, in reading poetry, a sense for the best, the really excellent, and of the strength and joy to be drawn from it, should be present in our minds and should govern our estimate of what we read. But this real estimate, the only true one, is liable to be superseded, if we are not watchful, by two other kinds of estimate, the historic estimate and the personal estimate, both of which are fallacious. A poet or a poem may count to us historically, they may count to us on grounds personal to ourselves, and they may count to us really. They may count to us historically. The course of development of a nation's language, thought, and poetry, is profoundly interesting; and by regarding a poet's work as a stage in this course of development we may easily bring ourselves to make it of more importance as poetry than in itself it really is, we may come to use a language of quite exaggerated praise in criticising it; in short, to overrate it.* So arises in our poetic judgements the fallacy caused by the estimate which we may call historic. Then, again, a poet or a poem may count to us on grounds personal to ourselves. Our personal affinities, likings, and circumstances have great power to sway our estimate of this or that poet's work, and to make us attach more importance to it as poetry than in itself it really possesses, because to us it is, or has been, of high importance. Here also we overrate the object of our interest, and apply to it a language of praise which is quite exaggerated. And thus we get the source of a second fallacy in our poetic judgements—the fallacy caused by an estimate which we may call personal.

Both fallacies are natural. It is evident how naturally the study of the history and development of a poetry may incline a man to pause over reputations and works once conspicuous but now obscure, and to quarrel with a careless public for skipping, in obedience to mere tradition and habit, from one famous name or work in its national poetry to another, ignorant of what it misses, and of the reason for keeping what it keeps, and of the whole process of growth in its poetry. The French have become diligent students of their own early poetry, which they long neglected; the study makes many of them dissatisfied with their so-called classical poetry, the court-tragedy of the seventeenth century, a poetry which Pellisson* long ago re-

***The course of development...:** 국어 변천사의 중요 자료가 되는 옛 시를 문학적으로 가치가 있는 작품이라고 판단할 위험이 많다는 것. 옛글의 가치는 반드시 문학적 가치는 아니다.

***Pellisson, Paul:** 17세기 프랑스의 시인, 비평가. 당시 신고전주의,비극을 "sterile and crawling politeness"라 비난.

proached with its want of the true poetic stamp, with its *politesse stérile et rampante*, but which nevertheless has reigned in France as absolutely as if it had been the perfection of classical poetry indeed. The dissatisfaction is natural; yet a lively and accomplished critic, M. Charles d'Héricault, the editor of Clément Marot,* goes too far when he says that 'the cloud of glory playing round a classic is a mist as dangerous to the future of a literature as it is intolerable for the purposes of history.' 'It hinders', he goes on, 'it hinders us from seeing more than one single point, the culminating and exceptional point; the summary, fictitious and arbitrary, of a thought and of a work. It substitutes a halo for a physiognomy, it puts a statue where there was once a man, and, hiding from us all trace of the labour, the attempts, the weaknesses, the failures, it claims not study but veneration; it does not show us how the thing is done, it imposes upon us a model. Above all, for the historian this creation of classic personages is inadmissible; for it withdraws the poet from his time, from his proper life, it breaks historical relationships, it blinds criticism by conventional admiration, and renders the investigation of literary origins unacceptable. It gives us a human personage no longer, but a God seated immovable amidst His perfect work, like Jupiter on Olympus; and hardly will it be possible for the young student, to whom such work is exhibited at such a distance from him, to believe that it did not issue ready made from that divine head.'

All this is brilliantly and tellingly said, but we must plead for a distinction. Everything depends on the reality of a poet's classic character. If he is a dubious classic,* let us sift him; if he is a false classic, let us explode him. But if he is a real classic, if his work belongs to the class of the very best (for this is the true and right meaning of the word *classic, classical*), then the great thing for us is to feel and enjoy his work as deeply as ever we can, and to appreciate the wide difference between it and all work which has not the same high character. This is what is salutary, this is what is formative; this is the great benefit to

* **classic:** 모범적 작가.
* **Marot :** 프랑스 시인(1496-1544)

be got from the study of poetry. Everything which interferes with it, which hinders it, is injurious. True, we must read our classic with open eyes, and not with eyes blinded with superstition; we must perceive when his work comes short,* when it drops out of the class of the very best, and we must rate it, in such cases, at its proper value. But the use of this negative criticism is not in itself, it is entirely in its enabling us to have a clearer sense and a deeper enjoyment of what is truly excellent. To trace the labour, the attempts, the weaknesses, the failures of a genuine classic, to acquaint oneself with his time and his life and his historical relationships, is mere literary dilettantism unless it has that clear sense and deeper enjoyment for its end. It may be said that the more we know about a classic the better we shall enjoy him; and, if we lived as long as Methuselah* and had all of us heads of perfect clearness and wills of perfect steadfastness, this might be true in fact as it is plausible in theory. But the case here is much the same as the case with the Greek and Latin studies of our schoolboys. The elaborate philological groundwork which we require them to lay is in theory an admirable preparation for appreciating the Greek and Latin authors worthily. The more thoroughly we lay the groundwork, the better we shall be able, it may be said, to enjoy the authors. True, if time were not so short, and schoolboys' wits not so soon tired and their power of attention exhausted; only, as it is, the elaborate philological preparation goes on, but the authors are little known and less enjoyed. So with the investigator of 'historic origins' in poetry. He ought to enjoy the true classic all the better for his investigations; he often is distracted from the enjoyment of the best, and with the less good he overbusies himself, and is prone to overrate it in proportion to the trouble which it has cost him.

The idea of tracing historic origins and historical relationships cannot be absent from a compilation like the present. And naturally the poets to be exhibited in it will be assigned to

---

*come short: 「부족하다」.

*Methuselah: 창세기 5 : 27에 나오는 969세까지 살았다는 인물.

those persons for exhibition who are known to prize them highly, rather than to those who have no special inclination towards them. Moreover, the very occupation with an author, and the business of exhibiting him, disposes* us to affirm and amplify his importance. In the present work, therefore, we are sure of frequent temptation to adopt the historic estimate, or the personal estimate, and to forget the real estimate; which latter, nevertheless, we must employ if we are to make poetry yield us its full benefit. So high is that benefit, the benefit of clearly feeling and of deeply enjoying the really excellent, the truly classic in poetry, that we do well, I say, to set it fixedly before our minds as our object in studying poets and poetry, and to make the desire of attaining it the one principle to which, as the *Imitation** says, whatever we may read or come to know, we always return. *Cum multa legeris et cognoveris, ad unum semper oportet redire principium.**

The historic estimate is likely in especial to affect our judgement and our language when we are dealing with ancient poets; the personal estimate when we are dealing with poets our contemporaries, or at any rate modern. The exaggerations due to the historic estimate are not in themselves, perhaps, of very much gravity. Their report hardly enters the general ear; probably they do not always impose even on the literary men who adopt them. But they lead to a dangerous abuse of language. So we hear Caedmon,* amongst our own poets, compared to Milton. I have already noticed the enthusiasm of one accomplished French critic for 'historic origins.' Another eminent French critic, M. Vitet, comments upon that famous document of the early poetry of his nation, the *Chanson de Roland.** It is indeed a most interesting document. The *joculator* or *jongleur**

*dispose: 「자세를 취하게 하다」.

**Imitation of Christ* (원명: *De Imitatione Christi*), by Thomas à Kempis (1380–1471)를 가리킨다.

**Cum malta*...: 'When you have read and known many things, it will behave thee always to return to the one beginning.' (BK Ⅲ, 43)

*Caedmon: 670년경에 종교시를 쓴 Anglo-Saxon 승려.

**Chanson de Ronland*: 11세기에 지어진 프랑스 무훈시의 하나.

**joculator, jongleur*: 중세 프랑스의 음유시인, 광대.

Taillefer, who was with William the Conqueror's army at Hastings,* marched before the Norman troops, so said the tradition, singing 'of Charlemagne and of Roland and of Oliver, and of the vassals who died at Roncevaux';* and it is suggested that in the *Chanson de Roland* by one Turoldus or Théroulde,* a poem preserved in a manuscript of the twelfth century in the Bodleian Library at Oxford, we have certainly the matter, perhaps even some of the words, of the chant which Taillefer sang. The poem has vigour and freshness; it is not without pathos. But M. Vitet is not satisfied with seeing in it a document of some poetic value, and of very high historic and linguistic value; he sees in it a grand and beautiful work, a monument of epic genius. In its general design he finds the grandiose conception, in its details he finds the constant union of simplicity with greatness, which are the marks, he truly says, of the genuine epic, and distinguish it from the artificial epic of literary ages. One thinks of Homer; this is the sort of praise which is given to Homer, and justly given. Higher praise there cannot well be, and it is the praise due to epic poetry of the highest order only, and to no other. Let us try, then, the *Chanson de Roland* at its best. Roland, mortally wounded, lays himself down under a pine-tree, with his face turned towards Spain and the enemy:—

> 'De plusurs choses a remembrer li prist,
> De tantes teres cume li bers cunquist,
> De dulce France, des humes de sun lign,
> De Carlemagne sun seignor ki l'nurrit.'*

That is primitive work, I repeat, with an undeniable poetic

***Hastings:** Normandy의 William 공이 Anglo-Saxon 군과 싸운 곳.

***Roncevaux:** 프랑크족의 왕 Charlemagne의 기사 Roland과 Oliver가 스페인 원정에서 돌아오다가 죽은(778) 곳으로, 피레네 산중에 위치.

***Turoldus or Théroulde:** *Chanson de Roland*의 말미에 나오는 인명. 저자 또는 필사자로 추정된다.

***De plusurs...:** 'Then began he to call many things to remembrance—all the lands which his valour conquered, and pleasant France, and the men of his lineage, and Charlemagne his liege lord who nourished him.' (*Chanson de Roland*, iii, 939—942).

quality of its own. It deserves such praise, and such praise is sufficient for it. But now turn to Homer:—

> Ὣς φάτο· τοὺς δ' ἤδη κατέχεν φυσίζοος αἶα
> ἐν Λακεδαίμονι αὖθι, φίλῃ ἐν πατρίδι γαίῃ.*

We are here in another world, another order of poetry altogether; here is rightly due such supreme praise as that which M. Vitet gives to the *Chanson de Roland.* If our words are to have any meaning, if our judgements are to have any solidity, we must not heap that supreme praise upon poetry of an order immeasurably inferior.

Indeed there can be no more useful help for discovering what poetry belongs to the class of the truly excellent, and can therefore do us most good, than to have always in one's mind lines and expressions of the great masters, and to apply them as a touchstone to other poetry. Of course we are not to require this other poetry to resemble them; it may be very dissimilar. But if we have any tact we shall find them, when we have lodged them well in our minds, an infallible touchstone for detecting the presence or absence of high poetic quality, and also the degree of this quality, in all other poetry which we may place beside them. Short passages, even single lines, will serve our turn quite sufficiently. Take the two lines which I have just quoted from Homer, the poet's comment on Helen's mention of her brothers;—or take his

> Ἆ δειλώ, τί σφῶϊ δόμεν Πηλῆϊ ἄνακτι
> θνητῷ; ὑμεῖς δ' ἐστὸν ἀγήρω τ' ἀθανάτω τε.
> ἦ ἵνα δυστήνοισι μετ' ἀνδράσιν ἄλγε' ἔχητον;*

the address of Zeus to the horses of Peleus;—or take finally this

*'So said she; they long since in Earth's soft arms were reposing,/There, in their own dear land, their fatherland, Lacedaemon' (Homer, *Iliad*, iii, 243—4 [translated by Dr. Hawtrey]). 앞의 p. 417 참조.

*'Ah, unhappy pair, why gave we you to King Peleus, to a mortal? but ye are without old age, and immortal. Was it that with men born in misery ye might have sorrow?' (*Iliad*, xvii, 443—5).

*καὶ σέ, γέρον, τὸ πρὶν μὲν ἀκούομεν ὄλβιον εἶναι·**

the words of Achilles to Priam, a suppliant before him. Take that incomparable line and a half of Dante, Ugolino's tremendous words:—

'Io no piangeva; sì dentro impietrai.
Piangevan elli . . .'*

take the lovely words of Beatrice to Virgil—

'Io son fatta da Dio, sua mercè, tale,
Che la vostra miseria non mi tange,
Nè fiamma d' esto incendio non m' assale . . .'*

take the simple, but perfect, single line—

'In la sua volontade è nostra pace.'*

Take of Shakespeare a line or two of Henry the Fourth's expostulation with sleep—

'Wilt thou upon the high and giddy mast
Seal up the ship-boy's eyes, and rock his brains
In cradle of the rude imperious surge . . .'*

and take, as well, Hamlet's dying request to Horatio—

'If thou didst ever hold me in thy heart,
Absent thee from felicity awhile,
And in this harsh world draw thy breath in pain
To tell my story . . .'*

Take of Milton that Miltonic passage—

---

*'Nay, and thou too, old man, in former days wast, as we hear, happy' (*Iliad*, xxiv, 543).

***Io no...**: 'I wailed not, so of stone grew I within; —*they* wailed' (Dante, *Inferno*, xxxiii, 39—40).

***Io son fatta...**: 'Of such sort hath God, thanked be His mercy, made me, that your misery toucheth me not, neither doth the flame of this fire strike me' (*Inferno*, ii, 91—93).

***In la sua...**: 'In His will is our peace' (*Paradiso*, iii, 85).

**Henry IV*, pt II, III, i, 13—15.

**Hamlet*, V, ii, 17—20.

> 'Darken'd so, yet shone
> Above them all the archangel; but his face
> Deep scars of thunder had intrench'd, and care
> Sat on his faded cheek . . .'*

add two such lines as—

> 'And courage never to submit or yield
> And what is else not to be overcome . . .'*

and finish with the exquisite close to the loss of Proserpine, the loss

> '. . . which cost Ceres all that pain
> To seek her through the world.'*

These few lines, if we have tact and can use them, are enough even of themselves to keep clear and sound our judgements about poetry, to save us from fallacious estimates of it, to conduct us to a real estimate.

The specimens I have quoted differ widely from one another, but they have in common this: the possession of the very highest poetical quality. If we are thoroughly penetrated by their power, we shall find that we have acquired a sense enabling us, whatever poetry may be laid before us, to feel the degree in which a high poetical quality is present or wanting there. Critics give themselves great labour to draw out what in the abstract constitutes the characters of a high quality of poetry. It is much better simply to have recourse to concrete examples;—to take specimens of poetry of the high, the very highest, quality, and to say: The characters of a high quality of poetry are what is expressed *there*. They are far better recognised by being felt in the verse of the master, than by being perused in the prose of the critic. Nevertheless if we are urgently pressed to give some critical account of them, we may safely, perhaps, venture on laying down, not indeed how and why the characters arise, but where and in what they arise. They are

---

**Paradise Lost*, I, 599—602.

**Ibid*, I, 109—110.

**Ibid*, IV, 271—2.

in the matter and substance of the poetry, and they are in its manner and style. Both of these, the substance and matter on the one hand, the style and manner on the other, have a mark, an accent, of high beauty, worth, and power. But if we are asked to define this mark and accent in the abstract, our answer must be: No, for we should thereby be darkening the question, not clearing it. The mark and accent are as given by the substance and matter of that poetry, by the style and manner of that poetry, and of all other poetry which is akin to it in quality.

Only one thing we may add as to the substance and matter of poetry, guiding ourselves by Aristotle's profound observation that the superiority of poetry over history consists in its possessing a higher truth and a higher seriousness (*φιλοσοφώτερον καὶ σπουδαιότερον*).* Let us add, therefore, to what we have said, this: that the substance and matter of the best poetry acquire their special character from possessing, in an eminent degree, truth and seriousness. We may add yet further what is in itself evident, that to the style and manner of the best poetry their special character, their accent, is given by their diction, and, even yet more by their movement. And though we distinguish between the two characters, the two accents, of superiority, yet they are nevertheless vitally connected one with the other. The superior character of truth and seriousness, in the matter and substance of the best poetry, is inseparable from the superiority of diction and movement marking its style and manner. The two superiorities are closely related, and are in steadfast proportion one to the other. So far as high poetic truth and seriousness are wanting to a poet's matter and substance, so far also, we may be sure, will a high poetic stamp of diction and movement be wanting to his style and manner. In proportion as this high stamp of diction and movement, again, is absent from a poet's style and manner, we shall find, also, that high poetic truth and seriousness are absent from his substance

*'Poetry is something more scientific and serious than history' (*Poetics*, IX, 3).

and matter.

So stated, these are but dry generalities; their whole force lies in their application. And I could wish every student of poetry to make the application of them for himself. Made by himself, the application would impress itself upon his mind far more deeply than made by me. Neither will my limits allow me to make any full application of the generalities above propounded; but in the hope of bringing out, at any rate, some significance in them, and of establishing an important principle more firmly by their means, I will, in the space which remains to me, follow rapidly from the commencement the course of our English poetry with them in my view.

Once more I return to the early poetry of France, with which our own poetry, in its origins, is indissolubly connected. In the twelfth and thirteenth centuries, that seed-time of all modern language and literature, the poetry of France had a clear predominance in Europe. Of the two divisions of that poetry, its productions in the *langue d'oil** and its productions in the *langue d'oc*,* the poetry of the *langue d'oc*, of southern France, of the troubadours, is of importance because of its effect on Italian literature;—the first literature of modern Europe to strike the true and grand note, and to bring forth, as in Dante and Petrarch it brought forth, classics. But the predominance of French poetry in Europe, during the twelfth and thirteenth centuries, is due to its poetry of the *langue d'oil*, the poetry of northern France and of the tongue which is now the French language. In the twelfth century the bloom of this romance-poetry* was earlier and stronger in England, at the court of our Anglo-Norman kings, than in France itself. But it was a bloom of French poetry; and as our native poetry formed itself, it formed itself out of this. The romance-poems which took

---

**Langue d'oil* 은 중세 프랑스어의 중부·북부의 방언으로 현대 프랑스어의 조상. *langue d'oc* 은 남부 프랑스의 방언으로 Provence 지방에 그 흔적이 남아 있으며, 이 방언은 이탈리아의 북부 방언에 영향을 끼쳤다.

***romance-poetry:** 프랑스어, 이탈리아어 등 로망스어로 쓰여진 시. 주로 환상적 내용.

possession of the heart and imagination of Europe in the twelfth and thirteenth centuries are French; 'they are,' as Southey* justly says, 'the pride of French literature, nor have we anything which can be placed in competition with them.' Themes were supplied from all quarters; but the romance-setting which was common to them all, and which gained the ear of Europe, was French. This constituted for the French poetry, literature, and language, at the height of the Middle Age, an unchallenged predominance. The Italian Brunetto Latini,* the master of Dante, wrote his *Treasure** in French because, he says, 'la parleure en est plus délitable et plus commune à toutes gens.'* In the same century, the thirteenth, the French romance-writer, Christian of Troyes,* formulates the claims, in chivalry and letters, of France, his native country, as follows:—

> 'Or vous ert par ce livre apris,
> Que Gresse ot de chevalerie
> Le premier los et de clergie;
> Puis vint chevalerie à Rome,
> Et de la clergie la some,
> Qui ore est en France venue.
> Diex doinst qu'ele i soit retenue,
> Et que li lius li abelisse
> Tant que de France n'isse
> L'onor qui s'i est arestée!'*

'Now by this book you will learn that first Greece had the renown for chivalry and letters: then chivalry and the primacy in letters passed to Rome, and now it is come to France. God grant it may be kept there; and that the place may please it so well, that the honour which has come to make stay in France may never depart thence!'

***Southey, Robert:** (1773—1843). 시인, 후에 계관시인.

***Brunetto Latini:** 13세기 플로렌스의 시인.

* ***Treasure*:** (Tresor). 프랑스어로 쓰인 일종의 백과전서.

***la parleur**...'the language is more delightful and commoner to all people'.

***Christian of Troyes:** (원명은 Chrétien de Troyes). 12세기 Arthur왕의 전설을 읊은 명작 장시들의 저자.

**Cligès* 의 서두.

Yet it is now all gone, this French romance-poetry, of which the weight of substance and the power of style are not unfairly represented by this extract from Christian of Troyes. Only by means of the historic estimate can we persuade ourselves now to think that any of it is of poetical importance.

But in the fourteenth century there comes an Englishman nourished on this poetry, taught his trade by this poetry, getting words, rhyme, metre from this poetry; for even of that stanza which the Italians used, and which Chaucer derived immediately from the Italians, the basis and suggestion was probably given in France. Chaucer (I have already named him) fascinated his contemporaries, but so too did Christian of Troyes and Wolfram of Eschenbach.* Chaucer's power of fascination, however, is enduring; his poetical importance does not need the assistance of the historic estimate; it is real. He is a genuine source of joy and strength, which is flowing still for us and will flow always. He will be read, as time goes on, far more generally than he is read now. His language is a cause of difficulty for us; but so also, and I think in quite as great a degree, is the language of Burns. In Chaucer's case, as in that of Burns, it is a difficulty to be unhesitatingly accepted and overcome.

If we ask ourselves wherein consists the immense superiority of Chaucer's poetry over the romance-poetry—why it is that in passing from this to Chaucer we suddenly feel ourselves to be in another world, we shall find that his superiority is both in the substance of his poetry and in the style of his poetry. His superiority in substance is given by his large, free, simple, clear yet kindly view of human life,—so unlike the total want, in the romance-poets, of all intelligent command of it. Chaucer has not their helplessness; he has gained the power to survey the world from a central, a truly human point of view. We have only to call to mind the Prologue to *The Canterbury Tales*. The right comment upon it is Dryden's: 'It is sufficient to say,

---

*Wolfram of Eschenbach: 13세기 초에 활약한 독일의 서사시인. *Parzival* 의 작가.

according to the proverb, that *here is God's plenty*.'* And again: 'He is a perpetual fountain of good sense.' It is by a large, free, sound representation of things, that poetry, this high criticism of life, has truth of substance; and Chaucer's poetry has truth of substance.

Of his style and manner, if we think first of the romance-poetry and then of Chaucer's divine liquidness of diction, his divine fluidity of movement, it is difficult to speak temperately. They are irresistible, and justify all the rapture with which his successors speak of his 'gold dew-drops of speech.'* Johnson misses the point entirely when he finds fault with Dryden for ascribing to Chaucer the first refinement of our numbers, and says that Gower* also can show smooth numbers and easy rhymes. The refinement of our numbers means something far more than this. A nation may have versifiers with smooth numbers and easy rhymes, and yet may have no real poetry at all. Chaucer is the father of our splendid English poetry; he is our 'well of English undefiled',* because by the lovely charm of his diction, the lovely charm of his movement, he makes an epoch and founds a tradition. In Spenser, Shakespeare, Milton, Keats, we can follow the tradition of the liquid diction, the fluid movement, of Chaucer; at one time it is his liquid diction of which in these poets we feel the virtue, and at another time it is his fluid movement. And the virtue is irresistible.

Bounded as is my space, I must yet find room for an example of Chaucer's virtue, as I have given examples to show the virtue of the great classics. I feel disposed to say that a single line is enough to show the charm of Chaucer's verse; that merely one line like this—

***'It is sufficient...'**; 'He is a perpetual....' Dryden's "*Preface to the Fables*" (1700)의 일절.

***'gold...speech'**: John Lydgate (1370-1451?)의 *The Life of Our Lady*의 일절.

***Johnson...easy rhymes:** Johnson, *Life of Dryden*을 참조.

***Gower, John:** (1330?-1408). *Confessio Amantis* (1390)의 작가.

***'well of English undefiled'**: Spenser가 그의 *Faerie Queene*, IV, ii, 32에서 Chaucer를 평한 말.

'O martyr souded* in virginitee!'

has a virtue of manner and movement such as we shall not find in all the verse of romance-poetry;—but this is saying nothing. The virtue is such as we shall not find, perhaps, in all English poetry, outside the poets whom I have named as the special inheritors of Chaucer's tradition. A single line, however, is too little if we have not the strain of Chaucer's verse well in our memory; let us take a stanza. It is from *The Prioress's Tale*, the story of the Christian child murdered in a Jewry—

'My throte is cut unto my nekke-bone
Saidè this child, and as by way of kinde*
I should have deyd, yea, longè time agone;
But Jesu Christ, as ye in bookès finde,
Will that his glory last and be in minde,
And for the worship of his mother dere
Yet may I sing *O Alma* loud and clere.'

Wordsworth has modernised this Tale, and to feel how delicate and evanescent is the charm of verse, we have only to read Wordsworth's first three lines of this stanza after Chaucer's—

'My throat is cut unto the bone, I trow,
Said this young child, and by the law of kind
I should have died, yea, many hours ago.'*

The charm is departed. It is often said that the power of liquidness and fluidity in Chaucer's verse was dependent upon a free, a licentious dealing with language, such as is now impossible; upon a liberty, such as Burns too enjoyed, of making words like *neck*, *bird*, into a dissyllable by adding to them, and words like *cause*, *rhyme*, into a dissyllable by sounding the *e* mute. It is true that Chaucer's fluidity is conjoined with this liberty, and is admirably served by it; but we ought not to say that it was dependent upon it. It was dependent upon his talent. Other

*O martyr...: '*The Prioress's Tale*, 127. 이 싯귀 중 souded=soldered, fixed fast.

*My throte...: *ibid*, 197—203. Kinde=nature.

*My throat...: "Selections from Chaucer Modernized" (1801), xxix.

poets with a like liberty do not attain to the fluidity of Chaucer; Burns himself does not attain to it. Poets, again, who have a talent akin to Chaucer's, such as Shakespeare or Keats, have known how to attain to his fluidity without the like liberty.

And yet Chaucer is not one of the great classics. His poetry transcends and effaces, easily and without effort, all the romance-poetry of Catholic Christendom; it transcends and effaces all the English poetry contemporary with it; it transcends and effaces all the English poetry subsequent to it down to the age of Elizabeth. Of such avail is poetic truth of substance, in its natural and necessary union with poetic truth of style. And yet, I say, Chaucer is not one of the great classics. He has not their accent.

What is wanting to him is suggested by the mere mention of the name of the first great classic of Christendom, the immortal poet who died eighty years before Chaucer,—Dante. The accent of such verse as

> 'In la sua volontade è nostra pace . . .'

is altogether beyond Chaucer's reach; we praise him, but we feel that this accent is out of the question for him. It may be said that it was necessarily out of the reach of any poet in the England of that stage of growth. Possibly; but we are to adopt a real, not a historic, estimate of poetry. However we may account for its absence, something is wanting, then, to the poetry of Chaucer, which poetry must have before it can be placed in the glorious class of the best. And there is no doubt what that something is. It is the *σπουδαιότης*, the high and excellent seriousness,* which Aristotle assigns as one of the grand virtues of poetry. The substance of Chaucer's poetry, his view of things and his criticism of life, has largeness, freedom, shrewdness, benignity; but it has not this high seriousness. Homer's criticism of life has it, Dante's has it, Shakespeare's has it. It is this chiefly which gives to our spirits what they can rest upon; and with the increasing demands of our modern ages upon

*Aristotle이 한 말. 「시학」 9장 참조(p. 736).

poetry, this virtue of giving us what we can rest upon will be more and more highly esteemed. A voice from the slums of Paris, fifty or sixty years after Chaucer, the voice of poor Villon* out of his life of riot and crime, has at its happy moments (as, for instance, in the last stanza of *La Belle Heaulmière**) more of this important poetic virtue of seriousness than all the productions of Chaucer. But its apparition in Villon, and in men like Villon, is fitful; the greatness of the great poets, the power of their criticism of life, is that their virtue is sustained.

To our praise, therefore, of Chaucer as a poet there must be this limitation; he lacks the high seriousness of the great classics, and therewith an important part of their virtue. Still, the main fact for us to bear in mind about Chaucer is his sterling value according to that real estimate which we firmly adopt for all poets. He has poetic truth of substance, though he has not high poetic seriousness, and corresponding to his truth of substance he has an exquisite virtue of style and manner. With him is born our real poetry.

For my present purpose I need not dwell on our Elizabethan poetry, or on the continuation and close of this poetry in Milton. We all of us profess to be agreed in the estimate

---

***Villon, François:** (1431-84), 프랑스의 부랑자 시인.

***the last stanza of La Belle Heaulmière:** [원주] The name Heaulmière is said to be derived from a head-dress (helm) worn as a mark by courtesans. In Villon's ballad, a poor old creature of this class laments her days of youth and beauty. The last stanza of the ballad runs thus—

'Ainsi le bon temps regretons
Entre nous, pauvres vieilles sottes.
Assises bas, à croppetons.
Tout en ung tas comme pelottes;
A petit feu de chenevottes
Tost allumées, tost estainstes.
Et jadis fusmes si mignottes!
Ainsi en prend à maintz et maintes.'

'Thus amongst ourselves we regret the good time, poor silly old things, low-seated on our heels, all in a heap like so many balls, by a little fire of hemp-stalks, soon lighted, soon spent. And once we were such darlings! So fares it with many and many a one.'

of this poetry; we all of us recognise it as great poetry, our greatest, and Shakespeare and Milton as our poetical classics. The real estimate, here, has universal currency. With the next age of our poetry divergency and difficulty begin. An historic estimate of that poetry has established itself; and the question is, whether it will be found to coincide with the real estimate.

The age of Dryden, together with our whole eighteenth century which followed it, sincerely believed itself to have produced poetical classics of its own, and even to have made advance, in poetry, beyond all its predecessors. Dryden regards as not seriously disputable the opinion 'that the sweetness of English verse was never understood or practised by our fathers'. Cowley could see nothing at all in Chaucer's poetry. Dryden heartily admired, and, as we have seen, praised its matter admirably; but of its exquisite manner and movement all he can find to say is that 'there is the rude sweetness of a Scotch tune in it, which is natural and pleasing, though not perfect.'* Addison,* wishing to praise Chaucer's numbers, compares them with Dryden's own. And all through the eighteenth century, and down even into our own times, the stereotyped phrase of approbation for good verse found in our early poetry has been, that it even approached the verse of Dryden, Addison, Pope, and Johnson.

Are Dryden and Pope poetical classics? Is the historic estimate, which represents them as such, and which has been so long established that it cannot easily give way, the real estimate? Wordsworth and Coleridge,* as is well known, denied it; but the authority of Wordsworth and Coleridge does not weigh much with the young generation, and there are many

*'there is the rude...': Dryden, *Preface to the Fables*.

*Addison: *An Account of the Great English poets*를 볼 것.

*Wordsworth and Coleridge: Wordsworth는 Dryden에 대해서 "I admire his talents and *Genius*, but he is not a poetical genius" (*Letter to Scott*, 1805), Pope에 대해서는 "Yet Cowley *was* a Poet, which...is more than (in the *strict* use of the term Poet) I can conscientiously say of Dryden". (*Marginalia in Pepys*)이라고 언급했다.

signs to show that the eighteenth century and its judgements are coming into favour again. Are the favourite poets of the eighteenth century classics?

It is impossible within my present limits to discuss the question fully. And what man of letters would not shrink from seeming to dispose dictatorially of the claims of two men who are, at any rate, such masters in letters as Dryden and Pope; two men of such admirable talent, both of them, and one of them, Dryden, a man, on all sides, of such energetic and genial power? And yet, if we are to gain the full benefit from poetry, we must have the real estimate of it. I cast about for* some mode of arriving, in the present case, at such an estimate without offence. And perhaps the best way is to begin, as it is easy to begin, with cordial praise.

When we find Chapman, the Elizabethan translator of Homer, expressing himself in his preface thus: 'Though truth in her very nakedness sits in so deep a pit, that from Gades to Aurora and Ganges few eyes can sound her, I hope yet those few here will so discover and confirm that, the date being out of her darkness in this morning of our poet, he shall now gird his temples with the sun',—we pronounce that such a prose is intolerable. When we find Milton writing: 'And long* it was not after, when I was confirmed in this opinion, that he, who would not be frustrate of his hope to write well hereafter in laudable things, ought himself to be a true poem',—we pronounce that such a prose has its own grandeur, but that it is obsolete and inconvenient. But when we find Dryden telling us: 'What Virgil* wrote in the vigour of his age, in plenty and at ease, I have undertaken to translate in my declining years; struggling with wants, oppressed with sickness, curbed in my genius, liable to be misconstrued in all I write,'—then we exclaim that here at last we have the true English prose, a

---

***cast about for:** search for.

***'And long...':** Milton, *Apology against a Pamphlet...Smectymnuus* (1642) 의 일절.

***'What Virgil...'** Dryden, *Postscript* to his translation, *The Works of Virgil* (1697).

prose such as we would all gladly use if we only knew how. Yet Dryden was Milton's contemporary.

But after the Restoration the time had come when our nation felt the imperious need of a fit prose. So, too, the time had likewise come when our nation felt the imperious need of freeing itself from the absorbing preoccupation which religion in the Puritan age had exercised. It was impossible that this freedom should be brought about without some negative excess, without some neglect and impairment of the religious life of the soul; and the spiritual history of the eighteenth century shows us that the freedom was not achieved without them. Still, the freedom was achieved; the preoccupation, an undoubtedly baneful and retarding one if it had continued, was got rid of. And as with religion amongst us at that period, so it was also with letters. A fit prose was a necessity· but it was impossible that a fit prose should establish itself amongst us without some touch of frost to the imaginative life of the soul. The needful qualities for a fit prose are regularity, uniformity, precision, balance. The men of letters, whose destiny it may be to bring their nation to the attainment of a fit prose, must of necessity, whether they work in prose or in verse, give a predominating, and almost exclusive attention to the qualities of regularity, uniformity, precision, balance. But an almost exclusive attention to these qualities involves some repression and silencing of poetry.

We are to regard Dryden as the puissant and glorious founder, Pope as the splendid high priest, of our age of prose and reason, of our excellent and indispensable eighteenth century. For the purposes of their mission and destiny their poetry, like their prose, is admirable. Do you ask me whether Dryden's verse, take it almost where you will, is not good?

> 'A milk-white Hind, immortal and unchanged,
> Fed on the lawns and in the forest ranged.'*

I answer: Admirable for the purposes of the inaugurator of an age of prose and reason. Do you ask me whether Pope's verse,

*'A milk-white...': "The Hind and the Panther", 1—2.

take it almost where you will, is not good?

> 'To Hounslow Heath I point, and Banstead Down;
> Thence comes your mutton, and these chicks my own.'*

I answer: Admirable for the purposes of the high priest of an age of prose and reason. But do you ask me whether such verse proceeds from men with an adequate poetic criticism of life, from men whose criticism of life has a high seriousness, or even, without that high seriousness, has poetic largeness, freedom, insight, benignity? Do you ask me whether the application of ideas to life in the verse of these men, often a powerful application, no doubt, is a powerful *poetic* application? Do you ask me whether the poetry of these men has either the matter or the inseparable manner of such an adequate poetic criticism, whether it has the accent of

> 'Absent thee from felicity awhile . . .'

or of

> 'And what is else not to be overcome . . .'

or of

> 'O martyr souded in virginitee!'

I answer: It has not and cannot have them; it is the poetry of the builders of an age of prose and reason. Though they may write in verse, though they may in a certain sense be masters of the art of versification, Dryden and Pope are not classics of our poetry, they are classics of our prose.

Gray is our poetical classic of that literature and age; the position of Gray is singular, and demands a word of notice here. He has not the volume or the power of poets who, coming in times more favourable, have attained to an independent criticism of life. But he lived with the great poets, he lived, above all, with the Greeks, through perpetually studying and enjoying them; and he caught their poetic point of view for regarding life, caught their poetic manner. The point of view and the manner are not self-sprung in him, he caught

*'To Hounslow...': "Imitations of Horace", II, ii, 143—4.

them of others; and he had not the free and abundant use of them. But whereas Addison and Pope never had the use of them, Gray had the use of them at times. He is the scantiest and frailest of classics in our poetry, but he is a classic.

And now, after Gray, we are met, as we draw towards the end of the eighteenth century, we are met by the great name of Burns. We enter now on times where the personal estimate of poets begins to be rife, and where the real estimate of them is not reached without difficulty. But in spite of the disturbing pressures of personal partiality, of national partiality, let us try to reach a real estimate of the poetry of Burns.

By his English poetry Burns in general belongs to the eighteenth century, and has little importance for us.

> 'Mark ruffian Violence, distain'd with crimes,
> Rousing elate in these degenerate times;
> View unsuspecting Innocence a prey,
> As guileful Fraud points out the erring way;
> While subtle Litigation's pliant tongue
> The life-blood equal sucks of Right and Wrong!'*

Evidently this is not the real Burns, or his name and fame would have disappeared long ago. Nor is Clarinda's love-poet, Sylvander,* the real Burns either. But he tells us himself: 'These English songs gravel me to death. I have not the command of the language that I have of my native tongue. In fact, I think that my ideas are more barren in English than in Scotch. I have been at *Duncan Gray** to dress it in English, but all I can do is desperately stupid.'* We English turn naturally, in Burns, to the poems in our own language, because we can read them easily; but in those poems we have not the real Burns.

The real Burns is of course in his Scotch poems. Let us boldly say that of much of this poetry, a poetry dealing

---

***'Mark ruffian...'**: Burns, "On the Death of Robert Dundas," 25—30.
***Sylvander:** Burns가 Clarinda (Mrs. Agnes Maclehose)와 서신을 주고 받을 때의 이름.
****Duncan Gray:*** Burns의 시.
***'These English...desperately stupid':** *The Letters of Robert Burns*에서.

perpetually with Scotch drink, Scotch religion, and Scotch manners, a Scotchman's estimate is apt to be personal. A Scotchman is used to this world of Scotch drink, Scotch religion, and Scotch manners; he has a tenderness for it; he meets its poet half-way. In this tender mood he reads pieces like the *Holy Fair* or *Halloween*. But this world of Scotch drink, Scotch religion, and Scotch manners is against a poet, not for him, when it is not a partial countryman who reads him; for in itself it is not a beautiful world, and no one can deny that it is of advantage to a poet to deal with a beautiful world. Burns's world of Scotch drink, Scotch religion, and Scotch manners, is often a harsh, a sordid, a repulsive world; even the world of his *Cottar's Saturday Night* is not a beautiful world. No doubt a poet's criticism of life may have such truth and power that it triumphs over its world and delights us. Burns may triumph over this world, often he does triumph over his world, but let us observe how and where. Burns is the first case we have had where the bias of the personal estimate tends to mislead; let us look at him closely—he can bear it.

Many of his admirers will tell us that we have Burns, convivial, genuine, delightful, here—

'Leeze me on drink! it gies us mair
Than either school or college;
It kindles wit, it waukens lair,
It pangs us fou o' knowledge.
Be't whisky gill or penny wheep
Or ony stronger potion,
It never fails, on drinking deep,
To kittle up our notion
By night or day.'*

There is a great deal of that sort of thing in Burns, and it is unsatisfactory, not because it is bacchanalian poetry, but be cause it has not that accent of sincerity which bacchanalian

*'Leeze me...': *The Holy Fair*의 일절. leeze me=commend me to, mair=more, waukens lear=awakens learning, pangs us fou=crams us full, Be't whiskey...wheep=Be it a measure of whiskey or small ale, ony=any, kittle=tickle.

poetry, to do it justice, very often has. There is something in it of bravado, something which makes us feel that we have not the man speaking to us with his real voice; something, therefore, poetically unsound.

With still more confidence, will his admirers tell us that we have the genuine Burns, the great poet, when his strain asserts the independence, equality, dignity, of men, as in the famous song *For a'**that and a' that*—

'A prince can mak' a belted knight,
A marquis, duke, and a' that;
But an honest man's aboon his might,
Guid faith he mauna fa' that!
For a' that, and a' that,
Their dignities, and a' that,
The pith o' sense, and pride o' worth,
Are higher rank than a' that.' *

Here they find his grand, genuine touches; and still more, when this puissant genius, who so often set morality at defiance* falls moralising—

'The sacred lowe o' weel-placed love
Luxuriantly indulge it;
But never tempt th' illicit rove,
Tho' naething should divulge it:
I waive the quantum o' the sin,
The hazard o' concealing,
But och! it hardens a' within,
And petrifies the feeling.'*

Or in a higher strain—

'Who made the heart, 'tis He alone
Decidedly can try us;
He knows each chord, its various tone;
Each spring, its various bias.
Then at the balance let's be mute,
We never can adjust it;

***a'**=all, **aboon**=above, **guid**=good, **mauna fa'**=must not attempt.

***set morality at defiance:** 「도덕율에 대항하다」.

***'The scared...':** *Epistle to a Young Friend.* **lowe**=flame, **weel**=well, **naething**=nothing.

What's *done* we partly may compute,
But know not what's resisted.'*

Or in a better strain yet, a strain, his admirers will say, unsurpassable—

'To make a happy fire-side clime
To weans and wife,
That's the true pathos and sublime
Of human life.'*

There is criticism of life for you, the admirers of Burns will say to us; there is the application of ideas to life! There is, undoubtedly. The doctrine of the last-quoted lines coincides almost exactly with what was the aim and end, Xenophon* tells us, of all the teaching of Socrates. And the application is a powerful one; made by a man of vigorous understanding, and (need I say?) a master of language.

But for supreme poetical success more is required than the powerful application of ideas to life; it must be an application under the conditions fixed by the laws of poetic truth and poetic beauty. Those laws fix as an essential condition, in the poet's treatment of such matters as are here in question, high seriousness;—the high seriousness which comes from absolute sincerity. The accent of high seriousness, born of absolute sincerity, is what gives to such verse as

'In la sua volontade è nostra pace . . .'

to such criticism of life as Dante's, its power. Is this accent felt in the passages which I have been quoting from Burns? Surely not; surely, if our sense is quick, we must perceive that we have not in those passages a voice from the very inmost soul of the genuine Burns; he is not speaking to us from these depths, he is more or less preaching. And the compensation for admiring such passages less, from missing the perfect poetic accent in them, will be that we shall admire more the poetry where that accent is found.

No; Burns, like Chaucer, comes short of the high seriousness

*'Who made...': *Address to the Unco Guid, or the Rigidly Righteous.*

*'To make...': *Epistle to Dr. Blacklock.* weans=children.

*Xenophon: *Memorabilia,* I, ii.

of the great classics, and the virtue of matter and manner which goes with that high seriousness is wanting to his work. At moments he touches it in a profound and passionate melancholy, as in those four immortal lines taken by Byron as a motto for *The Bride of Abydos*, but which have in them a depth of poetic quality such as resides in no verse of Byron's own—

'Had we never loved sae kindly,
Had we never loved sae blindly,
Never met, or never parted,
We had ne'er been broken-hearted.'*

But a whole poem of that quality Burns cannot make; the rest, in the *Farewell to Nancy*, is verbiage.

We arrive best at the real estimate of Burns, I think, by conceiving his work as having truth of matter and truth of manner, but not the accent or the poetic virtue of the highest masters. His genuine criticism of life, when the sheer poet in him speaks, is ironic; it is not—

'Thou Power Supreme, whose mighty scheme
These woes of mine fulfil,
Here firm I rest, they must be best
Because they are Thy will!'*

It is far rather: *Whistle owre the lave o't!** Yet we may say of him as of Chaucer, that of life and the world, as they come before him, his view is large, free, shrewd, benignant,—truly poetic, therefore; and his manner of rendering what he sees is to match. But we must note, at the same time, his great difference from Chaucer. The freedom of Chaucer is heightened, in Burns, by a fiery, reckless energy; the benignity of Chaucer deepens, in Burns, into an overwhelming sense of the pathos of things;—of the pathos of human nature, the pathos, also, of non-human nature. Instead of the fluidity of Chaucer's manner, the manner of Burns has spring, bounding swiftness. Burns is by far the

*'**Had we never...**': 여기서 제목을 *Farewell to Nancy* 라고 했지만, 원제목은 *Ae Fond Kiss* 이다. Byron 이 *The Bride of Abydos* 서두에 인용하고 있다. **sae**=so

*'**Thou Power...**': *Winter: a Dirge.*

* ***Whistle...o't***: 'Whistle over the rest of it'.

greater force, though he has perhaps less charm. The world of Chaucer is fairer, richer, more significant than that of Burns; but when the largeness and freedom of Burns get full sweep, as in *Tam o' Shanter*, or still more in that puissant and splendid production, *The Jolly Beggars*, his world may be what it will, his poetic genius triumphs over it. In the world of *The Jolly Beggars* there is more than hideousness and squalor, there is bestiality; yet the piece is a superb poetic success. It has a breadth, truth, and power which make the famous scene in Auerbach's Cellar, of Goethe's *Faust*,* seem artificial and tame beside it, and which are only matched by Shakespeare and Aristophanes.

Here, where his largeness and freedom serve him so admirably, and also in those poems and songs where to shrewdness he adds infinite archness and wit, and to benignity infinite pathos, where his manner is flawless, and a perfect poetic whole is the result,—in things like the address to the mouse* whose home he had ruined, in things like *Duncan Gray, Tam Glen, Whistle and I'll come to you my Lad, Auld Lang Syne* (this list might be made much longer)—here we have the genuine Burns, of whom the real estimate must be high indeed. Not a classic, nor with the excellent σπουδαιότης* of the great classics, nor with a verse rising to a criticism of life and a virtue like theirs; but a poet with thorough truth of substance and an answering* truth of style, giving us a poetry sound to the core. We all of us have a leaning towards the pathetic, and may be inclined perhaps to prize Burns most for his touches of piercing, sometimes almost intolerable, pathos; for verse like—

'We twa hae paidl't i' the burn
From mornin' sun till dine;
But seas between us braid hae roar'd
Sin auld lang syne . . .'*

***the famous scene**...*Faust*: *Faust*, pt. I, v(술잔치의 풍경).
*'To a Mouse' *'심각함'이란 뜻.
***answering**: 「그에 맞먹는」.
***'We twa...'**: *Auld Lang Syne*의 일절. **We twa...burn**=we two have paddled in the stream, **dine**=noon, **braid**=broad, **sin**=since.

where he is as lovely as he is sound. But perhaps it is by the perfection of soundness of his lighter and archer masterpieces that he is poetically most wholesome for us. For the votary misled by a personal estimate of Shelley, as so many of us have been, are, and will be,—of that beautiful spirit building his many-coloured haze of words and images

'Pinnacled dim in the intense inane'—*

no contact can be wholesomer than the contact with Burns at his archest and soundest. Side by side with the

'On the brink of the night and the morning
My coursers are wont to respire,
But the Earth has just whispered a warning
That their flight must be swifter than fire . . .'*

of *Prometheus Unbound*, how salutary, how very salutary, to place this from *Tam Glen*—

'My minnie does constantly deave me
And bids me beware o' young men;
They flatter, she says, to deceive me;
But wha can think sae o' Tam Glen?'*

But we enter on burning ground as we approach the poetry of times so near to us—poetry like that of Byron, Shelley, and Wordsworth—of which the estimates are so often not only personal, but personal with passion. For my purpose, it is enough to have taken the single case of Burns, the first poet we come to of whose work the estimate formed is evidently apt to be personal, and to have suggested how we may proceed, using the poetry of the great classics as a sort of touchstone, to correct this estimate, as we had previously corrected by the same means the historic estimate where we met with it. A collection like the present, with its succession of celebrated names and celebrated poems, offers a good opportunity to us for resolutely endeavouring to make our estimates of poetry

---

*'Pinnacled...': Shelley, *Prometheus Unbound*, Ⅲ, iv, 204.
*'On the brink...': *Ibid*, Ⅱ, v, 1—4.
*'My minnie...'에서, minnie=mother, deave=annoy, wha=who, sae=so.

real. I have sought to point out a method which will help us in making them so, and to exhibit it in use so far as to put any one who likes in a way of applying it for himself.

At any rate the end to which the method and the estimate are designed to lead, and from leading to which, if they do lead to it, they get their whole value,—the benefit of being able clearly to feel and deeply to enjoy the best, the truly classic, in poetry,—is an end, let me say it once more at parting, of supreme importance. We are often told that an era is opening in which we are to see multitudes of a common sort of readers, and masses of a common sort of literature; that such readers do not want and could not relish anything better than such literature, and that to provide it is becoming a vast and profitable industry. Even if good literature entirely lost currency with the world, it would still be abundantly worth while to continue to enjoy it by oneself. But it never will lose currency with the world, in spite of momentary appearances; it never will lose supremacy. Currency and supremacy are insured to it, not indeed by the world's deliberate and conscious choice, but by something far deeper,—by the instinct of self-preservation in humanity.

Walter Horatio Pater

(1839—1894)

런던에서 카톨릭 분위기가 농후한 의사 집안에 태어나 옥스포드에 진학, 한때에는 상당히 카톨릭 교회에 기울어졌으나, 플라톤과 독일 철학을 공부하는 사이에 차차 회의적으로 되어 대신 예술의 가치를 거의 종교적으로 신봉하다시피 하게 되었다. 옥스포드의 평의원(fellow)으로 있으면서 르네상스의 예술가와 작품들을 평한 *Studies in the History of the Renaissance* (1873), 인상주의적 비평집 *Appreciations*(1889), 예술과 종교의 합일점을 추구한 자전적 소설 *Marius the Epicurean*(개정판 1892) 등을 썼다(한국 독자에게 잘 알려진 "페이터의 산문"은 이 책의 일부분이다).

페이터는 다소 본의 아니게 "예술을 위한 예술"이라는 세기말의 심미주의의 사제격이 되어 있으나, 확실히 그는 예술 작품을 대하였을 때의 다른 철학적 종교적 견해가 개입되지 않은 순수한 인상을 강조한다. 순수한 인상이란, 순수한 상태의 "나"에게 순간적으로 포착되는 것이다. 그것은 이론적, 사상적이기에 앞서 단지 감각적 쾌감하고 관계가 있다. 이러한 감각적인 쾌감을 가질 수 있는 힘이야 말로 현대의 기계 문명에 대처할 수 있는 바람직한 자질이다. 그러한 경험은 순간적일 수밖에 없지만, 그런 순간들을 되도록 많이 가지는 심미적 인생이야 말로 부러운 것이다.

페이터의 이런 심미주의는 당시의 물질주의에 대한 하나의 반발이었지만 적극적인 예술관을 형성하기에는 모자라는 것이며, 또한 그의 추종자들에 의하여 기괴하게 왜곡되기도 하였다. 어쨌든 그의 비평은 이른바 창조적 비평, 인상주의 비평의 본보기를 제공한다.

From The Renaissance (1873)

PREFACE

MANY attempts have been made by writers on art and poetry to define beauty in the abstract, to express it in the most general terms, to find a universal formula for it. The value of these attempts has most often been in the suggestive and penetrating things said by the way.* Such discussions help us very little to enjoy what has been well done in art or poetry, to discriminate between what is more and what is less excellent in them, or to use words like beauty, excellence, art, poetry, with a more precise meaning than they would otherwise have. Beauty, like all other qualities presented to human experience, is relative; and the definition of it becomes unmeaning and useless in proportion to its abstractness. To define beauty, not in the most abstract, but in the most concrete terms possible, to find, not a universal formula for it, but the formula which expresses most adequately this or that special manifestation of it, is the aim of the true student of aesthetics.

"To see the object as in itself it really is, " has been justly said to be the aim of all true criticism whatever; and in aesthetic criticism the first step towards seeing one's object as it really is, is to know one's own impression as it really is, to discriminate it, to realise it distinctly. The objects with which aesthetic criticism deals — music, poetry, artistic and accomplished forms of human life — are indeed receptacles of so many powers or forces: they possess, like the products of nature, so many virtues or qualities. What is this song or picture, this engaging personality presented in life or in a book, to *me?* What effect does it really produce on me? Does

---

***by the way:** 「논의를 전개하는 도중에」.

it give me pleasure? and if so, what sort or degree of pleasure? How is my nature modified by its presence, and under its influence? The answers to these questions are the original facts with which the aesthetic critic has to do; and, as in the study of light, of morals, of number, one must realise such primary data for oneself, or not at all. And he who experiences these impressions strongly, and drives directly at the analysis and discrimination of them, has no need to trouble himself with the abstract question what beauty is in itself, or what its exact relation to truth or experience – metaphysical questions, as unprofitable as metaphysical questions elsewhere. He may pass them all by as being, answerable or not, of no interest to him.

The aesthetic critic, then, regards all the objects with which he has to do, all works of art, and the fairer forms of nature and human life, as powers or forces producing pleasurable sensations, each of a more or less peculiar or unique kind. This influence he feels, and wishes to explain, analysing it, and reducing it to its elements. To him, the picture, the landscape, the engaging personality in life or in a book, *La Gioconda,** the hills of Carrara,* Pico of Mirandola,* are valuable for their virtues, as we say, in speaking of a herb, a wine, a gem; for the property each has of affecting one with a special, a unique, impression of pleasure. Our education becomes complete in proportion as our susceptibility to these impressions increases in depth and variety. And the function of the aesthetic critic is to distinguish, analyse, and separate from its adjuncts, the virtue by which a picture, a landscape, a fair personality in life or in a book, produces this special impression of beauty or pleasure, to indicate what the source of that impression is, and under what conditions it is experienced. His end is reached when he has disengaged that virtue, and noted it, as a chemist notes some natural elements, for himself and others; and the rule for

---

******La Gioconda*:** da Vinci의 모나리자.

***Carrana:** 중부 이탈리아의 도시로 대리석 산지.

***Pico of Mirandola:** (1463-94). 이탈리아의 학자. 신비주의 사상가.

those who would reach this end is stated with great exactness in the words of a recent critic of Sainte-Beuve: *De se borner à connaître de près les belles choses, et à s'en nourrir en exquis amateurs, en humanistes accomplis.* *

What is important, then, is not that the critic should possess a correct abstract definition of beauty for the intellect, but a certain kind of temperament, the power of being deeply moved by the presence of beautiful objects. He will remember always that beauty exists in many forms. To him all periods, types, schools of taste, are in themselves equal. In all ages there have been some excellent workmen, and some excellent work done. The question he asks is always: — In whom did the stir, the genius, the sentiment of the period find itself? where was the receptacle of its refinement, its elevation, its taste? "The ages are all equal," says William Blake, "but genius is always above its age."

Often it will require great nicety to disengage this virtue from the commoner elements with which it may be found in combination. Few artists, not Goethe or Byron even, work quite cleanly, casting off all *débris,* and leaving us only what the heat of their imagination has wholly fused and transformed. Take, for instance, the writings of Wordsworth. The heat of his genius, entering into the substance of his work, has crystallised a part, but only a part, of it; and in that great mass of verse there is much which might well be forgotten. But scatterd up and down it, sometimes fusing and transforming entire compositions, like the stanzas on *Resolution and Independence,* and the Ode on the *Recollections of Childhood,* sometimes, as if at random, depositing a fine crystal here or there, in a matter it does not wholly search through and transform, we trace the action of his unique, incommunicable faculty, that strange, mystical sense of a life in natural things, and of man's life as a part of nature, drawing strength and colour and character from local influences, from the hills and streams, and from natural sights and

*De se borner...: 'To limit themselves to know lovely things near at hand, and to nourish themselves upon them, like refined amateurs, like accomplished humanists'.

sounds. Well! that is the *virtue,* the active principle in Wordsworth's poetry; and then the function of the critic of Wordsworth is to follow up that active principle, to disengage it, to mark the degree in which it penetrates his verse.

The subjects of the following studies are taken from the history of the Renaissance, and touch what I think the chief points in that complex, many-sided movement. I have explained in the first of them what I understand by the word, giving it a much wider scope than was intended by those who originally used it to denote only that revival of classical antiquity in the fifteenth century which was but one of many results of a general excitement and enlightening of the human mind, of which the great aim and achievements of what, as Christian art, is often falsely opposed to the Renaissance, were another result. This outbreak of the human spirit may be traced far into the Middle Age itself, with its qualities already clearly pronounced, the care for physical beauty, the worship of the body, the breaking down of those limits which the religious system of the Middle Age imposed on the heart and the imagination. I have taken as an example of this movement, this earlier Renaissance within the Middle Age itself, and as an expression of its qualities, two little compositions in early French; not because they constitute the best possible expression of them, but because they help the unity of my series, inasmuch as the Renaissance ends also in France, in French poetry, in a phase of which the writings of Joachim du Bellay* are in many ways the most perfect illustration; the Renaissance thus putting forth in France an aftermath, a wonderful later growth, the products of which have to the full* that subtle and delicate sweetness which belongs to a refined and comely decadence; just as its earliest phases have the freshness which belongs to all periods of growth in art, the charm of *ascèsis,** of the austere and serious girding of the loins in youth.

But it is in Italy, in the fifteenth century, that the interest

---

***Joachim du Bellay:** (1524-60). 프랑스의 시인, 비평가.

***to the full:** 「충만하게」.

****ascèsis*:** 'severe training', 'asceticism'.

of the Renaissance mainly lies, — in that solemn fifteenth century which can hardly be studied too much, not merely for its positive results in the things of the intellect and the imagination, its concrete works of art, its special and prominent personalities, with their profound aesthetic charm, but for its general spirit and character, for the ethical qualities of which it is a consummate type.

The various forms of intellectual activity which together make up the culture of an age, move for the most part from different starting-points, and by unconnected roads. As products of the same generation they partake, indeed, of a common character, and unconsciously illustrate each other; but of the producers themselves, each group is solitary, gaining what advantage or disadvantage there may be in intellectual isolation. Art and poetry, philosophy and the religious life, and that other life of refined pleasure and action in the open places of the world, are each of them confined to its own circle of ideas, and those who prosecute either of them are generally little curious of the thoughts of others. There come, however, from time to time, eras of more favourable conditions, in which the thoughts of men draw nearer together than is their wont, and the many interests of the intellectual world combine in one complete type of general culture. The fifteenth century in Italy is one of these happier eras; and what is sometimes said of the age of Pericles is true of that of Lorenzo:* — it is an age productive in personalities, many-sided, centralised, complete. Here, artists and philosophers and those whom the action of the world has elevated and made keen, do not live in isolation, but breathe a common air, and catch light and heat from each other's thoughts. There is a spirit of general elevation and enlightenment in which all alike communicate. It is the unity of this spirit which gives unity to all the various products of the Renaissance; and it is to this intimate alliance with mind, this participation in the best thoughts which that age produced,

---

*Lorenzo de' Medici: (1449-92). 이탈리아 피렌체의 지배자로 학예를 크게 진흥시킴.

that the art of Italy in the fifteenth century owes much of its grave dignity and influence.

I have added an essay on Winckelmann,* as not incongruous with the studies which precede it, because Winckelmann, coming in the eighteenth century, really belongs in spirit to an earlier age. By his enthusiasm for the things of the intellect and the imagination for their own sake, by his Hellenism, his life-long struggle to attain to the Greek spirit, he is in sympathy with the humanists of an earlier century. He is the last fruit of the Renaissance, and explains in a striking way its motive and tendencies.

CONCLUSION*

To regard all things and principles of things as inconstant modes or fashions has more and more become the tendency of modern thought. Let us begin with that which is without — our physical life. Fix upon it in one of its more exquisite intervals, the moment, for instance, of delicious recoil from the flood of water in summer heat. What is the whole physical life in that moment but a combination of natural elements to which science gives their names? But these elements, phosphorus and lime and delicate fibres, are present not in the human body alone: we detect them in places most remote from it. Our physical life is a perpetual motion of them — the passage of the blood, the wasting and repairing of the lenses of the eye, the modification of the tissues of the brain by every ray of light and sound — processes which science reduces to simpler and more elementary forces. Like the elements of which we are composed, the action of these forces extends beyond us; it rusts iron and ripens corn. Far out on every side of us those elements are broadcast, driven by many forces; and birth and gesture and death and the springing of violets from the grave are but a few out of ten thousand

---

***Winckelmann, Johann Joachim:** (1717-68). 독일의 고전학자.

*이 결론에 대해 Oxford를 비롯한 보수적 학계에서 큰 반발을 일으키자 제 2판에서는 삭제했다가 뒤에 다시 회복시켰다.

resultant combinations. That clear, perpetual outline of face and limb is but an image of ours, under which we group them — a design in a web, the actual threads of which pass out beyond it. This at least of flame-like our life has, that it is but the concurrence, renewed from moment to moment, of forces parting sooner or later on their ways.

Or if we begin with the inward world of thought and feeling, the whirlpool is still more rapid, the flame more eager and devouring. There it is no longer the gradual darkening of the eye and fading of colour from the wall, — the movement of the shoreside, where the water flows down indeed, though in apparent rest, — but the race of the mid-stream, a drift of momentary acts of sight and passion and thought. At first sight experience seems to bury us under a flood of external objects, pressing upon us with a sharp and importunate reality, calling us out of ourselves in a thousand forms of action. But when reflexion begins to act upon those objects they are dissipated under its influence; the cohesive force seems suspended like a trick of magic; each object is loosed into a group of impressions — colour, odour, texture — in the mind of the observer. And if we continue to dwell in thought on this world, not of objects in the solidity with which language invests them, but of impressions unstable, flickering, inconsistent, which burn and are extinguished with our consciousness of them, it contracts still further; the whole scope of observation is dwarfed to the narrow chamber of the individual mind. Experience, already reduced to a swarm of impressions, is ringed round for each one of us by that thick wall of personality through which no real voice has ever pierced on its way to us, or from us to that which we can only conjecture to be without. Every one of those impressions is the impression of the individual in his isolation, each mind keeping as a solitary prisoner its own dream of a world.

Analysis goes a step farther still, and assures us that that those impressions of the individual mind to which, for each one of us, experience dwindles down, are in perpetual flight; that each of them is limited by time, and that as time is infinitely divisible, each of them is infinitely divisible also; all that is actual in it being a single moment, gone while we try to apprehend it, of which it may ever be more truly said that it has ceased to be than that it is. To such a tremulous wisp constantly reforming itself on the stream, to a single sharp impression, with a sense in it, a relic more or less fleeting, of such moments gone by, what is real in our life fines* itself down. It is with this movement, with the passage and dissolution of impressions, images, sensations, that analysis leaves off — that continual vanishing away, that strange, perpetual weaving and unweaving of ourselves.

Philosophiren, says Novalis, *ist dephlegmatisiren vivificiren.** The service of philosophy, of speculative culture, towards the human spirit is to rouse, to startle it into sharp and eager observation. Every moment some form grows perfect in hand or face; some tone on the hills or the sea is choicer than the rest; some mood of passion or insight or intellectual excitement is irresistibly real and attractive for us, — for that moment only. Not the fruit of experience, but experience itself, is the end. A counted number of pulses only is given to us of a variegated, dramatic, life. How may we see in them all that is to be seen in them by the finest senses? How shall we pass most swiftly from point to point, and be present always at the focus where the greatest number of vital forces unite in their purest energy?

To burn always with this hard, gemlike flame, to maintain this ecstasy, is success in life. In a sense it might even be said that our failure is to form habits: for, after all, habit is relative to a stereotyped world, and meantime it is only the roughness of the eye that makes any two persons, things, situations, seem alike. While all melts under our feet, we may well catch at any exquisite passion, or any contribution to knowledge that seems by a lifted horizon to set the spirit free for a moment, or any stirring of the senses, strange dyes, strange colours, and curious odours, or work of the artist's

---

***fines:** fine itself down to...의 구문. 「스스로를 ...에다 한정시키다, ...에 한정되다」.

***Philosophiren...:** 'To philosophize is to throw off inertia, to come to life.' Novalis는 독일의 낭만파 시인.

hands, or the face of one's friend. Not to discriminate every moment some passionate attitude in those about us, and in the brilliancy of their gifts some tragic dividing of forces on their ways, is, on this short day of frost and sun, to sleep before evening.* With this sense of the splendour of our experience and of its awful brevity, gathering all we are into* one desperate effort to see and touch, we shall hardly have time to make theories about the things we see and touch. What we have to do is to be for ever curiously testing new opinions and courting new impressions, never acquiescing in a facile orthodoxy of Comte,* or of Hegel, or of our own Philosophical theories or ideas, as points of view, instruments of criticism, may help us to gather up what might otherwise pass unregarded by us. "Philosophy is the microscope of thought." The theory or idea or system which requires of us the sacrifice of some interest into which we cannot enter, or some abstract theory we have not identified with ourselves, or what is only conventional, has no real claim upon us.

One of the most beautiful passages in the writings of Rousseau is that in the sixth book of the *Confessions,* where he describes the awakening in him of the literary sense. An undefinable taint of death had always clung about him, and now in early manhood he believed himself smitten by mortal disease. He asked himself how he might make as much as possible of the interval that remained; and he was not biassed by anything in his previous life when he decided that it must be by intellectual excitement, which he found just then in the clear, fresh writings of Voltaire. Well! we are all *condamnés,* as Victor Hugo says: we are all under sentence of death but with a sort of indefinite reprieve — *les hommes sont tous condamnés à mort avec des sursis indéfinis:* we have an interval, and then our place knows us no more. Some spend this interval in listlessness, some in high passions, the wisest, at least among "the children of this world," in art and song. For our

---

*주변의 사물들을 면밀히 보지 않고 지나쳐버리는 것은 그렇지 않아도 짧은 인생을 중도에서 포기하는 것이나 마찬가지이다.

***gathering...into:** 「우리 존재의 전부를 합쳐서 ...으로 만들어」.

***Comte, Auguste:** (1798-1857). 프랑스의 실증주의 방법론의 창시자.

one chance lies in expanding that interval, in getting as many pulsations as possible into the given time. Great passions may give us this quickened sense of life, ecstasy and sorrow of love, the various forms of enthusiastic activity, disinterested or otherwise, which come naturally to many of us. Only be sure it is passion — that it does yield you this fruit of a quickened, multiplied consciousness. Of this wisdom, the poetic passion, the desire of beauty, the love of art for art's sake, has most; for art comes to you professing frankly to give nothing but the highest quality to your moments as they pass, and simply for those moments' sake.

Henry James

(1843—1916)

철학과 신학 연구에 심취한 부유한 아버지의 특이한 교육 방침에 따라 헨리 제임스는 출생지 뉴욕에서 가정교사에게 배우고, 12세 이후에는 유럽의 여러 곳으로 다니면서 교육을 받았다. 19세 때에 하버드 법과대학에 입학했으나 2년 후 퇴교, 직업이나 생활 걱정 없이 글 쓰는 일에 전념, 33세 이후에는 런던에 정착하여 유럽 작가들과 사귀며 그의 특이한 작품 세계를 열어나갔다. 1915년에 영국인으로 귀화, 이듬해에 죽었다.

헨리 제임스는 영미의 소설가 중에서 선구적으로 소설의 예술로서의 방법에 대하여 예리한 비평적 의식을 가졌던 사람이다. 그는 매우 비평적인 입장에서 창작을 한 「까다로운」 작가로 알려져 있다. 그는 또 만년에 전집("New York" Edition, 1907-9)을 내면서 각 작품들에 대한 비평적 서문을 달았다. 이 방대한 작업을 제외하고서도 그는 4권의 비평집을 냈고, 또 많은 잡지에 유럽 및 영미 작가, 시인에 관한 비평을 기고했다.

"The Art of Fiction"(1884)은 소설이 대중적 오락 또는 설교라는 당시의 관념에 이의를 제기하고 "의미 깊은 형식으로서의 소설"을 강조한 획기적 비평이다. 소설은 재미나 설교를 주기 위한 것이 아니라 "삶을 재현하는 것"으로서, 삶의 모습에 대하여 광대하고도 정교한 대응관계를 유지하는 자유로운 성격을 가진 웅장한 예술 형식이라고 주장한다. 이러한 예찬은 시, 그것도 서사시에게만 주어지던 것이었다. 소설은 서사시와 내용에 있어서뿐 아니라 형식상으로도 동등하다는 주장인 것이다. 소설의 형식은 작가의 내면을 표현하므로, 결국 형식도 작가 정신, 즉 윤리성을 내포한다. 형식은 그 만큼 의미 깊은 것이다.

The Art of Fiction (1884)

I should not have affixed so comprehensive a title to these few remarks, necessarily wanting in any completeness upon a subject the full consideration of which would carry us far, did I not seem to discover a pretext for my temerity in the interesting pamphlet lately published under this name by Mr. Walter Besant.* Mr. Besant's lecture at the Royal Institution —the original form of his pamphlet— appears to indicate that many persons are interested in the art of fiction, and are not indifferent to such remarks, as those who practice it may attempt to make about it. I am therefore anxious not to lose the benefit of this favorable association, and to edge in* a few words under cover of the attention which Mr. Besant is sure to have excited. There is something very encouraging in his having put into form certain of his ideas on the mystery of storytelling.

It is a proof of life and curiosity — curiosity on the part of the brotherhood of novelists as well as on the part of their readers. Only a short time ago it might have been supposed that the English novel was not what the French call *discutable.** It had no air of having a theory, a conviction, a consciousness of itself behind it — of being the expression of an artistic faith, the result of choice and comparison. I do not say it was necessarily the worse for that:* it would take much more courage than I possess to intimate that the form of the novel as Dickens and Thackeray (for instance) saw it had any taint of incompleteness. It was, however, *naïf** (if I may help

---

***Sir Walter Besant:** (1836-1901). 영국의 소설가, 평론가. 여기서 언급된 논문은 "The Art of Fiction".

***edge in:** (몇 마디) 「삽입하다, 끼워넣다」.

****discutable*:** 'discussable.'

***I do not say...for that:** 「그 때문에 반드시 더 나빴다고는 말하지 않는다」.

****naïf*:** naive, simple. ***naïveté*:** naïfe의 명사.

myself out with another French word); and evidently if it be destined to suffer in any way for having lost its *naïveté** it has now an idea of making sure of the corresponding advantages. During the period I have alluded to there was a comfortable, good-humored feeling abroad that a novel is a novel, as a pudding is a pudding, and that our only business with it could be to swallow it. But within a year or two, for some reason or other, there have been signs of returning animation — the era of discussion would appear to have been to a certain extent opened. Art lives upon discussion, upon experiment, upon curiosity, upon variety of attempt, upon the exchange of views and the comparison of standpoints; and there is a presumption that those times when no one has anything particular to say about it, and has no reason to give for practice or preference, though they may be times of honor, are not times of development — are times, possibly even, a little of dullness. The successful application of any art is a delightful spectacle, but the theory too is interesting; and though there is a great deal of the latter without the former I suspect there has never been a genuine success that has not had a latent core of conviction. Discussion, suggestion, formulation, these things are fertilizing when they are frank and sincere. Mr. Besant has set an excellent example in saying what he thinks, for his part, about the way in which fiction should be written, as well as about the way in which it should be published; for his view of the "art," carried on into an appendix, covers that too. Other laborers in the same field will doubtless take up the argument, they will give it the light of their experience, and the effect will surely be to make our interest in the novel a little more what it had for some time threatened to fail to be — a serious, active, inquiring interest, under protection of which* this delightful study may, in moments of confidence, venture to say a little more what it thinks of itself.

It must take itself seriously for the public to take it to. The old superstition about fiction being "wicked" has doubtless died out in England; but the spirit of it lingers in a certain

***which:** 선행사는 interest.

oblique regard directed toward any story which does not more or less admit that it is only a joke. Even the most jocular novel feels in some degree the weight of the proscription that was formerly directed against literary levity: the jocularity does not always succeed in passing for orthodoxy. It is still expected, though perhaps people are ashamed to say it, that a production which is after all only a "make-believe" (for what else is a "story"?) shall be in some degree apologetic — shall renounce the pretension of attempting really to represent life. This, of course, any sensible, wide-awake story declines to do, for it quickly perceives that the tolerance granted to it on such a condition is only an attempt to stifle it disguised in the form of generosity. The old evangelical hostility to the novel, which was as explicit as it was narrow, and which regarded it as little less favorable to our immortal part than a stage play, was in reality far less insulting. The only reason for the existence of a novel is that it does attempt to represent life. When it relinquishes this attempt, the same attempt that we see on the canvas of the painter, it will have arrived at a very strange pass.* It is not expected of the picture that it will make itself humble in order to be forgiven; and the analogy between the art of the painter and the art of the novelist is, so far as I am able to see, complete. Their inspiration is the same, their process (allowing for the different quality of the vehicle) is the same, their success is the same. They may learn from each other, they may explain and sustain each other. Their cause is the same, and the honor of one is the honor of another. The Mahometans think a picture an unholy thing, but it is a long time since any Christian did, and it is therefore the more odd that in the Christian mind the traces (dissimulated though they may be) of a suspicion of the sister art should linger to this day. The only effectual way to lay it to rest* is to emphasize the analogy to which I just alluded — to insist on the fact that as the picture is reality, so the novel is history. That is the only general description (which does it justice) that we

***pass:** 「난관」.
***lay it to rest:** 「그것(낡은 관념)을 잠재우다, 제거하다」.

may give of the novel. But history also is allowed to represent life; it is not, any more than painting, expected to apologize. The subject matter of fiction is stored up likewise in documents and records, and if it will not give itself away,* as they say in California, it must speak with assurance, with the tone of the historian. Certain accomplished novelists have a habit of giving themselves away which must often bring tears to the eyes of people who take their fiction seriously. I was lately struck, in reading over many pages of Anthony Trollope; with his want of discretion in this particular.* In a digression, a parenthesis or an aside, he concedes to the reader that he and this trusting friend* are only "making believe." He admits that the events he narrates have not really happened, and that he can give his narrative any turn the reader may like best. Such a betrayal of a sacred office seems to me, I confess, a terrible crime; it is what I mean by the attitude of apology, and it shocks me every whit as much in Trollope as it would have shocked me in Gibbon or Macaulay.* It implies that the novelist is less occupied in looking for the truth (the truth, of course I mean, that he assumes, the premises that we must grant him, whatever they may be) than the historian, and in doing so it deprives him at a stroke* of all his standing room. To represent and illustrate the past, the actions of men, is the task of either writer, and the only difference that I can see is, in proportion as he succeeds, to the honor of the novelist, consisting as it does in his having more difficulty in collecting his evidence, which is so far from being purely literary. It seems to me to give him a great character, the fact that he has at once so much in common with the philosopher and the painter; this double analogy is a magnificent heritage.

It is of all this evidently that Mr. Besant is full when he insists upon the fact that fiction is one of the *fine* arts, deserving

---

***give oneself away:** 「스스로를 배반하다, 자신을 포기하다」.

***in this particular:** 「바로 이 점에 있어서」.

***this trusting friend:** 독자를 지칭함.

***Gibbon, Macaulay:** 두 사람 다 이름난 역사가들. (역사가는 인생의 진실을 다룬다는 자부심이 있다.)

in its turn of all the honors and emoluments that have hitherto been reserved for the successful profession of music, poetry, painting, architecture. It is impossible to insist too much on so important a truth, and the place that Mr. Besant demands for the work of the novelist may be represented, a trifle less abstractly, by saying that he demands not only that it shall be reputed artistic, but that it shall be reputed very artistic indeed. It is excellent that he should have struck this note, for his doing so indicates that there was need of it, that his proposition may be to many people a novelty. One rubs one's eyes at the thought;* but the rest of Mr. Besant's essay confirms the revelation. I suspect in truth that it would be possible to confirm it still further, and that one would not be far wrong in saying that in addition to the people to whom it has never occurred that a novel ought to be artistic, there are a great many others who, if this principle were urged upon them, would be filled with an indefinable mistrust. They would find it difficult to explain their repugnance, but it would operate strongly to put them on their guard. "Art," in our Protestant communities, where so many things have got so strangely twisted about, is supposed in certain circles to have some vaguely injurious effect upon those who make it an important consideration, who let it weigh in the balance. It is assumed to be opposed in some mysterious manner to morality, to amusement, to instruction. When it is embodied in the work of the painter (the scupltor is another affair!) you know what it is: it stands there before you, in the honesty* of pink and green and a gilt frame; you can see the worst of it at a glance, and you can be on your *guard*. But when it is introduced into literature it becomes more insidious — there is danger of its hurting you before you know it. Literature should be either instructive or amusing, and there is in many minds an impression that these artistic preoccupations, the search for form, contribute to neither end, interfere indeed with both. They are too frivolous to be edifying, and too

***One...thought:** 「그 의견에 의아해 하다」.
***honesty:** 「숨김 없는 상태」.

serious to be diverting; and they are moreover priggish and paradoxical and superfluous. That, I think, represents the manner in which the latent thought of many people who read novels as an exercise in skipping would explain itself if it were to become articulate. They would argue, of course, that a novel ought to be "good," but they would interpret this term in a fashion of their own, which indeed would vary considerably from one critic to another. One would say that being good means representing virtuous and aspiring characters, placed in prominent positions; another would say that it depends on a "happy ending," on a distribution at the last of prizes, pensions, husbands, wives, babies, millions, appended paragraphs, and cheerful remarks. Another still would say that it means being full of incident and movement, so that we shall wish to jump ahead, to see who was the mysterious stranger, and if the stolen will was ever found, and shall not be distracted from this pleasure by any tiresome analysis or "description." But they would all agree that the "artistic" idea would spoil some of their fun. One would hold it accountable for all the description,* another would see it revealed in the absence of sympathy. Its hostility to a happy ending would be evident, and it might even in some cases render any ending at all impossible. The "ending" of a novel is, for many persons, like that of a good dinner, a course of dessert and ices, and the artist in fiction is regarded as a sort of meddlesome doctor who forbids agreeable aftertastes. It is therefore true that this conception of Mr. Besant's of the novel as a superior form encounters not only a negative but a positive indifference. It matters little that as a work of art it should really be as little or as much of its essence to supply happy endings, sympathetic characters, and an objective tone, as if it were a work of mechanics: the association of ideas, however incongruous, might easily be too much for it if an eloquent voice were not sometimes raised to call attention to the fact that it is at once as free and as serious a branch of

---

***One would...the description:** Artistic idea가 모두 (재미없는) 서술을 만들어내는 것이라고 주장할 것이다.

literature as any other.

Certainly this might sometimes be doubted in presence of the enormous number of works of fiction that appeal to the credulity of our generation, for it might easily seem that there could be no great character in a commodity so quickly and easily produced. It must be admitted that good novels are much compromised* by bad ones, and that the field at large suffers discredit from overcrowding. I think, however, that this injury is only superficial, and that the superabundance of written fiction proves nothing against the principle itself. It has been vulgarized, like all other kinds of literature, like everything else today, and it has proved more than some kinds accessible to vulgarization. But there is as much difference as there ever was between a good novel and a bad one: the bad is swept with all the daubed canvases* and spoiled marble* into some unvisited limbo, or infinite rubbish yard beneath the back windows of the world, and the good subsists and emits its light and stimulates our desire for perfection. As I shall take the liberty of making but a single criticism of Mr. Besant, whose tone is so full of the love of his art, I may as well have done with it at once. He seems to me to mistake in attempting to say so definitely beforehand what sort of an affair the good novel will be. To indicate the danger of such an error as that has been the purpose of these few pages; to suggest that certain traditions on the subject, applied *a priori*, have already had much to answer for,* and that the good health of an art which undertakes so immediately to reproduce life must demand that it be perfectly free. It lives upon exercise, and the very meaning of exercise is freedom. The only obligation to which in advance we may hold a novel, without incurring the accusation of being arbitrary, is that it be interesting. That general responsibility rests upon it, but it is the only one I can

---

***be compromised:** (남과 연루되어) 「명예가 손상되다」.
***daubed canvases:** 「때묻은 책 뚜껑」.
***spoiled marbles:** 「더러워진 대리석 무늬의 장식 뱃지」(대개 책 뚜껑 다음에 있음). 즉 헌 통속소설책을 의미함.
***have much to answer for:** 「책임져야 할 일(과오)이 많이 생기다」.

think of. The ways in which it is at liberty to accomplish this result (of interesting us) strike me as innumerable, and such as can only suffer from being marked out* or fenced in* by prescription. They are as various as the temperament of man, and they are successful* in proportion as they reveal a particular mind, different from others. A novel is in its broadest definition a personal, a direct impression of life: that, to begin with, constitutes its value, which is greater or less according to the intensity of the impression. But there will be no intensity at all, and therefore no value, unless there is freedom to feel and say. The tracing of a line to be followed, of a tone to be taken, of a form to be filled out, is a limitation of that freedom and a suppression of the very thing that we are most curious about. The form, it seems to me, is to be appreciated after the fact: then the author's choice has been made, his standard has been indicated; then we can follow lines and directions and compare tones and resemblances. Then in a word we can enjoy one of the most charming of pleasures, we can estimate quality, we can apply the test of execution. The execution belongs to the author alone; it is what is most personal to him, and we measure him by that. The advantage, the luxury, as well as the torment and responsibility of the novelist, is that there is no limit to what he may attempt as an executant — no limit to his possible experiments, efforts, discoveries, successes. Here it is especially that he works, step by step, like his brother of the brush, of whom we may always say that he has painted his picture in a manner best known to himself. His manner is his secret, not necessarily a jealous* one. He cannot disclose it as a general thing if he would; he would be at a loss to teach it to others. I say this with a due recollection of having insisted on the community* of method of the artist who paints a picture and the

---

***make out:** 「지적하다」.
***fence in:** 「제한하다」.
***successful:** 여기서의 뜻은 「틀렸음에도 불구하고 널리 통용되는」의 반어적 의미.
***jealous:** 「비밀스러운」.
***community:** 「공통성」.

artist who writes a novel. The painter *is* able to teach the rudiments of his practice, and it is possible, from the study of good work (granted the aptitude), both to learn how to paint and to learn how to write. Yet it remains true, without injury to *rapprochement,* that the literary artist would be obliged to say to his pupil much more than the other, "Ah, well, you must do it as you can!" It is a question of degree, a matter of delicacy. If there are exact sciences, there are also exact arts, and the grammar of painting is so much more definite that it makes the difference.

I ought to add, however, that if Mr. Besant says at the beginning of his essay that the "laws of fiction may be laid down and taught with as much precision and exactness as the laws of harmony, perspective, and proportion," he mitigates what might appear to be an extravagance by applying his remark to "general" laws, and by expressing most of these rules in a manner with which it would certainly be unaccommodating to disagree. That the novelist must write from his experience, that his "characters must be real and such as might be met with in actual life"; that "a young lady brought up in a quiet country village should avoid descriptions of garrison life," and "a writer whose friends and personal experiences belong to the lower middle class should carefully avoid introducing his characters into society"; that one should enter one's notes in a common-place book; that one's figures should be clear in outline; that making them clear by some trick of speech or of carriage is a bad method, and "describing them at length" is a worse one; that English fiction should have a "conscious moral purpose"; that "it is almost impossible to estimate too highly the value of careful workmanship—that is, of style"; that "the most important point of all is the story," that "the story is everything": these are principles with most of which it is surely impossible not to sympathize. That remark about the lower middle-class writer and his knowing his place is perhaps rather chilling; but for the rest I should find it difficult to dissent from any one of these recommendations. At the same time, I should find it difficult positively to assent to them, with the exception, perhaps, of the injunction as to entering one's notes in a common-place book. They scarcely seem to me to have the quality that Mr. Besant attributes to the rules of the novelist—the "precision and exactness" of "the laws of harmony, perspective, and proportion." They are suggestive, they are even inspiring, but they are not exact, though they are doubtless as much so as the case admits of: which is a proof of that liberty of interpretation for which I just contended. For the value of these different injunctions—so beautiful and so vague—is wholly in the meaning one attaches to them. The characters, the situation, which strike one as real will be those that touch and interest one most, but the measure of reality is very difficult to fix. The reality of Don Quixote or of Mr. Micawber* is a very delicate shade; it is a reality so colored by the author's vision that, vivid as it may be, one would hesitate to propose it as a model: one would as it may be, one would hesitate to propose it as a model: one would expose one's self to some very embarrassing questions on the part of a pupil. It goes without saying that you will not write a good novel unless you possess the sense of reality; but it will be difficult to give you a recipe for calling that sense into being.* Humanity is immense, and reality has a myriad forms; the most one can affirm is that some of the flowers of fiction have the odor of it, and others have not; as for telling you in advance how your nosegay should be composed, that is another affair. It is equally excellent and inconclusive to say that one must write from experience; to our supposititious aspirant such a declaration might savor of mockery. What kind of experience is intended, and where does it begin and end? Experience is never limited, and it is never complete; it is an immense sensibility, a kind of huge spiderweb of the finest silken threads suspended in the chamber of consciousness, and catching every air-borne particle in its tissue. It is the very atmosphere of the mind; and when the mind is imaginative—much more when it happens to be that of a man of genius—it takes to itself the faintest

---

***Mr. Micawber:** Dickens의 *David Copperfield*에 나오는 사실적 인물.
***call...into being:** (요술, 주문 따위로) 「...을 존재하게 하다, 나타나게 하다」.

hints of life, it converts the very pulses of the air into revelations. The young lady living in a village has only to be a damsel upon whom nothing is lost to make it quite unfair (as it seems to me) to declare to her that she shall have nothing to say about the military.* Greater miracles have been seen than that, imagination assisting,* she should speak the truth about some of these gentlemen.* I remember an English novelist, a woman of genius, telling me that she was much commended for the impression she had managed to give in one of her tales of the nature and way of life of the French Protestant youth. She had been asked where she learned so much about this recondite being, she had been congratulated on her peculiar opportunities. These opportunities consisted in her having once, in Paris, as she ascended a staircase, passed an open door where, in the household of a *pasteur,** some of the young Protestants were seated at table round a finished meal. The glimpse made a picture; it lasted only a moment, but that moment was experience. She had got her direct personal impression, and she turned out* her type. She knew what youth was, and what Protestantism; she also had the advantage of having seen what it was to be French, so that she converted these ideas into a concrete image and produced a reality. Above all, however, she was blessed with the faculty which when you give it an inch takes an ell,* and which for the artist is a much greater source of strength than any accident of residence or of place in the social scale. The power to guess the unseen from the seen, to trace the implication of things, to judge the whole piece by the pattern, the condition of feeling life in general so completely that you are well on your way

---

***The young lady...about the military:** 「무슨 사건이나 이야기든지 놓치지 않는 촌에 사는 아가씨이기만 하면 군대에 관해서는 그녀가 아무 말도 할 수 없다고 단언하는 것은 무척 부당한 일이 될 것이다」.

***imagination assisting:** 「상상력이 도움을 주면」.

***these gentlemen:** 「군인들」.

***pasteur:** (프랑스의 개신교) 「목사」.

***turn out:** 「만들어내다」.

***ell:** 「45 인치」.

to* knowing any particular corner of it — this cluster of gifts may almost be said to constitute experience, and they occur in country and in town, and in the most differing stages of education. If experience consists of impressions, it may be said that impressions *are* experience, just as (have we not seen it?) they are the very air we breathe. Therefore, if I should certainly say to a novice, "Write from experience and experience only," I should feel that this was rather a tantalizing monition if I were not careful immediately to add, "Try to be one of the people on whom nothing is lost!"

I am far from intending by this to minimize the importance of exactness—of truth of detail. One can speak best from one's own taste, and I may therefore venture to say that the air of reality (solidity of specification) seems to me to be the supreme virtue of a novel — the merit on which all its other merits (including that conscious moral purpose of which Mr. Besant speaks) helplessly and submissively depend. If it be not there, they are all as nothing, and if these be there, they owe their effect to the success with which the author has produced the illusion of life. The cultivation of this success, the study of this exquisite process, form, to my taste, the beginning and the end of the art of the novelist. They are his inspiration, his despair, his reward, his torment, his delight. It is here in very truth that he competes with life; it is here that he competes with his brother the painter in *his* attempt to render the look of things, the look that conveys their meaning, to catch the color, the relief, the expression, the surface, the substance of the human spectacle. It is in regard to this that Mr. Besant is well inspired when he bids him take notes. He cannot possibly take too many, he cannot possibly take enough.* All life solicits him, and to "render" the simplest surface, to produce the most momentary illusion, is a very complicated business. His case would be easier, and the rule would be more exact, if Mr. Besant had been able to tell him what notes to take. But this, I fear, he can never learn in any manual; it is the business of his life. He has to

---

***be well on one's way to...:** 「...의 길로 옳게 들어서다」.

***he cannot...enough:** note를 아무리 많이 해도 충분하지 못할 판이다.

take a great many in order to select a few, he has to work them up as he can, and even the guides and philosophers who might have most to say to him must leave him alone when it comes to the application of precepts, as we leave the painter in communion with his palette. That his characters "must be clear in outline," as Mr. Besant says — he feels that down to his boots*; but how he shall make them so is a secret between his good angel* and himself. It would be absurdly simple if he could be taught that a great deal of "description" would make them so, or that on the contrary the absence of description and the cultivation of dialogue, or the absence of dialogue and the multiplication of "incident," would rescue him from his difficulties. Nothing, for instance, is more possible than that he be of a turn of mind for* which this odd, literal opposition of description and dialogue, incident and description, has little meaning and light. People often talk of these things as if they had a kind of internecine distinctness, instead of melting into each other at every breath, and being intimately associated parts of one general effort of expression. I cannot imagine composition existing in a series of blocks, nor conceive, in any novel worth discussing at all, of a passage of description that is not in its intention narrative, a passage of dialogue that is not in its intention descriptive, a touch of truth of any sort that does not partake of the nature of incident, or an incident that derives its interest from any other source than the general and only source of the success of a work of art — that of being illustrative. A novel is a living thing, all one and continuous, like any other organism, and in proportion as it lives will it be found, I think, that in each of the parts there is something of each of the other parts. The critic who over the close texture of a finished work shall pretend to trace a geography of items will mark some frontiers as artificial, I fear, as any that have been known to history. There is an old-fashioned distinction between the novel of character and the novel of incident which must have cost

---

***down to one's boots:** 「철저하게」.

***good angel:** 그를 보살펴 주는 천사, 즉 영감.

***of a turn of mind for...:** 「...한 정신의 습성을 가진」.

many a smile to the intending fabulist* who was keen about his work. It appears to me as little to the point as the equally celebrated distinction between the novel and the romance — to answer as little to any reality. There are bad novels and good novels, as there are bad pictures and good pictures; but that is the only distinction in which I see any meaning, and I can as little imagine speaking of a novel of character as I can imagine speaking of a picture of character. When one says picture one says of character, when one says novel one says of incident, and the terms may be transposed at will. What is character but the determination of incident? What is incident but the illustration of character? What is either a picture or a novel that is *not* of character? What else do we seek in it and find in it? It is an incident for a woman to stand up with her hand resting on a table and look out at you in a certain way; or if it be not an incident I think it will be hard to say what it is. At the same time it is an expression of character. If you say you don't see it (character in *that — allons donc!**), this is exactly what the artist who has reasons of his own for thinking he *does* see it undertakes to show you. When a young man makes up his mind that he has not faith enough after all to enter the church* as he intended, that is an incident, though you may not hurry to the end of the chapter to see whether perhaps he doesn't change once more. I do not say that these are extraordinary or startling incidents. I do not pretend to estimate the degree of interest proceeding from them, for this will depend upon the skill of the painter. It sounds almost puerile to say that some incidents are intrinsically much more important than others, and I need not take this precaution after having professed my sympathy for the major ones in remarking that the only classification of the novel that I can understand is into that which has life and that which has it not.

The novel and the romance, the novel of incident and that of character — these clumsy separations appear to me to

***the intending fabulist:** 정작 소설을 쓰고자 하는 이. 즉, 뜻있는 소설가.
******allons donc*!: "come now!" 「자！」
***enter the church:** 「성직자가 되다」.

have been made by critics and readers for their own convenience, and to help them out of some of their occasional queer predicaments, but to have little reality or interest for the producer, from whose point of view it is of course that we are attempting to consider the art of fiction. The case is the same with another shadowy category which Mr. Besant apparently is disposed to set up — that of the "modern English novel"; unless indeed it be that in this matter he has fallen into an accidental confusion of standpoints. It is not quite clear whether he intends the remarks in which he alludes to it to be didactic or historical. It is as difficult to suppose a person intending to write a modern English as to suppose him writing an ancient English novel: that is a label which begs the question.* One writes the novel, one paints the picture, of one's language and of one's time, and calling it modern English will not, alas! make the difficult task any easier. No more, unfortunately, will calling this or that work of one's fellow artist a romance — unless it be, of course, simply for the pleasantness of the thing, as for instance when Hawthorne gave this heading to his story of *Blithedale*.* The French, who have brought the theory of fiction to remarkable completeness, have but one name for the novel, and have not attempted smaller things in it, that I can see, for that. I can think of no obligation to which the "romancer" would not be held equally with the novelist; the standard of execution is equally high for each. Of course it is of execution that we are talking — that being the only point of a novel that is open to contention. This is perhaps too often lost sight of,* only to produce interminable confusions and cross purposes. We must grant the artist his subject, his idea, his *donnée:** our criticism is applied only to what he makes of it. Naturally I do not mean that we are bound to like it or find it interesting: in case we do not, our course is perfectly simple — to let it alone. We may

---

***beg the question:** 「논점을 그대로 남겨두다, 선결조건을 내포하다」.

****Blithedale*:** 원명은 *The Blithedale Romance* (1852). 실제로 Hawthorne 자신이 novel과 romance를 구분했다.

***This is...sight of:** 「이 점은 우리가 잊을 때가 많다」.

****donnée*:** 「주어진 것」.

believe that of a certain idea even the most sincere novelist can make nothing at all, and the event* may perfectly justify our belief; but the failure will have been a failure to execute, and it is in the execution that the fatal weakness is recorded. If we pretend to respect the artist at all, we must allow him his freedom of choice, in the face,* in particular cases, of innumerable presumptions that the choice will not fructify. Art derives a considerable part of its beneficial exercise from flying in the face of presumptions, and some of the most interesting experiments of which it is capable are hidden in the bosom of common things. Gustave Flaubert has written a story about the devotion of a servant girl to a parrot,* and the production, highly finished as it is, cannot on the whole be called a success. We are perfectly free to find it flat, but I think it might have been interesting; and I, for my part, am extremely glad he should have written it; it is a contribution to our knowledge of what can be done — or what cannot. Ivan Turgenev has written a tale about a deaf and dumb serf and a lap dog,* and the thing is touching, loving, a little masterpiece. He struck the note of life where Gustave Flaubert missed it — he flew in the face of a presumption and achieved a victory.

Nothing, of course, will ever take the place of the good old fashion of "liking" a work of art or not liking it: the most improved criticism will not abolish that primitive, that ultimate test. I mention this to guard myself from the accusation of intimating that the idea, the subject, of a novel or a picture, does not matter. It matters, to my sense, in the highest degree, and if I might put up a prayer it would be that artists should select none but the richest. Some, as I have already hastened to admit, are much more remunerative than others, and it would be a world happily arranged in which persons intending to treat them should be exempt from confusions and mistakes. This fortunate condition will arrive only, I fear, on

***event:** 「실제의 결과」.
***in the face of...:** 「...에 직면하여, ...에도 불구하고」.
***a story about...to a parrot:** "Un Cœur Simple"이라는 중편소설.
***a tale about...a lap dog:** "Mumu"라는 소설.

the same day that critics become purged from error. Meanwhile, I repeat, we do not judge the artist with fairness unless we say to him, "Oh, I grant you your starting point, because if I did not I should seem to prescribe to you, and heaven forbid I should take that responsibility. If I pretend to tell you what you must not take, you will call upon me to tell you then what you must take; in which case I shall be prettily caught. Moreover, it isn't till I have accepted your data that I can begin to measure you. I have the standard, the pitch; I have no right to tamper with your flute and then criticize your music. Of course I may not care for your idea at all; I may think it silly, or stale, or unclean; in which case I wash my hands of you altogether.* I may content myself with believing that you will not have succeeded in being interesting, but I shall, of course, not attempt to demonstrate it, and you will be as indifferent to me as I am to you. I needn't remind you that there are all sorts of tastes: who can know it better? Some people, for excellent reasons, don't like to read about carpenters; others, for reasons even better, don't like to read about courtesans. Many object to Americans. Others (I believe they are mainly editors and publishers) won't look at Italians. Some readers don't like quiet subjects; others don't like bustling ones. Some enjoy a complete illusion, others the consciousness of large concessions. They choose their novels accordingly, and if they don't care about your idea they won't, *a fortiori,* * care about your treatment."

So that it comes back very quickly, as I have said, to the liking: in spite of M. Zola, who reasons less powerfully than he represents, and who will not reconcile himself to this absoluteness of taste, thinking that there are certain things that people ought to like, and that they can be made to like. I am quite at a loss to imagine anything (at any rate in this matter of fiction) that people *ought* to like or to dislike. Selection will be sure to take care of itself, for it has a constant motive behind it. That motive is simply experience. As people feel life, so they will feel the art that is most closely related to it.

***I wash...altogether:** 「너와는 완전히 결별이다」.

***a fortiori**: 'all the more'.

This closeness of relation is what we should never forget in talking of the effort of the novel. Many people speak of it as a factitious, artificial form, a product of ingenuity, the business of which is to alter and arrange the things that surround us, to translate them into conventional, traditional molds. This, however, is a view of the matter which carries us but a very short way, condemns the art to an eternal repetition of a few familiar *clichés,** cuts short its development, and leads us straight up to a dead wall. Catching the very note and trick, the strange irregular rhythm of life, that is the attempt whose strenuous force keeps Fiction upon her feet.* In proportion as in what she offers us we see life *without* rearrangement do we feel that we are touching the truth; in proportion as we see it *with* rearrangement do we feel that we are being put off* with a substitute, a compromise and convention. It is not uncommon to hear an extraordinary assurance of remark in regard to this matter of rearranging, which is often spoken of as if it were the last word of art. Mr. Besant seems to me in danger of falling into the great error with his rather unguarded talk about "selection." Art is essentially selection, but it is a selection whose main care is to be typical, to be inclusive. For many people art means rose-colored windowpanes, and selection means picking a bouquet for Mrs. Grundy.* They will tell you glibly that artistic considerations have nothing to do with the disagreeable, with the ugly; they will rattle off* shallow commonplaces about the province of art and the limits of art till you are moved to some wonder in return as to the province and the limits of ignorance. It appears to me that no one can ever have made a seriously artistic attempt

---

**clichés*: 「판에 박은 듯이 진부하고 상투적인 표현법」.

***keep...upon one's feet:** 「...을 계속 존립하게 하다」. Fiction은 여기서 여성으로 의인화되었다.

***put off:** 「푸대접하다」.

***Mrs. Grundy:** 도덕적인 이유를 들어 남을 비난하기 잘 하는 인물(Tom Morton의 희극 *Speed the Plough*(1798)에서 계속 언급되는 여인). 그러므로 통념상 이른바 selection은 도덕율에 저촉되지 않는 이야기만 골라 다룬다는 것.

***rattle off:** 「지껄여대다」.

without becoming conscious of an immense increase — a kind of revelation — of freedom. One perceives in that case — by the light of a heavenly ray — that the province of art is all life, all feeling, all observation, all vision. As Mr. Besant so justly intimates, it is all experience. That is a sufficient answer to those who maintain that it must not touch the sad things of life, who stick into its divine unconscious bosom little prohibitory inscriptions on the end of sticks, such as we see in public gardens — "It is forbidden to walk on the grass; it is forbidden to touch the flowers; it is not allowed to introduce dogs or to remain after dark; it is requested to keep to the right." The young aspirant in the line of fiction whom we continue to imagine will do nothing without taste, for in that case his freedom would be of little use to him; but the first advantage of his taste will be to reveal to him the absurdity of the little sticks and tickets. If he have taste, I must add, of course he will have ingenuity, and my disrespectful reference to that quality just now was not meant to imply that it is useless in fiction. But it is only a secondary aid; the first is a capacity for receiving straight impressions.

Mr. Besant has some remarks on the question of "the story" which I shall not attempt to criticize, though they seem to me to contain a singular ambiguity, because I do not think I understand them. I cannot see what is meant by talking as if there were a part of a novel which is the story and part of it which for mystical reasons is not — unless indeed the distinction be made in a sense in which it is difficult to suppose that anyone shoud attempt to convey anything. "The story," if it represents anything, represents the subject, the idea, the *donnée* of the novel; and there is surely no "school" — Mr. Besant speaks of a school — which urges that a novel should be all treatment and no subject. There must assuredly be something to treat; every school is intimately conscious of that. This sense of the story being the idea, the starting point, of the novel, is the only one that I see in which it can be spoken of as something different from its organic whole; and since in proportion as the work is successful the idea permeates and penetrates it, informs and animates it, so that every word and every punctuation point contribute directly to the expression, in that proportion do we lose our sense of the story being a blade which may be drawn more or less out of its sheath. The story and the novel, the idea and the form, are the needle and thread, and I never heard of a guild of tailors who recommended the use of the thread without the needle, or the needle without the thread. Mr. Besant is not the only critic who may be observed to have spoken as if there were certain things in life which constitute stories, and certain others which do not. I find the same odd implication in an entertaining article in the *Pall Mall Gazette,* devoted, as it happens, to Mr. Besant's lecture. "The story is the thing!"* says this graceful writer, as if with a tone of opposition to some other idea. I should think it was, as every painter who, as the time for "sending in"* his picture looms in the distance, finds himself still in quest of a subject — as every belated artist not fixed about his theme will heartily agree. There are some subjects which speak to us and others which do not, but he would be a clever man who should undertake to give a rule — an index expurgatorius* — by which the story and the no-story should be known apart. It is impossible (to me at least) to imagine any such rule which shall not be altogether arbitrary. The writer in the *Pall Mall* opposes the delightful (as I suppose) novel of *Margot la Balafrée** to certain tales in which "Bostonian nymphs" appear to have "rejected English dukes for psychological reasons."* I am not acquainted with the romance just designated, and can scarcely forgive the *Pall Mall* critic for not mentioning the name of the author, but the title appears to refer to a lady who may have received a

---

***"The story is the thing!":** "이야기야말로 중요한 것이다."

***the time for "sending in":** 「작품 제출 마감 일자」.

***index expurgatorius:** 「카톨릭의 금서목록」. (금서목록을 작성하듯 story와 no-story를 명확히 구분할 방법을 고안하는 사람은 똑똑한 친구이겠다) 〈비꼬는 말〉.

****Margot la Balafrée*:** Fortuné Du Boisgobey가 1884년에 발표한 소설. "Balafrée"는 "상처가 있는 여자"라는 뜻.

***Bostonian...psychological reasons:** James 자신의 소설 *An International Episode*(1879), *The Portait of a Lady*(1881)를 빗대어 언급하는 말.

scar in some heroic adventure. I am inconsolable at not being acquainted with this episode, but am utterly at a loss to see why it is a story when the rejection (or acceptance) or a duke is not, and why a reason, psychological or other, is not a subject when a cicatrix is. They are all particles of the multitudinous life with which the novel deals, and surely no dogma which pretends to make it lawful to touch the one and unlawful to touch the other will stand for a moment on its feet. It is the special picture that must stand or fall, according as it seem to possess truth or to lack it. Mr. Besant does not, to my sense, light up the subject* by intimating that a story must, under penalty of not being a story,* consist of "adventures." Why of adventures more than of green spectacles? He mentions a category of impossible things, and among them he places "fiction without adventure." Why without adventure, more than without matrimony, or celibacy, or parturition, or cholera, or hydropathy, or Jansenism? This seems to me to bring the novel back to the hapless little role of being an artificial, ingenious thing — bring it down from its large, free character of an immense and exquisite correspondence with life. And what *is* adventure, when it comes to that,* and by what sign is the listening pupil to recognize it? It is an adventure — an immense one — for me to write this little article; and for a Bostonian nymph to reject an English duke is an adventure only less stirring, I should say, than for an English duke is an adventure only less stirring, I should say, than for an English duke to be rejected by a Bostonian nymph. I see dramas within dramas in that, and innumerable points of view. A psychological reason is, to my imagination, an object adorably pictorial; to catch the tint of its complexion — I feel as if that idea might inspire one to Titianesque* efforts. There are few things more exciting to me, in short, than a psychological reason, and yet, I protest, the novel seems to me

---

***light up the subject:** 「그 문제를 밝히다」.

***under...story:** 「그렇지 않을 경우엔 이야기가 될 수 없다는 조건 하에서」.

***when...that:** 「그 문제에 관하여 말하자면」. 여기서 it=adventure.

***Titianesque:**: 르네상스 시대의 이탈리아의 화가 Titian 같은. Titian 은 육감적이고 극적인 화풍을 보여주고 있다.

the most magnificent form of art. I have just been reading, at the same time, the delightful story of *Treasure Island,* by Mr. Robert Louis Stevenson and, in a manner less consecutive, the last tale from M. Edmond de Goncourt, which is entitled *Chérie.** One of these works treats of murders, mysteries, islands of dreadful renown, hairbreadth escapes, miraculous coincidences, and buried doubloons. The other treats of a little French girl who lived in a fine house in Paris, and died of wounded sensibility because no one would marry her. I call *Treasure Island* delightful because it appears to me to have succeeded wonderfully in what it attempts; and I venture to bestow no epithet upon *Chérie,* which strikes me as having failed deplorably in what it attempts — that is, in tracing the development of the moral consciousness of a child. But one of these productions strikes me as exactly as much of a novel as the other, and as having a "story" quite as much. The moral consciousness of a child is as much a part of life as the islands of the Spanish Main, and the one sort of geography seems to me to have those "surprises" of which Mr. Besant speaks quite as much as the other. For myself (since it comes back in the last resort,* as I say, to the preference of the individual), the picture of the child's experience has the advantage that I can at successive steps (an immense luxury, near to the "sensual pleasure" of which Mr. Besant's critic in the *Pall Mall* speaks) say Yes or No, as it may be, to what the artist puts before me. I have been a child in fact, but I have been on a quest for a buried treasure only in supposition, and it is a simple accident that with M. de Goncourt I should have for the most part to say No. With George Eliot, when she painted that country with a far other intelligence, I always said Yes.

The most interesting part of Mr. Besant's lecture is unfortunately the briefest passage — his very cursory allusion to the "conscious moral purpose" of the novel. Here again it is not very clear whether he be recording a fact or laying down a principle; it is a great pity that in the latter case he should not

---

Chérie: 프랑스의 작가 Edmond de Concourt (1822-96) 의 작품.
***in the last resort:** 「마침내는, 끝에 가서는」.

have developed his idea. This branch of the subject is of immense importance, and Mr. Besant's few words point to considerations of the widest reach, not to be lightly disposed of. He will have treated the art of fiction but superficially who is not prepared to go every inch of the way that these considerations will carry him. It is for this reason that at the beginning of these remarks I was careful to notify the reader that my reflections on so large a theme have no pretension to be exhaustive. Like Mr. Besant, I have left the question of the morality of the novel till the last, and at the last I find I have used up my space. It is a question surrounded with difficulties, as witness the very first that meets us, in the form of a definite question, on the threshold. Vagueness, in such a discussion, is fatal, and what is the meaning of your morality and your conscious moral purpose? Will you not define your terms and explain how (a novel being a picture) a picture can be either moral or immoral? You wish to paint a moral picture or carve a moral statue: will you not tell us how you would set about it?* We are discussing the Art of Fiction; questions of art are questions (in the widest sense) of execution; questions of morality are quite another affair, and will you not let us see how it is that you find it so easy to mix them up? These things are so clear to Mr. Besant that he has deduced from them a law which he sees embodied in English fiction, and which is "a truly admirable thing and a great cause for congratulation." It is a great cause for congratulation indeed when such thorny problems become as smooth as silk. I may add that in so far as Mr. Besant perceives that in point of fact English fiction has addressed itself preponderantly to these delicate questions he will appear to many people to have made a vain discovery. They will have been positively struck, on the contrary, with the moral timidity of the usual English novelist; with his (or with her) aversion to face the difficulties with which on every side the treatment of reality bristles. He is apt to be extremely shy (whereas the picture that Mr. Besant draws is a picture of boldness),

---

*set about: 「착수하다」.

and the sign of his work, for the most part, is a cautious silence on certain subjects. In the English novel (by which of course I mean the American as well), more than in any other, there is a traditional difference between that which people know and that which they agree to admit that they know, that which they see and that which they speak of, that which they feel to be a part of life and that which they allow to enter into literature. There is the great difference, in short, between what they talk of in conversation and what they talk of in print. The essence of moral energy is to survey the whole field, and I should directly reverse Mr. Besant's remark and say not that the English novel has a purpose, but that it has a diffidence. To what degree a purpose in a work of art is a source of corruption I shall not attempt to inquire; the one that seems to me least dangerous is the purpose of making a perfect work. As for our novel, I may say lastly on this score that as we find it in England today it strikes me as addressed in a large degree to "young people," and that this in itself constitutes a presumption that it will be rather shy. There are certain things which it is generally agreed not to discuss, not even to mention, before young people. That is very well, but the absence of discussion is not a symptom of the moral passion. The purpose of the English novel – "a truly admirable thing, and a great cause for congratulation" – strikes me therefore as rather negative.

There is one point at which the moral sense and the artistic sense lie very near together; that is in the light of the very obvious truth that the deepest quality of a work of art will always be the quality of the mind of the producer. In proportion as that intelligence is fine will the novel, the picture, the statue partake of the substance of beauty and truth. To be constituted of such elements is, to my vision, to have purpose enough. No good novel will ever proceed from a superficial mind; that seems to me an axiom which, for the artist in fiction, will cover all needful moral ground: if the youthful aspirant take it to heart it will illuminate for him many of the mysteries of "purpose." There are many other useful things that might be said to him, but I have come to the end of my article, and can only touch them as I pass. The critic in the *Pall Mall Gazette,* whom I have already quoted, draws attention to the danger, in speaking of the art of fiction, of generalizing. The danger that he has in mind is rather, I imagine, that of particularizing, for there are some comprehensive remarks which, in addition to those embodied in Mr. Besant's suggestive lecture, might without fear of misleading him be addressed to the ingenuous student. I should remind him first of the magnificence of the form that is open to him, which offers to sight so few restrictions and such innumerable opportunities. The other arts, in comparison, appear confined and hampered; the various conditions under which they are exercised are so rigid and definite. But the only condition that I can think of attaching to the composition of the novel is, as I have already said, that it be sincere. This freedom is a splendid privilege, and the first lesson of the young novelist is to learn to be worthy of it. "Enjoy it as it deserves," I should say to him; "take possession of it, explore it to its utmost extent, publish it, rejoice in it. All life belongs to you, and do not listen either to those who would shut you up into corners of it and tell you that it is only here and there that art inhabits, or to those who would persuade you that this heavenly messenger wings her way outside of life altogether breathing a superfine air, and turning away her head from the truth of things. There is no impression of life, no manner of seeing it and feeling it, to which the plan of the novelist may not offer a place; you have only to remember that talents so dissimilar as those of Alexandre Dumas and Jane Austen, Charles Dickens and Gustave Flaubert have worked in this field with equal glory. Do not think too much about optimism and pessimism; try and catch the color of life itself. In France today we see a prodigious effort (that of Emile Zola,* to whose solid and serious work no explorer of the capacity of the novel can allude without respect), we see an extraordinary effort vitiated by a spirit of pessimism on a narrow basis. M. Zola is

*Zola에 대하여 James는 선구적 연구를 했다. 여기 나온 부분은 *Notes on Novelists* (1914)에 실림.

magnificent, but he strikes an English reader as ignorant; he has an air of working in the dark; if he had as much light as energy, his results would be of the highest value. As for the aberrations of a shallow optimism, the ground (of English fiction especially) is strewn with their brittle particles as with broken glass. If you must indulge in conclusions, let them have the taste of a wide knowledge. Remember that your first duty is to be as complete as possible — to make as perfect a work. Be generous and delicate and pursue the prize."

Thomas Earnest Hulme

(1883—1917)

케임브리지에 진학했으나 폭력 행위로 퇴학 당하여 혼자 철학 공부를 하는 한편 유럽을 널리 여행하였다. 오래 지난 후 그를 똑똑히 여긴 철학자 베르그송의 주선으로 케임브리지에 복교했으나, 곧 자퇴하여 계속 혼자 철학 공부를 하고 Ezra Pound와 사귀며 imagist 시를 몇 편 쓰고 젊은 지성인, 예술가들과 교유하며 철학 및 문학 평론을 전위적인 잡지에 기고했다. 1차 대전이 발발하자 지원 입대하여 전사했다.

그의 철학 및 문학 평론 중 중요한 것들을 그의 친구이자 비평가인 Herbert Read가 *Speculations*(1924)란 제목으로 출판했다. 나머지 평론 및 잡문은 S. Hynes가 ***Further Speculations*** (1955)에 모아놓았다.

흄은 전 세대의 낭만주의를 비판하는 입장에서 출발한다. 그에 의하면 낭만주의는 근본에 있어 오도된 인본주의로서, 개인 자신에 대한 과신, 인간의 완전성의 성취가 가능하다는 믿음, 막연하고 불확실한 사고, 감정에의 탐닉을 뜻한다고 보고, 이에 반하여 고전주의는 근본에 있어 종교적인 태도로서, 원죄의식으로 대표되는 인간의 제한성, 타락 가능성, 따라서 필요한 개인적 및 집단적 훈육, 경계가 뚜렷한 "기하학적"이고 정확한 사고 방식 등을 내세운다고 보았다. 자칫하면 낭만주의를 매우 종교적이라 보기 쉬운데, 이것은 종교의 진리를 오해한 결과라는 것이다.

흄의 문학사상은 세기말의 낭만주의의 퇴폐적 성향에 대한 반발의 한 형태이다. 개인의 감정적 자유는 퇴폐의 무질서를 낳았고, 그러한 무질서에서 견고한 문학은 나올 수 없다고 믿어졌다. 파운드, 엘리어트 등이 반낭만적인 문학을 수립하는 데에 흄의 영향은 다대하였다.

Romanticism and Classicism (1924)

I WANT to maintain that after a hundred years of romanticism, we are in for* a classical revival, and that the particular weapon of this new classical spirit, when it works in verse, will be fancy. And in this I imply the superiority of fancy — not superior generally or absolutely, for that would be obvious nonsense, but superior in the sense that we use the word good in empirical ethics — good for something, superior for something. I shall have to prove then two things, first that a classical revival is coming, and, secondly, for its particular purposes, fancy will be superior to imagination.

So banal have the terms Imagination and Fancy become that we imagine they must have always been in the language. Their history as two differing terms in the vocabulary of criticism is comparatively short. Originally, of course, they both mean the same thing; they first began to be differentiated by the German writers on aesthetics in the eighteenth century.*

I know that in using the words "classic" and "romantic" I am doing a dangerous thing. They represent five or six different kinds of antithesis, and while I may be using them in one sense you may be interpreting them in another. In this present connection I am using them in a perfectly precise and limited sense. I ought really to have coined a couple of new words, but I prefer to use the ones I have used, as I then conform to the practice of the group of polemical writers who make most use of them at the present day, and have almost succeeded in making them political catchwords. I mean Maurras, Lasserre and all the group connected with *L'Action*

---

*be in for...: 「~하게 되어 있다」.

*이것은 Hulme의 오해. 두 기능의 구별은 18세기 후반 영국에서 시작되었고, Coleridge는 그 이론적 근거를 확정했다.

Française. *

At the present time this is the particular group with which the distinction is most vital. Becuase it has become a party symbol. If you asked a man of a certain set whether he preferred the classics or the romantics, you could deduce from that what his politics were.

The best way of gliding into a proper definition of my terms would be to start with a set of people who are prepared to fight about it — for in them you will have no vagueness. (Other people take the infamous attitude of the person with catholic tastes who says he likes both.)

About a year ago, a man whose name I think was Fauchois gave a lecture at the Odéon* on Racine, in the course of which he made some disparaging remarks about his dullness, lack of invention and the rest of it. This caused an immediate riot: fights took place all over the house; several people were arrested and imprisoned, and the rest of the series of lectures took place with hundreds of gendarmes and detectives scattered all over the place. These people interrupted because the classical ideal is a living thing to them and Racine is the great classic. That is what I call a real vital interest in literature. They regard romanticism as an awful disease from which France had just recovered.

The thing is complicated in their case by the fact that it was romanticism that made the revolution. They hate the revolution, so they hate romanticism.

I make no apology for dragging in politics here; romanticism both in England and France is associated with certain political views, and it is in taking a concrete example of the working out of a principle in action that you can get its best definition.

What was the positive principle behind all the other principles of '89?* I am talking here of the revolution in as far as it

---

******L'Action Française*:** 프랑스의 극우왕당파운동. 이 운동의 주창자 Charles Maurras와 그의 추종자 Lassere는 문학에 있어서는 고전주의를 표방.

***Odéon:** 파리에 있는 극장 이름.

***'89:** 프랑스혁명이 일어난 해인 1789년.

was an idea; I leave out material causes — they only produce the forces. The barriers which could easily have resisted or guided these forces had been previously rotted away by ideas. This always seems to be the case in successful changes; the privileged class is beaten only when it has lost faith in itself, when it has itself been penetrated with the ideas which are working against it.

It was not the rights of man — that was a good solid practical war-cry. The thing which created enthusiasm, which made the revolution practically a new religion, was something more positive than that. People of all classes, people who stood to lose by it, were in a positive ferment about the idea of liberty. There must have been some idea which enabled them to think that something positive could come out of so essentially negative a thing. There was, and here I get my definition of romanticism. They had been taught by Rousseau that man was by nature good, that it was only bad laws and customs that had suppressed him. Remove all these and the infinite possibilities of man would have a chance. This is what made them think that something positive could come out of disorder, this is what created the religious enthusiasm. Here is the root of all romanticism: that man, the individual, is an infinite reservoir of possibilities; and if you can so rearrange society by the destruction of oppressive order then these possibilities will have a chance and you will get Progress.

One can define the classical quite clearly as the exact opposite to this. Man is an extraordinarily fixed and limited animal whose nature is absolutely constant. It is only by tradition and organisation that anything decent can be got out of him.

This view was a little shaken at the time of Darwin. You remember his particular hypothesis, that new species came into existence by the cumulative effect of small variations — this seems to admit the possibility of future progress. But at the present day the contrary hypothesis makes headway in the shape of De Vries's* mutation theory, that each

*De Vries, Hugo: (1848-1935). 네덜란드의 유전학자. 돌연변이설을 주장.

new species comes into existence, not gradually by the accumulation of small steps, but suddenly in a jump, a kind of sport, and that once in existence it remains absolutely fixed. This enables me to keep the classical view with an appearance of scientific backing.

Put shortly,* these are the two views, then. One, that man is intrinsically good, spoilt by circumstance; and the other that he is intrinsically limited, but disciplined by order and tradition to something fairly decent. To the one party man's nature is like a well, to the other like a bucket. The view which regards man as a well, a reservoir full of possibilities, I call the romantic; the one which regards him as a very finite and fixed creature, I call the classical.

One may note here that the Church has always taken the classical view since the defeat of the Pelagian heresy* and the adoption of the sane classical dogma of original sin.

It would be a mistake to identify the classical view with that of materialism. On the contrary it is absolutely identical with the normal religious attitude. I should put it in this way: That part of the fixed nature of man is the belief in the Deity. This should be as fixed and true for every man as belief in the existence of matter and in the objective world. It is parallel to appetite, the instinct of sex, and all the other fixed qualities. Now at certain times, by the use of either force or rhetoric, these instincts have been suppressed — in Florence under Savonarola,* in Geneva under Calvin, and here under the Roundheads.* The inevitable result of such a process is that the repressed instinct bursts out in some abnormal direction. So with religion. By the perverted rhetoric of Rationalism, your natural instincts are suppressed and you are converted into an agnostic. Just as in the case of the other instincts,

---

***put shortly:** 「간단히 말해서」.

***Pelagius:** (355–425). St. Augustine의 예정설과 원죄설에 반대하여 인간은 본래 선하게 태어났다고 주장. 나중에 이단으로 억압받음.

***Savonarola:** 15세기 이탈리아의 극단적 종교개혁가로서, 한때 플로렌스를 청교도적 원칙으로 엄격히 다스렸다.

***Roundhead:** 17세기 영국의 공화파(의회파). 머리를 짧게 깎는 관습에서 붙은 이름. 이들은 혁명을 거쳐 영국을 청교도적으로 지배했다.

Nature has her revenge. The instincts that find their right and proper outlet in religion must come out in some other way. You don't believe in a God, so you begin to believe that man is a god. You don't believe in Heaven, so you begin to believe in a heaven on earth. In other words, you get romanticism. The concepts that are right and proper in their own sphere are spread over, and so mess up, falsity and blur the clear outlines of human experience. It is like pouring a pot of treacle over the dinner table. Romanticism then, and this is the best definition I can give of it, is spilt religion.

I must now shirk the difficulty of saying exactly what I mean by romantic and classical in verse. I can only say that it means the result of these two attitudes towards the cosmos, towards man, in so far as it gets reflected in verse. The romantic, because he thinks man infinite, must always be talking about the infinite; and as there is always the bitter contrast between what you think you ought to be able to do and what man actually can, it always tends, in its later stages at any rate, to be gloomy. I really can't go any further than to say it is the reflection of these two temperaments, and point out examples of the different spirits. On the one hand I would take such diverse people as Horace, most of the Elizabethans and the writers of the Augustan age, and on the other side Lamartine,* Hugo, parts of Keats, Coleridge, Byron, Shelley and Swinburne.

I know quite well that when people think of classical and romantic in verse, the contrast at once comes into their mind between, say, Racine and Shakespeare. I don't mean this; the dividing line that I intend is here misplaced a little from the true middle. That Racine is on the extreme classical side I agree, but if you call Shakespeare romantic, you are using a different definition to the one I give. You are thinking of the difference between classic and romantic as being merely one between restraint and exuberance. I should say with Nietzsche that there are two kinds of classicism, the static and the dynamic. Shakespeare is the classic of motion.

***Lamartine, Alphonse de:** 19세기 프랑스의 낭만파 시인.

What I mean by classical in verse, then, is this. That even in the most imaginative flights there is always a holding back, a reservation. The classical poet never forgets this finiteness, this limit of man. He remembers always that he is mixed up with earth. He may jump, but he always returns back; he never flies away into the circumambient gas.

You might say if you wished that the whole of the romantic attitude seems to crystallise in verse round metaphors of flight. Hugo is always flying, flying over abysses, flying up into the eternal gases. The word infinite in every other line.

In the classical attitude you never seem to swing right along to the infinite nothing. If you say an extravagant thing which does exceed the limits inside which you know man to be fastened, yet there is always conveyed in some way at the end an impression of yourself standing outside it, and not quite believing it, or consciously putting it forward as a flourish. You never go blindly into an atmosphere more than the truth, an atmosphere too rarefied for man to breathe for long. You are always faithful to the conception of a limit. It is a question of pitch; in romantic verse you move at a certain pitch of rhetoric which you know, man being what he is, to be a little high-falutin. The kind of thing you get in Hugo or Swinburne. In the coming classical reaction that will feel just wrong. For an example of the opposite thing, a verse written in the proper classical spirit, I can take the song from Cymbeline beginning with "Fear no more the heat of the sun." I am just using this as a parable. I don't quite mean what I say here. Take the last two lines:

> Golden lads and lasses must,
> Like chimney sweepers come to dust.*

Now, no romantic would have ever written that. Indeed, so ingrained is romanticism, so objectionable is this to it, that people have asserted that these were not part of the original song.

Apart from the pun, the thing that I think quite classical

Cymbeline, Ⅳ, ii, 261—2. 여기서 must는 「～해야 한다」와 「곰팡이가 피다」의 뜻을 가진 pun.

is the word lad. Your modern romantic could never write that. He would have to write golden youth, and take up the thing at least a couple of notes in pitch.

I want now to give the reasons which make me think that we are nearing the end of the romantic movement.

The first lies in the nature of any convention or tradition in art. A particular convention or attitude in art has a strict analogy to the phenomena of organic life. It grows old and decays. It has a definite period of life and must die. All the possible tunes get played on it and then it is exhausted; moreover its best period is its youngest. Take the case of the extraordinary efflorescence of verse in the Elizabethan period. All kinds of reasons have been given for this — the discovery of the new world and all the rest of it. There is a much simpler one. A new medium had been given them to play with — namely, blank verse. It was new and so it was easy to play new tunes on it.

The same law holds in other arts. All the masters of painting are born into the world at a time when the particular tradition from which they start is imperfect. The Florentine tradition was just short of full ripeness when Raphael came to Florence, the Bellinesque* was still young when Titian was born in Venice. Landscape was still a toy or an appanage of figure-painting when Turner and Constable* arose to reveal its independent power. When Turner and Constable had done with landscape they left little or nothing for their successors to do on the same lines. Each field of artistic activity is exhausted by the first great artist who gathers a full harvest from it.

This period of exhaustion seems to me to have been reached in romanticism. We shall not get any new efflorescence of verse until we get a new technique, a new convention, to turn ourselves loose in.

Objection might be taken to this. It might be said that a

***Bellinesque:** 15세기, 16세기 초의 Bellini 3부자의 화풍. Bellini는 Titian의 스승.

***Turner, Constable:** 19세기 전반 영국의 최대의 풍경화가들.

century as an organic unity doesn't exist, that I am being deluded by a wrong metaphor, that I am treating a collection of literary people as if they were an organism or state department. Whatever we may be in other things, an objector might urge, in literature in as far as we are anything at all — in as far as we are worth considering — we are individuals, we are persons, and as distinct persons we cannot be subordinated to any general treatment. At any period at any time, an individual poet may be a classic or a romantic just as he feels like it. You at any particular moment may think that you can stand outside a movement. You may think that as an individual you observe both the classic and the romantic spirit and decide from a purely detached point of view that one is superior to the other.

The answer to this is that no one, in a matter of judgment of beauty, can take a detached standpoint in this way. Just as physically you are not born that abstract entity, man,* but the child of particular parents, so you are in matters of literary judgment. Your opinion is almost entirely of the literary history that came just before you, and you are governed by that whatever you may think. Take Spinoza's example of a stone falling to the ground. If it had a conscious mind it would, he said, think it was going to the ground because it wanted to. So you with your pretended free judgment about what is and what is not beautiful. The amount of freedom in man is much exaggerated. That we are free on certain rare occasions, both my religion and the views I get from metaphysics convince me. But many acts which we habitually label free are in reality automatic. It is quite possible for a man to write a book almost automatically. I have read several such products. Some observations were recorded more than twenty years ago by Robertson on reflex speech, and he found that in certain cases of dementia, where the people were quite unconscious so far as the exercise of reasoning went,* that

---

***Just as...man:** 「당신이 육체적으로 저 추상적 존재인 "인간"으로 태어나지 않고」.

***so far as...went:** 「추리작용에 관한 한」.

very intelligent answers were given to a succession of questions on politics and such matters. The meaning of these questions could not possibly have been understood. Language here acted after the manner of a reflex. So that certain extremely complex mechanisms, subtle enough to imitate beauty, can work by themselves — I certainly think that this is the case with judgments about beauty.

I can put the same thing in slightly different form. Here is a question of a conflict of two attitudes, as it might be of two techniques. The critic, while he has to admit that changes from one to the other occur, persists in regarding them as mere variations to a certain fixed normal, just as a pendulum might swing. I admit the analogy of the pendulum as far as movement, but I deny the further consequence of the analogy, the existence of the point of rest, the normal point.

When I say that I dislike the romantics, I dissociate two things: the part of them in which they resemble all great poets, and the part in which they differ and which gives them their character as romantics. It is this minor element which constitutes the particular note of a century, and which, while it excites contemporaries, annoys the next generation. It was precisely that quality in Pope which pleased his friends, which we detest. Now, anyone just before the romantics who felt that, could have predicted that a change was coming. It seems to me that we stand just in the same position now. I think that there is an increasing proportion of people who simply can't stand Swinburne.

When I say that there will be another classical revival I don't necessarily anticipate a return to Pope. I say merely that now is the time for such a revival. Given people of the necessary capacity, it may be a vital thing; without them we may get a formalism something like Pope. When it does come we may not even recognise it as classical. Although it will be classical it will be different because it has passed through a romantic period. To take a parallel example: I remember being very surprised, after seeing the Post Impressionists, to find in Maurice Denis's* account of the matter that they consider

***Maurice Denis:** (1870–1943). 프랑스의 벽화가, 평론가.

themselves classical in the sense that they were trying to impose the same order on the mere flux of new material provided by the impressionist movement, that existed in the more limited materials of the painting before.

There is something now to be cleared away before I get on with my argument, which is that while romanticism is dead in reality, yet the critical attitude appropriate to it still continues to exist. To make this a little clearer: For every kind of verse, there is a corresponding receptive attitude. In a romantic period we demand from verse certain qualities. In a classical period we demand others. At the present time I should say that this receptive attitude has outlasted the thing from which it was formed. But while the romantic tradition has run dry, yet the critical attitude of mind, which demands romantic qualities from verse, still survives. So that if good classical verse were to be written to-morrow very few people would be able to stand it.

I object even to the best of the romantics. I object still more to the receptive attitude. I object to the sloppiness which doesn't consider that a poem is a poem unless it is moaning or whining about something or other. I always think in this connection of the last line of a poem of John Webster's which ends with a request I cordially endorse:

End your moan and come away.*

The thing has got so bad now that a poem which is all dry and hard, a properly classical poem, would not be considered poetry at all. How many people now can lay their hands on their hearts and say they like either Horace or Pope? They feel a kind of chill when they read them.

The dry hardness which you get in the classics is absolutely repugnant to them. Poetry that isn't damp isn't poetry at all. They cannot see that accurate description is a legitimate object of verse. Verse to them always means a bringing in of some of the emotions that are grouped round the word infinite.

*John Webster (1580?-1625)의 비극 *The Duchess of Malfi*, IV, ii. moan이 아니고 groan이라야 옳다.

The essence of poetry to most people is that it must lead them to a beyond of some kind. Verse strictly confined to the earthly and the definite (Keats is full of it) might seem to them to be excellent writing, excellent craftsmanship, but not poetry. So much has romanticism debauched us, that, without some form of vagueness, we deny the highest.

In the classic it is always the light of ordinary day, never the light that never was on land or sea. It is always perfectly human and never exaggerated: man is always man and never a god.

But the awful result of romanticism is that, accustomed to this strange light, you can never live without it. Its effect on you is that of a drug.

There is a general tendency to think that verse means little else than the expression of unsatisfied emotion. People say: "But how can you have verse without sentiment?" You see what it is: the prospect alarms them. A classical revival to them would mean the prospect of an arid desert and the death of poetry as they understand it, and could only come to fill the gap caused by that death. Exactly why this dry classical spirit should have a positive and legitimate necessity to express itself in poetry is utterly inconceivable to them. What this positive need is, I shall show later. It follows from the fact that there is another quality, not the emotion produced, which is at the root of excellence in verse. Before I get to this I am concerned with a negative thing, a theoretical point, a prejudice that stands in the way and is really at the bottom of this reluctance to understand classical verse.

It is an objection which ultimately I believe comes from a bad metaphysic of art. You are unable to admit the existence of beauty without the infinite being in some way or another dragged in.

I may quote for purposes of argument, as a typical example of this kind of attitude made vocal, the famous chapters in Ruskin's *Modern Painters,* Vol. II, on the imagination. I must say here, parenthetically, that I use this word without prejudice to the other discussion with which I shall end the paper. I only use the word here because it is Ruskin's word.

All that I am concerned with just now is the attitude behind it, which I take to be the romantic.

"Imagination cannot but be serious; she sees too far, too darkly, too solemnly, too earnestly, ever to smile. There is something in the heart of everything, if we can reach it, that we shall not be inclined to laugh at. . . . Those who have so pierced and seen the melancholy deeps of things, are filled with intense passion and gentleness of sympathy." (Part III, Chap. III, § 9.)

"There is in every word set down by the imaginative mind an awful undercurrent of meaning, and evidence and shadow upon it of the deep places out of which it has come. It is often obscure, often half-told; for he who wrote it, in his clear seeing of the things beneath, may have been impatient of detailed interpretation; for if we choose to dwell upon it and trace it, it will lead us always securely back to that metropolis of the soul's dominion from which we may follow out all the ways and tracks to its farthest coasts." (Part II, Chap. III, § 5.)

Really in all these matters the act of judgment is an instinct, an absolutely unstateable thing akin to the art of the tea taster. But you must talk, and the only language you can use in this matter is that of analogy. I have no material clay to mould to the given shape; the only thing which one has for the purpose, and which acts as a substitute for it, a kind of mental clay, are certain metaphors modified into theories of aesthetic and rhetoric. A combination of these, while it cannot state the essentially unstateable intuition, can yet give you a sufficient analogy to enable you to see what it was and to recognise it on condition that you yourself have been in a similar state. Now these phrases of Ruskin's convey quite clearly to me his taste in the matter.

I see quite clearly that he thinks the best verse must be serious. That is a natural attitude for a man in the romantic period. But he is not content with saying that he prefers this kind of verse. He wants to deduce his opinion like his master, Coleridge, from some fixed principle which can be found by metaphysic.

Here is the last refuge of this romantic attitude. It proves itself to be not an attitude but a deduction from a fixed principle of the cosmos.

One of the main reasons for the existence of philosophy is not that it enables you to find truth (it can never do that) but that it does provide you a refuge for definitions. The usual idea of the thing is that it provides you with a fixed basis from which you can deduce the things you want in aesthetics. The process is the exact contrary. You start in the confusion of the fighting line, you retire from that just a little to the rear to recover, to get your weapons right. Quite plainly, without metaphor this — it provides you with an elaborate and precise language in which you really can explain definitely what you mean, but what you want to say is decided by other things. The ultimate reality is the hurlyburly, the struggle; the metaphysic is an adjunct to clear-headedness in it.

To get back to Ruskin and his objection to all that is not serious. It seems to me that involved in this is a bad metaphysical aesthetic. You have the metaphysic which in defining beauty or the nature of art always drags in the infinite. Particularly in Germany, the land where theories of aesthetics were first created, the romantic aesthetes collated all beauty to an impression of the infinite involved in the identification of our being in absolute spirit. In the least element of beauty we have a total intuition of the whole world. Every artist is a kind of pantheist.

Now it is quite obvious to anyone who holds this kind of theory that any poetry which confines itself to the finite can never be of the highest kind. It seems a contradiction in terms to them. And as in metaphysics you get the last refuge of a prejudice, so it is now necessary for me to refute this.

Here follows a tedious piece of dialectic, but it is necessary for my purpose. I must avoid two pitfalls in discussing the idea of beauty. On the one hand there is the old classical view which is supposed to define it as lying in conformity to certain standard fixed forms; and on the other hand there is the romantic view which drags in the infinite. I have got to find a metaphysic between these two which will enable me to hold consistently that a neo-classic verse of the type I have indicated involves no contradiction in terms. It is essential to prove that beauty may be in small, dry things.

The great aim is accurate, precise and definite description. The first thing is to recognise how extraordinarily difficult this is. It is no mere matter of carefulness; you have to use language, and language is by its very nature a communal thing; that is, it expresses never the exact thing but a compromise — that which is common to you, me and everybody. But each man sees a little differently, and to get out clearly and exactly what he does see, he must have a terrific struggle with language, whether it be with words or the technique of other arts. Language has its own special nature, its own conventions and communal ideas. It is only by a concentrated effort of the mind that you can hold it fixed to your own purpose. I always think that the fundamental process at the back of all the arts might be represented by the following metaphor. You know what I call architect's curves* — flat pieces of wood with all different kinds of curvature. By a suitable selection from these you can draw approximately any curve you like. The artist I take to be the man who simply can't bear the idea of that "approximately." He will get the exact curve of what he sees whether it be an object or an idea in the mind. I shall here have to change my metaphor a little to get the process in his mind. Suppose that instead of your curved pieces of wood you have a springy piece of steel of the same types of curvature as the wood. Now the state of tension or concentration of mind, if he is doing anything really good in this struggle against the ingrained habit of the technique, may be represented by a man employing all his fingers to bend the steel out of its own curve and into the exact curve which you want. Something different to what it would assume naturally.

***architect's curve:** 구름꼴 자. 도안용 자의 일종.

There are then two things to distinguish, first the particular faculty of mind to see things as they really are, and apart from the conventional ways in which you have been trained to see them. This is itself rare enough in all consciousness. Second, the concentrated state of mind, the grip over oneself which is necessary in the actual expression of what one sees. To prevent one falling into the conventional curves of ingrained technique, to hold on through infinite detail and trouble to the exact curve you want. Wherever you get this sincerity, you get the fundamental quality of good art without dragging in infinite or serious.

I can now get at that positive fundamental quality of verse which constitutes excellence, which has nothing to do with infinity, with mystery or with emotions.

This is the point I aim at, then, in my argument. I prophesy that a period of dry, hard, classical verse is coming. I have met the preliminary objection founded on the bad romantic aesthetic that in such verse, from which the infinite is excluded, you cannot have the essence of poetry at all.

After attempting to sketch out what this positive quality is, I can get on to the end of my paper in this way: That where you get this quality exhibited in the realm of the emotions you get imagination, and that where you get this quality exhibited in the contemplation of finite things you get fancy.

In prose as in algebra concrete things are embodied in signs or counters which are moved about according to rules, without being visualised at all in the process. There are in prose certain type situations and arrangements of words, which move as automatically into certain other arrangements as do functions* in algebra. One only changes the X's and the Y's back into physical things at the end of the process. Poetry, in one aspect at any rate, may be considered as an effort to avoid this characteristic of prose. It is not a counter language, but a visual concrete one. It is a compromise for a language of intuition which would hand over sensations bodily. It always endeavours to arrest you, and to make you continuously see a

*functions: 「함수」.

physical thing, to prevent you gliding through an abstract process. It chooses fresh epithets and fresh metaphors, not so much because they are new, and we are tired of the old, but because the old cease to convey a physical thing and become abstract counters. A poet says a ship "coursed the seas" to get a physical image, instead of the counter word "sailed." Visual meanings can only be transferred by the new bowl of metaphor; prose is an old pot that lets them leak out. Images in verse are not mere decoration, but the very essence of an intuitive language. Verse is a pedestrian taking you over the ground, prose — a train which delivers you at a destination.

I can now get on to a discussion of two words often used in this connection, "fresh" and "unexpected." You praise a thing for being "fresh." I understand what you mean, but the word besides conveying the truth conveys a secondary something which is certainly false. When you say a poem or drawing is fresh, and so good, the impression is somehow conveyed that the essential element of goodness is freshness, that it is good because it is fresh. Now this is certainly wrong, there is nothing particularly desirable about freshness *per se*. Works of art aren't eggs. Rather the contrary. It is simply an unfortunate necessity due to the nature of language and technique that the only way the element which does constitute goodness, the only way in which its presence can be detected externally, is by freshness. Freshness convinces you, you feel at once that the artist was in an actual physical state. You feel that for a minute. Real communication is so very rare, for plain speech is unconvincing. It is in this rare fact of communication that you get the root of aesthetic pleasure.

I shall maintain that wherever you get an extraordinary interest in a thing, a great zest in its contemplation which carries on the contemplator to accurate description in the sense of the word accurate I have just analysed, there you have sufficient justification for poetry. It must be an intense zest which hightens a thing out of the level of prose. I am using contemplation here just in the same way that Plato used it, only applied to a different subject: it is a detached interest. "The object of aesthetic contemplation is something framed apart by itself and regarded without memory or expectation, simply as being itself, as end not means, as individual not universal."

To take a concrete example. I am taking an extreme case. If you are walking behind a woman in the street, you notice the curious way in which the skirt rebounds from her heels. If that peculiar kind of motion becomes of such interest to you that you will search about until you can get the exact epithet which hits it off,* there you have a properly aesthetic emotion. But it is the zest with which you look at the thing which decides you to make the effort. In this sense the feeling that was in Herrick's mind when he wrote "the tempestuous petticoat"* was exactly the same as that which in bigger and vaguer matters makes the best romantic verse. It doesn't matter an atom that the emotion produced is not of dignified vagueness, but on the contrary amusing; the point is that exactly the same activity is at work as in the highest verse. That is the avoidance of conventional language in order to get the exact curve of the thing.

I have still to show that in the verse which is to come, fancy will be the necessary weapon of the classical school. The positive quality I have talked about can be manifested in ballad verse by extreme directness and simplicity, such as you get in "On Fair Kirkconnel Lea."* But the particular verse we are going to get will be cheerful, dry and sophisticated, and here the necessary weapon of the positive quality must be fancy.

Subject doesn't matter; the quality in it is the same as you get in the more romantic people.

It isn't the scale or kind of emotion produced that decides, but this one fact: Is there any real zest in it? Did the poet have an actually realised visual object before him in which he delighted? It doesn't matter if it were a lady's shoe or the

---

*hit off: 「적중하다」.

*Robert Herrick (1591-1674)의 "Delight in Disorder"의 일절. "A winning wave, deserving note,/In the tempestuous petticoat:"

*민요의 하나(?)

starry heavens.

Fancy is not mere decoration added on to plain speech. Plain speech is essentially inaccurate. It is only by new metaphors, that is, by fancy, that it can be made precise.

When the analogy has not enough connection with the thing described to be quite parallel with it, where it overlays the thing it described and there is a certain excess, there you have the play of fancy — that I grant is inferior to imagination.

But where the analogy is every bit of it necessary for accurate description in the sense of the word accurate I have previously described, and your only objection to this kind of fancy is that it is not serious in the effect it produces, then I think the objection to be entirely invalid. If it is sincere in the accurate sense, when the whole of the analogy is necessary to get out the exact curve of the feeling or thing you want to express — there you seem to me to have the highest verse, even though the subject be trivial and the emotions of the infinite far away.

It is very difficult to use any terminology at all for this kind of thing. For whatever word you use is at once sentimentalised. Take Coleridge's word "vital." It is used loosely by all kinds of people who talk about art, to mean something vaguely and mysteriously significant. In fact, vital and mechanical is to them exactly the same antithesis as between good and bad.

Nothing of the kind; Coleridge uses it in a perfectly definite and what I call dry sense. It is just this: A mechanical complexity is the sum of its parts. Put them side by side and you get the whole. Now vital or organic is merely a convenient metaphor for a complexity of a different kind, that in which the parts cannot be said to be elements as each one is modified by the other's presence, and each one to a certain extent is the whole. The leg of a chair by itself is still a leg. My leg by itself wouldn't be.

Now the characteristic of the intellect is that it can only represent complexities of the mechanical kind. It can only make diagrams, and diagrams are essentially things whose parts are separate one from another. The intellect always analyses — when there is a synthesis it is baffled. That is why the artist's work seems mysterious. The intellect can't represent it. This is a necessary consequence of the particular nature of the intellect and the purposes for which it is formed. It doesn't mean that your synthesis is ineffable, simply that it can't be definitely stated.

Now this is all worked out in Bergson, the central feature of his whole philosophy. It is all based on the clear conception of these vital complexities which he calls "intensive"* as opposed to the other kind which he calls "extensive,"* and the recognition of the fact that the intellect can only deal with the extensive multiplicity. To deal with the intensive you must use intuition.

Now, as I said before, Ruskin was perfectly aware of all this, but he had no such metaphysical background which would enable him to state definitely what he meant. The result is that he has to flounder about in a series of metaphors. A powerfully imaginative mind seizes and combines at the same instant all the important ideas of its poem or picture, and while it works with one of them, it is at the same instant working with and modifying all in their relation to it and never losing sight of their bearings on each other — as the motion of a snake's body goes through all parts at once and its volition acts at the same instant in coils which go contrary ways.

A romantic movement must have an end of the very nature of the thing. It may be deplored, but it can't be helped — wonder must cease to be wonder.

I guard myself here from all the consequences of the analogy, but it expresses at any rate the inevitableness of the process. A literature of wonder must have an end as inevitably as a strange land loses its strangeness when one lives in it. Think of the lost ecstasy of the Elizabethans. "Oh my America, my new found land," think of what it meant to

*여기서 말하는 **intensive, extensive**는 철학에서의 "내연적", "외연적"의 뜻.

them and of what it means to us. Wonder can only be the attitude of a man passing from one stage to another, it can never be a permanently fixed thing.

Thomas Stearns Eliot

(1888—1965)

미국 중부 쎈·루이에서 유복하고도 교양있는 집안에 태어난 그는 그의 조상이 살던 동부의 하버드에서 Babbit, Santayana 같은 위대한 스승들에게 문학과 철학을 배우고 철학박사 학위 논문을 쓰는 동안 소르본느, 옥스포드 등지에서 계속 수학하였다. 그러나 철학보다 시에 더 열중하게 되어 급기야는 다 쓴 철학박사 논문을 제껴두고 1915년 전쟁 중에 런던에 정착하여 빈곤한 생활 속에서 "현대시"와 "현대비평"의 새 시대를 열고 있었다. 1927년에 영국 시민으로 귀화했고, 또한 이어 영국 교회의 교인이 되었다. 그의 시인으로서의 성공은 여기서 언급하지 않는다.

런던에 정착한 엘리어트는 처음에는 시인으로서보다 평론가로 더 알려졌었다. 런던 타임즈 문예증보판(*T.L.S*)이나 작은 문예지에 발표한 글들이었으므로 비교적 짧은 평론들 중에서 골라서 *The Sacred Wood*(1920)란 책으로 냈다. 그의 초·중기의 비평은 *Selected Essays*(1932, 개정증보판 1950)에 수록되었으며, 하버드 대학에서의 강연록인 *The Use of Poetry and the Use of Criticism*(1933)은 영국의 비평과 시의 관계를 역사적으로 고찰한 글이다. 후기 비평은 *On Poetry and Poets*(1957)에 수록되어 있고, 사후에 그의 미망인이 나머지 비평들을 모아 *To Criticize the Critic*(1965)란 이름으로 출간했다. 그밖에 문명비평으로서 *The Idea of a Christian Society*(1939), *Notes Towards the Definition of Culture*(1948) 등이 있다.

엘리어트는 낭만주의적 경향에 반대하여 고전주의적 입장을 고수한 비평가로 알려져 있다. 이런 입장은 그의 하버드 시절의 스승 배빗트나, 거의 그의 동년배였던 런던 시절의 흄이나, 그의 좋은 충고자였던 시인 에즈러 파운드 등, 19세기 말의 영미 문학에 식상한 많은 문인들이 공통으로 취한 것이었다. 그러나 엘리어트는 낭만주의에의 반대 입장을 천명하는 데 있어서 남보다 훨씬 설득력이 있다.

그의 설득력은 어디서 오는가? 우선, 그것이 학술적 이론

체계나, 물샐틈 없는 논리성이나, 고고한 학덕이나 인격이 풍기는 카리스마가 아님은 분명하다. 오히려 이러한 설득, 설복의 요소들을 동원하지 않고서도 그는 "조용하고 매력적인 권위"를 발휘할 수 있었다.

그는 자기중심적, 자기주장적이 아니다. 그는 어떤 주장을 할 때에도——실제에 있어 그는 거의 언제나 굉장한 주장을 하곤 한다—— 그런 주장을 아니할 수 없어서 한다는 말투를 쓴다. 충격적인 말을 할 때에도 그것이 당연한 말인 것처럼 시침떼기가 일쑤이다. 독자는 「즐겁게 놀란다」. 즐겁게 놀란다는 것은 벌써 설득 당하는 것을 뜻한다.

엘리어트는 자기가 주장하고자 하는 바를 명확히 눈앞에 그려보면서, 서두르지도 않고 또는 반대로 방만하게 벌려놓지도 않는다. 그의 이름난 "일관성"은 논리성이라기보다는 바로 이러한 여유 있고도 한결같은 속도의 유지에서 온다고 보겠다.

그가 자기의 논지를 명확히 확정짓고 나아가고 있음은 그가 인용구를 적절히 끌어옴을 보아도 알 수 있다. 존 던, 웹스터, 마블 같은 17세기 문인들로부터 끌어온 기막히게 적절한 인용구들은 그가 전개하고 있는 논지의 타당성을 설득시키고도 남는다. 현재 우리가 기억하고 있는 17세기 문인들의 명구, 명언의 대부분은 엘리어트가 찾아낸 것들이며, 우리가 그것들을 명구, 명언으로 인용하는 한, 엘리어트는 계속 영향력을 발휘하는 셈이다. 이것은 보통의 비평가가 누릴 수 있는 권위가 아니다.

엘리어트는 구체적 작품에서의 인용문을 작가의 사상이나 독자에게 주는 교훈이나 감동의 면에서 해설하지 않고, 그 작품 전체와의 관련성과, 그 낱말, 심상, 리듬 등의 힘찬 결합의 양태를 예리하게 지적한다. 이러한 비평 방법은 비평을 심리학이나 윤리학이 아닌 "객관적으로" 문학적인 비평이라는 인상을 준다. 바로 이 방법이 후에 미국의 New Criticism, 영국의 "자세히 읽기"(close reading)의 원천이 되었던 것이다.

엘리어트는 적절한 인용뿐 아니라 적절한 용어와 비유의 재발굴 또는 발명으로도 유명하다. Tradition, historical sense, platinum catalysis, objective correlative, direct apprehension of thought, dissociation of sensibility 등등, 많은 용어가 현대 비평에서 일반 어휘처럼 쓰여지고 있다. 그 만큼 엘리어트는 이들 용어들을 적절히, 다시 말하면 설득력 있게 사용하였던 것이다.

엘리어트가 20세기의 다른 많은 비평가, 이론가들에 대하여 가지는 거의 절대적인 강점은 그가 20세기 최대 시인의 하나라는 사실이다. 그가 자신의 비평을 「작업실 비평」(workshop criticism)이라 하였듯이, 그의 비평은 학설이나 이론을 해설하기 위한 것이 아니라 창작을 위한 독서 체험과 작품 창작의 실제에서 얻어진 결과인 까닭에 생동감과 현장감이 넘친다.

결국 엘리어트는 시드니에서 아놀드에 이르기까지 창작의 실제를 체험한 바탕 위에서 문학의 문제를 논한 시인—비평가의 오랜 전통을 이은 인물임이 밝혀진다. 또한 잡다한 경험의 파편들이 결합하여 생긴 새로운 창조물에 지대한 관심을 가짐으로써, 상상력의 문제에 최대의 관심을 보이는 영국 비평의 전통을 이은 인물이기도 하다. 한편 그가 단지 문학에 대해서만이 아니라, 종교와 교육과 문화에 대한 끊임없는 관심을 보여 사회 윤리에 영향력을 행사한 것도 코울리지나 아놀드처럼 전통적 비평가의 안목을 계승한 「심각한」 비평가임을 보여준다. 결론적으로 그는 매우 전통적인, 따라서 권위있는 비평가인 것이다.

"Tradition and the Individual Talent" (1919)는 그의 가장 초창기에 속하지만 가장 잘 쓰여진 비평이다. 그러나 historical sense("역사 의식"이 아니라 "역사 감각"이라 번역함이 옳다)라든가, escape from emotion, life emotion이 아닌 art emotion 등의 개념은 제대로 이해되지 않은 채 인용되곤 한다.

"The Metaphysical Poets" (1921) 역시 잘 알려져 있는 비평이다. 17세기 시에 대한 관심이 높아져서 대학 교육 내용에 포합된 것은 이 글의 덕분이라 해도 과언이 아니다. "Dissociation of sensibility" 같은 명구, 연애, 스피노자, 타자 소리, 요리 냄새 등이 시인의 정신에서 하나로 결합할 수 있다는 말은 널리 기억되고 있다. 이상의 두 평론은 궁극적으로 상상력에 대한 재조명이라 할 수 있다.

"Religion and Literature" (1935)는 엘리어트의 중기 비평의 대표라 할 수 있는 것으로, 순수 문예비평은 윤리적, 신학적 비평으로 보완되어야 한다는 선언이다. 그는 "신앙적" 문학을 옹호하는 것이 아니라 Secularism 즉 세속적 물질주의에 반대하는 것이다. 아놀드도 이에 반대했지만, 엘리어트는 문학이 종교를 대신할 수 있대서가 아니라, 문학은 문학대로 그 특유의 정신적 사명이 있다고 보았기 때문이다.

후기 비평인 "The Social Function of Literature" (1945)는 언어의 순화가 시인이 사회에 이바지할 수 있는 최고의 특수 사명이며, 그 과업이 얼마나 "윤리적"인지를 천명한다.

Tradition and the Individual Talent (1917)

I

IN English writing we seldom speak of tradition, though we occasionally apply its name in deploring its absence. We cannot refer to 'the tradition' or to 'a tradition'; at most, we employ the adjective in saying that the poetry of So-and-so is 'traditional' or even 'too traditional'. Seldom, perhaps, does the word appear except in a phrase of censure. If otherwise, it is vaguely approbative, with the implication, as to the work approved, of some pleasing archaeological reconstruction.* You can hardly make the word agreeable to English ears without this comfortable reference to the reassuring science of archaeology.

Certainly the word is not likely to appear in our appreciations of living or dead writers. Every nation, every race, has not only its own creative, but its own critical turn of mind; and is even more oblivious of the shortcomings and limitations of its critical habits than of those of its creative genius. We know, or think we know, from the enormous mass of critical writing that has appeared in the French language the critical method or habit of the French; we only conclude (we are such unconscious people) that the French are 'more critical' than we, and sometimes even plume ourselves a little with the fact, as if the French were the less spontaneous.* Perhaps they are; but we might remind ourselves that criticism is as inevitable as breathing, and that we should be none the worse for articulating what passes in our minds when we read a book and feel an emotion about it, for criticizing our own minds in their work of criticism. One of the facts that might come to light in this process is our tendency to insist, when we praise a poet, upon those aspects of his work in which he least resembles anyone else. In these aspects or parts of his work we pretend to find what is individual, what is the peculiar essence of the man. We dwell with satisfaction upon the poet's difference from his predecessors, especially his immediate predecessors; we endeavour to find something that can be isolated in order to be enjoyed. Whereas if we approach a poet without this prejudice we shall often find that not only the best, but the most individual parts of his work may be those in which the dead poets, his ancestors, assert their immortality most vigorously. And I do not mean the impressionable period of adolescence, but the period of full maturity.

Yet if the only form of tradition, of handing down, consisted in following the ways of the immediate generation before us in a

---

***reconstruction:** (고전의) 「복원」.

***spontaneous:** 「창작력이 있는」.

blind or timid adherence to its successes, 'tradition' should positively be discouraged. We have seen many such simple currents soon lost in the sand; and novelty is better than repetition. Tradition is a matter of much wider significance. It cannot be inherited, and if you want it you must obtain it by great labour. It involves, in the first place, the historical sense, which we may call nearly indispensable to anyone who would continue to be a poet beyond his twenty-fifth year; and the historical sense involves a perception, not only of the pastness of the past, but of its presence; the historical sense compels a man to write not merely with his own generation in his bones, but with a feeling that the whole of the literature of Europe from Homer and within it the whole of the literature of his own country has a simultaneous existence and composes a simultaneous order. This historical sense, which is a sense of the timeless as well as of the temporal and of the timeless and of the temporal together, is what makes a writer traditional. And it is at the same time what makes a writer most acutely conscious of his place in time, of his own contemporaneity.

No poet, no artist of any art, has his complete meaning alone. His significance, his appreciation is the appreciation of his relation to the dead poets and artists. You cannot value him alone; you must set him, for contrast and comparison, among the dead. I mean this as a principle of aesthetic, not merely historical, criticism. The necessity that he shall conform, that he shall cohere, is not onesided; what happens when a new work of art is created is something that happens simultaneously to all the works of art which preceded it. The existing monuments form an ideal order among themselves, which is modified by the introduction of the new (the really new) work of art among them. The existing order is complete before the new work arrives; for order to persist after the supervention of novelty, the *whole* existing order must be, if ever so slightly, altered; and so the relations, proportions, values of each work of art toward the whole are readjusted; and this is conformity between the old and the new. Whoever has approved this idea of order, of the form of European, of English literature will not find it preposterous that the past should be altered by the present as much as the present is directed by the past. And the poet who is aware of this will be aware of great difficulties and responsibilities.

In a peculiar sense he will be aware also that he must inevitably be judged by the standards of the past. I say judged, not amputated, by them; not judged to be as good as, or worse or better than, the dead; and certainly not judged by the canons of dead critics. It is a judgement, a comparison, in which two things are measured by each other. To conform merely would be for the new work not really to conform at all; it would not be new, and would therefore not be a work of art. And we do not quite say that the new is more valuable because it fits in; but its fitting in is a test of its value—a test, it is true, which can only be slowly and cautiously applied, for we are none of us infallible judges of conformity. We say: it appears to conform, and is perhaps individual, or it appears individual, and may conform; but we are hardly likely to find that it is one and not the other.

To proceed to a more intelligible exposition of the relation of the poet to the past: he can neither take the past as a lump, an indiscriminate bolus, nor can he form himself wholly on one or two private admirations, nor can he form himself wholly upon one preferred period. The first course is inadmissible, the second is an important experience of youth, and the third is a pleasant and highly desirable supplement. The poet must be very conscious of the main current, which does not at all flow invariably through the most distinguished reputations. He must be quite aware of the obvious fact that art never improves, but that the material of art is never quite the same. He must be aware that the mind of Europe—the mind of his own country—a mind which he learns in time to be much more important than his own private mind—is a mind which changes, and that this change is a development which abandons nothing *en route*,*

---

*지성의 변화, 즉 발전은 옛것을 버리고 새것을 취함에 있는 과학의 그것이 아니라, 옛것을 축적하며 계속 새것을 받아들이는 형태, 즉 발전 도중(*en*

which does not superannuate either Shakespeare, or Homer, or the rock drawing of the* Magdalenian draughtsmen.* That this development, refinement perhaps, complication certainly, is not, from the point of view of the artist, any improvement. Perhaps not even an improvement from the point of view of the psychologist or not to the extent which we imagine; perhaps only in the end based upon a complication in economics and machinery. But the difference between the present and the past is that the conscious present is an awareness of the past in a way and to an extent which the past's awareness of itself cannot show.

Someone said: 'The dead writers are remote from us because we *know* so much more than they did'. Precisely, and they are that which we know.

I am alive to* a usual objection to what is clearly part of my programme for the *métier* of poetry. The objection is that the doctrine requires a ridiculous amount of erudition (pedantry), a claim which can be rejected by appeal to the lives of poets in any pantheon. It will even be affirmed that much learning deadens or perverts poetic sensibility. While, however, we persist in believing that a poet ought to know as much as will not encroach upon his necessary receptivity and necessary laziness, it is not desirable to confine knowledge to whatever can be put into a useful shape for examinations, drawing-rooms, or the still more pretentious modes of publicity. Some can absorb knowledge, the more tardy must sweat for it. Shakespeare acquired more essential history from Plutarch than most men could from the whole British Museum. What is to be insisted upon is that the poet must develop or procure the consciousness of the past and that he should continue to develop this consciousness throughout his career.

What happens is a continual surrender of himself as he is at

---

route)에 아무것도 폐기하지 않는 데 있다. 따라서 현재의 지성에는 과거가 축적되어 있다.

***the rock drawing...draughtsmen:** 구석기 최후시대 원시화가의 암굴 벽화.

***alive to:** 「잘 알고 있는, 의식하는」.

the moment to something which is more valuable. The progress of an artist is a continual self-sacrifice, a continual extinction of personality.

There remains to define this process of depersonalization and its relation to the sense of tradition. It is in this depersonalization that art may be said to approach the condition of science. I therefore invite you to consider, as a suggestive analogy, the action which takes place when a bit of finely filiated* platinum is introduced into a chamber containing oxygen and sulphur dioxide.*

II

Honest criticism and sensitive appreciation is directed not upon the poet but upon the poetry. If we attend to the confused cries of the newspaper critics and the susurrus* of popular repetition that follows, we shall hear the names of poets in great numbers; if we seek not Blue-book* knowledge but the enjoyment of poetry, and ask for a poem, we shall seldom find it. I have tried to point out the importance of the relation of the poem to other poems by other authors, and suggested the conception of poetry as a living whole of all the poetry that has ever been written. The other aspect of this Impersonal theory of poetry is the relation of the poem to its author. And I hinted, by an analogy, that the mind of the mature poet differs from that of the immature one not precisely in any valuation of 'personality', not being necessarily more interesting, or having 'more to say', but rather by being a more finely perfected medium in which special, or very varied, feelings are at liberty to enter into new combinations.

The analogy was that of the catalyst. When the two gases previously mentioned are mixed in the presence of a filament of

---

***filiated:** 「실같이 만든」.

***oxygen and sulphur dioxide:** 이산화유황 (SO_2).

***susurrus:** 「수근거림」.

***Blue-book:** 영국의 의회나 정부의 문서.

platinum, they form sulphurous acid.* This combination takes place only if the platinum is present; nevertheless the newly formed acid contains no trace of platinum, and the platinum itself is apparently unaffected: has remained inert, neutral, and unchanged. The mind of the poet is the shred of platinum. It may partly or exclusively operate upon the experience of the man himself; but, the more perfect the artist, the more completely separate in him will be the man who suffers* and the mind which creates; the more perfectly will the mind digest and transmute the passions which are its material.

The experience, you will notice, the elements which enter the presence of the transforming catalyst, are of two kinds: emotions and feelings. The effect of a work of art upon the person who enjoys it is an experience different in kind from any experience not of art. It may be formed out of one emotion, or may be a combination of several; and various feelings, inhering for the writer in particular words or phrases or images, may be added to compose the final result. Or great poetry may be made without the direct use of any emotion whatever: composed out of feelings solely. Canto XV of the *Inferno* (Brunetto Latini)* is a working up of the emotion evident in the situation; but the effect, though single as that of any work of art, is obtained by considerable complexity of detail. The last quatrain gives an image, a feeling attaching to an image, which 'came', which did not develop simply out of what precedes, but which was probably in suspension in the poet's mind until the proper combination arrived for it to add itself to. The poet's mind is in fact a receptacle for seizing and storing up numberless feelings, phrases, images, which remain there until all the particles which can unite to form a new compound

---

***surphurous acid:** 황산. 황산은 백금실을 촉매로 해서 합성된다.

***suffer:** (경험을) 「받아들이다」.

*선배학자 Brunetto Latini의 혼령이 Dante와 말을 주고 받은 후 다시 지옥의 제자리로 달려 돌아가는 모습에 대한 simile. (Verona에서의 경주에 비김). "He turned, and seemed like, in the field before/Verona, one of those who run the race/For the queen cloth; so seemed he running, nor/Seemed in the loser's but the winners' place."

are present together.

If you compare several representative passages of the greatest poetry you see how great is the variety of types of combination, and also how completely any semi-ethical criterion of 'sublimity' misses the mark. For it is not the 'greatness', the intensity, of the emotions, the components, but the intensity of the artistic process, the pressure, so to speak, under which the fusion takes place, that counts. The episode of Paolo and Francesca* employs a definite emotion, but the intensity of the poetry is something quite different from whatever intensity in the supposed experience it may give the impression of. It is no more intense, furthermore, than Canto XXVI, the voyage of Ulysses,* which has not the direct dependence upon an emotion. Great variety is possible in the process of transmutation of emotion: the murder of Agamemnon, or the agony of Othello, gives an artistic effect apparently closer to a possible original than the scenes from Dante. In the *Agamemnon*, the artistic emotion approximates to the emotion of an actual spectator; in *Othello* to the emotion of the protagonist himself. But the difference between art and the event is always absolute; the combination which is the murder of Agamemnon is probably as complex as that which is the voyage of Ulysses. In either case there has been a fusion of elements. The ode of Keats contains a number of feelings which have nothing particular to do with the nightingale, but which the nightingale, partly perhaps because of its attractive name, and partly because of its reputation, served to bring together.

The point of view which I am struggling to attack is perhaps related to the metaphysical theory of the substantial unity of the soul: for my meaning is, that the poet has, not a 'personality' to express, but a particular medium, which is only a medium and not a personality, in which impressions and experiences combine in peculiar and unexpected ways. Impressions

---

*Paolo and Francesca: *Inferno*, V, 73ff. 비련의 주인공들. Dante가 동정해 마지 않음.

*Ulysses가 자신이 나중에 다시 바다로 나가 죽은 이야기를 들려주는 장면.

and experiences which are important for the man may take no place in the poetry, and those which become important in the poetry may play quite a negligible part in the man, the personality.

I will quote a passage which is unfamiliar enough to be regarded with fresh attention in the light—or darkness—of these observations:

> And now methinks I could e'en chide myself
> For doating on her beauty, though her death
> Shall be revenged after no common action.
> Does the silkworm expend her yellow labours
> For thee? For thee does she undo herself?
> Are lordships sold to maintain ladyships
> For the poor benefit of a bewildering minute?
> Why does yon fellow falsify highways,
> And put his life between the judge's lips,
> To refine such a thing—keeps horse and men
> To beat their valours for her? . . .*

In this passage (as is evident if it is taken in its context) there is a combination of positive and negative emotions: an intensely strong attraction towards beauty and an equally intense fascination by the ugliness which is contrasted with it and which destroys it. This balance of contrasted emotion is in the dramatic situation to which the speech is pertinent, but that situation alone is inadequate to it. This is, so to speak, the structural emotion, provided by the drama. But the whole effect, the dominant tone, is due to the fact that a number of floating feelings, having an affinity to this emotion by no means superficially evident, have combined with it to give us a new art emotion.

It is not in his personal emotions, the emotions provoked by particular events in his life, that the poet is in any way remarkable, or interesting. His particular emotions may be simple, or crude, or flat. The emotion in his poetry will be a very complex thing, but not with the complexity of the emotions of people

---

*Cyril Tourneur, *The Revenger's Tragedy* (1607), III, iv.

who have very complex or unusual emotions in life. One error, in fact, of eccentricity in poetry is to seek for new human emotions to express; and in this search for novelty in the wrong place it discovers the perverse. The business of the poet is not to find new emotions, but to use the ordinary ones and, in working them up into poetry, to express feelings which are not in actual emotions at all. And emotions which he has never experienced will serve his turn as well as those familiar to him. Consequently, we must believe that 'emotion recollected in tranquillity' is an inexact formula. For it is neither emotion, nor recollection, nor, without distortion of meaning, tranquillity. It is a concentration, and a new thing resulting from the concentration, of a very great number of experiences which to the practical and active person would not seem to be experiences at all; it is a concentration which does not happen consciously or of deliberation. These experiences are not 'recollected', and they finally unite in an atmosphere which is 'tranquil' only in that it is a passive attending upon the event. Of course this is not quite the whole story. There is a great deal, in the writing of poetry, which must be conscious and deliberate. In fact, the bad poet is usually unconscious where he ought to be conscious, and conscious where he ought to be unconscious. Both errors tend to make him 'personal'. Poetry is not a turning loose of emotion, but an escape from emotion; it is not the expression of personality, but an escape from personality. But, of course, only those who have personality and emotions know what it means to want to escape from these things.

III

*ὁ δὲ νοῦς ἴσως θειότερόν τι καὶ ἀπαθές ἐστιν.**

This essay proposes to halt at the frontier of metaphysics or mysticism, and confine itself to such practical conclusions as

*'The mind may be too divine, and therefore unaffected.' (Aristotle, *On the Soul*, I. 4).

can be applied by the responsible person interested in poetry. To divert interest from the poet to the poetry is a laudable aim: for it would conduce to a juster estimation of actual poetry, good and bad. There are many people who appreciate the expression of sincere emotion in verse, and there is a smaller number of people who can appreciate technical excellence. But very few know when there is an expression of *significant* emotion, emotion which has its life in the poem and not in the history of the poet. The emotion of art is impersonal. And the poet cannot reach this impersonality without surrendering himself wholly to the work to be done. And he is not likely to know what is to be done unless he lives in what is not merely the present, but the present moment of the past, unless he is conscious, not of what is dead, but of what is already living.

The Metaphysical Poets (1921)

By collecting these poems* from the work of a generation more often named than read, and more often read than profitably studied, Professor Grierson has rendered a service of some importance. Certainly the reader will meet with many poems already preserved in other anthologies, at the same time that he discovers poems such as those of Aurelian Townshend or Lord Herbert of Cherbury here included. But the function of such an anthology as this is neither that of Professor Saintsbury's admirable edition of Caroline poets* nor that of the *Oxford Book of English Verse*. Mr. Grierson's book is in itself a piece of criticism, and a provocation of criticism; and we think that he was right in including so many poems of Donne, elsewhere (though not in many editions) accessible, as documents in the case of 'metaphysical poetry'. The phrase has long done duty as a term of abuse, or as the label of a quaint and pleasant taste. The question is to what extent the so-called metaphysicals formed a school (in our own time we should say a 'movement'), and how far this so-called school or movement is a digression from the main current.

Not only is it extremely difficult to define metaphysical poetry, but difficult to decide what poets practise it and in which of their verses. The poetry of Donne (to whom Marvell and Bishop King* are sometimes nearer than any of the other authors) is late Elizabethan, its feeling often very close to that of Chapman. The 'courtly' poetry is derivative from Jonson, who borrowed liberally from the Latin; it expires in the next

***these poems:** [원주] *Metaphysical Lyrics and Poems of the Seventeenth Century:* Donne to Butler. Selected and edited, with an Essay, by Herbert J.C. Grierson (Oxford: Clarendon Press, London: Milford).

**Minor Poets of the Caroline Period* (3vols., 1905-21), ed. by George Saintsbury.

***Henry King, Bishop of Chichester:** (1592-1669). 시인, 성직자.

century with the sentiment and witticism of Prior.* There is finally the devotional verse of Herbert, Vaughan, and Crashaw (echoed long after by Christina Rossetti and Francis Thompson); Crashaw, sometimes more profound and less sectarian than the others, has a quality which returns through the Elizabethan period to the early Italians. It is difficult to find any precise use of metaphor, simile, or other conceit, which is common to all the poets and at the same time important enough as an element of style to isolate these poets as a group. Donne, and often Cowley, employ a device which is sometimes considered characteristically 'metaphysical'; the elaboration (contrasted with the condensation) of a figure of speech to the furthest stage to which ingenuity can carry it. Thus Cowley develops the commonplace comparison of the world to a chessboard through long stanzas (*To Destiny*), and Donne, with more grace, in *A Valediction*,* the comparison of two lovers to a pair of compasses. But elsewhere we find, instead of the mere explication of the content of a comparison, a development by rapid association of thought which requires considerable agility on the part of the reader.

On a round ball
A workeman that hath copies by, can lay
An Europe, Afrique, and an Asia,
And quickly make that, which was nothing, *All*,
So doth each teare,
Which thee doth weare,
A globe, yea world by that impression grow,
Till thy tears mixt with mine doe overflow
This world, by waters sent from thee, my heaven dissolved so.*

Here we find at least two connexions which are not implicit in the first figure, but are forced upon it by the poet: from the geographer's globe to the tear, and the tear to the deluge. On the other hand, some of Donne's most successful and charac-

---

*Prior, Matthew: (1664-1721). 외교관, 시인.
A Valediction: Forbiding Mourning.
A Valediction: Of Weeping, 10-18.

teristic effects are secured by brief words and sudden contrasts:

> A bracelet of bright hair about the bone,*

where the most powerful effect is produced by the sudden contrast of associations of 'bright hair' and of 'bone'. This telescoping of images and multiplied associations is characteristic of the phrase of some of the dramatists of the period which Donne knew: not to mention Shakespeare, it is frequent in Middleton,* Webster, and Tourneur, and is one of the sources of the vitality of their language.

Johnson, who employed the term 'metaphysical poets', apparently having Donne, Cleveland, and Cowley chiefly in mind, remarks of them that 'the most heterogeneous ideas are yoked by violence together'. The force of this impeachment lies in the failure of the conjunction, the fact that often the ideas are yoked but not united;* and if we are to judge of styles of poetry by their abuse, enough examples may be found in Cleveland to justify Johnson's condemnation. But a degree of heterogeneity of material compelled into unity by the operation of the poet's mind is omnipresent in poetry. We need not select for illustration such a line as:

> Notre âme est un trois-mâts cherchant son Icarie;*

we may find it in some of the best lines of Johnson himself (*The Vanity of Human Wishes*):

> His fate was destined to a barren strand,
> A petty fortress, and a dubious hand;
> He left a name at which the world grew pale,
> To point a moral, or adorn a tale,

where the effect is due to a contrast of ideas, different in degree but the same in principle, as that which Johnson mildly reprehended. And in one of the finest poems of the age (a

---

* *The Relique*, 6.

***Middleton, Thomas:** (1570?-1627). 희곡작가. * 앞의 p. 249 참조.

***Notre âme...:** 'Our soul is a three-master seeking its Icarie' (Charles Baudelaire, *Le Voyage*, Ⅱ, 9). Icarie is a Utopia.

poem which could not have been written in any other age), the *Exequy* of Bishop King, the extended comparison is used with perfect success: the idea and the simile become one, in the passage in which the Bishop illustrates his impatience to see his dead wife, under the figure of a journey:

Stay for me there; I will not faile
To meet thee in that hollow Vale.
And think not much of my delay;
I am already on the way,
And follow thee with all the speed
Desire can make, or sorrows breed.
Each minute is a short degree,
And ev'ry houre a step towards thee.
At night when I betake to rest,
Next morn I rise nearer my West
Of life, almost by eight houres sail,
Than when sleep breath'd his drowsy gale . . .
But heark! My Pulse, like a soft Drum
Beats my approach, tells *Thee* I come;
And slow howere my marches be,
I shall at last sit down by *Thee*.

(In the last few lines there is that effect of terror which is several times attained by one of Bishop King's admirers, Edgar Poe.) Again, we may justly take these quatrains from Lord Herbert's Ode, stanzas which would, we think, be immediately pronounced to be of the metaphysical school:

So when from hence we shall be gone,
And be no more, nor you, nor I,
As one another's mystery,
Each shall be both, yet both but one.

This said, in her up-lifted face,
Her eyes, which did that beauty crown,
Were like two starrs, that having faln down,
Look up again to find their place:

While such a moveless silent peace
Did seize on their becalmed sense,
One would have thought some influence

Their ravished spirits did possess.*

There is nothing in these lines (with the possible exception of the stars, a simile not at once grasped, but lovely and justified) which fits Johnson's general observations on the metaphysical poets in his essay on Cowley. A good deal resides in the richness of association which is at the same time borrowed from and given to the word 'becalmed'; but the meaning is clear, the language simple and elegant. It is to be observed that the language of these poets is as a rule simple and pure; in the verse of George Herbert this simplicity is carried as far as it can go—a simplicity emulated without success by numerous modern poets. The *structure* of the sentences, on the other hand, is sometimes far from simple, but this is not a vice; it is a fidelity to thought and feeling. The effect, at its best, is far less artificial than that of an ode by Gray. And as this fidelity induces variety of thought and feeling, so it induces variety of music. We doubt whether, in the eighteenth century, could be found two poems in nominally the same metre, so dissimilar as Marvell's *Coy Mistress* and Crashaw's *Saint Teresa*; the one producing an effect of great speed by the use of short syllables, and the other an ecclesiastical solemnity by the use of long ones:

> Love, thou art absolute sole lord
> Of life and death.

If so shrewd and sensitive (though so limited) a critic as Johnson failed to define metaphysical poetry by its faults, it is worth while to inquire whether we may not have more success by adopting the opposite method: by assuming that the poets of the seventeenth century (up to the Revolution)* were the direct and normal development of the precedent age; and, without prejudicing their case by the adjective 'metaphysical', consider whether their virtue was not something permanently

*Lord Herbert of Cherbury (1583-1648, George Herbert 의 형), "Ode upon a Question moved, whether Love should continue forever?"

*1688 년의 Glorious Revolution 을 말함.

valuable, which subsequently disappeared, but ought not to have disappeared. Johnson has hit, perhaps by accident, on one of their peculiarities, when he observes that 'their attempts were always analytic'; he would not agree that, after the dissociation, they put the material together again in a new unity.

It is certain that the dramatic verse of the later Elizabethan and early Jacobean poets expresses a degree of development of sensibility which is not found in any of the prose, good as it often is. If we except Marlowe, a man of prodigious intelligence, these dramatists were directly or indirectly (it is at least a tenable theory) affected by Montaigne. Even if we except also Jonson and Chapman, these two were notably erudite, and were notably men who incorporated their erudition into their sensibility: their mode of feeling was directly and freshly altered by their reading and thought. In Chapman especially there is a direct sensuous apprehension of thought, or a recreation of thought into feeling, which is exactly what we find in Donne:

> in this one thing, all the discipline
> Of manners and of manhood is contained;
> A man to join himself with th' Universe
> In his main sway, and make in all things fit
> One with that All, and go on, round as it;
> Not plucking from the whole his wretched part.
> And into straits, or into nought revert,
> Wishing the complete Universe might be
> Subject to such a rag of it as he;
> But to consider great Necessity.*

We compare this with some modern passage:

> No, when the fight begins within himself,
> A man's worth something. God stoops o'er his head,
> Satan looks up between his feet—both tug—
> He's left, himself, i' the middle; the soul wakes
> And grows. Prolong that battle through his life!*

**Revenge of Bussy D'Ambois* (1607), IV, i, 137—46.

*Browning, *Bishop Blougram's Apology*, 693—97.

It is perhaps somewhat less fair, though very tempting (as both poets are concerned with the perpetuation of love by offspring), to compare with the stanzas already quoted from Lord Herbert's Ode the following from Tennyson:

> One walked between his wife and child,
> With measured footfall firm and mild,
> And now and then he gravely smiled.
>
> The prudent partner of his blood
> Leaned on him, faithful, gentle, good,
> Wearing the rose of womanhood.
>
> And in their double love secure,
> The little maiden walked demure,
> Pacing with downward eyelids pure.
>
> These three made unity so sweet,
> My frozen heart began to beat,
> Remembering its ancient heat.*

The difference is not a simple difference of degree between poets. It is something which had happened to the mind of England between the time of Donne or Lord Herbert of Cherbury and the time of Tennyson and Browning; it is the difference between the intellectual poet and the reflective poet. Tennyson and Browning are poets, and they think; but they do not feel their thought as immediately as the odour of a rose. A thought to Donne was an experience; it modified his sensibility. When a poet's mind is perfectly equipped for its work, it is constantly amalgamating disparate experience; the ordinary man's experience is chaotic, irregular, fragmentary. The latter falls in love, or reads Spinoza, and these two experiences have nothing to do with each other, or with the noise of the typewriter or the smell of cooking; in the mind of the poet these experiences are always forming new wholes.

We may express the difference by the following theory: The poets of the seventeenth century, the successors of the dramatists of the sixteenth, possessed a mechanism of sensibility

---

**The Two Voices*, 412—23.

which could devour any kind of experience. They are simple, artificial, difficult, or fantastic, as their predecessors were; no less nor more than Dante, Guido Cavalcanti, Guinicelli, or Cino.* In the seventeenth century a dissociation of sensibility set in,* from which we have never recovered; and this dissociation, as is natural, was aggravated by the influence of the two most powerful poets of the century, Milton and Dryden. Each of these men performed certain poetic functions so magnificently well that the magnitude of the effect concealed the absence of others.* The language went on and in some respects improved; the best verse of Collins, Gray, Johnson, and even Goldsmith satisfies some of our fastidious demands better than that of Donne or Marvell or King. But while the language became more refined, the feeling became more crude. The feeling, the sensibility, expressed in the *Country Churchyard** (to say nothing of Tennyson and Browning) is cruder than that in the *Coy Mistress*.

The second effect of the influence of Milton and Dryden followed from the first, and was therefore slow in manifestation. The sentimental age began early in the eighteenth century, and continued. The poets revolted against the ratiocinative, the descriptive; they thought and felt by fits, unbalanced; they reflected. In one or two passages of Shelley's *Triumph of Life*, in the second *Hyperion*,* there are traces of a struggle toward unification of sensibility. But Keats and Shelley died, and Tennyson and Browning ruminated.

After this brief exposition of a theory—too brief, perhaps, to carry conviction—we may ask, what would have been the fate of the 'metaphysical' had the current of poetry descended in a direct line from them, as it descended in a direct line to them? They would not, certainly, be classified as metaphysical. The

*13세기 또는 14세기 초에 활약한 이탈리아의 시인들.
*set in: 「시작되다」.
*others: other functions.
***Country Churchyard:** Gray의 *Elegy Written in a Country Churchyard*를 가리킴.
***Hyperion:** Keats의 *The Fall of Hyperion: A Dream*을 가리킴.

possible interests of a poet are unlimited; the more intelligent he is the better; the more intelligent he is the more likely that he will have interests: our only condition is that he turn them into poetry, and not merely meditate on them poetically. A philosophical theory which has entered into poetry is established, for its truth or falsity in one sense ceases to matter, and its truth in another sense is proved. The poets in question have, like other poets, various faults. But they were, at best, engaged in the task of trying to find the verbal equivalent for states of mind and feeling. And this means both that they are more mature, and that they wear better, than later poets of certainly not less literary ability.

It is not a permanent necessity that poets should be interested in philosophy, or in any other subject. We can only say that it appears likely that poets in our civilization, as it exists at present, must be *difficult*. Our civilization comprehends great variety and complexity, and this variety and complexity, playing upon a refined sensibility, must produce various and complex results. The poet must become more and more comprehensive, more allusive, more indirect, in order to force, to dislocate if necessary, language into his meaning. (A brilliant and extreme statement of this view, with which it is not requisite to associate oneself, is that of M. Jean Epstein, *La Poésie d'aujourd'hui*.)* Hence we get something which looks very much like the conceit—we get, in fact, a method curiously similar to that of the 'metaphysical poets', similar also in its use of obscure words and of simple phrasing.

> O géraniums diaphanes, guerroyeurs sortilèges,
> Sacrilèges monomanes!
> Emballages, dévergondages, douches! O pressoirs
> Des vendanges des grands soirs!
> Layettes aux abois,
> Thyrses au fond des bois!
> Transfusions, représailles,
> Relevailles, compresses et l'éternelle potion,

**La Poésie d'aujourd'hui*: The Poetry of Today (1921).

Angélus! n'en pouvoir plus
De débâcles nuptiales! de débâcles nuptiales!*

The same poet could write also simply:

Elle est bien loin, elle pleure,
Le grand vent se lamente aussi . . . *

Jules Laforgue, and Tristan Corbière* in many of his poems, are nearer to the 'school of Donne' than any modern English poet. But poets more classical than they have the same essential quality of transmuting ideas into sensations, of transforming an observation into a state of mind.

Pour l'enfant, amoureux de cartes et d'estampes,
L'univers est égal à son vaste appétit.
Ah, que le monde est grand à la clarté des lampes!
Aux yeux du souvenir que le monde est petit!*

In French literature the great master of the seventeenth century—Racine—and the great master of the nineteenth—Baudelaire—are in some ways more like each other than they are like anyone else. The greatest two masters of diction are also the greatest two psychologists, the most curious explorers of the soul. It is interesting to speculate whether it is not a misfortune that two of the greatest masters of diction in our

---

***O géraniums: ...:** 'O translucent geraniums, warriors casting spells,/Crazed and sacrilegious!/Packings, shameless act, shower baths! O wine-presses/For the sale of great entertainments!/Boxes at bay,/Thyrsis at the bottom of the woods!/Heady drinks, reprisals,/Clutching of hands, compresses, and the eternal potion,/Angelus! let there be no power more/For marital upheavals, for marital upheavals!' (Laforgue, *Derniers Vers*, X, 1—10).

***Elle est bien...:** 'She is far away, she weeps, /The great wind also laments...' (Laforgue, *Derniers Vers*, XI).

***Jules Laforgue** (1860-87)와 **Tristan Corbière** (1845-75)는 Eliot에게 큰 영향을 준 프랑스의 상징주의 시인. 이들의 시는 Metaphysical Poetry와 닮은 바가 적다.

***Pour l'enfant...:** 'For the child, in love with maps and prints, /The universe is equal to his vast appetite, /Ah, how large the world is by the light of lamps! /To the eyes of memory how little is the world!' (Baudelaire, *Le Voyage*, I, 1).

language, Milton and Dryden, triumph with a dazzling disregard of the soul. If we continued to produce Miltons and Drydens it might not so much matter, but as things are it is a pity that English poetry has remained so incomplete. Those who object to the 'artificiality' of Milton or Dryden sometimes tell us to 'look into our hearts and write'. But that is not looking deep enough; Racine or Donne looked into a good deal more than the heart. One must look into the cerebral cortex, the nervous system, and the digestive tracts.

May we not conclude, then, that Donne, Crashaw, Vaughan, Herbert and Lord Herbert, Marvell, King, Cowley at his best, are in the direct current of English poetry, and that their faults should be reprimanded by this standard rather than coddled by antiquarian affection? They have been enough praised in terms which are implicit limitations because they are 'metaphysical' or 'witty', 'quaint' or 'obscure', though at their best they have not these attributes more than other serious poets. On the other hand, we must not reject the criticism of Johnson (a dangerous person to disagree with) without having mastered it, without having assimilated the Johnsonian canons of taste. In reading the celebrated passage in his essay on Cowley we must remember that by wit he clearly means something more serious than we usually mean to-day; in his criticism of their versification we must remember in what a narrow discipline he was trained, but also how well trained; we must remember that Johnson tortures chiefly the chief offenders, Cowley and Cleveland. It would be a fruitful work, and one requiring a substantial book, to break up the classification of Johnson (for there has been none since) and exhibit these poets in all their difference of kind and of degree, from the massive music of Donne to the faint, pleasing tinkle of Aurelian Townshend*—whose *Dialogue between a Pilgrim and Time* is one of the few regrettable omissions from the excellent anthology of Professor Grierson.

***Aurelian Townshend:** (1583?-1643?). 극작가, 시인. 그의 시는 1912 년에야 수집됨.

Religion and Literature (1932)

WHAT I have to say is largely in support of the following propositions: Literary criticism should be completed by criticism from a definite ethical and theological standpoint. In so far as in any age there is common agreement on ethical and theological matters, so far can literary criticism be substantive. In ages like our own, in which there is no such common agreement, it is the more necessary for Christian readers to scrutinize their reading, especially of works of imagination, with explicit ethical and theological standards. The 'greatness' of literature cannot be determined solely by literary standards; though we must remember that whether it is literature or not can be determined only by literary standards.*

We have tacitly assumed, for some centuries past, that there is *no* relation between literature and theology. This is not to deny that literature — I mean, again, primarily works of imagination — has been, is, and probably always will be judged by some moral standards. But moral judgements of literary works are made only according to the moral code accepted by each generation, whether it lives according to that code or not. In an age which accepts some precise Christian theology, the common code may be fairly orthodox: though even in such periods the common code may exalt such concepts as 'honour,' 'glory' or 'revenge'* to a position quite intolerable to Christianity. The dramatic ethics of the Elizabethan Age offers an interesting study.

But when the common code is detached from its theological background, and is consequently more and more merely a matter of habit, it is exposed both to prejudice and

*[원주] As an example of literary criticism given greater significance by theological interests, I would call attention to Theodor Haecker: *Virgil* (Sheed and Ward).

*이들 개념들은 기독교적 윤리와는 반대되는, 주로 로마의 윤리개념들이다.

to change. At such times morals are open to being altered *by* literature; so that we find in practice that what is 'objectionable' in literature is merely what the present generation is not used to. It is a commonplace that what shocks one generation is accepted quite calmly by the next. This adaptability to change of moral standards is sometimes greeted with satisfaction as an evidence of human perfectibility: whereas it is only evidence of what unsubstantial foundations people's moral judgements have.

I am not concerned here with religious literature but with the application of our religion to the criticism of any literature. It may be as well, however, to distinguish first what I consider to be the three senses in which we can speak of 'religious literature'. The first is that of which we say that it is 'religious literature' in the same way that we speak of 'historical literature' or of 'scientific literature'. I mean that we can treat the Authorized translation of the Bible, or the works of Jeremy Taylor,* as literature, in the same way that we treat the historical writing of Clarendon or of Gibbon — our two great English historians — as literature; or Bradley's *Logic,** or Buffon's* *Natural History*. All of these writers were men who, incidentally to their religious, or historical, or philosophic purpose, had a gift of language which makes them delightful to read to all those who can enjoy language well written, even if they are unconcerned with the objects which the writers had in view. And I would add that though a scientific, or historical, or theological, or philosophic work which is also 'literature,' may become superannuated as anything but literature, yet it is not likely to be 'literature' unless it had its scientific or other value for its own time. While I acknowledge the legitimacy of this enjoyment, I am more acutely aware of its abuse.* The persons

---

***Jeremy Taylor:** 17세기 영국의 대 설교가.

***Bradley, Francis Herbert:** (1846-1924). 영국의 철학자로, *Principles of Logic* (1883)의 저자. Eliot는 이 철학자를 주제로 하여 자신의 박사학위 논문을 썼다.

***Buffon, Georges:** 18세기 프랑스의 박물학자.

***its abuse:** 철인, 사상가, 학자들의 저술을 단지 그 문장의 아름다움 때문에만 즐기는 것은 남용이라는 것.

who enjoy these writings *solely* because of their literary merit are essentially parasites; and we know that parasites, when they become too numerous, are pests. I could fulminate against the men of letters who have gone into ecstasies over 'the Bible as literature', the Bible as 'the noblest monument of English prose'. Those who talk of the Bible as a 'monument of English prose' are merely admiring it as a monument over the grave of Christianity. I must try to avoid the by-paths of my discourse: it is enough to suggest that just as the work of Clarendon, or Gibbon, or Buffon, or Bradley would be of inferior literary value if it were insignificant as history, science and philosophy respectively, so the Bible has had a *literary* influence upon English literature *not* because it has been considered as literature, but because it has been considered as the report of the Word of God. And the fact that men of letters now discuss it as 'literature' probably indicates the *end* of its 'literary' influence.

The second kind of relation of religion to literature is that which is found in what is called 'religious' or 'devotional' poetry. Now what is the usual attitude of the lover of poetry — and I mean the the person who is a genuine and first-hand enjoyer and appreciator of poetry, not the person who follows the admirations of other — towards this department of poetry? I believe, all that may be implied in his calling it a *department*. He believes, not always explicitly, that when you qualify poetry as 'religious' you are indicating very clear limitations. For the great majority of people who love poetry, '*religious* poetry' is a variety of *minor* poetry: the religious poet is not a poet who is treating the whole subjet matter of poetry in a religious spirit, but a poet who is dealing with a confined part of this subject matter: who is leaving out what men consider their major passions, and thereby confessing his ignorance of them. I think that this is the real attitude of most poetry lovers towards such poets as Vaughan, or Southwell,* or Crashaw, or George Herbert, or Gerard Hopkins.

***Southwell, Robert:** (1561?-1595). 카톨릭 승려이자 시인. 순교를 당함.

But what is more, I am ready to admit that up to a point these critics are right. For there is a kind of poetry, such as most of the work of the authors I have mentioned, which is the product of a special religious awareness, which may exist without the general awareness which we expect of the major poet. In some poets, or in some of their works, this general awareness may have existed; but the preliminary steps which represent it may have been suppressed, and only the end-product presented. Between these, and those in which the religious or devotional genius represents the *special* and limited awareness, it may be very difficult to discriminate. I do not pretend to offer Vaughan, or Southwell, or George Herbert, or Hopkins as major poets. I feel sure that the first three, at least, are poets of this limited awareness. They are not great religious poets in the sense in which Dante, or Corneile, or Racine, even in those of their plays which do not touch upon Christian themes, are great Christian religious poets. Or even in the sense in which Villon and Baudelaire, with all their imperfections and delinquencies, are Christian poets. Since the time of Chaucer, Christian poetry (in the sense in which I shall mean it) has been limited in England almost exclusively to minor poetry.

I repeat that when I am considering Religion and Literature, I speak of these things only to make clear that I am not concerned primarily with Religious Literature. I am concerned with what should be the relation between Religion and all Literature. Therefore the third type of 'religious literature' may be more quickly passed over. I mean the literary works of men who are sincerely desirous of forwarding the cause of religion: that which may come under the heading of Propaganda. I am thinking, of course, of such delightful fiction as Mr. Chesterton's* *Man Who Was Thursday,* or his *Father Brown.* No one admires and enjoys these things more than I do; I would only remark that when the same effect is aimed at by zealous persons of less talent than Mr. Chesterton the effect is negative. But my point is that such writings do

---

*Chesterton, Gilbert K.: (1874-1936). 가톨릭 작가. 평론가.

not enter into any serious consideration of the relation of Religion and Literature: because they are conscious operations in a world in which it is assumed that Religion and Literature are not related. It is a conscious and limited relating. What I want is a literature which should be *un*consciously, rather than deliberately and defiantly, Christian: because the work of Mr. Chesterton has its point from appearing in a world which is definitely not Christian.

I am convinced that we fail to realize how completely, and yet how irrationally, we separate our literary from our religious judgements. If there could be a complete separation, perhaps it might not matter: but the separation is not, and never can be, complete. If we exemplify literature by the novel — for the novel is the form in which literature affects the greatest number — we may remark this gradual secularization of literature during at least the last three hundred years. Bunyan, and to some extent Defoe, had moral purposes: the former is beyond suspicion, the latter may be suspect. But since Defoe the secularization of the novel has been continuous. There have been three chief phases. In the first, the novel took the Faith, in its contemporary version, for granted, and omitted it from its picture of life. Fielding, Dickens and Thackeray belong to this phase. In the second, it doubted, worried about, or contested the Faith. To this phase belong George Eliot, George Meredith and Thomas Hardy. To the third phase, in which we are living, belong nearly all contemporary novelists except Mr. James Joyce. It is the phase of those who have never heard the Christian Faith spoken of as anything but an anachronism.

Now, do people in general hold a definite opinion, that is to say religious or anti-religious; and do they read novels, or poetry for that matter,* with a separate compartment of their minds? The common ground between religion and fiction is behaviour. Our religion imposes our ethics, our judgement and criticism of ourselves, and our behaviour toward our fellow men. The fiction that we read affects our behaviour

---

***for that matter:** 「그에 관해서는, 그 말이 나왔으니 말이지」.

towards our fellow men, affects our patterns of ourselves. When we read of human beings behaving in certain ways, with approval of the author, who gives his benediction to this behaviour by his attitude towards the result of the behaviour arranged by himself, we can be influenced towards behaving in the same way.* When the contemporary novelist is an individual thinking for himself in isolation, he may have something important to offer to those who are able to receive it. He who is alone may speak to the individual. But the majority of novelists are persons drifting in the stream, only a little faster. They have some sensitiveness, but little intellect.

We are expected to be broadminded about literature, to put aside prejudice or conviction, and to look at fiction as fiction and at drama as drama. With what is inaccurately called 'censorship' in this country — with what is much more difficult to cope with than an official censorship, because it represents the opinions of individuals in an irresponsible democracy, I have very little sympathy; partly because it so often suppresses the wrong books, and partly because it is little more effective than Prohibition of Liquor; partly because it is one manifestation of the desire that state control should take the place of decent domestic influence; and wholly because it acts only from custom and habit, not from decided theological and moral principles. Incidentally, it gives people a false sense of security in leading them to believe that books which are *not* suppressed are harmless. Whether there *is* such a thing as a harmless book I am not sure: but there very likely are books so utterly unreadable as to be incapable of injuring anybody. But it is certain that a book is not harmless merely because no one is consciously offended by it. And if we, as readers, keep our religious and moral convictions in one compartment, and take our reading merely for entertainment, or on a higher plane, for aesthetic pleasure, I would point out that the author, whatever his conscious intentions in writing, in practice recognizes no such distinctions. The author of a

*[원주] Here and later I am indebted to Montgomery Belgion. *The Human Parrot* (chapter on The Irresponsible Propagandist).

work of imagination is trying to affect us wholly, as human beings, whether he knows it or not; and we are affected by it, as human beings, whether we intend to be or not. I suppose that everything we eat has some other effect upon us than merely the pleasure of taste and mastication; it affects us during the process of assimilation and digestion; and I believe that exactly the same is true of anything we read.

The fact that what we read does not concern merely something called out *literary taste,* but that it affects directly, though only amongst many other influences, the whole of what we are, is best elicited, I think, by a conscientious examination of the history of our individual literary education. Consider the adolescent reading of any person with some literary sensibility. Everyone, I believe, who is at all sensible to the seductions of poetry, can remember some moment in youth when he or she was completely carried away by the work of one poet. Very likely he was carried away by several poets, one after the other. The reason for this passing infatuation is not merely that our sensibility to poetry is keener in adolescence than in maturity. What happens is a kind of inundation, of invasion of the undeveloped personality by the stronger personality of the poet. The same thing may happen at a later age to persons who have not done much reading. One author takes complete possession of us for a time; then another; and finally they begin to affect each other in our mind. We weigh one against another; we see that each has qualities absent from others, and qualities incompatible with the qualities of others: we begin to be, in fact, critical; and it is our growing critical power which protects us from excessive possession by any one literary personality. The good critic — and we should all try to be critics, and not leave criticism to the fellows who write reviews in the papers — is the man who, to a keen and abiding sensibility, joins wide and increasingly discriminating reading. Wide reading is not valuable as a kind of hoarding, an accumulation of knowledge, or what sometimes is meant by the term 'a well-stocked mind'. It is valuable because in the process of being affected by one powerful personality after another, we cease to be dominated by any one, or by any small number. The very different views of life, cohabiting in our minds, affect each other, and our own personality asserts itself and gives each a place in some arrangement peculiar to ourself.

It is simply not true that works of fiction, prose or verse, that is to say works depicting the actions, thoughts and words and passions of imaginary human beings, *directly* extend our knowledge of life. Direct knowledge of life is knowledge directly in relation to ourselves, it is our knwledge of *how* people behave in general, of *what* they are like in general, in so far as that part of life in which we ourselves have participated gives us material for generalization. Knowledge of life obtained through fiction is only possible by another stage of self-consciousness.* That is to say, it can only be a knowledge of other people's knowledge of life, not of life itself. So far as we are taken up with* the happenings in any novel in the same way in which we are taken up with what happens under our eyes, we are acquiring at least as much falsehood as truth. But when we are developed enough to say: 'This is the view of life of a person who was a good observer within his limits, Dickens, or Thackeray, or George Eliot, or Balzac; but he looked at it in a different way from me, because he was a different man; he even selected rather different things to look at, or the same things in a different order of importance, because he was a different man; so what I am looking at is the world as seen by a particular mind' — then we are in a position to gain something from reading fiction. We are learning *something* about life from these authors direct, just as we learn something from the reading of history direct; but these authors are only really helping us when we can see, and allow for, their differences from ourselves.

Now what we get, as we gradually grow up and read more and more, and read a greater diversity of authors, is a variety of views of life. But what people commonly assume, I suspect,

---

*소설에서 배우는 인생의 지식은 소설가가 실제로 산 인생의 지식에서 배운 지식보다 많이 떨어져 있다.

***be taken up with:** 「...에 열중하다」.

is that we gain this experience of other men's views of life only by 'improving reading'. This, it is supposed, is a reward we get by applying ourselves to Shakespeare, and Dante, and Goethe, and Emerson, and Carlyle, and dozens of other respectable writers. The rest of our reading for amusement is merely killing time. But I incline to come to the alarming conclusion that it is just the literature that we read for 'amusement', or 'purely for pleasure' that may have the greatest and least suspected influence upon us. It is the literature which we read with the least effort that can have the easiest and most insidious influence upon us. Hence it is that the influence of popular novelists, and of popular plays of contemporary life, requires to be scrutinized most closely. And it is chiefly *contemporary* literature that the majority of people ever read in this attitude of 'purely for pleasure', of pure passivity.

The relation to my subject of what I have been saying should now be a little more apparent. Though we may read literature merely for pleasure, of 'entertainment' or of 'aesthetic enjoyment', this reading never effects simply a sort of special sense: it affects us as entire human beings; it affects our moral and religious existence. And I say that while individual modern writers of eminence can be improving, contemporary literature as a whole tends to be degrading. And that even the effect of the better writers, in an age like ours, may be degrading to some readers; for we must remember that what a writer does to people is not necessarily what he intends to do. It may be only what people are capable of having done to them.* People exercise an unconscious selection in being influenced. A writer like D. H. Lawrence may be in his effect either beneficial or pernicious. I am not sure that I have not had some pernicious influence myself.

At this point I anticipate a rejoinder from the liberal-minded, from all those who are convinced that if

---

***It may...to them:** 「사람들이 자신들에게 남의 영향이 끼치도록 내버려두는 것에 불과할지 모른다」. 여기서 having done은 과거완료형이 아니라 사역동사형임.

everybody says what he thinks, and does what he likes, things will somehow, by some automatic compensation and adjustment, come right in the end. 'Let everything be tried', they say, and if it is a mistake, then we shall learn by experience.' This argument might have some value, if we were always the same generation upon earth; or if, as we know to be not the case, people ever learned much from the experience of their elders. These liberals are convinced that only by what is called unrestrained individualism will truth ever emerge. Ideas, views of life, they think, issue distinct from independent heads, and in consequence of their knocking violently against each other, the fittest survive, and truth rises triumphant. Anyone who dissents from this view must be either a mediaevalist, wishful only to set back the clock, or else a fascist, and probably both.

If the mass of contemporary authors were really individualists, every one of them inspired Blakes,* each with his separate vision, and if the mass of the contemporary public were really a mass of *individuals* there might be something to be said for this attitude. But this is not, and never has been, and never will be. It is not only that the reading individual today (or at any day) is not enough an individual to be able to absorb all the 'views of life' of all the authors pressed upon us by the publishers' advertisements and the reviewers, and to be able to arrive at wisdom by considering one against another. It is that the contemporary authors are not individuals enough either. It is not that the world of separate individuals of the liberal democrat is undesirable; it is simply that this world does not exist. For the reader of contemporary literature is not, like the reader of the established great literature of all time, exposing himself to the influence of divers and contractory personalities; he is exposing himself to a mass movement of writers who, each of them, think that they have something individually to offer, but are really all working together in the same direction. And there never was a time, I believe, when the reading public was so large, or so

---

*William Blake 는 영국 시인 중에서 가장 유명한 개인주의적 신비론자.

helplessly exposed to the influences of its own time. There never was a time, I believe, when those who read at all, read so many more books by living authors than books by dead authors; there never was a time so completely parochial, so shut off from the past. There may be too many publishers; there are certainly too many books published; and the journals ever incite the reader to 'keep up' with what is being published. Individualistic democracy has come to high tide: and it is more difficult today to be an individual than it ever was before.

Within itself, modern literature has perfectly valid distinctions of good and bad, better and worse: and I do not wish to suggest that I confound Mr. Bernard Shaw with Mr. Noel Coward,* Mrs. Woolf with Miss Mannin.* On the other hand, I should like it to be clear that I am not defending a 'high'-brow against a 'low'-brow literature. What I do wish to affirm is that the whole of modern literature is corrupted by what I call Secularism, that it is simply unaware of, simply cannot understand the meaning of, the primacy of the supernatural over the natural life: of something which I assume to be our primary concern.

I do not want to give the impresion that I have delivered a mere fretful jeremiad against contemporary literature. Assuming a common attitude between my readers, or some of my readers, and myself, the question is not so much, what is to be done about it? as, how should we behave towards it?

I have suggested that the liberal attitude towards literature will not work. Even if the writers who make their attempt to impose their 'view of life' upon us were really distinct individuals, even if we as readers were distinct individuals, what would be the result? It would be, surely, that each reader would be impressed, in his reading, merely by what he was previously prepared to be impressed by; he would follow the 'line of least resistance', and there would be no assurance that he would be made a better man. For literary judgement

---

*Noel Coward: (1899-1980). 요즘 말로 쇼우 작가.

*Mannin, Ethel Edith: (1900-). 통속소설가.

we need to be acutely aware of two things at once: of 'what we like', and of 'what we *ought* to like'. Few people are honest enough to know either. The first means knowing what we really feel: very few know that. The second involves understanding our shortcomings; for we do not really know what we ought to like unless we also know why we ought to like it, which involves knowing why we don't yet like it. It is not enough to understand what we ought to be, unless we know what we are; and we do not understand what we are, unless we know what we ought to be. The two forms of self-consciousness, knowing what we are and what we ought to be, must go together.

It is our business, as readers of literature, to know what we like. It is our business, as Christians, *as well as* readers of literature, to know what we ought to like. It is our business as honest men not to assume that whatever we like is what we ought to like; and it is our business as honest Christians not to assume that we do like what we ought to like. And the last thing I would wish for would be the existence of two literatures, one for Christian consumption and the other for the pagan world. What I believe to be incumbent upon all Christians is the duty of maintaining consciously certain standards and criteria of criticism over and above those applied by the rest of the world; and that by these criteria and standards everything that we read must be tested. We must remember that the greater part of our current reading matter is written for us by people who have no real belief in a supernatural order, though some of it may be written by people with individual notions of a supernatural order which are not ours. And the greater part of our reading matter is coming to be written by people who not only have no such belief, but are even ignorant of the fact that there are still people in the world so 'backwrad' or so 'eccentric' as to continue to believe. So long as we are conscious of the gulf fixed between ourselves and the greater part of contemporary literature, we are more or less protected from being harmed by it, and are in a position to extract from it what good it has to offer us.

There are a very large number of people in the world today who believe that all ills are fundamentally economic. Some believe that various specific economic changes alone would be enough to set the world right; others demand more or less drastic changes in the social as well, changes chiefly of two opposed types. These changes demanded, and in some places carried out, are alike in one respect, that they hold the assumptions of what I call Secularism: they concern themselves only with changes of a temporal, material, and external nature; they concern themselves with morals only of a collective nature. In an exposition of one such new faith I read the following worlds:

'In our morality the one single test of any moral question is whether it impedes or destroys in any way the power of the Individual to serve the State. [The individual] must answer the questions: "Does this action injure the nation? Does it injure other members of the nation? Does it injure my ability to serve the nation?" And if the answer is clear on all those questions, the individual has absolute liberty to do as he will.'

Now I do not deny that this is a kind of morality, and that it is capable of great good within limits; but I think that we should all repudiate a morality which had no higher ideal to set before us than that. It represents, of course, one of the violent reactions we are witnessing, against the view that the community is solely for the benefit of the individual; but it is equally a gospel of this world, and of this world alone. My complaint against modern literature is of the same kind. It is not that modern literature is in the ordinary sense 'immoral' or even 'amoral'; and in any case to prefer that charge would not be enough. It is simply that it repudiates, or is wholly ignorant of, our most fundamental and important beliefs; and that in consequence its tendency is to encourage its readers to get what they can out of life while it lasts, to miss no 'experience' that presents itself, and to sacrifice themselves, if they make any sacrifice at all, only for the sake of tangible benefits to others in this world either now or in the future. We shall certainly continue to read the best of its kind, of what our time provides; but we must tirelessly criticize it according to our own principles, and not merely according to the prin-

ciples admitted by the writers and by the critics who discuss it in the public press.

The Social Function of Poetry (1943)

THE TITLE of this essay is so likely to suggest different things to different people, that I may be excused for explaining first what I do not mean by it before going on to try to explain what I do mean. When we speak of the 'function' of anything we are likely to be thinking of what that thing *ought* to do rather than of what it does do or has done. That is an important distinction, because I do not intend to talk about what I think poetry *ought* to do. People who tell us what poetry ought to do, especially if they are poets themselves, usually have in mind the particular kind of poetry that they would like to write. It is always possible, of course, that poetry may have a different task in the future from what it has had in the past; but even if that is so, it is worth while to decide first what function it has had in the past, both at one time or another in one language or another, and universally. I could easily write about what I do with poetry myself, or what I should like to do, and then try to persuade you that this is exactly what all good poets have tried to do, or ought to have done, in the past — only they have not succeeded completely, but perhaps that is not their fault. But it seems to me probable that if poetry — and I mean *all* great poetry — has had no social function in the past, it is not likely to have any in the future.

When I say *all* great poetry I mean to avoid another way in which I might treat the subject. One might take up the various kinds of poetry, one after another, and discuss the social function of each kind in turn without reaching the general question of what is the function of poetry as poetry. I want to distinguish between the general and particular functions, so that we shall know what we are not talking about. Poetry may have a deliberate, conscious social purpose. In its more primitive forms this purpose is often quite clear. There are, for example, early runes and chants, some of which had very practical magical purposes — to avert the evil eye,* to cure some disease, or to propitiate some demon. Poetry is early used in religious ritual, and when we sing a hymn we are still using poetry for a particular social purpose. The early forms of epic and saga may have transmitted what was held to be history before surviving for communal entertainment only; and before the use of written language a regular verse form must have been extremely helpful to the memory — and the memory of primitive bards, story-tellers and scholars must have been prodigious. In more advanced societies, such as that of ancient Greece, the recognized social functions of poetry are also very conspicuous. The Greek drama develops out of religious rites, and remains a formal public ceremony associated with traditional religious celebrations; the pindaric ode develops in relation to a particular social occasion. Certainly, these definite uses of poetry gave poetry a framework which made possible the attainment of perfection in particular kinds.

In more modern poetry some of these forms remain, such as that of the religious hymn which I have mentioned. The meaning of the term *didactic* poetry has undergone some change. *Didactic* may mean 'conveying information', or it may mean 'giving moral instruction', or it may mean something which comprehends both. Virgil's *Georgics,** for instance, are very beautiful poetry, and contain some very sound information about good farming. But it would seem impossible, at the present day, to write an up-to-date book about farming which should also be fine poetry: for one thing* the subject itself has become much more complicated and scientific; and for another,* it can be handled more readily in prose. Nor should we, as the Romans did, write astronomical and cosmological treatises in verse.* The poem, the ostensible aim of which is to convey information, has been

---

***the evil eye:** 「악의에 찬(악마같은) 눈초리」.

***Georgics:** 한국의 〈농가월령가〉처럼 전원시와 농사정보를 겸한 명작.

***for one thing:** 「한 예를 들자면」.

***for another:** 「또 다른 예를 들자면」.

*예컨대 Lucretius는 「자연 만물의 성질에 대하여」라는 우주과학 시를 썼다.

superseded by prose. Didactic poetry has gradually become limited to poetry of moral exhortation, or poetry which aims to *persuade* the reader to the author's point of view about something. It therefore includes a great deal of what can be called *satire,* though satire overlaps with burlesque and parody, the purpose of which is primarily to cause mirth. Some of Dryden's poems, in the seventeenth century, are satires in the sense that they aim to ridicule the objects against which they are directed, and also didactic in the aim to persuade the reader to a particular political or religious point of view; and in doing this they also make use of the allegorical method of disguising reality as fiction: *The Hind and the Panther,* which aims to persuade the reader that right was on the side of the Church of Rome against the Church of England, is his most remarkable poem in this kind. In the nineteenth century a good deal of the poetry of Shelley is inspired by a zeal for social and political reforms.

As for *dramatic* poetry, that has a social function of a kind now peculiar to itself. For whereas most poetry to-day is written to be read in solitude, or to be read aloud in a small company, dramatic verse alone has as its function the making an immediate, collective impression upon a large number of people gathered together to look at an imaginary episode acted upon a stage. Dramatic poetry is different from any other, but as its special laws are those of the drama its function is merged into that of the drama in general, and I am not here concerned with the special social function of the drama.

As for the special function of philosophical poetry, that would involve an analysis and an historical account of some length. I have, I think, already mentioned enough kinds of poetry to make clear that the special function of each is related to some other function: of dramatic poetry to drama, of didactic poetry of information to the function of its subject-matter, of didactic poetry of philosophy or religion or politics or morals to the function of these subjects. We might consider the function of any of these kinds of poetry and still leave untouched the question of the function of *poetry* For all these things can be dealt with in prose.

But before proceeding I want to dismiss one objection that may be raised. People somethimes are suspicious of any poetry that has a particular purpose: poetry in which the poet is advocating social, moral, political or religious views. And they are much more inclined to say that it isn't poetry when they dislike the particular views; just as other people often think that something is real poetry because it happens to express a point of view which they like. I should say that the question of whether the poet is using his poetry to advocate or attack a social attitude does not matter. Bad verse may have a transient vogue when the poet is reflecting a popular attitude of the moment; but real poetry survives not only a change of popular opinion but the complete extinction of interest in the issues with which the poet was passionately concerned. Lucretius' poem remains a great poem, though his notions of physics and astronomy are discredited; Dryden's, though the political quarrels of the seventeenth century no longer concern us, just as a great poem of the past may still give great pleasure, though its subject-matter is one which we should now treat in prose.

Now if we are to find the essential social function of poetry we must look first at its more obvious functions, those which it must perform if it is to perform any. The first, I think, that we can be sure about is that poetry has to give pleasure. If you ask what kind of pleasure then I can only answer, the kind of pleasure that poetry gives: simply because any other answer would take us far afield into aesthetics, and the general question of the nature of art.

I suppose it will be agreed that every good poet, whether he be a great poet or not, has something to give us besides pleasure: for if it were only pleasure, the pleasure itself could not be of the highest kind. Beyond any specific intention which poetry may have, such as I have already instanced in the various kinds of poetry, there is always the communication of some new experience, or some fresh understanding of the familiar, or the expression of something we have experienced but have no words for, which enlarges our consciousness or refines our sensibility. But it is not with such individual benefit from poetry, any more than it is with the quality of individual pleasure, that this paper is concerned. We all understand, I think, both the kind of pleasure which poetry can give, and the kind of difference, beyond the pleasure, which it makes to our lives. Without producing these two effects it simply is not poetry. We may acknowledge this, but at the same time overlook something which it does for us collectively, as a society. And I mean that in the widest sense. For I think it is important that every people should have its own poetry, not simply for those who enjoy poetry — such people could always learn other languages and enjoy their poetry — but because it actually makes a difference to the society as a whole, and that means to people who do not enjoy poetry. I include even those who do not know the names of their own national poets. That is the real subject of this paper.

We observe that poetry differs from every other art in having a value for the people of the poet's race and language, which it can have for no other. It is true that even music and painting have a local and racial character: but certainly the difficulties of appreciation in these arts, for a foreigner, are much less. It is true on the other hand that prose writings have significance in their own language which is lost in translation; but we all feel that we lose much less in reading a novel in translation than in reading a poem; and in a translation of some kinds of scientific work the loss may be virtually nil. That poetry is much more local than prose can be seen in the history of European languages. Through the Middle Ages to within a few hundred years ago Latin remained the language for philosophy, theology, and science. The impulse towards the literary use of the languages of the peoples began with poetry. And this appears perfectly natural when we realize that poetry has primarily to do with the expression of feeling and emotion; and that feeling and emotion are particular, whereas thought is general. It is easier to think in a foreign language than it is to feel in it. Therefore no art is more stubbornly national than poetry. A people may have its language taken away from it, suppressed, and another language compelled upon the schools; but unless you teach that people to *feel* in a new language, you have not eradicated the old one, and it will reappear in poetry, which is the vehicle of feeling. I have just said 'feel in a new language', and I mean something more than merely 'express their feelings in a new language'. A thought expressed in a different language may be practically the same thought, but a feeling or emotion expressed in a different language is not the same feeling or emotion. One of the reasons for learning at least one foreign language well is that we acquire a kind of supplementary personality; one of the reasons for not acquiring a new language *instead* of our own is that most of us do not want to become a different person. A superior language can seldom be exterminated except by the extermination of the people who speak it. When one language supersedes another it is usually because that language has advantages which commend it, and which offer not merely a difference but a wider and more refined range, not only for thinking but for feeling, than the more primitive language.

Emotion and feeling, then are best expressed in the common language of the people — that is, the language common to all classes: the structure, the rhythm, the sound, the idiom of a language, express the personality of the people which speaks it. When I say that it is poetry rather than prose that is concerned with the expression of emotion and feeling, I do not mean that poetry need have no intellectual content or meaning, or that great poetry does not contain more of such meaning than lesser poetry. But to develop this investigation would take me away from my immediate purpose. I will take it as agreed that people find the most conscious expression of their deepest feelings in the poetry of their own language rather than in any other art or in the poetry of other languages. This does not mean, of course, that true poetry is limited to feelings which everyone can recognize and understand; we must not limit poetry to *popular* poetry. It is enough that in a homogeneous people the feelings of the most refined and complex have something in common with those of the most crude and simple, which they have not in common with those of people of their own level speaking another language. And, when a civilization is healthy, the great poet will have something to say to his fellow countrymen at every level of education.

We may say that the duty of the poet, as poet, is only indirectly to his people: his direct duty is to his *language,* first to preserve, and second to extend and improve. In expressing what other people feel he is also changing the feeling by making it more conscious; he is making people more aware of what they feel already, and therefore teaching them something about themselves. But he is not merely a more conscious person than the others; he is also individually different from other people, and from other poets too, and can make his readers share consciously in new feelings which they had not experienced before. That is the difference between the writer who is merely eccentric or mad and the genuine poet. The former may have feelings which are unique but which cannot be shared, and are therefore useless; the latter discovers new variations of sensibility which can be appropriated by others. And in expressing them he is developing and enriching the language which he speaks.

I have said quite enough about the impalpable differences of feeling between one people and another, differences which are affirmed in, and developed by, their different languages. But people do not only experience the world differently in different places, they experience it differently at different times. In fact, our sensibility is constantly changing, as the world about us changes: ours is not the same as that of the Chinese or the Hindu, but also it is not the same as that of our ancestors several hundred years ago. It is not the same as that of our fathers; and finally, we ourselves are not quite the same persons that we were a year ago. This is obvious; but what is not so obvious is that this is the reason why we cannot afford to stop writing poetry. Most educated people take a certain pride in the great authors of their language, though they may never read them, just as they are proud of any other distinction of their country: a few authors even become celebrated enough to be mentioned occasionally in political speeches.

But most people do not realize that this is not enough; that unless they go on producing great authors, and especially great poets, their language will deteriorate, their culture will deteriorate and perhaps become absorbed in a stronger one.

One point is, of course, that if we have no living literature we shall become more and more alienated from the literature of the past; unless we keep up continuity, our literature of the past will become more and more remote from us until it is as strange to us as the literature of a foreign people. For our language goes on changing; our way of life changes, under the pressure of material changes in our environment in all sorts of ways; and unless we have those few men who combine an exceptional sensibility with an exceptional power over words, our own ability, not merely to express, but even to feel any but the crudest emotions, will degenerate.

It matters little whether a poet had a large audience in his own time. What matters is that there should always be at least a small audience for him in every generation. Yet what I have just said suggests that his importance is for his own time, or that dead poets cease to be of any use to us unless we have living poets as well. I would even press my first point and say that if a poet gets a large audience very quickly, that is a rather suspicious circumstance: for it leads us to fear that he is not really doing anything new, that he is only giving people what they are already used to, and therefore what they have already had from the poets of the previous generation. But that a poet should have the right, small audience in his own time *is* important. There should always be a small vanguard of people, appreciative of poetry, who are independent and somewhat in advance of their time or ready to assimilate novelty more quickly. The development of culture does not mean bringing everybody up to the front, which amounts to no more than making everyone keep step: it means the maintenance of such an *élite,* with the main, and more passive body of readers not lagging more than a generation or so behind. The changes and developments of sensibility which appear first in a few will work themselves into the language gradually, through their influence on other, and more readily popular authors; and by the time they have become well established, a new advance will be called for. It is, moreover, through the living authors that the dead remain alive. A poet like Shakespeare has influenced the English language very deeply, not only by his influence on his immediate successors. For the greatest poets have aspects which do not come to light at once; and by exercising a direct influence on other poets centuries later, they continue to affect the living language. Indeed, if an English poet is to learn how to use words in our time, he must devote close study to those who have used them best in *their* time; to those who, in their own day, have made the language new.

So far I have only suggested the final point to which I think the influence of poetry may be said to extend; and that can be put best by the assertion that, in the long run, it makes a difference to the speech, to the sensibility, to the lives of all the members of a society, to all the members of the community, to the whole people, whether they read and enjoy poetry or not: even, in fact, whether they know the names of their greatest poets or not. The influence of poetry, at the furthest periphery, is of course very diffused, very indirect, and very difficult to prove. It is like following the course of a bird or an aeroplane in a clear sky: if you have seen it when it was quite near, and kept your eye on it as it flew farther and farther away, you can still see it at a great distance, a distance at which the eye of another person, to whom you try to point it out, will be unable to find it. So, if you follow the influence of poetry, through those readers who are most affected by it, to those people who never read at all, you will find it present everywhere. At least you will find it if the national culture is living and healthy, for in a healthy society there is a continuous reciprocal influence and interaction of each part upon the others. And this is what I mean by the social function of poetry in its largest sense: that it does, in proportion to its excellence and vigour, affect the speech and the sensibility of the whole nation.

You must not imagine me to be saying that the language which we speak is determined exclusively by our poets. The structure of culture is much more complex than that. Indeed it will equally be true that the quality of our poetry is dependent upon the way in which the people use their language: for a poet must take as his material his own language as it is actually spoken around him. If it is improving, he will profit; if it is deteriorating, he must make the best of it.* Poetry can to some extent preserve, and even restore, the beauty of a language; it can and should also help it to develop, to be just as subtle and precise in the more complicated conditions and for the changing purposes of modern life, as it was in and for a simpler age. But poetry, like every other single element in that mysterious social personality which we call our 'culture', must be dependent upon a great many circumstances which are beyond its control.

This leads me to a few after-thoughts of a more general nature. My emphasis to this point has been upon the national and local function of poetry; and this must be qualified. I do not wish to leave the impression that the function of poetry is to divide people from people, for I do not believe that the cultures of the several peoples of Europe can flourish in isolation from each other. There have been, no doubt, in the past, high civilizations producing great art, thought and literature, which have developed in isolation. Of that I cannot speak with assurance, for some of them may not have been so isolated as at first appears. But in the history of Europe this has not been so. Even Ancient Greece owed much to Egypt, and something to the Asiatic frontiers; and in the relations of the Greek states to each other, with their different dialects and different manners, we may find a reciprocal influence and stimulus analogous to that of the countries of Europe upon each other. But the history of European literature will not show that any has been independent of the others; rather that there has been a constant give and take, and that each has in turn, from time to time, been revitalized by stimulation from outside. A general *autarky** in culture

---

*Shakespeare에 대한 예찬과 비교할 것.

***autarky:** (경제적) 「자급자족」.

simply will not work: the hope of perpetuating the culture of any country lies in communication with others. But if separation of cultures within the unity of Europe is a danger, so also would be a unification which led to uniformity. The variety is as essential as the unity. For instance, there is much to be said, for certain limited purposes, for a universal *lingua franca** such as Esperanto or Basic English.* But supposing that all communication between nations was carried on in such an artificial language, how imperfect it would be! Or rather, it would be wholly adequate in some respects, and there would be a complete lack of communication in others. Poetry is a constant reminder of all the things that can only be said in one language, and are untranslatable. The *spiritual* communication between people and people cannot be carried on without the individuals who take the trouble to learn at least one foreign language as well as one can learn any language but one's own, and who consequently are able, to a greater or less degree, to *feel* in another language as well as in their own. And one's understanding of another people, in this way, needs to be supplemented by the understanding of those individuals among that people who have gone to the pains to learn one's own language.

Incidentally, the study of another people's poetry is peculiarly instructive. I have said that there are qualities of the poetry of every language, which only those to whom the language is native can understand. But there is another side to this too. I have sometimes found, in trying to read a language which I did not know very well, that I did not understand a piece of prose until I understood it according to the standards of the school teacher: that is, I had to be sure of the meaning of every word, grasp the grammar and syntax, and then, I could think the passage out in English. But I have also found sometimes that a piece of poetry, which I could not

---

**lingua franca*: 「공용어」.

***Basic English:** 영국의 학자 C. K. Ogden 이 1930 년 창안한 것으로, 850 단어로 된 간이 영어. 세계 공용어 후보로 삼기 위해 창안했었다. British, American, Scientific, International, Commercial 의 머리글자를 따서 모은 것이다.

translate, containing many words unfamiliar to me, and sentences which I could not construe, conveyed something immediate and vivid, which was unique, different from anything in English — something which I could not put into words and yet felt that I understood. And on learning that language better I found that this impression was not an illusion, not something which I imagined to be in the poetry, but something that was really there. So in poetry you can, now and then, penetrate into another country, so to speak, before your passport has been issued or your ticket taken.

The whole question of the relation of countries of different language but related culture, within the ambit of Europe, is therefore one into which we are led, perhaps unexpectedly, by inquiring into the social function of poetry. I certainly do not intend to pass from this point into purely political questions; but I could wish that those who are concerned with political questions would more often cross the frontier into these which I have been considering. For these give the spiritual aspect of problems the material aspect of which is the concern of politics. On my side of the line one is concerned with living things which have their own laws of growth, which are not always reasonable, but must just be accepted by the reason: things which cannot be neatly planned and put into order any more than the winds and the rains and the seasons can be disciplined.

If, finally, I am right in believing that poetry has a 'social function' for the whole of the people of the poet's language, whether they are aware of his existence or not, it follows that it matters to each people of Europe that the others should continue to have poetry. I cannot read Norwegian poetry, but if I were told that no more poetry was being written in the Norwegian language I should feel an alarm which would be much more than generous sympathy. I should regard it as a spot of malady which was likely to spread over the whole Continent; the beginning of a decline which would mean that people everywhere would cease to be able to express, and consequently be able to feel, the emotions of civilized beings. This of course might happen. Much has been said everywhere about the decline of religious belief; not so much notice has been taken of the decline of religious sensibility. The trouble of the modern age is not merely the inability to believe certain things about God and man which our forefathers believed, but the inability to *feel* towards God and man as they did. A belief in which you no lnoger believe is something which to some extent you can still understand; but when religious feeling disappears, the words in which men have struggled to express it become meaningless. It is true that religious feeling varies naturally from country to country, and from age to age, just as poetic feeling does; the feeling varies, even when the belief, the doctrine, remains the same. But this is a condition of human life, and what I am apprehensive of is death. It is equally possible that the feeling for poetry, and the feelings which are the material of poetry, may disappear everywhere: which might perhaps help to facilitate that unification of the world which some people consider desirable for its own sake.*

*언어의 감각에 따라 민족이 구분되어 있는데, 그 감각이 없어지면 통일이 이루어지겠지만, 그렇게 되더라도 그것은 「죽은」 사람들의 통일일 것이다.

John Crowe Ransom

(1888—1974)

미국 테네시 주에서 목사의 아들로 태어나 명문 밴더빌트와 옥스포드를 졸업, 밴더빌트에서 가르치다가 1937년 이후에는 Kenyon 대학으로 옮겨, 이름 높은 문예지 *Kenyon Review*를 창간, 편집했다. 밴더빌트에 재직시에 *The Fugitive*라는 문예지를 주재하여 많은 남부 시인을 길러냈고, *Kenyon Review*를 통하여서는 New Criticism이라는 비평운동을 전개했다.

그는 시인으로서도 일급에 속하지만, 비평가로서의 영향은 훨씬 크다. 20세기의 최대의 비평운동의 하나인 New Criticism은 그와 그의 제자들에 의하여 주도된 것이다. *The World's Body*(1938, 개정판 1969), *The New Criticism*(1941)은 그의 대표적 비평집으로서, 이 뒤의 책에서 그가 주도한 비평 유파의 명칭이 생겼다.

랜섬은 작품의 자세한 분석을 중요시 하였지만, 그의 근본 비평 정신은 칸트적이다. 그는 무엇보다도 작품의 "존재론적" 구조에 관심이 있다. 즉 그 작품이 그 자체로서 무엇이냐 하는 문제에 주의를 집중하는 것이다.

"Poetry: A Note on Ontology" (1934)는 바로 그러한 랜섬의 문학관을 그대로 드러내는 비평 논문으로서, 관념적이고 추상적인 내용의 시를 배격하고 구체적이고 사물적인 시를 옹호하며, 사물에 대한 "육체적" 지각을 강조한다. 그는 과학의 언어(관념어)와 문학의 언어(구체어)를 구별하고 문학의 언어가 구현하는 특이한 인식적 가치를 주장한다. 그는 이미지를 강렬히 제시한 시를 "사물적"(physical)이라 하고, 사물을 통하여 관념을 전달코자 하는 시를 "플라톤적" 시라고 부른다. 여기에 대부분의 낭만파 시인과 빅토리아 시인이 포함된다. 그런데 metaphysical poetry는 구체적 image를 제시하는 데에서 그치지 않고 두 사물의 유사성을 완성시키는 일종의 기적(miraculism)이라고 본다. 즉 이것이야 말로 가장 시다운 시인 것이다.

Poetry: A Note on Ontology (1934)

A poetry may be distinguished from a poetry by virtue of subject-matter, and subject-matter may be differentiated with respect to its ontology, or the reality of its being. An excellent variety of critical doctrine arises recently out of this differentiation, and thus perhaps criticism leans again upon ontological analysis as it was meant to do by Kant. The recent critics remark in effect that some poetry deals with things, while some other poetry deals with ideas. The two poetries will differ from each other as radically as a thing differs from an idea.

The distinction in the hands of critics is a fruitful one. There is apt to go along with it a principle of valuation, which is the consequence of a temperament, and therefore basic. The critic likes things and intends that his poet shall offer them: or likes ideas and intends that he shall offer them: and approves him as he does the one or the other. Criticism cannot well go much deeper than this. The critic has carried to the last terms his analysis of the stuff of which poetry is made, and vlaued it frankly as his temperament or his need requires him to value it.

So philosophical a critic seems to be highly modern. He is; but this critic* as a matter of fact is peculiarly on one side of the question. (The implication is unfavorable to the other side of the question.) He is in revolt against the tyranny of ideas, and against the poetry which celebrates ideas, and which may be identified — so far as his usual generalization may be trusted — with the hateful poetry of the Victorians. His bias is in favor of the things. On the other hand the critic who likes Victorian verse, or the poetry of ideas, has probably not thought of anything of so grand a simplicity as electing

*this critic: 즉 Ransom 자신.

between the things and the ideas, being apparently not quite capable of the ontological distinction.

Therefore he does not know the real or constitutional ground of his liking, and may somewhat ingenuously claim that his predilection is for those poets who give him inspiration, or comfort, or truth, or honest metres, or something else equally "worth while." But Plato, who was not a modern, was just as clear as we are about the basic distinction between the ideas and the things, and yet stands far apart from the aforesaid conscious modern in passionately preferring the ideas over the things. The weight of Plato's testimony would certainly fall on the side of the Victorians, though they may scarcely have thought of calling him as their witness. But this consideration need not conclude the hearing.*

I. PHYSICAL POETRY

The poetry which deals with things was much in favor a few years ago with the resolute body of critics. And the critics affected the poets. If necessary, they became the poets, and triumphantly illustrated the new mode. The Imagists were important figures in the history of our poetry, and they were both theorists and creators. It was their intention to present things in their thinginess,* or *Dinge** in their *Dinglichkeit;** and to such an extent had the public lost its sense of *Dinglichkeit* that their redirection was wholesome. What the public was inclined to seek in poetry was ideas, whether large ones or small ones, grand ones or pretty ones, certainly ideas to live by and die by* but what the Imagists identified with the stuff of poetry was, simply, things.

Their application of their own principle was sufficiently heroic, though they scarcely consented to be as extreme in the practice as in the theory. They had artistic talent, every one

---

***hearing:** 청문회. 즉, 각자의 의견을 듣는 기회.
***thinginess:** 「물건스러움」. thingy-ness.
****Dinge*:** things. ***Dinglichkeit*:** thinginess. 둘 다 독일어.
***ideas to...by:** 「살고 죽기 위해 의존하는 사상」.

of the original group, and it was impossible that they should make of poetry so simple an exercise as in doctrine they seemed to think it was. Yet Miss Lowell* wrote a poem on *Thompson's Lunch Room, Grand Central Station;* it is admirable if its intention is to show the whole reach of the courage. Its detail goes like this:

> Jagged greenwhite bowls of pressed glass
> Rearing snow-peaks of chipped sugar
> Above the lighthouse-shaped castors
> Of gray pepper and gray-white salt.

For most of us as for the public idealist, with his "values," this is inconsequential. Unhappily it seems that the things as things do not necessarily interest us, and that in fact we are not quite constructed with the capacity for a disinterested interest. But it must be noted even here that the things are on their good behavior, looking rather well, and arranged by lines into something approaching a military formation. More technically, there is cross-imagery* in the snow-peaks of sugar, and in the lighthouse-shaped castors, and cross-imagery involves association, and will presently involve dissociation and thinking. The metre is but a vestige, but even so it means something, for metre is a powerful intellectual determinant marshalling the words and, inevitably, the things. The *Dinglichkeit* of this Imagist specimen, or the realism, was therefore not pure.* But it was nearer pure than the world was used to in poetry, and the exhibit was astonishing.

For the purpose of this note I shall give to such poetry, dwelling as exclusively as it dares upon physical things, the name Physical Poetry. It is to stand opposite to the poetry which dwells as firmly as it dares upon ideas.

But perhaps thing *versus* idea does not seem to name an opposition precisely. Then we might phrase it a little dif-

---

***Lowell, Amy Lawrence:** (1874-1925). 미국의 여류시인. Imagist 운동의 지도자.

***cross-imagery:** 「교차 심상」(심상들이 서로 연결되어 있는 상태).

***not pure:** 완전히 물건스럽지 못하고 지적 내용이 들어갔다는 것.

ferently: image *versus* idea. The idealistic philosophies are not sure that things exist,* but they mean the equivalent when they refer to images. (Or they may consent to perceptions; or to impressions, following Hume,* and following Croce,* who remarks that they are pre-intellectual and independent of concepts. It is all the same, unless we are extremely technical.) It is sufficient if they concede that image is the raw material of idea. Though it may be an unwieldy and useless affair for the idealist as it stands, much needing to be licked into shape,* nevertheless its relation to idea is that of a material cause, and it cannot be dispossessed of its priority.

It cannot be dispossessed of a primordial freshness, which idea can never claim. An idea is derivative and tamed. The image is in the natural or wild state, and it has to be discovered there, not put there, obeying its own law and none of ours. We think we can lay hold of image and take it captive, but the docile captive is not the real image but only the idea, which is the image with its character beaten out of it.

But we must be very careful: idealists are nothing if not dialectical. They object that an image in an original state of innocence is a delusion and cannot exist, that no image ever comes to us which does not imply the world of ideas, there is "no percept without a concept." There is something in it. Every property discovered in the image is a universal property, and nothing discovered in the image is marvellous in kind though it may be pinned down* historically or statistically as a single instance. But there is this to be understood too: the image which is not remarkable in any particular property is marvellous in its assemblage of many properties, a manifold of properties, like a mine or a field, something to be explored

---

***the idealistic...exist:** 관념철학에서는 사물 자체의 존재를 믿지 않는다. Image는 물론 허상으로 간주.

***Hume, David:** (1711-76). 영국의 철학자. 인식의 주관성을 주장.

***Croce, Benedetto:** (1866-1952). 이탈리아의 철학자. 예술에 있어서 직관과 표현은 동일한 것임을 주장.

***lick into shape:** 「고심하여 제대로 모습을 갖추게 하다」.

***pin down:** 「확정짓다」.

for the properties; yet science can manage the image, which is infinite in properties, only by equating it to the one property with which the science is concerned: for science at work is always *a science,* and committed to a special interest. It is not by refutation but by abstraction that science destroys the image. It means to get its "value" out of the image, and we may be sure that it has no use for the image in its original state of freedom. People who are engrossed with their pet "values" become habitual killers. Their game* is the images, or the things, and they acquire the ability to shoot them as far off as they can be seen, and do. It is thus that we lose the power of imagination, or whatever faculty it is by which we are able to contemplate things as they are in their rich and contingent materiality. But our dreams reproach us, for in dreams they come alive again. Likewise our memory; which makes light of* our science by recalling the images in their panoply of circumstance and with their morning freshness upon them.

It is the dream, the recollection, which compels us to poetry, and to deliberate aesthetic experience. It can hardly be argued, I think, that the arts are constituted automatically out of original images, and arise in some early age of innocence. (Though Croce seems to support this view, and to make art a pre-adult stage of experience.) Art is based on second love, not first love. In it we make a return to something which we had wilfully alienated. The child is occupied mostly with things, but it is because he is still unfurnished with systematic ideas, not because he is a ripe citizen by nature and comes along already trailing clouds of glory.* Images are clouds of glory for the man who has discovered that ideas are a sort of darkness. Imagism, that is, the recent historical movement, may resemble a naïve poetry of mere

---

***game:** 「사냥물, 사냥의 대상」. "가치"에 대한 idea로 가득찬 사람은 image를 사냥하는, 즉 죽이는 자이다. Image를 idea 때문에 죽이면 imagination은 불가능하게 된다.

***make light of…:** 「…을 가볍게 여기다」.

***he is a ripe…clouds of glory:** Wordsworth가 "Immorality Ode"에서 한 말. 어린이는 날 때부터 영광의 구름을 거느리는 시인이며 철학자라고 했다.

things, but we can read the theoretical pronouncements of Imagists, and we can learn that Imagism is motivated by a distaste or the systematic abstractedness of thought. It presupposes acquaintance with science; that famous activity which is "constructive" with respect to the tools of our economic role in this world, and destructive with respect to nature. Imagists wish to escape from science by immersing themselves in images.

Not far off the simplicity of Imagism was, a little later, the subtler simplicity of Mr. George Moore's* project shared with several others, in behalf of "pure poetry." In Moore's house on Ebury Street they talked about poetry, with an after-dinner warmth if not an early-morning discretion, and their tastes agreed almost perfectly and reinforced one another. The fruit of these conversations was the volume *Pure Poetry*. It must have been the most exclusive anthology of English poetry that had yet appeared, since its room was closed to all the poems that dallied visibly with ideas, so that many poems that had been coveted by all other anthologists do not appear there. Nevertheless the book is delicious, and something more deserves to be said for it.

First, that "pure poetry" is a kind of Physical Poetry. Its visible content is a thing-content. Technically, I suppose, it is effective in this character if it can exhibit its material in such a way that an image or set of images and not an idea must occupy the foreground of the reader's attention. Thus:

> Full fathom five thy father lies;
> Of his bones are coral made.*

Here it is difficult for anybody (except the perfect idealist who is always theoretically possible and who would expect to take a return from anything whatever) to receive any experience except that of a very distinct image, or set of images. It has the configuration of image, which consists in being

---

*George Moore: (1852-1933). 에이레 출신의 소설가. 1924에 *Pure Poetry: An Anthology*를 발표. "pure poetry"는 abstract idea를 시에서 제거하려는 운동.

*Shakespeare, *The Tempest*, I, ii, 398—9.

sharp of edges, and the modality of image, which consists in being given and non-negotiable,* and the density, which consists in being full, a plenum of qualities. What is to be done with it? It is pure exhibit; it is to be contemplated; perhaps it is to be enjoyed. The art of poetry depends more frequently on this faculty than on any other in its repertory; the faculty of presenting images so whole and clean that they resist the catalysis of thought.

And something else must be said, going in the opposite direction. "Pure poetry," all the same, is not as pure as it is claimed to be, though on the whole it is Physical Poetry. (All true poetry is a phase of Physical Poetry.) It is not as pure as Imagism is, or at least it is not as pure as Imagism would be if it lived up to* its principles; and in fact it is significant that the volume does not contain any Imagist poems, which argues a difference in taste somewhere. Imagism may take trifling things for its material; presumably it will take the first things the poet encounters, since "importance" and "interest" are not primary qualities which a thing possesses but secondary or tertiary ones which the idealist attibutes to it by virtue of his own requirements. "Pure poetry" as Moore conceives it, and as the lyrics of Poe and Shakespeare offer it, deals with the more dramatic materials, and here dramatic means human, or at least capable of being referred to the critical set of human interests. Employing this sort of material the poet cannot exactly intend to set the human economists in us actually into motion, but perhaps he does intend to comfort us with fleeting sense that it is potentially our kind of material.

In the same way "pure poetry" is nicely metred, where Imagism was free. Technique is written on it.* And by the way the anthology contains no rugged anonymous Scottish ballad either, and probably for a like reason: because it would not be technically finished. Now both Moore and de la Mare* are

---

***which...non-negotiable:** 그냥 주어진 것이고 다른 것으로 바꿀 수 없는 것.
***live up to:** (정해진 원칙 따위를) 「충실히 이행하다」.
***be written on it:** 「첫눈에 명백하다」.
***la Mare, Walter de:** (1873-1956). 영국의 시인. 동화작가.

accomplished conservative artists, and what they do or what they approve may be of limited range but it is sure to be technically admirable, and it is certain that they understand what technique in poetry is though they do not define it. Technique takes the thing-content and metres and orders it. Metre is not an original property of things. It is artificial, and conveys the sense of human control, even if it does not wish to impair the thinginess of the things. Metric is a science, and so far as we attend to it we are within the scientific atmosphere. Order is the logical arrangement of things. It involves the dramatic "form" which selects the things, and brings out their appropriate qualities, and carries them through a systematic course of predication until the total impression is a unit of logic and not merely a solid lump of thing-content. The "pure poems" which Moore admires are studied,* though it would be fatal if they look studious.* A sustained effort of ideation effected these composition. It is covered up, and communicates itself only on a subliminal plane of consciousness. But experiened readers are quite aware of it; they know at once what is the matter when they encounter a realism shamelessly passing for poetry, or a well-planned but blundering poetry.

As critics we should have every good will toward Physical Poetry: it is the basic constituent of any poetry. But the product is always something short of a pure or absolute existence, and it cannot quite be said that it consists of nothing but physical objects. The fact is that when we are more than usually satisfied with a Physical Poetry our analysis will probably disclose that it is more than usually impure.

II. PLATONIC POETRY

The poetry of ideas I shall denominate: Platonic Poetry. This also has grades of purity. A discourse which employed only abstract ideas with no images would be a scientific document and not a poem at all, not even a Platonic poem.

---

*studied: 「공을 들인」. studious: 「열성을 다하는」.

Platonic Poetry dips heavily into the physical. If Physical Poetry tends to employ some ideation surreptitiously while still looking innocent of idea,* Platonic Poetry more than returns the compliment, for it tries as hard as it can to look like Physical Poetry, as if it proposed to conceal its medicine, which is the idea to be propagated, within the sugar candy of objectivity* and *Dinglichkeit*. As an instance, it is almost inevitable that I quote a famous Victorian utterance:

> **The year's at the spring**
> **And day's at the morn;**
> **Morning's at seven;**
> **The hill-side's dew-pearled;**
> **The lark's on the wing;**
> **The snail's on the thorn:**
> **God's in his heaven—**
> **All's right with the world!***

which is a piece of transparent homiletics for in it six pretty, co-ordinate images are marched, like six little lambs to the slaughter, to a colon and a powerful text. Now the exhibits of this poetry in the physical kind are always large, and may take more of the attention of the reader than is desired, but they are meant mostly to be illustrative of the ideas. It is on this ground that idealists like Hegel detect something unworthy, like a pedagogical trick, in poetry after all, and consider that the race will abandon it when it has outgrown its childishness and is enlightened.

The ablest arraignment of Platonic Poetry that I have seen, as an exercise which is really science but masquerades as poetry by affecting a concern for physical objects, is that of Mr. Allen Tate* in a series of studies recently in *The New Republic*. I will summarize. Platonic Poetry is allegory, a

---

***innocent of ideas:** 「관념에 물들지 않은」.

***sugar candy:** 사탕발림 속에 idea를 약처럼 감추고 있다.

*Browning, *Pippa Passes*의 일절.

***Allen Tate:** (1899-). 시인, 비평가. *The New Republic*지에 "Three Types of Poetry"를 기고.

discourse in things, but on the understanding that they are translatable at every point into ideas. (The usual ideas are those which constitute the popular causes, patriotic, religious, moral, or social.) Or Platonic Poetry is the elaboration of ideas as such, but in proceeding introduces for ornament some physical properties after the style of Physical Poetry; which is rhetoric. It is positive when the poet believes in the efficacy of the ideas. It is negative when he despairs of their efficacy, because they have conspicuously failed to take care of him, and utters his personal wail:

> I fall upon the thorns of life! I bleed!*

This is "Romantic Irony," which comes at occasional periods to interrupt the march of scientific optimism. But it still falls under the category of Platonism; it generally proposes some other ideas to take the place of those which are in vogue. But why Platonism? To define Platonism we must remember that it is not the property of the historical person who reports dialogues about it in an Academy, any more than "pure poetry" is the property of the talkers who describe it from a house on Ebury Street.* Platonism, in the sense I mean, is the name of an impulse that is native to us all, frequent, tending to take a too complete possession of our minds. Why should the spirit of mortal be proud? The chief explanation is that modern mortal is probably a Platonist. We are led to believe that nature is rational and that by the force of reasoning we shall possess it. I have read upon high authority: "Two great forces are persistent in Plato: the love of truth and zeal for human improvement." The forces are one force. We love to view the world under universal or scientific ideas to which we give the name truth; and this is because the ideas seem to make not for* righteousness but for mastery. The Platonic view of the world is ultimately the predatory, for it reduces to the scientific, which we know. The Platonic Idea becomes the

---

*Shelley, "Ode to the West Wind"의 일절.

***a house on Ebury Street:** George Moore가 동료들과 pure poetry를 논하던 장소.

***make for…:** 「…으로 향하다」.

Logos which science worships, which is the Occidental God, whose minions we are, and whose children, claiming a large share in His powers for patrimony.

Now the fine Platonic world of ideas fails to coincide with the original world of perception, which is the world populated by the stubborn and contingent objects, and to which as artists we fly in shame. The sensibility manifested by artists makes fools of scientists, if the latter are inclined to take their special and quite useful form of truth as the whole and comprehensive article. A dandified pagan worldling like Moore can always defeat Platonism; he does it every hour; he can exhibit the savor of his fish and wines, the fragrance of his coffee and cigars, and the solidity of the images in his favorite verse. These are objects which have to be experienced, and cannot be reported, for what is their simple essence that the Platonist can abstract? Moore may sound mystical but he is within the literal truth when he defends "pure poetry" on the ground that the things are constant, and it is the ideas which change—changing according to the latest mode under which the species indulges its grandiose expectation of subjugating nature. The things are constant in the sense that the ideas are never emanacipated from the necessity of referring back to them as their original; and the sense that they are not altered nor diminished no matter which ideas may take off from them as a point of departure. The way to obtain the true *Dinglichkeit* of a formal dinner or a landscape or a beloved person is to approach the object as such, and in humility; then it unfolds a nature which we are unprepared for if we have put our trust in the simple idea which attempted to represent it.

The special antipathy of Moore is to the ideas as they put on their moral complexion, the ideas that relate everything to that insignificant centre of action, the human "soul" in its most Platonic and Pharisaic* aspect. Nothing can darken perception better than a repetitive moral earnestness, based on the reputed superiority and higher destiny of the human

---

***Pharisaic:** (성경에 나오는 위선적 열성파인) 「바리새 교인같은」.

species. If morality is the code by which we expect the race to achieve the more perfect possession of nature, it is an incitement to a more heroic science, but not to aesthetic experience, nor religious; if it is the code of humility, by which we intend to know nature as nature is, that is another matter; but in an age of science morality is inevitably for the general public the former; and so transcendent a morality as the latter is now unheard of. And therefore:

> O love, *they* die in yon rich sky,
> *They* faint on hill or field or river;
> *Our* echoes roll from soul to soul,
> And grow forever and forever.*

The italics are mine. These lines conclude an otherwise innocent poem, a candidate for the anthology, upon which Moore remarks: "The Victorian could never reconcile himself to finishing a poem without speaking about the soul, and the lines are particularly vindictive." Vindictive is just. By what right did the Laureate* exult in the death of the physical echoes and call upon his love to witness it, but out of the imperiousness of his savage Platonism? Plato himself would have admired this ending, and considered that it redeemed an otherwise vicious poem.

Why do persons who have ideas to promulgate risk the trial by poetry? If the poets are hired to do it, which is the polite conception of some Hegelians, why do their employers think it worth the money, which they hold in public trust for the cause? Does a science have to become a poetry too? A science is the less effective as a science when it muddies its clear waters with irrelevance, a sermon becomes less cogent when it begins to quote the poets. The moralist, the scientist, and the prophet of idealism think evidently that they must establish their conclusions in poetry, though they reach these conclusions upon quite other evidence. The poetry is likely to destroy the conclusions with a sort of death by drowning, if it is a free poetry.

---

*Tennyson, "The Splendor Falls"에서.

*Tennyson은 Poet Laureate였다.

When that happens the Platonists may be cured of Platonism. There are probably two cures, of which this is the better. One cure is by adversity, by the failure of the ideas to work, on account of treachery or violence, or the contingencies of weather, constitution, love, and economics; leaving the Platonist defeated and bewildered, possibly humbled, but on the other hand possibly turned cynical and worthless. Very much preferable is the cure which comes by education in the fine arts, erasing his Platonism more gently, leading him to feel that that is not a becoming habit of mind which dulls the perceptions.

The definition which some writers have given to art is: the reference of the idea to the image. The implication is that the act is not for the purpose of honest comparison so much as for the purpose of proving the idea by image. But in the event* the idea is not disproved so much as it is made to look ineffective and therefore foolish. The ideas will not cover the objects upon which they are imposed, they are too attenuated and threadlike; for ideas have extension and objects have intension, but extension is thin while intension is thick.*

There must be a great deal of genuine poetry which started in the poet's mind as a thesis to be developed, but in which the characters and the situations have developed faster than the thesis, and of their own accord.* The thesis disappears; or it is recaptured here and there and at the end, and lodged sententiously with the reader, where every successive reading of the poem will dislodge it again. Like this must be some plays, even some play out of Shakespeare, whose thesis would probably be disentangled with difficulty out of the crowded pageant; or some narrative poem with a moral plot but much pure detail; perhaps some "occasional" piece by a Laureate or official person, whose purpose is compromised but whose personal integrity is saved by his wavering between the sentiment which is a public duty and the ex-

---

***event:** 「결과」.

***intension, extension:** 「내연, 외연」. 또는 뭉치려는 성향과 퍼져나가려는 성향.

***of their own accord:** 「자기들 스스로」.

perience which he has in his own right;* even some proclaimed allegory, like Spenser's, unlikely as that may seem, which does not remain transparent and everywhere translatable into idea but makes excursions into the territory of objectivity. These are hybrid performances. They cannot possess beauty of design, though there may be a beauty in detailed passages. But it is common enough, and we should be grateful. The mind is a versatile agent, and unexpectedly stubborn in its determination not really to be hardened in Platonism. Even in an age of science like the nineteenth century the poetic talents are not so loyal to its apostolic zeal as they and it suppose, and do not deserve the unqualified scorn which it is fashionable to offer them, now that the tide has turned, for their performance is qualified.

But this may be not stern enough for concluding a note on Platonic Poetry. I refer again to that whose Platonism is steady and malignant. This poetry is an imitation of Physical Poetry, and not really a poetry. Platonists practice their bogus poetry in order to show that an image will prove an idea, but the literature which succeeds in this delicate mission does not contain real images but illustrations.

III. METAPHYSICAL POETRY

"Most men," Mr. Moore observes, "read and write poetry between fifteen and thirty and afterwards very seldom, for in youth we are attracted by ideas, and modern poetry being concerned almost exclusively with ideas we live on duty, liberty, and fraternity as chameleons are said to live on light and air, till at last we turn from ideas to things, thinking that we have lost our taste for poetry, unless, perchance, we are classical scholars."

Much is conveyed in this characteristic sentence, even in proportion to its length. As for the indicated chronology, the cart is put after the horse,* which is its proper sequence. And

*in his own right: 「자기 독자적으로」.

*the cart is...the horse: 「앞뒤가 바뀌다」.

it is pleasant to be confirmed in the belief that many men do recant from their Platonism and turn back to things. But it cannot be exactly a *volte-face,** for there are qualifications. If pure ideas were what these men turn from, they would have had no poetry at all in the first period, and if pure things were what they turn to, they would be having not a classical poetry but a pure imagism, if such a thing is possible, in the second.

The mind does not come unscathed and virginal out of Platonism. Ontological interest would have to develop curiously, or wastefully and discontinuously, if men through their youth must cultivate the ideas so passionately that upon its expiration they are done with* ideas forever and ready to become as little (and pre-logical) children. Because of the foolishness of idealists are ideas to be taboo for the adult mind? And, as critics, what are we to do with those poems (like *The Canonization* and *Lycidas*) which could not obtain admission by Moore into the anthology but which very likely are the poems we cherish beyond others?

The reputed "innocence" of the aesthetic moment, the "knowledge without desire" which Schopenhauer praises, must submit to a little scrutiny, like anything else that looks too good to be true. We come into this world as aliens come into a land which they must conquer if they are to live. For native endowment we have an exacting "biological" constitution which knows precisely what it needs and determines for us our inevitable desires. There can be no certainty that any other impulses are there, for why should they be? They scarcely belong in the biological picture. Perhaps we are simply an efficient animal species, running smoothly, working fast, finding the formula of life only too easy, and after a certain apprenticeship piling up power and wealth far beyond the capacity of our appetites to use. What will come next? Perhaps poetry, if the gigantic effort of science begins to seem disproportionate to the reward, according to a sense of diminishing returns.* But before this pretty event can come

---

**volte-face*: 「전향, 반대방향으로 바꿈」.

*be done with...: 「...와 관계를 끊다」.

*returns: (투자에 대한)「이득」.

to pass, it is possible that every act of attention which is allowed us is conditioned by a gross and selfish interest.

Where is innocence then? The aesthetic moment appears as a curious moment of suspension; between the Platonism in us, which is militant, always sciencing and devouring, and starved inhibited aspiration towards innocence which, if it could only be free, would like to respect and know the object as it might of its own accord reveal itself.

The poetic impulse is not free, yet it holds out stubbornly against science for the enjoyment of its images. It means to reconstitute the world of perceptions. Finally there is suggested some such formula as the following:

Science gratifies a rational or practical impulse and exhibits the minimum of perception. Art gratifies a perceptual impulse and exhibits the minimum of reason. . . .

What is Metaphysical Poetry? The term was added to the official vocabulary of criticism by Johnson, who probably took it from Pope, who probably took it from Dryden, who used it to describe the poetry of a certain school of poets, thus: "He [John Donne] affects the metaphysics, not only in his satires, but in his amorous verses, where nature only should reign. . . . In this Mr. Cowley has copied him to a fault."* But the meaning of metaphysical which was common in Dryden's time, having come down from the Middle Ages through Shakespeare, was simply: supernatural; *miraculous.* The context of the Dryden passage indicates it.

Dryden, then, noted a miraculism in poetry and repudiated it; except where it was employed for satire, where it was not seriously intended and had the effect of wit. Dryden himself employs miraculism wittily, but seems rather to avoid it if he will be really committed by it; he may employ it in his translations of Ovid, where the responsibility is Ovid's and not Dryden's, and in an occasional classical piece where he is making polite use of myths well known to be pagan errors. In his "amorous" pieces he finds the reign of nature sufficient, and it is often the worse for his amorous pieces. He is not

---

***"He affects...to a fault":** Dryden, *Discourse of the Original and Progress of Satire* (1692).

many removes from a naturalist. (A naturalist is a person who studies nature not because he loves it but because he wants to use it, approaches it from the standpoint of common sense, and sees it thin and not thick.) Dryden might have remarked that Donne himself had a change of heart and confined his miraculism at last to the privileged field of a more or less scriptural revelation. Perhaps Dryden found his way to accepting Milton because Milton's miraculism was mostly not a contemporary sort but classical and scriptural, pitched in a time when the age of miracles had not given way to the age of science. He knew too that Cowley had shamefully recanted from his petty miraculism, which formed the conceits, and turned to the scriptural or large order of miraculism to write his heroic (but empty) verses about David;* and had written a Pindaric ode in extravagant praise of "Mr. Hobs," whose naturalistic account of nature seemed to render any other account fantastic if not contrary to the social welfare.

Incidentally, we know how much Mr. Hobbes affected Dryden too, and the whole of Restoration literature. What Bacon with his disparagement of poetry had begun, in the cause of science and protestantism, Hobbes completed. The name of Hobbes is critical in any history that would account for the chill which settled upon the poets at the very moment that English poetry was attaining magnificently to the fullness of its powers. The name stood for common sense and naturalism, and the monopoly of the scientific spirit over the mind. Hobbes was the adversary, the Satan, when the latter first intimidated the English poets. After Hobbes his name is legion.*

"Metaphysics," or miraculism, informs a poetry which is the most original and exciting, and intellectually perhaps the most seasoned, that we know in our literature, and very probably it has few equivalents in other literatures. But it is evident that the metaphysical effects may be large-scale or they may be small-scale. (I believe that generically, or on-

---

***heroic verses about David:** Cowley의 *Davideis* (1656)을 말함.

***his name is legion:** 「그의 이름은 군대이니라」(마가복음 5 : 9). 여기서 군대는 "악령의 무리".

tologically, no distinction is to be made between them.) If Donne and Cowley illustrate the small-scale effects, Milton will illustrate the large-scale ones, probably as a consequence of the fact that he wrote major poems. Milton, in the *Paradise Lost,* told a story which was heroic and miraculous in the first place. In telling it he dramatized it, and allowed the scenes and characters to develop of their own native energy. The virtue of a long poem on a "metaphysical" subject will consist in the dramatization or substantiation of all the parts, the poet not being required to devise fresh miracles on every page so much as to establish the perfect "naturalism" of the material upon which the grand miracle is imposed. The *Paradise Lost* possesses this virtue nearly everywhere:

> Thus *Adam* to himself lamented loud
> Through the still Night, not now, as ere man fell,
> Wholsom and cool, and mild, but with black Air
> Accompanied, with damps and dreadful gloom,
> Which to his evil Conscience represented
> All things with double terror: On the ground
> Outstretcht he lay, on the cold ground, and oft
> Curs'd his Creation, Death as oft accus'd
> Of tardie execution, since denounc't
> The day of his offence. Why comes not Death,
> Said hee, with one thrice acceptable stroke
> To end me?*

This is exactly the sort of detail for a large-scale metaphysical work, but it would hardly serve the purpose with a slighter and more naturalistic subject: with "amorous" verses. For the critical mind Metaphysical Poetry refers perhaps almost entirely to the so-called "conceits" that constitute its staple. To define the conceit is to define small-scale Metaphysical Poetry.

It is easily defined, upon a little citation. Donne exhibits two conceits, or two branches of one conceit in the familiar lines:

*Milton, *Paradise Lost*, X, 845ff.

Our hands were firmly cemented
By a fast balm which thence did spring;
Our eye-beams twisted, and did thread
Our eyes upon one double string.*

The poem which follows sticks to the topic; it represents the loves in precisely that mode of union and no other. Cowley is more conventional yet still bold in the lines:

Oh take my Heart, and by that means you'll prove
    Within, too stor'd enough of love:
Give me but yours, I'll by that change so thrive
    That Love in all my parts shall live.
So powerful is this my change, it render can,
My outside Woman, and your inside Man.*

A conceit originates in a metaphor; and in fact the conceit is but a metaphor if the metaphor is meant; that is, if it is developed so literally that it must be meant, or predicated so baldly that nothing else can be meant. Perhaps this will do for a defintion.

Clearly the seventeenth century had the courage of its metaphors, and imposed them imperially on the nearest things, and just as clearly the nineteenth century lacked this courage, and was half-heartedly metaphorical, or content with similes. The difference between the literary qualities of the two periods is the difference between the metaphor and the simile. (It must be admitted that this like other generalizations will not hold without its exceptions.) One period was pithy and original in its poetic utterance, the other was prolix and predictable. It would not quite commit itself to the metaphor even if it came upon one. Shelley is about as vigorous as usual when he says in *Adonais:*

        Thou young Dawn,
Turn all thy dew to splendour . . .

But splendor is not the correlative of dew, it has the flat tone

*Donne, "The Extasy".
*Cowley, "The Change."

of a Platonic idea, while physically it scarcely means more than dew with sunshine upon it. The seventeenth century would have said: "Turn thy dew, which is water, into fire, and accomplish the transmutation of the elements." Tennyson in his boldest lyric sings:

> Come into the garden, Maud,
> For the black bat, night, has flown.*

and leaves us unpersuaded of the bat. The predication would be complete without the bat, "The black night has flown," and a flying night is not very remarkable. Tennyson is only affecting a metaphor. But later in the same poem he writes:

> The red rose cries, "She is near, she is near";
> And the white rose weeps, "She is late";
> The larkspur listens, "I hear, I hear";
> And the lily whispers, "I wait."

and this is a technical conceit. But it is too complicated for this author, having a plurality of images which do not sustain themselves individually. The flowers stand for the lover's thoughts, and have been prepared for carefully in an earlier stanza, but their distinctness is too arbitrary, and these are like a schoolgirl's made-up metaphors. The passage will not compare with one on a very similar situation in *Green Candles,* by Mr. Humbert Wolfe:*

> "I know her little foot," gray carpet said:
> "Who but I should know her light tread?"
> "She shall come in," answered the open door,
> "And not," said the room, "go out any more."

Wolfe's conceit works and Tennyson's does not, and though Wolfe's performance seems not very daring or important, and only pleasant, he employs the technique of the conceit correctly: he knows that the miracle must have a basis of verisimilitude.

Such is Metaphysical Poetry; the extension of a rhetorical

---

*Tennyson, "Maud", XXII.

***Humbert Wolfe:** (1886-1940). 영국의 시인, 비평가.

device; as one of the most brilliant successes in our poetry, entitled to long and thorough examination; and even here demanding somewhat by way of a more ontological criticism. I conclude with it.

We may consult the dictionary, and discover that there is a miraculism or supernaturalism in a metaphorical assertion if we are ready to mean what we say, or believe what we hear. Or we may read Mr. Hobbes, the naturalist, who was very clear upon it: "II. The second cause of absurd assertions I ascribe to the giving of names of 'bodies' to 'accidents,' or of 'accidents' to 'bodies,' as they do that say 'faith is infused' or 'inspired,' when nothing can be 'poured' or 'breathed' into anything but body . . . and that 'phantasms' are 'spirits,' etc."* Translated into our present terms, Hobbes is condemning the confusion of single qualities with whole things; or the substitution of concrete images for simple ideas.

Specifically, the miraculism arises when the poet discovers by analogy an identity between objects which is partial, though it should be considerable, and proceeds to an identification which is complete. It is to be contrasted with the simile, which says "as if" or "like," and is scrupulous to keep the identification partial. In Cowley's passage above, the lover is saying, not for the first time in this literature: "She and I have exchanged our hearts." What has actually been exchanged is affections, and affections are only in a limited sense the same as hearts. Hearts are unlike affections in being engines that pump blood and form body; and it is a miracle if the poet represents the lady's affection as rendering her inside into man. But he succeeds, with this mixture, in depositing with us the image of a very powerful affection.

From the strict point of view of literary criticism it must be insisted that the miraculism which produces the humblest conceit is the same miraculism which supplies to religions their substantive content. (This is said to assert the dignity not of the conceits but of the religions.) It is the poet and nobody else who gives to the God a nature, a form, faculties, and a

*Thomas Hobbes, *Leviathan.*

history; to the God, most comprehensive of all terms, which, if there were no poetic impulse to actualize or "find" Him, would remain the driest and deadest among Platonic ideas, with all intension sacrificed to infinite extension. The myths are conceits, born of metaphors. Religions are periodically produced by poets and destroyed by naturalists. Religion depends for its ontological validity upon a literary understanding, and that is why it is frequently misunderstood.

Ivor Armstrong Richards

(1893—1979)

케임브리지에서 윤리학과 영문학을 공부하고 대학 평의원이 되었다가 북경의 청화대학에서 초빙교수 노릇을 했고 그 후 생애의 대부분을 미국 하버드대학에서 보냈다. 850개 낱말로 된 Basic English의 창시자의 한 사람이며, 심리학자 C. K. Ogden과 *The Meaning of Meaning*(1923)을 써서 오늘날의 의미론을 창시하였으며, *Principles of Literary Criticism*(1925)에서는 행태주의 심리학을 원용한 비평 이론을 제시하였고, 또한 *Science and Poetry*(1926)에서는 낭만주의와 신비주의적 요소를 제거한 문학관을 말했으며, *Practical Criticism*(1929)에서는 선입견을 배제하고 작품 자체에 세심한 주의를 보내 옳게 해석하는 태도를 고창하였다. 그밖에도 문학 및 언어교육에 대한 여러 저서와 시집도 있다. 그의 자연주의적 심리 이론에 의거한 문학관은 널리 받아들여지지 않았다 해도, 예술이 사람의 정신에 최대한 긴장된 안정을 이루어 준다는 주장, 신비주의적 낭만주의의 불명확하고 무질서한 문학 해석 태도에 대한 날카로운 비판, 20세기의 과학 중심적 세계관에서의 문학의 가치에 대한 변호, 편견이나 관습에 지배되지 않고 한 문학 작품을 완결된 글로서 대하여 그 정확한 의미를 파악하고자 한 노력 등으로 그의 비평적 영향은 가위 세기적이라 하겠다. 엘리어트와 더불어 그를 20세기 비평의 창시자라 부르기도 한다. 특히 *Practical Criticism*에서 보여준, 그릇되게 작품을 읽는 원인에 대한 날카로운 분석은 후일 미국의 New Criticism의 중요한 방법으로 확대되었고, 영국의 이른바 practical criticism에 의한 문학 교육 방법의 기초가 되었다.

여기에 수록된 두 편의 글은 *Science and Poetry*의 2장과 6장으로서, 리쳐즈는 과학이 이른바 truth를 독점하고 있는 현실하에서, 문학이 전통적으로 주장한 truth에의 권리를 어떻게 유지할 수 있는가 하는 현대의 최대 문제를 솔직하게 제시한다. *Principles of Literary Criticism*에서 주장한 대로, 시는 가치 있는 경험을 이룩하여 줌으로써 계속 그 중요성을 유지할 수 있고, truth에의 권리 주장은 포기해야 한다고 그는 겁없이 말한다. 낭만주의자들이 과학을 경멸하는 듯이 말한 것은 실은 두려움의 도착된 표현인데, 이러한 태도가 20세기까지 지속될 수는 없다는 것이다. 시인의 말은 truth에 대한 statement가 아니라 pseudo-statement로서, 심리적 주체로서의 인간 생활을 질서있게 해주는 영향력을 행사한다는 것이다.

리처즈의 인간관 및 세계관은 확실히 현대적이다. 그러나 그의 예술관은, "Poetry brings the whole soul of man into activity"라고 주장하면서 충돌적 요소들을 화합으로 이끄는 상상력을 믿은 코울리지의 문학관을 몹시 닮고 있으며, 문학이 철학이나 종교를 대신하여 사람에게 정신적 위안을 가져올 것이라 믿은 아놀드의 사상과도 닮고 있다. 즉 리처즈는 영국 문학사상의 전통 위에 있는 것이다.

From Science and Poetry (1926)

THE POETIC EXPERIENCE

Extraordinary claims have often been made for poetry — Matthew Arnold's words quoted at the head of this essay are an example — claims which very many people are inclined to view with astonishment or with the smile which tolerance gives to the enthusiast. Indeed a more representative modern view would be that the future of poetry is *nil.* Peacock's conclusion in his *The Four Ages of Poetry* finds a more general acceptance. "A poet in our times is a semibarbarian in a civilized community. He lives in the days that are past. . . . In whatever degree poetry is cultivated, it must necessarily be to the neglect of some branch of useful study: and it is a lamentable thing to see minds, capable of better things, running to

seed* **in the specious indolence of these empty aimless mockeries of intellectual exertion. Poetry was the mental rattle that awakened the attention of intellect in the infancy of civil society: but for the maturity of mind to make a serious business of the playthings of its childhood, is as absurd as for a grown man to rub his gums with coral, and cry to be charmed asleep by the jingle of silver bells." And with more regret many others — Keats* was among them — have thought that the inevitable effect of the advance of science would be to destroy the possibility of poetry.**

What is the truth in this matter? How is our estimate of poetry going to be affected by science? And how will poetry itself be influenced? The extreme importance which has in the past been assigned to poetry is a fact which must be accounted for whether we conclude that it was rightly assigned or not, and whether we consider that poetry will continue to be held in such esteem or not. It indicates that the case for poetry, whether right or wrong, is one which turns on momentous issues. We shall not have dealt adequately with it unless we have raised questions of great significance.

Very much toil has gone to the endeavour to explain the high place of poetry in human affairs, with, on the whole, few satisfactory or convincing results. This is not surprising. For in order to show how poetry is important it is first necessary to discover to some extent what it is. Until recently this preliminary task could only be very incompletely carried out; the psychology of instinct and emotion was too little advanced; and, moreover, the wild speculations natural in prescientific enquiry definitely stood in the way.* Neither the professional psychologist, whose interest in poetry is frequently not intense, nor the man of letters, who as a rule has no adequate ideas of the mind as a whole, has been equipped for the investigation. Both a passionate knowledge of poetry and a capacity for dispassionate psychological analysis are required if it is to be satisfactorily prosecuted.

***running to seed:** 「시들어가는」.
***Keats:** 그는 *Lamia*에서 시에 대한 과학의 침해를 우화적으로 표현했다.
***stand in the way:** 「방해되다」.

It will be best to begin by asking "What *kind of a thing,* in the widest sense, is poetry?" When we have answered this we shall be ready to ask "How can we use and misuse it?" and "What reasons are there for thinking it valuable?"

Let us take an experience, ten minutes of a person's life, and describe it in broad outline. It is now possible to indicate its general structure, to point out what is important in it, what trivial and accessory, which features depend upon which, how it has arisen, and how it is probably going to influence his future experience. There are, of course, wide gaps in this description, none the less it *is* at last possible to understand in general how the mind works in an experience, and what sort of stream of events the experience is.

A poem, let us say Wordsworth's *Westminster Bridge* sonnet, is such an experience, it is the experience the right kind of reader has when he peruses the verses. And the first step to an understanding of the place and future of poetry in human affairs is to see what the general structure of such an experience is. Let us begin by reading it very slowly, preferably aloud, giving every syllable time to make its full effect upon us. And let us read it experimentally, repeating it, varying our tone of voice until we are satisfied that we have caught its rhythm as well as we are able, and — whether our reading is such as to please other people or not — we ourselves at least are certain how it should "go."

Earth has not anything to show more fair:
Dull would he be of soul who could pass by
A sight so touching in its majesty:
This City now doth like a garment wear
The beauty of the morning: silent, bare,
Ships, towers, domes, theatres and temples lie
Open to the fields, and to the sky;
All bright and glittering in the smokeless air.
Never did sun more beautifully steep
In his first splendour valley, rock or hill;
Ne'er saw I, never felt, a calm so deep!
The river glideth at its own sweet will:
Dear God! the very houses seem asleep

And all that mighty heart is lying still!

We may best make our analysis of the experience that arises through reading these lines from the surface inwards, to speak metaphorically. The surface is the impression of the printed words on the retina. This sets up an agitation which we must follow as it goes deeper and deeper.

The first things to occur (if they do not, the rest of the experience will be gravely inadequate) are the sound of the words "in the mind's ear" and the feel of the words imaginarily spoken. These together give the *full body,* as it were, to the words, and it is with the full bodies of words that the poet works, not with their printed signs. But many people lose nearly everything in poetry through these indispensable parts escaping them.

Next arise various pictures "in the mind's eye"; not of words but of things for which the words stand*; perhaps of ships, perhaps of hills; and together with them, it may be, other images of various sorts. Images of what it feels like to stand leaning on the parapet of Westminster Bridge. Perhaps that odd thing an image of "silence." But, unlike the image-bodies of the words themselves, those other images of things are not vitally important. Those who have them may very well think them indispensable, and *for them* they may be necessary; but other people may not require them at all. This is a point at which differences between individual minds are very marked.

Thence onwards the agitation which is the experience divides into a major and a minor branch, though the two streams have innumerable interconnections and influence one another intimately. Indeed it is only as an expositor's artifice that we may speak of them as two streams.

The minor branch we may call the intellectual stream; the other, which we may call the active, or emotional, stream, is made up of the play of our interests.

The intellectual stream is fairly easy to follow; it follows itself, so to speak; but it is the less important of the two. In

*stand for: 「대신하다, 나타내다」.

poetry it matters only *as a means;* it directs and excites the active stream. It is made up of thoughts, which are not static little entities that bob up into consciousness and down again out of it, but fluent happenings, events, which reflect or point to the things the thoughts are of.* Exactly how they do this is a matter which is still much disputed.

This pointing to or reflecting things is all that thoughts do. They appear to do much more; which is our chief illusion. The realm of thought is never a sovereign state. Our thoughts are the servants of our interests, and even when they seem to rebel it is usually our interests that are in disorder. Our thoughts are pointers and it is the other, the active, stream which deals with the things which thoughts reflect or point to.

Some people who read verse (they do not often read much of it) are so constituted that very little more happens than this intellectual stream of thoughts. It is perhaps superfluous to point out that they miss the real poem. To exaggerate this part of the experience, and give it too much importance on its own account, is a notable current tendency, and for many people explains why they do not read poetry.

The active branch is what really matters; for from it all the energy of the whole agitation comes. The thinking which goes on is somewhat like the play of an ingenious and invaluable "governor" run by, but controlling, the main machine. Every experience is essentially some interest or group of interests swinging back to rest.

To understand what an interest is we should picture the mind as a system of very delicately poised balances, a system which so long as we are in health is constantly growing. Every situation we come into disturbs some of these balances to some degree. The ways in which they swing back to a new equipoise are the impulses with which we respond to the situation. And the chief balances in the system are our chief interests.

Suppose that we carry a magnetic compass about in the neighbourhood of powerful magnets. The needle waggles as we move and comes to rest pointing in a new direction

---

***the things...are of:** 「생각들의 내용인 사물들」.

whenever we stand still in a new position. Suppose that instead of a single compass we carry an arrangement of many magnetic needles, large and small, swung so that they influence one another, some able only to swing horizontally, others vertically, others hung freely. As we move, the perturbations in this system will be very complicated. But for every position in which we place it there will be a final position of rest for all the needles into which they will in the end settle down, a general poise for the whole system. But even a slight displacement may set the whole assemblage of needles busily readjusting themselves.

One further complication. Suppose that while all the needles influence one another, some of them respond only to some of the outer magnets among which the system is moving. The reader can easily draw a diagram if his imagination needs a visual support.

The mind is not unlike such a system if we imagine it to be incredibly complex. The needles are our interests, varying in their importance, that is in the degree to which any movement they make involves movement in the other needles. Each new disequilibrium, which a shift of position, a fresh situation, entails, corresponds to a need: and the wagglings which ensue as the system rearranges itself are our responses, the impulses through which we seek to meet the need. Often the new poise is not found until long after the original disturbance. Thus states of strain can arise which last for years.

The child comes into the world as a comparatively simple arrangement. Few things affect him comparatively speaking, and his responses also are few and simple, but he very quickly becomes more complicated. His recurrent needs for food and for various attentions are constantly setting all his needles swinging. Little by little separate needs become departmentalized as it were, sub-systems are formed; hunger causes one set of responses, the sight of his toys another, loud noises yet another, and so on. But the sub-systems never become quite independent. So he grows up, becoming susceptible to ever more numerous and more delicate influences.

He grows more discriminating in some respects, he is

thrown out of equilibrium by slighter differences in his situation. In other respects he becomes more stable. From time to time, through growth, fresh interests develop; sex is the outstanding example. His needs increase, he becomes capable of being upset by quite new causes, he becomes responsive to quite new aspects of the situation.

This development takes a very indirect course. It would be still more erratic if society did not mould and remould him at every stage, reorganising him incompletely two or three times over before he grows up. He reaches maturity in the form of a vast assemblage of major and minor interests, partly a chaos, partly a system, with some tracts of his personality fully developed and free to respond, others tangled and jammed in all kinds of accidental ways. It is this incredibly complex assemblage of interests to which the printed poem has to appeal. Sometimes the poem is itself the influence which disturbs us, sometimes it is merely the means by which an already existing disturbance can right itself. More usually perhaps it is both at once.

We must picture then the stream of the poetic experience as the swinging back into equilibrium of these disturbed interests. We are reading the poem in the first place only because we are in some way interested in doing so, only because some interest is attempting to regain its poise thereby. And whatever happens as we read happens only for a similar reason. We understand the words (the intellectual branch of the stream goes on its way successfully) only because an interest is reacting through that means, and all the rest of the experience is equally but more evidently our adaptation working itself out.*

The rest of the experience is made up of emotions and attitudes. Emotions are what the reaction, with its reverberations in bodily changes, feels like. Attitudes are the impulses towards one kind of behaviour or another which are set ready by the response. They are, as it were, its outward going part. Sometimes, as here in *Westminster Bridge*, they are very easi-

***work itself out:** 「힘들여 완성하다」.

ly overlooked. But consider a simpler case — a fit of laughter which it is absolutely essential to conceal, in Church or during a solemn interview, for example. You contrive not to laugh; but there is no doubt about the activity of the impulses in their restricted form. The much more subtle and elaborate impulses which a poem excites are not different in principle. They do not show themselves as a rule, they do not come out into the open, largely because they are so complex. When they have adjusted themselves to one another and become organized into a coherent whole, the needs concerned may be satisfied. *In a fully developed man a state of readiness for action will take the place of action when the full appropriate situation for action is not present.* The essential peculiarity of poetry as of all the arts is that the full appropriate situation is *not* present. It is an *actor* we are seeing upon the stage, not Hamlet. So readiness for action takes the place of actual behaviour.

This is the main plan then of the experience. Signs on the retina, taken up by sets of needs (remember how many other impressions all day long remain entirely *unnoticed* because no interest responds to them); thence an elaborate agitation of impulses, one branch of which is *thoughts* of what the words mean, the other an emotional response leading to the development of *attitudes,* preparations, that is, for action which may or may not take place; the two branches being in intimate connection.

We must look now a little more closely at these connections. It may seem odd that we do not more definitely make the thoughts the rulers and causes of the rest of the response. To do just this has been in fact the grand error of traditional psychology. Man prefers to stress the features which distinguish him from monkey, and chief among these are his intellectual capacities. Important though they are, he has given them a rank to which they are not entitled. Intellect is an adjunct to the interests, a means by which they adjust themselves more successfully. Man is not in any sense primarily an intelligence; he is a system of interests. Intelligence helps man but does not run him.

Partly through this natural mistake, and partly because intellectual operations are so much easier to study, the whole traditional analysis of the working of the mind has been turned upside down. It is largely as a remedy from the difficulties which this mistake involves that poetry may have so much importance in the future. But let us look again more closely at the poetic experience.

In the first place, why is it essential in reading poetry to give the words their full imagined sound and body? What is meant by saying that the poet works with this sound and body? The answer is that even before the words have been intellectually understood and the thoughts they occasion formed and followed, the movement and sound of the words is playing deeply and intimately upon the interests.* How this happens is a matter which has yet to be successfully investigated, but that it happens no sensitive reader of poetry doubts. A good deal of poetry and even some great poetry exists (e.g., some of Shakespeare's Songs and, in a different way, much of the best of Swinburne) in which the sense of the words can be *almost* entirely missed or neglected without loss. Never perhaps entirely without effort, however; though sometimes with advantage. But the plain fact that the relative importance of grasping the sense of the words may vary (compare Browning's *Before* with his *After* is enough for our purpose here.

In nearly all poetry the sound and feel of the words, what is often called the *form* of the poem in opposition to its *content,* get to work first, and the sense in which the words are taken is subtly influenced by this fact. Most words are ambiguous as regards their plain sense, especially in poetry. We can take them as we please in a variety of senses. The sense we are pleased to choose is the one which most suits the impulses already stirred through the form of the verse. The same thing can be noticed in conversation. Not the strict logical sense of what is said, but the tone of voice and the occasion are the primary factors by which we interpret. Science, it is worth noting, endeavours with increasing success to bar out these factors. We believe a scientist because he can substantiate his remarks, not because he is eloquent or forcible in his enunciation. In fact, we distrust him when he seems to be influencing us by his manner.

In its use of words poetry is just the reverse of science. Very definite thoughts do occur, but not because the words are so chosen as logically to bar out all possibilities but one.* No. But because the manner, the tone of voice, the cadence and the rhythm play upon our interests and make *them* pick out from among an indefinite number of possibilities the precise particular thought which they need. This is why poetical descriptions often seem so much more accurate than prose descriptions. Language logically and scientifically used cannot describe a landscape or a face. To do so it would need a prodigious apparatus of names for shades and nuances, for precise particular qualities. These names do not exist, so other means have to be used. The poet, even when, like Ruskin or De Quincey, he writes in prose, makes the reader pick out the precise particular sense required from an indefinite number of possible senses which a word, phrase or sentence may carry. The means by which he does this are many and varied. Some of them have been mentioned above, but the way in which he uses them is the poet's own secret, something which cannot be taught. He knows how to do it, but he does not himself know how it is done.

Misunderstanding and under-estimation of poetry is mainly due to over-estimation of the thought in it. We can see still more clearly that thought is not the prime factor if we consider for a moment not the experiencer of the reader but that of the poet. Why does the poet use these words and no others? Not because they stand for a series of thoughts which in themselves are what he is concerned to communicate. It is never what a poem *says* which matters, but what it *is*. The poet is not writing as a scientist. He uses these words because the interests which the situation calls into play combine to bring them, just in this form, into his consciousness *as a means*

*시에서도 사상이 나타나는 게 사실이지만, 단 한 가지만을 제외하고는 모든(의미 해석의) 가능성들을 봉쇄하도록 낱말들이 논리적으로 선택된 까닭이 아니다.

of ordering, controlling and consolidating the whole experience. The experience itself, the tide of impulses sweeping through the mind, is the source and the sanction of the words. They represent this experience itself, not any set of perceptions or reflections, though often to a reader who approaches the poem wrongly they will seem to be only a series of remarks about other things. But to a suitable reader the words — if they actually spring from experience and are not due to verbal habits, to the desire to be effective, to factitious excogitation, to imitation, to irrelevant contrivances, or to any other of the failings which prevent most people from writing poetry — the words will reproduce in his mind a similar play of interests putting him for the while into a similar situation and leading to the same response.

Why this should happen is still somewhat of a mystery. An extraordinarily intricate concourse of impulses brings the words together. Then in another mind* the affair in part reverses itself, the words bring into being a similar concourse of impulses. The words which seem to be the effect of the experience in the first instance, seem to become the cause of a similar experience in the second. A very odd thing to happen, not exactly paralleled outside communication.* But this description is not quite accurate. The words, as we have seen, are not simply the effect in one case, nor the cause in the other. In both cases they are the part of the experience which binds it together, which gives it a definite structure and keeps it from being a mere welter of disconnected impulses. They are *the key,* to borrow a useful metaphor from McDougall,* for this particular combination of impulses. So regarded, it is less strange that what the poet wrote should reproduce his experience in the mind of the reader.

POETRY AND BELIEFS

The business of the poet, as we have seen, is to give order

*__another mind:__ 즉 독자의 정신.

*그런 일이 생기다니 기이한 일이다. 의사전달 행위 이외에서는 정확한 유례가 없다.

*__McDougall, William:__ (1871-1938). 영국 태생의 미국 심리학자.

and coherence, and so freedom, to a body of experience. To do so through words which act as its skeleton, as a structure by which the impulses which make up the experience are adjusted to one another and act together. The means by which words do this are many and varied. To work them out is a problem for psychology. A beginning has been indicated above, but only a beginning. What little can be done shows already that most critical dogmas of the past are either false or nonsense. A little knowledge is not here a danger, but clears the air in a remarkable way.

Roughly and inadequately, even in the light of our present knowledge, we can say that words work in the poem in two main fashions. As sensory stimuli and as (in the *widest* sense) symbols. We must refrain from considering the sensory side of the poem, remarking only that it is *not* in the least independent of the other side, and that it has for definite reasons prior importance in most poetry. We must confine ourselves to the other function of words in the poem, or rather, omitting much that is of secondary relevance, to one form of that function, let me call it *pseudo-statement.* *

It will be admitted — by those who distinguish between scientific statement, where truth is ultimately a matter of verification as this is understood in the laboratory, and emotive utterance, where "truth" is primarily acceptability *by* some attitude, and more remotely is the acceptability *of* this attitude itself — that it is *not* the poet's business to make true statements. Yet poetry has constantly the air of making statements, and important ones; which is one reason why some mathematicians cannot read it. They find the alleged statements to be *false*. It will be agreed that their approach to poetry and their expectations from it are mistaken. But what exactly is the other, the right, the poetic, approach and how does it differ from the mathematical?

The poetic approach evidently limits the framework of possible consequences into which the pseudo-statement is taken. For the scientific approach this framework is

***pseudo-statement:** 「가짜 진술」. "사랑은 아름다운 것이다"처럼 진술 비슷하지만 아닌 것.

unlimited. Any and every consequence is relevant. If any of the consequences of a statement conflicts with acknowledged fact then so much the worse for the statement. Not so with the pseudo-statement when poetically approached. The problem is — just how does the limitation work? The usual account is in terms of a supposed universe of discourse, a world of make-believe, of imagination, of recognised fictions common to the poet and his readers. A pseudo-statement which fits into this system of assumptions would be regarded as "poetically true"; one which does not, as "poetically false." This attempt to treat "poetic truth" on the model of general "coherence theories" is very natural for certain schools of logicians; but is inadequate, on the wrong lines from the outset. To mention two objections out of many; there is no means of discovering what the "universe of discourse" is on any occasion, and the kind of coherence which must hold within it, supposing it to be discoverable, is not an affair of logical relations. Attempt to define the system of propositions into which

O Rose, thou art sick!*

must fit, and the logical relations which must hold between them if it is to be "poetically true"; the absurdity of the theory becomes evident.

We must look further. In the poetic approach the relevant consequences are not logical or to be arrived at by a partial relaxation of logic. Except occasionally and by accident logic does not enter at all. They are the consequences which arise through our emotional organisation. The acceptance which a pseudo-statement receives is entirely governed by its effects upon our feelings and attitudes. Logic only comes in, if at all, in subordination, as a servant to our emotional response. It is an unruly servant, however, as poets and readers are constantly discovering. A pseudo-statement is "true" if it suits and serves some attitude or links together attitudes which on other grounds are desirable. This kind of truth is so opposed to scientific truth that it is a pity to use so similar a word, but at present it is difficult to avoid the malpractice.

*Blake, "The Sick Rose".

This brief analysis may be sufficient to indicate the fundamental disparity and opposition between pseudo-statements as they occur in poetry and statements as they occur in science. A pseudo-statement is a form of words which is justified entirely by its effect in releasing or organising our impulses and attitudes (due regard being had for the better or worse organisations of these *inter se*)*; a statement, on the other hand, is justified by its truth, i.e. its correspondence, in a highly technical sense, with the fact to which it points.

Statements true and false alike do of course constantly touch off* attitudes and action. Our daily practical existence is largely guided by them. On the whole true statements are of more service to us than false ones. None the less we do not and, at present, cannot order our emotions and attitudes by true statements alone. Nor is there any probability that we ever shall contrive to do so. This is one of the great new dangers to which civilisation is exposed. Countless pseudo-statements — about God, about the universe, about human nature, the relations of mind to mind, about the soul, its rank and destiny — pseudo-statements which are pivotal points in the organisation of the mind, vital to its well-being, have suddenly become, for sincere, honest and informal minds, impossible to believe. For centuries they have been believed; now they are gone, irrecoverably; and the knowledge which has killed them is not of a kind upon which an equally fine organisation of the mind can be based.

This is the contemporary situation. The remedy, since there is no prospect of our gaining adequate knowledge, and since indeed it is fairly clear that genuine knowledge cannot serve us here and can only increase our practical control of Nature, is to cut our pseudo-statements free from belief, and yet retain them, in this released state, as the main instruments by which we order our attitudes to one another and to the world. Not so desperate a remedy as may appear, for poetry conclusively shows that even the most important among our attitudes can be aroused and maintained without any belief

---

***inter se**: 'among themselves.'

***touch off**: 「생기게 하다」.

entering in at all. Those of Tragedy, for example. We need no beliefs, and indeed we must have none, if we are to read *King Lear*. Pseudo-statements to which we attach no belief and statements proper such as science provides cannot conflict. It is only when we introduce illicit beliefs into poetry that danger arises. To do so is from this point of view a profanation of poetry.

Yet an important branch of criticism which has attracted the best talents from prehistoric times until today consists of the endeavour to persuade men that the functions of science and poetry are identical, or that the one is a "higher form" of the other, or that they conflict and we must choose between them.

The root of this persistent endeavour has still to be mentioned; it is the same as that from which the Magical View* of the world arose. If we give to a pseudo-statement the kind of unqualified acceptance which belongs by right only to certified scientific statements, if we can contrive to do this, the impulses and attitudes with which we respond to it gain a notable stability and vigour. Briefly, if we can contrive to believe poetry, then the world *seems,* while we do so, to be transfigured. It used to be comparatively easy to do this, and the habit has become well established. With the extension of science and the neutralisation of nature it has become difficult as well as dangerous. Yet it is still alluring; it has many analogies with drug-taking. Hence the endeavours of the critics referred to. Various subterfuges have been devised along the lines of regarding Poetic Truth as figurative, symbolic; or as more immediate, as a truth of Intuition, not of reason; or as a higher form of the same truth as reason yields. Such attempts to use poetry as a denial or as a corrective of science are very common. One point can be made against

***the Magical View of the world:** "The central dominant change may be described as the *Neutralization of Nature,* the transference from the Magical View of the world to the scientific.... By the Magical View I mean, roughly, the belief in a world of spirits and powers which control events, and which can be evoked and to some extent controlled themselves by human practices." (*Science and Poetry,* 5)

them all: they are never worked out in detail. There is no equivalent to Mill's *Logic** expounding any such view. The language in which they are framed is usually a blend of obsolete psychology and emotive exclamations.

The long-established and much-encouraged habit of giving to emotive utterances — whether pseudo-statements simple, or looser and larger wholes taken as saying something figuratively — the kind of assent which we give to established facts, has for most people debilitated a wide range of their responses. A few scientists, caught young and brought up in the laboratory, are free from it; but then, as a rule, they pay no *serious* attention to poetry. For most men the recognition of the neutrality of nature brings about — through this habit — a divorce from poetry. They are so used to having their responses propped up by beliefs, however vague, that when these shadowy supports are removed they are no longer able to respond. Their attitudes to so many things have been forced in the past, over-encouraged. And when the world-picture ceases to assist there is a collapse. Over whole tracts of natural emotional response we are today like a bed of dahlias whose sticks have been removed. And this effect of the neutralisation of nature is only in its beginnings. Consider the probable effects upon love-poetry in the near future of the kind of enquiry into basic human constitution exemplified by psychoanalysis.

A sense of desolation, of uncertainty, of futility, of the groundlessness of aspirations, of the vanity of endeavour, and a thirst for a life-giving water which seems suddenly to have failed, are the signs in consciousness of this necessary reorganisation of our lives.* Our attitudes and impulses are

---

*Mill's *Logic*: John Stuart Mill (1806–73)의 저서 *System of Logic* (1843)

*To those familiar with Mr. Eliot's *The Waste Land*, my indebtedness to it at this point will be evident. He seems to me by this poem, to have performed two considerable services for this generation. He has given a perfect emotive description of a state of mind which is probably inevitable for a while to all meditative people. Secondly, by effecting a complete severance between his poetry and *all* beliefs, and this without any weakening of the poetry, he has realised what might otherwise have

being compelled to become self-supporting; they are being driven back upon their biological justification, made once again sufficient to themselves. And the only impulses which seem strong enough to continue unflagging are commonly so crude that, to more finely developed individuals, they hardly seem worth having. Such people cannot live by warmth, food, fighting, drink and sex alone. Those who are least affected by the change are those who are emotionally least removed from the animals. As we shall see at the close of this essay, even a considerable poet may attempt to find relief by a reversion to primitive mentality.

It is important to diagnose the disease correctly and to put the blame in the right quarter. Usually it is some alleged "materialism" of science which is denounced. This mistake is due partly to clumsy thinking, but chiefly to relics of the Magical View. For even if the Universe were "spiritual" all through (whatever that assertion might mean; all such assertions are probably nonsense), that would not make it any more accordant to human attitudes. It is not what the universe is made of but how it works, the law it follows, which makes knowledge of it incapable of spurring on our emotional responses, and further the nature of knowledge itself makes it inadequate. The contact with things which we therein establish is too sketchy and indirect to help us. We are beginning to know too much about the bond which unites the mind to its object in knowledge for that old dream of a perfect knowledge which would guarantee perfect life to retain its sanction. What was thought to be pure knowledge, we see now to have been shot through with* hope and desire, with fear and wonder, and these intrusive elements indeed gave it all its power to support our lives. In knowledge, in the "How?" of events, we can find hints by which to take advantage of circumstances in our favour and avoid mischances. But we cannot get from it a *raison d'être* or a justification of more than a

---

remained largely a speculative possibility, and has shown the way to the only solution of these difficulties. "In the destructive element immerse, That is the way."

*shot through with...: 「...이 가득 스며든」.

relatively lowly kind of life.

The justification, or the reverse, of any attitude lies, not in the object, but in itself, in its serviceableness to the whole personality. Upon its place in the whole system of attitudes, which is the personality, all its worth depends. This is true equally for the subtle, finely compounded attitudes of the civilised individual as for the simpler attitudes of the child.

In brief, experience is its own justification; and this fact must be faced, although sometimes — by a lover, for example — it may be very difficult to accept. Once it is faced, it is apparent that all the attitudes to other human beings and to the world in all its aspects, which have been serviceable to humanity, remain as they were, as valuable as ever. Hesitation felt in admitting this is a measure of the strength of the evil habit we have described. But many of these attitudes, valuable as ever, are, now that they are being set free, more difficult to maintain, because we still hunger after a basis in belief.

Frank Raymond Leavis

(1895—1981)

케임브리지에서 태어나 케임브리지를 다니고 후에 케임브리지에서 오래 가르쳤다. 1930년대에 리비스는 영국의 가장 영향력 있는 비평가로 군림하여 케임브리지의 영문학 교수로 많은 추종자를 가르쳤고 또 문학 평론지 *The Scrutiny*(1932-53)를 통하여 젊은 학도와 비평가들을 상대하였다.

그는 대학 교수로서 *D.H. Lawrence*(1930)를 써서 말썽 많던 그 작가를 처음으로 심각하게 다루었고, *New Bearings in English Poetry*(1932)에서는 역시 말썽 많던 시인들인 Eliot, Pound, Hopkins의 문학적 성취를 예찬하였다. *Revaluation* (1936)은 영시의 새로운 전통론, *The Great Tradition*(1948)은 영소설의 전통을 새롭게 부각한 명저들이다. 로렌스에 대해서는 2권의 책을 더 냈으며, *The Common Pursuit*(1950), *English in Our Time and the University*(1969) 등의 문학평론집과 사회, 교육 평론집도 많이 발표하였다.

리비스는 전통을 중시하는 대학에서 고전 문학 교육에서 현대 문학 교육으로 옮겨가는 과도기에 현대 문학이 학술적·교육적 가치가 있음을 보여준 공로자이기도 하다. 그러기 위하여 그는 현대 문학을 단순한 저널리스트의 입장이 아닌 확고한 전통사상의 입장에서 세밀하게 읽었고, 과거의 문학 역시 새로운 입장에서 그 전통성을 강조하였다. 엘리어트와 로렌스가 대학 교육 내용에 포함된 것은 그의 공적이라고 한다.

그는 개별 작품을 매우 주의깊게 면밀히 읽는 습관을 가르쳤다. 그래서 그는 가끔 미국의 New Critics와 비슷한 비평가로 지목되기도 하지만, 실제에 있어 그는 영국 비평의 전통에 따라 작품의 도덕적 감각과 방향을 가장 중요하게 여긴다. 간혹 지나치게 자신의 도덕적 해석을 고집하여 완고하다는 평을 듣기도 한다.

*New Bearings in English Poetry*는 그의 비평가로서의 명성을 확립해준 짧은 평론집으로, 여기 수록된 "Poetry and the Modern World"는 제1장이다. 19세기적인 낡은 개념을 타파하고 현대시를 수용할 것을 촉구하고 있다.

Poetry and the Modern World (1932)

POETRY matters little to the modern world. That is, very little of contemporary intelligence concerns itself with poetry. It is true that a very great deal of verse has come from the press in the last twenty years, and the uninterested might take this as proving the existence both of a great deal of interest in poetry and of a great deal of talent. Indeed, anthologists do. They make, modestly, the most extravagant claims on behalf of the age. 'It is of no use asking a poetical renascence to conform to type,' writes Mr J. C. Squire* in his *Prefatory Note* to *Selections from Modern Poets.* 'There are maked differences in the features of all those English poetical movements which have chiefly contributed to the body of our "immortal" poetry.... Should our literary age be remembered by posterity solely as an age during which fifty men had written lyrics of some durability for their truth and beauty, it would not be remembered with contempt. It is in that conviction that I have compiled this anthology.' Mr Harold Monro,* introducing *Twentieth Century Poetry,* is more modest and more extravagant: 'Is it a great big period, or a minutely small? Reply who can! Somebody with whom I was talking said: "They are all of them only poetical persons — *not* poets. Who will be reading them a century hence?" To which I answered: "There are so many of them that, a century hence, they may appear a kind of Composite Poet; there may be 500 excellent poems proceeding from 100 poets mostly not so very great, but well worth remembering a century hence."'

Such claims are symptoms of the very weakness that they

***Squire, Sir John Collins:** (1884–1958). 시인, 편집인. 이른바 "Georgian Poets"의 하나.

***Monro, Harold Edward:** (1879–1932). 시인, 편집인. "Georgian Poets"의 하나.

deny: they could have been made only in an age in which there were no serious standards current, no live tradition of poetry, and no public capable of informed and serious interest. No one *could* be seriously interested in the great bulk of the verse that is culled and offered to us as the fine flower of modern poetry. For the most part it is not so much bad as dead — it was never alive.* The words that lie there arranged on the page have no roots: the writer himself can never have been more than superficially interested in them. Even such genuine poetry as the anthologies of modern verse do contain is apt, by its kind and quality, to suggest that the present age does not favour the growth of poets. A study of the latter end of *The Oxford Book of Victorian Verse* leads to the conclusion that something has been wrong for forty or fifty years at the least.

For it seems unlikely that the number of potential poets born varies as much from age to age as literary history might lead one to suppose. What varies is the use made of talent. And the use each age makes of its crop of talent is determined largely by the preconceptions of 'the poetical' that are current, and the corresponding habits, conventions and techniques. There are, of course, other very important conditions, social, economic, philosophical and so on; but my province is that of literary criticism, and I am confining myself as far as possible to those conditions which it rests with the poet and the critic to modify — those which are their immediate concern.

Every age, then, has its preconceptions and assumptions regarding poetry: these are the essentially poetical subjects, these the poetical materials, these the poetical modes. The most influential are apt to be those of which we are least aware. The preconceptions coming down to us from the last century were established in the period of the great Romantics, Wordsworth, Coleridge, Byron, Shelley and Keats. To attempt to define them is to risk misrepresenting them, for it

*당시의 Georgian Poetry 에 대한 혹평. George V 가 국왕이던 1910-36 년에 걸쳐, 전통적인 시형으로 잘 길들여진 전통적 주제를 다룬 시의 경향을 Georgian Poetry 라 한다.

is largely in their being vague and undefined that their power has lain. Their earliest formulation is to be found, perhaps, in the *Dedication* (dated 1756) of Joseph Warton's *Essay on the Genius and Writings of Pope.* * What Warton, consciously challenging the prevailing ideas, puts explicity, afterwards came to be implicitly assumed.

> We do not, it should seem, sufficiently attend to the difference there is between a MAN OF WIT, a MAN OF SENSE, and a TRUE POET Donne and Swift were undoubtedly men of wit, and men of sense: but what traces have they left of PURE POETRY?

The question would seem to determine the spirit of the affirmation: any doubt that may remain, both affirmation and question in the following combine to settle:

> The sublime and the pathetic are the two chief nerves of all genuine poesy. What is there transcendently sublime or pathetic in Pope?

Warton goes on to classify the English Poets:

> In the first class I would place our only three sublime and pathetic poets: SPENSER, SHAKESPEARE, MILTON.

The collocation is decisive: it defines with sufficient precision the nineteenth-century idea of the poetical. Donne, we may note, Warton places in the third class. The reign of the idea is challenged when Donne comes to be associated with Shakespeare in contrast to Spenser and Milton. How universal and unquestioned it had become in the Victorian Age Matthew Arnold may be cited to prove. His evidence is the more significant in that it was unwitting, for he regarded himself as a critic of the ideas about poetry current in his day.

> Though they may write in verse, though they may in a certain sense be masters of the art of versification, Dryden and Pope are not classics of our poetry, they are classics of our prose.*

---

*Joseph Warton (1722-1800) 은 *Essay on the Genius and Writings of Pope* (1756) 에서 신고전주의를 배격하고 "낭만적" 요소를 옹호하였다.

*Arnold, "The Study of Poetry". 앞의 p. 480 참조.

> The difference between genuine poetry and the poetry of Dryden, Pope, and all their school, is briefly this: their poetry is conceived and composed in their wits, genuine poetry is conceived and composed in the soul.*

Arnold, that is, shares with his age a prejudice against recognizing as poetry anything that is not, in the obvious sense of Milton's formula, 'simple, sensuous, and passionate.'* Poetry, it was assumed, must be the direct expression of simple emotions, and these of a limited class; the tender, the exalted, the poignant, and, in general, the sympathetic. (It is still quite common to come to the University from school doubting whether satire can be poetry.) Wit, play of intellect, stress of cerebral muscle had no place: they could only hinder the reader's being 'moved' — the correct poetical response.*

There is something further to be noted of 'the poetical' in the nineteenth century. It comes out if one considers these half-a-dozen well-known and representative poems: *La Belle Dame Sans Merci, Mariana, The Lady of Shalott, The Blessed Damozel,* Morris's *The Nymph's Song to Hylas, A Forsaken Garden,* O'Shaughnessy's *Ode.** Nineteenth-century poetry, we realize, was characteristically preoccupied with the creation of a dream-world.* Not all of the poetry, or all of the poets: but the preoccupation was characteristic. So that when a poetaster like O'Shaughnessy, with nothing personal to communicate, was moved by the desire to write poetry he pro-

---

*"Thomas Gray" in *Essays in Criticism*, 2nd Series.

*Milton, *Tractate of Education* (1644) 의 일절.

**cf.* 'Poetry tells about things that have happened long ago, and it tells you about them in language that is rich with an antique idiom. ...The poet must, I think, be regarded as striving after the simplicity of a childish utterance. His goal is to think as a child, to understand as a child. He must deliver himself—and the poetic task is the same in every age—from the burden of the intellect of his day and the the complexity of the forms of speech which it involves.'—J. M. Thorburn, *Art and the Unconscious*, p. 70.

*열거된 시편들 중에서 *Mariana* 와 *The Lady of Shalott* 은 Tennyson, *The Blessed Damozel* 은 Rossetti 의 작품.

duced this:

We are the music-makers,
And we are the dreamers of dreams,
Wandering by lone sea-breakers,
And sitting by desolate streams:
World-losers and world forsakers,
On whom the pale moon gleams....*

The preoccupation, the habit, then, became a dominant element in the set of ideas, attitudes and sentiments constituting 'the poetical' for the nineteenth century, and may often be seen to be present and potent when it is not avowed or even wittingly entertained. Consider, for instance, Andrew Lang's sonnet, *The Odyssey*. Lang* (born in 1844) was a scholar and a man of taste, with a feeling for language and a desire to write poetry — with, in short, all the qualifications of a poet except the essential one, the need to communicate something of his own. His sonnet is one of the most interesting of the many documents of like value that are to be found in *The Oxford Book of English Verse*. It illustrates very neatly the kind of thing that cultured people in the latter part of the nineteenth century took poetry to be.

As one that for a weary space has lain
Lull'd by the song of Circe and her wine
In gardens near the pale of Proserpine,
Where that Aeaean isle forgets the main,
And only the low lutes of love complain,
And only shadows of wan lovers pine —
As such an one were glad to know the brine
Salt on his lips, and the large air again —
So gladly from the songs of modern speech
Men turn, and see the stars, and feel the free
Shrill wind beyond the close of heavy flowers,
And through the music of the languid hours

---

*Arthur William O'Shaughnessy (1841-81)의 "Ode"의 첫 연. 이 한 편의 시로 알려짐.

***Lang, Andrew:** (1844-1912). 고전학자, 인류학자. 시를 쓰기도 했다.

They hear like Ocean on a western beach
The surge and thunder of the Odyssey.

This is a very representative document. To begin with, there is about the whole thing an atmosphere such as we have learnt to associate with the 'nineties. It is quite in keeping,* then, that Swinburne should be very much in evidence: 'gardens near the pale of Proserpine,' 'the low lutes of love,' 'the close of heavy flowers,' etc. Morris,* too, is there, suggesting a general Pre-Raphaelite collaboration. Then, as we should expect in late Victorian poetastry,* we are aware of the pervasive presence of Tennyson. And When Lang wishes to escape from 'the music of the languid hours' into the 'larger air' of 'a western beach' he naturally has recourse to Matthew Arnold. But in spite of the explicit intention to end in the larger air and the success with which Lang achieves 'the traditional trumpet blast of the close' (as the reviewers say), it is the music of the languid hours that predominates in his sonnet.

We are the music-makers
And we are the dreamers of dreams,

and if we dream of Homer and of waking up, it is still dreaming. And there is in the sonnet yet another presence, that of Keats — the Keats of *La Belle Dame Sans Merci* ('And only shadows of wan lovers pine') which counts for so much in 'the poetical' of the nineteenth century.

It is not only in the practice of poetasters that such preconceptions, habits and conventions assert themselves: they exercise a decisive influence over the use of genuine talent. Poetry tends in every age to confine itself by ideas of the essentially poetical which, when the conditions which gave rise to them have changed, bar the poet from his most valuable material, the material that is most significant to sensitive and adequate minds in his own day; or else sensitive and

---

***in keeping:** 「어울리는」.

***Morris, William:** (1836-96). 시인, 미술가, 사업가, 사회운동가.

***poetastry:** poetaster (3류시인)의 작품, 즉 못난 시.

adequate minds are barred out of poetry. Poetry matters because of the kind of poet who is more alive than other people, more alive in his own age. He is, as it were, at the most conscious point of the race in his time. ('He is the point at which the growth of the mind shows itself,' says Mr I. A. Richards.*) The potentialities of human experience in any age are realized only by a tiny minority, and the important poet is important because he belongs to this (and has also, of course, the power of communication). Indeed, his capacity for experiencing and his power of communicating are indistinguishable; not merely because we should not know of the one without the other, but because his power of making words express what he feels is indistinguishable from his awareness of what he feels. He is unusually sensitive, unusually aware, more sincere and more himself than the ordinary man can be. He knows what he feels and knows what he is interested in. He is a poet because his interest in his experience is not separable from his interest in words; because, that is, of his habit of seeking by the evocative use of words to sharpen his awareness of his ways of feeling, so making these communicable. And poetry can communicate the actual quality of experience with a subtlety and precision unapproachable by any other means. But if the poetry and the intelligence of the age lose touch with each other, poetry will cease to matter much, and the age will be lacking in finer awareness. What this last prognostication means it is perhaps impossible to bring home to any one who is not already convinced of the importance of poetry. So that it is indeed deplorable that poetry should so widely have ceased to interest the intelligent.

The mischievousness of the nineteenth-century conventions of 'the poetical' should by now be plain. They had behind them the prestige of the Romantic achievement and found their sanction in undoubted poetic successes. But as the situation changed and the incidence of stress for the adult sensitive mind shifted, more and more did they tend to get between such a mind and its main concerns. It clearly could

*_The Principles of Literary Criticism_, p. 61.

not take the day-dream habit seriously, though to cut free from the accompanying conventions and techniques would not be so easy as one might think. The other habits and conventions that have been indicated would be still harder to escape. But they would be equally disabling. For a sensitive adult in the nineteenth century could not fail to be preoccupied with the changed intellectual background, and to find his main interests inseparable from the modern world. Tennyson did his best. But, in spite of a great deal of allusion to scientific ideas ('If that hypothesis of theirs be sound'*), and in spite of the approval of contemporary savants, his intellectual interests (of which, therefore, we need not discuss the quality) have little to do with his successful poetry, which answers to the account of 'the poetical' given above. Indeed, there could be no better illustration. To justify his ambition would have taken a much finer intelligence and a much more robust original genius than Tennyson's — much greater strength and courage. He might wrestle solemnly with the 'problems of the age,' but the habits, conventions and techniques that he found congenial are not those of a poet who could have exposed himself freely to the rigours of the contemporary climate. And in this he is representative. It was possible for the poets of the Romantic period to believe that the interests animating their poetry were the forces moving the world, or that might move it. But Victorian poetry admits implicitly that the actual world is alien, recalcitrant and unpoetical, and that no protest is worth making except the protest of withdrawal.

A comparison between any comparable passages of Tennyson and Keats will suggest readily how even Keats, who might at first seem to resist this generalized distinction, may be reconciled with it: Tennyson, in the comparison, will show as literary and Alexandrian,* a senior contemporary of the Pre-Raphaelites. His case is well put by *The Palace of Art*: the

---

* [원주] There is no need to insist on the significance of the revised *Hyperion* and Keats's reasons for the revision. 인용구는 *In Memoriam*의 일절.

***Alexandrian:** 헬레니즘의 말기 현상을 보인 에집트의 「Alexanderia 풍의」(세련되고 퇴폐적인 예술 경향).

explicit moral of this poem is that withdrawal will not do; but when he comes to the moral Tennyson's art breaks down: the poetry belongs to the palace. Pre-Raphaelite art is frankly withdrawn — the appropriate metaphor would suggest something not only beglamoured, but also ritualistic and religiose. Swinburne sings Liberty and Revolution, but it would be difficult to illustrate more forcibly the distinction I have pointed to than by comparing him with Shelley.

The causes of this peculiar other-worldliness of Victorian poetry are sufficiently indicated by Matthew Arnold's recurrent note — his references to

> . . . this strange disease of modern life,
> With its sick hurry, its divided aims,
> Its heads o'ertaxed, its palsied hearts . . .*

and to this age that

> had bound
> Our souls in its benumbing round*

and

> . . . this iron time
> Of doubts, disputes, distractions, fears.*

The frankness of this explicit recognition distinguishes Arnold from among his fellow poets, but it is not enough to constitute the poetic 'criticism of life' that he desiderated. Alas! the past was out of date, the future not yet born, and Arnold's response to these conditions does not differ fundamentally from that of his fellows. Whatever reasons of discipline he may give for valuing Wordsworth and the Greeks, it is plain that he frequents them largely as means of escape to 'the freshness of the early world.' His debt to Wordsworth,* in

*"The Scholar Gipsy", 203—5.

*"Resignation", 209—10.

*"Memorial Verses", 43—5.

*And of Wordsworth he says: 'The gravest of them, Wordsworth, retired (in Middle-Age phrase) into a monastery. I mean, he plunged himself in the inward life, he voluntarily cut himself off from the modern spirit.'—*Essays in Criticism*, First Series: *Heinrich Heine*.

fact, is hardly separable from a debt to Coleridge, and he bears much the same kind of relation to these two as Tennyson bears to Coleridge and Keats. If we note further the relation of *Sohrab and Rustum, for instance, to the 'ineffectual angel'* we shall have a fair idea of Arnold's general relation to the Romantic period. He derives from it in the same kind of way as Tennyson and the Pre-Raphaelites do. This obvious point seems worth dwelling on because he certainly aimed to be a very different kind of poet from these, and his unwitting testimony to the strength of the prevailing atmosphere and conventions is even more striking in his poetry than in his criticism.**

I am not thinking of his frankly romantic poems so much as of his work in the manner of *A Summer Night,* in which he is explicitly concerned with 'this strange disease of modern life.' Except as the explicit occasion of his thin, sweet, meditative melancholy, 'modern life,' 'its sick hurry,' 'its divided aims,' 'its heads o'ertaxed'* are not there. They could have been put there only by genius of the order of Gerard Manley Hopkins — genius, that is, in which technical originality is inseparable from the rare adequacy of mind, sensibility and spirit that it vouches for. Arnold — and we have no reason to say that will and intelligence more than technical abilities were lacking — slips away from 'this uncongenial place, this human life' to moonlight transformations, and the iron time dissolves in wistful, melodious sentiment.

To explain why moonlight appears so often in Arnold's poetry is to explain why, in *Empedocles on Etna, it should**

Sobrab and Rustum: Arnold가 Homer를 흉내내어 지은 짧은 epic episode (1853).

*"Shelley" in *Essays in Criticism*, 2nd Series. 〔Shelley〕 is "*a beautiful and ineffectual angel*, beating in the void his luminous wings in vain."

*열거된 인용어구들은 다 Arnold의 "the Scholar Gipsy"에 나온다.

Empedocles on Etna: 시극 형식으로 쓴 장시. 1852년 작. Callicles는 등장인물의 하나로 a young harp-player. 음울한 내용이 전개되는 가운데 이 harp-player만이 달콤한 노래를 부른다. 아래의 인용된 부분은 427—28, 443, 453행.

be in the two songs of Callicles that the sap suddenly flows. One of these songs is so obviously significant that a phrase or two from it will be enough to clinch the argument:

Far, far from here
The Adriatic breaks in a warm bay . . .

There those two live, far in the Illyrian brakes.

. . . but were rapt, far away . . .

Arnold's manner of evasion distinguishes him from his fellows mainly in the cool, meditative lucidity of his waking dream. In his poems of the English countryside his quest is the Scholar-Gypsy's — sanctuary from the modern world, 'its sick hurry, its divided aims.' And even in poems that do not fall naturally under the head of 'evasion' the sentiment has the same well-bred innocence as always, the same sweet, limpid solemnity: one could hardly have divined in the poet the scourge of the Philistines.*

No, Matthew arnold was not qualified either as critic or poet to give English poetry a new direction. When he predicted that poetry would — advocated that it should — more and more take the place of religion, he intended something very different from an indulging of religious sentiment in a hushed cult of Beauty, a religiose sensuality, a retreat out of the profane world into an exquisite cloistral art; but this describes fairly enough the development from the Pre-Raphaelites and Swinburne through Pater and Oscar Wilde to the 'nineties.

Where, it might be asked, does Browning come in these generalizations? His can hardly be described as a poetry of withdrawal. It belongs to the world he lives in, and he lives happily in the Victorian world with no sense of disharmony. But is this altogether by reason of qualities that should recommend a poet? There are kinds of strength a poet is best without. And it is too plain that Browning would have been less robust if he had been more sensitive and intelligent. He

*Arnold의 비평의 논조는 그의 시의 가락과 걸맞지 않다는 평을 많이 듣는다.

did indeed bring his living interests into his poetry, but it is too plain that they are not the interests of an adult sensitive mind. He did not need to withdraw into a dream-world, because he was able to be a naîve romantic of love and action on the waking plane. If he lived in the Victorian world, it was only as *l'homme moyen sensuel** might live there; unaware of disharmonies because for him there were none, or, rather, only such as were enough to exhilarate, to give him a joyous sense of physical vitality. It is possible to consider him as a philosophical or psychological poet only by confusing intelligence with delight in the exercise of certain grosser cerebral muscles. When he is a poet he is concerned merely with simple emotions and sentiments: the characteristic corrugation* of his surface is merely superficial, and not the expression of a complex sensibility. And yet it was a truly remarkable force that broke as Browning did with the current poetical habits. His use, if only it had been finer, of spoken idiom in verse might have been worth a great deal to later poets: at the end of the century Mr Pound found it worth study. But so inferior a mind and spirit as Browning's could not provide the impulse needed to bring back into poetry the adult intelligence.

As for Meredith,* if any one should comment that I have taken no account of him I can only say that *Modern Love* seems to me the flashy product of unusual but vulgar cleverness working upon cheap emotion: it could serve later poets, if at all, only as a warning.

The further on we go in *The Oxford Book* the more apparent does it become that the age did not make full use of its talent. Who, for instance, would guess from his poetry that William Morris was one of the most versatile, energetic and original men of his time, a force that impinged decisively in the world of practice? He reserved poetry for his day-dreams.

**l'homme moyen sensuel*: 'a man of average sense'

***corrugation:** "주름살". 그의 시의 style은 까다롭고 꼬아 쓴 것으로 알려져 있다.

***Meredith, George:** (1828-1909). Pre-Raphaelites와 교유. *Modern Love* (1862)는 16행시 50편을 모은 시집.

And if we look through any anthologies covering the last fifty years, it becomes impossible to doubt that distinguished minds that should have gone into poetry have gone elsewhere. It is hard to explain otherwise the dearth of original talent in any form or degree. When original talent of a minor order does manifest itself, as, for instance, in Mr A. E. Housman, or, though the collocation is unfair to Mr Housman, Rupert Brooke, it is apt to exert a disproportionate influence. The books of 'Georgian' verse abound with tributes, more or less unconscious, to these two poets (not to insist on R. L. Stevenson's part): indeed it was largely in terms of them that the Victorian bequest of habits and conventions was brought up to date. But these remained essentially the same, as a perusal of the representative anthology, Mr J. C. Squire's *Selections from Modern Poets,* will show. The modernity manifests itself, for the most part, in a complacent debility; the robust, full-blooded emotional confidence of the Victorians is lacking, a modest quietness being the Georgian study; and technical liberation, accordingly, takes the form of loose, careless, unconvinced craftsmanship.

To make a fresh start in poetry under such conditions is a desperate matter. It is easy enough to say that poetry must be adequate to modern life, and it has often been said. But nothing has been done until such generalities have been realized in particulars, that is, in the invention of new techniques, and this, in an age when the current conventions will not serve even to provide a start, is something beyond any but a very unusually powerful and original talent. The established habits form a kind of atmosphere from which it is supremely difficult to escape. Mr J. C. Squire, for instance, reviewing in *The Observer* the late Poet Laureate's* *The Testament of Beauty,* wrote:

> . . . the old poet has done triumphantly what none of his juniors have managed to do — he has, assisted by courage, a natural sincerity, a belief in the function of

---

*1913년부터 계관시인을 지냈던 Robert Bridges(1844-1930)를 말함. 그의 작품 *The Testament of Beauty*(1929)는 철학적 장시.

poetry, contrived to bring within the borders of a poem, and avoiding flatness, all his feelings, knowledge, speculations, interests, hopes and fears. For generations, owing to the reaction of the aesthetic against the new scientific, industrial and largely materialistic world, we have become accustomed to the idea that certain things are 'not poetical,' that a poet can mention a rose, but not a Rolls-Royce, that poetry is a refuge and not an attack, that a poet is a sensitive refugee and not a man facing life, the whole of it, and sounding a clarion call to his more speechless and encumbered fellows.

The first sentence might seem to be in the spirit of this essay, though the phrase 'bring within the borders of a poem' should put us on our guard.* On the next sentence — 'we have become accustomed to the idea that certain things are not poetical' — our commentary runs: worse, we have become accustomed to the idea that certain things *are* poetical, e.g. flowers, dawn, dew, birds, love, archaisms and country place-names;* 'that a poet can mention a rose, but not a Rolls-Royce' — suspicious; 'that poetry is a refuge and not an attack, that a poet is a sensitive refugee and not a man facing life, the whole of it, and sounding a clarion call' — this will not do: it is plain by now that the critic is trying to put a misconception right by turning it upside-down. For we are no more justified in demanding that poetry shall be an attack than in demanding that it shall be a refuge. Indeed, it is very unlikely that a significant modern poem will be anything in the nature of a clarion call. The passage betrays a total misconception of the way in which such a poem will exhibit modernity. It will not be by mentioning modern things, the apparatus of modern civilization, or by being about modern subjects or topics. If the Rolls-Royce enters significantly into poetry it will be, perhaps, in some such

---

*put...our guard: 「우리의 경계심을 자극하다, 조심하게 하다」.

*If it be remarked that the cultivated no longer hold this idea, then the cultivated are reduced to a very small minority indeed.

way as Mr T. S. Eliot suggests* when he says that probably the modern's perception of rhythm has been affected by the internal combustion engine. All that we can fairly ask of the poet is that he shall show himself to have been fully alive in our time. The evidence will be in the very texture of his poetry.

Mr Alfred Noyes* wrote (is still writing?) a long work in verse, *The Torch-Bearers,* about the succession of great astronomers. A few glances were enough to establish its complete insignificance as poetry. For such an undertaking would have to justify itself in the texture of the verse, by an unmistakable newness of tone, rhythm and imagery, by an utterly unfamiliar 'feel.' Mr Noyes's verse is such as any one with a feeling for language, and a close acquaintance with the poets of the past, could learn to write. On like grounds a subtler performance, Mr Laurence Binyon's* *The Sirens,* an ode on the questing spirit of man, must be dismissed. The ode has been praised for its technical accomplishment, and in a sense it does exhibit skilled craftsmanship. But the only technique that matters is that which compels words to express an intensely personal way of feeling, so that the reader responds, not in a general way that he knows beforehand to be 'poetical,' but in a precise, particular way that no frequenting of *The Oxford Book* could have made familiar to him. To invent techniques that shall be adequate to the ways of feeling, or modes of experience, of adult, sensitive moderns is difficult in the extreme. Until it has been once done it is so difficult as to seem impossible. One success makes others more probable because less difficult.

That is the peculiar importance of Mr T. S. Eliot. For, though there is, inevitably, a great deal of snobbism in the cult he suffers from, mere snobbism will not account for his

---

******Savonorala,* Charlotte Eliot. *Introduction,* xi.

***Alfred Noyes:** (1880–1958). 그는 "이야기"를 많이 지었다. *The Torch-Bearers* (1922–30)는 그 중의 한 가지.

***Laurence Binyon:** (1869–1943). 시인, 동양미술학자.

prestige among the young. Having a mind unquestionably of rare distinction he has solved his own problem as a poet, and so done more than solve the problem for himself. His influence has been the more effective in that he is a critic as well as a poet, and his criticism and his poetry reinforce each other. It is mainly due to him that no serious poet or critic today can fail to realize that English poetry in the future must develop (if at all) along some other line than that running from the Romantics through Tennyson, Swinburne, *A Shropshire Lad,** and Rupert Brooke. He has made a new start, and established new bearings.

To justify these contentions and enforce the general account given above it will be necessary first to make a closer survey of the situation as it was just after the war, before Mr Eliot impinged.

*A. E. Housman (1859–1936)의 시집 (1896).

Cleanth Brooks

(1906—　　)

미국 남부에 속하는 켄터키 주에서 태어나 남부 명문 밴더빌트와 툴레인대학에서 공부, 이어 옥스포드를 마쳤다. 밴더빌트에서 랜섬의 영향을 깊이 받았다. 루이지애너 주립대학에서 오래 가르쳤고, 1947 이후에는 예일대학에서 가르쳤다. Robert Penn Warren과 문예지 *Southern Review*를 편집, 이른바 「남부 문학」의 부흥을 도왔고, 워른 또는 Robert Heilman과 같이 낸 *Understandiry Poetry*(1938), *Understanding Fiction*(1943), *Understanding Drama*(1947)는 한국에까지도 널리 알려진 문학 교재로서 수많은 모방작을 낳게 했으며, *Modern Poetry and the Tradition*(1939), *The Well-Wrought Urn*(1947) 등의 평론집은 이른바 New Criticism의 방법의 묘미를 최대한도로 보여준 실제 비평들을 싣고 있다. 주로 그에 의해 뉴 크리티시즘의 개념들인 아이러니, 파라독스, 윗트, 상징, 애매성, 극적 구성 등의 용어가 널리 퍼지고, 그것들에 의한 작품 분석의 방법이 많은 사람들에게 알려졌다. 윔서트와 함께 쓴 *Literary Criticism: A Short History*(1957)는 비평의 개념들을 역사적으로 정확히 분석 음미한 명저다.

"Irony as a Principle of Structure"(1949)는 그의 명징한 분석적 실제비평의 하나로, 시의 언어적 구조에, 그 다양한 각 부분의 상호 연관성에, 그것들의 힘겨운, 그러나 힘있는 통일에 주의한다. 이러한 힘의 오고 감에 있어서 가장 중요한 구조적인 역할을 하는 요소를 그는 아이러니라 부르고, 그것의 작용의 실제를 여러 편의 잘 알려진 영시 작품에서 보여주고 있다. 아이러니는 일상생활에서는 주로 농담에 쓰이니까 전혀 시답지 않으나, 브룩스의 분석에 따르면 그것이야 말로 모든 좋은 시의 기본 요소인 것이다.

Irony as a Principle of Structure (1949)

ONE can sum up modern poetic technique by calling it the rediscovery of metaphor and the full commitment to metaphor. The poet can legitimately step out into the universal only by first going through the narrow door of the particular. The poet does not select an abstract theme and then embellish it with concrete details. On the contrary, he must establish the details, must abide by the details, and through his realization of the details attain to whatever general meaning he can attain. The meaning must issue from the particulars; it must not seem to be arbitrarily forced upon the particulars. Thus, our conventional habits of language have to be reversed when we come to deal with poetry. For here it is the tail that wags the dog. Better still,* here it is the tail of the kite — the tail that makes the kite fly — the tail that renders the kite more than a frame of paper blown crazily down the wind.

The tail of the kite, it is true, seems to negate the kite's function: it weights down something made to rise; and in the same way, the concrete particulars with which the poet loads himself seem to deny the universal to which he aspires. The poet wants to "say" something. Why, then, doesn't he say it directly and forthrightly? Why is he willing to say it only through his metaphors? Through his metaphors, he risks saying it partially and obscurely, and risks not saying it at all. But the risk must be taken, for direct statement leads to abstraction and threatens to take us out of poetry altogether.

The commitment to metaphor thus implies, with respect to general theme, a principle of indirection. With respect to

---

*Better still: 「더 적절히 표현하자면」.

particular images and statements, it implies a principle of organic relationship. That is, the poem is not a collection of beautiful or "poetic" images. If there really existed objects which were somehow intrinsically "poetic," still the mere assemblage of these would not give us a poem. For in that case, one might arrange bouquets of these poetic images and thus create poems by formula. But the elements of a poem are related to each other, not as blossoms juxtaposed in a bouquet, but as the blossoms are related to the other parts of a growing plant. The beauty of the poem is the flowering of the whole plant, and needs the stalk, the leaf, and the hidden roots.

If this figure seems somewhat highflown, let us borrow an analogy from another art: the poem is like a little drama. The total effect proceeds from all the elements in the drama, and in a good poem, as in a good drama, there is no waste motion and there are no superfluous parts.

In coming to see that the parts of a poem are related to each other organically, and related to the total theme indirectly, we have come to see the importance of *context*. The memorable verses in poetry — even those which seem somehow intrinsically "poetic" — show on inspection* that they derive their poetic quality from their relation to a particular context. We may, it is true, be tempted to say that Shakespeare's "Ripeness is all"* is poetic because it is a sublime thought, or because it possesses simple eloquence; but that is to forget the context in which the passage appears. The proof that this is so becomes obvious when we contemplate such unpoetic lines as "vitality is all," "serenity is all," "maturity is all," — statements whose philosophical import in the abstract is about as defensible as that of "ripeness is all." Indeed, the commonplace word "never" repeated five times becomes one of the most poignant lines in *Lear,** but it becomes so because of the supporting context. Even the "meaning" of any particular item is modified by the context.

***on inspection:** 「자세히 관찰하면」.

**King Lear*

**King Lear*, V, iii, 308.

For what is said is said in a particular situation and by a particular dramatic character.

The last instances adduced can be most properly regarded as instances of "loading" from the context. The context endows the particular word or image or statement with significance. Images so charged become symbols; statements so charged become dramatic utterances. But there is another way in which to look at the impact of the context upon the part. The part is modifed by the pressure of the context.

Now the *obvious* warping of a statement by the context we characterize as "ironical." To take the simplest instance, we say "this is a fine state of affairs," and in certain contexts the statement means quite the opposite of what it purports to say literally. This is sarcasm, the most obvious kind of irony. Here a complete reversal of meaning is effected: effected by the context, and pointed, probably, by the tone of voice. But the modification can be most important even though it falls far short of sarcastic reversal, and it need not be underlined by the tone of voice at all. The tone of irony can be effected by the skillful disposition of the context. Gray's *Elegy* will furnish an obvious example.

> Can storied urn or animated bust
> Back to its mansion call the fleeting breath?
> Can Honour's voice provoke the silent dust,
> Or Flatt'ry soothe the dull cold ear of death?

In its context, the question is obviously rhetorical. The answer has been implied in the characterization of the breath as fleeting and of the ear of death as dull and cold. The form is that of a question, but the manner in which the question has been asked shows that it is no true question at all.

These are obvious instances of irony, and even on this level, much more poetry is ironical than the reader may be disposed to think. Many of Hardy's poems and nearly all of Housman's, for example, reveal irony quite as definite and overt as this. Lest these examples, however, seem to specialize irony in the direction of the sardonic, the reader ought to be reminded that irony, even in its obvious and conventionally recognized forms, comprises a wide variety of modes: tragic irony, self-irony, playful, arch, mocking, or gentle irony, etc. The body of poetry which may be said to contain irony in the ordinary senses of the term stretches from *Lear*, on the one hand, to "Cupid and Campaspe Played,"* on the other.

What indeed would be a statement wholly devoid of an ironic potential — a statement that did not show any qualification of the context? One is forced to offer statements like "Two plus two equals four," or "The square on the hypotenuse of a right triangle is equal to the sum of the squares on the two sides." The meaning of these statements is unqualified by any context; if they are true, they are equally true in any possible context.* These statements are properly abstract, and their terms are pure denotations. (If "two" or "four" actually happened to have connotations for the fancifully minded, the connotations would be quite irrelevant: they do not participate in the meaningful structure of the statement.)

But connotations are important in poetry and do enter significantly into the structure of meaning which is the poem. Moreover, I should claim also — as a corollary of the foregoing proposition — that poems never contain abstract statements. That is, any "statement" made in the poem bears the pressure of the context and has its meaning modified by the context. In other words, the statements made — including those which appear to be philosophical generalizations — are to be read as if they were speeches in a drama. Their relevance, their propriety, their rhetorical force, even their

*John Lyly의 서정시. 정확히는 "Cupid and my Campaspe Played"

*This is not to say, of course, that such statements are not related to a particular "universe of discourse." They are indeed, as are all statements of whatever kind. But I distinguish here between "context" and universe of discourse." "Two plus two equals four" is not dependent on a special dramatic context in the way in which a "statement" made in a poem is. Compare "two plus two equals four" and the same "statement" as contained in Housman's poem:

—To think that two and two are four
And neither five nor three
The heart of man has long been sore
And long 'tis like to be.

meaning, cannot be divorced from the context in which they are imbedded.

The principle I state may seem a very obvious one, but I think that it is nonetheless very important. It may throw some light upon the importance of the term *irony* in modern criticism. As one who has certainly tended to overuse the term *irony* and perhaps, on occasion, has abused the term, I am closely concerned here. But I want to make quite clear what that concern is: it is not to justify the term *irony* as such, but rather to indicate why modern critics are so often tempted to use it. We have doubtless stretched the term too much, but it has been almost the only term available by which to point to a general and important aspect of poetry.

Consider this example: The speaker in Matthew Arnold's "Dover Beach" states that the world, "which seems to lie before us like a land of dreams . . . hath really neither joy nor love nor light. . . ." For some readers the statement will seem an obvious truism. (The hero of a typical Hemingway short story or novel, for example, will say this, though of course in a rather different idiom.) For other readers, however, the statement will seem false, or at least highly questionable. In any case, if we try to "prove" the proposition, we shall raise some very perplexing metaphysical questions, and in doing so, we shall certainly also move away from the problems of the poem and, finally, from a justification of the poem. For the lines are to be justified in the poem in terms of the context: the speaker is standing beside his loved one, looking out of the window on the calm sea, listening to the long withdrawing roar of the ebbing tide, and aware of the beautiful delusion of moonlight which "blanches" the whole scene. The "truth" of the statement, and of the poem itself, in which it is imbedded, will be validated, not by a majority report of the association of sociologists, or a committee of physical scientists, or of a congress of metaphysicians who are willing to stamp the statement as proved. How is the statement to be validated? We shall probably not be able to do better than to apply T.S. Eliot's test: does the statement seem to be that which the mind of the reader can accept as coherent, mature, and founded on the facts of experience?* But when we raise such a question, we are driven to consider the poem as drama. We raise such further questions as these: Does the speaker seem carried away with his own emotions? Does he seem to oversimplify the situation? Or does he, on the other hand, seem to have won to a kind of detachment and objectivity? In other words, we are forced to raise the question as to whether the statement grows properly out of a context; whether it acknowledges the pressures of the context; whether it is "ironical" — or merely callow, glib, and sentimental.

I have suggestd elsewhere* that the poem which meets Eliot's test comes to the same thing as I. A. Richards' "poetry of synthesis" — that is, a poetry which does not leave out what is apparently hostile to its dominant tone, and which, because it is able to fuse the irrelevant and discordant, has come to terms with itself and is invulnerable to irony. Irony, then, in this further sense, is not only an acknowledgment of the pressures of a context. Invulnerability to irony is the stability of a context in which the internal pressures balance and mutually support each other. The stability is like that of the arch: the very forces which are calculated to drag the stones to the ground actually provide the principle of support — a principle in which thrust and counterthrust become the means of stability.

In many poems the pressures of the context emerge in obvious ironies. Marvell's "To His Coy Mistress" or Releigh's "Nymph's Reply" or even Gray's "Elegy" reveal themselves as ironical, even to readers who use irony strictly in the conventional sense.

But can other poems be subsumed under this general principle, and do they show a comparable basic structure? The test case would seem to be presented by the lyric, and particularly the simple lyric. Consider, for example, one of Shakespeare's songs:

**The Use of Poetry and the Use of Criticism* (London, 1933), p. 96.

**The Well-Wrought Urn* (New York, 1947), pp. 254—56; Richards, *Principle of Literary Criticism* (London, 1924), pp. 246—50.

Who is Silvia: what is she
    That all our swains commend her?
Holy, fair, and wise is she;
    The heavens such grace did lend her,
That she might admired be.

Is she kind as she is fair?
    For beauty lives with kindness.
Love doth to her eyes repair,
    To help him of his blindness,
And, being help'd, inhabits there.

Then to Silvia let us sing,
    That Silvia is excelling;
She excels each mortal thing
    Upon the dull earth dwelling:
To her let us garlands bring.*

On one level the song attempts to answer the question "Who is Silvia?" and the answer given makes her something of an angel and something of a goddess. She excels each mortal thing "Upon the dull earth dwelling." Silvia herself, of course, dwells upon that dull earth, though it is presumably her own brightness which makes it dull by comparison. (The dull earth, for example, yields bright garlands which the swains are bringing to her.) Why does she excel each mortal thing? Because of her virtues ("Holy, fair, and wise is she"), and these are a celestial gift. She is heaven's darling ("The heavens such grace did lend her").

Grace, I suppose, refers to grace of movement, and some readers will insist that we leave it at that. But since Silvia's other virtues include holiness and wisdom, and since her grace has been lent from above, I do not think that we can quite shut out the theological overtones. Shakespeare's audience would have found it even more difficult to do so. At any rate, it is interesting to see what happens if we are aware of these overtones. We get a delightful richness, and we also get something very close to irony.

**The Two Gentlemen of Verona*, IV, ii, 39—53.

The motive for the bestowal of grace — that she might admired be — is oddly untheological. But what follows is odder still, for the love that "doth to her eyes repair" is not, as we might expect, Christian "charity" but the little pagan god Cupid ("Love doth to her eyes repair, / To help him of his blindness.") But if Cupid lives in her eyes, then the second line of the stanza takes on another layer of meaning. "For beauty lives with kindness" becomes not merely a kind of charming platitude — actually often denied in human experience. (The Petrarchan lover, for example, as Shakespeare well knew, frequently found a beautiful and *cruel* mistress.) The second line, in this context, means also that the love god lives with the kind Silvia, and indeed has taken these eyes that sparkle with kindness for his own.

Is the mixture of pagan myth and Christian theology, then, an unthinking confusion into which the poet has blundered, or is it something wittily combined? It is certainly not a confusion, and if blundered into unconsciously, it is a happy mistake. But I do not mean to press the issue of the poet's self-consciousness (and with it, the implication of a kind of playful irony). Suffice it to say that the song is charming and delightful, and that the mingling of elements is proper to a poem which is a deft and light-fingered attempt to suggest the quality of divinity with which lovers perennially endow maidens who are finally mortal. The touch is light, there is a lyric grace, but the tone is complex, nonetheless.

I shall be prepared, however, to have this last example thrown out of court since Shakespeare, for all his universality, was a contemporary of the metaphysical poets, and may have incorporated more of their ironic complexity than is necessary or normal. One can draw more innocent and therefore more convincing examples from Wordsworth's Lucy poems.

> She dwelt among the untrodden ways
>   Beside the springs of Dove,
> A maid whom there were none to praise
>   And very few to love;
>
> A violet by a mossy stone
>   Half hidden from the eye!

Fair as a star, when only one
    Is shining in the sky.

She lived unknown, and few could know
    When Lucy ceased to be;
But she is in her grave, and, oh,
    The difference to me.

Which is Lucy really like — the violet or the star? The context in general seems to support the violet comparison. The violet, beautiful but almost unnoticed, already half hidden from the eye, is now, as the poem ends, completely hidden in its grave, with none but the poet to grieve for its loss. The star comparison may seem only vaguely relevant — a conventional and here a somewhat anomalous compliment. Actually, it is not difficult to justify the star comparison: to her lover's eyes, she is the solitary star. She has no rivals, nor would the idea of rivalry, in her unselfconscious simplicity, occur to her.

The violet and the star thus balance each other and between themselves define the situation: Lucy was, from the viewpoint of the great world, unnoticed, shy, modest, and half hidden from the eye, but from the standpoint of her lover, she is the single star, completely dominating that world, not arrogantly like the sun, but sweetly and modestly, like the star. The implicit contrast is that so often developed ironically by John Donne in his poems where the lovers, who amount to nothing in the eyes of the world, become, in their own eyes, each the other's world — as in "The Good-Morrow," where their love makes "one little room an everywhere," or as in "The Canonization," where the lovers drive into the mirrors of each other's eyes the "towns, countries, courts" — which make up the great world; and thus find that world in themselves. It is easy to imagine how Donne would have exploited the contrast between the violet and the star, accentuating it, developing the irony, showing how the violet was really like its antithesis, the star, etc.

Now one does not want to enter an Act of Uniformity*

***enter an Act of Uniformity:** 일종의 기도방식의 통일 법령같은 것을 제기하다. 즉, "시인들은 모두 꼭같은 방식으로 시를 쓰라고 요청한다' 라는 뜻.

against the poets. Wordsworth is entitled to his method of simple juxtaposition with no underscoring of the ironical contrast. But it is worth noting that the contrast with its ironic potential is there in his poem. It is there in nearly all of Wordsworth's successful lyrics. It is certainly to be found in "A slumber did my spirit seal."

> A slumber did my spirit seal;
> I had no human fears:
> She seemed a thing that could not feel
> The touch of earthly years.
>
> No motion has she now, no force;
> She neither hears nor sees,
> Rolled round in earth's diurnal course,
> With rocks, and stones, and trees.

The lover's insensitivity to the claims of mortality is interpreted as a lethargy of spirit — a strange slumber. Thus the "human fear" that he lacked are apparently the fears normal to human beings. But the phrase has a certain pliability. It could mean fears *for* the loved one as a mortal human being; and the lines that follow tend to warp the phrase in this direction: it does not occur to the lover that he needs to fear for one who cannot be touched by "earthly years." We need not argue that Wordsworth is consciously using a witty device, a purposed ambiguity; nor need we conclude that he is confused. It is enough to see that Wordworth has developed, quite "normally," let us say, a context calculated to pull "human fears" in opposed directions, and that the slightest pressure of attention on the part of the reader precipitates an ironical effect.

As we move into the second stanza, the potential irony almost becomes overt. If the slumber has sealed the lover's spirit, a slumber, immersed in which he thought it impossible that his loved one could perish, so too a slumber has now definitely sealed *her* spirit: "No motion has she now, no force; / She neither hears nor sees." It is evident that it is her unnatural slumber that has waked him out of his. It is curious to speculate on what Donne or Marvell would have made of this.

Wordsworth, however, still does not choose to exploit the contrast as such. Instead, he attempts to suggest something of the lover's agonized shock at the loved one's present lack of motion — of his response to her utter and horrible inertness. And how shall he suggest this? He chooses to suggest it, not by saying that she lies as quiet as marble or as a lump of clay; on the contrary, he attempts to suggest it by imagining her in violent motion — violent, but imposed motion, the same motion indeed which the very stones share, whirled about as they are in earth's diurnal course. Why does the image convey so powerfully the sense of something inert and helpless? Part of the effect, of course, resides in the fact that a dead lifelessness is suggested more sharply by an object's being whirled about by something else than by an image of the object in repose. But there are other matters which are at work here: the sense of the girl's falling back into the clutter of things, companioned by things chained like a tree to one particular spot, or by things completely inanimate, like rocks and stones. Here, of course, the concluding figure leans upon the suggestion made in the first stanza, that the girl once seemed something not subject to earthly limitations at all. But surely, the image of the whirl itself is important in its suggestion of something meaningless — motion that mechanically repeats itself. And there is one further element: the girl, who to her lover seemed a thing that could not feel the touch of earthly years, is caught up helplessly into the empty whirl of the earth which measures and makes time. She is touched by and held by earthly time in its most powerful and horrible image. The last figure thus seems to me to summarize the poem — to offer to almost every facet of meaning suggested in the earlier lines a concurring and resolving image which meets and accepts and reduces each item to its place in the total unity.

Wordsworth, as we have observed above, does not choose to point up specifically the ironical contrast between the speaker's former slumber and the loved one's present slumber. But there is one ironical contrast which he does stress: this is the contrast between the two senses in which the girl becomes insulated against the "touch of earthly years." In the first stanza, she "could not feel / The touch of earthly years" because she seemed divine and immortal. But in the second stanza, now in her grave, she still does not "feel the touch of earthly years," for, like the rocks and stones, she feels nothing at all. It is true that Wordsworth does not repeat the verb "feels"; instead he writes "She neither *hears* nor *sees.*" But the contrast, though not commented upon directly by any device of verbal wit, is there nonetheless, and is bound to make itself felt in any sensitive reading of the poem. The statement of the first stanza has been literally realized in the second, but its meaning has been ironically reversed.

Ought we, then, to apply the term *ironical* to Wordsworth's poem? Not necessarily. I am trying to account for my temptation to call such a poem ironical — not to justify my yielding to the temptation — least of all to insist that others so transgress. Moreover, Wordsworth's poem seems to me admirable, and I entertain no notion that it might have been more admirable still had John Donne written it rather than William Wordsworth. I shall be content if I can make a much more modest point: namely, that since both Wordsworth and Donne are poets, their work has at basis a similar structure, and that the dynamic structure — the pattern of thrust and counterthrust — which we associate with Donne has its counterpart in Wordsworth. In the work of both men, the relation between part and part is organic, which means that each part modifies and is modified by the whole.

Yet to intimate that there are potential ironies in Wordsworth's lyric may seem to distort it. After all, is it not simple and spontaneous? With these terms we encounter two of the critical catchwords of the nineteenth century, even as *ironical* is in danger of becoming a catchword of our own period. Are the terms *simple* and *ironical* mutually exclusive? What after all do we mean by *simple* or by *spontaneous*? We may mean that the poem came to the poet easily and even spontaneously: very complex poems may — indeed have — come just this way. Or the poem may seem in its effect on the reader a simple and spontaneous utterance: some poems of great complexity possess this quality. What is likely to cause trouble here is the intrusion of a special theory of composition. It is fairly represented as an intrusion since a theory as to how a poem is written is being allowed to dictate to us how the poem is to be read. There is no harm in thinking of Wordsworth's poem as simple and spontaneous unless these terms deny complexities that actually exist in the poem, and unless they justify us in reading the poem with only half our minds. A slumber ought not to seal the *reader's* spirit as he reads this poem, or any other poem.

I have argued that irony, taken as the acknowledgment of the pressures of context, is to be found in poetry of every period and even in simple lyrical poetry. But in the poetry of our own time, this pressure reveals itself strikingly. A great deal of modern poetry does use irony as its special and perhaps its characteristic strategy. For this there are reasons, and compelling reasons. To cite only a few of these reasons: there is the breakdown of a common symbolism; there is the general scepticism as to universals; not least important, there is the depletion and corruption of the very language itself, by advertising and by the mass-produced arts of radio, the moving picture, and pulp fiction. The modern poet has the task of rehabilitating a tired and drained language so that it can convey meanings once more with force and with exactitude. This task of qualifying and modifying language is perennial; but it is imposed on the modern poet as a special burden. Those critics who attribute the use of ironic techniques to the poet's own bloodless sophistication and tired scepticism would be better advised to refer these vices to his potential readers, a public corrupted by Hollywood and the Book of the Month Club.* For the modern poet is not addressing simple primitives but a public sophisticated by commercial art.

At any rate, to the honor of the modern poet be it said that he has frequently succeeded in using his ironic techniques to win through to clarity and passion. Randall

*매달 선정된 책을 사 보는 독서클럽. 주로 대중문학을 취급하고, 책을 싼 값에 많이 팔기 위한 상업적 방법에서 생겼으며, 여러가지 형태가 있다.

Jarrell's* "Eighth Air Force" represents a success of this sort.

If, in an odd angle of the hutment,
A puppy laps the water from a can
Of flowers, and the drunk sergeant shaving
Whistles *O Paradiso!* — shall I say that man
Is not as men have said: a wolf to man?

The other murderers troop in yawning;
Three of them play Pitch, one sleeps, and one
Lies counting missions, lies there sweating
Till even his heart beats: One; One; One.
O murderers! . . . Still, this is how it's done:

This is a war. . . . But since these play, before they die,
Like puppies with their puppy; since, a man,
I did as these have done, but did not die —
I will content the people as I can
And give up these to them: Behold the man!

I have suffered, in a dream, because of him,
Many things; for this last saviour, man,
I have lied as I lie now. But what is lying?
Men wash their hands, in blood, as best they can:
I find no fault in this just man.

There are no superfluous parts, no dead or empty details. The airmen in their hutment are casual enough and honest enough to be convincing. The raw building is domesticated: there are the flowers in water from which the mascot, a puppy, laps. There is the drunken sergeant, whistiling an opera aria as he shaves. These " murderers," as the poet is casually to call the airmen in the next stanza, display a touching regard for the human values. How, then, can one say that man is a wolf to man, since these men "play before they die, like puppies with their puppy." But the casual presence of the puppy in the hutment allows us to take the stanza both ways, or the dog is a kind of tamed and domesticated wolf, and his presence may prove on the contrary that the hutment is the

*Randall Jarrell: (1914-65). 미국의 시인.

wolf den. After all, the timber wolf plays with its puppies.

The second stanza takes the theme to a perfectly explicit conclusion. If three of the men play pitch, and one is asleep, at least one man is awake and counts himself and his companions murderers. But his unvoiced cry "O murderers" is met, countered, and dismissed with the next two lines: ". . . Still this is how it's done: / This is a war. . . ."

The note of casuistry and cynical apology prepares for a brilliant and rich resolving image, the image of Pontius Pilate,* which is announced specifically in the third stanza:

> I will content the people as I can
> And give up these to them: behold the man!

Yet if Pilate,* as he is first presented, is a jesting Pilate, who asks "What is truth?" it is a bitter and grieving Pilate who concludes the poem. It is the integrity of Man himself that is at stake. Is man a cruel animal, a wolf, or is he the last savior, the Christ of our secular religion of humanity?

The Pontius Pilate metaphor, as the poet uses it, becomes a device for tremendous concentration. For the speaker (presumably the young airman who cried "O murderers") is himself the confessed murderer under judgment, and also the Pilate who judges, and, at least as a representative of man, the savior whom the mob would condemn. He is even Pilate's better nature, his wife, for the lines "I have suffered, in a dream, because of him, / Many things" is merely a rearrangement of *Matthew* 27:19, the speech of Pilate's wife to her husband. But this last item is more than a reminiscence of the scriptural scene. It reinforces the spaker's present dilemma. The modern has had high hopes for man; are the hopes merely a dream? Is man incorrigible, merely a cruel beast? The speaker's present torture springs from that hope and from his reluctance to dismiss it as an empty dream. This Pilate is even harder-pressed than was the Roman magistrate. For he must convince himself of this last savior's innocence. But he has lied for him before. He will lie for him now.

***Pontius Pilate:** 예수를 재판한 유태 총독인 본디오 빌라도. 마태복음 27장 참조.

Men wash their hands in blood, as best they can:
I find no fault in this just man.

What is the meaning of "Men wash their hands in blood, as best they can"? I can mean: Since my own hands are bloody, I have no right to condemn the rest. It can mean: I know that man can love justice, even though his hands are bloody, for there is blood on mine. It can mean: Men are essentially decent: they try to keep their hands clean even if they have only blood in which to wash them.

None of these meanings cancels out the others. All are relevant, and each meaning contributes to the total meaning. Indeed, there is not a facet of significance which does not receive illumination from the figure.

Some of Jarrell's weaker poems seem weak to me because they lean too heavily upon this concept of the goodness of man. In some of them, his approach to the theme is too direct. But in this poem, the affirmation of man's essential justness by a Pilate who contents the people as he washes his hands in blood seems to me to supply every qualification that is required. The sense of self-guilt, the yearning to believe in man's justness, the knowledge of the difficulty of so believing — all work to render accurately and dramatically the total situation.

It is easy at this point to misapprehend the function of irony. We can say that Jarrell's irony pares his theme down to acceptable dimensions. The theme of man's goodness has here been so qualified that the poet himself does not really believe in it. But this is not what I am trying to say. We do not ask a poet to bring his peom into line with our personal beliefs — still less to flatter our personal beliefs. What we do ask is that the poem dramatize the situation so accurately, so honestly, with such fidelity to the total situation that it is no longer a question of our beliefs, but of our participation in the poetic experience. At his best, Jarrell manages to bring us, by an act of imagination, to the most penetrating insight. Participating in that insight, we doubtless become better citizens. (One of the "uses" of poetry, I should agree, is to make us better citizens.) But poetry is not the eloquent rendition of the citizen's creed. It is not even the accurate rendition of his creed. Poetry must carry us beyond the abstract creed into the very matrix out of which, and from which, our creeds are abstracted. That is what "The Eighth Air Force" does. That is what, I am convinced, all good poetry does.

For the theme in a genuine poem does not confront us as abstraction — that is, as one man's generalization from the relevant particulars. Finding its proper symbol, defined and refined by the participating metaphors, the theme becomes a part of the reality in which we live — an insight, rooted in and growing out of concrete experience, many-sided, three-dimensional. Even the resistance to generalization has its part in this process — even the drag of the particulars away from the universal — even the tension of opposing themes — play their parts. The kite properly loaded, tension maintained along the kite string, rises steadily *against* the thrust of the wind.

William Kurtz Wimsatt, Jr.

(1907—1975)

예일 대학에서 박사 학위를 받고 죽을 때까지 그곳에서 가르쳤다. 18세기 영문학 연구로 학자 생활을 시작하였으나, 곧 문학 비평의 이론적 고찰에 예리한 분석력을 기울여, 1946년에 철학자인 친구 Monroe C. Beardsley와의 공저로 유명한 "The Intentional Fallacy"와 "The Affective Fallacy"를 발표함으로써, 굉장한 반응을 일으켰다. 이 두 논문은 한국인에게도 상당히 잘 알려져 있고, 앞의 것은 번역도 되어 있다(삼성판 세계 문학 전집 90 〈세계평론선〉에 이상섭 역으로 수록되어 있으나, 본인이 번역한 것이 아님을 밝힌다). 계속하여 비평에 관련된 여러 문제들에 대하여 유례를 찾기 힘들 정도의 날카로운 분석력을 발휘한 문제의 논문들을 연이어 발표함으로써 가장 중요한 이론가의 하나로 지목받게 되었다. 초기의 논문들은 *The Verbal Icon* (1954)에 수록되었고, 그후의 논문들은 각각 *Hateful Contraries*(1965)와 *Day of the Leopards*(1976)에 실려 있다. 뉴 크리티시즘의 대표자인 동료 브룩스와의 공저 *Literary Criticism; A Short History*(1956)는 명저이다.

윔서트는 철학과 논리학의 기본 훈련이 뛰어난 비평가로서 문학작품의 언어, 그 비유적 성질과 극적 구조를 개인적, 사회적 문맥에서 떼어내어 고찰하였다. 말하자면 뉴 크리티시즘의 이론적 기틀을 마련한 셈이나, 바로 그 이론적 성격 때문에 정작 뉴 크리틱들과는 구별된다.

「의도」와 「영향」에 관한 두 논문은 너무나도 잘 알려져서——오해, 곡해가 많지만—— 제외하고, 역시 중요한 문제를 잘 다룬 "The Concrete Universal"(1947)을 읽기로 한다. 문학은 보편성을 제시한다는 주장이 있는 반면, 문학은 특수성을 표현한다는 주장이 있는데, 이런 상반된 주장이 문학의 언어의 어떤 성질과 관계가 있는지를 따지는 논문이다.

The Concrete Universal (1947)

1

THE CENTRAL agrument of this essay, concerning what I shall, taking a term from Hegel, call the "concrete universal," proceeds from the observation that literary theorists have from early times to the present persisted in making statements which in their contexts seem to mean that a work of literary art is in some peculiar sense a very individual thing or a very universal thing or both. What that paradox can mean, or what important fact behind the paradox has been discerned by such various critics as Aristotle, Plotinus, Hegel, and Ransom, it will be the purpose of the essay to inquire, and by the inquiry to discuss not only a significant feature of metaphysical poetics from Aristotle to the present day but the relation between metaphysical poetics and more practical and specific rhetorical analysis. In the brief historical survey which forms one part of this essay it will not be my purpose to suggest that any of these writers meant exactly what I shall mean in later parts where I describe the structure of poetry. Yet throughout the essay I shall proceed on the theory not only that men have at different times used the same terms and have meant differently, but that they have sometimes used different terms and have meant the same or somewhat the same. In other words, I assume that there is continuity in the problems of criticism, and that a person who studies poetry today has a legitimate interest in what Plato said about poetry.

The view of common terms and their relations to classes of things from which I shall start is roughly that which one may read in the logic of J. S. Mill, a view which is not much different from the semantic view of today and for most purposes not much different from the Aristotelian and scholastic view.

Mill speaks of the word and its denotation and connotation (the term, referent and reference of Ogden and Richards; the sign, denotatum and designatum of Charles W. Morris).* The denotation is the *it*, the individual thing or the aggregate of things to which the term may refer; the connotation is the *what*, the quality or classification inferred for the it, or implicitly predicated by the application of the term or the giving of the name.* The main difference between all modern positivistic, nominalistic and semantic systems and the scholastic and classical systems is that the older ones stress the similarity of the individuals denoted by the common term and hence the real universality of meaning, while the modern systems stress the differences in the individuals, the constant flux even of each individual in time and space and its kinetic structure, and hence infer only an approximate or nominal universality of meaning and a convenience rather than a truth in the use of general terms. A further difference lies in the view of how the individual is related to the various connotations of terms which may be applied to it. That is, to the question: What is it? the older writers seem to hold there is but one (essentially right) answer, while the moderns accept as many answers as there are classes to which the individual may be assigned (an indefinite number). The older writers speak of a proper essence or whatness of the individual, a quality which in some cases at least is that designated by the class name most commonly applied to the individual: a bench is a bench, essentially a bench, accidentally a heavy wooden object or something covered with green paint. "When we say *what* it is," observes Aristotle, "we do not say 'white' or 'hot' or 'three cubits long,' but 'a man' or 'a god.'"* And this view is

---

***Charles W. Morris,** "Ethics and the Theory of Signs," *Journal of Unified Science,* Ⅷ (1939), 131—50.

*The terms "denotation" and "connotation" are commonly and loosely used by literary critics to distinguish the dictionary meaning of a term (denotation) from the vaguer aura of suggestion (connotation). But both these are parts of the connotation in the legal sense. [Wimsatt 자신의 주: 이하 W로 표시함].

**Metaphysics*, Ⅶ (Z), 1 (1028). *cf*. Mortimer J. Adler, *The Problem of Species* (New York, 1940), pp. 24—25. [W]

also a habit scarcely avoidable in our own daily thinking, especially when we think of living things or of artifacts, things made by us or our fellows for a purpose. What is it? Bench, we think, is an adequate answer. An assemblage of sticks painted green, we consider freakish.

2

Whether or not one believes in universals, one may see the persistence in literary criticism of a theory that poetry presents the concrete and the universal, or the individual and the universal, or an object which in a mysterious and special way is both highly general and highly particular. The doctrine is implicit in Aristotle's two statements that poetry imitates actions and that poetry tends to express the universal. It is implicit again at the end of the classic period in the mystic doctrine of Plotinus, who in his later writing on beauty reverses the Platonic objection that art does not know the ultimate reality of the forms. Plotinus arrives at the view that the artist by a kind of bypass of the inferior natural productions of the world soul reaches straight to the forms that lie behind in the divine intelligence.* Another version of the classic theory, with affinities for Plotinus, lies in the scholastic phrase *resplendentia formae*. *

Cicero's account of how Zeuxis painted an ideal Helen from the five most beautiful virgins of Crotona* is a typical development of the less mystic Aristotelian theory, in effect the familiar neo-classic theory found in Du Fresnoy's *Art of*

*"The arts are not to be slighted on the ground that they create by imitation of natural objects; for, to begin with, these natural objects are themselves imitations; then, we must recognize that they give no bare reproduction of the thing seen but go back to the ideas from which Nature itself derives" (*Enneads*, v, viii, 1, *Plotinus—The Fifth Ennead*, trans. Stephen MacKenna [London, 1926], p. 74). [W]

****resplendentia formae*:** 'resplendence of form'

***Zeuxis...virgins of Crotona:** 그리이스의 화가 Zeuxis 가 Crotona 의 다섯 아가씨들을 모델로 하여 미인 Helen 의 초상을 그렸다고 함.

*Painting,** in the writings of Johnson, especially in the tulip passage in *Rasselas,* and in the *Discourses* and *Idlers** of Reynolds. The business of the poet is not to number the streaks of the tulip; it is to give us not the individual, but the species. The same thing is stated in a more complicated way by Kant in telling how the imagination constructs the "aesthetical normal Idea":

It is the image for the whole race, which floats among all the variously different intuitions of individuals, which nature takes as archetype in her productions of the same species, but which seems not to be fully reached in any individual case.*

And Hegel's account is as follows:

The work of art is not only for the *sensuous* apprehension as sensuous object, but its position is of such a kind that as sensuous it is at the same time essentially addressed to the *mind.**

In comparison with the show or semblance of immediate sensuous existence or of historical narrative, the artistic semblance has the advantage that in itself it points beyond self, and refers us away from itself to something spiritual which it is meant to bring before the mind's eye. . . . The hard rind of nature and the common world give the mind more trouble in breaking through to the idea than do the products of art.*

The excellence of Shakespeare, says Coleridge, consists in a "union and interpenetration of the universal and particular."* In one terminology or another this idea of a concrete universal is found in most metaphysical aesthetic of the eighteenth

---

*Du Fresnoy's *Art of Painting*: 프랑스의 화가. 비평가 Charles Alphonse du Fresnoy의 라틴 운문 *De arte graphica* (1668)을 John Dryden이 번역함 (1695).

**Idler*: Johnson의 잡지. Reynolds가 기고함.

*Kant's *Critique of Judgment*, J. H. Bernard, tr. (London, 1931), 88—89. [W]

**The Introduction to Hegel's Philosophy of Fine Art*, Bernard Bosanquet, tr. (London, 1886), p. 67. *cf.* Walter T. Stace, *The Meaning of Beauty* (London, 1929), p. 16. [W]

**The Introduction to Hegel's Philosophy of Fine Art*. p. 16. *cf.* pp. 72—78, 133—37. [W]

**The Friend* (1818), Ⅱ, p. 150.

and nineteenth centuries.

A modern literary critic, Mr. John Crowe Ransom, speaks of the argument of a poem (the universal) and a local texture or tissue of concrete irrelevance.* Another literary critic, Mr. Allen Tate, manipulating the logical terms "extension" and "intension," has arrived at the concept of "tension" in poetry.* "Extension," as logicians use the word, is the range of individuals denoted by a term (denotation); "intension" is the total of qualities connoted (connotation). In the ordinary or logical use of the terms, extension and intension are of inverse relationship—the wider the one, the shallower the other. A poem, says Mr. Tate, as I interpret him, is a verbal structure which in some peculiar way has both a very wide extension and a very deep intension.

Not all these theories of the concrete universal lay equal stress on the two sides of the paradox, and it seems indicative of the vitality of the theory and of the truth implicit in it that the two sides have been capable of exaggeration into antithetic schools and theories of poetry. For Du Fresnoy, Johnson and Reynolds poetry and painting give the universal; the less said about the particulars the better. This is neoclassic theory, the illustrations of which we seek in Pope's *Essay on Man* or in Johnson's *Rambler,** where the ideas are moral and general and concerned with "nature," "one clear, unchanged, and universal light."* The opposite theory had notable expression in England, a few years before Johnson wrote *Rasselas,* in Joseph Warton's *Essay on Pope:**

A minute and particular enumeration of circumstances judiciously selected, is what chiefly discriminates poetry from history, and renders the former, for that reason, a more close and faithful

---

*그의 비평, "Criticism as Pure Speculation" (1941)의 논지. 이 비평은, Sangsup Lee, *et al.* eds., *Selected Modern Critical Essays* (서울, 한국영어영문학회, 1969)에서 쉽게 볼 수 있음.

*그의 비평, "Tension in Poetry". 비평집 *Reason in Madness* (1941)에 수록됨.

****Ramblers*:** Johnson이 발간한 잡지 (1749-52). 그의 비평이 많이 실려 있다.

***one clear...light*:** Pope, *Essay on Criticism*, 71행.

****Essay on Pope*:** 비평가 Joseph Warton의 저작 (1756). 고전주의에 반대.

representation of nature than the latter.

And Blake's marginal criticism of Reynolds was: "THIS Man was Hired to Depress art." "To Generalize is to be an Idiot. To Particularize is the Alone Distinction of Merit. General Knowledges are those Knowledges that Idiots possess." "Sacrifice the Parts: What becomes of the whole?"* The line from Warton's *Essay* to Croce's *Aesthetic seems a straight and obvious one, from Thomson's* specific descriptions of flowers to the individual act of intuition-expression which is art—its opposite and enemy being the concept or generality.* The two views of art (two that can be held by different theorists about the same works of art) may be startlingly contrasted in the following passages about fictitious character—one a well-known statement by Johnson, the other by the philosopher of the *élan vital.****

[Shakespeare's] characters are not modified by the customs of particular places, unpractised by the rest of the world; by the peculiarities of studies or professions, which can operate but upon small numbers; or by the accidents of transient fashions or temporary opinions: they are the genuine progeny of common humanity, such as the world will always supply, and observation will always find. His persons act and speak by the influence of those general passions and principles by which all minds are agitated, and the whole system of life is continued in motion. In the writings of other poets a character is too often an individual; in those of Shakespeare it is commonly a species.

Hence it follows that art always aims at what is *individual.* What the artist fixes on his canvas is something he has seen at a certain spot, on a certain day, at a certain hour, with a colouring that will

---

*이 비평들은 Blake가 Reynolds의 *Discourses*의 책장 여백에다 써넣은 것들.

***Croce's *Aesthetic*:** 이탈리아의 철학자 Benedetto Croce (1866-1952)의 명저. 예술은 독특한 "intuition-expression"이라는 미학이론을 전개.

***Thomson:** 장편서경시 *The Seasons*(1726-30)을 쓴 시인 James Thomson (1700-48)을 가리킴.

*...the main drift of Croce's aesthetic, in being against conceptualization, is radically against the universal. [W]

***the philosopher of *élan vital*:** 프랑스의 철학자 Henri Bergson(1859-1941). *élan vital*(생명력)의 철학을 주창함.

never be seen again. What the poet sings of is a certain mood which was his, and his alone, and which will never return. . . . Nothing could be more unique than the character of Hamlet. Though he may resemble other men in some respects, it is clearly not on that account that he interests us most.*

Other critics, notably the most ancient and the most modern (Aristotle, Morris, Whitehead, Ransom), have tried to hold the extremes together. Neither of the extremes gives a good account of art and each leads out of art. The theory of particularity leads to individuality and originality (Edward Young was another eighteenth century Crocean), then to the idiosyncratic and the unintelligible and to the psychology of the author, which is not in the work of art and is not a standard for judgment. The theory of universality as it appears in Johnson and Reynolds leads to platitude and to a standard of material objectivity, the average tulip, the average human form, some sort of average.

3

"Just representations of general nature," said Johnson, and it ought to be noted, though it perhaps rarely is, that two kinds of generality are involved, as indeed they are in the whole neo-classic theory of generality. There is the generality of logic or classification, of the more general as opposed to the more specific, "essential" generality, one might say. And there is the generality of literal truth to nature, "existential" generality. The assumption in neo-classic theory seems to be that these two must coincide. As a matter of fact they may and often do, but need not. Thus: "purple cow" is a more general (less specific) term and concept than "tan cow with a broken horn," yet the latter is more general or true to nature. We have, in short, realism or fantasy, and in either there may be various degrees of the specific or the general. We have *A Journal of the Plague Year* and *The Rambler*, *Gulliver's Travels* and *Rasselas*. The fact that there are a greater

*Henri Bergson, *Laughter, An Essay on the Meaning of the Comic* (New York, 1928), pp. 161—62.

number of "vicissitudes" and "miscarriages" (favorite *Rambler* events) in human experience than plagues at London, that there are more tan cows than tan cows with broken horns, makes it true in a sense that a greater degree of essential generality involves a greater degree of existential. But in this sense the most generally reliable concept is simply that of "being."

The question is how a work of literature can be either more individual (unique) or more universal than other kinds of writing, or how it can combine the individual and the universal more than other kinds. Every description in words, so far as it is a direct description (The barn is red and square) is a generalization. That is the nature of words. There are no individuals conveyed in words but only more or less specific generalizations, so that Johnson is right, though we have to ask him what degree of verbal generality makes art, and whether "tulip" is a better or more important generality than "tulip" with ten streaks," or whether "beauty" is not in fact a much more impressive generality than "tulip." On the other hand, one cannot deny that in some sense there are more tulips in poetry than pure abstracted beauty. So that Bergson is right too; only we shall have to ask him what degree of specificity in verbal description makes art. And he can never claim complete specificity or individuality, even for Hamlet.

If he could, if a work of literary art could be looked on as an artifact or concrete physical work, the paradox for the student of universals would return from the opposite direction even more forcibly—as it does in fact for theorists of graphic art. If Reynolds' picture "The Age of Innocence" presents a species or universal, what species does it present? Not an Aristotelian essence — "man," or "humanity," nor even a more specific kind of being such as "womanhood." For then the picture would present the same universal as Reynolds' portrait of Mrs. Siddons* as "The Tragic Muse," and all dif-

*Mrs. Sarah Siddons: 18세기 최대의 여배우. 비극에 능했음. Reynolds의 그림 "The Tragic Muse"의 모델. "The Age of Innocence"도 Reynolds의 이름난 그림.

ferences between "The Age of Innocence" and "The Tragic Muse" would be aesthetically irrelevant. Does the picture then present girlhood, or barefoot girlhood, or barefoot girlhood in a white dress against a gloomy background? All three are equally valid universals (despite the fact that makeshift phrases are required to express two of them), and all three are presented by the picture. Or is it the title which tells us what universal is presented, "The Age of Innocence," and without the title should we not know the universal? The question will be: What in the individual work of art demands that we attribute to it one universal rather than another?

We may answer that for poetry it is the generalizing power of words already mentioned, and go on to decide that what distinguishes poetry from scientific or logical discourse is a degree of irrelevant concreteness in descriptive details. This is in effect what Mr. Ransom says in his doctrine of argument and local irrelevance, but the doctrine bears a suspicious resemblance to an ancient and now rather theoroughly discredited theory, that of ornamental metaphor. The argument, says Mr. Ransom, is the prose or scientific meaning, what the poem has in common with other kinds of writing. The irrelevance is a texture of concreteness which does not contribute anything to the argument but is somehow enjoyable or valuable for its own sake, the vehicle of a metaphor which one boards heedless of where it runs, whether crosstown or downtown—just for the ride. So Mr. Ransom nurses and refines the argument, and on one page he makes the remark that the poet searches for "suitability" in his particular phrases, and by suitability Mr. Ransom means "the propriety which consists in their denoting the particularity which really belongs to the logical object."* But the dif-

---

**The New Criticism* (Norfolk, 1941), p. 315. Mr. Maritain, coming from a different direction, arrives at somewhat the same poser. "If it pleases a futurist to paint a lady with only one eye, or a quarter of an eye, nobody denies him such a right: all one is entitled to require—and here is the whole problem—is that the quarter eye is all the lady needs *in the given case*" (*Art and Scholasticism* [New York, 1937], p. 28). Here indeed is the whole problem. Long ago Aristotle said, "Not to know that a hind

ference between "propriety" and relevance in such a context is not easy to see. And relevance is logic. The fact is that all concrete illustration has about it something of the irrelevant. An apple falling from a tree illustrates gravity, but apple and tree are irrelevant to the pure theory of gravity. It may be that what happens in a poem is that the apple and the tree are somehow made more than usually relevant.

Such a theory, not that of Johnson and Reynolds, not that of Warton and Bergson, not quite that of Mr. Ransom, is what I would suggest—yet less as a novelty than as something already widely implicit in recent poetical analyses and exegeses, in those of Mr. Empson, for instance, Mr. Tate, Mr. Blackmur, Mr. Brooks, and Mr. R. P. Warren*. If a work of literature is not in a simple sense either more individual or more universal than other kinds of writing, it may yet be such an individual or such a complex of meaning that it has a special relation to the world of universals. Some acute remarks on this subject were made by Ruskin in a chapter of *Modern Painters* neglected today perhaps because of its distasteful ingredient of "noble emotion." Poetry, says Ruskin in criticizing Reynolds' *Idlers,* is not distinguished from history by the omission of details, nor for that matter by the mere addition of details. "It is not the multiplication of details which constitutes history—there must be something either in the nature of the details themselves, or the method of using them, which invests them with poetical power." Their nature, one may add, as assumed through their relation to one another, a relation which may also be called the method of using them. The poetic character of details consists not in what they say directly and explicitly (as if roses and moonlight were poetic) but in what by their arrangement they *show* implicitly.

has no horns is a less serious matter than to paint it inartistically" (*Poetics*, xxv, 5). [W]

***Mr. Empson...Warren:** New Critics 들임.

4

"One," observes Ben Jonson, thinking of literature, "is considerable two waies: either, as it is only separate, and by it self: or as being compos'd of many parts it beginnes to be one as those parts grow or are wrought together." A literary work of art is a complex of detail (an artifact, if we may be allowed that metaphor for what is only a verbal object), a composition so complicated of human values that its interpretation is dictated by the understanding of it, and so complicated as to seem in the highest degree individual—a concrete universal. We are accustomed to being told, for example, that what makes a character in fiction or drama vital is a certain fullness or rotundity: that the character has many sides. Thus E. M. Forster:

> We may divide characters into flat and round. Flat characters were called "humours" in the seventeenth century, and are sometimes called types, and sometimes caricatures. In their purest form, they are constructed round a single idea or quality: when there is more than one factor in them, we get the beginning of the curve towards the round. The really flat character can be expressed in one sentence such as "I never will desert Mr. Micawber."*

It remains to be said, however, that the many traits of the round character (if indeed it is one character and not a hodge-podge) are harmonized or unified, and that if this is so, then all the traits are chosen by a principle, just as are the traits of the flat character. Yet it cannot be that the difference between the round and flat character is simply numerical; the difference cannot be merely that the presiding principle is illustrated by more examples in the round character. Something further must be supposed—a special interrelation in the traits of the round character. Bobadil is an example of the *miles*

**Aspects of the Novel* (London, 1927), Ch.4. Flat, round, character 란 용어는 Forster 의 발명.

*gloriosus,** a flat humour. He swears by "The foot of Pharaoh," takes tobacco, borrows money from his landlady, is found lying on a bench fully dressed with a hangover, brags about his feats at the siege of Strigonium, beats Cob a poor water carrier, and so on. It is possible that he has numerically as many traits as Falstaff, one of the most vital of all characters. But one of the differences between Falstaff and Bobadil is that the things Falstaff says are funny; the things Bobadil says are not. Compared to Falstaff, Bobadil is unconscious, an opaque butt. There is the vitality of consciousness in Falstaff. And further there is the crowning complexity of self-consciousness. The fact that Morgann* could devote a book to arguing that Falstaff is not a coward, that lately Professor Wilson* has argued that at Gadshill Falstaff may exhibit "'all the common symptoms of the malady' of cowardice" and at the same time persuade the audience that he has "'never once lost his self-possession,'" the fact that one can conceive that Falstaff in the Gadshill running-away scene really knows that his assailants are the Prince and Poins—all this shows that in Falstaff there is a kind of interrelation among his attributes, his cowardice, his wit, his debauchery, his presumption, that makes them in a special way an organic harmony. He is a rounded character not only in the sense that he is gross (a fact which may have tempted critics to speak of a rounded character) or in the sense that he is a bigger bundle of attributes, stuffed more full, than Bobadil or Ralph Roister Doister;* but in the sense that his attributes make a circuit and connection. A kind of awareness of self (a very high and human characteristic), with a pleasure in the fact, is perhaps the central principle which instead of simplifying the

---

Bobadil**은 Ben Jonson의 *Every Man in His Humour* (1598)에 나오는 허풍선이 군인 (miles gloriosus***: 'boastful soldier')으로, 이른바 a flat character.

Maurice Morgann:** 18세기 영국의 정치인. ***Essay on the Dramatic Character of Falstaff (1777)을 지음.

John Dover Wilson:** Shakespeare 학자로, ***The Fortunes of Falstaff (1943)을 저술.

***Ralph Roister Doister:** 16세기 영국의 극작가 Nicholas Udall이 지은 동명의 희극(1553?)의 주인공.

attributes gives each one a special function in the whole, a double or reflex value. Falstaff or such a character of self-conscious "infinite variety"* as Cleopatra are concrete universals because they have no class names, only their own proper ones, yet are structures of such precise variety and centrality that each demands a special interpretation—which none can name—in the realm of human values.

Character is one type of concrete universal; there are other types, as many perhaps as the central terms of criticism; but most can be learned I believe by examination of metaphor—the structure most characteristic of concentrated poetry. The language of poets, said Shelley, "is vitally metaphorical: that is, it marks the before unapprehended relations of things and perpetuates their apprehension*." Wordsworth spoke of the abstracting and modifying powers of the imagination. And long ago Aristotle said that the greatest thing was the use of metaphor, because it meant an eye for resemblances.* Even the simplest form of metaphor or simile ("My love is like a red, red rose") presents us with a special and creative, in fact a concrete, kind of abstraction different from that of science. For behind a metaphor lies a resemblance between two classes, and hence a more general third class (perhaps bridging a gap wide in the pattern of actual things), but nevertheless and most likely remains unnamed and is apprehended only through the metaphor. It is a new conception for which there is no other expression. Keats discovering Homer is like a traveler in the realms of gold, like an astronomer who discovers a planet, like Cortez gazing at the Pacific. The title of the sonnet, "On First Looking into Chapman's Homer," seems to furnish not so much the subject of the poem as a fourth member of a central metaphor, the real subject of the poem being an abstraction, a certain kind of thrill in discovering, for which there is no name and no other description, only the four members of the metaphor pointing, as to

---

*I do not mean that self-consciousness is the only principle of complexity in character, yet a degree of it I suspect will be found in all the richest characters. [W] .*앞의 p. 366 참조.

**Poetics*, 22 장, 9 절.

the center of their pattern. The point of the poem seems to lie somewhere outside both vehicle and tenor.*

To take a more complicated instance, Wordsworth's "Solitary Reaper" has the same basic metaphorical structure, the girl alone reaping and singing, and the two bird images, the nightingale in Arabian sands and the cuckoo among the Hebrides, the three figures serving the parallel or metaphorical function of bringing out the abstraction of loneliness, remoteness, mysterious charm in the singing. But there is also a kind of third-dimensional significance, in the fact that one bird is far out in the northern sea, the other far off in southern sands, a fact which is not part of the comparison between the birds and the girl. By an implication cutting across the plane of logic of the metaphor, the girl and the two birds suggest extension in space, universality and world communion—an effect supported by other details of the poem such as the overflowing of the vale profound, the mystery of the Erse song,* the bearing of the song away in the witness' heart, the past and future themes which the girl may be singing. Thus a central abstraction is created, of communion, telepathy in solitude, the prophetic soul of the wide world dreaming on things to come—an abstraction which is the effect not wholly of the metaphor elaborated logically (in a metaphysical way) but of a working on two axes, by association rather than by logic, by a three-dimensional complexity of structure.

To take yet a third instance, metaphoric structure may appear where we are less likely to realize it explicitly—in poetic narratives, for example, elliptically concealed in the more obvious narrative outlines. "I can bring you," writes Mr. Max Eastman,* "examples of diction that is metrical but not metaphoric—a great part of the popular ballads, for ex-

---

***vehicle and tenor:** metaphor를 이루는 두 요소. vehicle은 실제로 사용된 말(rose), tenor는 그 말의 비유적인 뜻(sweet heart).

***Erse song:** Wordsworth는 스콧트랜드의 Highland를 여행하던 중에, Gaelic의 일종인 Erse 방언으로 노래하는 처녀를 보았던 것이다.

***Max Eastman:** (1883-). 미국의 평론가.

ample—and you can hardly deny that they too are poetic." But the best story poems may be analyzed, I believe, as metaphors without expressed tenors, as symbols which speak for themselves. "La Belle Dame Sans Merci," for example (if a literary ballad may be taken), is about a knight, by profession a man of action, but sensitive, like the lily and the rose, and about a faery lady with wild, wild eyes. At a more abstract level, it is about the loss of self in the mysterious lure of beauty—whether woman, poetry, or poppy. It sings the irretrievable departure from practical normality (the squirrel's granary is full), the wan isolation after ecstasy. Each reader will experience the poem at his own level of experience or at several. A good story poem is like a stone thrown into a pond, into our minds, where ever widening concentric circles of meaning go out—and this because of the structure of the story.

"A poem should not mean but be."* It is an epigram worth quoting in every essay on poetry. And the poet "nothing affirmeth, and therefore never lieth." "Sit quidvis," said Horace, "simplex dumtaxat et unum."* It seems almost the reverse of the truth. "Complex dumtaxat et unum"* would be better. Every good poem is a complex poem and may be demonstrated so by rhetorical analysis. And further it is only in virtue of its complexity that it has artistic unity. Without complexity it could have the unity of a cobblestone but not that of a typewriter. A newspaper poem by Edgar Guest* does not have such heterogeneous unity, and hence does not have unity in the artistic sense. It is this truth which is expressed by Aristotle when he says that ontological beauty is based on unity in variety, and by Coleridge when he says that "The Beautiful, contemplated in its essentials, that is, in *kind* and not in *degree,* is that in which the *many,* still seen as many becomes one," and that a work of art is "rich in propor-

---

*미국의 시인 Archibald McLeish의 시 "Ars Poetica"의 일절.

**Sit quidvis*...: 'Let each thing be only simple and a unit', *Ars poetica.*

**Complex*...: 'Only complex and a unit.'

***Edgar Albert Guest:** (1881-1959). "famous bad poet". 통속적 도덕을 강조하는 운문작가.

tion to the variety of parts which it holds in unity."*

5

The discussion so far has been a rhetorical one, that is, one about the relations of parts and whole, and most objective analysis of poetry is in fact rhetorical. It is easier to show how poetry works than to show why anyone should want it to work in a given way; it is easier to show its structure than its value. Rhetorical theory of poetry has always tended to separate from evaluation, technique from worth. But the very structure of poems as concrete and universal, it seems to me, is the principle by which the two may be kept together. If it be granted that the "subject matter" of poetry is in a broad sense the moral realm, human actions as good or bad, with all their associated feelings, all the cognition and imagination that goes with happiness and suffering (if poetry submits "the shews of things to the desires of the Mind")*, then the rhetorical structure of the concrete universal, the complexity and unity of the poem, is also its maturity and sophistication or richness or depth, hence its value. Complexity of form is sophistication of content. The unity and maturity of good poems are two sides of the same thing. The kind of unity which we look for and find in poetry (that of the typewriter rather than that of the cobblestone) is attained only through a degree of complexity in design which itself involves maturity and richness. For a visual diagram of the metaphysics of poetry one might write vertically the word complexity, a column, and give it a head with Janus faces, one looking in the rhetorical direction, unity, and the other in the axiological, maturity.

A final point to be made is that a criticism of structure and of value is an objective criticism. It rests on facts of human psychology (as that a man may love a woman so well as to give up empires), facts, which though psychological, yet are so

*"On the Principles of Genial Criticism concerning the Fine Art" (1814). Essay 3rd. *앞의 p. 80 참조.

well acknowledged as to lie in the realm of what may be called public psychology—a realm which one should distinguish from the private realm of the author's psychology and from the equally private realm of the individual reader's psychology (the vivid pictures which poetry or stories are supposed to create in the imagination, or the venerable action of catharsis—all that poetry is said to *do* rather than to *be*). Such a criticism, again, is objective and absolute, as distinguished from the relative criticism of idiom and period. I mean that this criticism will notice that Pope is different from Shakespeare, but will notice even more attentively that Shakespeare is different from Taylor the Water Poet and Pope different from Sir Richard Blackmore.* Such a criticism will be interested to analyze the latter two differences and see what these differences have in common and what Shakespeare and Pope have in common, and it will not despair of describing that similarity (that formula or character of great poetry) even though the terms be abstract and difficult—for the proof will always be found in specific analysis of a good poem. Or, if we are told that there is no universal agreement about what is good—that Pope has not been steadily held in esteem, that Shakespeare has been considered a barbarian, the objective analyst of structures can at least say (and it seems much to say) that he is describing a class of poems, those which through a peculiar complexity possess unity and maturity and in a special way can be called both individual and universal. Among all recorded "poems," this class is a relative rarity, and further the members of this class will be found in an impressive way to coincide with the members of the class "poems which have by some body of critics, some age of educated readers, been called great."

The function of the objective critic is by approximate descriptions of poems, or multiple restatements of their meaning, to aid other readers to come to an intuitive and full realization of poems themselves and hence to know good poems and distinguish them from bad ones. It is of course impossible to tell all about a poem in other words. Croce tells us

---

*18세기의 3류시인들.

as we should expect him to, of the "impossibility of ever rendering in logical terms the full effect of any poetry or of other artistic work." "Criticism, nevertheless," he tells us, "...performs its own office, which is to discern and to point out exactly where lies the poetical motive and to formulate the divisions which aid in distinguishing what is proper to every work."* The situation is something like this: In each poem there is something (an individual intuition—or a concept) which can never be expressed in other terms. It is like the square root of two or like pi, which cannot be expressed by rational numbers, but only as their *limit*. Criticism of poetry is like 1.414 . . . . or 3.141. . . . , not all it would be, yet all that can be had and very useful.

---

*Croce, *Ariosto, Shakespeare and Corneille* (London, 1920), pp. 146—147. [W]

Northrop Frye

(1912—　　)

캐나다의 퀘벡 주에서 태어나 터론토 대학에서 신학을 전공, 목사가 되었다가 1939년에 영문학 교수가 되었다. 놀라우리만큼 해박한 인문학적 지식과 막힘없는 해석능력을 구사하여 쓴 *The Fearful Symmetry*(1947, 블레이크 연구서)를 발표하면서 명성을 날리기 시작했다.

이어서 인류의 신화와 개인의 상상, 그 둘을 연결시키는 핵인 "원형"(archetype)의 본질을 파헤치는 이론적 논문이 계속 발표되었다. 그중 크게 주목을 끈 것은 "The Archetypes of Literature"(1951)으로서, 4계절에 관한 신화와 문학의 장르와의 관계를 설명한 논문이다. 이 생각은 치밀하고도 상상적인 체계를 이루어 드디어 *Anatomy of Criticism*(1957)에서 그 결실을 본다.

이 책의 서문에서 프라이는 비평의 목적은 작품의 평가에 있지 않고 문학에 관한 지식에 있다고 주장한다. 평가는 개인적·시대적 취향에 좌우되나 참지식은 변하지 않는 것이다. 비평도 인문과학이 되어야 한다고 그는 주장한다. 문학에 관한 지식에 도달하기 위하여서는 외형의 변화에도 불구하고 변하지 않는 근본 구조를 추적해내야 한다. 프라이 자신은 그 구조가 신화의 구조라고 믿는다. 그는 넓은 의미의 "구조주의자"이다.

"Myth, Fiction, and Displacement"(1961)는 신화와 문학의 관계를 쉽게 풀이한 글로서 비평집 *Fables of Identity*(1963)에 수록되어 있다. 그의 문학론에 대한 썩좋은 안내문이라고 생각된다.

The Stubborn Structure(1970), *Spiritus Mundi*(1976) 등은 그후의 비평집들이고, *The Educated Imagination*(1964), *The Well-Tempered Critic*(1966), *The Secular Scripture*(1975) 등은 각각 한 주제에 대한 일련의 강연록들이다.

프라이는 아마도 뉴 크리틱들 이후 가장 주목받는 비평가일 것이다. 그는 사람을 근본에 있어 상상적인 존재로 본다. 사람은 자연히 세계에서의 모든 경험을 그의 상상의 틀에다 비추어 해석한다. 그러므로 경험의 의미는 상상적일 수밖에 없다. 개인의 상상적 틀이란 결국 하나의 거대한 신화체계에 속함으로써만 그 뜻을 갖게 된다. 이러한 인간론은 칸트주의(코울리지도 믿은 바 있는) 계열에 속한 것이지만, 프라이의 독창성은 자기가 아는 세계의 모든 문학 작품을 그 거대한 체계의 각 지점에다 거침없이 배열할 수 있다는 점이다. 즉 그는 모든 문학 현상을 설명할 수 있는 방대한 상상적 틀을 가지고 있다. 그는 시를 쓰지 아니하였으되 스펜서나 밀튼같은 백과사전적 서사시인을 상상적으로 닮은 비평가이다.

Myth, Fiction, and Displacement

'MYTH' is a conception which runs through many areas of contemporary thought: anthropology, psychology, comparative religion, sociology, and several others. What follows* is an attempt to explain what the term means in literary criticism today. Such an explanation must begin with the question: Why did the term ever get into literary criticism? There can be only one legitimate answer to such a question: because myth is and has always been an integral element of literature, the interest of poets in myth and mythology having been remarkable and constant since Homer's time.

There are two broad divisions of literary works, which may be called the fictional and the thematic. The former comprises works of literature with internal characters, and includes novels, plays, narrative poetry, folk tales, and everything that tells a story. In thematic literature the author and the reader are the only characters involved: this division

---

***What follows:** 「다음에서 다루는 것은」.

includes most lyrics, essays, didactic poetry and oratory. Each division has its own type of myth, but we shall be concerned here only with the fictional part of literature, and with myth in its more common and easily recognized form as a certain kind of narrative.

When a critic deals with a work of literature, the most natural thing for him to do is to freeze it, to ignore its movement in time and look at it as a completed pattern of words, with all its parts existing simultaneously. This approach is common to nearly all types of critical techniques: here new and old-fashioned critics are at one. But, in the direct experience of literature, which is something distinct from criticism, we are aware of what we may call the persuasion of continuity, the power that keeps us turning the pages of a novel and that holds us in our seats at the theatre. The continuity may be logical, or pseudo-logical, or psychological, or rhetorical: it may reside in the surge and thunder of eipc verse or in some donkey's carrot* like the identity of the murderer in a detective story or the first sexual act of the heroine in a romance. Or we may feel afterwards that the sense of continuity was pure illusion, as though we had been laid under a spell.

The continuity of a work of literature exists on different rhythmical levels. In the foreground, every word, every image, even every sound made audibly or inaudibly by the words, is making its tiny contribution to the total movement. But it would take a portentous concentration to attend to such details in direct experience: they belong to the kind of critical study that is dealing with a simultaneous unity. What we are conscious of in direct experience is rather a series of larger groupings, events and scenes that make up what we call the story. In ordinary English the word "plot" means this latter sequence of gross events. For a term that would include the total movement of sounds and images, the word "narrative" seems more natural than "plot," though the choice is a

---

***donkey's carrot:** 당나귀 입 앞에 홍당무를 갖다 대면 그것을 먹으려고 계속 따라간다. 다음에 무슨 일이 벌어지는지 계속 흥미를 느끼게 만드는 이야기 수법(탐정소설이나 통속연애소설 등에서 자주 이용된다).

matter of usage and not of inherent correctness. Both words translate Aristotle's *mythos,* but Aristotle meant mainly by *mythos* what we are calling plot: narrative, in the above sense, is closer to his *lexis.** The plot, then, is like the trees and houses that we focus our eyes on through a train window: the narrative is more like the weeds and stones that rush by in the foreground.

We now run into a curious difficulty. Plot, Aristotle says, is the life and soul of tragedy* (and by implication of fiction generally): the essence of fiction, then, is plot or imitation of action, and characters exist primarily as functions of the plot. In our direct experience of fiction we feel how central is the importance of the steady progression of events that holds and guides our attention. Yet afterwards, when we try to remember or think about what we have seen, this sense of continuity if one of the most difficult things to recapture. What stands out in our minds is a vivid characterization, a great speech or striking image, a detached scence, bits and pieces of unusually convincing realization. A summary of a plot, say of a Scott novel, has much the same numbing effect on a hearer as a summary of last night's dream. That is not how we remember the book; or at least not why we remember it. And even with a work of fiction that we know thoroughly, such as *Hamlet,* while we keep in mind a sequence of senes, and know that the ghost comes at the beginning and the duel with Laertes at the end, still there is something oddly discontinuous about our possession of it. With the histories this disappearance of continuity is even more striking. *The Oxford Companion to English Literature** is an invaluable reference work largely because it is so good at summarizing all the fictional plots that one has forgotten, but here is its summary of *King John:**

The play, with some departures from historical ac-

***lexis:** (그리이스 어) word. Aristotle이 *Poetics*에서 쓴 *mythos*는 plot 또는 narrative 라는 뜻.

**Poetics,* 6장 14절.

*Sir Paul Harvey가 편찬한 영문학 사전.

***King John:** Shakespeare의 초기 역사극.

> curacy, deals with various events in King John's reign, and principally with the tragedy of young Arthur. It ends with the death of John at Swinstead Abbey. It is significant that no mention of Magna Carta appears in it. The tragic quality of the play, the poignant grief of Constance, Arthur's mother, and the political complications depicted, are relieved by the wit, humour, and gallantry of the Bastard of Faulconbridge.

This is, more or less, how we remember the play. We remember Faulconbridge and his great speech at the end; we remember the death scene of Prince Arthur; we remember Constance; we remember nothing about Magna Carta; we remember in the background the vacillating, obstinate, defiant king. But what *happened* in the play? What were the incidents that made it an imitation of an action? Does it matter? If it doesn't matter, what becomes of the principle that the characters exist for the sake of the action, the truth of which we felt so vividly while watching the play? If it does matter, are we going to invent some silly pedantic theory of unity that would rule out *King John* as legitimate drama?

Whatever the final answer, we may tentatively accept the principle that, in the direct experience of fiction, continuity is the center of our attention; our later memory, or what I call the possession of it, tends to become discontinuous. Our attention shifts from the sequence of incidents to another focus: a sense of what the work of fiction was all *about,* or what criticism usually calls its theme. And we notice that as we go on to study and reread the work of fiction, we tend, not to reconstruct the plot, but to become more conscious of the theme, and to see all incidents as manifestations of it. Thus the incidents themeselves tend to remain, in our critical study of the work, discontinuous, detached from one another and regrouped in a new way. Even if we know it by heart this is still true, and if we are writing or lecturing on it, we usually start with something other than its linear action.

Now in the conception "theme," as in the conception "narrative," there are a number of distinguishable elements. One of them is "subject," which criticism can usually express by some kind of summarized statement. If we are asked what Arthur Miller's *The Crucible** is about, we say that it is about — that is, its subject is — the Salem witch trials. Similarly, the subject of *Hamlet* is Hamlet's attempt at revenge on an uncle who has murdered his father and married his mother. But the Olivier movie of *Hamlet** began with the statement (quoted from an unreliable memory): "This is the strory of a man who could not make up his mind." Here is a quite different conception of theme: it expresses the theme in terms of what we may call its allegorical value. To the extent that it is an adequate statement of the theme of *Hamlet,* it makes the play into an allegory and the chief character into a personification of Indecision. In his illuminating study of *The Ancient Mariner,* Robert Penn Warren* says that the poem is written out of, and about, the general belief that the truth is implicit "in the poetic act as such, that the moral concern and the aesthetic concern are aspects of the same activity, the creative activity, and that this activity is expressive of the whole mind" (italicized in the original). Here again is allegorization, of a kind that takes the theme to be what Aristotle appears to have meant primarily by *dianoia,* the "thought" or sententious reflexion that the poem suggests to a meditative reader.

It seems to me that a third conception of "theme" is possible, less abstract than the subject and more direct than an allegorical translation. It is also, however, a conception for which the primitive vocabulary of contemporary criticism is ill adapted. Theme in this third sense is the *mythos* or plot examined as a simultaneous unity, when the entire shape of it is clear in our minds.* In *Anatomy of Criticism* I use *dianoia* in

---

*Arthur Miller의 1953년 작. 1690년 Massachusetts 주 Salem에서 일어난 마녀사냥(witch-hunting)사건을 소재로 다룬 작품.

*명배우 Sir Lawrence Oliver가 주연한 *Hamlet* 영화.

***Robert Penn Warren:** (1905-). 미국의 시인, 비평가, 소설가. *The Ancient Mariner* 연구는 *Selected Essays* (1958)에 수록되어 있다.

*전체적 주제(subject)도 아니고, 도덕적 의미도 아니며, 계속적으로 파악되는 이야기의 흐름도 아닌 이야기 전체의 순간적인(simultaneous' 또는 공시적) 모습. 이를 나타내는 비평용어가 없다(현대의 이론에서는 plot이라고 부르기도 한다).

this sense: an extension of Aristotle's meaning, no doubt, but in my opinion a justifiable one. The theme, so considered, differs appreciably from the moving plot: it is the same in substance, but we are now concerned with the details in relation to a unity, not in relation to suspense and linear progression. The unifying factors assume a new and increased importance, and the smaller details of imagery, which may escape conscious notice in direct experience, take on their proper significance. It is because of this difference that we find our memory of the progression of events dissolving as the events regroup themselves around another center of attention. Each event or incident, we now see, is a manifestation of some underlying unity, a unity that it both conceals and reveals, as clothes do the body in *Sartor Resartus.***

Further, the plot or progress of events as a whole is also a manifestation of the theme, for the same story (i.e., theme in our sense) could be told in many different ways. It is, of course, impossible to say how extensive the changes of detail would have to be before we had a different theme, but they can be surprisingly extensive. Chaucer's *Pardoner's Tale is a folk tale that started in India and must have reached Chaucer from some West-European source. It also stayed in India, where Kipling picked it up and put it into the *Second Jungle Book.** Everything is different — setting, details, method of treatment — yet I think any reader, on whatever level of sophistication, would say that it was recognizably the same "story" — story as theme, that is, for the linear progression is what is different. More often we have only smaller units in common, of a kind that students of folklore call motifs. Thus in Hawthorne's *The Marble Faun* we have the motifs of the two heroines, one dark and one light, that we have in *Ivanhoe***

****Sartor Resartus*:** Thomas Carlyle의 "옷"철학을 담은 명저 (1838).

***Pardoner's Tale:** *Canterbury Tales*의 하나인 이 이야기는 황금을 발견한 세 사람의 친구가 각각 그것을 독차지하려고 서로 죽이는 내용을 담고 있다(한국 민담에도 그런 내용이 있다).

*Scott의 *Ivanhoe*에 희고 키가 큰 Rowena 공주와 가무잡잡하고 키가 작은 Rebecca가 등장하고, *Marble Faun*에서는 Hilda와 Miriam이란 두 여자가 등장. 이들은 "희고 검은 두 여자"의 motif 또는 archetype이다.

and elsewhere;* in *Lycidas* we have the motif of the "sanguine flower inscrib'd with woe," the red or purple flower that turns up everywhere in pastoral elegy, and so on. These smaller units I have elsewhere called archetypes, a word which has been connected since Plato's time with the sense of a pattern or model used in creation.

In most works of fiction we are at once aware that the *mythos* or sequence of events which holds our attention is being shaped into a unity. We are continually, if often unconsciously, attempting to construct a larger pattern of simultaneous significance out of what we have so far read or seen. We feel confident that the beginning implies an end, and that the story is not like the soul in natural theology,* starting off at an arbitrary moment in time and going on forever. Hence we often keep on reading even a tiresome novel "to see how it turns out." That is, we expect a certain point near the end at which linear suspense is resolved and the unifying shape of the whole design becomes conceptually visible. This point was called *anagnorisis* by Aristotle, a term for which "recognition" is a better rendering than "discovery." A tragic or comic plot is not a straight line: it is a parabola* following the shapes of the mouths on the conventional masks. Comedy has a U-shaped plot, with the action sinking into deep and often potentially tragic complications, and then suddenly turning upward into a happy ending. Tragedy has an inverted U, with the action rising in crisis to a peripety* and then plunging downward to catastrophe through a series of recognitions, usually of the inevitable consequences of previous acts. But in both cases what is recognized is seldom anything new; it is something which has been there all along, and which, by its reappearance or manifestation, brings the end into line with the beginning.

Recognition, and the unity of theme which it manifests, is

***natural theology:** 원시종교, 범신론 따위.

***parabola:** parable.「우화, 이야기」.

***shapes of the mouths...masks:** 옛 희극의 가면은 입 모양이 U형, 비극은 ∩형을 하고 있었다. 이것은 곧 이야기의 줄거리를 닮았던 것임.

***peripety:**「사태의 뒤바뀜」.

often symbolized by some kind of emblematic object. A simple example is in the sixteenth-century play, *Gammer Gurton's Needle,** the action of which is largely a great to-do over the loss of the needle, and which ends when a clown named Hodge gets it stuck in his posterior, bringing about what *Finnegans Wake* would call a culious epiphany.* Fans, rings, chains and other standard props of comedy are emblematic talismans of the same kind. Nearly always, however, such an emblem has to do with the identification of a chief character. Birthmarks and their symbolic relatives have run through fiction from Odysseus' scar to the scarlet letter,* and from the brand of Cain to the rose tattoo.* In Greek romance and its descendants we have infants of noble birth exposed on a hillside with birth-tokens beside them; they are found by a shepherd or farmer and brought up in a lower station of life, and the birth-tokens are produced when the sotry has gone on long enough. In more complex fiction the emblem may be an oblique comment on a character, as with Henry James's golden bowl;* or, if it is only a motif, it may serve as what T. S. Eliot calls an objective correlative.*

In any case, the point of recognition seems to be also a point of identification, where a hidden truth about something or somebody emerges into view. Besides the emblem, the hero may discover who his parents or children are, or he may go through some kind of ordeal (*basanos*) that manifests his true character, or the villain may be unmasked as a hypocrite, or, as in a detective story, identified as a murderer. In the

---

*작자 미상.

***culious epiphany:** "small" epiphany. James Joyce에 있어 epiphany는 작품의 말미에 가서 순간적으로 제시되는 상징적 의미를 뜻함.

*scarlet letter의 archetype가 가장 잘 나타난 작품은 Hawthorne의 동명 소설.

*rose tattoo의 archetype가 가장 잘 나타난 작품은 Tennessee Williams의 동명 희곡.

*Henry James의 소설에 동명의 소설 *The Golden Bowl* (1904)이 있다.

***objective correlative:** 이 말은 T. S. Eliot가 그의 평론 "Hamlet" (1919)에서 썼다. "The only way of expressing emotion in the form of art is by finding an 'objective correlative'; in other words, a set of objects, a chain of events which shall be the formula of that particular emotion."

Chinese play *The Chalk Circle* we have almost every possible form of recognition in the crucial scene. A concubine bears her master a son and is then accused of having murdered him by the wife, who has murdered him herself, and who also claims the son as her own. The concubine is tried before a foolish judge and condemned to death, then tried again before a wise one, who performs an experiment in a chalk circle resembling that of the judgment of Solomon in the Bible, and which proves that the concubine is the mother. Here we have: (a) the specific emblematic device which gives the play its name; (b) an ordeal or test which reveals character; (c) the reunion of the mother with her rightful child; and (d) the recognition of the true moral natures of concubine and wife. There are several other elements of structural importance, but these will do to go on with.*

So far, however, we have been speaking of strictly controlled forms, like comedy, where the end of the linear action also manifests the unity of the theme. What shall we find if we turn to other works where the author has just let his imagination go? I put the question in the form of this very common phrase because of the way that it illustrates a curious critical muddle. Usually, when we think of "imagination" psychologically, we think of it in its Renaissance sense as a faculty that works mainly by association and outside the province of judgment. But the associative faculty is not the creative one, though the two are frequently confused by neurotics. When we think of imagination as the power that produces art, we often think of it as the designing or structural principle in creation, Coleridge's "esemplastic" power. But imagination in this sense, left to itself, can only design. Random fantasy is exceedingly rare in the arts, and most of what we do have is a clever simulation of it. From primitive cultures to the *tachiste* and action paintings* of today, it has been a regular rule that the uninhibited imagination, in the

***these will do to go on with:** 「논의를 진행시키기 위해서는 이것으로 충분하다」.

****tachiste* and action painting:** 신 인상파의 점묘화와 행동화(둘 다 자유를 강조).

structural sense, produces highly conventionalized art.

This rule implies, of course, that the main source of inhibitions is the need to produce a credible or plausible story, to come to terms with things as they are and not as the storyteller would like them to be for his convenience. Removing the necessity for telling a credible story enables the teller to concentrate on its structure, and when this happens, characters turn into imaginative projections, heroes becoming purely heroic and villains purely villainous. That is, they become assimilated to their functions in the plot. We see this conventionalizing of structure very clearly in the folk tale. Folk tales tell us nothing credible about the life or manners of any society; so far from giving us dialogue, imagery or complex behavior, they do not even care whether their characters are men or ghosts or animals. Folk tales are simply abstract story-patterns, uncomplicated and easy to remember, no more hampered by barriers of language and culture than migrating birds are by customs officers, and made up of interchangeable motifs that can be counted and indexed.

Nevertheless, folk tales form a continuum with other literary fictions. We know, vaguely, that the story of Cinderella has been retold hundreds of thousands of times in middle-class fiction, and that nearly every thriller we see is a variant of Bluebeard.* But it is seldom explained why even the greatest writers are interested in such tales: why Shakespeare put a folk-tale motif into nearly every comedy he wrote; why some of the most intellectualized fiction of our day, such as the later works of Thomas Mann,* are based on them. Writers are interested in folk tales for the same reason that painters are interested in still-life arrangements: because they illustrate essential principles of storytelling. The writer who uses them then has the technical problem of making them sufficiently plausible or credible to a sophisticated audience. When he succeeds, he produces, not realism, but a

---

***Bluebeard:** 옛날 이야기에 나오는 기사로, 일곱 명의 아내를 살해하여 감추었다.

*Thomas Mann은 구약의 요셉에 관한 설화를 바탕으로 *Joseph und seine Brüder* (3부작)을 썼다.

distortion of realism in the interests of structure. Such distortion is the literary equivalent of the tendency in painting to assimilate subject-matter to geometrical form, which we see both in primitive painting and in the sophisticated primitivism of, say, Léger or Modigliani.*

What we see clearly in the folk tale we see less clearly in popular fiction. If we want incident for its own sake, we turn from the standard novelists to adventure stories, like those of Rider Haggard or John Buchan,* where the action is close to if not actually across the boundary of the credible. Such stories are not looser or more flexible than the classical novels, but far tighter. Gone is all sense of the leisurely acquiring of incidental experience, of exploring all facets of a character, of learning something about a specific society. A hazardous enterprise is announced at the beginning and everything is rigorously subordinated to that. In such works, while characters exist for the sake of the action, the two aspects of the action which we have defined as plot and theme are very close together. The story could hardly have been told in any other narrative shape, and our attention has so little expanding to do when it reaches the recognition that we often feel that there would be no point in reading it a second time. The subordination of character to linear action is also a feature of the detective story, for the fact that one of the characters is capable of murder is the concealed clue on which every detective story turns. Even more striking is the subordinating of moral attitude to the conventions of the story. Thus in Robert Louis Stevenson's tale, *The Body-Snatcher,* which is about the smuggling of corpses from cemeteries into medical classrooms, we read of bodies being "exposed to uttermost indignities before a class of gaping boys," and much more to the same effect. It is irrelevant to inquire whether this is really Stevenson's attitude to the use of cadavers in medical study or whether he expects it to be ours. The more sinister the crime

---

*Fernand Léger는 현대 프랑스 회가. Amedeo Modigliani는 20세기 초의 이탈리아 화가.

*Rider Haggard, John Buchan: 둘 다 20세기 초반 모험소설을 쓴 영국의 소설가.

can be felt to be, the more thrilling the thriller, and the moral attitude is being deliberately talked up to thicken the atmosphere.

The opposite extreme from such conventionalized fiction is represented by Trollope's *Last Chronicle of Barset*. Here the main story line is a kind of parody of a detective novel — such parodies of suspense are frequent in Trollope. Some money has been stolen, and suspicion falls on the Reverend Josiah Crawley, curate of Hogglestock. The point of the parody is that Crawley's character is clearly and fully set forth, and if you imagine him capable of stealing money you are simply not attending to the story. The action, therefore, appears to exist for the sake of the characters, reversing Aristotle's axiom. But this is not really true. Characters still exist only as functions of the action, but in Trollope the "action" resides in the huge social panorama that the linear events build up. Recognition is continuous: it is in the texture of characterization, the dialogue and the comment itself, and needs no twist in the plot to dramatize a contrast between appearance and reality. And what is true of Trollope is roughly true of most mimetic fiction between Defoe and Arnold Bennett. When we read Smollett or Jane Austen or Dickens, we read them for the sake of the texture of characterization, and tend to think of the plot, when we think of it at all, as a conventional, mechanical, or even (as occasionally in Dickens) absurd contrivance included only to satisfy the demands of the literary market.

The requirement of plausibility, then, has the apparently paradoxical effect of limiting the imagination by making its design more flexible. Thus in a Dutch realistic interior the painter's ability to render the sheen of satin or the varnish of a lute both limits his power of design (for a realistic painter cannot, like Braque or Juan Gris,* distort his object in the interest of pictorial composition) and yet makes that design less easy to take in at a glance. In fact we often "read" Dutch pictures instead of looking at them, absorbed by their technical virtuosity but unaffected by much conscious sense of their

---

***Braque, Juan Gris:** 현대 화가들.

total structure.

By this time the ambiguity in our word "imagination" is catching up with us. So far we have been using it in the sense of a structural power which, left to itself, produces rigorously predictable fictions. In this sense Bernard Shaw spoke of the romances of Marie Corelli* as illustrating the triumph of imagination over mind. What is implied by "mind" here is less a structural than a reproductive power, which expresses itself in the texture of characterization and imagery. There seems no reason why this should not be called imagination too: in any case, in reading fiction there are two kinds of recognition. One is the continuous recognition of credibility, fidelity to experience, and of what is not so much lifelikeness as lifeliveliness.* The other is the recognition of the identity of the total design, into which we are initiated by the technical recognition in the plot.

The influence of mimetic fiction has thrown the main emphasis in criticism on the former kind of recognition. Coleridge, as is well known, intended the climax of the *Biographia Literaria* to be a demonstration of the "esemplastic" or structural nature of the imagination, only to discover when the great chapter arrived that he was unable to write it. There were doubtless many reasons for this, but one was that he does not really think of imagination as a constructive power at all. He means by imagination what we have called the reproductive power, the ability to bring to life the texture of characterization and imagery. It is to this power that he applies his favorite metaphor of an organism, where the unity is some mysterious and elusive "vitality." His practical criticism of work he admires is concerned with texture: he never discusses the total design, or what we call the theme, of a Shakespeare play. It is really fancy which is his "esemplastic" power, and which he tends to think of as mechanical. His conception of fancy as a mode of memory, emancipated from time and space and playing with fixities

***Marie Corelli:** 20세기 초 영국의 통속소설가.

***life-liveliness:** 인생의 닮음 (like-likeness) 이라기보다는 "인생처럼 활기있음".

and definites, admirably characterizes the folk tale, with its remoteness from society and its stock of interchangeable motifs. Thus Coleridge is in the tradition of critical naturalism, which bases its values on the immediacy of contact between art and nature that we continuously feel in the texture of mimetic fiction.

There is nothing wrong with critical naturalism, as far as it goes, but it does not do full justice to our feelings about the total dsign of a work of fiction. We shall not improve on Coleridge, however, by merely reversing his perspective, as T. E. Hulme did, and giving our favorable value-judgments to fancy, wit, and highly conventionalized forms. This can start a new critical trend, but not develop the study of criticism. In the direct experience of a new work of fiction we have a sense of its unity which we derive from its persuasive continuity. As the work becomes more familiar, this sense of continuity fades out, and we tend to think of it as a discontinuous series of episodes, held together by something which eludes critical analysis. But that this unity is available for critical study as well seems clear when it emerges as a unity of "theme," as we call it, which we can study all at once, and to which we are normally initiated by some crucial recognition in the plot. Hence we need a supplementary form of criticism which can examine the total design of fiction as something which is neither mechanical nor of secondary importance.

By a myth, as I said at the beginning, I mean primarily a certain type of story. It is a story in which some of the chief characters are gods or other beings larger in power than humanity. Very seldom is it located in history: its action takes place in a world above or prior to ordinary time, *in illo tempore,** in Mircea Eliade's* phrase. Hence, like the folk tale, it is an abstract story-pattern. The characters can do what they like, which means what the story-teller likes: there is no need to be plausible or logical in motivation. The things that happen in myth are things that happen only in stories; they are in a self-contained literary world. Hence myth would naturally

---

****in illo tempore***: 'at that time.'

***Mircea Eliade:** 현대의 저명한 신화학자, 민속학자.

have the same kind of appeal for the fiction writer that folk tales have. It presents him with a ready-made framework, hoary with antiquity, and allows him to devote all his energies to elaborating its design. Thus the use of myth in Joyce or Cocteau, like the use of folk tale in Mann, is parallel to the use of abstraction and other means of emphasizing design in contemporary painting; and a modern writer's interest in primitive fertility rites is parallel to a modern sculptor's interest in primitive woodcarving.

The differences between myth and folk tale, however, also have their importance. Myths, as compared with folk tales, are usually in a special category of seriousness: they are believed to have "really happened," or to have some exceptional significance in explaining certain features of life, such as ritual. Again, whereas folk tales simply interchange motifs and develop variants, myths show an odd tendency to stick together and build up bigger structures. We have creation myths, fall and flood myths, metamorphosis and dying-god myths, divine-marriage and hero-ancestry myths, etiological myths, apocalyptic myths; and writers of sacred scriptures or collectors of myth like Ovid tend to arrange these in a series. And while myths themselves are seldom historical, they seem to provide a kind of containing form of tradition, one result of which is the obliterating of boundaries separating legend, historical reminiscence, and actual history that we find in Homer and the Old Testament.

As a type of story, myth is a form of verbal art, and belongs to the world of art. Like art, and unlike science, it deals, not with the world that man contemplates, but with the world that man creates. The total form of art, so to speak, is a world whose content is nature but whose form is human; hence when it "imitates" nature it assimilates nature to human forms. The world of art is human in perspective, a world in which the sun continues to rise and set long after science has explained that its rising and setting are illusions. And myth, too, makes a systematic attempt to see nature in human shape: it does not simply roam at large in nature like the folk tale.

The obvious conception which brings together the human

form and the natural content in myth is the god. It is not the connexion of the stories of Phaethon and Endymion* with the sun and moon that makes them myths, for we could have folk tales of the same kind: it is rather their attachment to the body of stories told about Apollo and Artemis which gives them a canonical place in the growing system of tales that we call a mythology. And every developed mythology tends to complete itself, to outline an entire universe in which the "gods" represent the whole of nature in humanized form, and at the same time show in perspective man's origin, his destiny, the limits of his power, and the extension of his hopes and desires. A mythology may develop by accretion, as in Greece, or by rigorous codifying and the excluding of unwanted material, as in Israel; but the drive toward a verbal circumference of human experience is clear in both cultures.

The two great conceptual principles which myth uses in assimilating nature to human form are analogy and identity. Analogy establishes the parallels between human life and natural phenomena, and identity conceives of a "sun-god" or a "tree-god." Myth seizes on the fundamental element of design offered by nature — the cycle, as we have it daily in the sun and yearly in the seasons — and assimilates it to the human cycle of life, death, and (analogy again) rebirth. At the same time the discrepancy between the world man lives in and the world he would like to live in develops a dialectic in myth which, as in the New Testament and Plato's *Phaedo*, separates reality into two contrasting states, a heaven and a hell.

Again, myths are often used as allegories of science or religion or morality: they may arise in the first place to account for a ritual or a law, or they may be *exempla* or parables which illustrate a particular situation or argument, like the myths in Plato or Achilles' myth of the two jars of Zeus at the end of the Iliad. Once established in their own right, they may then be interpreted dogmatically, or allegorically, as all the standard myths have been for cen-

*__Phaethon__ 은 태양신 Apollo(또는 Helios)의 아들, **Endymion** 은 달의 여신 Artemis의 사랑을 받은 미남으로, Keats의 시의 주제가 되었다.

turies, in innumerable ways. But because myths are stories, what they "mean" is inside them, in the implications of their incidents. No rendering of any myth into conceptual language can serve as a full equivalent of its meaning. A myth may be told and retold: it may be modified or elaborated, or different patterns may be discovered in it; and its life is always the poetic life of a story, not the homiletic life of some illustrated truism. When a system of myths loses all connexion with belief, it becomes purely literary, as Classical myth did in Christian Europe. Such a development would be impossible unless myths were inherently literary in structure. As it makes no difference to that structure whether an interpretation of the myth is believed in or not, there is no difficulty in speaking of a Christian mythology.

Myth thus provides the main outlines and the circumference of a verbal universe which is later occupied by literature as well. Literature is more flexible than myth, and fills up this universe more completely: a poet or novelist may work in areas of human life apparently remote from the shadowy gods and gigantic story-outlines of mythology. But in all cultures mythology merges insensibly into, and with, literature. The Odyssey is to us a work of literature, but its early place in the literary tradition, the importance of gods in its action, and its influence on the later religious thought of Greece, are all features common to literature proper and to mythology, and indicate that the difference between them is more chronological than structural. Educators are now aware that any effective teaching of literature has to recapitulate its history and begin, in early childhood, with myths, folk tales and legends.

We should expect, therefore, that there would be a great many literary works derived directly from specific myths, like the poems by Drayton* and Keats about Endymion which are derived from the myth of Endymion. But the study of the relations between mythology and literature is not confined to such one-to-one relationships. In the first place, mythology as

---

***Drayton, Michael:** (1563-1631). 영국의 시인. Endymion의 신화를 다룬 작품 *Endymion and Phoebe* (1595)가 있다.

a total structure, defining as it does a society's religious beliefs, historical traditions, cosmological speculations — in short, the whole range of its verbal expressiveness — is the matrix of literature, and major poetry keeps returning to it. In every age poets who are thinkers (remembering that poets think in metaphors and images, not in propositions) and are deeply concerned with the origin or destiny or desires of mankind — with anything that belongs to the larger outlines of what literature can express — can hardly find a literary theme that does not coincide with a myth. Hence the imposing body of explicitly mythopoeic poetry in the epic and encyclopaedic forms* which so many of the greatest poets use. A poet who accepts a mythology as valid for belief, as Dante and Milton accepted Christianity, will naturally use it; poets outside such a tradition turn to other mythologies as suggestive or symbolic of what might be believed, as in the adaptations of Classical or occult mythological systems made by Goethe, Victor Hugo, Shelley, or Yeats.

Similarly, the structural principles of a mythology, built up from analogy and identity, become in due course the structural principles of literature. The absorption of the natural cycle into mythology provides myth with two of these structures; the rising movement that we find in myths of spring or the dawn, of birth, marriage and resurrection, and the falling movement in myths of death, metamorphosis, or sacrifice. These movements reappear as the structural principles of comedy and tragedy in literature. Again, the dialectic in myth that projects a paradise or heaven above our world and a hell or place of shades below it reappears in literature as the idealized world of pastoral and romance and the absurd, suffering, or frustrated world of irony and satire.

The relation between myth and literature, therefore, is established by studying the genres and conventions of literature. Thus the convention of the pastoral elegy in *Lycidas* links it to Virgil and Theocritus, and thence with the myth of Adonis. Thus the convention of the foundling plot,

---

***encyclopaedic forms:** Homer, Dante, Milton 등 mythopoetic poets의 작품은 "신화백과사전"처럼 많은 신화가 체계적으로 집대성되어 있다.

which is the basis of *Tom Jones* and *Oliver Twist*, goes back to Menandrine comedy* formulas, thence to Euripides, and so back to such myths as the finding of Moses and Perseus. In myth criticism, when we examine the theme or total design of a fiction, we must isolate that aspect of the fiction which is conventional, and held in common with all other works of the same category. When we begin, say, *Pride and Prejudice*, we can see at once that a story which sustains that particular mood or tone is most unlikely to end in tragedy or melodrama or mordant irony or romance. It clearly belongs to the category represented by the word "comedy," and we are not surprised to find in it the conventional features of comedy, including a foolish lover, with some economic advantages, encouraged by one of the parents, a hypocrite unmasked, misunderstandings between the chief characters eventually cleared up and happy marriages for those who deserve them. This conventional comic form is in *Pride and Prejudice* somewhat as the sonata form is in a Mozart symphony. Its presence there does not account for any of the merits of the novel, but it does account for its conventional, as distinct from its individual, structure. A serious interest in structure, then, ought naturally to lead us from *Pride and Prejudice* to a study of the comic form which it exemplifies, the conventions of which have presented much the same features from Plautus* to our own day. These conventions in turn take us back into myth. When we compare the conventional plot of a play of Plautus with the Christian myth of a son appeasing the wrath of a father and redeeming his bride,* we can see that the latter is quite accurately described, from a literary point of view, as a divine comedy.

Whenever we find explicit mythologizing in literature, or a writer trying to indicate what myths he is particularly interested in, we should treat this as confirmatory or supporting

---

***Menandrine comedy:** BC 4세기경 로마의 희극 작가 Menander는 "주워온 아이"의 motif를 많이 사용했다. 여기에 언급된 작중의 인물들도 "주워온 아이"들이었다.

***Plautus:** BC 2,3세기 로마의 희극 작가. 유럽 희극의 원형을 만든 사람.

***Christian myth...his bride:** 하나님의 아들 예수가 인류(그의 아내)를 하나님의 노여움에서 구원하신다는 믿음.

evidence for our study of the genres and conventions he is using. Meredith's *The Egoist* is a story about a girl who narrowly escapes marrying a selfish man, which makes many references, both explicitly and indirectly in its imagery, to the two best-known myths of female sacrifice, the stories of Andromeda and Iphigeneia.* Such allusions would be pointless or unintelligible except as indications by Meredith of an awareness of the conventional shape of the story he is telling. Again, it is as true of poetry as it is of myth that its main conceptual elements are analogy and identity, which reappear in the two commonest figures of speech, the simile and the metaphor. Literature, like mythology, is largely an art of misleading analogies and mistaken identities. Hence we often find poets, especially young poets, turning to myth because of the scope it affords them for uninhibited poetic imagery. If Shakespeare's *Venus and Adonis* had been simply a story about a willing girl and an unwilling boy, all the resources of analogy and identity would have been left unexplored: the fanciful imagery appropriate to the mythical subject would have been merely tasteless exaggeration. Especially is this true with what may be called sympathetic imagery, the association of human and natural life:

> No flower was nigh, no grass, herb, leaf, or weed,
> But stole his blood and seem'd with him to bleed.*

The opposite extreme from such deliberate exploiting of myth is to be found in the general tendency of realism or naturalism to give imaginative life and coherence to something closely resembling our own ordinary experience. Such realism often begins by simplifying its language, and dropping the explicit connexions with myth which are a sign of an awareness of literary tradition. Wordsworth, for example, felt that in his day Phoebus and Philomela were getting to be mere trade slang for the sun and the nightingale,

---

*Andromeda는 신에 대한 어머니의 죄값을 곤욕으로 치른 여자. Iphigeneia는 아버지의 야망을 달성시키기 위해 제사의 제물로 희생된 여자.

**Venus aud Adonis*, 1055—56.

and that poetry would do better to discard this kind of inorganic allusion. But, as Wordsworth himself clearly recognized, the result of turning one's back on explicit myth can only be the reconstructing of the same mythical patterns in more ordinary words:

> Paradise, and groves
> Elysian, Fortunate Fields — like those of old
> Sought in the Atlantic Main — why should they be
> A history only of departed things,
> Or a mere fiction of what never was?
> For the discerning intellect of Man,
> When wedded to this goodly universe
> In love and holy passion, shall find these
> A simple produce of the common day.

To this indirect mythologizing I have elsewhere given the name of displacement.* By displacement I mean the techniques a writer uses to make his story credible, logically motivated or morally acceptable — lifelike, in short. I call it displacement for many reasons, but one is that fidelity to the credible is a feature of literature that can affect only content. Life presents a continuum, and a selection from it can only be what is called a *tranche de vie:** plausibility is easy to sustain, but except for death life has little to suggest in the way of plausible conclusions. And even a plausible conclusion does not necessarily round out a shape. The realistic writer soon finds that the requirements of literary form and plausible content always fight against each other. Just as the poetic metaphor is always a logical absurdity, so every inherited convention of plot in literature is more or less mad. The king's rash promise, the cuckold's jealousy, the "lived happily ever after" tag to a concluding marriage, the manipulated happy endings of comedy in general, the equally manipulated ironic endings of modern realism — none of these was suggested by any observation of human life or behavior: all exist solely as

**Anatomy of Criticism* (Princeton, 1957), pp. 136—38, 155—56, 188, 190 참조.

**tranche de vie*: 'slice of life'. 사실주의자들의 구호의 하나.

story-telling devices. Literary shape cannot come from life; it comes only from literary tradition, and so ultimately from myth. In sober realism, like the novels of Trollope, the plot, as we have noted, is often a parody plot. It is instructive to notice, too, how strong the popular demand is for such forms as detective stories, science fiction, comic strips, comic formulas like the P. G. Wodehouse* stories, all of which are as rigorously conventional and stylized as the folk tale itself, works of pure "esemplastic" imagination, with the recognition turning up as predictably as the caesura in minor Augustan poetry.

One difficulty in proceeding from this point comes from the lack of any literary term which corresponds to the word "mythology." We find it hard to conceive of literature as an order of words, as a unified imaginative system that can be studied as a whole by criticism. If we had such a conception, we could readily see that literarure as a whole provides a framework or context for every work of literature, just as a fully developed mythology provides a framework or context for each of its myths. Further, because mythology and literature occupy the same verbal space, so to speak, the framework or context of every work of literature can be found in mythology as well, when its literary tradition is understood. It is relatively easy to see the place of a myth in a mythology, and one of the main uses of myth criticism is to enable us to understand the corresponding place that a work of literature has in the context of literature as a whole.

Putting works of literature in such a context gives them an immense reverberating dimension of significance. (If anyone is worrying about value-judgements, I should add that establishing such a context tends to make the genuine work of literature sublime and the pinchbeck one ridiculous.) This reverberating significance, in which every literary work catches the echoes of all other works of its type in literature, and so ripples out into the rest of literature and thence into life, is often, and wrongly, called allegory. We have allegory when one literary work is joined to another, or to a myth, by a

*P.G. Wodehouse: 현대 영국의 소설가로, 미국에 거주.

certain interpretation of meaning rather than by structure. Thus *The Pilgrim's Progress* is related allegorically to the Christian myth of redemption, and Hawthorne's story, *The Bosom Serpent,* is related allegorically to various moral serpents going back to the Book of Genesis. Arthur Miller's *The Crucible,* already mentioned, deals with the Salem witch trials in a way that suggested McCarthyism to most of its original audience. This relation in itself is allegorical. But if *The Crucible* is good enough to hold the stage after McCarthyism has become as dead an issue as the Salem trials, it would be clear that the theme of *The Crucible* is one which can always be used in literature, and that any social hysteria can form its subject matter. Social hysteria, however, is the content and not the form of the theme itself, which belongs in the category of the purgatorial or triumphant tragedy. As so often happens in literature, the only explicit clue to its mythical shape is provided by the title.

To sum up. In the direct experience of a new work of literature, we are aware of its continuity or moving power in time. As we become both more familiar with and more detached from it, the work tends to break up into a discontinuous series of felicities, bits of vivid imagery, convincing characterization, witty dialogue, and the like. The study of this belongs to what we have called critical naturalism or continuous recognition, the sense of the sharply focused reproduction of life in the fiction. But there was a feeling of unity in the original experience which such criticism does not recapture. We need to move from a criticism of "effects" to what we may call a criticism of causes, specifically the formal cause which holds the wok together. The fact that such unity is available for critical study as well as for direct experience is normally symbolized by a crucial recognition, a point marking a real and not merely apparent unity in the design. Fictions like those of Trollope which appeal particularly to critical naturalism often play down or even parody such a device, and such works show the highest degree of displacement and the least conscious or explicit relationship to myth.

If, however, we go on to study the theme or total shape of the fiction, we find that it also belongs to a convention or category, like those of comedy and tragedy. With the literary category we reach a dead end, until we realize that literature is a reconstructed mythology, with its structural principles derived from those of myth. Then we can see that literature is in a complex setting what a mythology is in a simpler one: a total body of verbal creation. In literature, whatever has a shape has a mythical shape, and leads us toward the center of the order of words. For just as critical naturalism studies the counterpoint of literature and life, words and things, so myth criticism pulls us away from "life" toward a self-contained and autonomous literary universe. But myth, as we said at the beginning, means many things besides literary structure, and the world of words in not so self-contained and autonomous after all.

Excerpts from Classical Criticism

Aristotle
Poetics

INTRODUCTION

Poetry as Imitation

UNDER the general heading of the art of poetry, I propose not only to speak about this art itself, but also to discuss the various kinds of poetry and their characteristic functions, the types of plot-structure that are required if a poem is to succeed, the number and nature of its constituent parts, and similarly any other matters that may be relevant to a study of this kind. I shall begin in the natural way, that is, by going back to first principles.

Epic and tragic poetry, comedy too, dithyrambic poetry, and most music composed for the flute and the lyre, can all be described in general terms as forms of imitation or representation. However, they differ from one another in three respects: either in using different media for the representation, or in representing different things, or in representing them in entirely different ways.

CHAPTER I

The Media of Poetic Imitation

SOME artists, whether by theoretical knowledge or by long practice, can represent things by imitating their shapes and colours, and others do so by the use of the voice; in the arts I have spoken of the imitation is produced by means of rhythm, language, and music, these being used either separately or in combination. Thus the art of the flute and of the lyre consists only in music and rhythm, as does any other of the same type, such as that of the pipes. The imitative medium of dancers is rhythm alone, unsupported by music, for it is by the manner in which they arrange the rhythms of their movements that they represent men's characters and feelings and actions.

The form of art that uses language alone, whether in prose or verse, and verse either in a mixture of metres or in one particular kind, has up to the present been without a name. For we have no common name that we can apply to the prose mimes of Sophron and Xenarchus and the Socratic dialogues, or to compositions employing iambic trimeters or elegiac couplets or any other metres of these types. We can say only that people associate poetry with the metre employed, and speak, for example, of elegiac poets and epic poets; they call them poets, however, not from the fact that they are making imitations, but indiscriminately from the fact that they are writing in metre. For it is customary to describe as poets even those who produce medical and scientific works in verse. Yet Homer and Empedocles have nothing in common except their metre, and therefore, while it is right to call the one a poet, the other should rather be called a natural philosopher than a poet. In the same way, an author composing his imitation in a mixture of all the metres, as Chaeremon did in his *Centaur*, a rhapsody employing just such a mixture, would also have to be called a poet. Such are the distinctions I would make.

Again, there are some arts which make use of all the media I have mentioned, that is, rhythm, music, and formal metre;

such are dithyrambic and nomic poetry,[1] tragedy and comedy. They differ, however, in that the first two use all these media together, while the last two use them separately, one after another.

These, then, are what I mean by the differences between the arts as far as the media of representation are concerned.

CHAPTER 2

The Objects of Poetic Imitation

SINCE imitative artists represent men in action, and men who are necessarily either of good or of bad character (for as all people differ in their moral nature according to the degree of their goodness or badness, characters almost always fall into one or other of these types), these men must be represented either as better than we are, or worse, or as the same kind of people as ourselves. Thus among the painters Polygnotus represented his subjects as better, and Pauson as worse, while Dionysius painted them just as they were. It is clear that each of the kinds of imitation I have referred to will admit of these variations, and they will differ in this way according to the differences in the objects they represent. Such diversities may occur even in dancing, and in music for the flute and the lyre; they occur also in the art that is based on language, whether it uses prose or verse unaccompanied by music. Homer, for example, depicts the better types of men, and Cleophon normal types, while Hegemon of Thasos, the first writer of parodies, and Nicochares, the author of the *Deiliad*, show them in a bad light. The same thing happens in dithyrambic and nomic poetry; for instance, the Cyclops might be represented in different ways, as was done by Timotheus and Philoxenus. This is the difference that marks the distinction between comedy and tragedy; for comedy aims at representing men as worse than they are nowadays, tragedy as better.

1. The Nome, or nomic song, was an ancient type of ode, akin to the dithyramb, sung to the lyre or flute in honour of some god, usually Apollo.

CHAPTER 3

The Manner of Poetic Imitation

THERE remains the third point of difference in these arts, that is, the manner in which each kind of subject may be represented. For it is possible, using the same medium, to represent the same subjects in a variety of ways. It may be done partly by narration and partly by the assumption of a character other than one's own, which is Homer's way; or by speaking in one's own person without any such change; or by representing the characters as performing all the actions dramatically.

These, then, as I pointed out at the beginning, are the three factors by which the imitative arts are differentiated: their media, the objects they represent, and their manner of representation. Thus in one sense Sophocles might be called an imitator of the same kind as Homer, for they both represent good men; in another sense he is like Aristophanes, in that they both represent men in action, men actually doing things. And this, some say, is why their works are called dramas, from their representing men doing things.[1] For this reason too the Dorians claim the invention of both tragedy and comedy. Comedy is claimed by the Megarians, both by those here in Greece on the grounds that it came into being when they became a democracy, and by those in Sicily because the poet Epicharmus, who was much earlier than Chionides and Magnes, came from there; certain Dorians of the Peloponnese lay claim also to tragedy. They regard the names as proof of their belief, pointing out that, whereas the Athenians call outlying villages δῆμοι (*dēmoi*), they themselves call them κῶμαι (*kōmai*); so that comedians take their name, not from κωμάζειν (*kōmazein*, 'to revel'), but from their touring in the κῶμαι when lack of appreciation drove them from the city. Furthermore, their

1. The word 'drama' means literally 'a thing done', and is derived from the verb δρᾶν (*drān*, 'to do') which here provides the translation 'doing things'. Cf. the last sentence of the paragraph.

word for 'to do' is δρᾶν (*drān*), whereas the Athenian word is πράττειν (*prattein*).

So much then for the number and character of the different kinds of imitation.

CHAPTER 4

The Origins and Development of Poetry

THE creation of poetry generally is due to two causes, both rooted in human nature. The instinct for imitation is inherent in man from his earliest days; he differs from other animals in that he is the most imitative of creatures, and he learns his earliest lessons by imitation. Also inborn in all of us is the instinct to enjoy works of imitation. What happens in actual experience is evidence of this; for we enjoy looking at the most accurate representations of things which in themselves we find painful to see, such as the forms of the lowest animals and of corpses. The reason for this is that learning is a very great pleasure, not for philosophers only, but for other people as well, however limited their capacity for it may be. They enjoy seeing likenesses because in doing so they acquire information (they reason out what each represents, and discover, for instance, that 'this is a picture of so and so'); for if by any chance the thing depicted has not been seen before, it will not be the fact that it is an imitation of something that gives the pleasure, but the execution or the colouring or some other such cause.

The instinct for imitation, then, is natural to us, as is also a feeling for music and for rhythm – and metres are obviously detached sections of rhythms. Starting from these natural aptitudes, and by a series of for the most part gradual improvements on their first efforts, men eventually created poetry from their improvisations.

However, poetry soon branched into two channels, according to the temperaments of individual poets. The more serious-minded among them represented noble actions and the doings of noble persons, while the more trivial wrote about the meaner sort of people; thus while the one type wrote hymns and panegyrics, these others began by writing invectives. We know of no poems of this kind by any poet earlier than Homer, though it is likely enough that many poets wrote them; but from Homer onwards examples may be found, his own *Margites*, for instance, and poems of the same type. It was in such poems that the iambic metre was brought into use because of its appropriateness for the purpose, and it is still called iambic today, from being the metre in which they wrote 'iambs', or lampoons, against one another.

In this way it came about that some of our early poets became writers of heroic, and some of iambic verse. But just as Homer was the supreme poet in the serious style, standing alone both in excellence of composition and in the dramatic quality of his representations of life, so also, in the dramatic character that he imparted, not to invective, but to his treatment of the ridiculous, he was the first to indicate the forms that comedy was to assume; for his *Margites* bears the same relationship to our comedies as his *Iliad* and *Odyssey* bear to our tragedies. When tragedy and comedy appeared, those whose natural aptitude inclined them towards the one kind of poetry wrote comedies instead of lampoons, and those who were drawn to the other wrote tragedies instead of epics; for these new forms were both grander and more highly regarded than the earlier.

It is beyond my scope here to consider whether or not tragedy is now developed as far as it can be in its various forms, and to decide this both absolutely and in relation to the stage.

Both tragedy and comedy had their first beginnings in improvisation. The one originated with those who led the dithyramb, the other with the leaders of the phallic songs which still survive today as traditional institutions in many of our cities. Little by little tragedy advanced, each new element being developed as it came into use, until after many changes it attained its natural form and came to a standstill. Aeschylus was the first to increase the number of actors from one to two, cut down the role of the chorus, and give the first place to the dialogue. Sophocles introduced three actors and painted scenery. As for the grandeur of tragedy, it was not until late that it acquired its characteristic stateliness, when, progressing beyond the methods of satyric drama,[1] it discarded slight plots and comic diction, and its metre changed from the trochaic tetrameter to the iambic. At first the poets had used the tetrameter because they were writing satyr-poetry, which was more closely related to the dance; but once dialogue had been introduced, by its very nature it hit upon the right measure, for the iambic is of all measures the one best suited to speech. This is shown by the fact that we most usually drop into iambics in our conversation with one another, whereas we seldom talk in hexameters, and then only when we depart from the normal tone of conversation. Another change was the increased number of episodes, or acts. We must pass over such other matters as the various embellishments of tragedy and the circumstances in which they are said to have been introduced, for it would probably be a long business to go into them in any detail.

CHAPTER 5

The Rise of Comedy. Epic Compared with Tragedy

As I have remarked, comedy represents the worse types of men; worse, however, not in the sense that it embraces any and every kind of badness, but in the sense that the ridiculous is a species of ugliness or badness. For the ridiculous consists in some form of error or ugliness that is not painful or injurious; the comic mask, for example, is distorted and ugly, but causes no pain.

Now we know something of the successive stages by which tragedy developed, and of those who were responsible for them; the early history of comedy, however, is obscure, because it was not taken seriously. It was a long time before the archon granted a chorus to comedies; until then the performers were volunteers.[2] Comedy had already acquired

1. Satyric drama is described on p. 86–7, footnote 3.
2. The Greek dramatist submitted his play to the archon, or magistrate,

certain clear-cut forms before there is any mention of those who are named as its poets. Nor is it known who introduced masks, or prologues, or a plurality of actors, and other things of that kind. Properly worked out plots originated in Sicily with Epicharmus and Phormis; of Athenian poets Crates was the first to discard the lampoon pattern and to adopt stories and plots of a more general nature.

Epic poetry agrees with tragedy to the extent that it is a representation, in dignified verse, of serious actions. They differ, however, in that epic keeps to a single metre and is in narrative form. Another point of difference is their length: tragedy tries as far as possible to keep within a single revolution of the sun, or only slightly to exceed it, whereas the epic observes no limits in its time of action – although at first the practice in this respect was the same in tragedies as in epics. Of the constituent parts, some are common to both kinds, and some are peculiar to tragedy. Thus anyone who can discriminate between what is good and what is bad in tragedy can do the same with epic; for all the elements of epic are found in tragedy, though not everything that belongs to tragedy is to be found in epic.[1]

CHAPTER 6

A Description of Tragedy

I SHALL speak later about the form of imitation that uses hexameters and about comedy, but for the moment I propose to discuss tragedy, first drawing together the definition of its essential character from what has already been said.

Tragedy, then, is a representation of an action that is worth

1. Herein, it is perhaps worth pointing out, lies the justification of the far fuller treatment that Aristotle gives to drama.

---

in charge of the religious festival at which he hoped to have it performed. If the play was chosen for performance, the archon 'granted it a chorus'; that is, he provided a choregus, a wealthy citizen who, as a form of public service, paid the expenses of the production. The earlier 'volunteers' presumably paid their own expenses.

serious attention, complete in itself, and of some amplitude; in language enriched by a variety of artistic devices appropriate to the several parts of the play; presented in the form of action, not narration; by means of pity and fear bringing about the purgation of such emotions. By language that is enriched I refer to language possessing rhythm, and music or song; and by artistic devices appropriate to the several parts I mean that some are produced by the medium of verse alone, and others again with the help of song.

Now since the representation is carried out by men performing the actions, it follows, in the first place, that spectacle is an essential part of tragedy, and secondly that there must be song and diction, these being the medium of representation. By diction I mean here the arrangement of the verses; song is a term whose sense is obvious to everyone.

In tragedy it is action that is imitated, and this action is brought about by agents who necessarily display certain distinctive qualities both of character and of thought, according to which we also define the nature of the actions. Thought and character are, then, the two natural causes of actions, and it is on them that all men depend for success or failure. The representation of the action is the plot of the tragedy; for the ordered arrangement of the incidents is what I mean by plot. Character, on the other hand, is that which enables us to define the nature of the participants, and thought comes out in what they say when they are proving a point or expressing an opinion.

Necessarily, then, every tragedy has six constituents, which will determine its quality. They are plot, character, diction, thought, spectacle, and song. Of these, two represent the media in which the action is represented, one involves the manner of representation, and three are connected with the objects of the representation; beyond them nothing further is required. These, it may be said, are the dramatic elements that have been used by practically all playwrights; for all plays alike possess spectacle, character, plot, diction, song, and thought.

Of these elements the most important is the plot, the ordering of the incidents; for tragedy is a representation, not of men, but of action and life, of happiness and unhappiness – and happiness and unhappiness are bound up with action. The purpose of living is an end which is a kind of activity, not a quality; it is their characters, indeed, that make men what they are, but it is by reason of their actions that they are happy or the reverse. Tragedies are not performed, therefore, in order to represent character, although character is involved for the sake of the action. Thus the incidents and the plot are the end aimed at in tragedy, and as always, the end is everything. Furthermore, there could not be a tragedy without action, but there could be without character; indeed the tragedies of most of our recent playwrights fail to present character, and the same might be said of many playwrights of other periods. A similar contrast could be drawn between Zeuxis and Polygnotus as painters, for Polygnotus represents character well, whereas Zeuxis is not concerned with it in his painting. Again, if someone writes a series of speeches expressive of character, and well composed as far as thought and diction are concerned, he will still not achieve the proper effect of tragedy; this will be done much better by a tragedy which is less successful in its use of these elements, but which has a plot giving an ordered combination of incidents. Another point to note is that the two most important means by which tragedy plays on our feelings, that is, 'reversals' and 'recognitions', are both constituents of the plot. A further proof is that beginners can achieve accuracy in diction and the portrayal of character before they can construct a plot out of the incidents, and this could be said of almost all the earliest dramatic poets.

The plot, then, is the first essential of tragedy, its life-blood, so to speak, and character takes the second place. It is much the same in painting; for if an artist were to daub his canvas with the most beautiful colours laid on at random, he would not give the same pleasure as he would by drawing a recognizable portrait in black and white. Tragedy is the representation of an action, and it is chiefly on account of the action that it is also a representation of persons.

The third property of tragedy is thought. This is the ability to say what is possible and appropriate in any given circumstances; it is what, in the speeches in the play, is related to the arts of politics and rhetoric. The older dramatic poets made their characters talk like statesmen, whereas those of today make them talk like rhetoricians. Character is that which reveals personal choice, the kinds of thing a man chooses or rejects when that is not obvious. Thus there is no revelation of character in speeches in which the speaker shows no preferences or aversions whatever. Thought, on the other hand, is present in speeches where something is being shown to be true or untrue, or where some general opinion is being expressed.

Fourth comes the diction of the speeches. By diction I mean, as I have already explained, the expressive use of words, and this has the same force in verse and in prose.

Of the remaining elements, the music is the most important of the pleasurable additions to the play. Spectacle, or stage-effect, is an attraction, of course, but it has the least to do with the playwright's craft or with the art of poetry. For the power of tragedy is independent both of performance and of actors, and besides, the production of spectacular effects is more the province of the property-man than of the playwright.

CHAPTER 7

The Scope of the Plot

Now that these definitions have been established, I must go on to discuss the arrangement of the incidents, for this is of the first importance in tragedy. I have already laid down that tragedy is the representation of an action that is complete and whole and of a certain amplitude – for a thing may be whole and yet lack amplitude. Now a whole is that which has a beginning, a middle, and an end. A beginning is that which does not necessarily come after something else, although something else exists or comes about after it. An end, on the contrary, is that which naturally follows something else either as a necessary or as a usual consequence, and is not itself followed by anything. A middle is that which follows something else, and is itself followed by something. Thus well-constructed plots must neither begin nor end in a haphazard way, but must conform to the pattern I have been describing.

Furthermore, whatever is beautiful, whether it be a living creature or an object made up of various parts, must necessarily not only have its parts properly ordered, but also be of an appropriate size, for beauty is bound up with size and order. A minutely small creature, therefore, would not be beautiful, for it would take almost no time to see it and our perception of it would be blurred; nor would an extremely large one, for it could not be taken in all at once, and its unity and wholeness would be lost to the view of the beholder – if, for example, there were a creature a thousand miles long.

Now in just the same way as living creatures and organisms compounded of many parts must be of a reasonable size, so that they can be easily taken in by the eye, so too plots must be of a reasonable length, so that they may be easily held in the memory. The limits in length to be observed, in as far as they concern performance on the stage, have nothing to do with dramatic art; for if a hundred tragedies had to be performed in the dramatic contests, they would be regulated in length by the water-clock, as indeed it is said they were at one time.[1] With regard to the limit set by the nature of the action, the longer the story is the more beautiful it will be, provided that it is quite clear. To give a simple definition, a length which, as a matter either of probability or of necessity, allows of a change from misery to happiness or from happiness to misery is the proper limit of length to be observed.

CHAPTER 8

Unity of Plot

A PLOT does not possess unity, as some people suppose, merely because it is about one man. Many things, countless things indeed, may happen to one man, and some of them will not contribute to any kind of unity; and similarly he may

1. There is no evidence elsewhere that this was ever done, and it seems an improbable proceeding. One is almost tempted to accept Schmidt's emendation (*εἰώθασιν* for *φασιν*) and translate, 'as is regularly done at certain other times', i.e., with pleas in the law-courts.

carry out many actions from which no single unified action will emerge. It seems, therefore, that all those poets have been on the wrong track who have written a *Heracleid*, or a *Theseid*, or some other poem of this kind, in the belief that, Heracles being a single person, his story must necessarily possess unity. Homer, exceptional in this as in all other respects, seems, whether by art or by instinct, to have been well aware of what was required. In writing his *Odyssey* he did not put in everything that happened to Odysseus, that he was wounded on Mount Parnassus, for example, or that he feigned madness at the time of the call to arms, for it was not a matter of necessity or probability that either of these incidents should have led to the other; on the contrary, he constructed the *Odyssey* round a single action of the kind I have spoken of, and he did this with the *Iliad* too. Thus, just as in the other imitative arts each individual representation is the representation of a single object, so too the plot of a play, being the representation of an action, must present it as a unified whole; and its various incidents must be so arranged that if any one of them is differently placed or taken away the effect of wholeness will be seriously disrupted. For if the presence or absence of something makes no apparent difference, it is no real part of the whole.

CHAPTER 9

Poetic Truth and Historical Truth

IT will be clear from what I have said that it is not the poet's function to describe what has actually happened, but the kinds of thing that might happen, that is, that could happen because they are, in the circumstances, either probable or necessary. The difference between the historian and the poet is not that the one writes in prose and the other in verse; the work of Herodotus might be put into verse, and in this metrical form it would be no less a kind of history than it is without metre. The difference is that the one tells of what has happened, the other of the kinds of things that might happen. For this reason poetry is something more philosophical and more worthy of serious attention than history; for while poetry is concerned with universal truths, history treats of particular facts.

By universal truths are to be understood the kinds of thing a certain type of person will probably or necessarily say or do in a given situation; and this is the aim of poetry, although it gives individual names to its characters. The particular facts of the historian are what, say, Alcibiades did, or what happened to him. By now this distinction has become clear where comedy is concerned, for comic poets build up their plots out of probable occurrences, and then add any names that occur to them; they do not, like the iambic poets, write about actual people.[1] In tragedy, on the other hand, the authors keep to the names of real people, the reason being that what is possible is credible. Whereas we cannot be certain of the possibility of something that has not happened, what has happened is obviously possible, for it would not have happened if this had not been so. Nevertheless, even in some tragedies only one or two of the names are well known, and the rest are fictitious; and indeed there are some in which nothing is familiar, Agathon's *Antheus*, for example, in which both the incidents and the names are fictitious, and the play is none the less well liked for that. It is not necessary, therefore, to keep entirely to the traditional stories which form the subjects of our tragedies. Indeed it would be absurd to do so, since even the familiar stories are familiar only to a few, and yet they please everybody.

What I have said makes it obvious that the poet must be a maker of plots rather than of verses, since he is a poet by virtue of his representation, and what he represents is actions. And even if he writes about things that have actually happened, that does not make him any the less a poet, for there is nothing to prevent some of the things that have happened from being in accordance with the laws of possibility and probability, and thus he will be a poet in writing about them.

1. The old iambic or lampooning poets, of whom the earliest and greatest was Archilochus (seventh century B.C.), wrote about real people, as did the poets of the Old Comedy, such as Aristophanes. In the New Comedy, of which Menander is the greatest representative, the names were stock names which, though they might sometimes by association or etymology have a certain appropriateness, were not those of real people.

Of simple plots and actions those that are episodic are the worst. By an episodic plot I mean one in which the sequence of the episodes is neither probable nor necessary. Plays of this kind are written by bad poets because they cannot help it, and by good poets because of the actors; writing for the dramatic competitions, they often strain a plot beyond the bounds of possibility, and are thus obliged to dislocate the continuity of events.

However, tragedy is the representation not only of a complete action, but also of incidents that awaken fear and pity, and effects of this kind are heightened when things happen unexpectedly as well as logically, for then they will be more remarkable than if they seem merely mechanical or accidental. Indeed, even chance occurrences seem most remarkable when they have the appearance of having been brought about by design – when, for example, the statue of Mitys at Argos killed the man who had caused Mitys's death by falling down on him at a public entertainment. Things like this do not seem mere chance occurrences. Thus plots of this type are necessarily better than others.

CHAPTER 10

Simple and Complex Plots

SOME plots are simple, and some complex, for the obvious reason that the actions of which they are representations are of one or other of these kinds. By a simple action I refer to one which is single and continuous in the sense of my earlier definition, and in which the change of fortune comes about without a reversal or a discovery. A complex action is one in which the change is accompanied by a discovery or a reversal, or both. These should develop out of the very structure of the plot, so that they are the inevitable or probable consequence of what has gone before, for there is a big difference between what happens as a result of something else and what merely happens after it.

CHAPTER II

Reversal, Discovery, and Calamity

As has already been noted, a reversal is a change from one state of affairs to its opposite, one which conforms, as I have said, to probability or necessity. In *Oedipus*, for example, the Messenger who came to cheer Oedipus and relieve him of his fear about his mother did the very opposite by revealing to him who he was. In the *Lynceus*, again, Lynceus is being led off to execution, followed by Danaus who is to kill him, when, as a result of events that occurred earlier, it comes about that he is saved and it is Danaus who is put to death.

As the word itself indicates, a discovery is a change from ignorance to knowledge, and it leads either to love or to hatred between persons destined for good or ill fortune. The most effective form of discovery is that which is accompanied by reversals, like the one in *Oedipus*. There are of course other forms of discovery, for what I have described may happen in relation to inanimate and trifling objects, and moreover it is possible to discover whether a person has done something or not. But the form of discovery most essentially related to the plot and action of the play is the one described above, for a discovery of this kind in combination with a reversal will carry with it either pity or fear, and it is such actions as these that, according to my definition, tragedy represents; and further, such a combination is likely to lead to a happy or an unhappy ending.

As it is persons who are involved in the discovery, it may be that only one person's identity is revealed to another, that of the second being already known. Sometimes, however, a natural recognition of two parties is necessary, as for example, when the identity of Iphigenia was made known to Orestes by the sending of the letter, and a second discovery was required to make him known to Iphigenia.

Two elements of plot, then, reversal and discovery, turn upon such incidents as these. A third is suffering, or calamity.

Of these three, reversal and discovery have already been defined. A calamity is an action of a destructive or painful nature, such as death openly represented, excessive suffering, wounding, and the like.

CHAPTER 12

The Main Parts of Tragedy

I SPOKE earlier of the various elements that are to be employed as the constituents of tragedy. The separate sections into which the work is divided are as follows: prologue, episode, exode, and choral song, the last being subdivided into parode and stasimon. These are common to all tragedies; songs from the actors and 'commoi', however, are a characteristic only of some tragedies.

The prologue is the whole of that part of a tragedy that precedes the parode, or first entry of the Chorus. An episode is the whole of that part of a tragedy that comes between complete choral songs. The exode is the whole of that part of a tragedy which is not followed by a song of the Chorus. In the choral sections the parode is the whole of the first utterance of the Chorus, and a stasimon is a choral song without anapaests or trochees. A 'commos' is a passage of lament in which both Chorus and actors take part.

These then are the separate sections into which the body of the tragedy is to be divided; I mentioned earlier the elements of which it must be composed.

CHAPTER 13

Tragic Action

FOLLOWING upon the points I have already made, I must go on to say what is to be aimed at and what guarded against in the construction of plots, and what are the sources of the tragic effect.

We saw that the structure of tragedy at its best should be complex, not simple, and that it should represent actions capable of awakening fear and pity – for this is a characteristic function of representations of this type. It follows in the first place that good men should not be shown passing from prosperity to misery, for this does not inspire fear or pity, it merely disgusts us. Nor should evil men be shown progressing from misery to prosperity. This is the most untragic of all plots, for it has none of the requisites of tragedy; it does not appeal to our humanity, or awaken pity or fear in us. Nor again should an utterly worthless man be seen failing from prosperity into misery. Such a course might indeed play upon our humane feelings, but it would not arouse either pity or fear; for our pity is awakened by undeserved misfortune, and our fear by that of someone just like ourselves – pity for the undeserving sufferer and fear for the man like ourselves – so that the situation in question would have nothing in it either pitiful or fearful.

There remains a mean between these extremes. This is the sort of man who is not conspicuous for virtue and justice, and whose fall into misery is not due to vice and depravity, but rather to some error, a man who enjoys prosperity and a high reputation, like Oedipus and Thyestes and other famous members of families like theirs.

Inevitably, then, the well-conceived plot will have a single interest, and not, as some say, a double. The change in fortune will be, not from misery to prosperity, but the reverse, from prosperity to misery, and it will be due, not to depravity, but to some great error either in such a man as I have described or in one better than this, but not worse. This is borne out by existing practice. For at first the poets treated any stories that came to hand, but nowadays the best tragedies are written about a handful of families, those of Alcmaeon, for example, and Oedipus and Orestes and Meleager and Thyestes and Telephus, and others whom it has befallen to suffer or inflict terrible experiences.

The best tragedies in the technical sense are constructed in this way. Those critics are on the wrong tack, therefore, who criticize Euripides for following such a procedure in his tragedies, and complain that many of them end in misfortune;

for, as I have said, this is the right ending. The strongest evidence of this is that on the stage and in the dramatic competitions plays of this kind, when properly worked out, are the most tragic of all, and Euripides, faulty as is his management of other points, is nevertheless regarded as the most tragic of our dramatic poets.

The next best type of structure, ranked first by some critics, is that which, like the *Odyssey*, has a double thread of plot, and ends in opposite ways for the good and the bad characters. It is considered the best only because of the feeble judgement of the audience, for the poets pander to the taste of the spectators. But this is not the pleasure that is proper to tragedy. It belongs rather to comedy, where those who have been the bitterest of enemies in the original story, Orestes and Aegisthus, for example, go off at the end as friends, and nobody is killed by anybody.

CHAPTER 14

Fear and Pity

FEAR and pity may be excited by means of spectacle; but they can also take their rise from the very structure of the action, which is the preferable method and the mark of a better dramatic poet. For the plot should be so ordered that even without seeing it performed anyone merely hearing what is afoot will shudder with fear and pity as a result of what is happening – as indeed would be the experience of anyone hearing the story of Oedipus. To produce this effect by means of stage-spectacle is less artistic, and requires the cooperation of the producer. Those who employ spectacle to produce an effect, not of fear, but of something merely monstrous, have nothing to do with tragedy, for not every kind of pleasure should be demanded of tragedy, but only that which is proper to it; and since the dramatic poet has by means of his representation to produce the tragic pleasure that is associated with pity and fear, it is obvious that this effect is bound up with the events of the plot.

Let us now consider what kinds of incident are to be

regarded as fearful or pitiable. Deeds that fit this description must of course involve people who are either friends to one another, or enemies, or neither. Now if a man injures his enemy, there is nothing pitiable either in his act or in his intention, except in so far as suffering is inflicted; nor is there if they are indifferent to each other. But when the sufferings involve those who are near and dear to one another, when for example brother kills brother, son father, mother son, or son mother, or if such a deed is contemplated, or something else of the kind is actually done, then we have a situation of the kind to be aimed at. Thus it will not do to tamper with the traditional stories, the murder of Clytemnestra by Orestes, for instance, and that of Eriphyle by Alcmaeon; on the other hand, the poet must use his imagination and handle the traditional material effectively.

I must explain more clearly what I mean by 'effectively'. The deed may be done by characters acting consciously and in full knowledge of the facts, as was the way of the early dramatic poets, when for instance Euripides made Medea kill her children. Or they may do it without realizing the horror of the deed until later, when they discover the truth; this is what Sophocles did with Oedipus. Here indeed the relevant incident occurs outside the action of the play; but it may be a part of the tragedy, as with Alcmaeon in Astydamas's play, or Telegonus in *The Wounded Odysseus*. A third alternative is for someone who is about to do a terrible deed in ignorance of the relationship to discover the truth before he does it. These are the only possibilities, for the deed must either be done or not done, and by someone either with or without knowledge of the facts.

The least acceptable of these alternatives is when someone in possession of the facts is on the point of acting but fails to do so, for this merely shocks us, and, since no suffering is involved, it is not tragic. Hence nobody is allowed to behave like this, or only seldom, as when Haemon fails to kill Creon in the *Antigone*. Next in order of effectiveness is when the deed is actually done, and here it is better that the character should act in ignorance and only learn the truth afterwards, for there is nothing in this to outrage our feelings, and the revelation comes as a surprise. However, the best method is the last, when, for example, in the *Cresphontes* Merope intends to kill her son, but recognizes him and does not do so; or when the same thing happens with brother and sister in *Iphigenia in Tauris*; or when, in the *Helle*, the son recognizes his mother when he is just about to betray her.

This then is the reason why, as I said before, our tragedies keep to a few families. For in their search for dramatic material it was by chance rather than by technical knowledge that the poets discovered how to gain tragic effects in their plots. And they are still obliged to have recourse to those families in which sufferings of the kind I have described have been experienced.

I have said enough now about the arrangement of the incidents in a tragedy and the type of plot it ought to have.

CHAPTER 15

The Characters of Tragedy

In characterization there are four things to aim at. First and foremost, the characters should be good. Now character will be displayed, as I have pointed out, if some preference is revealed in speech or action, and if it is a preference for what is good the character will be good. There can be goodness in every class of person; for instance, a woman or a slave may be good, though the one is possibly an inferior being and the other in general an insignificant one.

In the second place the portrayal should be appropriate. For example, a character may possess manly qualities, but it is not appropriate that a female character should be given manliness or cleverness.

Thirdly, the characters should be lifelike. This is not the same thing as making them good, or appropriate in the sense in which I have used the word.

And fourthly, they should be consistent. Even if the person who is being represented is inconsistent, and this trait is the basis of his character, he must nevertheless be portrayed as consistently inconsistent.

As an example of unnecessary badness of character, there is Menelaus in the *Orestes*. The character who behaves in an unsuitable and inappropriate way is exemplified in Odysseus' lament in the *Scylla*, and in Melanippe's speech. An inconsistent character is shown in *Iphigenia at Aulis*, for Iphigenia as a suppliant is quite unlike what she is later.

As in the arrangement of the incidents, so too in characterization one must always bear in mind what will be either necessary or probable; in other words, it should be necessary or probable that such and such a person should say or do such and such a thing, and similarly that this particular incident should follow on that.

Furthermore, it is obvious that the unravelling of the plot should arise from the circumstances of the plot itself, and not be brought about *ex machina*, as is done in the *Medea* and in the episode of the embarkation in the *Iliad*. The *deus ex machina* should be used only for matters outside the play proper, either for things that happened before it and that cannot be known by the human characters, or for things that are yet to come and that require to be foretold prophetically – for we allow to the gods the power to see all things. However, there should be nothing inexplicable about what happens, or if there must be, it should be kept outside the tragedy, as is done in Sophocles's *Oedipus*.[1]

Since tragedy is a representation of people who are better than the average, we must copy the good portrait-painters. These, while reproducing the distinctive appearance of their sitters and making likenesses, paint them better-looking than they are. In the same way the poet, in portraying men who are hot-tempered, or phlegmatic, or who have other defects of character, must bring out these qualities in them, and at the same time show them as decent people, as Agathon and Homer have portrayed Achilles.

These points must be carefully watched, as too must those means used to appeal to the eye, which are necessarily dependent on the poet's art; for here too it is often possible to make mistakes. However, enough has been said about these matters in my published works.

1. Aristotle is here referring to the fact that Oedipus remained for many years ignorant of the circumstances of Laius's death. Cf. Chapter 24, p. 70.

CHAPTER 16

The Different Kinds of Discovery

I HAVE already explained what I mean by discovery. Of the different kinds of discovery, the first is the least artistic, and is mostly used from sheer lack of invention; this is discovery by means of visible signs or tokens. These may be congenital marks, like 'the spearhead that the Earthborn bear', or 'stars', such as those that Carcinus uses in his *Thyestes*; or they may be acquired, whether marks on the body such as scars, or external objects such as necklaces – or, in the *Tyro*, the discovery by means of the cradle. However, some ways of using these tokens are better than others; for example, the discovery of Odysseus through his scar is made in one way by his nurse and in another way by the swineherds. These discoveries, when made merely to gain credence, are less effective, as are all types of discovery used for such intentions; better are those that are unexpected, as happens in the Washing Episode in the *Odyssey*.

The second class of discoveries are those which are manufactured by the poet, and which are inartistic for that reason. An example occurs in *Iphigenia in Tauris* when Orestes reveals who he is. While the identity of Iphigenia is revealed by means of the letter, Orestes himself is made to say what the poet here requires instead of its being done through the plot; and this is not far removed from the fault I spoke about a moment ago, for he might have brought some tokens as well. Another example is 'the voice of the shuttle' in Sophocles's *Tereus*.

A third kind is the discovery that is due to memory, when the sight of something leads to the required understanding. Thus in *The Cyprians*, by Dicaeogenes, Teucer bursts into tears on seeing the portrait, and in *The Tale of Alcinous* Odysseus also weeps when the sound of the minstrel's harp reawakens the past for him, and this is how these two are recognized.

The fourth kind is the result of reasoning, such as is found in *The Choephori*: 'Someone who is like me has come; no one is like me except Orestes; therefore it is Orestes who has come.'

Another example is what the sophist Polyidus suggests for the *Iphigenia*, for it is likely enough that Orestes should reason that, as his sister was sacrificed, so too it was his fate to be sacrificed. Then there is the episode in the *Tydeus* of Theodectes when the father has come to find his son, and realizes that he is himself to die; or that in the *Phineidae* where, on seeing a particular place, the women infer that they are fated to die there, for it was there that they had been exposed at birth.

There is also a fictitious form of discovery arising from the fallacious reasoning of the parties concerned, as in *Odysseus the False Messenger*; he said that he would know the bow, which he had not seen; but it was false reasoning to suppose from this that he would know it again.[1]

Of all the forms of discovery, the best is that which is brought about by the incidents themselves, when the startling disclosure results from events that are probable, as happens in Sophocles's *Oedipus*, and again in the *Iphigenia* – for it was quite probable that she should wish to send off a letter. Discovery scenes of this kind are the only ones that dispense with such artificial aids as tokens and necklaces. The next best are those that depend on reasoning.

CHAPTER 17

Some Rules for the Tragic Poet

IN putting together his plots and working out the kind of speech to go with them, the poet should as far as possible keep the scene before his eyes. In this way, seeing everything very vividly, as though he were himself an eyewitness of the events, he will find what is appropriate, and will be least likely to overlook inconsistencies. Evidence of this is the censure laid on Carcinus, by whom Amphiaraus was made to come out of a temple; this would have escaped notice if the episode had not

1. The text here seems to be defective, and it is difficult to render it satisfactorily. Bywater translates: 'He said he should know the bow – which he had not seen; but to suppose from that that he would know it again (as though he had once seen it) was bad reasoning.'

been actually seen, but the audience took offence at it, and the play was not a success on the stage.

As far as possible, too, the dramatic poet should carry out the appropriate gestures as he composes his speeches, for of writers with equal abilities those who can actually make themselves feel the relevant emotions will be the most convincing – agitation or rage will be most vividly reproduced by one who is himself agitated or in a passion. Hence poetry is the product either of a man of great natural ability or of one not wholly sane; the one is highly responsive, the other possessed.

As for the stories, whether he is taking over something ready-made or inventing for himself, the poet should first plan in general outline, and then expand by working out appropriate episodes. What I mean by planning in outline may be illustrated from the *Iphigenia*, as follows: A young girl was offered as a sacrifice, and mysteriously disappeared from the view of her sacrificers; she was set down in another country, where it was the custom to sacrifice strangers to the goddess, and became the priestess of this rite. Some time later it happened that the priestess's brother arrived (the fact that the oracle had for a certain reason told him to go there and the purpose of his journey are matters that lie outside the plot). On his arrival he was seized, and was about to be sacrificed, when he revealed who he was, either in the way that Euripides makes it happen or, as Polyidus suggests, by making the not unnatural remark that not only his sister, it seemed, was fated to be sacrificed, but himself too; and thus he was saved.

When he has reached this stage the poet may supply the proper names and fill in the episodes, making sure that they are appropriate, like the fit of madness in Orestes which led to his capture, and his escape by the device of the purification.

In plays the episodes are of course short; in epic poetry they are what supply the requisite length. The story of the *Odyssey*, for example, is not a long one. A man is kept away from his home for many years; Poseidon is watching him with a jealous eye, and he is alone. The state of affairs at home is that his wealth is being squandered by his wife's suitors, and plots are being laid against his son's life. After being buffeted by many storms he returns home and reveals his identity; he falls upon his enemies and destroys them, but preserves his own life. There you have the essential story of the *Odyssey*; the rest of the poem is made up of episodes.

CHAPTER 18

Further Rules for the Tragic Poet

EVERY tragedy has its complication and its denouement. The complication consists of the incidents lying outside the plot, and often some of those inside it, and the rest is the denouement. By complication I mean the part of the story from the beginning to the point immediately preceding the change to good or bad fortune; by denouement the part from the onset of this change to the end. In the *Lynceus* of Theodectes, for instance, the complication is what happened before the events of the play proper, together with the seizure of the boy and that in turn of the parents, and the denouement extends from the accusation of murder to the end.

Properly speaking, tragedies should be classed as similar or dissimilar according to their plots, that is to say, according to their similarity in complication and denouement. Many poets are skilful in complicating their plots but clumsy in unravelling them; a constant mastery of both techniques is what is required.

There are four kinds of tragedy, a number corresponding to that of the constituent parts that I spoke about. There is complex tragedy, which depends entirely on reversal and discovery; tragedy of suffering, as in the various plays on Ajax or Ixion; tragedy of character, as in *The Phthiotides* and the *Peleus*; and fourthly, spectacular tragedy, as in *The Phorcides*, in the *Prometheus*, and in plays with scenes in Hades. The poet should try to include all these elements, or, failing that, as many as possible of the most important, especially since it is the fashion nowadays to find fault with poets; just because there have been poets who excelled in the individual parts of tragedy, the critics expect that a single man should outdo each of them in his special kind of excellence.

Bearing in mind what has often been said, the dramatic poet

must be careful not to give his tragedy an epic structure, by which I mean one with a multiplicity of stories – as though one were to attempt a plot covering the whole story of the *Iliad.* By reason of its length, the *Iliad* can allow the proper development of its various parts, but in plays the results of such attempts are disappointing, as is proved by experience. For all the poets who have dramatized the destruction of Troy in its entirety, and not, like Euripides, only parts of it, or the whole of the story of Niobe, and not as Aeschylus did it, have either failed utterly or done badly in the dramatic competitions; and indeed even a play by Agathon was a failure for this alone. And yet in the handling of reversals and of simple plots these poets may succeed wonderfully in getting the effect they want, that is, one which is tragic and appeals to our humanity. This happens when the clever man who is also wicked is outwitted, as Sisyphus was, or when the brave man who is also unscrupulous is worsted; and this is a likely enough result, as Agathon points out, for it is quite likely that many things should happen contrary to likelihood.

The Chorus should be regarded as one of the actors; it should be a part of the whole, and should assume a share in the action, as happens in Sophocles, but not in Euripides. With other playwrights the choral songs may have no more to do with the plot in hand than with any other tragedy; they are mere choral interludes, according to the practice first introduced by Agathon. But what difference is there between the singing of interpolated songs like these and the transference of a speech or a whole episode from one play to another?

CHAPTER 19

Thought and Diction

Now that the other parts of tragedy have been dealt with, it remains to say something about diction and thought. As far as thought is concerned, enough has been said about it in my treatise on rhetoric, for it more properly belongs to that study. Thought includes all the effects that have to be produced by means of language; among these are proof and refutation, the awakening of emotions such as pity, fear, anger, and the like, and also exaggeration and depreciation. It is clear, too, that in the action of the play the same principles should be observed whenever it is necessary to produce effects of pity or terror, or of greatness or probability – with this difference, however, that here the effects must be made without verbal explanation, while the others are produced by means of language coming from the lips of a speaker, and are dependent on the use of language. For where would be the need of a speaker if the required effects could be conveyed without the use of language?

As for diction, one branch of study is the various forms of expression, an understanding of which belongs to the art of elocution and is necessary to the practitioner of this art: I refer to such things as a command, a prayer, a statement, a threat, a question, an answer, and so on. The poet's art is not seriously criticized according to his knowledge or ignorance of these things. For what would anyone think is wrong about the words which Protagoras censures on the grounds that the poet, intending a prayer, actually gives a command when he says, 'Sing of the wrath, Goddess'? For, says Protagoras, to order a person to do or not to do something is a command. However, we may pass this topic over as one which, though it may be relevant to some other art, is not so to the art of poetry.

CHAPTER 20

Some Linguistic Definitions

LANGUAGE in general is made up of the following parts: the letter, the syllable, the connecting-word, the article, the noun, the verb, the inflexion or case, and the phrase or proposition.

A letter is an indivisible sound, not just any such sound, but one from which intelligible language may be produced; animals also, it is true, utter indivisible sounds, but none that I should describe as a letter. The different forms of this sound are the vowel, the semi-vowel, and the mute letter or consonant. A vowel is a letter which has an audible sound without any contact between two of the organs of speech. A semi-vowel (S or R, for instance) is given audible sound by such a contact. A mute is a letter which even with such contact has no sound of its own, but which becomes audible when combined with letters which possess sound; examples are G and D. The letters differ in sound according to the shape of the mouth and the places where they are produced; according as they are aspirated or not aspirated; according to their length or shortness; according as they have an acute, a grave, or a circumflex accent. However, the detailed study of these matters is the province of the metrist.

A syllable is a sound-unit without meaning, made up of a mute and a sounded letter; for GR without an A is as much a syllable as it is with an A, as in GRA. But these distinctions are also the concern of metrical theory.

A connecting-word is a sound-unit without significance which neither hinders nor helps the production of a single significant utterance from the combination of several sounds, and which should not be put at the beginning of a phrase standing by itself; examples are *μέν*, *δή*, *τοί*, and *δέ*.[1] Alternatively it is a sound without significance capable of producing a single significant utterance from the combination of several sounds which are themselves significant; examples are *ἀμφί* and *περί* and similar words.[2]

An article is a sound without significance which indicates the beginning or the end of a speech, or a dividing-point in it, and its natural position is at either end or in the middle.

A noun is a composite of sounds with a meaning; it is independent of time, and none of its individual parts has a meaning in its own right. For in compounds we do not give separate meanings to the parts; in the name 'Theodore', for instance, the *dore* part has in itself no meaning.

A verb is a composite of sounds with a meaning; it is concerned with time, and, as was the case with nouns, none of its

1. These particles, though virtually untranslatable by single English words, indicate particular relationships between the phrases or clauses that they link.

2. Both words (*amphi, peri*) mean 'about', 'around', and they are presumably connecting-words in that they are prepositions linking words in special relationships.

individual parts has a meaning in its own right. The words 'man' and 'white' give no indication of time, but 'walks' and 'has walked' indicate respectively present and past time.

Case or inflexion in a noun or verb is that which gives the sense of 'of' or 'to' a thing, and the like, or indicates whether it relates to one or many, as with 'man' and 'men'. Alternatively it may signify types of intonation, as in question or command; 'walked?' and 'walk!' represent verbal inflexions of this kind.

A phrase or proposition is a composite of sounds with a meaning, and some parts of it have a meaning of their own. Not every proposition is made up of verbs and nouns – the definition of a man, for example; it is possible for a proposition to exist without verbs, and yet some part of it will always have a meaning of its own, as 'Cleon' has in the proposition 'Cleon walks'. A proposition may represent unity in one of two ways, either in that it implies one thing, or in that it achieves unity by a conjunction of several factors; the unity of the *Iliad*, for example, results from such a conjunction, that of the definition of a man from its signifying one thing.

CHAPTER 21

Poetic Diction

NOUNS may be classified as simple, by which I mean those made up of elements which individually have no meaning, like the word 'earth' (γῆ), or as double or compound. These compounds may take the form either of a part which has a meaning combined with one which has no meaning – although within the compound no part has a separate meaning – or of parts which all have meanings. A noun may be triple or quadruple or multiple in form, like many of our more grandiose names, for example, Hermocaïcoxanthus.

Every noun is either a word in current use or a foreign loan-word, a metaphor or an ornamental word, a poetic coinage or a word that has been expanded or abbreviated or otherwise altered.

By a word in current use I mean a word that everybody uses,

and by a loan-word one that other peoples use. Obviously the same word can be both current and a loan-word, though not in relation to the same people; to the Cypriots, for example, *sigunon* is the current word for a spear, but to us it is a loan-word.

Metaphor is the application to one thing of a name belonging to another thing; the transference may be from the genus to the species, from the species to the genus, or from one species to another, or it may be a matter of analogy. As an example of transference from genus to species I give 'Here lies my ship', for lying at anchor is a species of lying. Transference from species to genus is seen in 'Odysseus has indeed performed ten thousand noble deeds', for 'ten thousand', which is a particular large number, is used here instead of the word 'many'. Transference from one species to another is seen in 'Draining off the life with the bronze' and 'Severing with the unyielding bronze'; here 'draining off' is used for 'severing', and 'severing' for 'draining off', and both are species of 'taking away'.

I explain metaphor by analogy as what may happen when of four things the second stands in the same relationship to the first as the fourth to the third; for then one may speak of the fourth instead of the second, and the second instead of the fourth. And sometimes people will add to the metaphor a qualification appropriate to the term which has been replaced. Thus, for example, a cup stands in the same relationship to Dionysus as a shield to Ares, and one may therefore call the cup Dionysus's shield and the shield Ares's cup. Or again, old age is to life as evening is to day, and so one may call the evening the old age of the day, or name it as Empedocles named it[1]; and one may call old age the evening of life or the sunset of life. In some cases there is no name for some of the terms of the analogy, but the metaphor can be used just the same. For example, to scatter corn is called sowing, but there is no word for the sun's scattering of its flame; however, this stands in the same relationship to sunlight as sowing does to corn, and hence the expression, 'sowing his god-created flame'.

This kind of metaphor can also be used in another way;

1. The words that Empedocles used in this connexion are not extant; they must have been something like, but not identical with, 'the old age of the day'.

having called an object by the name of something else, one can deny it one of its attributes – for example, call the shield, not Ares's cup, but a wineless cup.

A poetic coinage is a word which has not been in use among a people, but has been invented by the poet himself. There seem to be words of this kind, such as 'sprouters' for horns, and 'supplicator' for priest.

A word is expanded when it uses a longer vowel than is normal to it or takes on an extra syllable, and it is abbreviated when some part of it has been removed. Examples of expansion are *πόληος* for *πολέως* and *Πηληιάδεω* for *Πηλείδου*, and of abbreviation *κρῖ* and *δῶ*, and *ὄψ* in *μία γίνεται ἀμφοτέρων ὄψ* ('the faces of the pair become as one').[1] An altered word is one in which part is left unchanged and part is coined, as when *δεξιτερόν* is used for *δεξιόν* in *δεξιτερὸν κατὰ μαζόν* ('on the right breast').

Of the nouns themselves some are masculine, some feminine, and some neuter. Masculine are all that end in N (n), P (r), and *Σ* (s), and in the compounds of *Σ*, that is, the two letters *Ψ* (ps) and *Ξ* (x). Feminine are all those ending in the vowels that are always long, such as H (ē) and *Ω* (ō), and in A among the vowels which may be lengthened. Thus there are equal numbers of masculine and feminine endings, for *Ψ* and *Ξ* are equivalent to *Σ*. No noun ends in a mute consonant or in a short vowel. Only three end in *i*: *μέλι* ('honey'), *κόμμι* ('gum'), and *πέπερι* ('pepper'); and five end in *Υ* (u). The neuters may end in these vowels, and in N (n), P (r), and *Σ* (s).

CHAPTER 22

Diction and Style

THE greatest virtue of diction is to be clear without being commonplace. The clearest diction is that which consists of words in everyday use, but this is commonplace, as can be seen

1. The expanded and normal genitive singular forms of *πόλις* ('city') and *Πηλείδης* ('son of Peleus') and the abbreviated *κρῖ* for *κριθή* ('barley'), *δῶ* for *δῶμα* ('house'), and *ὄψ* for *ὄψις* ('eye', 'face').

in the poetry of Cleophon and Sthenelus. On the other hand, a diction abounding in unfamiliar usages has dignity, and is raised above the everyday level. By unfamiliar usages I mean loan-words, metaphors, expanded forms, and anything else that is out of the ordinary. However, the exclusive use of forms of this kind would result either in a riddle or in barbarism – a riddle if they were all metaphorical, barbarism if they were all importations. The very essence of a riddle is to express facts in an impossible combination of language. This cannot be done by a mere succession of ordinary terms, but it can by the use of metaphors, as in the riddle, 'I saw a man welding bronze on another man with fire'[1] and similar examples. In the same way, the use of importations leads to barbarism. What is needed, then, is some mixture of these various elements. For the one kind will prevent the language from being mean and commonplace, that is, the unusual words, the metaphors, the ornamental terms, and the other figures I have described, while the everyday words give the necessary clarity.

Among the most effective means of achieving both clarity of diction and a certain dignity is the use of expanded, abbreviated, and altered forms of words; the unfamiliarity due to this deviation from normal usages will raise the diction above the commonplace, while the retention of some part of the normal forms will make for clarity. It is not good criticism, therefore, to censure this type of language and to ridicule the poet for using it, as the elder Eucleides did when he said that it would be easy to write poetry if one were allowed to lengthen syllables whenever one liked, and when he burlesqued this style in the lines, *'Επιχάρην εἶδον Μαραθῶναδε βαδίζοντα*, and *οὐκ ἄν γ' ἐράμενος τὸν ἐκείνου ἐλλέβορον.*[2]

1. The solution to this riddle is a bronze cupping-bowl. Heated and placed over a small incision, it would as it cooled draw out the blood.

2. The text is corrupt, and translators usually make no attempt to translate the two quotations, though the first may perhaps be rendered, 'I saw Epichares on his way to Marathon.' However, Aristotle's point is probably clear enough without translation. Homer occasionally lengthens a short vowel 'by position', as when he begins *Odyssey* XII, 423 with *ἐπίτονος*; no doubt other poets did so more frequently. Eucleides burlesques this practice by devising passages which can be read as verse if several short vowels are lengthened.

The too obvious use of these tricks, then, is ridiculous; moderation is necessary in all kinds of writing alike. The same effect would be produced by anyone using metaphors, unfamiliar loan-words and other such devices ineptly and for the mere sake of raising a laugh. How great a difference is made by their being used properly may be seen in epic poetry if one replaces them with ordinary everyday words in the verse; anyone substituting common words for the unfamiliar words or for the metaphors and other devices mentioned would see the truth of what I am saying. For instance, Aeschylus and Euripides wrote the same line of iambics, with the change only of a single word; an unfamiliar word was substituted for an ordinary one, and the new line is beautiful where the old was commonplace. This was the line as Aeschylus wrote it in his *Philoctetes*:

φαγέδαινα ἥ μου σάρκας ἐσθίει ποδός.[1]

For ἐσθίει ('eats') Euripides put θοινᾶται ('feasts upon'). Just suppose that in the line

νῦν δέ μ' ἐὼν ὀλίγος τε καὶ οὐτιδανὸς καὶ ἀεικής[2]

one were to use everyday words and say,

νῦν δέ μ' ἐὼν μικρός τε καὶ ἀσθενικὸς καὶ ἀειδής.

Or suppose that for this line,

δίφρον ἀεικέλιον καταθεὶς ὀλίγην τε τράπεζαν,[3]

one were to read

δίφρον μοχθηρὸν καταθεὶς μικράν τε τράπεζαν.

Or that for ἠιόνες βοόωσιν ('the sea-shore is thundering') one were to read ἠιόνες κράζουσιν ('the sea-shore is crying out').

1. 'The ulcer that eats the flesh of my foot.' The Philoctetes plays of Aeschylus and Euripides are lost.

2. *Odyssey* IX, 515 (except that ἄκικυς has been misquoted as ἀεικής). 'And now a puny fellow, ungoodly and of no account, [has blinded me].' Aristotle's inferior version might be rendered, 'And now a little, weak, ugly fellow ...'.

3. *Odyssey* XX, 259. 'Having placed for him an unseemly stool and an insignificant table.' In the inferior version, 'Having placed for him a shabby stool and a little table.'

Then again, Ariphrades ridiculed the tragedians for using expressions that no one would use in ordinary speech, such as *δωμάτων ἄπο* ('from the houses away') instead of *ἀπὸ δωμάτων* ('away from the houses'), and *σέθεν* ('thine'), and *ἐγὼ δέ νιν* ('I [married] her'), and *Ἀχιλλέως πέρι* instead of *περὶ Ἀχιλλέως* ('about Achilles'), and the like. By the very fact of not being normal idiom, all such usages as these raise the diction above the level of the commonplace; but Ariphrades failed to see this.

It is a fine thing to be able to make proper use of all the devices I have mentioned, as also of compound words and unfamiliar importations, but far the most important thing to master is the use of metaphor. This is the one thing that cannot be learnt from anyone else, and it is the mark of great natural ability, for the ability to use metaphor well implies a perception of resemblances.

Of the different types of words, compound forms are best suited to dithyrambs, unfamiliar borrowings to heroic verse, and metaphorical usages to iambic verse. All these may, indeed, be fittingly used in heroic verse; but in iambic verse, which as far as possible models itself on speech, the only appropriate terms are those that anyone might use in speeches, and these are words in current use, metaphors, and ornamental words.

I need say no more now about tragedy and the art of representation by means of action.

CHAPTER 23

Epic Poetry

As for the art of representation in the form of narrative verse, clearly its plots should be dramatically constructed, like those of tragedies; they should centre upon a single action, whole and complete, and having a beginning, a middle, and an end, so that like a single complete organism the poem may produce its own special kind of pleasure. Nor should epics be constructed like the common run of histories, in which it is not the exposition of a single action that is required, but of a single period, and of everything that happened to one or more persons during this period, however unrelated the various events may have been. For just as the sea-battle at Salamis and the engagement with the Carthaginians in Sicily took place at the same time, but did not work towards the same end, so too in any sequence of time events may follow one another without producing any one single result. Yet most of our poets use the methods of the historian.

In this respect, too, Homer seems, as I have already described him, divinely inspired beyond all other poets, in that, although the Trojan War had a beginning and an end, he did not attempt to put the whole of it into his poem; it would have been too large a subject to be taken in all at once, and, if he had limited its length, the diversity of its incident would have made it too complicated. As it is, he has selected one part of the story, and has introduced many incidents from other parts as episodes, such as the Catalogue of Ships and other episodes with which he gives variety to the poem. Other epic poets write about one man, or a single period of time, or a single action made up of many separate incidents; among such poets are the authors of the *Cypria* and *The Little Iliad*. Thus, while only one tragedy could be made out of the *Iliad* or the *Odyssey*, several might be made out of the *Cypria*, and more than eight out of *The Little Iliad*: an *Award of the Arms*, a *Philoctetes*, a *Neoptolemus*, an *Eurypylus*, an *Odysseus the Beggar*, a *Laconian Women*, a *Sack of Troy*, and a *Departure of the Fleet*, not to mention a *Sinon* and a *Trojan Women*.

CHAPTER 24

Epic Poetry (Continued)

FURTHERMORE, epic poetry must divide into the same types as tragedy, that is, the simple, the complex, that which turns on character, and that which turns on suffering. With the exception of song and spectacle, its constituent parts must also be the same, for it needs reversals and discoveries and tragic incidents, and moreover the thought and diction must be of good quality. All these things Homer was the first to use, and he did so with skill. Of his two poems the one, the *Iliad*, is simple in structure and a story of suffering, the other, the *Odyssey*, is complex (for it has discovery scenes throughout) and turns on character; moreover, they surpass all other poems in diction and in quality of thought.

Epic differs from tragedy both in the length of the composition and in the metre used. The limitations as to length that have already been indicated will suffice; that is to say, it must be possible for the beginning and the end to be embraced within a single view, and this will be the case if the poems are shorter than the ancient epics, but stretch to the length of a group of tragedies offered at a single hearing. It is the special advantage of epic that it may be of considerable length. In tragedy it is not possible to represent several parts of the story as taking place simultaneously, but only the part that is actually being performed on the stage by the actors; epic poetry, on the other hand, being narrative, is able to represent many incidents that are being simultaneously enacted, and, provided they are relevant, they increase the weight of the poem, and give it the merits of grandeur, variety of interest, and diversity in its episodes. Monotony will soon bore an audience and ruin the effect of a tragedy on the stage.

Experience has shown that the heroic hexameter is the right metre for epic. If anyone were to write a narrative poem in some other metre, or in a variety of metres, the incongruity would be glaring, for of all metres, the heroic hexameter has the greatest weight and stability, which enables it most readily to admit unfamiliar borrowings and metaphorical usages; and in this respect, too, the narrative form of representation is better than any other. The iambic and the trochaic tetrameter are metres suitable to the expression of movement, the latter being a dancing measure, while the former lends itself to the dramatic representation of action. However, it would be even more out of place to mix several metres, as Chaeremon did. And so no one has ever written a poem on the grand scale in any other than the heroic measure; as I have said, nature herself teaches us to choose the right metre for our purposes.

Admirable as he is in so many other respects, Homer is especially so in this: he is the only poet who recognizes what part he himself ought to play in his poems. The poet should speak as little as possible in his own person, for it is not in that way that he represents actions. Other poets appear in their own character throughout their poems, and little of what they write is impersonal representation. But after a few prefatory words, Homer at once introduces a man, a woman, or some other person, no one of them lacking in character but each with distinctive characteristics.

The marvellous should of course be represented in tragedy, but epic poetry, where the persons acting the story are not before our eyes, may include more of the inexplicable, which is the chief element in the marvellous. If it were brought on to the stage there would be something ridiculous about the pursuit of Hector, with the Greeks merely standing there instead of pursuing him, and Achilles restraining them with a shake of the head; in the poem the absurdity is not apparent. The marvellous is a source of pleasure, as is shown by the fact that in passing on a piece of news everyone will add something of his own as an agreeable extra.

Above all, Homer has taught other poets how to tell untruths as they ought to be told, that is, by the use of fallacy. If one thing exists because another exists, or happens because this other happens, people think that, if the consequent exists or happens, the antecedent will also exist; but this is not the case. Thus if a proposition were untrue, but there was something else which must be true or must happen if the proposition were true, then it is this something else that we should lay down as a fact; for the mind, knowing it to be true, may fallaciously infer the truth of the original proposition. There is an example of this in the episode of the Washing in the *Odyssey*.[1]

Probable impossibilities are to be preferred to improbable possibilities. Stories should not be made up of irrational incidents; anything irrational should as far as possible be excluded,

1. *Odyssey* XIX, 164–260. Odysseus tells Penelope that he is one Aethon, a Cretan, who entertained Odysseus when he was blown off his course on the way to Troy. She believes him because he accurately describes Odysseus's dress and appearance and his squire Eurybates. The fallacy is that she infers the truth of the antecedent from the truth of the consequent.

or if not, at least kept out of the tale proper, like Oedipus's not knowing how Laius died; not admitted into the play, as in the *Electra* we have the messenger's report of the Pythian Games, or in the *Mysians* the business of the man's coming from Tegea to Mysia without speaking. To say that otherwise the plot would have been spoilt is ridiculous; plots like these should not be devised in the first instance, but if a poet does employ such a plot and it appears that it could have been worked out more reasonably, then his endeavour is entirely misplaced. Even in the *Odyssey* the irrational elements in the episode of Odysseus's being set ashore in Ithaca would obviously not have been acceptable if they had been treated by an inferior poet; as it is, Homer has managed to disguise their absurdity, charming it away by his other excellences.[1]

The diction should be elaborated only in 'neutral' sections, that is, in passages where neither character nor thought is in question, for diction that is too brilliant may obscure the presentation of character and thought.

CHAPTER 25

Critical Objections and their Answers

THE way to get a clear idea of the various critical problems – their number, their nature, and the solutions to be offered – is to look at them as follows. Like the painter or any other artist, the poet aims at the representation of life; necessarily, therefore, he must always represent things in one of three ways: either as they were or are, or as they are said to be or seem to be, or as they ought to be. His medium is language, with the possible admixture of unfamiliar terms and metaphors and the various other modifications of language that we allow to poets. We must remember, too, that there are not the same standards of correctness in poetry as in political theory or any

1. *Odyssey* XIII, 116 ff. The critics considered it irrational that Odysseus should not have awakened when the Phaeacians ran their ship aground in the harbour of Phorcys in Ithaca and lifted him out on to the sand.

other art. In poetry there are two kinds of fault, the one kind essential, the other incidental. If the poet has undertaken to represent some particular fact, and has gone astray through sheer lack of skill, that is an essential fault. But if his error lies in what he sets out to do, if for instance he represents a horse with both its offside legs thrown forward, then that is an error in some special branch of knowledge (it could perhaps be medicine or some other technical subject); or alternatively impossibilities of some other kind may have been depicted, but no essential fault is involved. These then are the points to be considered in resolving problems of criticism.

Taking first problems relating to the essentials of the poetic art: if the poet has depicted something impossible, he is at fault indeed, but he is justified in doing it as long as the art attains its true end, as I have described it, that is, as long as it makes this or some other part of the poem more striking. The pursuit of Hector is a case in point. If, however, this end could have been achieved just as well, or better, by conforming to the requirements of the art, then there is no justification for the fault, for if possible a poem should be entirely free of faults. Then again, which of the two kinds of fault is actually in question, one that concerns the essentials of the poetic art or one that is merely incidental? It is a less serious fault not to know that a female deer has no horns than to make an unrecognizable picture of one.

Suppose next that a description is criticized as not being true. The answer might be, 'No, but it ought to be like that' – just as Sophocles said that he drew men as they ought to be, whereas Euripides drew them as they are. However, if neither of these claims fits the case, then an appeal might be made to tradition, as for example with the tales about the gods. Now it is possible that these tales are neither true nor improve on the truth, but are what Xenophanes said of them;[1] nevertheless they are in accordance with tradition. In other cases the answer might be, not that it is better than the truth, but that it represents things as they used to be – for instance in the matter of the

1. Xenophanes (sixth century B.C.) attacked the polytheism and anthropomorphism of the traditional Greek religion.

spears: 'Their spears stood upright on their butt ends'; for that was then the custom, as it still is among the Illyrians.

In deciding whether something that has been said or done is morally good or bad, not only should we pay regard to the goodness or badness of the saying or deed itself, but we should also take into account the persons by whom and to whom it was said or done, the occasion, the means, and the reason – whether, for example, to bring about a greater good, or to avert a greater evil.

Some criticisms may be answered by examining the diction; an example is the rare word in *οὐρῆας μὲν πρῶτον*, where it is possible that by *οὐρῆας* Homer means 'sentinels', not 'mules'. Then there is Dolon, *ὅς ῥ' ἦ τοι εἶδος μὲν ἔην κακός* ('who indeed was evil of form'); here the reference is perhaps not to his deformed body but to his ugly face, for the Cretans use *εὐειδές* ('fair-formed') with the sense of *εὐπρόσωπον* ('fair-faced'). Then again, *ζωρότερον δὲ κέραιε* ('stronger mix the wine') may mean 'more quickly mix the wine', and not have the sense of 'unmixed', as though for drunkards.

Other expressions are metaphorical. For example, in Homer's words, *ἄλλοι μέν ῥα θεοί τε καὶ ἀνέρες εὗδον* <*ἅπαντες*> *παννύχιοι*,[1] bearing in mind that he also says, *ἦ τοι ὅτ' ἐς πεδίον τὸ Τρωικὸν ἀθρήσειεν, αὐλῶν συρίγγων τε ὅμαδόν*, the word *ἅπαντες* ('all') is metaphorically used instead of *πολλοί* ('many'), for *πᾶν* ('all') is a species of *πολύ* ('much'). So too *οἴη δ' ἄμμορος* ('alone without a share)'[2] is metaphorical, for the best-known representative is referred to as the only one.

Again, the solution of the difficulty may be a matter of how to read a word, as with the changes of Hippias of Thasos in

1. *Iliad* II, 1–2. 'Then all other gods and men slept through the night.' The quotation differs slightly from our text of the *Iliad*; moreover, Aristotle seems to be confusing it with the very similar opening to *Iliad* X, since the quotation that follows ('And indeed when he gazed at the Trojan plain [Agamemnon wondered at] the sound of flutes and pipes and the noise [of men]') comes from lines 11–13 of that book. Aristotle's point is that 'all' is used metaphorically for 'many', for if the Trojans are revelling all men cannot be asleep.

2. *Iliad* XVIII, 489. 'She that alone has no share in the baths of the Ocean.' The reference is to the Great Bear; but as the other northern constellations also do not set, the reference to the Great Bear as the only one is metaphorical.

δίδομεν δέ οἱ ('and we grant him')[1] and τὸ μὲν οὗ καταπύθεται ὄμβρῳ ('part of which rots in the rain');[2] or again of word-grouping, as in Empedocles: αἶψα δὲ θνήτ' ἐφύοντο, τὰ πρὶν μάθον ἀθάνατα ζωρά τε πρὶν κέκρητο;[3] or of ambiguity, as in παρῴχηκεν δὲ πλέω νύξ,[4] where πλέω is ambiguous; or, finally, of normal linguistic usage – wine mixed with water, for example, is normally called wine, and so one finds the phrase 'a greave of newly-wrought tin'[5] and workers of metal are called blacksmiths, and so too Ganymede is said to pour wine for Zeus, although the gods do not drink wine.[6] But this may perhaps be explained as a metaphorical usage.

Whenever a word seems to involve some inconsistency of meaning, we ought to consider in how many ways it may be interpreted in the context – in, for example, τῇ ῥ' ἔσχετο χάλκεον ἔγχος ('there the brazen spear was stopped'), how many ways there are of taking 'there ... was stopped'.[7] We

1. The reference is to *Iliad* II, 15 – where, however, our text is different. Zeus is telling the Dream-god how to lure Agamemnon to disaster. By reading δίδομεν as διδόμεν Hippias turns it into an infinitive used as an imperative, which transfers the telling of a falsehood from Zeus to the Dream-god and thus preserves Zeus's reputation for veracity.

2. *Iliad* XXIII, 328. The reference is to an old withered stump which, Homer says, does not rot in the rain. This seems incredible. However, if Homer's οὐ ('not') is changed to οὗ ('of which'), as Aristotle quotes it, the difficulty is removed.

3. 'And soon they grew mortal that formerly learned immortal ways, and pure formerly intermingled.' This necessarily awkward translation illustrates what appears to be the problem of word-order at issue – whether 'formerly' is to be taken with 'pure' (as seems preferable), or with 'intermingled'. Empedocles is speaking of the elements.

4. *Iliad* X, 253. 'And the night has advanced more [than two thirds, but the third part is still left].' The difficulty is that, if *more* than two thirds had passed, a third could not be left. It has been suggested that πλέω is to be taken, not as 'more', but as 'full': 'the night has advanced full two thirds.'

5. The greaves are made of bronze, an alloy of tin and copper, which is here called by the name of the more important metal.

6. The gods drink nectar, not wine; but in accordance with what is said in Chapter 21, the drink is metaphorically called 'wine'.

7. *Iliad* XX, 272 – at the end of a passage describing how Achilles took on his shield a spear hurled with great force by Aeneas. The shield consisted of a layer of gold, two of bronze, and two of tin. Homer says

should think how best we shall avoid the fault described by Glaucon when he says that critics make unreasonable presuppositions, and go on to draw conclusions from their own adverse comments on the poet; if his words conflict with the conclusions they have thus reached, they censure him as though he had actually said what they ascribe to him. This is what has happened in the case of Icarius. Some critics believe that he was a Spartan, and therefore think it strange that Telemachus should not have met him when he went to Sparta. But the truth of the matter may be, as the Cephallenians say, that Odysseus married in their country, and that the name was Icadius, not Icarius. Thus it is probably through a mistake that this particular difficulty has arisen.

Generally speaking, then, the 'impossible' has to be justified on grounds either of poetic effect, or of an attempt to improve on reality, or of accepted tradition. As far as poetic effect is concerned, a convincing impossibility is preferable to an unconvincing possibility. Even though it is impossible that there should be such people as Zeuxis used to paint, yet it would be better if there were, for the ideal type ought to be surpassingly good.

Accepted tradition may justify the use of the irrational, as may the plea that there are times when it is not irrational, for it is probable enough that things should happen contrary to probability. Verbal inconsistencies should be examined in the same way as refutations in dialectical exercises in order to see whether the poet means the same thing, in the same relation and with the same significance as you mean yourself, before you blame him for contradicting either what he has himself said or what an intelligent man would assume to be true. However, irrationality and depravity are rightly censured when there is no need for them and they are not properly used, as no good use is made of the irrationality in Euripides's introduction of Aegeus in the *Medea*, or of the depravity of Menelaus in the *Orestes*.

There are, then, five grounds on which a passage may be

---

that the spear drove through two layers, but was held by the gold – which would presumably be the outside layer. Bywater's solution of the difficulty is the suggestion that the spear was in fact held by the gold, even though its point pierced to the layers beneath.

censured: that it is impossible, irrational, immoral, inconsistent, or technically at fault. And the answers are to be studied in the light of the twelve criteria that I have already enumerated.

CHAPTER 26

Epic and Tragedy Compared

It may be asked which of the two forms of representation is the better, the epic or the tragic. If the better form is the less vulgar, and the less vulgar is always that which is designed to appeal to the better type of audience, then it is obvious that the form that appeals to everybody is extremely vulgar. And indeed, as though you will not see them unless they thrust themselves on your notice, performers are apt to go in for a great deal of unnecessary movement; bad flute-players, for instance, throw themselves about if they have to represent throwing a discus, and keep pulling at the leader of the Chorus if they are performing 'Scylla'. This is what tragedy is like, we are told; it corresponds with what the older actors thought of their successors – for Mynniscus used to call Callipides 'the Ape' on the grounds that he overacted grossly, and the same was said of Pindarus. The tragic art as a whole, then, stands in the same relationship to the epic as these more recent actors do to the earlier. Thus epic is said to appeal to cultivated readers who do not need the help of visible forms, while tragedy appeals to meaner minds. If then it is a vulgar art, it is obviously inferior to epic.

Now in the first place, this way of arguing is a criticism of acting, not of poetry, for it is also possible for a bard to exaggerate his gestures while reciting, as Sosistratus used to do, and for a singer too, like Mnasitheus the Opuntian. No more than every kind of dancing is every kind of movement to be rejected, but only that of the meaner types of people; Callipides was subjected to the same criticism that is levelled against some modern actors, that is, that they cannot act the parts of respectable women. For another thing, tragedy fulfils its own special function even without the help of action, and in just the same way as epic, for its quality can be seen from reading it. So that if tragedy is in other respects the higher of the two arts, this disadvantage is not necessarily inherent in it.[1]

In the second place, tragedy has everything that epic has, and it can even use the epic measure; and as a not inconsiderable addition, it offers scenic effects and music, the source of a distinct feeling of pleasure. Then the effect is as vivid when a play is read as when it is acted. Moreover, this form of imitation achieves its ends in shorter compass, and what is more compact gives more pleasure than what is extended over a long period. Just imagine the *Oedipus* of Sophocles spread out over as many lines as there are in the *Iliad*. Then there is less unity in the imitation of the epic poets, as is shown by the fact that any one work of this kind contains matter for several tragedies, so that, if these poets deal with a single plot, either it will appear truncated if it is briefly set out, or it will give the impression of being watered down if it observes the usual length of such poems; I mean one composed of several actions, such as the *Iliad* or the *Odyssey*, which have many parts, and each of a certain amplitude – and yet these poems are constructed as well as they could be, and each is, as far as this is possible, the representation of a single action.

If, therefore, tragedy is superior to epic in all these respects, and also in fulfilling its artistic function – for these forms of art ought to give, not just any kind of pleasure, but the kinds I have described – then obviously, in achieving its ends better than epic, it must be the better form of art.

This is all I have to say about tragedy and epic poetry, whether in general terms or in relation to their various forms and constituent parts; about the number and the characteristics of these parts; about the causes of their success or failure; and about the various critical problems and their solutions.

1. The disadvantage claimed for it, that it appeals to meaner minds

Plato
From The Republic

§ 1. ART AND ILLUSION

The Greek word mimesis, *'representation', used in Part III to describe dramatic as opposed to narrative poetry, is now used to describe artistic creation as a whole, and interpreted to mean a rather literal imitation. The productions both of the painter and the poet are imitations of a life which has itself only secondary reality, and neither painter nor poet have any knowledge of what they imitate. Pictures and poems are secondhand, unreal, and tell us nothing about life.*

'YOU know,' I said, 'among all the excellent features of our ideal state, there's none I rank higher than its treatment of poetry.'

'Why exactly?'

'Because it excluded all dramatic representation. Now that we have distinguished the various elements in the mind, we can see even more clearly how essential it is to exclude it.'

'What do you mean?'

'Between ourselves – and you mustn't give me away to the tragedians and other writers of the kind – such representations definitely harm the minds of their audiences, unless they're inoculated against them by knowing their real nature.'

'What exactly have you in mind?'

'I must tell you, I suppose; yet the love and respect I've always had from a boy for Homer makes me hesitate – for I think he's the original master and guide of all the great tragic poets. But one must not respect an individual more than the truth, and so, as I say, I must tell you.'

'You must,' he said.

'Listen, then; or, rather, answer my questions.'

'Ask away.'

'Can you tell me in general terms what representation *is*? I'm not sure that I know, myself, exactly how to describe its purpose.'

'Then it's not very likely I shall!'

'Oh, I don't know,' I said. 'It isn't always the sharpest eyes that see things first.'

'True enough,' he replied. 'But with you here, if I did see anything, I shouldn't much want to say so. You must use your own eyes.'

'Then shall we start by following our usual procedure? You know that we always postulate in each case a single form for each set of particular things, to which we apply the same name?'

'Yes, I know.'

'Then let us take any set you choose. For example, there are many particular beds and tables.'

'Yes.'

'But there are only two forms, one of bed and one of table.'

'Yes.'

'Then we normally say that the maker of either of these kinds of furniture has his eye on the appropriate form when he makes the beds and tables we use; and similarly with other things. For no craftsman could possibly make the form itself, could he?'

'No.'

'Well now, I wonder what you would call a craftsman of the following kind.'

'Describe him.'

'One who can make all the objects produced by other particular crafts.'

'He would be a wonderfully clever man.'

'Just a minute, and you'll be more surprised still. For this same craftsman can not only make all artificial objects, but also create all plants and animals, himself included, and, in addition, earth and sky and gods, the heavenly bodies and everything in the underworld.'

'An astonishing exhibition of skill!' he exclaimed.

'You don't believe me?' I asked. 'Tell me, do you think that a craftsman of this sort couldn't exist, or (in one sense, if not in another) create all these things? Do you know that there's a sense in which you could create them yourself?'

'What sense?'

'It's not difficult, and can be done in various ways quite

quickly. The quickest way is to take a mirror and turn it round in all directions; before long you will create sun and stars and earth, yourself and all other animals and plants, and furniture and the other objects we mentioned just now.'

'Yes, but they would only be reflections,' he said, 'not real things.'

'Quite right,' I replied, 'and very much to the point. For a painter is a craftsman of just this kind, I think. Do you agree?'

'Yes.'

'You may perhaps object that the things he creates are not real; and yet there *is* a sense in which the painter creates a bed, isn't there?'

'Yes,' he agreed, 'he produces an appearance of one.'

'And what about the carpenter? Didn't you agree that what he produces is not the form of bed which according to us is what a bed really is, but a particular bed?'

'I did.'

'If, then, what he makes is not "what a bed really is", his product is not "what is", but something which *resembles* "what is" without *being* it. And anyone who says that the products of the carpenter or any other craftsman are ultimately real can hardly be telling the truth, can he?'

'No one familiar with the sort of arguments we're using could suppose so.'

'So we shan't be surprised if the bed the carpenter makes is a shadowy thing compared to reality?'

'No.'

'Then shall we try to discover just what the activity of representation is, on the basis of this example?'

'Yes, please.'

'We have seen that there are three sorts of bed. The first exists in nature, and we would say, I suppose, that it was made by god. No one else could have made it, could they?'

'I think not.'

'The second is made by the carpenter.'

'Yes.'

'And the third by the painter?'

'Granted.'

'So painter, carpenter, and god are each responsible for one kind of bed.'

'Yes.'

'God, then, created only one real bed-in-itself in nature, either because he wanted to or because some necessity prevented him from making more than one; at any rate he didn't produce more than one, and more than one could not possibly be produced.'

'Why?'

'Because, suppose he created two only, another would emerge whose form the other two shared, and it, not the other two, would be the real bed-in-itself.'

'That's true.'

'And I suppose that god knew it, and as he wanted to be real creator of a real bed, and not just a carpenter making a particular bed, produced in nature a single bed-in-itself.'

'I suppose so.'

'Then do you think we might call him author of its nature or some such name?'

'We could do so with justice; for it and all other things in nature are his creation.'

'And what about the carpenter? Doesn't he manufacture a bed?'

'Yes.'

'And what about the artist? Does he make or manufacture?'

'No.'

'Then what does he do?'

'I think that we may fairly claim that he represents what the other two make.'

'Good,' said I. 'Then you say that the artist's representation stands at third remove from reality?'

'I do.'

'So the tragic poet, if his art is representation, is by nature at third remove from the throne of truth; and the same is true of all other representative artists.'

'So it seems.'

'We are agreed about representation, then. But, tell me, which does the painter try to represent? The thing-itself as it is in nature or the things the craftsman makes?'

'The things the craftsman makes.'

'As they are, or as they appear? There is still that distinction to make.'

'I don't understand,' he said.

'What I mean is this. If you look at a bed, or anything else, sideways or endways or from some other angle, does it make any difference to the bed? Isn't it merely that it *looks* different, without *being* different? And similarly with other things.'

'Yes, it's the same bed, but it looks different.'

'Then consider – when the painter makes his representation, does he do so by reference to the object as it actually is or to its superficial appearance? Is his representation one of an apparition or of the truth?'

'Of an apparition.'

'The art of representation is therefore a long way removed from truth, and it is able to reproduce everything because it has little grasp of anything, and that little is of a mere phenomenal appearance. For example, a painter can paint a portrait of a shoemaker or a carpenter or any other craftsman without understanding any of their crafts; yet, if he is skilful enough, his portrait of a carpenter may, at a distance, deceive children or simple people into thinking it is a real carpenter.'

'Yes, it may.'

'In all such cases,' I went on, 'we should bear the following considerations in mind. When someone tells us that he has met someone who is a master of every craft and has a more exact understanding about all subjects than any individual expert, we must answer that he is a simple-minded fellow who seems to have been taken in by the work of a charlatan, whose apparent omniscience is due entirely to his own inability to distinguish knowledge, ignorance, and representation.'

'Very true.'

'We must go on to examine the claims of the tragedians

and their chief, Homer. We are told that they are masters of all forms of skill, and know all about human excellence and defect and about religion; for – so the argument runs – a good poet must, if he's to write well, know all about his subject, otherwise he can't write about it. We must ask ourselves whether those who have met the poets have, when they see or hear their works, failed to perceive that they are representations at the third remove from reality, and easy to produce without any knowledge of the truth, because they are appearances and not realities; or are they right, and do good poets really know about the subjects on which the public thinks they speak so well?'

'It's a question we should certainly examine.'

'Suppose, then, a man could produce both the original and the copy. Do you think he would seriously want to devote himself to the manufacture of copies and make it the highest object in life?'

'No, I don't.'

'Of course not. If he really knew about the things he represented, he would devote himself to them and not to their representations; he would try to leave behind him the memory of many deeds well done, and be more anxious to be praised himself than to write in praise of others.'

'I agree; his reputation and effectiveness would both be greater.'

'We won't, then, expect Homer or any of the poets to explain medicine or any similar skilled activity to us; for example, if they claim to be real doctors and not merely to imitate doctors' talk, we won't ask them to name any poet, ancient or modern, who has performed cures like Aesculapius, or founded a school of medicine to follow him as he did. But we *have* a right to cross-question Homer when he tries to deal with matters of such supreme importance as military strategy, political administration and human education. "My dear Homer," we shall say, "if our definition of representation is wrong and you are not merely manufacturing copies at third remove from reality, but are a stage nearer the truth about human excellence, and really capable of judging what kind of conduct will make the individual or the community better or worse, tell us any state whose constitution you have reformed, as Lycurgus did at Sparta and others have done elsewhere on a larger or smaller scale. What city attributes the benefit of its legal system to your skill? Italy and Sicily owe theirs to Charondas, we owe ours to Solon. Tell us who is similarly indebted to you?" '

'I don't think,' said Glaucon, 'that Homer's most devoted admirers could claim there was anyone.'

'Well, then, is there any record of a successful war being fought in Homer's day either under his command or with his advice?'

'No.'

'Then had he any practical skill? Is he said to have invented any ingenious technical or practical devices like Thales of Miletus or Anacharsis the Scythian?'

'He did nothing of that sort.'

'Well, if he did no public service, do we hear of him founding a school of his own, where enthusiastic pupils came to hear him while he lived and to hand on a Homeric way of life to their successors? That was how Pythagoras got his great reputation, and his successors still talk of a Pythagorean way of life which distinguishes them in the eyes of the world from other people.'

'We hear nothing of that sort about Homer. Indeed, if the stories about Homer are true, his friend Creophylus is an even more absurd example of education than his name suggests, as he is said to have paid very little attention to Homer in his own day, when he was still alive.'

'Yes, that's the story,' I said. 'But do you think, Glaucon, that if Homer had really been able to bring men the benefits of education, instead of merely representing it, he would not have had many enthusiastic followers and admirers? Protagoras of Abdera and Prodicus of Ceos and a whole lot of other individual teachers have managed to persuade their contemporaries that no one who has not studied under *them* is fit to manage either private or public affairs; and they are so admired for this expert knowledge that their pupils are almost ready to carry them about shoulder-high. Would the contemporaries of Homer and Hesiod have let them continue as wandering minstrels, if they had really been able to make them better men? Wouldn't they have clung to them like solid gold and tried to keep them at home, and if they wouldn't stay, gone to school with them wherever they were till they had learnt what they could from them?'

'I think that's perfectly true, Socrates.'

'We may assume, then, that all the poets from Homer downwards have no grasp of truth but merely produce a superficial likeness of any subject they treat, including human excellence. For example, as we said just now, the painter paints what looks like a shoemaker, though neither he nor his public know about shoemaking, but judge merely by colour and form.'

'True.'

'In the same way the poet can use words and phrases as a medium to paint a picture of any craftsman, though he knows nothing except how to represent him, and the metre and rhythm and music will persuade people who are as ignorant as he is, and who judge merely from his words, that he really has something to say about shoemaking or generalship or whatever it may be. So great is the natural magic of poetry. Strip it of its poetic colouring, reduce it to plain prose, and I think you know how little it amounts to.'

'Yes, I've noticed that.'

'Like a face which relied on the bloom of youth for its charm, and whose lack of beauty is plain to see when youth deserts it.'

'Yes.'

'Now to another point. The artist who makes a likeness of a thing knows nothing about the reality but only about the appearance – that was what we said, wasn't it?'

'Yes.'

'But that is only half the story. Let us look at it more fully.'

'Go on.'

'The painter may paint a picture of bridle and bit.'

'Yes.'

'But aren't they made by the harness-maker and smith?'

'Yes.'

'Then does the painter know what the bridle and bit ought to be like? Isn't this something that even the makers – the harness-maker and the smith – don't know, but only the horseman who knows how to use them?'

'True.'

'Isn't the same thing always true?'

'Your meaning?'

'You always have the three techniques – use, manufacture, and representation.'

'Yes.'

'And isn't the quality, beauty and fitness of any implement or creature or action judged by reference to the use for which man or nature produced it?'

'Yes.'

'It must follow, then, that the user of a thing has the widest experience of it and must tell the maker how well it has performed its function in the use to which he puts it. For example, the flute-player reports to the flute-maker on the performance of his flutes, and will give specifications for their manufacture which the flute-maker will follow.'

'Of course.'

'The player, in fact, knows about the merits and defects of his instruments, and the manufacturer will rely on the player's judgement?'

'Yes.'

'The maker of an implement, therefore, has a correct *belief* about its merits and defects, but he is obliged to get this by associating with and listening to someone who *knows*. And the person with the relevant knowledge is the user.'

'That is so.'

'What about the artist and his representations? Has he the user's direct experience of the things he paints to enable him to know whether or not his pictures are good or right? Or has he the correct opinion that springs from enforced acquaintance with and obedience to someone who knows what he ought to paint?'

'He has neither.'

'So the artist has neither knowledge nor correct opinion about the goodness or badness of the things he represents.'

'Apparently not.'

'So the poet too, as artist, will be beautifully ill-informed about the subjects of his poetry.'

'Completely.'

'None the less he'll go on writing poetry, in spite of not knowing whether what he produces is good or bad: and what he will represent will be anything that appeals to the taste of the ignorant multitude.'

'What else can he do?'

'Well,' I concluded, 'we seem to be pretty well agreed that the artist knows little or nothing about the subjects he represents and that the art of representation is something that has no serious value; and that this applies above all to all tragic poetry, epic or dramatic.'

'Yes, entirely agreed.'

§2. THE APPEAL OF ART AND POETRY

Art and poetry appeal to, and represent, the lower, less rational part of our nature.

'Now, look here,' I said; 'we have said that this process of representation deals with something at third remove from the truth, haven't we?'

'Yes.'

'Then on what part of the human being does it exercise its power?'

'What do you mean by part?'

'Something like this. The apparent size of an object, as you know, varies with its distance from our eye.'

'Yes.'

'So also a stick will look bent if you put it in the water, straight when you take it out, and deceptive differences of shading can make the same surface seem to the eye concave or convex; and our minds are clearly liable to all sorts of confusions of this kind. It is this natural weakness of ours that the scene-painter and conjurer and their fellows exploit with magical effect.'

'True.'

'Measuring, counting, and weighing have happily been discovered to help us out of these difficulties, and to ensure that we should not be guided by apparent differences of size, quantity and heaviness, but by calculations of number, measurement, and weight.'

'Of course.'

'And these calculations are performed by the element of reason in the mind.'

'Yes, that's true.'

'Yet when reason informs us, as the result of frequent measurements, that one thing is greater than or less than or equal to another, it may be contradicted by appearances.'

'It may be.'

'Yet we said that the same part of us cannot hold different opinions about the same thing at the same time.'

'And we were quite right.'

'So the part of the mind which contradicts the measurements cannot be the same as the part which agrees with them.'

'No.'

'But the part which relies on measurement and calculation must be the best part of us.'

'Of course.'

'So is not the part which contradicts them an inferior one?'

'Inevitably.'

'That was the conclusion I had in mind when I said that the work of the painter and of all other representative artists was far removed from the truth and associated with elements in us equally far removed from reason, in a fond liaison without health or truth.'

'Absolutely true.'

'So representative art is an inferior child born of inferior parents.'

'I suppose so.'

'And does this apply to the visual arts only, or also to the art which appeals to the ear which we call poetry?'

'I should think it probably applies to poetry too.'

'We mustn't rely on probabilities drawn from painting,' I said, 'but consider the part of the mind to which dramatic poetry appeals, and ask what serious worth it has.'

'Yes, that's what we should do,' he agreed.

'Then let us put it like this,' I went on: 'drama represents human beings in action, either voluntarily or under compulsion; in that action they fare, as they think, well or ill, and experience joy or sorrow. Is that a fair summary?'

'Yes.'

'And does a man remain at unity in himself in all these experiences? We saw that there could be conflict and contrary opinions about the same objects in the realm of vision; isn't there a similar conflict and internal struggle in the realm of action? There is really no need to ask the question, because, as I remember, we have already earlier in our discussion agreed well enough that our mind is full of innumerable conflicts of this sort.'

'We were quite right about that.'

'Yes, but there's an omission we must now make good.'

'What is it?'

'Didn't we then say that a good man who loses his son, or anything else dear to him, will bear the misfortune more equably than other people?'

'Yes.'

'Now consider: is it because he will feel no grief? or is that impossible, and is it because he will moderate his sorrow?'

'The second alternative is nearer the truth.'

'Then tell me, will he be more inclined to resist and fight against his grief when his fellows can see him, or when he is alone by himself?'

'Much more inclined when others can see him.'

'On the other hand, when he is alone he will not mind saying and doing things which he would be ashamed to let other people hear or see.'

'That is true.'

'Reason and principle demand restraint, while his very

feeling of sorrow prompts him to give way to grief.'

'True.'

'And the simultaneous presence of opposite impulses about the same thing implies that there are two elements in his nature.'

'Of course.'

'Of these, one is prepared to obey the direction of principle.'

'How do you mean?'

'Well, of course, custom and principle say that it is best, so far as we can, to bear misfortune patiently and without complaint; for we cannot tell whether it will turn out well or ill, and nothing is gained by impatience, nor is anything in human life of great consequence; besides, grief prevents us getting just the help we need.'

'And what is that?'

'That of deliberation,' I said, 'which reflects on what has happened and then makes what reason picks as the best move that the fall of the dice allows. We must learn not to hold our hurts and waste our time crying, like children who've bumped themselves, but to train our mind to cure our ills and rectify our lapses as soon as it can, banishing sorrow by healing it.'

'That is the right way to deal with misfortune.'

'And the highest part of us is ready to follow this reasoning.'

'Yes, obviously.'

'The other part of us, which remembers our sufferings and is never tired of bemoaning them, we may, I think, call irrational and lazy and inclined to cowardice.'

'Yes, we may.'

'And this recalcitrant element in us gives plenty of material for dramatic representation; but the reasonable element and its unvarying calm are difficult to represent, and difficult to understand if represented, particularly by the motley audience gathered in a theatre, to whose experience it is quite foreign.'

'Very true.'

'The dramatic poet will not therefore naturally turn to this element, nor will his skill be directed to please it, if he wants to win a popular reputation; but he will find it easy to represent a character that is unstable and refractory.'

'Obviously.'

'Then we can fairly take the poet and set him beside the painter. He resembles him both because his works have a low degree of truth and also because he deals with a low element in the mind. We are therefore quite right to refuse to admit him to a properly run state, because he wakens and encourages and strengthens the lower elements in the mind to the detriment of reason, which is like giving power and political control to the worst elements in a state and ruining the better elements. The dramatic poet produces a similarly bad state of affairs in the mind of the individual, by encouraging the unreasoning part of it, which cannot distinguish greater and less but thinks the same things are now large and now small, and by creating images far removed from the truth.'

'I agree.'

§ 3. THE EFFECTS OF POETRY AND DRAMA

Poetry, dramatic poetry in particular, has a bad effect on its audiences, who learn to admire and imitate the faults it represents. We cannot, therefore, allow poetry in our ideal state.

'The gravest charge against poetry still remains. It has a terrible power to corrupt even the best characters, with very few exceptions.'

'It is indeed terrible if it can do that.'

'Then listen. When we hear Homer or one of the tragic poets representing the sufferings of a hero and making him bewail them at length, perhaps with all the sounds and signs of tragic grief, you know how even the best of us enjoy it and let ourselves be carried away by our feelings; and we are full of praises for the merits of the poet who can most powerfully affect us in this way.'

'Yes, I know.'

'Yet in our private griefs we pride ourselves on just the opposite, that is, on our ability to bear them in silence like men, and we regard the behaviour we admired on the stage as womanish.'

'Yes, I'm aware of that.'

'Then is it really right,' I asked, 'to admire, when we see him on the stage, a man we should ourselves be ashamed to resemble? Is it reasonable to feel enjoyment and admiration rather than disgust?'

'It seems most unreasonable,' he said.

'Particularly,' I added, 'if you look at it in this way.'

'How?'

'If you consider that the poet gratifies and indulges the instinctive desires of a part of us, which we forcibly restrain in our private misfortunes, with its hunger for tears and for an uninhibited indulgence in grief. Our better nature, being without adequate intellectual or moral training, relaxes its control over these feelings, on the grounds that it is someone else's sufferings it is watching and that there's nothing to be ashamed of in praising and pitying another man with some claim to goodness who shows excessive grief; besides, it reckons the pleasure it gets as sheer gain, and would certainly not consent to be deprived of it by condemning the whole poem. For very few people are capable of realizing that what we feel for other people must infect what we feel for ourselves, and that if we let our pity for the misfortunes of others grow too strong it will be difficult to restrain our feelings in our own.'

'That is very true.'

'Does not the same argument apply to laughter as to pity? For the effect is similar when you enjoy on the stage – or even in ordinary life – jokes that you would be ashamed to make yourself, instead of detesting their vulgarity. You are giving rein to your comic instinct, which your reason has restrained for fear you may seem to be playing the fool, and bad taste in the theatre may insensibly lead you into becoming a buffoon at home.'

'It may indeed.'

'Poetry has the same effect on us when it represents sex and anger, and the other desires and feelings of pleasure and pain which accompany all our actions. It waters them when they ought to be left to wither, and makes them control us when we ought, in the interests of our own greater welfare and happiness, to control them.'

'I can't deny it,' he said.

'And so, Glaucon,' I continued, 'when you meet people who admire Homer as the educator of Greece, and who say that in the administration of human affairs and education we should study him and model our whole lives on his poetry, you must feel kindly towards them as good men within their limits, and you may agree with them that Homer is the best of poets and first of tragedians. But you will know that the only poetry that should be allowed in a state is hymns to the gods and paeans in praise of good men; once you go beyond that and admit the sweet lyric or epic muse, pleasure and pain become your rulers instead of law and the rational principles commonly accepted as best.'

'Quite true.'

'Our defence, then, when we are reminded that we banished poetry from our state, must be that its character was such as to give us good grounds for so doing and that our argument required it. But in case we are condemned for being insensitive and bad mannered, let us add that there is an old quarrel between philosophy and poetry. One can quote many examples of this ancient antagonism: remarks about the "bitch that growls and snarls at her master", and "a reputation among empty-headed fools", or "the crowd of heads that know too much" and the "subtle thinkers" who are "beggars" none the less. However, let us freely admit that if drama and poetry written for pleasure can prove to us that they have a place in a well-run society, we will gladly admit them, for we know their fascination only too well ourselves; but it would be wicked to abandon what seems to be the truth. I expect you feel the fascination of poetry yourself, don't you,' I asked, 'especially when it's Homer exercising it?'

'I do indeed.'

'It is only fair, then, that poetry should return, if she can make her defence in lyric or other metre.'

'Yes.'

'And we should give her defenders, men who aren't poets themselves but who love poetry, a chance of defending her in prose and proving that she doesn't only give pleasure but brings lasting benefit to human life and human society. And we will listen favourably, as we shall gain much if we find her a source of profit as well as pleasure.'

'Yes, we shall gain a lot.'

'But if they fail to make their case, then we shall have to follow the example of the lover who renounces a passion that is doing him no good, however hard it may be to do so. Brought up as we have been in our own admirably constituted societies, we are bound to love poetry, and we shall be glad if it proves to have high value and truth; but in the absence of such proof we shall, whenever we listen to it, recite this argument of ours to ourselves as a charm to prevent us falling under the spell of a childish and vulgar passion. Our theme shall be that such poetry has no serious value or claim to truth, and we shall warn its hearers to fear its effects on the constitution of their inner selves, and tell them to adopt the view of poetry we have described.'

'I entirely agree.'

'Yes, my dear Glaucon,' I said, 'because the issues at stake, the choice between becoming a good man or a bad, are even greater than they appear, and neither honour nor wealth nor power, nor poetry itself, should tempt us to neglect the claims of justice and excellence of every kind.'

'I agree,' he said; 'your argument convinces me, as I think it would anyone else.'

Horace
Art of Poetry

SUPPOSING a painter chose to put a human head on a horse's neck, or to spread feathers of various colours over the limbs of several different creatures, or to make what in the upper part is a beautiful woman tail off into a hideous fish, could you help laughing when he showed you his efforts? You may take it from me, my friends, that a book will have very much the same effect as these pictures if, like a sick man's dreams, the author's idle fancies assume such a shape that it is impossible to make head or tail of what he is driving at. 'But,' you will say, 'the right to take liberties of almost any kind has always been enjoyed by painters and poets alike.' I know that; we poets do claim this licence, and in our turn we concede it to others, but not to the point of associating what is wild with what is tame, of pairing snakes with birds or lambs with tigers.

Works that begin impressively and with the promise of carrying on in the heroic strain often have one or two purple passages tacked on to catch the eye, giving a description of Diana's grove and altar, the meanderings of a stream through a picturesque countryside, the River Rhine, or a rainbow. But this is not the right place for things of that kind. Perhaps, too, you know how to paint a cypress; but what is the point of that if you are being paid to paint a shipwrecked man swimming for dear life? A potter sets out to make a two-handled wine-flagon: why, as his wheel spins, does it turn into an ordinary water-jug? In short, whatever you set your hand to, you must be single-minded about it and keep to the point.

Most of us poets, my friends, are led astray by our notions of the right way to go to work. I try my hardest to be succinct, and merely succeed in being obscure; I aim at smoothness, only to find that I am losing fire and energy. One poet sets out to achieve the sublime, and falls into turgidity; another is over-cautious, and, nervous of spreading his wings, never leaves the ground. Yet another, wishing to vary the monotony of his subject with something out of the ordinary, introduces a dolphin into his woods, or puts a boar among his waves. If art is lacking, the avoidance of a petty fault may lead to a serious imperfection.

At the end of the row of stalls down by the Aemilian gladiatorial school there is a craftsman in bronze who will mould fingernails and reproduce wavy hair to the life, but the total effect of his work is unsatisfactory because he cannot put together a complete figure. Now if I set out to write a poem, I would no more want to be like him than to have a crooked nose, much though I might be admired for my dark eyes and black hair.

Choose a subject that is suited to your abilities, you who aspire to be writers; give long thought to what you are capable of undertaking, and what is beyond you. A man who chooses a subject within his powers will never be at a loss for words, and his thoughts will be clear and orderly. The virtue and attraction of order, I think I am right in saying, is that the poet will at any moment be saying exactly what his poem at that moment requires; he will be keeping back points for the time being or leaving them out altogether, and showing what he thinks admirable and what beneath notice.

Furthermore, you will make an excellent impression if you use care and subtlety in placing your words and, by the skilful choice of setting, give fresh meaning to a familiar word. If it happens that you have to invent new terms for the discussion of abstruse topics, you will have a chance to coin words that were unknown to earlier generations of Romans,[1] and no one will object to your doing this, as long as you do it with discretion. New and recently-coined words will win acceptance if they are borrowed from Greek sources and drawn upon sparingly. And indeed, why should we Romans allow this privilege to Caecilius and Plautus, and refuse it to Virgil and Varius? Why should I be grudged the right to add a few words

1. Horace's words are *cinctutis . . . Cethegis*, 'the girdled Cethegi'. He is referring to the time, some 200 years earlier, when such men as M. Cornelius Cethegus (censor B.C. 209, consul 204) wore a kind of girdle or loin-cloth (*cinctus*) under the toga instead of the tunic of later, more effeminate times.

to the stock if I can, when the language of Cato and Ennius has enriched our native speech by the introduction of new terms? It has always been accepted, and always will be, that words stamped with the mint-mark of the day should be brought into currency. As the woods change their foliage with the decline of each year, and the earliest leaves fall,[1] so words die out with old age; and the newly born ones thrive and prosper just like human beings in the vigour of youth. We are all destined to die, we and all our works. Perhaps the land has been dug out and an arm of the sea let in, to give protection to our fleets from the northern gales (and what a royal undertaking this was!);[2] or a marsh, long a barren waste on which oars were plied, has been put under the plough and produces food for the neighbouring towns;[3] or a river has been made to change a course ruinous to the cornfields and turned into a straighter channel:[4] whatever they are, the works of men will pass away. How much less likely are the glory and grace of language to have an enduring life! Many terms that have now dropped out of use will be revived, if usage so requires, and others which are now in repute will die out; for it is usage which regulates the laws and conventions of speech.

Homer showed us in what metre the exploits of kings and commanders and the miseries of war were to be recorded. The elegiac couplet was first used as the vehicle for lament, but was later adopted for verses of thanksgiving; however, scholars argue about who devised this slighter elegiac form, and the case so far rests undecided. Archilochus invented the iambic measure as the weapon for furious satire; it was adopted both for comedy and for high tragedy, since it is appropriate for

1. In warm countries deciduous trees do not necessarily shed all their foliage in autumn, but the oldest leaves are likely to fall.

2. This may be a reference to the Portus Julius, an artificial harbour which Agrippa, the friend of Augustus and his admiral in the Battle of Actium, formed on the coast of Campania by constructing strong channels between Lake Lucrinus and the sea and between Lake Lucrinus and Lake Avernus.

3. Probably a reference to the draining of the Pontine Marshes, projected by Julius Caesar and perhaps partly carried out by Augustus.

4. Probably a reference to the straightening of the course of the Tiber – another of Julius Caesar's schemes carried out in the time of Augustus.

dialogue, is capable of drowning the noises of the audience,[1] and is by its nature well suited to accompany action. To lyrical poetry the Muse assigned the task of celebrating the gods and their offspring, the winner in a boxing-match, and the horse that led the field; the task, too, of singing the woes of young lovers and the pleasures of wine.[2] If I have not the ability and skill to adhere to these well-defined functions and styles of poetic forms, why should I be hailed as a poet? Why out of false shame should I prefer to remain ignorant rather than to learn my craft? A comic subject is not susceptible of treatment in a tragic style, and similarly the banquet of Thyestes cannot be fitly described in the strains of everyday life or in those that approach the tone of comedy. Let each of these styles be kept for the role properly allotted to it. Yet even comedy at times uses elevated language, and an angry Chremes rails in bombastic terms;[3] while in tragedy Telephus and Peleus often express their grief in prosaic language, and each of them in his poverty-stricken exile renounces his usual rant and his sesquipedalian words[4] when he wants to move the spectator's pity with his lamentation.

It is not enough that poems should have beauty; if they are to carry the audience with them, they must have charm as well. Just as smiling faces are turned on those who smile, so is sympathy shown with those who weep. If you want to move me to tears, you must first feel grief yourself; then, Telephus and Peleus, your misfortunes will grieve me too, whereas, if your speeches are out of harmony with your feelings, I shall either fall asleep or burst out laughing. Pathetic language is appropriate to the face of sorrow, and violent language to the

1. The murmur of an audience might drown any but the clearest elocution; the regularly recurring stress of the iambic line would contribute towards the required clarity.

2. Greek lyrical poetry included hymns to the gods and heroes, odes (such as those of Pindar) celebrating victories in the games, and amatory and convivial poems (such as those of Sappho, Alcaeus, and Anacreon).

3. Terence uses the name Chremes four times in his comedies, three times for old men. The reference is probably to the *Heautontimorumenos* V, iv, where the old man Chremes rails at his son.

4. *Sesquipedalia verba*: literally 'words a foot and a half long'. Telephus and Peleus provided subjects for several tragedies.

face of anger; a sportive diction goes with merry looks, and a serious with grave looks. For nature has so formed us that we first feel inwardly any change in our fortunes; it is she that cheers us or rouses us to anger, she that torments us and bows us to the ground with a heavy burden of sorrow, and it is only afterwards that she expresses these feelings in us by means of the tongue. If the speaker's words are out of key with his fortunes, a Roman audience will cackle and jeer to a man. It will make a great difference whether a god or a hero is speaking, a man of ripe years or a hot-headed youngster in the pride of youth, a woman of standing or an officious nurse, a roving merchant or a prosperous farmer, a Colchian or an Assyrian, a man from Thebes or one from Argos.

Either follow the beaten track, or invent something that is consistent within itself. If in your play you happen to be representing the illustrious Achilles, let him be energetic, passionate, ruthless, and implacable; let him say that laws are not meant for him, and think that everything must yield to the force of arms. See to it that Medea is fierce and indomitable, Ino tearful, Ixion faithless, Io a wanderer, and Orestes sorrowful. If you introduce an untried subject to the stage, or are so bold as to invent a new character, be sure that it remains the same all the way through as it was at the beginning, and is entirely consistent.

It is hard to be original in treating well-worn subjects,[1] and it is better for you to be putting a Trojan tale into dramatic form than that you should be first in the field with a theme hitherto unknown and unsung.[2] A theme that is familiar can be made your own property as long as you do not waste your time on a hackneyed treatment; nor should you try to render your original word for word like a slavish translator, or in imitating another writer plunge yourself into difficulties from which shame, or the rules you have laid down for yourself, prevent you from extricating yourself. And you must not, like

1. *Difficile est proprie communia dicere*. Some editors would translate *communia* as 'subjects of general interest', others as 'subjects not treated before'.

2. This passage suggests that the young Piso is actually writing, or intending to write, a play on a Homeric theme.

the cyclic poet of old,[1] begin: 'Of Priam's fate I'll sing and war's renown.' What will emerge that can live up to such extravagant promises? The mountains will fall into labour, and there will be born – an absurd little mouse. How much more to the purpose are the words of the man who makes no foolish undertakings: 'Sing for me, Muse, the man who, after the fall of Troy, made himself acquainted with the ways of many men and their cities.' This poet does not mean to let his flash of fire die away in smoke, but to make the smoke give way to light, when he may with striking effect relate his tales of wonder, tales of Antiphates and Scylla and Charybdis and the Cyclops. He does not trace Diomede's return right back to the death of Meleager, or the Trojan War to the twin eggs of Leda.[2] All the time he is hurrying on to the crisis, and he plunges his hearer into the middle of the story as if it were already familiar to him; and what he cannot hope to embellish by his treatment he leaves out. Moreover, so inventive is he, and so skilfully does he blend fact and fiction, that the middle is not inconsistent with the beginning, nor the end with the middle.

I will tell you what I, and with me the public as a whole, look for in a play. If you want an appreciative hearer who will wait for the curtain and remain in his seat until the player calls out, 'Give us your applause', you must note the behaviour of people of different ages, and give the right kind of manners to characters of varying dispositions and years. The child who has just learnt to speak and to plant his feet firmly on the ground loves playing with his friends, will fly into a temper and with as little reason recover from it, and will change every hour. The beardless youth who has at last got rid of his tutor finds his pleasures in horses and dogs and the grassy sports-fields of the Campus Martius; pliant as wax, he is easily persuaded to vicious courses, is irritable with his counsellors, slow to pro-

1. The cyclic poets were epic poets, probably later than Homer, who wrote upon legends connected with the Trojan and Theban wars. Their poems were arranged into cycles by the Alexandrian scholars.

2. That is, to the birth of Helen. Leda was visited by Zeus in the form of a swan, and brought forth two eggs, from one of which Helen issued, and from the other Castor and Pollux.

vide for his needs, lavish with his money, of high aspirations and passionate desires, and quick to abandon the objects of his fancy. When he is become a man in years and spirit, his inclinations change; he sets out to acquire wealth and influential connexions, aims at securing public offices, and is careful to avoid doing anything which he might later wish had been done otherwise. The old man is beset by many troubles; either he tries to make money, but holds back miserably when it comes his way and is afraid to use it, or he is cautious and faint-hearted in all his dealings; he puts things off, clings to his hopes, and remains inactive in an eager desire to prolong his life; he is obstinate, too, and querulous, and given to praising the days when he was a boy and criticizing and rebuking his juniors. Advancing years bring with them many blessings, but many of these are taken away in the decline of life. Thus, in order not to give a young man the characteristics of old age, or the child those of a grown man, we shall always dwell upon the qualities that are appropriate to a particular time of life.

An episode is either acted on the stage, or reported as having taken place. However, the mind is less actively stimulated by what it takes in through the ear than by what is presented to it through the trustworthy agency of the eyes – something that the spectator can see for himself. But you will not bring on to the stage anything that ought properly to be taking place behind the scenes, and you will keep out of sight many episodes that are to be described later by the eloquent tongue of a narrator. Medea must not butcher her children in the presence of the audience, nor the monstrous Atreus cook his dish of human flesh within public view, nor Procne be metamorphosed into a bird, nor Cadmus into a snake. I shall turn in disgust from anything of this kind that you show me.

If you want your play to be called for and given a second performance, it should not be either shorter or longer than five acts. A *deus ex machina* should not be introduced unless some entanglement develops which requires such a person to unravel it. And there should not be more than three speaking characters on the stage at the same time.[1]

The Chorus should sustain the role and function of an

1. Literally, 'And let not a fourth character strive to speak.'

actor, and should not sing anything between the acts that does not contribute to the plot and fit appropriately into it. It should side with the good characters and give them friendly advice, and should control those who are out of temper and show approval to those who are anxious not to transgress. It should commend moderation in the pleasures of the table, the blessings of law and justice, and times of peace when the gates lie open; it should respect confidences, and should pray and beseech the gods to let prosperity return to the wretched and desert the proud.

At one time the flute – not as now bound with brass and a rival to the trumpet, but simple and delicate in tone and with only a few stops – was of service in giving the note to the Chorus and accompanying it; and its soft music filled rows of seats that were not yet overcrowded, where an audience small enough to be counted came together – simple, thrifty folk, modest and virtuous in their ways. But when a conquering race began to extend its territories, and cities grew in size, and the tutelary deity could be propitiated without fear of censure by drinking in the daytime on festal occasions, a greater freedom was allowed in the choice both of rhythms and melodies. For what taste could be expected in a crowd of uneducated men enjoying a holiday from work, when country bumpkins rubbed shoulders with townsfolk, and slum-dwellers with men of rank? Thus the flute-player introduced wanton movements that were unknown in the style of earlier days, and trailed his robe as he made his way over the stage. The grave lyre, too, acquired new notes,[1] and a more abrupt type of eloquence brought with it a new style of speech in which wise saws and prophecies of the future caught the very manner of the Delphic oracle.[2]

The poet originally competed in tragic verse for the paltry prize of a goat;[3] soon he introduced wild and naked satyrs on to the stage, and without loss of dignity tried his hand at a

1. By the addition of further strings.

2. They became as obscure and unhelpful as the utterances of the Delphic oracle.

3. The derivation of the word 'tragedy' from τράγος (*tragos*, 'he-goat'), because the prize in the competition for tragedy was a he-goat, is no longer accepted. However, in the earliest stages of Greek tragedy the Chorus consisted of satyrs, the primitive, goat-like followers of Dionysus,

form of crude jesting; for an audience that was tipsy after observing the Bacchic rites and in a lawless mood could only be held by the attraction of some enticing novelty. But if jesters and mocking satyrs are to win approval, and a transition made from the serious to the light-hearted, it must be done in such a way that no one who has been presented as a god or hero, and who a moment ago was resplendent in purple and gold, is transported into a dingy hovel and allowed to drop into the speech of the back streets, or alternatively to spout cloudy inanities in an attempt to rise above vulgarity. Tragedy scorns to babble trivialities, and, like a married woman obliged to dance at a festival, will look rather shamefaced among the wanton satyrs. If ever I write satyric dramas, my dear fellows, I shall not be content to use merely the plain, unadorned language of everyday speech; I shall try not to depart so far from the tone of tragedy as to make no distinction between the speech of a Davus, or of a bold-faced Pythias who has managed to trick Simo out of a talent, and that of Silenus, who after all was the guardian and attendant of the young god Bacchus. I shall aim at a style that employs no unfamiliar diction, one that any writer might hope to achieve, but would sweat tears of blood in his efforts and still not manage it – such is the power of words that are used in the right places and in the right relationships, and such the grace that they can add to the commonplace when so used. If you are going to bring woodland fauns on to the stage, I do not think you should ever allow them to speak as though they had been brought up in the heart of the city; do not let them be too youthfully indiscreet in the lines you give them, or crack any filthy or obscene jokes. For such things give offence to those of knightly or freeborn rank and the more

---

no doubt clad in goat-skins. The satyr-play, which Horace goes on to discuss, was a short play appended to a tragic trilogy, usually dealing in comic fashion with a theme related to that of the trilogy, and having a Chorus of satyrs. The only complete surviving satyr-play is the *Cyclops* of Euripides, best known in Shelley's version and recently translated for the Penguin Classics by Roger Lancelyn Green. It is doubtful whether, as Horace suggests, the satyric drama came into being later than tragedy; the two forms seem rather to be different developments of the same origins. Little is known of satyric drama in Rome; perhaps Piso, or even Horace himself, was hoping to revive it.

substantial citizens; these men do not take kindly to what meets with the approval of the masses, the buyers of roast beans and chestnuts, nor do they give it a prize.

A long syllable following a short one is called an iambus, which is a fast-moving foot. From this the name 'trimeters' became attached to the iambic line, since it produced six beats; and the metre was the same throughout the line.[1] But not so very long ago, so that it might fall upon the ear with rather more weight and deliberation, the iambic line obligingly opened its ranks to the steady spondee, but did not extend its welcome to the point of giving way to it in the second or fourth foot. The true iambic measure is rarely found in the 'noble' trimeters of Accius; and on the verse, too, with which Ennius so ponderously burdened the stage lies the reproach of over-hasty and careless composition, or of ignorance of his art. Not everyone is critical enough to be aware of rhythmical faults in verse, and an indulgence has been shown to our Roman poets that true poets should not need. Is that a reason for loose and lawless writing on my part? Or should I assume that everyone will notice my transgressions, and therefore proceed cautiously, keeping within the bounds in which I may safely hope for indulgence? If I do so, I shall have escaped censure, indeed, but shall not have deserved any praise. For yourselves, my friends, you must give your days and nights to the study of Greek models. But, you will say, your grandfathers were enthusiastic about the versification and wit of Plautus. They were altogether too tolerant, not to say foolish, in their admiration of both these things in him, if you and I have any idea of how to discriminate between coarseness and graceful wit, and how to pick out the right rhythm both by counting and by ear.

Thespis is given the credit for having invented tragedy as a new genre;[2] he is said to have taken his plays about to be sung

1. *Cum* ... *redderet* is usually translated '*although* it produced'. But Horace has called the iambus a fast-moving or light foot, and he seems to be saying that because of this lightness the six iambics give the effect of a trimeter, two iambics forming a *metrum*.

2. He did this by introducing an actor who was independent of the Chorus, and who could speak a prologue and engage in dialogue with the leader of the Chorus. Thus he made tragedy dramatic.

and acted on wagons by players whose faces were smeared with the lees of wine. After him came Aeschylus, who devised the mask and the dignified robe of tragedy; it was he who laid down a stage with planks of moderate size, and who introduced the grand style into tragedy and increased the actor's height with buskins. These playwrights were succeeded by those of the Old Comedy, which enjoyed a fairly considerable favour; but its freedom degenerated into an offensive violence of language which had to be curbed by law. This law was observed, and the Chorus, deprived of its right to be abusive, fell into a shamed silence.

Our own poets have tried their hand in every style; and they have enjoyed some of their greatest successes when they have had the courage to turn aside from the paths laid down by the Greeks and sing of deeds at home, and this in both tragedies and comedies with Roman backgrounds. Indeed Italy would be no less renowned in the arts of language than she is in valour and the arts of war, were it not that her poets, one and all, shrink from the tedious task of polishing their work. But you, my dear fellows, the descendants of Numa Pompilius, you must have nothing to do with any poem that has not been trimmed into shape by many a day's toil and much rubbing out, and corrected down to the smallest detail.

Because Democritus believes that native genius is worth any amount of piddling art, and will not allow a place on Mount Helicon to poets with rational minds, a good many will not take the trouble to trim their nails and their beards; they haunt solitary places, and keep away from the public baths. For they will gain the repute and title of poets, they think, if they never submit to the ministrations of the barber Licinus a head that all the hellebore of all the Anticyras in the world could never reduce to sanity.[1] What an ass I am to purge the bile out of my system as the season of spring comes along! Otherwise no man would write better poetry. But the game's not worth the candle. So I will play the part of a whetstone, which can put an edge on a blade, though it is not itself capable of cutting. Even if I write nothing myself, I will teach the poet his duties and

1. Hellebore, which grew abundantly at Anticyra in Phocis, was prescribed as a cure for madness.

obligations; I will tell him where to find his resources, what will nourish and mould his poetic gift, what he may, and may not, do with propriety, where the right course will take him, and where the wrong.

The foundation and fountain-head of good composition is a sound understanding. The Socratic writings will provide you with material, and if you look after the subject-matter the words will come readily enough. The man who has learnt his duty towards his country and his friends, the kind of love he should feel for a parent, a brother, and a guest, the obligations of a senator and of a judge, and the qualities required in a general sent out to lead his armies in the field – such a man will certainly know the qualities that are appropriate to any of his characters. I would lay down that the experienced poet, as an imitative artist, should look to human life and character for his models, and from them derive a language that is true to life. Sometimes a play that has a few brilliant passages showing a true appreciation of character, even if it lacks grace and has little depth or artistry, will catch the fancy of an audience, and keep its attention more firmly than verse which lacks substance but is filled with well-sounding trifles.

To the Greeks the Muses gave native wit and the ability to turn phrases, and there was nothing they craved more than renown. We Romans in our schooldays learn long calculations for dividing the pound into dozens of parts. 'Here, young Albinus, you tell me: if you take an ounce from five-twelfths of a pound, what's left? Come on now, you could have answered by now.' 'A third of a pound.' 'Good! You'll be able to look after yourself all right. If you add an ounce, what does that come to?' 'A half.' When once this corroding lust for profit has infected our minds, can we hope for poems to be written that are worth rubbing over with cedar oil[1] and storing away in cases of polished cypress?

Poets aim at giving either profit or delight, or at combining the giving of pleasure with some useful precepts for life. When you are giving precepts of any kind, be succinct, so that receptive minds may easily grasp what you are saying and retain it firmly; when the mind has plenty to cope with, anything

1. As a preservative.

superfluous merely goes in one ear and out of the other. Works written to give pleasure should be as true to life as possible, and your play should not demand belief for just anything that catches your fancy; you should not let the ogress Lamia gobble up a child, and later bring it out of her belly alive. The centuries of the elder citizens will disapprove of works lacking in edification, while the haughty Ramnes will have nothing to do with plays that are too serious.[1] The man who has managed to blend profit with delight wins everyone's approbation, for he gives his reader pleasure at the same time as he instructs him. This is the book that not only makes money for the booksellers, but is carried to distant lands and ensures a lasting fame for its author.

However, there are faults that we should be ready to forgive; for the lute-string does not always give the note intended by the mind and hand, but often returns a high note when a low one is required, and the bow will not always hit the mark aimed at. When there are plenty of fine passages in a poem, I shall not take exception to occasional blemishes which the poet has carelessly let slip, or which his fallible human nature has not guarded against. What then is our conclusion about this? Just as the literary scribe gets no indulgence if he keeps on making the same mistake however often he is warned, and the lutenist is laughed at if he always goes wrong on the same string, so the poet who is often remiss seems to me another Choerilus,[2] whose two or three good lines I greet with an amused surprise; at the same time I am put out when the worthy Homer nods, although it is natural that slumber should occasionally creep over a long poem.

A poem is like a painting: the closer you stand to this one the more it will impress you, whereas you have to stand a good distance from that one; this one demands a rather dark corner, but that one needs to be seen in full light, and will stand up to the keen-eyed scrutiny of the art-critic; this one only pleased you

1. The Ramnes were one of the three centuries of knights. They seem here to stand, in contrast to the centuries of elders, as representatives of the aristocratic young bloods of the day.

2. Choerilus of Iasos, an inferior epic poet of the time of Alexander the Great. Acron, the commentator on Horace, says that there were only seven good lines in his poem on the exploits of Alexander.

the first time you saw it, but that one will go on giving pleasure however often it is looked at.

A word to you, the elder of the Piso boys. Though you have been trained by your father to form sound judgements and have natural good sense, take this truth to heart and do not forget it: that only in certain walks of life does the second-rate pass muster. An advocate or barrister of mediocre capacity falls short of the eloquent Messalla in ability, and knows less than Aulus Cascellius, yet he is not without his value; on the other hand, neither gods nor men – nor, for that matter, booksellers – can put up with mediocrity in poets. Just as at a pleasant dinner-party music that is out of tune, a coarse perfume, or poppy-seeds served with bitter Sardinian honey give offence, for the meal could just as well have been given without them, so is it with a poem, which is begotten and created for the soul's delight; if it falls short of the top by ever so little, it sinks right down to the bottom. A man who does not understand the games keeps away from the weapons of the Campus Martius, and if he has no skill with the ball or quoit or hoop, he stands quietly aside so that the crowds round the side-lines will not roar with laughter at his expense; yet the man who knows nothing about poetry has the audacity to write it. And why not? he says. He is his own master, a man of good family, and above all he is rated as a knight in wealth and there is nothing against him.

You, I am sure, will not say or do anything counter to the will of Minerva; you have judgement and sense enough for that. But if at any time you do write anything, submit it to the hearing of the critic Maecius, and your father's and mine as well; then put the papers away and keep them for nine years. You can always destroy what you have not published, but once you have let your words go they cannot be taken back.

While men still roamed the forests, they were restrained from bloodshed and a bestial way of life by Orpheus, the sacred prophet and interpreter of the divine will – that is why he is said to have tamed tigers and savage lions. Amphion, too, the founder of Thebes, is credited with having moved stones by the strains of his lyre, and led them where he would with this sweet blandishment. At one time this was the way of the wise man: to distinguish between public and personal rights and between things sacred and profane, to discourage indiscriminate sexual union and make rules for married life, to build towns, and to inscribe laws on tablets of wood. For this reason honour and fame were heaped upon the bards, as divinely inspired beings, and upon their songs. After them the illustrious Homer and Tyrtaeus fired the hearts of men to martial deeds with their verses. In song, too, oracles were delivered, and the way to right living taught; the favour of kings was sought in Pierian strains; and singing-festivals were devised as a close to the year's long toils. So there is no need for you to blush for the Muse, with her skill in song, and for Apollo the god of singers.

The question has been asked whether a fine poem is the product of nature or of art. I myself cannot see the value of application without a strong natural aptitude, or, on the other hand, of native genius unless it is cultivated – so true is it that each requires the help of the other, and that they enter into a friendly compact with each other. The athlete who strains to reach the winning-post has trained hard as a boy and put up with a great deal, sweating, and shivering in the cold, and keeping away from women and wine; the flautist who plays at the Pythian games has first had to learn his art under a stern master. Yet nowadays it is enough for a man to say: 'I write marvellous poems – the devil take the hindmost![1] It would be dreadful if I fell behind and had to admit that I know absolutely nothing about what, after all, I've never learnt.'

Like the auctioneer who gathers a crowd round him anxious to buy his wares, the poet who has plenty of property and plenty of money accumulating interest is a standing invitation to flatterers to swarm round for what they can make out of him. But if he is a man who can put on a first-class dinner in proper style, or stand security for a poor man of little credit, or rescue him when he is tied up in a dismal lawsuit, I shall be surprised if, for all his apparent happiness, he can tell a true friend from a false. And you, if you have given or intend to give anyone a present, do not ask him in the first flush of his delight to listen

1. An allusion to a game like 'Touch me' or tag in which the children cried out, 'The devil take the hindmost.' Horace implies that some people merely play at writing poetry.

to your own poems. 'Lovely!' he will exclaim. 'That's excellent – it's absolutely first-rate!' He will turn quite pale with emotion, and will even be so amiable as to squeeze out a tear or two; he will dance with excitement, or tap out his approval with his foot. Just as at a funeral the paid mourners are on the whole more active and vocal than those who are really suffering deeply, so the mock admirer shows more appreciation than the man who is sincere in his praise. It is said that when kings are anxious to test thoroughly whether a man is worthy of their friendship, they put him to the trial with wine, and ply him with many bumpers. If you are going to write poetry, see to it that you are never put upon by people with the hidden cunning of the fox.

When anything was read to Quintilius Varus, he would say: 'You must put this right – and this too, please.' If after two or three ineffectual attempts you said you could not do any better, he would tell you to get rid of the passage; the lines were badly turned and would have to be hammered out again. If you chose to defend a weakness rather than correct it, he would not say another word, nor waste any effort in trying to prevent you from regarding yourself and your work as unique and unrivalled. An honest, sensible man will condemn any lines that are lifeless, will find fault with them if they are rough, and will run his pen through any that are inelegant; he will cut out any superfluous adornment, will force you to clarify anything that is obscure, and will draw attention to ambiguities; in fact he will prove another Aristarchus and point out everything that requires changing.[1] He will not say, 'Why should I quarrel with a friend over trifles?' Those trifles will bring his friend into serious trouble when once his efforts have been taken amiss and he has become an object of ridicule.

Just as happens when a man is plagued by a nasty rash, or by jaundice, or a fit of lunacy, so men of sense are afraid to have any dealings with a mad poet, and keep clear of him; but children boldly follow him about and tease him. While he is wandering about, spouting his lines with his head in the air like a fowler intent on his game, he can fall into a well or pit, and no one will

1. Aristarchus, an Alexandrian critic of the second century B.C., has been described as 'the greatest critic of antiquity'. His work on the Homeric poems has been the basis of all later texts.

bother to pull him out however long he goes on shouting to the passers-by for help. And if anyone should take the trouble to lend a hand and let down a rope, 'How do you know he didn't jump down there on purpose,' I shall say, 'and doesn't want to be rescued?' and I shall tell the story of the Sicilian poet Empedocles' death. Eager to be regarded as one of the immortal gods, Empedocles in cold blood leapt into the flames of Etna. And poets should have the right to take their own lives. To save a man who does not want to be saved is as good as murdering him. This is not the first time he has tried, and if he is pulled out he will not immediately become a normal human being and abandon his desire to win notoriety by his death. Nor is it very clear why he goes on trying to write poetry – whether because he has defiled his father's ashes, or sacrilegiously violated a place struck by lightning. It is certain, at any rate, that he is raving mad, and like a bear that has been strong enough to burst the bars of its cage, he makes everyone, learned and ignorant alike, take to their heels when he embarks on his detestable recitations. He will fasten on to anyone he manages to catch, and read him to death – just like a leech that will not drop off your skin until it is gorged with blood.

Longinus
From On the Sublime

INTRODUCTION

Cecilius's Treatise and Its Shortcomings

As you will remember, my dear Postumius Terentianus, when we were working together on Cecilius's little treatise on the sublime, it seemed to us too trivial a handling of the subject as a whole; it showed no grasp of the main points, and offered its readers little of the practical help that it should be the writer's main object to supply. In any systematic treatise two things are essential: first, there must be some definition of the subject; second in order of treatment, but of greater importance, there must be some indication of the methods by which we may ourselves reach the desired goal. Now Cecilius, assuming us to be ignorant, sets out to establish the nature of the sublime by means of innumerable examples; but he leaves out of account, apparently considering it unnecessary, the means by which we may be enabled to raise our faculties to the proper pitch of grandeur. However, we ought perhaps rather to praise him for the industry he has shown in carrying out his purpose than find fault with him for his deficiencies.

CHAPTER I

First Thoughts on Sublimity

SINCE you have urged me in my turn to write down my thoughts on the sublime for your gratification, we should consider whether my views contain anything of value to men in public life. And as your nature and your sense of fitness prompt you, my dear friend, you will help me to form the truest possible judgements on the various details; for it was a sound answer that was given by the man who, when asked what we have in common with the gods, replied, 'Benevolence and truth'.

As I am writing for you, Terentianus, who are a man of some erudition, I almost feel that I can dispense with a long preamble showing that sublimity consists in a certain excellence and distinction in expression, and that it is from this source alone that the greatest poets and historians have acquired their preeminence and won for themselves an eternity of fame. For the effect of elevated language is, not to persuade the hearers, but to entrance them; and at all times, and in every way, what transports us with wonder is more telling than what merely persuades or gratifies us. The extent to which we can be persuaded is usually under our own control, but these sublime passages exert an irresistible force and mastery, and get the upper hand with every hearer. Inventive skill and the proper order and disposition of material are not manifested in a good touch here and there, but reveal themselves by slow degrees as they run through the whole texture of the composition; on the other hand, a well-timed stroke of sublimity scatters everything before it like a thunderbolt, and in a flash reveals the full power of the speaker. But I should think, my dear Terentianus, that you could develop these points and others of the same kind from your own experience.

CHAPTER 2

Is there an Art of the Sublime?

BEFORE going any farther, I must take up the question whether there is such a thing as an art of sublimity or profundity, for some people think that those who relate matters of this kind to a set of artistic precepts are on a completely wrong track. Genius, they say, is innate; it is not something that can be learnt, and nature is the only art that begets it. Works of natural genius are spoilt, they believe, are indeed utterly debased, when they are reduced to the bare bones of rules and systems. However, I suggest that there is a case for the opposite point of view when it is considered that, although nature is in the main subject only to her own laws where sublime feelings are concerned, she is not given to acting at random and wholly without system. Nature is the first cause and the fundamental creative principle in all activities, but the function of a system is to prescribe the degree and the right moment for each, and to lay down the clearest rules for use and practice. Furthermore, sublime impulses are exposed to greater dangers when they are left to themselves without the ballast and stability of knowledge; they need the curb as often as the spur.

Speaking of the life of mankind as a whole, Demosthenes declares that the greatest of all blessings is good fortune, and that next to it comes good counsel, which, however, is no less important, since its absence leads to the complete destruction of what good fortune brings. Applying this to diction, we might say that nature fills the place of good fortune, and art that of good counsel. Most important, we must remember that the very fact that certain linguistic effects derive from nature alone cannot be learnt from any other source than art. If then the critic who censures those who want to learn this art would take these points into consideration, he would no longer, I imagine, regard the study of the topic I am treating as superfluous and unprofitable.

(Here two pages of the manuscript are missing)

CHAPTER 3

Defects that Militate against Sublimity

... Quell they the oven's far-flung splendour-glow!
Ha, let me but one hearth-abider mark –
One flame-wreath torrent-like I'll whirl on high;
I'll burn the roof, to cinders shrivel it! –
Nay, now my chant is not of noble strain.[1]

SUCH things as this are not tragic, but pseudo-tragic – the 'flame-wreaths', the 'vomiting forth to heaven', the representation of Boreas as a flute-player, and all the rest. They are turbid in expression, and the imagery is confused rather than suggestive of terror; each phrase, when examined in the light of day, sinks gradually from the terrible to the contemptible.

Now even in tragedy, which by its very nature is majestic and admits of some bombast, misplaced tumidity is unpardonable; still less, I think, would it be appropriate to factual narration. This is why people laugh at Gorgias of Leontini[2] when he writes of 'Xerxes the Zeus of the Persians', or of 'vultures, animated sepulchres'. Similarly certain expressions of Callisthenes[3] are ridiculed as being high-flown and not sublime; still more are some of Cleitarchus's[4] – a frivolous fellow who, in the words of Sophocles,[5] blows 'on wretched pipes without control of breath'. Such effects will be found also in Amphicrates and Hegesias and Matris,[6] for often when

1. I have adopted the translation provided by A. S. Way for Roberts's edition, since it brings out so well the bombastic, pseudo-tragic quality to which Longinus takes exception. The lines probably come from a lost *Orithyia* by Aeschylus.

2. A Sicilian rhetorician of the fifth century B.C.

3. A historian who wrote at the end of the fourth and beginning of the third centuries B.C.

4. Another historian, contemporary with Callisthenes; celebrated the deeds of Alexander the Great.

5. The words, probably from a lost *Orithyia* by Sophocles, are quoted in a fuller form by Cicero (*Ad Atticum*).

6. Amphicrates of Athens (*fl.* 90 B.C.), Hegesias of Magnesia (*fl.* 270 B.C.), and Matris of Thebes (*fl.* ? 200 B.C.) were rhetoricians.

they believe themselves to be inspired they are not really carried away, but are merely being puerile.

Tumidity seems, on the whole, to be one of the most difficult faults to guard against. For somehow or other, all those who aim at grandeur in the hope of escaping the charge of feebleness and aridity fall naturally into this very fault, putting their trust in the maxim that 'to fall short of a great aim is at any rate a noble failure'. As in the human body, so also in diction swellings are bad things, mere flabby insincerities that will probably produce an effect opposite to that intended; for as they say, there is nothing drier than a man with dropsy.

Tumidity, then, arises from the desire to outdo the sublime. Puerility, on the other hand, is the complete antithesis of grandeur, for it is entirely low and mean-spirited, and is indeed the most ignoble of faults. What then is puerility? Is it not, surely, a thought which is pedantically elaborated until it tails off into frigidity? Writers slip into this kind of fault when they strive for unusual and well-wrought effects, and above all for attractiveness, and instead flounder into tawdriness and affectation.

Related to this there is a third type of fault in impassioned writing which Theodorus[1] called *parenthyrsus*, or false sentiment. This is misplaced, hollow emotionalism where emotion is not called for, or immoderate passion where restraint is what is needed. For writers are often carried away, as though by drunkenness, into outbursts of emotion which are not relevant to the matter in hand, but are wholly personal, and hence tedious. To hearers unaffected by this emotionalism their work therefore seems atrocious, and naturally enough, for while they are themselves in an ecstasy, their hearers are not. However, I am leaving this matter of the emotions for treatment in another place.

1. Theodorus of Gadara, a rhetorician (*fl.* 30 B.C.).

CHAPTER 4

Frigidity

OF the second fault I mentioned, that is, frigidity, there are plenty of examples in Timaeus,[1] in other respects a writer of some ability, and not incapable of occasional grandeur – a man, indeed, of much learning and inventiveness. However, while he was very fond of criticizing the failings of others, he remained blind to his own, and his passion for continually embarking upon odd conceits often led him into the most trifling puerilities. I shall give you only one or two examples from this author, since Cecilius has anticipated me with most of them. In his eulogy of Alexander the Great he says of him that 'he gained possession of the whole of Asia in fewer years than Isocrates[2] took to write his *Panegyric* advocating war against the Persians.' How remarkable is this comparison of the great Macedonian with the rhetorician! For it is obvious, Timaeus, that, seen in this light, the Spartans were far inferior in prowess to Isocrates, since they took thirty years over the conquest of Messene, whereas he took no more than ten over the composition of his *Panegyric*. Then look at the way in which he speaks of the Athenians captured in Sicily: 'They had behaved sacrilegiously towards Hermes and mutilated statues of him, and it was for this reason that they were punished, very largely through the efforts of a single man, Hermocrates the son of Hermon, who on his father's side was descended from the outraged god.' I am surprised, my dear Terentianus, that he does not write of the tyrant Dionysius that, 'having been guilty of impious conduct towards Zeus and Heracles, he was therefore

1. Timaeus of Tauromenium (*fl.* 310 B.C.), a Sicilian historian who was so fond of finding faults in the work of other writers that he was nicknamed Epitimaeus, i.e., 'fault-finder'.

2. Isocrates (436–338 B.C.), the great Athenian orator and rhetorician. In his *Panegyric* (380 B.C.) he urged the Athenians and the Spartans to lay aside their rivalry and unite against Persia.

deprived of his sovereignty by Dion and Heracleides.'[1]

But why speak of Timaeus when even such demigods as Xenophon and Plato, trained as they were in the school of Socrates, forget themselves at times for the sake of such trivial effects? In his *Constitution of Sparta* Xenophon writes: 'In fact you would hear their voices less than those of marble statues, and would turn aside their gaze less easily than those of bronze figures; and you would think them more modest even than the maidens in their eyes.'[2] It would have been more characteristic of Amphicrates[3] than Xenophon to speak of the pupils of our eyes as modest maidens. And good heavens, to ask us to believe that every single one of them had modest eyes, when it is said that the shamelessness of people is revealed in nothing so much as in their eyes! 'You drunken sot with the eyes of a dog,' as the saying goes.[4] However, Timaeus could not let Xenophon keep even this frigid conceit to himself, but laid his thieving hands on it. At all events, speaking of Agathocles, and how he abducted his cousin from the unveiling ceremony when she had been given in marriage to another man, he asks, 'Who would have done this if he had not had strumpets in his eyes instead of maidens?'

As for the otherwise divine Plato, he says, when he means merely wooden tablets, 'They will inscribe memorials of cypress-wood and place them in the temples;'[5] and again, 'With regard to walls, Megillus, I would agree with Sparta that the walls be allowed to remain lying asleep in the ground, and not rise again.'[6] And Herodotus's phrase for beautiful women, when he calls them 'tortures for the eyes',[7] is not much better. However, Herodotus can in some measure be defended, for it is barbarians who use this phrase in his book, and they in their cups. All the same, it is not proper to put low terms into the

1. The genitive of Zeus is Dios, and Longinus ironically bases on this a conceit in the manner of Timaeus's far-fetched pun on Hermes and Hermocrates the son of Hermon.

2. Because it reflects a tiny image of the person gazing into it, the pupil of the eye was called *korē*, or maiden.

3. An Athenian rhetorician at the beginning of the first century B.C.

4. *Iliad* I, 225.

5. *Laws* V, 741 C.

6. ibid. VI, 778 D.

7. Herodotus, V, 18.

mouths even of such people as these, and thereby lay oneself open to the censure of later ages.

CHAPTER 5

The Origins of Literary Impropriety

ALL these ignoble qualities in literature arise from one cause – from that passion for novel ideas which is the dominant craze among the writers of today; for our faults spring, for the most part, from very much the same sources as our virtues. Thus while a fine style, sublime conceptions, yes, and happy turns of phrase, too, all contribute towards effective composition, yet these very factors are the foundation and origin, not only of success, but also of its opposite. Something of the kind applies also to variations in manner, to hyperbole, and to the idiomatic plural, and I shall show later the dangers which these devices seem to involve. At the moment I must cast about and make some suggestions how we may avoid the defects that are so closely bound up with the achievement of the sublime.

CHAPTER 6

Criticism and the Sublime

THE way to do this, my friend, is first of all to get a clear understanding and appreciation of what constitutes the true sublime. This, however, is no easy undertaking, for the ability to judge literature is the crowning achievement of long experience. Nevertheless, if I am to speak by way of precept, we can perhaps learn discrimination in these matters from some such considerations as those which follow.

CHAPTER 7

The True Sublime

It must be understood, my dear friend, that, as in everyday life nothing is great which it is considered great to despise, so is it with the sublime. Thus riches, honours, reputation, sovereignty, and all the other things which possess in marked degree the external trappings of a showy splendour, would not seem to a sensible man to be great blessings, since contempt for them is itself regarded as a considerable virtue; and indeed people admire those who possess them less than those who could have them but are high-minded enough to despise them. In the same way we must consider, with regard to the grand style in poetry and literature generally, whether certain passages do not simply give an impression of grandeur by means of much adornment indiscriminately applied, being shown up as mere bombast when these are stripped away – passages which it would be more noble to despise than to admire. For by some innate power the true sublime uplifts our souls; we are filled with a proud exaltation and a sense of vaunting joy, just as though we had ourselves produced what we had heard.

If an intelligent and well-read man can hear a passage several times, and it does not either touch his spirit with a sense of grandeur or leave more food for reflection in his mind than the mere words convey, but with long and careful examination loses more and more of its effectiveness, then it cannot be an example of true sublimity – certainly not unless it can outlive a single hearing. For a piece is truly great only if it can stand up to repeated examination, and if it is difficult, or, rather, impossible to resist its appeal, and it remains firmly and ineffaceably in the memory. As a generalization, you may take it that sublimity in all its truth and beauty exists in such works as please all men at all times. For when men who differ in their pursuits, their ways of life, their ambitions, their ages, and their languages all think in one and the same way about the same works, then the unanimous judgement, as it were, of men who have so little in common induces a strong and unshakeable faith in the object of admiration.

CHAPTER 8

Five Sources of Sublimity

IT may be said that there are five particularly fruitful sources of the grand style, and beneath these five there lies as a common foundation the command of language, without which nothing worth while can be done. The first and most important is the ability to form grand conceptions, as I have explained in my commentary on Xenophon. Second comes the stimulus of powerful and inspired emotion. These two elements of the sublime are very largely innate, while the remainder are the product of art – that is, the proper formation of the two types of figure, figures of thought and figures of speech, together with the creation of a noble diction, which in its turn may be resolved into the choice of words, the use of imagery, and the elaboration of the style. The fifth source of grandeur, which embraces all those I have already mentioned, is the total effect resulting from dignity and elevation.

We must consider, then, what is involved under each of these heads, with a preliminary reminder that Cecilius has left out of account some of the five divisions, one of them obviously being that which relates to emotion. Now if he thought that these two things, sublimity and emotion, were the same thing, and that they were essentially bound up with each other, he is mistaken. For some emotions can be found that are mean and not in the least sublime, such as pity, grief, and fear; and on the other hand many sublime passages convey no emotion, such as, among countless examples, the poet's daring lines about the Aloadae:

> Keenly they strove to set Ossa upon Olympus, and upon Ossa, the forest-clad Pelion, that they might mount up to heaven;

and the still greater conception that follows:

> And this would they have accomplished.[1]

With the orators, again, their eulogies, ceremonial addresses,

1. *Odyssey* XI, 315–16; 317.

and occasional speeches contain touches of majesty and grandeur at every point, but as a rule lack emotion; thus emotional speakers are the least effective eulogists, while, on the other hand, those who excel as panegyrists avoid emotionalism. But if Cecilius believed that emotion contributes nothing at all to the sublime, and for this reason considered it not worth mentioning, once again he was making a very serious mistake; for I would confidently maintain that nothing contributes so decisively to the grand style as a noble emotion in the right setting, when it forces its way to the surface in a gust of frenzy, and breathes a kind of divine inspiration into the speaker's words.

CHAPTER 9

Nobility of Soul

Now since the first of these factors, that is to say, nobility of soul,[1] plays the most important part of them all, here too, even though it is a gift rather than an acquired characteristic, we should do all we can to train our minds towards the production of grand ideas, perpetually impregnating them, so to speak, with a noble inspiration. By what means, you will ask, is this to be done? Well, I have written elsewhere to this effect: 'Sublimity is the echo of a noble mind.' Thus, even without being spoken, a simple idea will sometimes of its own accord excite admiration by reason of the greatness of mind that it expresses; for example, the silence of Ajax in 'The Calling Up of the Spirits'[2] is grand, more sublime than any words.

First, then, it is absolutely necessary to indicate the source of this power, and to show that the truly eloquent man must have a mind that is not mean or ignoble. For it is not possible that those who throughout their lives have feeble and servile thoughts and aims should strike out anything that is remarkable, anything that is worthy of an immortality of fame; no,

1. The first of the five sources of sublimity, listed in the previous chapter as 'the ability to form grand conceptions'.

2. *Odyssey* XI, 543 ff.

greatness of speech is the province of those whose thoughts are deep, and stately expressions come naturally to the most high-minded of men. Alexander's reply to Parmenio when he said, 'I would have been content . . .'[1]

(Here six pages of the manuscript are missing)

. . . the distance from earth to heaven; and it might be said that this is the stature of Homer as much as of Strife.[2]

Quite different from this is Hesiod's description of Trouble – if indeed *The Shield* is to be ascribed to Hesiod:[3]

> Rheum was running from her nostrils.

The image he has presented is not powerful, but offensive. But see how Homer exalts the heavenly powers:

> And as far as a man can see with his eyes into the hazy distance as he sits upon a mountain-peak and gazes over the wine-dark sea, even so far is the leap of the loudly-neighing steeds of the gods.[4]

He measures their mighty leap in terms of cosmic distances. Might one not exclaim, from the supreme grandeur of this, that if the steeds of the gods make two leaps in succession they will no longer find room on the face of the earth? And vast also are the images he conjures up for the Battle of the Gods:

> And round them rolled the trumpet-tones of the wide heavens and of Olympus. And down in the underworld Hades, monarch of the realm of the shades, leapt from his throne and cried aloud in dread, lest the earth-shaker Poseidon thereafter should cleave the earth apart, and reveal to the gaze of mortals and immortals

1. Arrian (II, 25, 2) records that Parmenio said to Alexander that, if he had been Alexander, he would have been content to end a war on the terms offered without wishing to go further, to which Alexander replied that, if he had been Parmenio, he would have done so.

2. Evidently Longinus has referred to Homer's description of Strife (*Iliad* IV, 442).

3. Hesiod, who belongs probably to the eighth century B.C., is best known for his *Works and Days*. *The Shield of Heracles*, on the authorship of which Longinus casts doubt, is probably the work of an imitator.

4. *Iliad* V, 770 ff.

alike those grim and festering abodes which the very gods look upon with abhorrence.[1]

You see, my friend, how the earth is split from its foundations upwards, how Tartarus itself is laid bare, how the whole universe is turned upside down and torn apart, and everything alike, heaven and hell, things mortal and immortal, shares in the conflict and peril of the combat.

And yet, awe-inspiring as these things are, from another aspect, if they are not taken as allegory, they are altogether ungodly, and do not preserve our sense of what is fitting. In his accounts of the wounds suffered by the gods, their quarrels, their vengeful actions, their tears, their imprisonment, and all their manifold passions, Homer seems to me to have done everything in his power to make gods of the men fighting at Troy, and men of the gods. But while for us mortals, if we are miserable, death is appointed as a refuge from our ills, Homer has given the gods immortality, not only in their nature, but also in their misfortunes.

But far superior to the passages on the Battle of the Gods are those which represent the divine nature as it really is, pure, majestic, and undefiled; for example, the lines on Poseidon, in a passage on which many others before me have commented:

> And the far-stretched mountains and woodlands, and the peaks, and the Trojan city and the ships of the Achaeans trembled beneath the immortal feet of Poseidon as he strode forth. And he went on to drive over the swelling waters, and from all round the monsters of the deep came from their hiding-places and gambolled about him, for they knew their lord. And in rapture the sea parted her waves, and onwards they flew.[2]

So too the lawgiver of the Jews, no ordinary person, having formed a high conception of the power of the Divine Being, gave expression to it when at the very beginning of his Laws he wrote: 'God said' – what? 'Let there be light, and there was light; let there be land, and there was land.'

I should not, I think, seem a bore, my friend, if I were to put before you still one more passage from Homer – one dealing

1. A conflation of *Iliad* XXI, 388 and XX, 61–5.
2. Another conflation: *Iliad* XIII, 18; XX, 60; XIII, 19; 27–9.

with human affairs – in order to show how he habitually associates himself with the sublimity of his heroic themes. All of a sudden the battle of the Greeks is plunged into the impenetrable darkness of night, and then Ajax, utterly at a loss what to do, cries out:

> Father Zeus, do but rescue the sons of Achaea from out of the gloom, give us fair weather, and grant that we may see with our eyes. So long as it be in the light of day, even destroy us.[1]

These are truly the feelings of an Ajax. He does not beg for life, for this plea would be too base for the hero: but since in the crippling darkness he can turn his valour to no noble purpose, he is annoyed that this prevents him from getting on with the fight, and prays for the immediate return of daylight, resolved at least to find a death worthy of his courage, even though Zeus should be fighting against him. Here indeed Homer breathes in the inspiration of the fray, and is affected by it just as if he himself

> is raging madly, like Ares the spear-hurler, or as when ruinous flames rage among the hills, in the thickets of a deep forest, and foam gathers about his lips.[2]

However, throughout the *Odyssey*, which for a number of reasons must be taken into consideration, Homer shows that when a great genius is falling into decline, it is a special mark of his old age that he should be fond of fables. For it is clear on many grounds that he produced this work as his second composition, besides the fact that throughout the *Odyssey* he introduces remnants of the experiences at Troy as episodes from the Trojan War. And indeed he there pays a debt of mourning and lamentation to his heroes as something long due to them. In fact the *Odyssey* is nothing more than an epilogue to the *Iliad*:

> There lies Ajax the great warrior, there Achilles, there too Patroclus, peer of the gods in counsel; and there too my own dear son.[3]

1. *Iliad* XVII, 645–7.
2. *Iliad* XV, 605–7.
3. *Odyssey* III, 109–11. Nestor is telling Telemachus about the siege of Troy.

It was, I suppose, for the same reason that, writing the *Iliad* in the prime of life, he filled the whole work with action and conflict, whereas the greater part of the *Odyssey* is narrative, as is characteristic of old age. Thus in the *Odyssey* Homer may be likened to the setting sun, whose grandeur remains without its intensity; for no longer there does he maintain the same pitch as in those lays of Troy. The sublime passages have not that consistency which nowhere lapses into mediocrity, nor is there the same closely-packed profusion of passions, nor the versatile and oratorical style studded with images drawn from real life. As though the ocean were withdrawing into itself and remaining quietly within its own bounds, from now on we see the ebbing of Homer's greatness as he wanders in the realms of the fabulous and the incredible. In saying this I have not forgotten the storms in the *Odyssey* and the episode of the Cyclops and other things of the kind. I am speaking indeed of old age, but after all it is the old age of a Homer. Nevertheless, in every one of these passages the fabulous predominates over the actual.

As I said, I have digressed in this way in order to show how very easily a great spirit in his decline may at times be misled into writing nonsense; examples are the episodes of the wine-skin,[1] of the men whom Circe fed like swine, and whom Zoilus[2] described as 'wailing piglets', of Zeus nurtured by the doves like a nestling, and of the man remaining without food on the wreck for ten days,[3] and the incredible story of the killing of the suitors. For how else are we to describe these things than as veritable dreams of Zeus?

There is another reason why these comments should be made on the *Odyssey*, and that is that you should understand how the decline of emotional powers in poets and prose-writers leads to the study of character. For of this kind are the facts, given from the point of view of character, of the way of life in Odysseus's household; they constitute what is in effect a comedy of character.

1. *Odyssey* X, 17. The wine-skin in which Aeolus enclosed for Odysseus the unfavourable winds, which were released by his followers.

2. A grammarian and critic of the fourth century B.C. who was nick-named 'Homer's Scourge' for his carping criticism of Homer.

3. A reference to Odysseus's ten-day swim at the end of *Odyssey* XII.

CHAPTER 10

The Selection and Organization of Material

NEXT we must consider whether there is anything else that makes for sublimity of style. Now as we naturally associate with all things certain elements that are inherent in their substance, so it necessarily follows that we shall find one source of the sublime in the unerring choice of the most felicitous of these elements, and in the ability to relate them to one another in such a way as to make of them a single organism, so to speak.

CHAPTER 11

Amplification

A MERIT associated with those already presented is that which is called amplification, that is, when the matters under discussion or the points of an argument allow of many pauses and many fresh starts from section to section, and the grand phrases come rolling out one after another with increasing effect.

This may be managed either by the rhetorical development of a commonplace, or by exaggeration, whether facts or arguments are to be stressed, or by the orderly disposition of factual points or of appeals to the feelings. There are, indeed, countless forms of amplification. Yet the speaker must be aware that, without the help of sublimity, none of these methods can of itself form a complete whole, unless indeed in the expression of pity or disparagement. In other forms of amplification, when you take away the element of the sublime, it will be like taking the soul out of the body; for their vigour will be completely drained away without the sustaining power of the sublime.

However, in the interests of clarity I must briefly indicate how my present precepts differ from those about which I have just spoken, that is, the marking-out of the most striking points and their organization into a single whole, and in what general respects sublimity is to be distinguished from the effects of amplification.

CHAPTER 12

Amplification Defined

Now the definition of the writers on rhetoric is not, in my view, acceptable. Amplification, they say, is language which invests the subject with grandeur. But obviously this definition could apply equally well to sublimity and to the emotional and the figurative styles, since these too invest language with some degree of grandeur. As I see it, they are to be distinguished from one another by the fact that sublimity consists in elevation, amplification in quantity; thus sublimity is often contained in a single idea, whereas amplification is always associated with quantity and a certain amount of redundancy. To sum it up in general terms, amplification is the accumulation of all the small points and incidental topics bearing on the subject-matter; it adds substance and strength to the argument by dwelling on it, differing from proof in that, while the latter demonstrates the point at issue . . .

(Here two pages of the manuscript are lost)

. . . extremely rich; like some ocean, he[1] often swells into a mighty expanse of grandeur. From this I should say that, where language is concerned, the orator,[2] being more concerned with the emotions, shows much fire and vehemence of spirit, whilst

1. Chapter 13 makes it clear that this refers to Plato.
2. Demosthenes.

Plato, standing firmly based upon his supreme dignity and majesty, though indeed he is not cold, has not the same vehemence.

It seems to me that it is on these same grounds, my dear Terentianus – if we Greeks may be allowed an opinion in this matter – that Cicero is to be differentiated from Demosthenes in his use of the grand style. Demosthenes is characterized by a sublimity which is for the most part rugged, Cicero by profusion. Demosthenes, by reason of his force, yes, and his speed and power and intensity, may be likened to a thunderbolt or flash of lightning, as it were burning up or seizing as his own all that he falls upon. But Cicero is, in my opinion, like a wide-spreading conflagration that rolls on to consume everything far and wide; he has within him an abundance of steady and enduring flame which can be let loose at whatever point he desires, and which is fed from one source after another.

However, you Romans should be able to form a better judgement in this matter. But the right place for the Demosthenean sublimity and intensity is in passages where hyperbole and powerful emotions are involved, and where the audience are to be swept off their feet. On the other hand, profusion is in order when it is necessary to flood them with words. It is for the most part appropriate to the treatment of rhetorical commonplaces, and of perorations and digressions; well suited, too, to all descriptive and epideictic[1] writings, to works of history and natural philosophy, and to a number of other types of literature.

CHAPTER 13

Plato and the Sublime. Imitation

Now although Plato – for I must return to him – flows with such a noiseless stream, he none the less achieves grandeur. You are familiar with his *Republic* and know his manner. 'Those,

1. Epideictic orations were one of the types of set speech defined in the rhetorical systems of the ancients – in Latin *genus demonstrativum*; they include such things as funeral orations, panegyrics, and speeches of dispraise.

therefore,' he says,[1] 'who have no experience of wisdom and goodness, and are always engaged in feasting and similar pleasures, are brought down, it would seem, to a lower level, and there wander about all their lives. They have never looked up towards the truth, nor risen higher, nor tasted of any pure and lasting pleasure. In the manner of cattle, they bend down with their gaze fixed always on the ground and on their feeding-places, grazing and fattening and copulating, and in their insatiable greed for these pleasures they kick and butt one another with horns and hoofs of iron, and kill one another if their desires are not satisfied.'

Provided that we are ready to give him due attention, this author shows us that, in addition to those already mentioned, there is another way that leads to the sublime. And what kind of a way is this? It is the imitation and emulation of the great historians and poets of the past. Let us steadfastly keep this aim in mind, my dear fellow. For many authors catch fire from the inspiration of others – just as we are told that the Pythian priestess, when she approaches the tripod standing by a cleft in the ground from which, they say, there is breathed out a divine vapour, is impregnated thence with the heavenly power, and by virtue of this afflatus is at once inspired to speak oracles. So too, as though also issuing from sacred orifices, certain emanations are conveyed from the genius of the men of old into the souls of those who emulate them, and, breathing in these influences, even those who show very few signs of inspiration derive some degree of divine enthusiasm from the grandeur of their predecessors.

Was Herodotus alone an extremely Homeric writer? No, for even earlier there was Stesichorus,[2] and Archilochus, and above all others Plato, who for his own use drew upon countless tributary streams from the great Homeric river. I should perhaps have had to prove this had not Ammonius[3] and his followers selected and recorded the facts.

1. *Republic* IX, 586.
2. Stesichorus (*c.* 640 – *c.* 555 B.C.), one of the great lyrical poets.
3. Ammonius (*fl.* 140 B.C.) carried on at Alexandria the work of his master Aristarchus, who has been described as 'the founder of scientific scholarship'.

Now this procedure is not plagiarism; rather it is like taking impressions from beautiful pictures or statues or other works of art. I do not think there would have been so fine a bloom on Plato's philosophical doctrines, or that he would so often have embarked on poetic subject-matter and phraseology, had he not been striving heart and soul with Homer for first place, like a young contestant entering the ring with a long-admired champion, perhaps showing too keen a spirit of emulation in his desire to break a lance with him, so to speak, yet getting some profit from the endeavour. For as Hesiod says,[1] 'This strife is good for mortals.' And indeed the fight for fame and the crown of victory are noble and very well worth the winning where even to be worsted by one's predecessors carries no discredit.

CHAPTER 14

Imagery and the Power of the Imagination

FURTHERMORE, my dear boy, dignity, grandeur, and powers of persuasion are to a very large degree derived from images – for that is what some people call the representation of mental pictures. In a general way the term 'image' is used of any mental conception, from whatever source it presents itself, which gives rise to speech; but in current usage the word is applied to passages in which, carried away by your feelings, you imagine you are actually seeing the subject of your description, and enable your audience as well to see it. You will have noticed that imagery means one thing with orators and another with poets – that in poetry its aim is to work on the feelings, in oratory to produce vividness of description, though indeed in both cases an attempt is made to stir the feelings.

> Mother, I beseech you, do not set upon me those blood-boltered and snake-like hags. See there, see there, they approach, they leap upon me![2]

1. *Works and Days* 24.
2. Euripides, *Orestes* 255–7.

and again,

> Ah! She will slay me! Whither shall I fly?[1]

In these passages the poet himself had 'seen' the Furies, and he almost compelled his audience, too, to see what he had imagined.

CHAPTER 15

Rhetorical Figures: Adjuration

We now come to the place which I have duly set aside for rhetorical figures, for they too, when properly handled, will contribute in no small measure, as I have said, to the effect of grandeur. However, since it would be a toilsome and indeed endless business to consider them all closely at this stage, I shall merely, in order to confirm my proposition, run over a few of those which make for grandeur of utterance.

In the following passage Demosthenes is putting forward an argument in support of his policy. What was the natural procedure for doing this? 'You were not wrong, you who undertook the struggle for the freedom of the Greeks, and you have a precedent for this here at home. For those who fought at Marathon were not wrong, nor those at Salamis, nor those at Plataea.'[2] But when, as though carried away by a divine enthusiasm and by the inspiration of Phoebus himself, he uttered his oath by the champions of Greece, 'By those who stood the shock at Marathon, it cannot be that you were wrong,' it would seem that, by his use of this single figure of adjuration, which I here give the name of apostrophe, he has deified his ancestors by suggesting that we ought to swear by men who have died such deaths as we swear by gods; he has instilled into his judges the spirit of the men who stood there in the forefront of the danger, and has transformed the natural flow of his

1. Euripides, *Iphigenia in Tauris* 291.

2. *De Corona* 208. Demosthenes is defending, by reference to the past, his aggressive policy which resulted in the Athenian defeat at Chaeronea.

argument into a passage of transcending sublimity, endowing it with the passion and the power of conviction that arise from unheard-of and extraordinary oaths. At the same time he has infused into the minds of his audience words which act in some sort as an antidote and a remedy, so that, uplifted by these eulogies, they come to feel just as proud of the war against Philip as of the triumphs at Marathon and Salamis. By all these means he has been able to carry his hearers away with the figure he has employed.

It is said, indeed, that Demosthenes found the germ of this oath in Eupolis:[1]

> For by the fight I fought at Marathon, no one of them shall vex my heart and not pay for it.

But there is nothing grand about the mere swearing of an oath; we must take into account the place, the manner, the circumstances, and the motive. In the Eupolis there is nothing but an oath, and that addressed to the Athenians while they were still enjoying prosperity and in no need of consolation. Moreover, the poet has not in his oath deified the warriors in order to engender in his audience a high opinion of their valour, but has wandered away from those who stood the shock to something inanimate, that is, the fight. In Demosthenes the oath is designed for men who have suffered defeat, so that the Athenians may no longer regard Chaeronea as a disaster; and at the same time it is, as I said, a proof that no wrong has been done, an example, a demonstration of the efficacy of oaths, a eulogy, and an exhortation. And since the orator was likely to be faced with the objection, 'You are speaking of a defeat that resulted from your policy, yet your oath relates to victories,' in what follows he keeps on the safe side and measures every word, showing that even in orgies of the imagination it is necessary to remain sober. 'Those who stood in the forefront of the battle at Marathon,' he says, 'and those who fought aboard ship at Salamis and Artemisium, and those who stood shoulder to

1. Eupolis (*c.* 446 – *c.* 411 B.C.) was a poet of the Old Comedy. The lines come from his lost comedy *Demi.*

shoulder at Plataea.' Nowhere does he speak of the 'victors'; everywhere he cunningly avoids mention of the result, since it was a happy one and the reverse of what happened at Chaeronea. Thus he anticipates objections and carries his audience with him. 'To all of whom, Aeschines,' he adds, 'the state gave a public funeral, not only to those who were successful.'

CHAPTER 16

Asyndeton, or the Omission of Conjunctions

. . . the words come gushing out, as it were, set down without connecting links, and almost outstripping the speaker himself. 'And, locking their shields,' says Xenophon,[1] 'they pressed forward, fought, slew, were slain.' Then there are the words of Eurylochus:

> We came through the oak-coppice, as you bade, renowned Odysseus. We saw amid the forest-glens a beautiful palace.[2]

The phrases, disconnected, but none the less rapid, give the impression of an agitation which at the same time checks the utterance and urges it on. And the poet has produced such an effect by his use of asyndeton.

CHAPTER 17

The Accumulation of Figures

A COMBINATION of figures for a common purpose usually has a very moving effect – when two or three unite in a kind of partnership to add force, persuasiveness, and beauty. Thus in Demosthenes' speech against Meidias you will find examples of asyndeton interwoven with the figures of anaphora and diatyposis:[3] 'For the aggressor might do many things, some

1. Xenophon, *Historia Graeca* IV, 3, 19.
2. *Odyssey* X, 251–2.
3. Anaphora is the repetition of words; diatyposis is vivid description.

of which the victim would be unable to describe to anyone else, by his manner, his looks, his voice.' Then, in order that the speech may not, as it proceeds, remain at a standstill as far as these particular effects are concerned (for standing still connotes calm, whereas emotion, being an upheaval or agitation of the soul, connotes disorder), he at once hurries on to fresh examples of asyndeton and anaphora: 'By his manner, his looks, his voice, when he acts with insolence, when he acts with hostility, when he strikes you with his fists, when he strikes you like a slave.' In this way the orator does just the same as the aggressor; he belabours the judges' minds with blow after blow. He goes on from here to make yet another hurricane onslaught: 'When he strikes you with his fists,' he says, 'when he beats you about the face – this rouses you, this drives men out of their wits when they are not used to being trampled underfoot. No one describing this could bring out the strength of its effect.' Thus all the way through, although with continual variations, he preserves the essential character of the repetitions and the asyndeta, and thus too his order is disordered, and similarly his disorder embraces a certain element of order.

CHAPTER 18

The Figure of Hyperbaton, or Inversion

HYPERBAT , or inversions, must be put into the same class. These consist in the arrangement of words or ideas out of their normal sequence, and they carry, so to speak, the genuine stamp of powerful emotion. There are people who, when they are angry or frightened or irritated or carried away by jealousy or any other feeling – for there are innumerable forms of emotion, and indeed no one would be able to say just how many – will sometimes let themselves be deflected; and often, after they have brought forward one point, they will drop in others without rhyme or reason, and then, under the stress of their agitation, they will come right round to their original position just as though they were being chased by a whirlwind. Dragged in every direction by their rapid changes of mood, they will keep altering the arrangement of their words and ideas, losing their natural sequence and introducing all sorts of variations. In the same way the best authors will use inversion in such a way that their representations will assume the aspect of natural processes at work. For art is perfect only when it looks like nature, and again, nature hits the mark only when she conceals the art that is within her.

This may be exemplified by the words of Dionysius the Phocaean in Herodotus:[1] 'For our affairs stand on a razor's edge, men of Ionia, whether we are to be free men or slaves, and runaway slaves at that. Now, therefore, if you are prepared to accept hardships, straightway there is toil for you, but you will be able to overcome your enemies.' Here the normal order would have been, 'O men of Ionia, now is the time for you to take toil upon you; for our affairs stand on a razor's edge.' However, the speaker has transposed 'men of Ionia', starting at once with the thought of the fear, as though in this pressing danger he would not even address his hearers first. Furthermore, he has inverted the order of his ideas; for instead of saying that they must endure toil, which is the point of his exhortation, he first gives them the reason why they must toil when he says, 'Our affairs stand on a razor's edge.' Thus what he says does not seem premeditated, but forced out of him.

CHAPTER 19

Polyptoton: Interchange of Singular and Plural

THE figures called polyptota[2] (accumulations, variations, and climaxes) are, as you know, very powerful auxiliaries in the production of elegance and of every kind of sublime and emotional effect. Observe, too, how greatly an exposition is

1. Herodotus, VI, 11.
2. Strictly speaking, polyptoton is the use of more than one case of the same word, but Longinus seems to apply it also to rhetorical effects gained by changes in number, person, tense, or gender.

diversified and enlivened by changes in case, tense, person, number, and gender. In the matter of number, I can say that the decorative quality of a passage is not enhanced only by words which are singular in form, but which on close examination are found to have a plural meaning, as in

> Straightway a countless host ranged along the beaches send out a cry, 'Tunny!'[1]

But it is more noteworthy that at times the use of the plural in place of the singular has a more resounding effect, and impresses us by the very idea of multitude implied in the plural number.

CHAPTER 20

Polyptoton: Conversion of Plural to Singular

FURTHERMORE, the opposite process, the contraction of plural ideas into a singular form, sometimes achieves an outstanding effect of sublimity. 'Afterwards,' says Demosthenes,[2] 'the whole Peloponnese was at variance.' Again, 'And when Phrynicus produced his play *The Capture of Miletus* the theatre burst into tears.'[3] To compress the number from multiplicity into unity gives a stronger impression of a single entity. In both examples the reason for the striking effect is, I think, the same. Where the words are singular, to turn them into the plural suggests an unexpected burst of feeling; where they are plural, and are fused into a fine-sounding singular, the change in the opposite direction produces an effect of surprise.

1. Author unknown. Presumably the passage refers to a crowd of fisherfolk hailing the appearance of a shoal of tunny.

2. *De Corona* 18.

3. Herodotus, VI, 21. Phrynicus was a tragic playwright contemporary with Aeschylus. Herodotus continues the anecdote quoted here by recounting that the Athenians fined Phrynicus 1000 drachmas for reminding them in *The Capture of Miletus* of a disaster which had befallen a friendly state, and ordered that the play should never again be performed.

CHAPTER 21

Polyptoton: Interchange of Tenses

AGAIN, if you introduce circumstances that are past in time as happening at the present moment, you will turn the passage from mere narrative into vivid actuality. 'Someone,' says Xenophon, 'has fallen under Cyrus's horse, and being trampled on, strikes the horse in the belly with his sword. It rears and throws Cyrus, and he falls to the ground.'[1] Thucydides is particularly fond of this device.

CHAPTER 22

Polyptoton: Variations of Person, or Personal Address

IN the same way the change of person is striking, and often makes the hearer feel that he is moving in the thick of the danger:

> You would say that they met in the shock of war, all unwearied and undaunted, so impetuously did they rush into the fray.[2]

Then there is Aratus's

> Do not in that month entrust yourself to the surges of the ocean.[3]

Herodotus does much the same kind of thing: 'From the city of Elephantine you will sail upwards, until you come to a level plain; and after you have crossed this tract, you will board again another ship and sail for two days, and then you will come to a great city whose name is Meroe.'[4] You see, my friend, how, as he takes you in imagination through the places in question,

1. Xenophon, *Cyropaedia* VII, i, 37.
2. *Iliad* XV, 697–8.
3. Aratus (*fl.* 270 B.C.), one of the didactic poets of Alexandria. This is line 299 of his *Phaenomena*.
4. Herodotus, II, 29.

he transforms hearing into sight. All such passages, by their direct personal form of address, bring the hearer right into the middle of the action being described. When you seem to be addressing, not the whole audience, but a single member of it –

> But you would not have known of Tydeus's son for which of the armies he fought –[1]

you will affect him more profoundly, and make him more attentive and full of active interest, if you rouse him by these appeals to him personally.

CHAPTER 23

Polyptoton: Conversion to the First Person

AGAIN, there are times when a writer, while speaking of a character, suddenly breaks off and converts himself into that character. A figure of this kind is in a way an outburst of emotion:

> And with a far-echoing shout Hector cried out to the Trojans to rush against the ships and leave the blood-spattered spoils. And if I spy anyone who of his own will holds back from the ships, I will surely bring about his death.[2]

Here the poet has taken upon himself the presentation of the narrative, as is appropriate, and then suddenly, without any warning, has attributed the abrupt threat to the angry chieftain. Had he inserted, 'Hector said so and so', it would have given a frigid effect; as it is, the change in form of the passage has anticipated the sudden change of speakers. Accordingly this figure should be used for preference when a sudden crisis will not give the author time to linger, but compels him to change at once from one character to another.

1. *Iliad* V, 85.
2. *Iliad* XV, 346–9.

There is another example in Hecataeus:[1] 'Ceyx took this badly and at once ordered the descendants of Heracles to depart. For it is not in my power to help you. Therefore, in order that you may not perish yourselves and injure me, take yourselves off to some other country.'

CHAPTER 24

Metaphor

WITH regard to the appropriate number of metaphors, Cecilius appears to side with those who lay down that two, or at most three, should be brought together in the same passage. Demosthenes is again the standard in this context. The appropriate occasion for their use is when the emotions come pouring out like a torrent, and irresistibly carry along with them a host of metaphors. 'Men,' he says, 'who are steeped in blood, who are flatterers, who have each of them mutilated the limbs of their own fatherlands, who have pledged their liberty by drinking first to Philip, and now to Alexander, measuring their happiness by their bellies and their basest appetites, and who have uprooted that liberty and that freedom from despotism which were to the Greeks of earlier days the rules and standards of integrity.'[2] Here the orator's indignation against the traitors casts a veil over the number of figurative expressions he has used.

Now Aristotle and Theophrastus declare that the following phrases have a softening effect on bold metaphors: 'as if', and 'as it were', and 'if one may put it like this', and 'if one may venture the expression'; for the qualifications, they say, mitigate the boldness. I accept this, but at the same time, as I said when I was talking about rhetorical figures, the timely expression of violent emotions, together with true sublimity, is the

1. Hecataeus of Miletus (*fl.* 520 B.C.), historian and geographer.
2. *De Corona* 296.

appropriate antidote for the number and boldness of metaphors. For the onward rush of passion has the property of sweeping everything before it, or rather of requiring bold imagery as something altogether indispensable; it does not allow the hearer leisure to consider the number of metaphors, since he is carried away by the enthusiasm of the speaker.

Furthermore, in the handling of commonplaces and of description nothing so much confers distinction as a continuous series of metaphors. It is by this means that the anatomy of the human body is superbly depicted in Xenophon,[1] and still more divinely in Plato.[2] The head, says Plato, is a citadel, and the neck is constructed as an isthmus between the head and the breast; and the vertebrae, he says, are set below like pivots. Pleasure tempts men to evil, and the tongue is the touchstone of taste. The heart is the fuel-store of the veins, the fountain from which the blood begins its vigorous course, and it keeps its station in the guard-house of the body. The various passages he calls the lanes. 'And for the thumping of the heart which takes place when danger is imminent or when anger is rising, when it becomes fiery-hot, the gods,' he says, 'have devised some relief by implanting the lungs, which, being soft and bloodless, and pierced inwardly with pores, serve as a kind of buffer, so that when anger boils up in the heart, it may throb against a yielding substance and not be damaged.' The seat of the desires he compares with the women's apartments, and that of anger with the men's. Then the spleen is the napkin of the entrails, from which it is filled with waste matter, and swells and festers. 'And after this,' he says, 'they covered everything over with flesh, which they put there, like felt matting, as a protection against attacks from outside.' And he called the blood the fodder of the flesh, adding that, 'in order to provide nourishment, they irrigated the body, cutting channels as is done in gardens, so that, the body being perforated with conduits, the rivulets of the veins might flow on as though from some never-failing source.' And when the end comes, he

1. *Memorabilia* I, iv, 5.
2. The descriptions are drawn from the *Timaeus* 65 C – 85 E.

says, the cables of the soul, like those of a ship, are loosed, and she is set free. These and innumerable similar metaphors form a continuous succession. But those I have mentioned are enough to show that figurative language is a natural source of grandeur, and that metaphors contribute to sublimity; and also that it is emotional and descriptive passages that most gladly find room for them.

However, it is obvious, even without my stating it, that the use of metaphors, like all the other beauties of style, is liable to lead to excess. In this respect even Plato is severely criticized, on the ground that he is often carried away by a kind of linguistic frenzy into harsh and intemperate metaphors and bombastic allegory. 'For it is not easy to see,' he says, 'that a city needs to be mixed like a bowl of wine, in which the strong, raging wine seethes as it is poured in, but when it is chastened by another god who is sober, its association with such good company turns it into an excellent and temperate drink.'[1] To call water 'a sober god', say the critics, and to describe mixing as 'chastening', is to use the language of some poet who is not in fact sober.

Cecilius, too, has picked on such defects as these, and in the works he has written in praise of Lysias he has actually dared to represent Lysias as being in all respects superior to Plato. But here he has given way to two uncritical impulses; for although he is even fonder of Lysias than of himself, his hatred for Plato altogether surpasses his love for Lysias. However, he is merely being contentious, and his premisses are not, as he thought, admitted. For he prefers the orator, whom he regards as faultless and without blemish, to Plato, who often made mistakes. But this is not the truth of the matter, nor anything like the truth.

1. Plato, *Laws* 773 C.

CHAPTER 25

Composition, or Disposition of Material

THE fifth of the factors contributing to the sublime which I specified at the beginning remains to be dealt with, my friend, and that is the arrangement of the words in due order. On this matter I have already in two treatises given an adequate account of such conclusions as I could reach; for my present purpose I need only add the essential fact that men find in a harmonious arrangement of sounds, not only a natural medium of persuasion and pleasure, but also a marvellous instrument of grandeur and passion. For does not the flute instil certain emotions into those that hear it, seeming to carry them away and fill them with a divine frenzy? Does it not give rhythmic movement, and compel the hearer to conform to the melody and adapt his own movements to this rhythm, even if he is not in the least musical? Then the tones of the harp, in themselves meaningless, often cast a wonderful spell, as you know, by their variations in sound and the throbbing interplay and harmonious blending of the notes struck.

Yet these are mere semblances, spurious counterfeits of the art of persuasion, and not, as I have mentioned, a genuine expression of human nature. Now composition is a kind of harmony of the words which are implanted in man at his birth, and which affect not his hearing alone but his very soul, and it is my belief that it brings out manifold patterns of words, thoughts, deeds, beauty, and melody, all of them originally born and bred in us; moreover, by the blending of its myriad tones it brings into the hearts of the bystanders the actual emotion of the speaker, and always induces them to share it; and finally it builds up an accumulation of phrases into a grand and harmonious structure. Are we not to believe that by these means it casts a spell on us, and draws our thoughts towards what is majestic and dignified and sublime, and towards any other potentialities which it embraces, gaining a complete mastery over our minds? But it is madness to dispute on matters which are the subject of such general agreement, since experience is sufficient proof.

An idea which appears sublime, and which is certainly to be admired, is that which Demosthenes associates with his decree: 'This decree caused the peril which at that time encompassed the city to pass away just like a cloud.'[1] But its ring owes no less to the harmony than to the thought, for its delivery rests entirely on the dactylic rhythms, which are the noblest of rhythms and make for grandeur – which is why the heroic measure, the most beautiful of known measures, is composed of dactyls. And indeed, if you moved it wherever you liked away from its proper place,[2] and said, 'this decree, just like a cloud, caused the peril at that time to pass away', or if you cut out a single syllable and said, 'caused to pass away like a cloud', you would realize how far the harmony of sound chimes in with the sublimity. For 'just like a cloud' starts off with a long rhythm, consisting of four metrical beats, and if you remove a single syllable and write 'like a cloud', by this abbreviation you at once mutilate the effect of grandeur. And again, if you stretch the phrase out with 'caused to pass away just as if a cloud', the meaning is the same, but it no longer falls on the ear with the same effect because, by the drawing out of the final beats, the sheer sublimity of the passage is robbed of its solidity and of its tension.

1. *De Corona* 188.

2. The awkwardness here is due to corruption in the text, the loss perhaps of a phrase, perhaps of a preceding sentence, which would have indicated that 'it' refers to the last phrase of the decree, 'just like a cloud'. It is difficult to find English equivalents for most of the technicalities of this paragraph.

CHAPTER 26

The Structure of the Sentence

AMONG the chief agents in the formation of the grand style is the proper combination of the constituent members – as is true of the human body and its members. Of itself no single member, when dissociated from any other, has anything worthy of note about it, but when they are all mutually interconnected they make up a perfect whole. Similarly, when the elements of grandeur are separated from one another, they carry the sublimity along with them, dispersing it in every direction; but when they are combined into a single organism, and, moreover, enclosed within the bonds of harmony, they form a rounded whole, and their voice is loud and clear, and in the periods thus formed the grandeur receives contributions, as it were, from a variety of factors. I have, however, sufficiently demonstrated that many writers both of prose and verse who have no natural gift of sublimity, or even of grandeur, and who for the most part employ common and popular words which carry no extraordinary associations, have nevertheless, by merely combining and fitting these words together in the right order, achieved dignity and distinction and an appearance of grandeur – among many others Philistus,[1] for example, Aristophanes at times, and Euripides as a rule.

After the slaughter of his children Heracles says,

> I am stowed to the hatches with woes, and there is no room for more.[2]

The expression is extremely vulgar, but it becomes sublime by reason of its aptness to its setting. If you fit the passage together in any other way, you will realize that Euripides is a poet rather by virtue of his power of composition than of his ideas. Writing of Dirce being dragged away by the bull, he says:

> And wheresoever he chanced to wheel around, he seized and dragged along at once woman or rock or oak, now this, now that.[3]

1. A Sicilian historian of the fourth century.
2. Euripides, *Hercules Furens* 1245.
3. From the lost *Antiope* of Euripides.

This idea is excellent in itself, but gains further strength from the fact that the rhythm is not hurried or as it were carried along on rollers, but the words offer resistance to one another and derive support from the pauses, and take their stand in a firmly-based grandeur.

CHAPTER 27

Conciseness

FURTHERMORE, excessive conciseness in expression reduces sublimity, for grandeur is marred when it is too closely compressed. You must take this to mean, not compression that is properly used, but what is entirely broken up into fragments and thus frittered away. For excessive conciseness curtails the sense where brevity goes straight to the point. On the other hand, it is clear that prolixity is lifeless, since it entails an unseasonable length.

CHAPTER 28

Triviality of Expression, and Amplification

THE use of trivial words terribly disfigures passages in the grand style. For example, as far as content is concerned, the storm in Herodotus is marvellously described, but the description contains certain details which are, heaven knows, too far below the dignity of the subject. One might perhaps instance 'when the sea boiled', where the word 'boiled' is so cacophonous as to detract greatly from the sublimity. Then 'the wind,' he says, 'grew fagged'; and 'an unpleasant end' awaited those who were clinging to the wreck.[1] The phrase 'grew fagged' is uncouth, and lacks dignity, and 'unpleasant' is inappropriate

1. Herodotus, VII, 188; VII, 191; VIII, 13.

to so great a disaster.

Similarly, when Theopompus had given a marvellous account of the Persian King's descent into Egypt, he spoiled the whole description by the use of some trivial words. 'For which city and which tribe of all those in Asia,' he says, 'did not send envoys to the King? And which of the products of the earth or of the beautiful or precious achievements of art was not brought to him as an offering? Were there not many costly coverlets and mantles, purple and white and multi-coloured, many pavilions of gold furnished with all things needful, many robes of state and costly couches? Further, there was silver and gold plate richly wrought, goblets and mixing-bowls, some of which you might have seen studded with jewels, others embellished in a cunning and costly fashion. In addition to these there were countless myriads of weapons, both Greek and barbarian, and beasts of burden beyond number, and sacrificial victims fattened for the slaughter; and many bushels of spices, and bags and sacks and sheets of papyrus and all other useful things; and such a store of preserved flesh from every kind of victim as to form piles so large that anyone approaching them from a distance took them for mounds and hills confronting them.'

Here Theopompus runs from the sublime to the trivial where he ought, on the contrary, to have been heightening his effects. By mixing bags and spices and sacks with the wonderful report of the equipment as a whole, he has almost given the impression of a cook-shop. Suppose that among all those decorative objects, among the golden and jewelled mixing bowls, the silver plate, the pavilions of pure gold, and the goblets – suppose that someone had actually brought paltry bags and sacks and placed them in the midst of all these, his action would have produced an effect that offended the eye. Well, in the same way the untimely introduction of such words as these as it were disfigures and debases the description. He could have given a general account, as he speaks of the 'hills' of flesh being built up, and with regard to the rest of the provisions have spoken of wagons and camels and a host of baggage-animals laden with everything that ministers to the luxury and the pleasures of the table; or he could have called them piles of all kinds of grain and of all that conduces to fine cooking and good living; or if he had to put it so explicitly, he could have spoken of all the delicacies of caterers and good cooks.

In sublime passages we ought not to resort to sordid and contemptible terms unless constrained by some extreme necessity. We should use words that suit the dignity of the subject, and imitate nature, the artist who has fashioned man, for she has not placed in full view our private parts or the means by which our whole frame is purged, but as far as possible has concealed them, and, as Xenophon says,[1] has put their passages into the farthest background so as not to sully the beauty of the whole figure.

However, there is no urgent need to enumerate and classify the things that lead to triviality. For as I have previously indicated the qualities that furnish style with nobility and sublimity, it is obvious that their opposities will for the most part make it mean and ugly.

CHAPTER 29

The Decay of Eloquence

HOWEVER, as in view of your love of learning I will not hesitate to add, my dear Terentianus, there remains to be cleared up a problem to which a certain philosopher has recently applied his wits. 'I wonder,' he said, 'as no doubt do many other people, why it is that in our age there are men well fitted for public life who are extremely persuasive, who are keen and shrewd, and especially well endowed with literary charm, and yet really sublime and transcendent natures are, with few exceptions, no longer produced. Such a great and world-wide dearth of literature attends our age! Are we,' he went on, 'are we to accept the well-worn view that democracy is the kindly nurse of great men, and that great men of letters may be said to have flourished only under democracy and perished with it? For freedom, they say, has the power to foster the imaginations of high-souled men and to inspire them with hope, and with it there spreads the

1. *Memorabilia* I, iv, 6.

keenness of mutual rivalry and an eager competition for the first place. Furthermore, by reason of the prizes which are open to all in republics, the intellectual gifts of orators are continually sharpened by practice and as it were kept bright by rubbing, and, as might be expected, these gifts, fostered in freedom, help to shed light on the affairs of state. Nowadays,' he continued, 'we seem to absorb from our childhood onwards the lessons of the slavery to which we are accustomed, all but swaddled in the infancy of our minds as we are in slavish customs and observances, and never tasting of the finest and most productive source of eloquence, by which I mean freedom; and thus we emerge as nothing but sublime flatterers.'

This, he maintained, was the reason why, although all other faculties may fall to the lot even of menials, no slave ever becomes an orator; for the fact that he has no freedom of speech, that he lives as it were a dungeoned life, and that he is always liable to be beaten, comes bubbling up to the surface. As Homer puts it, 'The day of our enslavement takes away half our manhood.'[1] 'And so,' went on the philosopher, 'just as the cages in which they keep the Pygmies, or dwarfs, as they call them, not only stunt the growth of these who are imprisoned in them, if what I hear is true, but also shrink them by reason of the fetters fixed round their bodies, so all slavery, however just it may be, could well be described as a cage of the soul, a common prison-house.'

However, I took him up and said: 'It is easy, my good sir, and a characteristic of human nature, always to be finding fault with the present state of affairs. But consider whether it may be that it is not the peace of this world of ours that corrupts great natures, but much rather this endless war which holds our desires in its grasp, yes, and further still the passions that garrison our lives nowadays and utterly devastate them. For the love of money, that insatiable craving from which we all now suffer, and the love of pleasure make us their slaves, or rather, one might say, sink our lives (body and soul) into the depths, the love of money being a disease that makes us

1. *Odyssey* XVII, 332.

petty-minded, and the love of pleasure an utterly ignoble attribute.

'On further reflection, indeed, I do not see how, if we value the possession of unlimited wealth, or, to give the truth of the matter, make a god of it, we can avoid allowing the evils that naturally attend its entry into our souls. For vast and unlimited wealth is closely followed – step by step, as they say – by extravagance, and no sooner has the one opened the gates of cities and houses than the other comes in and joins it in setting up house there. With the passing of time, according to the philosophers, they build nests in our lives, and soon set about begetting offspring, giving birth to pretentiousness, vanity, and luxury – no bastards these, but very much their true-born issue. And if these children of wealth are allowed to reach maturity they soon breed in our hearts implacable masters, insolence and lawlessness and shamelessness. This will inevitably happen, and then men will no longer lift up their eyes nor take any further thought for their good name; the ruin of their lives will gradually be completed as their grandeur of soul withers and fades until it sinks into contempt, when they become lost in admiration of their mortal capabilities and neglect to develop the immortal.

'A man who has accepted a bribe for a verdict would never be a sound and unbiased judge of what is just and honourable, for a corrupt judge must necessarily regard his own private interests as honourable and just. And where bribery now governs all our lives, and we hunt others to death, and lay traps for legacies, and bargain our souls for gain from any and every source, having become slaves to [luxury], can we expect, in this pestilential ruin of our lives, that there should still remain an unbiased and incorruptible judge of works which possess grandeur or enduring life, and that he would not be overcome by his passion for gain? For such men as we are, indeed, it is perhaps better that we should be ruled than live in freedom. If we were given complete liberty, like released prisoners, our consuming greed for out neighbours' possessions might set the world on fire with our deeds of evil.'

In short, I maintained that what wears down the spirit of the present generation is the apathy in which, with few exceptions, we all pass our lives; for we do no work nor show any enterprise from any other motives than those of being praised or being able to enjoy our pleasures – never from an eager and honourable desire to serve our fellows.

'It is best to leave such things at a guess',[1] and to pass on to the next problem, that is, the emotions, about which I previously undertook to write in a separate treatise, for they seem to me to share a place in literature generally, and especially in the sublime . . .

(*The rest is lost*)

1. Euripides, *Electra* 379.

이상섭

연세대학교 영문학과 졸업
연세대학교 대학원 영문학과 졸업
미국 애모리대 대학원 문학박사
미국 하바드대학 초빙 연구원
미국 버지니아대학 방문학자
연세대학교 영문과 교수 역임
연세대학교 명예교수

저서

Elizabethan Literary Opinion(연대 대학원), 문학의 이해(서문당), 문학연구의 방법(탐구당), 문학이론의 역사적 전개(연대출판부), 문학비평용어사전(민음사), 언어와 상상(문학과 지성사), '님의 침묵'의 어휘와 그 활용구조(탐구당), 르네상스와 신고전주의 비평(민음사), 복합성의 시학: 뉴 크리티시즘 연구(민음사)

Selected English Critical Texts
WITH EXCERPTS FROM CLASSICAL CRITICISM

1판 1쇄 발행 _ 1982년 9월 10일
1판 6쇄 발행 _ 2018년 8월 31일

편 저 자 • 이 상 섭
발 행 인 • 정 현 걸
발　 행 • 신 아 사
인　 쇄 • 대명프린팅
출판등록 • 1956년 1월 5일 (제9–52호)
주　 소 • 서울시 은평구 통일로 59길 4 (2F)
전　 화 • 02)382–6411 · 팩스 02)382–6401
홈페이지 • www.shinasa.co.kr
E – MAIL • shinasa@daum.net

ISBN 89–8396–230–5(93840)

정가 *22,000* 원